PROUST

Ronald Hayman has worked in
the theatre as an actor and director.
His books include biographies of
Kafka, Brecht and Sartre. He also
writes the Radio 3 comedy series
Such Rotten Luck. He lives in
London.

Proust

A BIOGRAPHY

Ronald Hayman

Minerva

A Minerva Paperback
PROUST

First published in Great Britain 1990
by William Heinemann Ltd
This Minerva edition published 1991
by Mandarin Paperbacks
Michelin House, 81 Fulham Road, London SW3 6RB

Minerva is an imprint of the Octopus Publishing Group

Copyright © Ronald Hayman 1990

A CIP catalogue record for this title
is available from the British Library
ISBN 0 7493 9902 3

Printed and bound in Great Britain
by Cox & Wyman Ltd, Reading, Berks

IN MEMORIAM

John Hayman (1890–1954)
and
Sadie Hayman (1905–89)

CONTENTS

V: 1910–14 Reclusion

VI: 1914–22 Rehearsals for Dying

ACKNOWLEDGMENTS

Each time, after finishing a biography, I sit down to formulate an acknowledgment for the help received from friends and acquaintances who have been endlessly tolerant and generous with their time, I feel like a spendthrift customer lunching with an indulgent bank manager. The debts of gratitude add up to an enormous overdraft, but no pressure is put on me to start making repayments.

The first word of thanks must go to Catharine Carver, who has often been helpful in the past, reading work in progress and making insightful suggestions. This time I was greedier than ever for help, which she gave unstintingly.

Altogether I had so many conversations which exerted influence on the book and have received so much help of so many different kinds from so many people that it will seem churlish to list them alphabetically. But I feel more grateful than will be apparent to Mona Abboud, John Ardagh, Gigi Ashe, Frank Barrett, Sally Belfrage, Anne Borrel, Gilles Chouraqui, Erica Cumming, Comte Ghislain de Diesbach, Elsie Birch Donald, Jane Dorrell, Lord Eccles, Jean Gimpel, Shusha Guppy, Gabriel Josipovici, Philip Kolb, Sir Bernard Ledwidge, Richard Mayne, Colin Nears, Gary O'Connor, Jenny Pepper, Frances Porter of the Wildenstein Gallery, Sue Standing, Elizabeth Russell Taylor, Dr Estella Welldon and Robert Winder.

I have also received invaluable help from my two editors, Tom Weldon of Heinemann and Kathy Walton Banks of Edward Burlingame Books.

CHRONOLOGY

1870
19.7   Franco–Prussian War begins
2.9   Napoleon III defeated at Sedan
3.9   wedding of Dr Adrien Proust (b. 18.3.1834) and
         Jeanne-Clémence Weil (b. 21.3.1849)
4.9   Second Republic proclaimed
19.9   siege of Paris begins

1871
28.1   Paris capitulates and armistice signed with Germany
15.2   Thiers elected president
18.3   rising of Commune
?3 or 4 Dr Proust almost killed by a bullet
10.7   Marcel Proust born
5.8   baptised

1873
24.4   Thiers resigns and MacMahon elected president
         Robert Proust born
1.8   the family moves to 9, boulevard Malesherbes
19.12   Dr Proust appointed director of Hospice de Sainte-
         Perrine at Auteuil

1877
20.6   appointed medical director of the Lariboisière hospital

1878
9   the family holidays at Illiers

1879
30.1   MacMahon resigns and Jules Grévy elected president
1.5   Proust falls over in the Champs-Élysées and breaks his
         nose

1880
?   starts at the Pape–Carpentier school

1881
?3 or 4   first asthma attack on the way back from the Bois de
             Boulogne
6.9   goes to Dieppe
?autumn   his first visit to the theatre

1882
2.10   starts at the Lycée Fontanes, which is renamed the
             Lycée Condorcet on 27.1.83

1883
3.8   second prize in natural science, fourth runner-up in
             Latin composition and fifth in French language
5–7   absent from school
8.8   *certificat d'études de grammaire*
8   holidays in Houlgate. Takes Greek lessons
10   moved up to third class in the *lycée*

1885
14.2   *tableau d'honneur*
31.3   last day at school: absent throughout summer term
9   Proust at Salies-de-Béarn
10   moved up to second class but absent for most of the
             term
28.12   Grévy re-elected president
31.12   Proust leaves the *lycée*

1886
3   being tutored by his mother; writes 'Les Nuages' and
             'L'Eclipse', an essay about Christopher Columbus
autumn   in Illiers
10   goes back into second class

1887
7   makes friends with Marie Benardaky in the Champs-
             Élysées
14.7   watches a parade in honour of General Boulanger
2.8   second prizes in history and geography
10   starts two years of preparation for *baccalauréat*; gets to
             know Robert Dreyfus, Jacques Bizet, Daniel Halévy
             and Pierre Lavallée

1888

31.7	first prize for French composition
7.9	stays with Éduard Joyant in L'Isle–Adam
9	takes dancing lessons
1.10	in M. Darlu's philosophy class
10?	the *Revue lilas* and the *Revue verte* are started at the *lycée*. Proust writes a theatre column for the *Revue lilas*
12	meets Laure Hayman

1889

19.3	his paternal grandmother dies
1.4	Tour Eiffel completed in time for the International Fair
15.7	*certificat d'aptitude au grade de bachelier ès lettres*
30.7	first prize in French composition
9	stays with the Finalys in Ostende
10	meets Mme Arman de Caillavet and Anatole France; makes friends with Gaston de Caillavet
11.11	signs on for military service

1890

3.1	death of his maternal grandmother
2	meets Robert de Billy
summer	learns to ride, has a fall, gives up riding
9	on leave joins his mother in Cabourg
22.9	back to camp
14.11	returns to Paris
11	enrols first for law school and then for political science friendship with Mme Straus begins

1891

21.3	sees Réjane in *Germinie Lacerteux*
9	in Cabourg
1.10	at 'Les Frémonts' in Trouville with M. and Mme Arthur Baignères
11/12	meets Oscar Wilde

1892

7.1	*garçon d'honneur* at wedding of Henri Bergson and Louise Neuberger
1	friendship with Fernand Gregh, who founds the review *Le Banquet* with Proust, Robert Dreyfus, Jacques Bizet, Horace Finaly, Louis de la Salle and Daniel Halévy

8–9	spends four weeks with Reynaldo Hahn at Mme Lemaire's château, Reveillon
14 or 15–23.9	stays in Trouville with his mother
23–25.9	stays on alone
27.12?	Reynaldo takes him to the Daudets for the first time

1895

5.1	Dreyfus stripped of his rank
15–17.1	Casimir-Périer resigns as president and Félix Faure elected
29.5	applies for unpaid job at Bibliothèque Mazarine
7	goes to Kreuznach with his mother, works on *Jean Santeuil*
end of 7	given two months' leave from library
7/8	stays with the Daudets at Champrosay and, together with Reynaldo, with Mme Lemaire at Dieppe
8	submits his story 'La Mort de Baldassare Silvande' to the *Revue hebdomadaire*
9	goes with Reynaldo to Belle-Île-en-Mer and Begmeil
31.10	in Reveillon, writes 'Les Maronniers'
11	writes an essay on Chardin after looking at his paintings in the Louvre

1896

ca 31.1	reviews Lemaître's *La Bonne Hélène* at the Vaudeville
28.3	galley proofs of his book 'Château de Reveillon' (later retitled *Les Plaisirs et les jours*)
15–17.4	page proofs
10.5	Louis Weil dies
9.6	Anatole France's preface to *Les Plaisirs et les jours* published in *Le Figaro*
12.6	the book published
30.6	Nathé Weil dies
8.8	goes to Mont-Dore with his mother for almost three weeks; works on *Jean Santeuil*
19.10	moves to Fontainebleau
25/6.10	returns to Paris
11	developing relationship with Lucien Daudet
12	meets Marie Nordlinger

1897

6.2	fights duel with Jean Lorrain, whose review of *Les Plaisirs et les jours* implied a homosexual relationship with Lucien Daudet

13.10	goes back to Venice
mid-10	his parents move into a new flat at 45, rue de Courcelles
late 10	returns to Paris and settles in the new flat

1901

6.?5	gives a soirée at which poems by Anna de Noailles are recited
19.6	gives a dinner party in honour of Anna de Noailles
7.9	expedition with the Yeatmans to Amiens and Abbeville

1902

spring	working on notes for Ruskin translation
May/June	friendship with Fénelon; dinners at Larue's
6.9	visit to the Daudets at Prey
3.10	leaves with Fénelon for Holland
19 or 20.10	returns to Paris
11.11	enlists in territorial army
11	quarrels with mother about dissipating energy
6.12	accepts commission from the *Mercure de France* to finish Ruskin translation by 1.2
8.12	Fénelon posted to Constantinople

1903

2.2	Robert Proust marries
15.2	excerpt from translation published in Constantin de Brancovan's *La Renaissance latine*
25.2	first of Proust's articles on salons published in *Le Figaro*
7.3	threatens to move out
1.4	gives a dinner party
21.4	motoring expedition with friends
11.5	article on Mme Lemaire's salon published pseudonymously
6	writes postscript to preface for translation
18.6	incipient friendship with Albufera and Louisa de Mornand celebrated in long poem about her charms
16.7	gives dinner party with Gaston Calmette, editor of *Le Figaro*, as guest of honour
31.8	leaves for Evian, where he stays from 1.9 till 10.10
26.11	father dies, not quite seventy
2 or 3.12	Proust starts work again, correcting proofs

1904

18.1   pastiche of Balzac published pseudonymously in *Le Figaro*
2   Marie Nordlinger helps him with translation
?10.4   spends a night with Louisa
end 6   gives a party for Fénelon
17.7   consults Dr Merklen, who suggests German clinic to cure asthma habit
16.8   'La Mort des cathédrales' published in *Le Figaro*
8.11   Louisa opens in the role Proust has secured for her in Henry Bataille's *Maman Colibri*

1905

5.1   gives dinner party for Fénelon
2   starts on translation of Ruskin's *Sesame and Lilies*
2.6   gives a soirée at which Montesquiou reads
15.6   'Sur la lecture' published in *La Renaissance latine*
28.6   sees the comtesse Greffulhe at princesse Murat's
28.7   consultation with Dr Brissaud
8   article on Montesquiou appears in *Les Arts de la vie*
6 or 7.9   arrives with his mother at Evian. Both are ill. Robert arrives to take her home
13.9   Proust returns to Paris
26.9   she dies, aged fifty-six
ca 2.12   consultation with Dr Sollier
ca 3.12   moves into clinic in Boulogne

1906

ca 24.1   returns to flat
3   friendship with Illan de Casa-Fuerte
5.5   his review of Ruskin's *The Stones of Venice* (trans. Mme Crémieux) published in the *Chronique des arts*
12.5   copies of *Sesame and Lilies* ready
6   starts routine of sleeping by day and working at night
6.8   moves into Hôtel des Réservoirs at Versailles, taking Félicie Fitau as servant
7.8   his uncle Georges dies
9   plans for collaboration with René Peter on play
10   decides to rent flat in boulevard Haussmann
27.12   moves in

1907

24.1   Henri van Blarenberghe kills his mother and himself
1.2   Proust's 'Sentiments filiaux d'un parricide' published in *Le Figaro*

3   employs a valet, Nicolas Cottin

9.3   his review of Gabriel Mouray's *Gainsborough* published in the *Chronique des arts*

mid-3   writes review of Anna de Noailles' *Les Éblouissements* for *Le Figaro*, where it finally appears on 15.6

20.3   'Journées de lecture' published in *Le Figaro*

4   sponsors Illan de Casa-Fuerte for membership of the Cercle de l'Union

11.4   attends the princesse de Polignac's ball

early 5   employs Nicolas' wife Céline

1.7   Félicie Fitau leaves; gives big dinner party at Ritz for Calmette

23.7   'Une Grandmère' published in *Le Figaro*

early 8   leaves for Cabourg

?.9   returns to Paris

19.11   'Impressions de route en automobile' published in *Le Figaro*

26.12   his obituary of Gustave de Borda published in *Le Figaro*

1908

     starts essay 'Contre la méthode de Sainte-Beuve'

early 1   drafts 'Robert et le chevreau'

9.1   Lemoine scandal breaks

22.1   pastiches of Balzac, the Goncourts, Michelet and Faguet published in *Le Figaro*'s literary supplement

late 2   visits Helleu

14.3   pastiches of Flaubert and Sainte-Beuve published in *Le Figaro*

21.3   pastiche of Renan published in *Le Figaro*

late 4   starts on the novel

spring   thanks to Guiche he is elected a member of the Polo de Paris

18.7   leaves for Cabourg

8   meets Gaston Gallimard and invites him to dinner in Cabourg with Robert Gangnat and Louisa

9   friendship with Marcel Plantevignes

8.9   writes pseudonymous review of Lucien Daudet's *Le Chemin mort* for *L'Intransigeant*

end 9   moves into Hôtel des Réservoirs at Versailles

early 11   returns to Paris flat

12   works on study of Sainte-Beuve, parodies Chateaubriand and reads Saint-Simon

1909

1–2	ill but working on book
6.3	pastiche of Régnier published in *Le Figaro*
6	working flat out on book but writes pastiche of Ruskin
8	submits book to *Mercure de France*, who reject it, but Calmette offers to publish it serially in *Le Figaro*
15.8	leaves for Cabourg
end 9	returns
mid-11	reads parts of book to Reynaldo and Georges de Lauris
early 12	delivers manuscript to *Le Figaro*

1910

28.1	flooding in Paris
3	reworks opening of book to accommodate criticisms by Beaunier
18.3	meets Jean Cocteau
early 6	sees Nijinsky in *Scheherazade*
11.6	sees *Cléopâtre* and *Les Sylphides* with the comtesse Greffulhe
17.7	collects manuscript from *Le Figaro*
17.7	leaves for Cabourg
8	friendship with the vicomte d'Alton
end 9	returns to Paris in a taxi
11	working on *Swann* and 'Matinée chez la princesse de Guermantes'

1911

10.1	Théâtrophone installed in his room
late 2	listens to an act of *Die Meistersinger* and to *Pelléas et Mélisande*
3	friendship with Louis de Robert
11.7	leaves for Cabourg with Albert Nahmias
end 9	returns to Paris
12	sustains heavy losses through a stock-exchange speculation

1912

21.3	extract from *Swann* published in *Le Figaro*
end 4	submits novel to publishers
4	drives in Odilon Albaret's taxi to see apple blossom at Rueil
24.5	observes contrasting dresses of comtesse Greffulhe and Mme Standish
4.6	more excerpts in *Le Figaro*
7.8	leaves for Cabourg

3.9	'L'Église de village' in *Le Figaro*; visit to Honfleur with Mme Straus
5.9	returns to Paris
28.10	sends typescript of novel to Fasquelle
early 11	sends it to Gallimard, and an extract to Copeau for the *NRF*
ca 23.12	Gallimard rejects it
24.12	Fasquelle rejects it; Proust asks de Robert to approach Ollendorff

1913

early 1	sends manuscript to Ollendorff
end 1	studies the Sainte-Anne door of Notre Dame
mid-2	Ollendorff rejects novel
ca 20.2	Proust asks René Blum to approach Grasset
11.3	contract with Grasset signed
25.3	'Vacances de Pâques' published in *Le Figaro*
31.3	first proofs printed
19.4	hears the César Franck violin sonata
end 4	heavy loss on stock exchange
mid-5	returns first set of corrected proofs
17.5	sees Nijinsky in *L'Après-midi d'un faune*, and dines with him
29.5	sees première of *Le Sacre du printemps*; dines with Stravinsky and Cocteau
30.5	Alfred Agostinelli and Anna move in
26.7	they all go to Cabourg
4.8	they return to Paris
8	sends proofs of *Swann* to Louis de Robert and Lucien Daudet
13.11	interview with Élie-Joseph Bois published in *Le Temps*
14.11	*Swann* appears in the bookshops
11	Proust uses Céleste Albaret to deliver copies to friends
1.12	Agostinelli leaves

1914

11.1	Gide writes, supporting the novel against review in the *NRF* by Henri Ghéon
end 1	Fasquelle offers to publish remainder of novel
20.3	Gide makes same offer for NRF
5	Proust offers to write a regular column for *Le Figaro*
30.5	Agostinelli crashes his plane into sea and drowns
6.6	proofs begin to arrive but he is too depressed to correct them
6 & 7	excerpts in *Le Figaro*

28.7–4.8   war breaks out
8   Nicolas is conscripted and Céleste moves in
3.9   leaves for Cabourg with her and her new valet Ernst
           Forssgren
ca 13.10 returns to Paris after running out of cash – banks
           immobilised by war
10   telephone disconnected
17.12   Fénelon killed at front but death not confirmed till
           3.15

1915
14.1   Gaston de Caillavet dies
1   publication of the novel suspended, Grasset being at
           the front
9   army doctors give him six months' reprieve on call-
           up
11   has fully plotted out the Albertine relationship and
           summarises it for Mme Scheikévitch

1916
24.2   Gide calls on him offering to have novel published by
           the NRF
14.4   editorial committee sanctions this offer
spring   visits to Le Cuziat's male brothel and finishes *Le Temps
           retrouvé*
31.5   claims to be bankrupt and to have had no money from
           the five editions of *Swann* which have appeared since
           1914
6   stays with Blanche in Auteuil
29.8   Grasset releases him
11   Poulet quartet gives him a private performance of
           César Franck

1917
           works on *Le Temps retrouvé*
1   friendship with Paul Morand
3   meets Morand's friend the princesse Soutzo and starts
           dining at the Ritz, where she has a suite
spring   expresses fears for Laon cathedral and relocates
           Combray and Tansonville near Laon; friendship with
           Emmanuel Berl
12.4   last meeting with Emmanuel Bibesco
5   writes on Dostoevsky; incorporates piece in novel
27.7   watches air-raid from a balcony at the Ritz
late 8   Proust gives no sign of life for two days

13.10	Morand appointed as secretary to Rome embassy
11	sells furniture to pay interest on a loan taken out in 1911
31.12	long nocturnal walk with two young American soldiers

1918

	employs new secretary, Henri Rochat
30.1	walks about Paris during air-raid
2	friendship with the abbé Mugnier
early 4	facial paralysis and speech difficulties make him consult Dr Babinski
mid-4	receives final proofs for *Jeunes Filles*
5	works on preface for Blanche's *Propos de peintres*
mid-5	receives rest of *Jeunes Filles* proofs
6	discusses with Gallimard a collection of pastiches and articles
9	daily meetings with Robert, convalescent after car accident at front
30.11	printing of *Jeunes Filles* completed
12	receives first galleys of *Guermantes*. *Pastiches et mélanges* sent to printer

1919

mid-1	learns aunt has sold house: he will have to move
3	speech difficulties
25.4	agrees to have publication delayed till after excerpt has appeared in first post-war *NRF* (1.6)
30.5	moves to furnished flat in house belonging to Réjane
1.6	excerpt of *Jeunes Filles* in *NRF*
9	decides to try for Prix Goncourt
1.10	moves to flat in rue Hamelin
10.12	announcement he has won Goncourt

1920

1.1	his essay on Flaubert in the *NRF*
3	writes article on Léon Daudet
end 3	agrees to have first half of *Guermantes* published separately
early 4	de-luxe edition of *Jeunes Filles* published
ca 23.5	returns final proofs for first half of *Guermantes*
25.9	made Chevalier de la Légion d'honneur
30.9	arranges for Jacques Rivière to be awarded Blumenthal prize

I

1871–88
Fragile Boyhood

ONE

MY LITTLE WOLF

Auteuil was still a rustic village, and the house was a large one, set in a big park with tall chestnut trees, lawns, flowerbeds, well-kept gravel paths, a fountain and a fishpond. A stronghold of bourgeois taste, it was furnished in the Louis-Philippe style, with upholstered armchairs and heavy curtains on the windows. It belonged to Proust's fifty-four-year-old great-uncle, Louis Weil, who'd made his fortune from a button factory employing 5,000 workers, but in November 1870, when his wife died, he retired to Auteuil and devoted his life mainly to actresses and courtesans. His young niece's new husband, Dr Adrien Proust, disapproved strongly, but their baby was born in this house at Auteuil.

Since their wedding on 3 September, Adrien and Jeanne Proust had been living in the rue Roy, a small street linking the boulevard Haussmann to the rue la Boétie. The flat cost 2,500 francs a month, but this was a time in which wealth could buy neither comfort nor security. The pregnancy, which began a few weeks after the wedding, coincided with one of the most turbulent periods in the history of Paris. The Second Empire had ended a day before the wedding, when Napoleon III surrendered to Bismarck's army at Sedan, but, defying the leaders of the new republic, Paris held out against the Prussians though the winter was so severe that the Seine and the fountains froze. Supplies of coal and wood ran out; food was in such short supply that people were eating cats, dogs and even rats. Adrien Proust, who'd been active during the 1866 cholera epidemic in promoting the idea of a *cordon sanitaire*, was half expecting a new outbreak of the disease.[1]

On 28 January 1871 an armistice was signed, but the ordeal of Proust's pregnant mother wasn't over. In March, after the Prussian army paraded down the Champs-Élysées, the humiliated city erupted in four months of the worst street-fighting it had seen since 1848, and one day while Adrien Proust was

on his way to the Hôpital de la Charité, where he was head
of clinical medicine, a bullet narrowly missed him. The Commune, which was set up on the day of the armistice, ruled Paris
viciously for two months, shooting hostages and demolishing
buildings. Though the pregnant wife was reluctant to be parted
from her husband, she took refuge in her uncle's house on the
far side of the Bois de Boulogne, and it was here, at 96 rue de
Lafontaine, that the baby was born on 10 July 1871, a boy.
He'd been weakened so severely by psychological and physical
pressures she'd suffered throughout the pregnancy that he
wasn't expected to survive. His hold on life remained precarious, and if it hadn't been for his father's professional skills, his
life might have been extremely short. As it was, his pre-natal
experience left marks on his constitutional make-up, and on
his relationship with his mother, who felt it was her fault he'd
emerged from her womb in such a pitiful condition.

It was probably in government circles that she'd met Adrien
Proust, a thirty-six-year-old doctor, son of an Illiers grocer
who'd intended him for the priesthood. As a schoolboy he'd
relished the idea, and a sense of vocation survived in his energetic devotion to medical work and especially in his concern
for public hygiene. In 1869 he travelled to Russia and Persia
on a government mission to investigate how cholera spread,
and on his return in 1870 he was decorated with a Légion
d'honneur.

Fifteen years his junior, good-looking, well-read, shy, intelligent, his wife was the daughter of a rich Jewish stockbroker,
Nathé Weil; her mother, Adèle Berncastel, was the great-niece
of Adolphe Crémieux, who'd been minister of justice in 1848
and had fought in 1851 against the Napoleonic *coup d'état* which
turned the Second Republic into the Second Empire. He
resumed his role as minister of justice in the new republican
government.

Marriages between well-connected Jewish and gentile families were quite common. The arrangement between the Prousts
was that, while she wouldn't convert, the children would be
brought up as Catholics. At the age of four weeks, the baby
was baptised at the local church, St-Louis d'Antin. His given
names were Marcel-Valentin-Louis-Eugène-Georges.

They didn't live long enough in the rue Roy for the flat to
leave any traces in Marcel's memory. He was only just over a
year old when his mother became pregnant again, and the

doctor decided they should move to a big second-floor flat in
the boulevard Malesherbes, between the Madeleine and the rue
de Courcelles. It was shortly after Marcel's second birthday
that they made the move. Their new home had all the latest
luxuries – running water, gas lighting, coal-fired central heating (when most of the central heating in Paris was based on
wood fires), a bathroom, a lavatory, a gas-cooker with a pilot-
light, a hotplate in the service hatch in the wall of the dining-
room. The flat had 'the sumptuous spaciousness of the homes
of the moneyed bourgeoisie in the years 1890–1900. The
impression I have kept,' wrote Proust's friend Fernand Gregh,
'is of a rather dark interior, chock-full of bulky furniture,
draught-proofed with curtains, suffocated with carpets, the
whole black and red, the flat typical of the period, which was
not so distant as we used to believe from the sombre Balzacian
bric-à-brac.'² The drawing-room had what Proust was to call
'a wholly medical ugliness . . . in which the bronzes, the palm
trees, the plush and the mahogany played their respective
parts'.³

The building even boasted a lift. Only a few blocks away
from the rue Roy, the boulevard was just twelve years old.
On each of its seven storeys the house had a wide balcony
fronted by an iron balustrade. In the forecourt was a row of
small lean-to workshops. Closest to the imposing double doors
was a cobbler's shop, where the concierge mended shoes. He
also worked as a tailor and reared poultry and rabbits in the
courtyard. Living at the far end of it was a comtesse. Wearing
a hat trimmed with irises, and driving out behind two big
horses in a barouche that raised her liveried footman's head to
the level of the first-floor windows, she waved to the water-
carrier, to neighbours, to the concierge's children. She stopped
frequently as she drove along the boulevard, sending the footman to leave visiting cards and fetch shopkeepers to the carriage door for orders.

This was the infant Marcel's first experience of the aristocracy, but during the first three years of his life nothing made
so much impact on him as the loss of undivided attention from
his mother. He was too young to know what was going on,
but it became more difficult to nestle into a comfortable position on her lap. The soft, warm, welcoming stomach was
getting bigger. He was still being cuddled, but something was
pushing him further away from the middle of her body, and

preparations were being made for an event which had nothing
to do with him. Then, on 24 May 1873, another baby boy
was born. It was incomprehensible that anyone should have
thought another baby was needed, but they all seemed to like
him, and there was no way to get rid of him. He was christened
Robert-Émile-Sigismond-Léon, and at first he had more of a
hold on his mother's attention than his sickly sibling, who
knew instinctively she felt responsible for his frailty, and,
partly because the new baby was normal and healthy, it was
soon possible to get more attention from her by producing a
new symptom or emphasising an old one.

Fierce and possessive, the mutual adoration of young mother
and ailing boy made the placid, healthy baby a pig-in-the-
middle. She called Marcel 'mon petit loup' and Robert 'mon
autre loup'. In *Contre Sainte-Beuve* Robert appears in his high-
chair, saying Marcel has been given more blancmange than he
has, and the siblings squabbled endlessly. Robert was never to
forget a quarrel in which they came to blows and Marcel tried
to break his drum. Marcel's jealousy was the more deadly,
though repressed and compensated by a protectiveness towards
his younger brother modelled on his mother's towards him.
Recalling life at the age of three, Robert wrote: 'I find constantly the image of my brother, watching over me with a
gentleness that was infinite, enveloping and almost maternal.'[4]
But Robert, instinctively realising he'd lost his mother to his
rival, went all out to win love from his father.

The boys were dressed like characters in a costume drama.
Jeanne Proust's love of theatre increased her pleasure in choosing clothes for the small supporting actors who graced her
appearances in the park, in shops and in front of visitors.
Unintentionally, she was encouraging their childish exhibition-
ism. One photograph shows them carrying little canes and
dressed like princes in clothes trimmed with fur and lace. In
another photograph, taken when Marcel was six, they're
dressed almost identically in long jackets that end in kilt-like
skirts and are decorated with a double row of brass buttons
down the front. There are more buttons on the sleeves and on
the deep, wide, sporran-like pockets. Marcel has a wide Eton
collar, and Robert a lace collar, both with big silk cravats.
Both boys are beautifully coiffured; both wear white handkerchiefs in their breast pocket. In cold weather, when the boys

wore fur muffs, the cook baked jacket potatoes to keep their hands warm.[5]

Their father held strong views about the way children should be reared. In the two books on hygiene he published in 1881 and 1883,[6] he maintained that people – especially children – were harmed by impure air, noise and contact with crowds. In December 1873, he was appointed medical director of the Hospice de Sainte-Perrine at Auteuil. Always energetic, and unscared of a heavy workload, he was still clinical director of the Hôpital de la Charité, as well as being a consultant at Parvis Notre-Dame and the Hôtel-Dieu, and serving on the *corps médical* at the Opéra-Comique. But, overcoming his misgivings about Louis Weil's way of life, he got the children out of Paris during spring and early summer by staying in the house at Auteuil. You could go there on a *bateau-mouche* decorated with flags and streamers. Laundry-boats were still to be seen moored at quays along the Seine, with brightly coloured washing hanging up to dry. While the family was holidaying in Auteuil, the doctor could go to the Hôpital de la Charité or the Hôtel-Dieu by bus: it was less than an hour's journey. Nathé Weil came to dine in Auteuil every evening, but always went back to sleep in Paris. In eighty-five years he left Paris only once – when the city was under siege and he went to instal his wife at Étampes.[7]

For Marcel the pleasure of arriving in Auteuil was inseparable from the scent of the lime trees in the street outside the house. The bedroom he was given there had Empire-blue satin curtains, and he never forgot the wardrobe with its mirror doors or the characteristic smells of the house – the soap, the gruyère cheese, the cherries and apricots in the fruit dish. He drank cider 'from tumblers so thick one was tempted to bite the glass', and in the dining-room the knives and forks were propped on cut-glass prisms which threw iridescent peacock-feather patterns on the walls.[8]

The house and the park at Auteuil were important in Proust's childhood, but less important than the grey sandstone market-town fifteen miles to the south-west of Chartres. It was then called Illiers, and the family regularly spent the Easter holidays there, but, writing about it as if a major part of his childhood had been spent there, he called it Combray, and Illiers-Combray is now its official name.

In Paris the boys saw relatively little of their busy father, but when he joined them on holiday, even if it was only for the weekend, they saw more of their parents together. Jeanne Proust adored her husband and in *Swann*, when the family goes for a long moonlight walk around Combray the husband stops abruptly to ask his wife where they are. When she lovingly confesses she has no idea, he shrugs and points to the gate of his sister's house.[9]

Dr Proust's invalid sister, Élisabeth, was married to Jules Amiot, a prosperous draper, twelve years her senior. Their servant, Ernestine, who stayed with them for thirty-three years, cooked elaborate meals. Amiot, whose shop was 'permeated with the smell of Holland cloth', was a keen amateur painter, shutting himself away to work in the extension to the house, decorated with souvenirs of his travels in Algeria – rugs, carved coconuts, photographs of mosques and palm trees.

On the edge of the town he'd created a large private park in the English style, and called it the Pré Catalan, after the park in the Bois de Boulogne. When I visited it in 1989, the outside of the octagonal summer house had been disfigured by the words 'SEX PISTOLS' sprayed in black paint, but the park has been well preserved, with trees drooping opulently over hilly but extensive lawns, well-tended flowerbeds colourfully interrupting the broad stretches of green, neatly trimmed hedges, and domed, oriental-looking dovecotes. The young Marcel must have felt privileged to be playing in a private park bigger than any garden in the town.

Sometimes the boys would be taken to the swimming baths. When Jean Santeuil, Proust's *alter ego* in his first novel, stands on the raft, staring at the huge liquid cavern which bellies out in front of him under plunging bodies, he almost thinks he's at the entrance to the underworld. Normally Jean never sees his mother in a state of undress, but when she swims in the pool, laughing, splashing, blowing kisses up to him, and when she climbs out, 'beautiful under her little rubber helmet with water dripping off her body, he would not have been surprised if he had been told he was the son of a goddess and that he had therefore been allowed to see the entrance to this fantastic world, unknown to everyone else'.[10]

Marcel was impressed by his invalid Aunt Élisabeth. It would never have occurred to him that his life was going to repeat the pattern of hers, but he admired the control she could exert over other people without stirring from her bed. In the novel Aunt Léonie regularly gives the little boy a piece of madeleine dipped in lime-blossom tea. Since her husband's death she's been increasingly immobile, and now stirs from her bed only when the room is being aired, spending most of her time staring out of the windows at the road which, 'monotonous and greyish, with three high sandstone steps in front of almost each door, seemed like a gorge created by some sculptor of Gothic images from the same stone he could have used for a crib or a calvary'. Her two rooms are 'saturated with the fine essence of a silence so nourishing, so succulent, that I could never go in without a sort of greed'.

But there was no hunger to rival his constant need for his mother. The moment he was separated from her, he felt impatient to be with her again, and if his parents went out for dinner or spent an evening at the theatre, the little boy would lie awake, torturing himself. What if the theatre caught fire while they were inside? What if the horse ran away with the carriage?[11] In 1905, when Jeanne Proust was dying, and her elder son was thirty-four, she was still – according to the nurse looking after her – treating him like a four-year-old,[12] and for the rest of his life he went on seeing himself partly through her eyes. To himself he'd always be 'little Marcel'. 'When I'm dead,' he told his housekeeper, Céleste Albaret, 'you'll always go on thinking about little Marcel.'

His habit of holding his hand against his cheek may have derived from the feeling of his mother's fingers caressing him. She gave the impression of being more concerned about his welfare than her own, though he often felt jealous of the time she devoted to his father and his brother. Believing he could always discover himself 'at the root of her intentions'[13] he used her as his mirror, and they were never closer than during childhood illnesses, when she read to him and took complete charge of his routine. When his father was away or wanted a second opinion and other doctors were called in, she didn't give Marcel the medicines they prescribed, dieting him instead on milk until his temperature went down and his pulse steadied. Then a sole would be cooked for him.[14]

Robert was given no chance to become so dependent on her, but at Illiers in 1879, when Marcel was going to be left with his father for a few days after she went away with Robert, the five-year-old child made as much fuss about being separated from his pet kid as his seven-year-old brother did about separation from their mother, who was already in the habit of using classical allusions to give him courage. 'Leonidas could face calamities with fortitude. I hope my threepenny-piece is going to prove his equal.'[15] He made an effort, only to find, for once, that he was upstaged by his brother, who threw a tantrum. Robert had been dressed up to have his photograph taken. He was wearing his best frock and his lace petticoat. His hair had been set with curling tongs and dressed with large bows. His biscuits, his hairbrush and his comb, together with two or three pocket mirrors, had been packed for him into several small satin bags. Upset at the prospect of being separated from the kid, he talked to it, sang to it, smashed the mirrors, trampled on the bags and scared his mother by sitting down on the railway track at an ungated crossing where a train might pass any minute.

Both boys would have liked to punish their mother by making her miss the train, but it was Marcel who was going to be separated from her. For fear of the fuss he'd make, his parents didn't want to take him to the station, but they let themselves be persuaded, and, out of consideration for her feelings, Marcel kissed her less than he wanted to. Leaning out of the carriage window and beckoning him back when his father wasn't looking, she said: 'We understand each other's feelings, don't we, my lamb? If my dear boy behaves sensibly, he'll get a little letter from his mamma tomorrow. *Sursum corda.*'[16]

If, for Jeanne Proust, there was nothing odd in talking about Leonidas and using Latin tags when talking to children, the explanation is to be found in the influence of her highly educated mother, Adèle Weil, who never went anywhere without a volume of Mme de Sévigné's letters or Mme de Beausergent's memoirs.[17] Like many of the girls growing up into rich Jewish bourgeois families in nineteenth-century Paris, Adèle had been educated by parents under the influence of Saint-Simon, who believed society could be transformed through industrial progress and the aristocracy could be intellectualised. Nathanaël Berncastel and Rose Silny wanted Adèle to be capable of shining in literary salons.

Adéle Weil was ten years younger than her husband, and only ten years older than Dr Proust. Marcel loved being with her, and in *Swann* the grandmother is described as 'so humble of heart and so gentle that her tenderness to other people and her lack of concern for herself and her own sufferings were combined on her face in a smile which, unlike the one seen on most human faces, had no irony in it, except towards herself, and for all of us it was like a kiss from those eyes which could not look at those she loved without caressing them passionately with their glances'.[18]

Well versed in the arts and passionately literary, she had learnt a good deal from her great uncle, Adolphe Crémieux, and had attended his wife's salon, where she met Victor Hugo, George Sand, Musset, Lamartine, Rossini and the actress Rachel. By giving Marcel George Sand's novels, Adèle Weil helped to inculcate 'a nostalgia for impossible journeys through time'.[19] Believing adventure stories to be as damaging to children as pastries and sweets, she helped to make her grandsons precocious. The earliest of Marcel's extant letters, written from Auteuil when he was nine to a second cousin, Pauline Neuberger, thanks her for sending him books,[20] and a letter written when Robert was nine says he and Marcel, having already read the first two novels in Lucien Biart's series *Les Voyages involuntaires*, were looking forward to the third. Adèle Weil, who'd brought up her daughter to take as much pleasure in books as she did, soon introduced both grandsons to Musset, Rousseau and Saint-Simon.[21] Her conversations with her daughter were enthusiastically literary; Marcel and Robert heard them both quoting freely from Racine and Mme de Sévigné,[22] while Jeanne Proust copied into a notebook favourite passages from books she read.

She read a great deal to Marcel in a voice which seemed to caress both him and the words. In *Swann* Mamma leaves out all the love scenes when she reads from George Sand's *François le champi*. 'If my mother was an unfaithful reader, she was also, for books where she found the tone of true feeling, an admirable reader in the respectfulness and simplicity of the interpretation, in the beauty and sweetness of the sound.' Reading George Sand she was 'careful to exclude from her voice all pettiness and affectation which could have held up the powerful flow, she supplied all the natural tenderness, all the succulent sweetness required by sentences which seemed to have been written for her voice and which were all, so to speak, within the range of her sensitivity'.[23] She also read poetry to him – 'verses which dealt with the noblest simplicities, summer and wind, sunsets and church bells and the sea'[24] but she fails to arouse any enthusiasm in him for Victor Hugo's *Les Contemplations* or Corneille's *Horace*.

Associating literature with the mother he loved so passionately, he soon developed an insatiable appetite for it, and the pleasures of reading were scarcely less sensuous than the pleasures of eating, drinking and being tucked up in bed.

> When we were young there was always one book we carried to the park and read with a passion no other book could quite supplant. In those days we were never so absorbed by the contents of the book as to be indifferent to the actual feel of the pages we turned. . . . Holding it in our hands and looking at its pages, we never, in our mind, separated its contents from the softness of its thin pages, from its lovely smell, from the fine, stiff, binding with the gilded corners. . . . The thin pages with their wide margins on which here and there a date had been scribbled, as in a notebook of the same shape, made us feel we were imbibing instruction during those delicious hours and that the thrilling objects, from which we would not willingly have been parted, were the very treasury of truth. I remember that smell as being just as sweet as the smell of the great press in which clean linen and pink biscuits were kept.[25]

With his sensitivity to smells and his keen ability to remember them, he went on associating clean linen with the favourite moment of being tucked up. 'You have only to take a handkerchief from a drawer and smell the subtle fragrance of fresh linen, to know, to feel again, that moment of arriving in the country, that moment when, dinner done, your mother put you to bed after first dressing you in a fine white nightshirt, in white sheets, with a white pillow for your head, in a room where the window gave on to a little garden which you could not see because you had arrived so late. . . .'[26]

It was with his Jewish mother and his Jewish grandmother that Marcel felt most at ease. Both father and son were so shy that neither could break through the other's reserve. In *Swann* the father's 'unpredictable acts of kindness had given me when they occurred such a strong desire to kiss the red cheeks above the beard that if I did not give in, it was only from fear of displeasing him'.[27] Wanting his son to grow into a strong, manly man, the father is 'irritated by what he called sob-stuff'.[28] But it was probably the doctor who intervened in his son's favour when his wife sent the boy to bed without a goodnight kiss – a deprivation which has become more notorious than any act of cruelty to children in Dickens' novels.

It was one night when Marcel was about seven that she deviated from the routine of tucking him up. We'll never know exactly what happened, though the incident monopolises both the first chapter of *Jean Santeuil*, which he wrote in his late twenties, and the opening of *À la recherche*. In *Jean Santeuil*, which is more directly autobiographical, the boy's health is delicate, his disposition nervous, and both parents, eager to make him more manly, take care not to give in too often. Together with his grandfather, the gruff M. Sandré, and their visitor, a doctor, they're sitting in the garden. The light in the boy's bedroom is switched off, but it goes on again, and they see him in his white nightgown, opening the window to call his mother, who warns him he's in danger of catching a cold.

As he snuggles back under the blankets, knowing she'll come, he also knows she'll be angry. The kiss will be meaningless and though she'll conceal her mood, he'll pay tomorrow for tonight's misdemeanour. His nervousness disappears as he's kissed, but, jumping out of bed when she's about to go, he tearfully clings to her. The sobbing brings on a feeling of tightness in his chest and she resigns herself to lying down next to him. When she finally rejoins the adults on the lawn, the doctor remarks that, at the age of seven, unhappiness is fortunately not a serious matter. Part of Proust's purpose is to expose this as nonsense. 'Jean was right to take his misery seriously.'[29]

The strokes endured in those hours of childhood fell on the very metal of his heart and the sounds they gave off might well reverberate with a fuller, a more cracked or a deeper note as age set a harder crust upon his feelings. . . . The reader would be much mistaken should he think that, even in so trivial a matter as has been described, Jean ever changed completely. Habit, the only one of all the ancient powers of this world which is stronger than suffering, might overcome, little by little, the cruel torments . . . which through all his early years he still endured whenever evening came. But each time in youth, or even in maturity, that some circumstance occurred to suspend temporarily the anaesthetising effects of

habit . . . he would feel deep down within himself . . . the
awakening of a trouble old as his very life.

The main change in Marcel's life was that his parents lost faith
in their campaign to toughen him by imposing a discipline.
He'd learnt how to get his own way through a display of
weakness. In fact his willpower was formidably strong, but,
seeing it as weak, his parents and grandmother were ready to
be intimidated by weakness, and he wasn't slow in learning
how to use this powerful weapon, but he was right to be
saddened and frightened by his success.

The crux lies in his unconscious desire to monopolise his
mother, and the upset produces a climax in the struggle against
dependence on her. Irrationally guilty about his frailty, Jeanne
Proust has been innocently but irresistibly seductive: reacting
over-generously to physiological and emotional needs, she's
made him incurably dependent. In the tantrum the jealous
aggression was aimed partly at the seductive woman and partly
at the two main rivals – the smaller brother and the formidable
father who could speak with professional authority about the
danger of spoiling a boy by giving in. But in the fantasy world
he created in *Jean Santeuil* the younger rival is eliminated, while
the older one is deprived of his medical authority, and the
boy's name hints at an identification with Jeanne Proust.

Unable to monopolise her, the boy resents his dependence.
Telling himself the kiss is meaningless, he's trying to break
free, but he feels guilty about this, and in clinging to her he's
trying to wipe out his progress towards independence. If fiction
is always, as Flaubert says, 'the response to a deep and always
hidden wound', the chapter in *Jean Santeuil* is a prodigiously
elaborate response to the wound his mother inflicted when she
expected him to manage without a goodnight kiss.

With his faith in the value of fresh air and exercise, the
doctor liked the boys to play in the Champs-Élysées every day
unless it was raining. The playground there was much the
same as when Sigmund Freud described it in 1885: 'One side
of the avenue is formed by an extensive park in which the
prettiest children spin their tops, ride on merry-go-rounds,
watch the Punch-and-Judy show, or drive themselves about in
little carriages drawn by goats. Sitting on the benches are wet-
nurses feeding babies and nursemaids to whom the children
rush screaming when they have quarrelled.'[30] Nearby were

eight wooden booths selling barley-sugar, gingerbread, toy drums, marbles and windmills. During the spring of 1880, throwing himself too enthusiastically into a game of prisoners' base, Marcel fell over and broke his nose.

But if the doctor had legislative authority over the lives of his sons, the administration was in the hands of his wife, who had a striking physical and temperamental affinity with Marcel. Alphonse Daudet's son Lucien said she had 'the same long, full face, the same silent laughter when anything amused her, the same attentiveness to every word one uttered, that kind of attentiveness, which, in Marcel Proust, was taken for absent-mindedness because he looked as though his thoughts were elsewhere'.[31] Underlying his symbiotic relationship with his mother was his conviction they were both made of the same material, while his father was different. A minor government official, Jean Santeuil's father is inferior to his wife in intelligence, tact, artistic taste and sensitivity. He is unimpressed when she tells him Jean will have a feeling for poetry,[32] while she, convinced of his superiority to her, questions the value of artistic qualities since he gets on so well without them. With his respect for opinions expressed by members of the government, M. Santeuil is more likely to be influenced by the new foreign minister's high opinion of writers than by his wife's.[33]

Generally Marcel tried to forget that his parents' families were involved in traditions with different rituals and symbols. Occasionally the boys were taken to a synagogue, as when, in November 1881, their mother's first cousin Daniel Mayer, married Marguerite Lévy. That Proust wasn't proud of his half-Jewishness can be inferred from his avoidance of the subject in both fiction and letters. Neither the narrator's mother in *À la recherche* nor Jean Santeuil's mother is Jewish. Jean's is a blonde from an anti-Semitic family, but, except in the references to Dreyfus, the book has as little to say about anti-Semitism as it has about Jews and Jewishness. The first reference to anti-Semitism comes halfway through.

In all his writing about childhood, religious practice and belief play almost no part. In *Contre Sainte-Beuve* he complains about 'our old priest' who was always pulling his curls, 'an event which had been the terror and tyranny of my childhood'. It made him glad when his curls were cut off.[34] Generally, though, priests and religious services are rarely mentioned. This doesn't mean he was temperamentally irreligious. His

capacity for religious devotion filtered into his worship of his
mother and into the pleasure he took in domestic rituals. He
gave a quasi-religious edge to his pleasure in the taste of his
favourite foods and in things he loved, such as clean bed-linen,
or a fire in the cold bedroom where he had to get dressed. It
was an almost fetishistic fixation on pleasure-giving things that
etched them indelibly in his mind long before he thought of
writing about them.

Though there was still a streak of Puritanism in Adrien
Proust, whose temperament had been conditioned by his boyhood ambition to be a priest, he never tried to deprive his sons
of the basic pleasures, but his missionary devotion to medical
work left him with little time or enthusiasm for literature and
the arts. His connection with the Opéra-Comique brought him
into occasional contact with actors and actresses, and in
October 1881, Marie van Zandt, an American opera singer,
sent him a photograph of herself in male apparel: she is wearing
knee-length pantaloons with frills. But generally he regarded
actresses as no better than prostitutes. If an actress's name was
mentioned during mealtime conversations, he was liable to
turn disapprovingly to his wife: 'One of your uncle's friends.'[35]

Adrien Proust's Puritanism conflicted with the love of theatre his wife and her mother implanted in Marcel long before
he had his first experience of theatregoing at the age of ten.
His grandmother talked about the theatre a lot, and he formed
a vivid but inaccurate picture of the pleasures available in it.
As the Narrator tells us in *À la recherche*, 'I almost believed
that each of the spectators looked, as through a stereoscope,
at a scene that existed for himself alone.'[36] On the corner
opposite the house in the boulevard Malesherbes there was –
there still is – a column covered in advertisements.

Every morning I ran to the Morris column to see the advertisements for plays. Nothing was more disinterested or happier than the daydreams which were offered to my imagination
by each play announced and which were conditioned not
only by the images inseparable from the words forming the
titles but also by the colour of the posters still damp and
wrinkled with paste, on which the title stood out. Unless it
were one of such strange works as *Le Testament de César
Girodot* or *Oedipe-Roi*, which were printed not on the green
posters of the Opéra-Comique but on the wine-coloured

posters of the Comédie-Française, nothing seemed to me more different from the sparkling white plume of *Les Diamants de la couronne* than the sleek mysterious satin of *Le Domino noir*, and, my parents having told me that when I went to the theatre for the first time I would have to choose between these two pieces, trying to study each of the titles in turn, since that was all I had to go on, trying to apprehend in each the pleasure it promised and to compare it with the pleasure concealed in the other, I succeeded in picturing so vividly on the one hand a dazzling and arrogant play and on the other a gentle and velvety play that I was as incapable of deciding which one I preferred as if, for dessert, I had been given a choice between rice *à l'Impératrice* and *crème au chocolat.*'[37]

Le Testament de César Girodot was a play by Belot and Villetard; both *Les Diamants de la couronne* and *Le Domino noir* were comic operas by Scribe and Auber. He talked to friends about actors and compiled mental lists, arranging actors in order of merit. It was exciting to see the names of stars in big letters outside theatres, to watch an actor coming out of the stage door or to glimpse a beautiful woman in a passing brougham: perhaps she was an actress. Marcel was, as he later put it, a Platonic lover of the theatre.

Excited greed for future pleasures was inseparable from the excitement of living from day to day, but the rhythm of his life was shattered when he wasn't quite ten. One day in the spring of 1881, while the family was staying at Auteuil, they went for a walk with friends in the Bois de Boulogne. On the way back Marcel suddenly succumbed to a panicking attack of breathlessness, so severe that his father didn't expect him to survive it. Like most little boys in France, he was being brought up not to cry in the presence of his father, and this asthma attack may have developed out of suppressing the urge when he was desperate. Subsequent attacks were equally violent, and sometimes both distraught parents would sit up all night by his bed, doubtful whether he'd still be alive in the morning. During one of the worst attacks the doctor supported the suffocating child by propping up his pillows with big medical dictionaries and, during another, he sent for a colleague who gave the boy a morphine injection. The asthma was to stay with him, a constant if not entirely malleable factor in his complicated emotional transactions with his over-protective mother.

His life was permanently changed. 'A child who since birth has breathed without being careful about it is unaware how essential to his life is the air which swells his chest so gently that he does not even notice. Will he suffocate in a convulsion during a feverish attack? In the most desperate effort of his life, it is almost for survival that he is struggling, and for the vanished calm he will rediscover only with the air from which he did not know it to be inseparable.' This is Proust's account of his asthmatic breathlessness in an 1893 story which describes the asthma which is asphyxiating 'the poor suffocating patient who, through eyes filled with tears, smiles at the people who are sympathising without being able to help him'.[38]

TWO

ABSENTEE SCHOOLBOY

Proust grew up in a Paris which had undergone changes unparalleled in London, Vienna or Rome. The revolutions of 1789 and 1848 had left the old buildings and bridges intact: afterwards dirty water still flowed unhealthily through narrow, crooked, gutterless streets. But in 1853 baron Haussmann was given almost unlimited powers as préfet de la Seine, and he soon began to demolish neighbourhoods of cluttered houses in favour of the spacious tree-lined boulevards which gave Paris the configuration it still has. One advantage for the state was that wide thoroughfares made it harder for rebellious citizens to erect barricades and easier for cavalry to charge.

The Second Empire was a period of paternalistic encouragement for investment and the accumulation of capital. At the international exhibition staged in Paris during 1867, an American visitor was impressed by 'the fresh tint of nearly every structure along the principal thoroughfares – the effect of whitewash, paint or the mason's hammer renewing the stonework, and giving a singular lightness to the streets'. Eight new bridges had been built, and superstructures of ancient shops removed from old bridges. Industry, commerce and tourism flourished, benefiting from improvements in transport, while the city's population almost doubled between 1840 and 1870. The horse-drawn omnibuses, which had 40 million passengers in 1855, had 116 million in 1873, and nearly 200 million in 1882.[1] Haussmann and Louis Napoleon claimed they were giving Paris light, air and space, while making nature available in the new parks and gardens. Though Renoir was later to deplore the ruthless destruction of old buildings and monuments, impressionism – the term dates from 1874 – threw most of its weight behind the claim, celebrating the brightness and airiness of the new Paris.

More cars were on the roads than in New York, though

they were still outnumbered by horse-drawn carriages. Public telephone boxes functioned from 1885, and the Tour Eiffel was opened in 1889, when Proust was eighteen, to celebrate the centenary of the revolution. The Métro started operating in 1900 – the same year as the Grand Palais was opened to the public – but the Champs-Élysées were still unpaved, and, in spite of the whitewash, the paint, the wide thoroughfares and the new parks, Proust was to recall a Paris dark in comparison with the brightly lit city of his adult life. 'Even in the centre there was no electric light in the public thoroughfares, and very little in private houses. The lamps of a drawing-room situated on the ground floor or a low mezzanine were enough to lighten the street, making the passer-by raise his eyes and connect with the glow from the windows, as with its apparent though veiled cause, the presence outside the door of a string of smart broughams.'[2]

For Marcel, the atmosphere of prosperity in the city was inseparable from the atmosphere of prosperity brought by the success of his father's career. There were always domestic servants and nursemaids, and later there were tutors and governesses, but his mother and grandmother had more to do with his early education. They were both literary in their inclinations, but Robert, while exposed to the same early influences, developed a passion for mathematics, to which Marcel was always resistant. The governess who taught him geometry failed to interest him in how to prove one triangle could be equal to another, and he exhausted her patience by asking why it should be.[3]

When he was nine or ten he was finally sent to a preparatory school, the Cours Pape-Carpentier, where his fellow-pupils included Robert Dreyfus and two cousins – Jacques Bizet and Daniel Halévy. All three were younger than he was. Jacques was the son of Georges Bizet, who'd died in 1875, and Geneviève Halévy, granddaughter of another composer, Fromental Halévy, who wrote La Juive. His son, Ludovic Halévy, a writer and member of the Académie, was Daniel's father.

There was nothing abnormal about Marcel's classroom alternation between hard work and daydreaming, but his image of himself was conditioned by his parents' conviction that he was weak-willed, which in turn derived partly from his skill in exaggerating symptoms, making himself out to be unhealthier than he was. He was congenitally frail, but the display of weakness gave him extra strength. When the Santeuils discuss their son's disappointing achievements at school, his mother says it's not his health

> that's holding him back, as we used to believe, nor, thank God, a passionate temperament. Nor is he too imaginative, as his French master says, nor lazy, which is what his physics teacher thinks. The snag is the lack of willpower which, when he was six, should have stopped him from crying in bed instead of going to sleep . . . and which should now keep him on the right road instead of writing nonsense, daydreaming, reading novels and poetry, and above all stuffing himself with ten pastries from the *pâtisserie* and spoiling his appetite for dinner as well as ruining his stomach for the future.[4]

Adrien Proust's theories about neurasthenia and his disapproval of 'sob-stuff' increased his wife's anxieties about their sickly elder son. If they wanted to make him more manly, they must stop mollycoddling him. But their campaign to impose discipline precipitated a deterioration in his relationship with his father. One day, aiming to please his mother by winning a prize at school, Jean Santeuil completes a set of Latin verses. Pleased with himself, he goes out to play briefly in the sun, and he's on his way back, about to start work on an essay in his room, when he meets his father, who accuses him of breaking his promise to work harder.[5] M. Santeuil has the male sex's usual 'indifference to the illusions and sensitivities' of children.[6]

Jeanne Proust went with Marcel when he was being tutored in the catechism, and intervened when the priest was being severe. 'He's only a child.'[7] She was a gentle, reticent, self-effacing woman, firm with the servants but generally liable to behave as if she weren't entitled to have her own opinions – her husband was always right. But she could be more assertive about the children's rights than she could about her own. She could no longer protect Marcel, though, when, at the beginning of October 1882, he was sent against his will to the Lycée Fontanes in the rue de Caumartin – the well-known school which changed its name three months later to Lycée Condorcet. Built as a Capuchin monastery in the late eighteenth century, the austere building had undergone little conversion, though discipline was milder than at rival Left Bank institutions

such as the Henri IV and the Louis-le-Grand, where more
pressure was put on the boys. As it was, Marcel never overcame his resistance to maths and German. Even Robert was
better at maths, but when he tried to help his elder brother
with maths homework, Marcel would say: 'Stop, I'm out of
my depth.'[8] Generally he seems to have found it harder than
his younger brother did to adjust to classroom work after so
many years of learning in the loving presence of mother and
grandmother, and with no experience of the classroom. In *Jean
Santeuil* the Narrator asks whether Jean was suffering from 'the
first, blighting effects of the squalid, dank atmosphere of
school' or whether his 'over-responsive mind and body' were
being forced to protect themselves from 'the devastating
attacks of life' by growing an impervious hide 'abounding in
coarse knots and scales'.[9]

At the *lycée* Marcel started in section D of the fifth form,
where he failed to impress the teachers with his ability to recite
long passages of de Musset and Hugo by heart. At the end of
the year he was fourth runner-up (*accessit*) in Greek composition and fifth in French language, but his best results were in
natural science, as they were during his second year at the
school. His natural aptitude for the subject stemmed from his
intense pleasure in observing and his interest in the possibility
of bridging between specific facts and general laws.

His early school career was hindered by ill health and
absences. Hearing that cauterisation could, by destroying erec-
tile tissue, make the nose immune to the action of pollen,
Adrien Proust put Marcel in the hands of Dr Martin, who
painfully cauterised the boy's nose over a hundred times. Finally Marcel was told he'd never again suffer from hay-fever
and was taken into the country. He immediately suffered such
a severe attack that he was taken straight back to Paris 'with
violet hands and feet, like the corpse of a drowned man'.[10]

In was in Illiers, at the age of twelve, that he discovered
how to masturbate. He locked the door of the lavatory, but
the window was always open, and a lilac, rooted in the wall,
had pushed a bough into the room. Scared he was going to
kill himself by interfering with natural processes, he was also
exuberant, feeling as if his consciousness were bigger than the
world outside the open window, while the overpowering scent
of lilac was like a caress. Afterwards he pictured the devil as a

lengthening silvery thread he could spin out from inside himself. It left a trail like a snail-track on the lilac.[11]

The account of masturbation in *Swann* is probably the first in any novel. The scent of lilac is replaced with the mixed scents of orris root and wild-currant bush. The reason for the change is that both plants contain trimethalymine; present in both semen and urine, the substance helps to give them their characteristic smell.[12] Virtually none of Proust's readers would be aware of this, and the change indicates a compulsion to find connections between private life and the natural environment. The word 'lavatory' isn't mentioned in *Swann* but, 'destined for a more special and more vulgar use', the little room at the top of the house is for a long time the Narrator's place of refuge because it's the only room where he's allowed to lock himself in. He therefore used it 'for all my occupations which required an inviolable solitude: reading, reverie, tears and sensual pleasure'.[13] Through the half-opened window of the room he sees nothing but the tower of the prison at Roussainville, 'while with the heroic hesitations of a traveller setting out on an expedition or of a desperate man killing himself, faltering, I broke into myself, clearing an unknown route I believed to be fatal, until a natural trail, like that of a snail, appeared on the leaves of the wild currant which reached towards me'.[14]

Even if the boy had been able to discuss the question with his father, the doctor would have passed on the prevalent view (endorsed by Krafft-Ebing) that masturbation weakened the will. At this time, that would have seemed self-evident to the addict. Clearly, he was caught in a vicious circle: if his willpower was already too weak for him to give up the habit, this must be because he'd already weakened it too much, and he was continually depleting his reserves of strength each time he gave in to temptation. To Proust, already accused by his parents of being weak-willed, the accumulation of toxic guilt-feelings was overpowering. We are told in *Swann* – one piece of information comes on the heels of the last – that the boy has a delicate constitution, little stamina, a weak will and masturbates regularly.

He of course tried to keep his parents in ignorance of the habit, but when his father, coming unexpectedly into the room, discovered his son's secret, he reacted more realistically and more sympathetically than the guilt-ridden boy would have expected. He was asked to promise that he'd go for four days without doing it again.

Though he went on believing he was jeopardising his life and weakening not only his willpower but his resistance to the illness that so often kept him in bed, he was unable to give up the habit. At school, though, his frequent and prolonged absences didn't stop him from doing well in history, French, Latin and Greek.[15] The 'certificate of studies' he received on 8 August 1884 says he'd achieved the standard required for the fourth form in French, Latin, Greek, German, Roman history, French geography, simple arithmetic, elementary geometry, geology and botany.

Absence played havoc with his third year, especially during the spring, when his asthma was at its worst. He did better in Latin than Greek, and best in French.[16] His December 1884 composition on 'The Dying Gladiator' shows a precocious rhetorical skill, making the reader into a member of the crowd acclaiming the dying man's adversary: 'He hears your applause only as a confused murmur, like a last echo of life while his soul is already fleeing towards the dead. It does not concern him; you bloodied people, it is not to you he owes his last thoughts. He carries them down there, far from the flowering banks of the Danube, towards the rough-hewn hut he glimpses in his mind like a gentle and cruel image of his past life. Ivy crowns the roof. . . .'[17]

Marcel was cultivating his literary instincts with a mixture of self-discipline and self-indulgence, tentativeness and self-assurance. In each of Jean Santeuil's French essays,

in which the pupil was expected to produce a short narrative, correctly, if not elegantly written, he feverishly released the love or the pity inspired in him by the character given to him as a subject. He covered page after page, intoxicated by his fluency, expressing the infinite and delicious sadness he felt about the torture of Jeanne d'Arc or the words of the connétable de Bourbon, and he decorated them, to impress his teachers with the width of his reading, with images borrowed from the poets he read. So his essays, conceived in tears, aroused laughter when they were read out to the class.[18]

But in February 1885 Proust's name appears on the *tableau d'honneur*.

Throughout his childhood Jean Santeuil has seen more of his mother than his busy father; now, expelled from the paradise of childhood freedom, he tries to reassess his psycho-physiological make-up. Has he inherited more than he realised of his father's 'inoffensive self-love'?[19] But what alienated Marcel's teachers and moved his classmates to laughter was a preciosity modelled on his mother's. Nothing seemed more desirable than to talk and write as she did, with a maximum of quotations and classical allusions. It seemed more important to resemble her than to excel at school. Robert Dreyfus, who was two years his junior, describes him as 'full of fantasy, an elusive apprentice of meditation and daydreams, inspired more by delight in reading, thinking and feeling than by any ambition to shine on prize-days'.[20] This addiction to reading and daydreaming is confirmed by the answers he wrote early in 1886 to questions in a young girl's confession-book.

A year older than he was, Antoinette Faure became his friend in the Champs-Élysées, where he still played every day after school ended at three o'clock, and on Thursday afternoons, when there was no school. Aristocratic children from the west end of Paris played games with bourgeois children from the centre and formed friendships which were unlikely to last for long.

Antoinette had grey eyes and long eyelashes. She was the daughter of Félix Faure, deputy for Le Havre and, later, president of the republic. His wife was a close friend of Jeanne Proust, and they often went for walks together in the Bois de Boulogne.[21] In Antoinette's album the fourteen-year-old Marcel declares his favourite occupations to be 'reading, dreaming and writing in verse'. His idea of happiness is 'to live close to all the people I love, with the beauties of nature, plenty of books and music, and a French theatre in the vicinity'. He would like to live in the country of the ideal, 'or rather of my ideal'. The key words in his answers are 'ideal', 'beauty', 'genius', 'intelligence' and 'naturalness'. To the question 'For what faults do you have the most indulgence?' his answer is: 'For the private life of geniuses.' The qualities he values in men are intelligence and the moral sense; in women naturalness, gentleness and 'sentilligence' (possibly a meaningful slip of the pen). His 'pet aversion' is people who have no feeling for goodness and do not know 'the pleasures of affection', while his 'idea of the depths of misery' is 'to be separated from

Mother'. His favourite prose writers are George Sand and
Augustin Thierry, and his favourite poet de Musset. The only
composers he lists are Mozart and Gounod, the only painter
Ernest Meissonier, who often depicts cavalrymen on
manoeuvre or soldiers relaxing off duty.[22]

In a photograph of Antoinette and Marcel she's wearing a
plumed hat and carrying an umbrella, while he wears a striped
straw hat. Comtesse de Martel, a friend of the Faures who'd
seen them together, met him in Calmann-Lévy's bookshop
buying the complete works of Molière and Lamartine. His
literary precocity assorts oddly with the pleasure he took in
Meissonier's military uniforms and parades. He used to recite
his favourite poems to Antoinette, who reciprocated by teaching him how to make caramels.[23]

He was absent for so much of the school year 1885–6 that
he had to stay in the second class for an extra year, but his
health had improved, and he did well. He won no prizes, but
ended the year with good marks in everything but maths. He
was first runner-up in Latin language and fourth in French
composition.[24]

Boyhood holidays were mostly spent with his brother and
mother or grandmother on the Normandy coast – at Cabourg
or Dieppe or Trouville. In Illiers he knew most of the villagers,
but the seaside world was tantalisingly full of children who
didn't invite him to play with them and adults he had no
chance to charm. Watching them eat and chatter in the dining-
room of the Grand Hôtel at Cabourg, or staring out through
its huge windows at the people on the promenade, he felt
frustrated. 'Whether they were going home to some unknown
villa or coming out, racquet in hand, to meet for a game of
tennis, or mounting horses whose hooves trampled on my
heart, I watched with passionate curiosity, in the blinding light
of the beach where social relations are changed, I followed all
their movements through the transparency of that great glassed
bay which admitted so much light.'[25]

During one of these summer holidays he stayed with his
mother at the Hôtel de la Paix in the Pyrenees, at Salies-de-
Béarn. His style of letter-writing suggests he'd been more
influenced by her and the reading habits she'd inculcated than
by schoolteachers. This is sophistication which has been cultivated in a greenhouse. The style, though not unhumorous, is
self-conscious and affected. In a letter to his grandmother, he

describes a twenty-seven-year-old friend of his mother's, Marie-Marguerite Catusse, whose husband, Anatole, was later a senator. She'd promised to sing an aria by Massenet or Gounod if Marcel showed her the portrait he'd penned of her. The resultant letter shows that pastiche came naturally to him. He paraphrases a declaration of love in a de Musset comedy, and echoes the oaths in Leconte de Lisle's translations of Homer.

> I swear to you by Artemis, the white goddess, and by Pluto of the burning eyes . . . that I feel a certain shame in telling her I find her charming. But it's the sad truth. Mme Catusse must be between 22 and 25. A delightful face, two gentle, bright eyes, fine, white skin, a face that deserves to be dreamed about by a painter in love with perfect beauty, framed in beautiful black hair. (Oh! what an unbearable task to defy Musset and tell you, especially when one thinks that, Madame, that you are pretty, extremely pretty. . . .) The waist is slender, pleasantly shaped. But nothing matches the face, which one can't stop looking at. . . . Madame Catusse's conversation has come to me as a consolation for my plentiful vexations and for the boredom exuded by Salies for anyone without enough 'double muscles', as Tartarin would put it, to search among the freshness of the neighbouring countryside for the grain of poetry which is necessary to existence and which, alas, is totally absent on the terrace full of chatter and tobacco-smoke where we pass the time.[26]

Mme Catusse found him irritating. Travelling with her on the horse-drawn bus from Auteuil to the Madeleine, he thought he was charming her with his conversation when she asked: 'Are you going to talk like that all the way?'[27] But, according to Robert Dreyfus, Marcel generally made a good impression on the grown-ups, 'who were unanimous in their rapture at the refinements of his courtesy, the complications of his good intentions. I see him now, very handsome and very sensitive to cold, smothered in jerseys and mufflers, rushing to meet our mothers or grandmothers, bowing at their approach and always finding the right words to touch their hearts, whether he broached subjects usually reserved for his elders or merely enquired after their health.'[28]

Many of them treated him like an equal. He was barely fifteen when he was taken out to dinner at the Ritz by a friend of the family, Dr Pozzi, a fashionable and fashion-conscious doctor who'd been Mme Straus' lover.[29] The evening helped to arouse Marcel's appetite for contact with rich and fashionable people in elegant surroundings.

But with his peers he was bad at gauging how much intimacy he was entitled to expect. Of the boys in the class the three who mattered to him most were the three he'd known longest – Robert Dreyfus, Jacques Bizet and Daniel Halévy. He would confide in Dreyfus, but, more attracted to the other two, he behaved erratically, confusing them as much as they confused him by their reactions. 'There was something about him we found unpleasant,' Halévy recalled. 'His kindness and tender attentiveness looked like mere affectation and posing, and we missed no opportunity to tell him so. Poor, miserable boy, we were beastly to him.'[30] No doubt he demanded too much affection, and no doubt there was something effeminate about him, even if he didn't yet understand his own sexual proclivities.

No one knows at first that he is an invert, or a poet or a snob, or wicked. The schoolboy who had just been studying love poetry or looking at obscene pictures would, if he pressed up against a classmate, only think himself to be sharing with him the same desire for a woman. Why should he think he is not like everybody else when the substance of his feelings corresponds to what he reads in Mme de Lafayette, Racine, Baudelaire, Walter Scott?[31]

Halévy thought of Proust 'with his enormous oriental eyes, his big white collar and flying cravat, as a sort of disturbed and disturbing archangel'. When he talked about sex to Bizet and Halévy, he only succeeded in shocking the two younger boys. He might be a genius, but he was certainly a masturbator, and already he was possibly a fornicator and possibly a pederast. They never beat him up, but teased him mercilessly, making his big eyes brim with sadness.[32] Long after his schooldays are over, Jean Santeuil thinks regretfully about the three 'intelligent boys' who'd thought him 'insincere and affected'.[33] All three had at first seemed to like him. Writing to Dreyfus about Halévy, Marcel asks:

Why, after being on the whole very nice to me, does he drop me *completely*, making me very aware that he's doing so, and why, a month later, does he come up to say 'good morning' when he hadn't even been speaking to me? . . . And his cousin Bizet? Why does he say he feels friendship for me and then cut me dead? What do they want? To get rid of me, infuriate me, mystify me, what? I thought they were so nice! . . . When one doesn't know where one stands, it's easy to be either too stand-offish or too importunate.[34]

His relationships with them were complicated at the beginning of 1887, when Halévy took the initiative in founding *Lundi*, an 'artistic and literary review'. It was either duplicated or handwritten into an exercise book. It soon expired, but in February 1888 Halévy started a new one called *Revue de seconde*. Feeling they needed an *ism*, the boys opted for 'subtilism', a word which served to unite the contributors until the thirteenth issue appeared in March 1888.[35] Though the sixteen-year-old Marcel wasn't equipped to be the driving editorial force, the others relied on his literary taste, and when Halévy wrote a long poem, he submitted it to Marcel, whose detailed comments concluded: 'And now, my dear Daniel, that you have forced me to read these verses, so full of talent, but so painful, boring and sometimes execrable, and to write these ineptitudes, I say *Ouf*, put down my critical pen, take off my pedantic mask.' He listed twenty-three writers from Homer to Anatole France whom he recommended: 'You will learn that if your mind is original and powerful, your works will not have these qualities until you are absolutely sincere.'[36]

But the stern critic was still using baby-talk to his mother and still playing games in the Champs-Élysées, where he enjoyed chatting with boys of his own age and reciting poetry to them. He enthused mainly about Racine, Hugo, Baudelaire, de Musset, Leconte de Lisle and Lamartine. He also talked about actors, especially Mounet-Sully and Bernhardt.[37] But he was happier still when he was with girls.[38] His combination of good looks and frailty helped him to make a favourable impression on the first girl who aroused jealousy in his mother. Marie de Benardaky was the dark-haired daughter of a rich Russian nobleman who'd been master of ceremonies at the Tsar's court. With his handsome wife and their two daughters he lived in the rue de Chaillot. In a 1918 letter Proust will call Marie 'the intoxication and the despair of my youth', and though he remembers her as being fifteen when they met in the Champs-Élysées, she was probably only thirteen. In the middle of July 1887, when he'd just turned sixteen and was playing there almost every day, he wrote to Antoinette, describing Marie as 'very pretty and increasingly exuberant'. She'd been involved in a fist fight with another girl, and had won.[39] In *Jean Santeuil*, the little Russian girl, Marie Kossichef, has a mass of black hair, rosy cheeks, dark, mocking eyes, and the extravert vivacity Jean lacks. Each day, when she arrives with her governess and her younger sister, his heart beats faster. Comparatively ignorant of French literature, they seemed to enjoy listening when he explained it to them, while he, emotionally immature and vulnerable, felt sure of himself when he was talking about literature.

Jean Santeuil is too agitated in Marie's presence to feel happy, but he's agonised when she leaves. He thinks about her every day on waking up and before going to sleep. One day, when there's snow on the ground, he feels like hitting his mother after she guesses accurately at his unspoken thoughts and says Marie won't be in the Champs-Élysées today. He goes, anyway, with the maid, and the Kossichef sisters arrive, swaddled in fur. They all slide and play snowballs. To please Marie, Jean stuffs snow down the neck of a boy she doesn't like. When they're alone together, he can think of nothing to say, but in her absence he's always holding imaginary conversations with her.

At the stall which sold marbles, there were two kinds. Stone marbles cost a sou each, while the larger transparent marbles cost six sous. 'The only boys who had them were those he wasn't allowed to play with – boys in long trousers, who smoked cigarettes.'[40] When Marie gives him one of these marbles, he treasures it. 'He asked it whether Marie loved him. He moistened it with his tears, saying: "You see – you're staying with me." At night he took it to bed with him, and, before going to sleep, slipped it under his pillow, clasped it in his palm, or let it roll to the bottom of the bed, between his feet, which played with it.'[41] And when he goes down to dinner with his parents, he takes the marble with him, secretly kissing it while pretending to put a piece of bread in his mouth.

One day, when it is her younger sister's turn to pick sides for prisoners' base, she tells Jean: 'You belong to Marie,' which makes a smile spread over Marie's face, and when she's ordered by the doctor to stay indoors for two months because of the extreme winter cold, she sends Jean a letter, inviting him to tea at her home. He pretends he never drinks chocolate at teatime and that the chairs in his parents' drawing-room are always in loose covers, just like the drawing-room chairs in her home. The darkness on the staircase adds to the romance of this aristocratic house, and he's impressed by

> the solemn shades of the ante-room, where you couldn't tell whether the man standing in front of the Gothic mystery of an old oak chest was a footman waiting for his mistress, who had gone out to pay a call, or the master of the house . . . while in the drawing-room, which couldn't be entered without manoeuvring several door-hangings, the ermined canopies of the tapestry hangings, the stained-glass windows, the lapdog, the tea-table and the painted ceiling seemed like vassals and prerogatives of its feudal Dame.[42]

His friendship with Marie ends when his parents, apprehensive about his permanent over-excitement, decide to separate him from her, and, in spite of desperate pleading, threats of disobedience and unprecedented declarations that he hates his mother, he isn't allowed to go on seeing her. For a time Marcel thought of killing himself by jumping off the balcony, but his symbiotic relationship with his mother soon resumed.

She wanted to share everything in his life. She read the letters he wrote, and tore up one to Antoinette, ostensibly because the handwriting wasn't good enough, but possibly because it expressed admiration for General Boulanger, who'd won great popularity by making jingoistic speeches against the Prussians. On Bastille Day he led a parade through the streets of Auteuil. Though the sixteen-year-old Marcel criticised him as 'very common, and a vulgar beater of the big drum',[43] the boy was excited by the crowd's hysteria. 'This great enthusiasm, so unpredictable, so *romantic* in the banal life which is always the same, arouses everything in the heart which is primitive, untamed, warlike.'[44] Writing another letter to Antoinette, Proust blames his mother's misgivings on her mixture of royalist and republican sentiments.

He pleased her, at any rate, by the efforts he made to catch up with schoolwork he'd missed through absence. In the autumn of 1886, when he'd been put back into the second class, he did well in the exams. By winning second prize in both history and geography he'd won the right to compete in a history exam held at the Sorbonne. There were about 125 candidates – two or three from each division in each of the *lycées*, and in the same letter of July 1887 to Antoinette he describes writing non-stop for five hours. At the *lycée*, besides winning the second *accessit d'excellence*, he was first runner-up in Latin and fourth in French composition.

He could no longer enjoy holidays among the lilacs and hawthorns of Illiers, but, spending time with his sixty-four-year-old grandmother at Auteuil and on the Normandy coast, he developed a great rapport with her. Later he'd write about 'those seaside holidays when Grandmother and I, lost in one another, walked battling against the wind and talking'. Whenever they travelled to Illiers together, she insisted on breaking the journey at Chartres. She loved the two belfry towers: 'My dears, you may laugh at me – they don't match, they may not be beautiful according to the rules, but their asymmetrical old faces please me. . . . I think if they played the piano, they'd have a nice touch.'[45]

During September 1887, when Marcel was in Auteuil with her, he sent his mother detailed bulletins about his health. Already he was suffering from '*transparent* nights with the sensation one has when asleep that one is about to wake up soon, etc., dreams and a bad taste in the mouth on waking up'. One evening, after visiting the Louvre and driving through the Bois de Boulogne in a closed carriage, he had a particularly indigestible meal, indulging his love of sweet things by eating three desserts. Waking up after an undisturbed night with a clean taste in his mouth, he was so surprised that he let out a cry of delight. He felt well the next day, but after going for a walk in the Bois, slept badly and again woke up with an unpleasant taste in his mouth. But the next day he again appeared to benefit from not going for a walk and from eating such a heavy dinner that his grandmother was alarmed.[46]

At the end of the holiday, in the autumn of 1887, he had to start on two years of preparation for the *baccalauréat*. The first year, known as the *rhétorique*, he called 'a circular tour from Homer to Chénier via Petronius'.[47] The three teachers who dominated the year were Oswald Dauphiné, who'd just been appointed as head of rhetoric at the *lycée*, Victor Cucheval-Clarigny, the Latin master, and Maxime Gaucher, who besides teaching Greek and French wrote literary criticism for *La Revue bleue*. Gaucher recognised an extraordinary talent in his pupil. Proust's classmate, Pierre Lavallée, remembered his friend's essays as being 'rich in impressions and images, already very "Proustian", with their sentences packed with digressions and parentheses, which exasperated M. Cucheval and so intrigued M. Gaucher. I can still see and hear Marcel reading out his work, and the admirable, charming M. Gaucher commenting, praising, criticising, then suddenly laughing helplessly at some stylistic audacity which basically delighted him.'[48] Robert Dreyfus called Gaucher 'the wittiest and most generous of the teachers'.[49] He often made Proust read his essays out to the other boys, who booed and applauded derisively. 'If it hadn't been for Gaucher, they'd have massacred me.'[50] But many of them imitated his style: 'I did homework which didn't look at all like homework. The result was that within two months two dozen imbeciles were writing in a decadent style, and Cucheval thought I was poisoning their minds and causing civil war in the class and some of them thought I was a poseur. Luckily it did not go on for more than two months.'[51] Towards the end of the year, though, Cucheval was predicting: 'He'll get through because it was only a practical joke, but, thanks to him, fifteen of them will fail.'[52]

At first Cucheval had little to say in Proust's favour. 'Unsteady and a daydreamer', he was making only 'mediocre' progress in Latin. But the pupil respected the teacher. Though he was 'coarse', 'crude', 'ferocious', liable to make idiotic jokes and unable to appreciate 'exquisite combinations of syllables and contours', he was 'excellent in all other respects and a refreshing change from the imbeciles who speak in well-rounded phrases. . . . He is the ideal teacher, and never boring.'[53]

M. Dauphiné was

a small man, thin, dry and fussy. Extremely intelligent and cultivated. A mind of marvellous agility and acuity. . . . Lessons very *distinguished*, very rich, very *alive*. His mind is rigorous and virtuous. Much more intelligent and, above all, intellectual than artistic. Though he admires Leconte de Lisle. But finds him 'bizarre'! I can see him from here, all movement, all flame, his little eyes 'alive', looking like a vivisector-psychologist. But on the whole it is a very strong and flexible mental discipline, a remarkable course, full of things and ideas.[54]

Towards the end of the school year, M. Gaucher, seriously ill, was replaced by M. Dupré, who was friendlier than M. Cucheval, but boring. Though familiar with the work of Leconte de Lisle and the other Parnassians, such as Léon Dierx, he infuriated Proust by entering into 'endless discussions' about their limitations. Proust summed up the three teachers by calling Dauphiné 'a course', Cucheval 'a class' and Dupré 'often a conversation'.[55] At the end of the year he won one of the *prix d'honneur* for French composition.[56]

The discontinuity between school life, games in the Champs-Élysées and life at home was already helping him towards an insight crucial to his writing. Wasn't the self more plural than singular? If the Marcel who dined at the Ritz was different from the one who played prisoners' base, the one who held back his tears when classmates teased him was different from the one who wrote poems they learnt by heart, and the lovelorn son, driven almost mad by his mother's absence, was hardly the same Marcel as the one who joined in schoolboy conversations about sex and girls. He could move from babyishness to dandyish posturing, and the more insecurity he felt about cracks in his wholeness, the more inclined he was to overplay differences between the various Marcels, sending himself up, exaggerating his feelings, satirising himself as a way of taking out insurance against the possibility of being rebuffed.

'Among the various gentlemen of whom I consist,' he wrote, when his feelings towards Halévy were becoming dangerously ardent,

> the romantic gentleman, whose voice inspires my mistrust, tells me: 'He's trying to tease you, to amuse himself, to test you, and then, not wanting to lose you, he's full of remorse.' But the cynical gentleman, whom I prefer, tells me it's much simpler – that Halévy can't bear me, that to someone so restrained my ardour seems at first ridiculous and then insufferable, that he wanted me to know I was being importunate and to get rid of me . . . This gentleman doesn't know whether the behaviour is motivated by pity or indifference or moderation.[57]

Even in his letters there are striking contrasts between childish declarations of love for his mother and sophisticated attempts to hedge his bets. Oscillations in his behaviour were no less violent. One day, in the place de l'Opéra, lisping and with one finger in his mouth, he asked a friend how to find the rue de Richelieu.[58] But he could also astonish friends with a show of manliness. Even if he was only play-acting, wanting to contradict rumours about his effeminacy, at least he could put on a convincing performance. When Halévy told him about a beautiful shopkeeper in the rue de Fontanes, he wanted to see her. The shop was a dairy and together they watched admiringly through the window while the lovely black-haired Mme Chirade served her customers. After pronouncing her magnificent, as beautiful as Flaubert's Salammbo, Marcel asked: 'Do you think it would be possible to sleep with her?' Halévy was so flabbergasted that it was Marcel who broke the silence: 'It would be best to bring her some flowers.' They agreed on a day for the experiment, left the *lycée* together, called at a florist in the rue Pigalle, bought an armful of roses and went to the dairy. Halévy waited outside, not expecting Marcel even to make the attempt, but he went into the shop and, holding the bouquet in front of him, approached Mme Chirade. Amused, she shook her head. He held his ground. Gently but firmly she advanced, and, reluctantly, he backed towards the door. 'I think it is impossible to be thrown out more graciously than he was.'[59]

He received friendlier treatment from the famous courtesan Laure Hayman when he found her with his great-uncle Louis in Auteuil. This encounter is reproduced in *Swann*. A carriage and pair is waiting outside the house, and the manservant seems reluctant to admit the boy, who hears a woman asking for him to be received, just for a second. The pretty lady, who looks like an actress, is wearing a pink silk dress and a pearl necklace. Her glance is rapid and kindly, her manner candid. When the three of them go into the study, she refuses the cigarette her lover offers her. ' "No dear," she said, "you know I'm used to the ones the Grand Duke sends me. I told him they made you jealous." '[60]

Louis Weil was now seventy; Laure Hayman was thirty-seven, and her lovers had included the King of Greece, the duc d'Orléans and Prince Karl Egon von Fürstenberg. An intelligent, witty and accomplished woman, blonde with dark eyes, she lived in the rue de la Pérouse and held a literary salon, where she received mainly people of the previous generation. Among her regulars was the fashionable novelist Paul Bourget, one of the lovers no older than she was. Proust spent so much on buying flowers for her that she spoke to his father about it. 'He scolded me for my extravagance . . . but Papa himself admired Laure Hayman for her sensitivity and intelligence, and he encouraged me to keep up a friendship with her.'[61] She gave him a copy of a book she'd inspired – Bourget's *Gladys Harvey*. The heroine is praised for having about her 'something of the eighteenth-century harlot and not too much of the ferociously calculating harlot of our brutal and positivist period'.[62] The copy she gave Proust in October 1888 was signed by Bourget, bound in silk from one of her petticoats and inscribed: 'Do not love a Gladys Harvey.' Proust told Dreyfus that, though he'd exchanged photographs and letters with her, the relationship was Platonic.

The letter to Dreyfus was written on 25 September from L'Isle-Adam, where he was staying with a classmate, Édouard Joyant. Other recent experiences, he claimed, included 'a very uncomplicated intrigue which ended very tamely with the obligatory ending and which gave birth to an absorbing liaison which is threatening to last for at least a year, much to the profit of the café-concerts and places of that kind where one takes this sort of person'.[63] The friendship, which was with a Viennese girl he'd met at a dancing class near the *lycée*, was less absorbing than he wanted Dreyfus to believe, and less durable than his friendship with Laure Hayman.

Because his mother was in Salies with Robert when Marcel returned from L'Isle-Adam, he was sent to Auteuil. Though he enjoyed the company of her lawyer brother Georges, who was two years her senior, he complained so much about not being with her that he was reprimanded by his great-uncle, 'who told me this grief was "egoism". This little psychological discovery led him to taking such unadulterated pleasure in his pride and satisfaction that he went on moralising relentlessly. Grandfather, much gentler, only called me an idiot, quietly, and Grandmother just shook her head, laughing and saying it didn't at all prove that I loved my mother.'[64] Marcel had never seen much of his grandfather, who'd chosen to stay at home while his wife took their grandson on holiday. Nathé Weil was a hard-faced, white-bearded, sharp-nosed old man, with clean-shaven spaces around the tight lips. He had a reputation for meanness, and kept a bottle of good wine under the table, pouring from it into his own glass, while the rest of the family drank from the bottle of cheap wine on the table, but his attempts to be strict with Marcel alternated with kindliness.

In the morning the boy consoled himself by taking a book – *Le Mariage de Loti*, published anonymously by Julien Viaud, who afterwards used the *nom de plume* Pierre Loti – and walking to the Bois de Boulogne. 'Oh, my little Mamma, how wrong I was not to do that before, and how often I will in future. From the first moment it felt good, sunshine, cool, and soon I was laughing with joy all by myself; it was a pleasure to breathe, to smell, to move my limbs.'

In his letters he was already theorising about 'character' and about the 'play-acting' involved in converting experiences into narrative. He profited from brooding about discontinuity in his reactions to Halévy's real or apparent indifference. Comparing Halévy's unpredictability with that of Molière's misanthrope, Proust observed that one actor might interpret Alceste's stand-offishness as malicious while another could make it look noble. 'I do not believe a type is a character. In my opinion, what we think we know about a character is only an effect of association of ideas. . . . All we are doing is constructing in our minds a character based on a few features we have observed while presupposing others are there. But this construction is very hypothetical.'[65] This was probably written before the letter about 'the different gentlemen of whom I consist'. One advantage of multiplying himself into the plural was that he could side with his friends against some of his other selves.

While play-acting and being someone else, I can revile them with impunity. Myself too. I'd willingly draw a self-portrait . . . 'I can tell you that for my part I rather dislike him, with his eternal grand manner, his appearance of being busy, his great passions and his adjectives. Above all he seems to me quite insane or quite insincere. . . . After knowing you just a week, he pretends to feel something for you, and while claiming to love a friend like a father, he loves him like a woman. . . . He writes febrile letters to you. . . . Pretending he's not being serious, just making phrases, writing pastiche, he tells you your eyes are divine and your lips are tempting him. The worst thing, *ma chère*, is that after making a fuss of B, he drops him to flirt with D, soon abandoning him to throw himself at E's feet and then into F's lap. . . .' If this is a portrait, it's not very flattering and it would flatter

me less than the portrait I make myself of you – according
to you. . . .[66]

Seizing quickly on the comic and dramatic potential of his new
insight, he was having fun and challenging himself at the same
time. This is writing which interrogates itself as it goes along;
he is more penetratingly and amusingly self-critical than in any
previous letter. But his main intention is to make indirect
advances to Halévy. Dreyfus is allowed – almost encouraged
– to show him the letter, but if Halévy dismisses it as 'so
sincere that it is insincere', he'll be quite right. Suddenly Proust
is much more like a novelist, both acknowledging emotion
and standing back at a safe distance.

Returning to the *lycée* at the beginning of October, he met
his new philosophy teacher, Alphonse Darlu, who on the
second day of term talked about the way consciousness splits
when a man can neither act nor think without analysing his
actions and thoughts. In the evening Proust wrote to Darlu,
asking for help. What remedy was there for this disorder?

Marie-Alphonse Darlu was thirty-nine – small, bearded, brilliant and sarcastic. In *Jean Santeuil* he's portrayed as M. Beulier,
who makes his first appearance in the classroom red-faced, out
of breath from running, wearing spectacles and a silk scarf.[67]
The preface to *Les Plaisirs et les jours* acknowledges how Darlu's
'inspired words, more certain to survive than many a book,
made me, like so many others, start thinking', and in one of
the notes to his translation of Ruskin's *Sesame and Lilies* Proust
called Darlu 'the most admirable master I have known, the
man who has had the greatest influence on my thought'. Darlu
would leave his top hat on his desk and use it to illustrate his
philosophy lessons. Expounding Leibniz's theories, he made
the hat represent a Monad and dropped his handkerchief into
it.[68] As another pupil put it, 'He brought the whole of philosophy, like a conjurer, out of that hat.'[69] Criticising Proust's
prose, Darlu accused him of picking up bad habits from magazines and pounced derisively on phrases that were pretentious
or hackneyed. How could he talk about 'the red conflagration
of the sunset'? And when Proust wrote on a question that was
to remain important to him – how factual knowledge leads
scientists to conclusions from which laws can be formulated –
Darlu commented: 'Extremely vague and superficial.'[70] But
Jean Santeuil soon becomes inordinately fond of Beulier. This

man, who was worse than badly dressed, knew neither how to enter a room nor how to greet an acquaintance, but there was in his deportment something striking and gentle which would have been lacking in that of a prince. He 'was neither handsome nor ugly, but Jean looked at his red cheeks, his strong nose and the swollen veins on his hands with such a tender respect that if M. Beulier's coldness hadn't discouraged it, he would have kissed them with the same loving care as the cheeks, the nose, the hands of his mother'.[71]

Darlu was above all a moralist. 'Morality is central to philosophy,' he maintained.[72] His lessons on happiness, society and formal logic seem to have been seminal. In the notes Proust scribbled he was penetrating into the paradoxes and ambivalences that would be crucial to his work. On happiness he noted: 'Object of desire, sort of dream . . . fundamentally morality of happiness = pessimism. True for man, for children (what is a spoiled child) even for populace; danger of doctrines which make promises to crowds. Therefore, happiness principle of sadness, principle of unhappiness.'[73]

With Darlu as their teacher, the boys had even more incentive to create literary reviews than in the second form. Written on green paper, the *Revue verte* had Proust as its editorial secretary, but he threatened to resign when Halévy, with Bizet's support, asked for permission to copy part of the text. It must be protected, Proust countered, against the criticism of readers for whom it was not intended. For the *Revue lilas*, which they launched in the same month, October 1888, and named after the colour of the exercise books, bought in the stationer's shop in the passage du Havre, Proust wrote a piece dedicated 'to my dear friend Jacques Bizet'. Proust pictures himself as a fifteen-year-old in his bedroom, oppressed by the banality of the lamp, the noise of crockery in the adjacent room, the dark violet sky with gleaming stains of moon and stars. Then, two years later, everything is acceptable – 'the blue moonbeams dripping from the chestnut trees' in the boulevard Malesherbes, and 'the fresh, chill breathing of all these sleeping things'. Ordinary objects are no longer repulsive. 'I've made them sacred, and Nature too, because I couldn't conquer them. I've clothed them with my soul, with the inner splendour of images. I inhabit a sanctuary surrounded by a pageant. I'm the centre of things, and each brings me sensations or sentiments that are magnificent or melancholy.'[74]

This was a period of awakening. The intellectual stimulation
from Darlu interpenetrated with his confused and excited sexuality. If the advances he'd been making to Halévy had previously been ambiguous, they were explicitly homosexual by
the beginning of the new school year, and, hurt at being
accused of pederasty, Proust started a self-justifying letter
during one of Darlu's classes.

> My moral principles allow me to believe the pleasures of the
> senses are good. . . . You take me for someone who is blasé
> and demoralised, but you are wrong. If you are delicious, if
> you have pretty bright eyes which reflect the fine delicacy of
> your mind so purely that I feel I cannot love your mind fully
> unless I kiss your eyes, if your body and your eyes are, like
> your thoughts, so supple and fine that it seems to me that I
> could mingle better with your thoughts by sitting on your
> knees, if, finally, I feel that the charm of your self, your self
> in which I can't separate your lively mind from your lithe
> body, would refine and increase for me 'the sweete joies of
> love', there is nothing in this that justifies the contemptuous
> words which could more aptly have been addressed to a man
> who is fed up with women and searching for new pleasures
> in pederasty.[75]

He goes on to cite Socrates and (erroneously) Montaigne as
men who loved only men and believed male love to be less
damaging than heterosexual love. But he knew there was no
hope of persuading Halévy.

Proust's homosexuality was rooted in his mother-fixation.
The hothouse protectiveness and possessiveness of her love
stopped him from maturing into autonomy. Though he was
far from indifferent to women, the sexual excitement they
aroused would invariably be transferred to male objects. In
Freud's conjectures about Leonardo da Vinci's mother and the
way she depleted his masculinity, the pattern that emerges is
of homosexuality that develops in two stages. In the first an
excessive maternal tenderness produces excessive filial devotion. In the second the son represses this love by putting himself in his mother's place and takes his own person as a model
for the new love objects he chooses. He starts to love boys in
the way his mother seemed to love him.[76] Proust's development followed the same pattern, and by this time there could
hardly have been more contrast between the two brothers.

Robert was robustly built, ruddy-complexioned and fond of sport, especially boating. Marcel, incessantly feeling cold and wrapping himself in pullovers and rugs, lived as if his life were in constant danger, while his mother, with an endearing mixture of tenderness and irony, joined in the game of keeping him safe.[77]

Nearing the end of his schooldays and approaching the beginnings of adult life, he was increasingly aware of tensions between his various selves. He'd been presenting a different face to his mother from the one he presented to boys of his own age, and the face he let them see revealed little of the emotions they made him feel. He was already sinking deeply into habits of dissimulation. His parents must never be allowed to find out the truth, but there were moments when their suspicions were aroused. This happened when he made some progress in his friendship with Jacques Bizet. Early in 1889, Proust wrote a portrait of him in sonnet form, and he gave Proust a photograph of himself. When he started absenting himself from his home overnight, his stepfather, Émile Straus, became suspicious about his relationship with Marcel and called on the Prousts to say their son was exerting a harmful influence on Jacques.[78]

It was a relief when he could go away on holiday, and after graduating as *bachelier ès lettres* in July 1889, and doing well at the annual prizegiving, where he received the *prix d'honneur* in French composition, and was acclaimed as third runner-up in general excellence, he went to stay in Ostende with a new friend he'd made in Darlu's philosophy class. Horace Finaly was the son of a German-speaking banker, and, being in another country and carrying on conversations in another language, Proust could feel that he'd temporarily escaped from most of his problems. Except that his anxious mother was pressing him in her letters to supply full details about what he was eating, what time he was going to bed and getting up, how much time he spent in the fresh air and how much he was resting.[79]

II

1889–96
Pleasure and Daylight

THREE

SOLDIERING AND SALONS

The French Revolution failed to make the country into a democracy: in 1815 only about 90,000 male landowners had the right to vote, while aristocrats still owned roughly a fifth of the land in France – they had owned a quarter before 1789 – and they dominated the bureaucracy, accepting status and salary in lieu of the seigneurial rights they'd forfeited. In the past their power had depended on maintaining hierarchical and authoritarian political structures, with support from the Catholic Church. So long as the republic remained conservative, the old attitudes survived in the tendency to interpret social problems as symptoms of moral decline and in the fear that universal suffrage would put power into the hands of men unredeemed by education. It was heredity that had given wealth and status to the absentee landlords who lived in the Faubourg Saint-Germain and visited their estates only during the shooting season. While the money, pride and traditional values which alienated them from the mass society also helped them to survive, their political power was substantially reduced by the constitutional changes which followed the revolution of July 1830. Seats in the upper chamber no longer depended on heredity, and new peers were created to emphasise the change. Instead of needing to pay 300 francs each year in direct taxation to qualify for a vote, a man needed to pay only 200 francs. Censorship was abolished, and links between Church and state loosened. When the infant Marcel Proust watched the comtesse in her flower-trimmed hat driving out in her barouche with her liveried footman, the aristocracy still had a great deal of wealth but much less power than was implied by its displays of grandeur.

Not that the class system had been destroyed by the series of revolutions, though both conservative and radical politicians claimed it had. 'Today,' wrote Louis Napoleon before he became Napoleon III, 'the rule of the classes is over, and we can govern only with the masses.' The Third Republic, too, was designed to transcend class conflict, and in 1892 Léon Gambetta claimed it marked the political début of 'nouvelles couches sociales'. He didn't want to use the word 'classes'. But in the 1890s, when radical propagandists said France was controlled by an oligarchy of 200 families, this was only an overstatement. The old upper crust was still on top, though it wasn't quite the same. The Napoleons had issued new titles, while aristocratic wealth had been eroded by the agricultural depression of the 1880s. Lowering rents and land values, it pushed young noblemen from old families into marrying heiresses from newly ennobled families and the bourgeoisie, while others made money from investment or banking or by joining boards of management in commerce or industry. By 1902 30 per cent of the railway directors were noble.[1] There had been a brief spell when the duc de Broglie served as prime minister, with two other monarchist ducs, Decazes and Audiffet-Pasquier, in his cabinet, but after this, the aristocracy virtually withdrew from politics. While the army wasn't predominantly aristocratic, its higher echelons were largely filled with refugees from noble Catholic families, and most of the bishops were appointed by the aristocracy.

The French aristocracy was less anti-intellectual than its English counterpart, and salons not only provided a forum in which ideas could be exchanged but helped to break down some of the barriers between classes. Writers, artists, musicians and academics were invited to aristocratic salons, while aristocrats were invited to bourgeois salons. The young Proust was highly susceptible to the magnetism of the Faubourg Saint-Germain. Stylish, self-confident, elegant, rich, blessed with all the graces he lacked or thought he lacked, proud owners of names that had become familiar from history lessons, good-looking young noblemen seemed extremely glamorous. If he couldn't have them as his lovers, nothing was more desirable than having them as his friends, but he didn't know he was preparing the ground for his novel, penetrating into the world he was going to describe, while overvaluing its inhabitants enough to make disillusionment inevitable. Both disillusionment and the interpenetration of nobility and upper bourgeoisie were to be dominant themes.

Seeing the interior of the Ritz when he was fifteen, he'd been given a foretaste of a fashionable milieu, and he was still a schoolboy when, invited to the homes of schoolfriends, he met some of the most fashionable hostesses. Though he couldn't yet meet the glamorous and famous people who attended their salons, it was like being taken backstage in a theatre between performances of a successful play, sitting down on the imposing set, drinking tea on the empty stage. Jacques Bizet's mother, Geneviève Straus, was now forty. She'd been twenty when she married Georges Bizet, a former student of her father, Jacques-Fromental Halévy, in composition classes at the Conservatoire. After Bizet died in 1875, she let fourteen years elapse before she married Émile Straus, a lawyer five years her senior and said to be an illegitimate half-brother of the three barons de Rothschild, who employed him.

The Strauses lived luxuriously in the boulevard Haussmann with paintings by Monet and Nattier next to the portrait of Mme Straus by Delaunay. Jacques was her only son, and Proust was one of the schoolfriends invited to the flat for lunch. After the meal Mme Straus would sing fashionable songs to the boys. Every day for two months (or so he later told her) Proust promised himself to kiss her hand the next day, but never found the courage.[2] Though he'd been to the flat many times, he wasn't yet invited either to her salon or to the one run by the mother of another schoolfriend, Jacques Baignères.

The first salons he attended were those of his great-uncle's mistress, Laure Hayman, and Mme Arman de Caillavet. He was eighteen when he was introduced to Mme Arman, who almost immediately invited him. She'd been born with the name Léontine Lippmann but at the insistence of her husband, Albert Arman, added to their marital name the name of the vineyard château he owned, de Caillavet. They lived near the Étoile, in the avenue Hoche, where she held her salon on Sundays. Among the guests – mostly writers and politicians – the most prominent was Anatole France. She'd been his patroness since 1886 and his mistress since 1888. France was usually to be seen leaning against the mantelpiece and holding forth. 'Entering Mme Arman's drawing-room', one of her guests wrote, 'was like being in a railway station with Anatole France as station-master.'[3] Trying to make France's dominating presence into a joke, Albert Arman would introduce himself to newcomers either by saying he wasn't Anatole France or by calling himself 'the master', adding 'of the house' and then shouting to tell France that another of his admirers had arrived.[4] After lunch Mme Arman made France work in her husband's study and at tea parties she could never resist letting her guests into the secret that the famous writer was in the house. Later on, coming downstairs with his hat and cane, he'd open the door and say: 'Good afternoon, my dear friend. It's over a week since I had the pleasure of seeing you.'[5]

In May 1889, not knowing how soon he'd meet Anatole France, Proust sent him a flattering letter signed 'A Student of Philosophy'. Claiming to know some of France's books by heart and to be an avid reader of his weekly chronicle in *Le Temps*, Proust said he'd been reading France's work 'to the more intelligent of my comrades at Condorcet. I have won some firm friendships for you there, Monsieur.' Another contributor to *Le Temps*, M. Chantavoine, had written harshly about France, and this letter was being sent to 'comfort' him.[6] The forty-five-year-old writer turned out to be a small man 'with a red nose like a snail's shell and a pointed black beard'.[7] Hiding his disappointment, the eighteen-year-old boy made such a favourable impression that France soon had designs on him as a son-in-law.

Other regulars at the salon included Alexandre Dumas *fils*, the reactionary critic Jules Lemaître, the playwright Édouard Pailleron and Victor Brochard, a professor at the Sorbonne. These four also attended Mme Aubernon de Nerville's prestigious salon, where France had been a regular until he transferred his allegiance to Mme Arman. Guy de Maupassant also came to her salon, though he'd been rebuffed when he made advances to her, and Proust met him there twice.[8]

He also met Colette, who wasn't impressed by 'his extreme politeness, the excessive attention he paid to his interlocutors, especially if they were women, an attentiveness which emphasised the difference in age between them and him. He looked singularly young, younger than any of the men or any of the women. Large, melancholy, blackish-brown eye sockets, a complexion sometimes rosy and sometimes pale, anxious eyes, the mouth, when it was silent, tight and puckered, as if for a kiss, formal clothes and one intransigent lock of hair.'[9]

Proust's young friend Maurice Duplay was sometimes invited to stay with him while he was getting ready to go out.

'How kind you are, my dear Maurice, to have taken the trouble to come! I've been almost suffocating, recently, but this evening I feel better. So I'm going to a soirée. As it's so near, I thought you might like to stroll across with me . . .'

He was trying to conceal a pullover underneath his waist-coat. He did up one button on his boots. He sat down, out of breath. He knotted his cravat. He talked. He quoted Racine in connection with a thought which had struck him about a cab-driver, introduced Leibniz or Confucius into a story about servants, and he had great relish for consorting with them. His cravat came undone. He tied it again. He did up another button on his boots . . .

Suddenly Mme Proust came in. 'Will you soon be ready, my little booby? Your soirée is at ten and it's eleven already.'

'Mamma, little Mamma, don't hustle me . . .'

'My God, my dear Marcel, how scruffy you look! Your boots! . . . This lining!' She pointed at the buttonholes on his boots, mostly gaping open, and tucked the lining back inside.

This son, whose astonishing gifts she was almost alone in recognising, whose genius she appreciated, how she treated him like a backward child! But didn't her protectiveness betoken her tenderness and her admiration? She knew that great minds are always badly adapted to material living and that, after falling out of the skies, the albatross finds it hard to walk, because of 'its giant wings'.

Breathing heavily from exertion, Marcel did up one more button. Mme Proust went out.[10]

Though he was almost invariably late at salons and soirées, sometimes arriving when most of the other guests had left, he seldom failed to conciliate both hosts and waiters who had to stay on late to look after him. One of the new friends he made at this time was Mme Arman's son, Gaston, who was serving in the army for a year as a volunteer. Since 1872 most young Frenchmen had been conscripted for five years of compulsory service, but until July 1889, when the period was reduced to three, volunteers served for only one year if they'd passed the *baccalauréat* and could pay for their uniform and maintenance. Though they served in the ranks, they were treated more or less like cadets, and passed out as non-commissioned officers in the reserve. They would be called back for stretches of a month, and would be commissioned as officers if they met the required standard. This system of voluntary service was now to be abolished, but though the new law had been passed in July, Proust could volunteer before it came into force.

As an asthmatic and as the son of a doctor well placed to pull strings, he could easily have got exemption from military service. But, after eighteen years of living with his parents, he was impatient for a change. He could postpone for a year the arguments he was inevitably going to have with his father about a career, and he could escape from his possessive mother into a relatively independent existence, living at close quarters with young men from all classes. She was a woman who'd never shake hands with a valet or a footman; he was a man who often wished he could make love to men she'd never touch. Here was his chance to fraternise freely with boys of his own age at a safe distance from her. It would have been understandable if he'd felt as scared of barrack-room life as he might once have felt of boarding-school, but on Monday 11 November he signed on, and four days later presented himself at the barracks in Orléans, where he was vaccinated and enlisted as a second-class soldier in the first battalion of the second company of the 76th Infantry. He's described in his army pay-book as having an oval face with chestnut hair, dark chestnut eyebrows, low forehead, medium-sized nose and mouth and a round chin. His height was five feet six inches.[11]

He was as pleased as he'd hoped to be with 'the simplicity of some of my peasant comrades whose bodies were more beautiful and more agile, their minds more original, their hearts more spontaneous, their characters more natural than in the case of the young men I had known before or knew after-wards'.[12] But his nervousness brought on persistent asthma attacks. Normally, volunteers weren't allowed to take lodgings in town, but because other men in the barracks were being kept awake at night, Proust's captain made him apply for permission, which was granted, and he found lodgings near the cathedral in the rue des Bons Enfants. His commanding officer, Colonel Arvers, also exempted him from early-morning parades.

He met Gaston de Caillavet mainly at weekends, when they both had passes to leave camp, and they wrote each other letters. Though most of Gaston's friends disliked Proust – some of them wouldn't even speak to him – their friendship developed so quickly that on Sunday evenings, when Proust had to catch the 7.40 train to Orléans, Gaston would regularly drive him to the station.[13] As a recruit, he was trained in swordsmanship and in 'third-class gymnastics'. He enjoyed 'the peacefulness of a life where one's occupations are more strictly regulated and one's imagination less trammelled than in any other, where pleasure is more constantly present because we have not time in rushing about looking for it to run away from it'.[14] As Robert Proust has suggested, the experience widened his brother's horizons and gave a new orientation to his field of observation.[15] The scenes from military life which stayed in Proust's memory were, he says, like Dutch paintings 'in which the people are usually of modest station, caught at some ordinary moment . . . in a setting that is not at all extraordinary'. He lived these scenes 'naturally, without much pleasure and without great sorrow, and I remember them with tenderness'.[16] In *Jean Santeuil* he makes occasional references to route marches and military discipline, but the emphasis in the army episodes is on camaraderie, eating and drinking. Officers and sergeants most often look away when rules are being broken.

Some of the officers were young noblemen, and the comte Walewski, a company commander, was the grandson of Napoleon Bonaparte and his Polish mistress, Marie Walewska, while the comte's mother had been a mistress of Napoleon III; Proust was thrilled to notice his facial resemblance to both emperors. Observing his behaviour at close quarters, Proust could compare the manners of the old nobility with those of the new aristocracy, and in *Guermantes*, modelling the prince de Borodino on the comte, Proust characterises the aristocrats of the Second Empire as inclined to put on a greater show of friendliness towards bourgeois acquaintances, and the old noblemen as majestically affable but deliberately stiff.[17]

There was no rigidity in separating the officers from the men, and one evening Proust dined with a captain who offered to put him up for the night. After accepting he was given a room in which he found a pile of blankets and sheets on the bed. He'd never had to make a bed, and, after a half-hearted attempt, slept on the bare mattress.[18]

His elegant young lieutenant, the comte de Cholet, would later give him a photograph inscribed 'To Marcel Proust, from one of his torturers'. He served as the model for two characters in *Jean Santeuil* – the comte de Saintré and Lieutenant de Brucourt. Vain and competitive, Saintré has found that fashionable life in the Faubourg Saint-Germain was using up his inherited fortune too quickly, and has re-entered the army to cut a dash and throw spectacular parties more economically in a garrison town. Despite his snobbery he's keen 'to show that he and his friends were ready to be on good terms with republicans and commoners, provided they were neither dirty, stupid nor blasphemous'.[19]

Jean is invited to his parties, as he is to those of Lieutenant de Brucourt, who occupies a big house facing the parade ground, and enjoys 'all the prestige with which his rank, his exceptional position in society, his fine appearance on parade and his kindliness had endowed him'.[20]

If the lieutenant seems to miss the point of what Jean says, or makes remarks which seem mindless, Jean always gives him the benefit of the doubt, assuming him to be a man 'whose intelligent outlook must have long ago resolved and dissipated every problem which was interesting Jean at that time. "I too wrote poetry when I was your age." – "I've given up reading novels." ' He boasts of being related to the Queen of Serbia, and makes Jean feel crushed, humble, ugly, ill-dressed and foolishly talkative.[21] An incident in which Cholet cut Proust is reprised when Jean is cut dead when saluting the lieutenant. But it was easy to take literary revenge. Years later, in Paris, the lieutenant, wanting to ask a favour, starts a letter 'My dear Jean'.[22]

In the middle of December he received a visit from Horace Finaly, who was all the more welcome as Proust's leave had been cancelled.[23] His mother was not only disappointed at being unable to see him but upset that her mother, dying of uraemia, forfeited her last chance of seeing her beloved grandson. The doctor had ordered Mme Weil to take nothing but milk, but she hated the taste. She was to die on the third day of the new year.

On 16 December Proust was admitted into the instructional platoon, where he had to train for ten weeks before his six months of instruction at the company's school on 3 March. He'd have liked to emerge as a non-commissioned officer, but it was impossible for him to make himself into a good soldier. In February, when, thanks to an introduction from his father, he was invited to dinner with M. Boegner, the préfet of the Loiret, the other guests included an intelligent and highly cultured young man from the 30th Artillery. Two years Proust's senior, Robert de Billy was soon to become a friend, and he wasn't the only witness to find Proust's bearing and speech unmilitary. He often wore his greatcoat unbuttoned, and the shako looked strange on him, while his hair and his oval face assorted oddly with his uniform.[24]

He had big, questioning eyes, and he seemed full of curiosity, eagerly interrogating friends, apparently in search of new viewpoints. He talked about philosophy and about Darlu, about poetry, painting, aesthetics and society. When he went to the Louvre with Billy – who got the impression he was driven there by Baudelaire's art criticism – Proust reacted most enthusiastically to van Dyck and the Cuyps.[25]

He was missing his mother. Though he often went home at weekends – the train journey lasted less than two hours – they exchanged letters almost every other day. When he referred her to Loti's semi-autobiographical *Roman d'un enfant*, which had just been published, she focused on Loti's earliest memories of his mother: 'And for the first appearance in this memoir of this blessed figure, I should like to greet her with special words, words made for her, words like none that exist, words which would alone be enough to make soothing tears flow, bringing I know not what consoling sweetness.' Mme Proust was enchanted. 'I am, my darling, impregnated with Loti.' But, never forgetting her son's health, she passed on Dr Proust's advice – no swimming or riding for the time being.[26] In another letter he was told to cut down on his consumption of cream-cheese. Her letters often end with loverlike endearments. Thousands of kisses or a quotation from Racine. 'Ah, que ce temps est long à mon impatience!'[27]

In June he still hadn't accustomed himself to the idea that his grandmother was dead, but his mother urged him not to let grief stop him from writing to her. 'I'm never saddened by thinking you're thinking of your grandmother; on the contrary, it pleases me greatly. . . . So, my darling, don't get into the habit of not writing so as to avoid saddening me, because the effect is the opposite. And then, my darling, think about her, love her with me, but don't go through days of weeping, which enervate you, and which she wouldn't want.'[28]

For her it was like a double bereavement. She'd never been separated for long from either of the two people she loved most – her mother and her elder son – but in the weeks and months after the funeral she was seeing almost nothing of him, while he, in spite of her black clothes, had little idea of how painful it was for her to accept the new situation. In *Sodome et*

Gomorrhe the Narrator is slow to realise how much his bereaved mother has been suffering.

> For the first time I understood that this fixed and tearless look . . . was stuck at the incomprehensible contradiction between memory and nothingness. . . . It is not enough to say she had lost all her gaiety; dissolved, paralysed in a sort of image of entreaty, she seemed nervous of upsetting by too brusque a movement, by too high a tone of voice, the sorrowful presence that never left her. But above all, as soon as I saw her come in wearing her mourning crape overcoat, I saw what had escaped my notice in Paris: it was no longer my mother I was looking at but my grandmother.[29]

But in Paris he still saw relatively little of her. His life was becoming so busy. On many of his Sundays he had tea at Mme Arman's. But when Gaston became engaged to a pretty twenty-five-year-old, Jeanne Pouquet, Proust bombarded her with disconcertingly effusive compliments. Habituated to overstating the fondness he felt for middle-aged women, he used the same tactics on Jeanne. Ignoring the reactions of Gaston and his mother, he kept asking Jeanne for a photograph, and he invited her and her mother to visit the churches and museums in Orléans with him. He often went to the Pouquets' house, and when Gaston devised a revue starring Jeanne as Cleopatra, Proust acted as prompter until the dress-rehearsal, when his enthusiasm for the performers distracted him from his duties.[30] When Gaston wrote a Colombine play for Jeanne, Proust refused to be cast as Pierrot: this was the role he was always playing in reality, he said.[31]

In the summer, while learning to mount a horse, he had a fall. After making one more attempt, he refused to go on learning, and when he completed the course in August, he was graded sixty-third out of sixty-four soldiers. Even this didn't deter him for applying to stay on in the army for a few extra months after his year of service ended. His colonel turned him down.

On his August leave in Paris, he missed seeing his father, who'd been sent, as inspector-general of the health services, to investigate the cholera outbreak in Spain. And in September, after spending his leave in Cabourg with his mother, who was staying mostly in bed, he wrote to his father on his first day back in Orléans: 'I am not feeling so bad (except for my stomach) and am not even suffering the general melancholy which, if it is not caused by this year of absence, is at least occasioned and therefore excused by it. But I am finding it extremely difficult to focus my attention, to read, to learn by heart, to remember.'[32]

The stage was now set for the conflict with his father which had only been postponed by the year of military service. Adrien Proust not only wanted his son to have a secure career, he saw it as his duty to fortify the boy against laziness, neurasthenic tendencies and addiction to the pleasures of high society. Like many worried and well-meaning parents, he enlisted friends to argue with his recalcitrant son. When a Foreign Office acquaintance of M. Santeuil's proffers commonsensical advice, Jean explains his priorities: 'What I need is to make myself concentrate, go into myself more deeply, search for the truth, express the whole of my soul, dealing with what is true and not with things that are really futile.'[33]

Monsieur Santeuil also consults the rector of the University, who recommends diplomacy as the best career for a young man with a philosophical disposition. Jean, he says, should study at the School of Political Science. 'Imagination is all right in its way,' concedes M. Boisard, the lecturer who's especially commended, 'but what really counts is sound critical judgment.'[34] Proust rates his father's willpower so high and his own so low that, although he wanted to become neither a lawyer nor a diplomat, he meekly enrolled on 20 November 1890 as a law student at the Sorbonne, and, almost simultaneously, as a student of political science. His lecturers included the historian Albert Sorel and the philosopher Henri Bergson, while Robert de Billy was among the students.

Proust's ambition and energy went mainly into his social life while his semi-incestuous love for his mother was diverted into passionate but puppyish efforts to win affection from his friends' mothers and other alluring ladies of the same age. The glamour of Mme Arman, Laure Hayman, Mme Straus and Mme Baignères was almost inseparable from the glamour of their salons. He enjoyed the sumptuously furnished drawing-rooms, the showy clothes, the deferential servants in livery, the mixture among the guests of formal politeness and pushy competitiveness. While hostesses competed for the most desirable guests – the most distinguished aristocrats, the most fashionable women, the most famous writers, artists,

musicians – some of the guests were secretly wishing they'd
been invited to a more exclusive salon. For the young bourgeois with beauty or talent, the salons provided a means to
find out how high they'd be able to fly.

The sense of belonging to an elite compensated Proust for
the old sense of inferiority to the Benardakys and the current
sense of inferiority to his forceful, competent, successful father.
Middle-aged ladies were delighted to receive extravagant compliments from a well-groomed, good-looking, soft-spoken,
soulful young man, no less charming than if he hoped to seduce
them, but more confident than he would have been if he had.
Quickwittedness and precocious erudition combined with his
skill as a mimic to make him entertaining in conversation. The
gift for mimicry derived partly from insecurity: if he could
caricature people he secretly envied, they became less enviable
when laughter confirmed his success in recreating their voice
and mannerisms. But he was so dissatisfied with himself that
he genuinely wanted to resemble them. In *Jean Santeuil* it is
envy of M. Perrotin's success in drawing-room conversation
that makes Jean model himself on the man.[35]

The diffident Mme Proust, who seldom went out in the
evenings, shared her husband's critical disapproval of their
son's new habit of squandering time and money on what
looked like social climbing, but neither of them understood
the desperation behind the ambition. He was soon venturing
into society whenever he had the opportunity, and going to
the theatre. In October he saw *Athalie, Pièd de Mouton*, a fairy
play by Cogniard and Crémieux, *Mimi*, a comedy by Raymond
and Boucheron, *L'Amante du Christ* by Darzens, and Ambroise
Thomas' opera *Mignon*. At the end of the month he wrote a
theatre chronicle for the *Revue lilas*, partly emulating and partly
parodying Jules Lemaître, whose reviews were appearing in
La Revue bleue and *La Revue des deux mondes*.

The most important of the middle-aged women in Proust's
life was Mme Straus, who finally invited him to her salon after
he'd completed his military service. Still in the process of
buying clothes for civilian life, he had to delay his first appearance there until after one o'clock, unable to appear in his jacket,
and needing to collect a new frock-coat from the tailor.[36] Mme
Straus was considered to be a beauty and was renowned for
her wit. Among her admirers were the painters Degas and
Jean-Louis Forain. Her salon attracted a mixture of highly

intelligent people from the nobility and from the arts. The regulars included Bonaparte's septuagenarian niece, princesse Mathilde, the English ambassador, Lord Lytton, the comtesse de Chevigné, comtesse Greffulhe, prince Auguste d'Arenberg, comte Othenin d'Haussonville, Henri Meilhac, who collaborated with her cousin, Ludovic Halévy, on librettos for Offenbach, Laure Hayman's lover Paul Bourget, Louis Ganderax, literary editor of the *Revue de Paris*, and Charles Haas.

Haas was a good-looking man of fifty-six whose Jewishness – his father was a stockbroker – hadn't stopped him from achieving stardom in the Faubourg Saint-Germain. In his middle thirties he'd posed with a prince, a baron, four marquis and three comtes for Tissot's 1868 *Le Cercle de la rue Royale*, which had been commissioned by its members. He was blackballed four times by the Jockey Club, but, sponsored by the comte de Saint-Priest and comte Albéric de Bernis, his fifth attempt to join was successful, partly because of his bravery in the war of 1870. Combining erudition with dandyism, Haas was a connoisseur of Italian painting, but his achievements were mainly social, and Proust's admiration was ambivalent. As a Jew who'd endeared himself to King Edward VII, to the comte de Paris, the pretender to the French throne, and to the most desirable hostesses, Haas was enviable; as a brilliant man who'd wasted his talents, he signalled the consequences of taking soft options. According to Jacques Blanche, though, Proust used him as a model not only for Swann but for his own way of speaking and behaving.[37] If his anti-socialite and formidably energetic father was an impossible role model for a boy who believed himself to be lazy and weak-willed, here was the ideal alternative. While the doctor's success resulted from hard work and self-denial, Haas' rested on good looks, wit, charm, elegance and courage.

One of Mme Straus' guests, the marquise de Clermont-Tonnerre, has written about the impression Proust made on her.

His pale thin face with a long, aquiline nose, gave him an oriental appearance which became frankly Assyrian when he let his beard grow. Vast black pupils, which divulged no personal sentiment but looked like two receptacles ready to receive all the waves of space, let their orbs glisten round the interlocutors, and from the mouth which was often twisted by a one-sided smile came an extraordinary voice, rather puerile, caressing, pleasing, charged with a thousand gracious inflections, giving the impression of those little soft paws, smeared with jam, which children put on your clothes, it is tender, sticky, you are both flattered and slightly irritated. Phrases you are not used to hearing – 'I hope you are not angry.' 'Your goodness towards me.' 'He is so kind to me.'

She found his humility all the more surprising because it was impossible, even at a first meeting, to 'measure the heavy tonnage of this powerful personality who travelled graciously under white sails which were always spread'.[38] At the same time he was visibly taking note of 'imperceptible differences between people who were at ease in a salon and those who were obliged to remind themselves they were in a salon'.[39]

Like Mme Straus' salon, that of Mme Baignères attracted a mixture of nobility and haute bourgeoisie. Hoping to win her friendship, Proust invited her and her son, Jacques, together with Mme Straus and Jacques Bizet, to share a box at the Odéon on 15 December, the first night of Edmond de Goncourt's *Germinie Lacerteux*, starring Réjane. Thirty-four years later he remembered how much it had made him weep. 'I came out with my eyes so red that sympathetic members of the audience thought I had been attacked.'[40] In March 1891 he was paying intensive court to Mme Straus: 'I have found in de Vigny things you should like, since they were apparently written to glorify you. He had anticipated you.'[41]

Later in the month he asked Mme Straus whether she was going to see Stanislas Rzewuski's play *L'Impératrice Faustine* on Friday 27 March. He had a ticket for that performance, he said, but did not want to go unless he'd be able to look at her. Irked by his wife's tolerance towards the young man who courted her in such an exaggerated way, and intensely irritated when she called him 'my dear little Marcel', Émile Straus would fidget in his chair, get up, pace about, pick up the tongs, poke at the fire, throw them down noisily, warn his wife not to overtire herself by talking too much.[42]

Later Proust seems to have annoyed her with either the extravagance of his compliments or his extravagance in buying flowers. French horticulturalists had begun to grow Japanese-style chrysanthemums, and he enjoyed sending these gigantic blooms to friends, male and female. Robert de Billy received some, to the astonishment of his parents,[43] and, to ward off a protest from Mme Straus, Proust flatteringly wrote: 'You will, for once and for all, surely be grateful for the infrequent flowers when I tell you that they always mean you are being spared a letter from me. And, however humble, they will always be prettier and less nuanced than my prose. When my willpower is too weak for me to concentrate my affectionate thoughts, I have to write or do something.'[44] When she tried to stop his effusive declarations of affection, his response shows that anger was good for his prose:

> I believe you love only a certain style of life which brings out your intelligence less than your wit, your wit less than your tact, your tact less than your wardrobe. You are some-one who loves this style of life more than anything – and who charms. And it is because you charm that one must not oblige you by leading you to suppose I love you less. To convince you of the opposite . . . I shall send you more pretty flowers, and you will be angry.[45]

A period of coolness ensued, but in mid-November he told her he was in 'ecstasy' to hear she felt as well disposed as she had before. 'I am too happy with yesterday's divine words which show you are unique – as in everything else – in the art of making hearts swell, as well as in breaking them.'[46]

When we read his letters today, it's easy to feel repelled by the exorbitant flattery, but his feeling of plurality helped him to feel justified. Two Marcels watched from the wings – one amused, one disapproving – while the obsequious Marcel on stage succeeded in ingratiating himself. When he spoke to friends, the half-joking tone in his soft voice left them free to choose how seriously to take the flattery, while in his letters the handwritten words – almost audible in his voice – were steeped in his personal charm.

> First he was beautiful, with a rather Italian beauty – he laughed complacently when I said he looked like an Italian prince for a Bourget novel. His long slim figure with cheeks however which were full, with a straight nose, slightly arched with a bump which made him coquettishly despairing . . . his eyes inherited from his admirable mother, black liquid eyes, with heavy brown lids which lowered like a beautiful veil of flesh on an oriental hearth of light and

dreams – everything about him was princely. He felt it, he lingered voluptuously on summer evenings to stroll along, going 'into society', a light overcoat half-open over his shirt-front, a flower in his buttonhole – the flowers in fashion at that time were white camellias – he enjoyed his adolescent grace reflected in the eyes of passers-by with a little juvenile fatuity and a hint of that 'consciousness of evil' which he already possessed at eighteen and which was his Muse. He sometimes exaggerated this gracefulness in a simpering manner, but always amusingly, as he sometimes exaggerated his affability in flattery, but always intelligently; and we had even created among ourselves the verb *proustify* to express a slightly too conscious attitude of geniality together with what would vulgarly have been called affectations, interminable and delicious.[47]

The compulsion to proustify stemmed from the same insecurity as the compulsion to overtip waiters and reward friends with gigantic bouquets and extravagant presents. No less deep-rooted than the princely self-assurance was an agonising uncertainty about whether he was likeable. Desperate for affection and unwilling to trust his intrinsic qualities, he couldn't stop himself from trying to bribe the world with compliments and gifts.

He always did it stylishly, and with his beauty, his affability and his wit, he impressed the princesse Mathilde, who invited him to her salon. About seventy, she was still handsome, with a thick, almost growling voice and an engaging way of dismissing flattery. 'She has a tough, almost masculine candour, a German bluntness softened by an Italian languor which appears in her smile.' 'The sum of the parts was enveloped in an outfit so typical of the Second Empire that although the princesse wore it, no doubt, only from attachment to the fashions she had loved, it looked as though she had wanted to avoid any error in historic colour and to satisfy the expectations of those who wanted her to evoke another era.'[48]

Her fondness for Proust was so apparent that her friends nicknamed him Popelin Junior after her last lover, Claudius Popelin. Her appearance in *À la recherche* is a reminder of his excitement whenever history flickered into visibility. Swann describes her as 'the friend of Flaubert, of Sainte-Beuve, of Dumas. Just think, she's Napoleon I's niece. Napoleon III and the Tsar of Russia both wanted to marry her.' Nothing stimulated Proust more than what felt like direct confrontation with history. When he started going to balls, he sometimes saw the octogenarian duchesse de Maille, who had grey, upswept hair, like a judge's wig. She was the niece of Mme de Boigne, who'd been dandled on the laps of Louis XVI and Marie-Antoinette. In 1907, when he thought of writing an article on 'Snobbery and Posterity', it was to explore his excitement about direct contact with the nobility, which seemed to involve personal contact with history.[49] He was thrilled by the names of noble families and even thrilled by the antique Christian names they still favoured – Odon, Ghislain, Adhéaume, Josselin.

It's all too easy, when looking back at Proust's career, to erect a misleading barrier between his life in high society and his literary activity. But the qualities which made him a darling of the salons are qualities evident in his early writings, and in 1892–3 the principal showcase for these was a review conceived in Mme Straus' home. Proust founded *Le Banquet* with Jacques Bizet, Daniel Halévy, Robert Dreyfus, comte Louis de la Salle, vicomte Robert de Flers and Fernand Gregh. De la Salle, de Flers and Gregh had all been at the *lycée*, but in lower forms. All three made friends with Proust after Jacques Bizet brought him home for the inaugural meeting. Writing to de Billy, Proust described de Flers as charming, intelligent, good and sweet.[50] Later, he and Lucien Daudet were photographed together with Proust, whose mother forbade him to show anyone the photograph for fear it might arouse suspicions about the purity of their friendship.

It was in tribute to their former teacher Darlu that they named the new review after Plato's *Le Banquet* (*Symposium*). Each of the founder-editors would contribute ten francs a month to have it printed by a friend of Bizet's. At first 400 copies of each issue were printed; later 200. The main object was to publish their own work, but there were also contributions from outsiders. When Proust met Henri Barbusse in March 1882 at one of the Saturdays held in the house of the Parnassian poet José Maria de Heredia, he invited Barbusse to contribute verse to *Le Banquet*. The first issue had come out in March. But Proust was disappointed with the work by some of the outsiders. The fourth issue, which appeared in June, contained an essay by the twenty-year-old Léon Blum (later socialist prime minister). It struck Proust as a cheap imitation of the thirty-year-old Boulangiste deputy Maurice Barrès, who'd been elaborating his *culte du moi* in essayistic novels. In May Barrès was the guest of honour at a party held by Léon Yeatman, a fellow-student of Proust in the law school at the Sorbonne.

Proust's first contribution to *Le Banquet* was a review of *Les Petits Souliers* by Louis Ganderax, and in March, after meeting the eyes of the fair-haired comtesse de Mailly-Nesles when she was wearing a red velvet gown at princesse Mathilde's salon, he wrote: 'They were like eyes that had seen nothing of what all human eyes ordinarily reflect, eyes still virginal to earthly experience. But when I looked at you more carefully, you suggested something affectionate and suffering, as if you were someone the fairies had denied what she most wanted, even before she was born.'[51]

In other pieces for *Le Banquet* Proust depicted some of the mother-figures he was courting. Mme Straus was one of the 'indifferent and cheerful people with big eyes, dark as grief, as if a funnel had been held between their soul and their eyes and as if they had, so to speak, passed the whole living content of their soul into their eyes'.[52] She was also the model for the 'woman who betrayed her intelligence only in a subtler grace, who was content to live and did not dissipate in excessively precise conversations the charming mystery of her nature. She was as gentle as those graceful, agile animals with deep eyes and as disconcerting as the memory which is almost effaced at daybreak of our dreams. But she did not bother to do what the two others had done for him – love him.'[53] Proust later confided to her: 'I love mysterious women, since that is what you are, and I have often said so in *Le Banquet*, where I would often have liked you to recognise yourself.'[54] It was a lifelong habit to portray friends in his work, hoping they'd recognise themselves when the portrait was favourable. When it was critical, he lived in fear of their reactions.

If there was a perverse obstinacy in his infatuations, there was a mixture of impulse and calculation in his attempts to cure himself of them by writing. Another lady he portrayed in *Le Banquet* was the blonde and witty comtesse Laure de Chevigné, one of Mme Straus' regulars. Descended from the de Sade family, she was in her thirties and had been married since 1879 to the comte Adhéaume de Chevigné, gentleman in waiting to the Bourbon pretender to the French throne. In

March, not content with raising his hat to the comtesse when he met her in the street, Proust started to wait near her house in the rue de Miromesnil or in the avenue de Marigny or the avenue Gabriel, knowing she'd soon pass on her daily visit to her lover, comte Robert de FitzJames. When Proust finally found the courage to address her, he was curtly rebuffed: 'FitzJames is expecting me.'[55]

FOUR

AMBIVALENCE

In the summer of 1892 Proust didn't know whether he was capable of fighting for the future he wanted. His twenty-first birthday was approaching, but manhood wasn't going to bring manliness like his father's, or like his nineteen-year-old brother's. Perhaps he'd never escape from the consequences of his surrender to his father's superior willpower. He'd spent two years studying political sciences and law, putting a good deal of effort into his work. At the end of June 1892 he passed the oral examinations on 'Diplomatic History from 1818 to 1878', 'Eastern Affairs' and 'A Portrait of Contemporary Europe'. His marks ranged from 4¼ to 5 out of 6, and the comments included 'extremely intelligent' and 'good answers in general'.[1] At the beginning of August he passed the first part of his exams at the law faculty, but failed in the oral.

Unable to do himself justice when arguing with his parents, he was more outspoken in the discussions he held with himself in the stories he wrote, but even here he didn't quarrel with their view that he was lacking in willpower. It was like a sentence they'd passed on him and, instead of appealing against it, he issued warnings to himself about the dangers of wasting time in high society – the dangers of emulating Charles Haas instead of Adrien Proust.

The doctor was neither a martinet nor unenlightened; judged by the standards of the period, his books about the upbringing of children were progressive, and his practice as a father was broadly in line with his theories. Attempts to impose discipline, he contended, could be counterproductive; it was wrong to undermine a child's self-confidence 'by telling him brutally that he does not understand, does not know, cannot do this or that'.[2] But he had strong misgivings about the life Marcel was leading. To him it seemed neurasthenic. In fact his views on neurasthenia had been influenced by watching his son's behaviour, but the influence was reciprocal: reading his father's articles and books about neurasthenia, Proust could hardly fail to recognise himself in them, and they had an effect on both his self-image and his early fiction. Neurasthenia was still a novel concept. The pioneering monograph had been written by George M. Beard in 1880: one of the main symptoms was lack of willpower.

But the doctor's misgivings about his son's social life were only partly medical. Adrien Proust's experience seemed to confirm his Puritanical belief in achieving salvation through hard work. Elected to the Académie de Médecine in 1879, made inspector-general of sanitary services in 1884 and appointed the next year as professor of hygiene in the Medical Faculty, he'd been richly rewarded for his high-stamina medical labour, and had become one of the most fashionable doctors in Paris. 'I should never dare to consult your father,' said Anatole France. 'I'm not important enough for him. These days the only patients he takes are river basins.' Inveterately ambitious, Dr Proust enjoyed having some of the most powerful men in France, including well-known government ministers, among his friends and dinner guests: their company was enjoyable and their goodwill helpful. But it wasn't just his shyness and his residual priestly Puritanism that made him ambivalent about high society. He not only disapproved of the idle life but saw it as a cause of neurasthenia. To most fathers Marcel's social success would have seemed enviable. Adrien Proust wasn't immune to envy, but he was more interested in symptom and causation. In the book he wrote in collaboration with Gilbert Ballet, life in high society is listed among the causes of nervous exhaustion and depression. Without demanding an excessive outlay of mental energy, they argued, society left little time for relaxation or domesticity. 'No man is busier, it has been said, than the one who does nothing. . . . More than anyone, men about town and society women are absorbed throughout the day by exigencies imposed on them by conventions and vain concern for their reputation: visits, dinner parties, balls, soirées give them a life of constant and unremitting pressure and obligation.' In high society, people slipped into 'a kind of existence at odds with all the rules of hygiene', habituating themselves 'to excitements of all kinds . . . to meals at which they sit too long and eat too much in rooms which are often overheated, to long evenings, to lack of sleep, or at least of sleep taken at the normal times'. This routine often led to 'a sort of moral exhaustion which results from paltry efforts to realise the fantasies of vanity'.[3]

Whether Adrien Proust argued like this when talking and writing to Marcel, or whether his books acted as a safety valve for the points he stopped himself from making out of fear that they'd be counterproductive, the lines were being laid down for the battle which was to be fought between father and son. Moral disapproval of the idle life merged with paternal fears for the future of a son who seemed to have inordinate social ambitions and unrealistic literary ambitions, but none of any other kind. If only he could be persuaded into a sensible career, the routine of hard work might prove salutary.

The diffident son had never felt altogether comfortable with his diffident father. In spite of the mutual affection, they were awkward about touching each other. During childhood, the sickly Marcel had seen his father's powers as infinite: he had the omniscience of a doctor and the godlike power to make rules in the sickroom, while some of the most powerful men in France were his friends. Measuring himself against this man, the boy felt incompetent, untalented. The powerful father could always keep him out of trouble, but it would be impossible to impress him or achieve comparable success.

Instead of trying to block his ears against his father's forceful arguments, Marcel incorporated them into his dispute with himself. In August 1892 he wrote a story about a conflict between social and spiritual impulses, 'Violante ou la mondanité'. The first two of the four chapters have captions from *The Imitation of Christ* by Thomas à Kempis. 'Have little traffic with young folk and people of the world. . . . Never seek to be seen in the company of the great.' 'Never lean on a reed which is shaken by the wind, and place no trust in it, for all flesh is as grass, and its glory passes like the flower in the field.' Proust's self-doubt is projected into a viscount's daughter, who's brought up in Styria, which he describes as a rustic domain 'far from the world'. Though 'beautiful and lively, like her father, and as benevolent and mysteriously seductive as her mother',[4] Violante lacks willpower.

Orphaned at fifteen, she learns more from her dreams than from her tutor. She has 'a feeling of happiness, of still unknown power, the feeling she was arranging her life a little according to her caprice and for the sake of her pleasure, that at the wheels of their two destinies, which seemed to imprison them

mechanically at a distance from each other, she could nevertheless apply pressure with her thumb'.[5] She inherits neither her
father's vulgarity nor his insensitivity, but she can't resist the
temptations of high society, though, before setting out for the
Austrian court, she says: 'The world to me is only a means. It
offers weapons which are vulgar but invincible, and if some
day I want to be loved, I need to possess them. . . . I need
both a rest and a training. . . . At a precise moment, not far
away, I shall stop going down this slope and return to Styria.'

She finds people 'so mediocre that as soon as she deigned to
mix with them, she eclipsed nearly all of them. . . . She alone
had wit, taste and a bearing which suggested perfection in
everything.'[6] She reflects both Proust's contempt for the chit-
chat of fashionable salons and his pleasure at being accepted in
them. Bored though she is in society, she never turns the
conversation to 'concerns which by their very superiority are
unpleasing and incomprehensible to the people who live in the
world'. In spite of making enemies, including a Lesbian princess who tries to seduce her, she cannot make up her mind to
go home. She's too tempted by 'a reception which would be
more enjoyable, perhaps, than the others, a prettier gown to
display'. When she dies, she's still trying to be a leader of
fashion in the *beau monde*. She's the victim of the habit she has
formed, and habit is 'a force which, if nourished from the
outset by vanity, can overcome disgust, contempt and even
boredom'.[7]

Ambivalent though Proust was about high society, he was
so alert to the dangers of squandering time that, according to
Jacques-Émile Blanche, he never made that mistake. Blanche
was a thirty-one-year-old painter whose parents had a villa
in Dieppe, and, having sketched Proust during October in
Trouville, he was now seeing him every Saturday to work on
his portrait in oil. After the sessions they'd have dinner with
Blanche's father, a well-known psychiatrist, Antoine-Émile
Blanche, who kept a private lunatic asylum not far from Louis
Weil's villa in Auteuil. Guy de Maupassant was currently one
of the inmates.

When the portrait was finished, Blanche disliked it so much
he tore the canvas up. Proust rescued the head, but couldn't
salvage the rest of his body.[8] But Blanche's attitude to the
painting didn't reflect his feelings towards the sitter. Proust,
he says, read a great deal, going around with books and reviews

stuffed into his pockets, and had an unusual capacity for storing impressions and information in his memory. 'The exceptional quality of this recording apparatus enabled him to retain sensations and fugitive perceptions which escape most of us almost as soon as they are formed.' At receptions older people were impressed by his knowledge and erudition, and though he often accompanied ladies to their dressmaker or their hairdresser, he wasn't idle even then. He was always brimming with curiosity, posing questions, reciting poetry, quoting from novels, checking artistic valuations. Wasn't Delaunay's portrait of Mme Straus more beautiful than *La Gioconda*? Wasn't Madeleine Lemaire more talented than Rosalba? And he was slightly hurt if you didn't agree.[9]

Blanche's evidence reinforces a point François Mauriac has made: there was no real dichotomy between Proust's social life and his literary activity. Irresistibly attracted by elegant, arrogant aristocrats, good-looking men and women, finely dressed, well coiffured, he was intrigued by the social games they played and convinced that mysterious laws were at work, just as they were in nature. Wanting to understand everything that was going on, Proust had to observe carefully.

Blanche's first sketch for the portrait had been done at 'Les Frémonts', the hilltop villa in Trouville where Proust had been staying with the Baignères. He liked the villa so much that he recommended it to the Finalys, who rented it for the summer of 1893, and later, when they bought it from the Baignères, he was presented with a cane to thank him for the part he'd played. In August, the month he wrote 'Violante', he and Louis de la Salle went there to stay with the Finalys. If Proust was already half in love with Horace, he now fell equally for the pretty, green-eyed, nineteen-year-old sister, Mary. Gregh describes her as 'the centre of the family . . . a delightful girl, alternately laughing and serious. We were all a little in love with her.'[10] Proust was amazed at her 'moral, almost religious preoccupations'.[11] Oscillating between happiness and melancholy, he was sometimes enervated by her apparent indifference, sometimes moved by her ability to share his moods. She appears in another story he wrote for *Le Banquet*: 'During the day, Assunta's companionship, her singing, her sweetness towards me, whom she barely knew, her white, brown and pink beauty, her perfume lingering in the gusts of wind from the sea, the feather in her hat, the pearls around her neck, had distracted me.' Most of the piece is about an alfresco feeling of euphoria which supervenes on an oppressive dream refracting unrequited love and everyday anxieties, but Assunta reappears in the final section, worried he may be feeling cold. 'I went up to her; I shivered, she took me under her cloak, and to keep it folded around me, put her arm around my neck.' When they tread on a piece of the moon, he nestles against her head, and they both weep. The moon weeps too.[12]

His aestheticism and his premature world-weariness are partly genuine, but also parts of an attempt to conform with fin-de-siècle disillusionment about what he called 'the incurable imperfection of the present'. It was easy for him to identify with 'the man bored with the ways of the world or who guesses, before trying them, how bitter and vulgar they are'.[13] Proust's problem was that when he tried them, he was liable to be less critical than this, and, like 'Violante', this story is written partly as a warning to himself against the dangers of addiction to social pleasures. His ambivalence is equally visible in the portraits he created, trying to view people critically, as if they were works of art, but unable to repress his affection and admiration. Writing about the twenty-two-year-old Mme Guillaume Beer, who owned the pavilion de Voisins at Louveciennes, he praised her for combining Italian grace with Nordic mystery. Leconte de Lisle celebrated her charm in the poem 'La Rose de Louveciennes', and Proust claimed that a flower in her hands or between her breasts, a banal compliment from her lips or the gesture of holding her arm when walking in to the dinner table acquired 'a grace as disturbing as an artistic emotion. Around her all things soften themselves into a delicious harmony which continues into the folds of her gown.' Her charm seemed to be 'perfumed with a holy odour'.[14] If the emotion in these early stories seems uncontrolled, it's largely because he couldn't bring his ambivalence into focus.

It's equally visible in the answers he wrote late in 1892 or early in 1893 to a questionnaire in a confessional album. His principal character trait, he says, is 'the need to be loved, or, to be more precise, the need to be appreciated and spoiled rather than the need to be admired', and what he values most in his friends is evidence of their affection for him 'if their person is exquisite enough for me to set a high value on their affection'. What he'd most like to be is himself 'as the people I admire would like me to be'. What he hates most is 'the bad in myself', and the natural gifts he most covets are 'willpower and seductiveness'. His main fault is 'not knowing how to, not being able to "will" '. His greatest misfortune would have been not to know his mother and his grandmother, while the lower value he set on his father is again revealed when he says the qualities he most admires in a man are feminine charm and, in a woman, 'masculine virtues and openness in friendship'. His favourite occupation is loving, and his favourite poets are now Baudelaire and de Vigny. De Musset, who was his favourite eight years ago when he replied to the questions in Antoinette Faure's album, no longer rates a mention. His favourite prose writers are Anatole France and Pierre Loti, his favourite composers Beethoven, Wagner and Schumann, and his favourite painters Leonardo and Rembrandt. His hero from fiction is Hamlet, his heroine from history Cleopatra, and his heroes from real life M. Darlu and M. Boutroux. Émile Boutroux was his favourite professor at the Sorbonne, a historian.

In contrast to the answers of eight years ago, these emphasise the need to be loved. At thirteen he could take it for granted that people cared for him; at twenty-one he was suffering from the insecurity which made him compulsive about plying friends with flowers and flattery, giving extravagant presents and overtipping. Desperate for affection, he felt sure he'd never get enough of it unless he paid generously. And it was almost like making a payment to his parents when, a week after passing his law exam in November, he again enrolled at the law school, registering at the same time for a third year of political science. He also started to take private lessons in law from Pierre Lavallée.

It is doubtful whether the Third Republic was any more corrupt than the monarchy before 1848 or the empire until 1871, but, given the new power of the press, it was easier for opponents of the regime to uncover malpractice, and France was never so badly rocked by scandals as it was during the 1890s. In November 1892, three years before the Dreyfus affair, a scandal broke over fraudulence practised by the Panama Canal Company, and Proust introduced this into *Jean Santeuil* through Charles Marie, whose Jewish wife seems to be modelled on Mme Proust – she's described as 'an exquisite creature, a ravishing and witty woman, a superb wife and mother'.[15] As minister of finance, Marie had consorted with unscrupulous bankers and dabbled in shady enterprises. Proust sympathetically describes the crisis in which a politician accustomed to applause has to address a hostile chamber. His downfall is advantageous to the 'poor party, called socialist' in its struggle against 'the capitalist and opportunist party'.[16] M. Santeuil, who's Marie's oldest friend, goes on supporting him, but comes under attack in a left-wing paper. Jean then tries to persuade a former friend of his father's, a prominent left-winger, to stand up in defence of M. Santeuil's probity. Marie loses his seat and impotently watches the government pursuing policies that can only, he believes, lead to disaster. Proust couldn't integrate the political material satisfactorily, but what he was witnessing was the opportunistic exploitation of a scandal and a widening of the cracks that were to divide France into reactionary and progressive factions three years later.

If the material seemed attractive to him, this was partly because it involved people at the top of the social spectrum. He never made any serious attempt to integrate the working classes into his fiction, though he often spoke up in favour of servants. 'All in all,' he told Maurice Duplay, 'I like domestic servants better than people in society. Servants are spontaneous and picturesque in a different way! In fact, because of their profession, they are much better brought up, much politer.'[17] Like many homosexuals, he often took servants as his lovers, but he made no serious attempt in his fiction to represent working-class experience or to discuss the emotional discontinuity between affairs with servants and affairs with men of his own class. Even when the baron de Charlus enters into sexual liaisons with social inferiors, the event is described from outside, with no penetration into the emotion involved.

Most of the time, neither emotion nor jealousy was involved in Proust's liaisons with footmen, waiters and male secretaries, but in his friendships with young men who were socially his equals or superiors, jealousy was integral to the pleasure, even when sexual intimacy wasn't integral to the friendship. He was also pleasurably jealous of friendships his friends had. De Billy's liaison, for instance, with an elegant and cultivated young visitor from Geneva, Edgar Aubert. The three of them went for walks in the Tuileries, and Aubert gave Proust his photograph. The relationship seemed particularly romantic in retrospect, for Aubert died suddenly of appendicitis in September 1892, only a few days after a holiday with de Billy.

Proust had been frustrated when he fell in love with a young American, Edward Cachard, the son of a lawyer, but at the end of 1892 or the beginning of 1893 he was more fortunate, entering happily into a liaison with the young comte Robert de Flers. They'd known each other for years. Eighteen months his junior, Robert had been at the Condorcet and had studied both law and literature. It was through working together on *Le Banquet* that they became intimate. In January Robert was coming to see Proust almost every day[18] and was given a photograph. 'Nothing has changed much in my emotional life,' Proust wrote on 10 January, 'except that I have found a friend, someone who is for me what I could perhaps have been for Cachard if he had not been so cold. It is the young and charming and intelligent and good and sweet Robert de Flers.'[19] In February Robert took Proust with him to the abbé Pierre Vignot's Lenten sermons at the École Fénelon. Robert's grandmother, Mme de Rozière, told Proust: 'Robert loves you like a brother,' which he took to mean: 'You should try to be worthy of him.'[20]

The affair was soon eclipsed by one with a young Englishman, Willie Heath. In June, when Proust's parents gave a dinner party for ten of his friends – including four comtes and two vicomtes – he sat between Robert and François de Carbonnel de Mongival, while Willie sat on Mme Proust's left. Blond, good-looking, elegant, dandyish, he had melancholy eyes which reminded Proust of cavaliers in portraits by van Dyck, and he had what Proust called a 'moral elegance', conveyed by his soul to his body. When they went for walks in the Bois de Boulogne, they shared a fantasy of a future in which they'd live together in a small community of 'high-minded men and women, somewhere too far away from stupidity, vice and malice for their vulgar arrows ever to reach us'.[21] But, like Aubert's life, Willie's was cut brutally short. He died of typhoid at the beginning of October.

One of Proust's hostesses was the fashionable society painter Madeleine Lemaire, who was known as la Patronne. She lived in the rue de Monceau, where, from April till June, she held musical evenings in a glass-roofed studio. They were attended by the nobility and by well-known artists including Puvis de Chavannes. A tall, rouged woman with false hair and arching eyebrows, Mme Lemaire was fashionable as a painter of flower-pieces, which were sold for about 500 francs. 'No one except God', said Dumas *fils*, 'has created more roses,' and Proust called her salon 'the lilac court and the rose studio'. She had electricity installed in her home early enough for the event to be worth mentioning in the newspapers.[22]

On 14 April 1893 *Le Gaulois* reported: 'Mme Lemaire has just resumed her Thursday receptions. Yesterday evening's was preceded by an elegant dinner. The salon of this great artist is known to be one of the Parisian world's intellectual centres, and it was before a distinguished audience that Mlle Bartet yesterday evening gave an exquisite recitation of several poems by M. José de Heredia and by comte Robert de Montes-quiou-Fezensac.' Julia Bartet was a star of the Comédie Fran-çaise.

Proust could do an effective imitation of Mme Lemaire taking leave of her guests. 'Madame de Maupeou, you sang like an angel this evening! This Brandes is amazing, she's always twenty! And this little creature is such an artissst! Au revoir, Montesquiou, dear, great, sublime poet. . . . Ochoa, don't catch cold.' Then she'd say 'Come on, Suzette' to her daughter, and, going upstairs, tell her dogs what she was really thinking.[23]

Montesquiou came from one of the noblest families in France. Descended from Blaise de Montluc, the sixteenth-century author of the *Commentaires*, and from Charles de Batz, the seventeenth-century original of D'Artagnan in *Les Trois Mousquetaires*, he was related through aristocratic intermar-riages to many of the great ducal families, including La Roche-foucauld, Gramont and Béthune. Now thirty-eight, tall, slim, elegant, arrogant, handsome, brilliant, with rouged cheeks and thick black hair, permanently waved, Mephistophelian eye-brows, a wavy moustache (modelled on Whistler's) with pointed, upturned ends and a tiny pointed beard poking out-wards from between the lower lip and the chin, he had a fluting voice and grotesque affectations. He'd served as the model for the duc Jean des Esseintes in Huysmans' novel *À Rebours*. 'Anaemic and highly strung, he had hollow cheeks, cold, steel-blue eyes, a nose that was retroussé but straight, and thin papery hands.'[24] The comte used the château d'Artagnan as his country seat, and called his Neuilly house the Palais des Muses. He was reputed to have been one of Sarah Bernhardt's lovers, but now took more pleasure in relationships with male

secretaries and attractive young men. Since he was in demand
at the most exclusive salons, he was in a position to give Proust
entrée to them, while Proust, quite apart from his own appeal,
could give the comte introductions to young men.

He was invited to call at the house in rue Franklin which
had been described by the Goncourts as 'crammed with a
mixture of incongruous objects, old family portraits, Empire
furniture, Japanese kakemonos and etchings by Whistler'.[25] The
bathroom was decorated with representations of the hydrangea
'in every possible material and every conceivable art-form' and
he had a sledge on a white bearskin, church furniture and a
gilded tortoise. He also possessed a plaster-cast of Castiglione's
knees.

The reading at Mme Lemaire's was part of a campaign he'd
just launched to make his poetry fashionable in high society,
and when Proust, after visiting him, sent flowers, he reciprocated by sending a de-luxe edition of his 1892 collection, Les
Chauves-souris (The Bats), inscribed with a quotation from it:
'I am the sovereign of the transitory.' He was thanked in the
third of many flattering letters Proust wrote to him: 'Be assured
it will remain for me an everlasting bouquet.'[26] In a July letter,
praising two of Montesquiou's lines as being on a par with
Corneille's, Proust told him that in a period lacking in genius,
'you excel through the twofold force of your reflectiveness and
your energy'. He wasn't just the sovereign of the transitory
but the sovereign of things eternal, and he could count on
having a place 'in a very selective anthology of philosophical
poetry in France'.[27]

It's hard to be sure whether the comte wanted the twenty-
two-year-old Proust as a lover. Montesquiou's narcissism was
a more potent force than his homosexuality, while Proust,
more articulate, intelligent and sensitive than most flatterers,
would have been an ideal disciple. Proust's memories of their
early meetings are filtered into his portrayal of baron Charlus,
who seems almost as uncertain of what he wants from the
Narrator as of what he can get. At their first encounter, Charlus
stares with eyes that seem to be starting out of his head,[28]
and his subsequent behaviour alternates dauntingly between
brusqueness and friendliness, between imperious formality and
suggestive intimacy. The Narrator is confused, while Charlus,
often hesitating and making false starts, oscillates between
haughtiness and diffidence. He continues behaving enigmati-

cally, going out of his way to befriend the young man, and suggesting he could be helpful, but modulating into angry complaints about ingratitude. After the party given by his aunt, Mme de Villeparisis, he explicitly asks: 'Are you worth my trouble or not?' Talking about his influence, his connections, his importance, he says they should see each other every day,[29] but never makes an unambiguous pass and often, as if feeling rejected, switches into infuriated reprimands.

Unpredictable though it was, Montesquiou's friendship helped Proust to penetrate into more exclusive circles. He was soon receiving invitations from both the duchesse de Gramont and her sister the princesse de Wagram. His social success caused both conflict with his parents and awkwardness with his friends. His parents rationalised their displeasure by saying he wasn't concentrating on things that mattered, and punished him by making it harder for him to present himself as stylishly as he would have liked at exclusive soirées. He'd have to manage with a simple rose from the garden in his buttonhole instead of one wrapped in silver paper; instead of lending him the family carriage, they had the horses unharnessed at seven in the evening and refused to pay for him to travel by cab. During the spring and early summer, when they were in Auteuil, he went to Paris by bus, trying to hide his white tie and tails under his overcoat.[30]

Not wanting to make fellow-students jealous, he tried to give the impression he never went into society and was no better off than they were. At the Gare Saint-Lazare, meeting friends who were on their way to Auteuil, he hid his first-class ticket and travelled with them in a third-class compartment. One afternoon in Auteuil, on his way home from a session with Blanche, who was still working at his portrait, he called at the house of a young man, only to find himself hustled downstairs to the basement. 'Forgive me, my dear chap, it's impossible to ask you in, as you'll understand. You see, the Dutilleuls are coming to tea.' Proust would have been less unwelcome if the young man had known he'd been invited that evening to the princesse de Wagram's ball, and, coincidentally, they met on the bus to Paris. The young man apologised for having no time to spare in the afternoon but, when he caught sight of the white tie under the lapel of the overcoat, he asked why Proust was in evening dress. He had to admit he was going to a ball, and, not wanting to use the word 'princesse' when the young man asked which one, answered: 'The Wagram ball.' He didn't know a ball was held at the Salle Wagram for waiters and servants. 'My dear chap, at least you shouldn't make out you've been receiving invitations when you're so lacking in connections that you're reduced to going to servants' balls and paying for admission!'[31]

It was in the princesse de Wagram's house at the beginning of July that he saw a superbly beautiful woman with magnetic agate eyes. She impressed him so much he didn't ask to be introduced. 'It seems to me that in speaking to her I would experience rather a painful agitation. But I would like her to know what a great impression she made on me.' She was wearing orchids in her hair. 'Her coiffure had a Polynesian grace, and mauve orchids were hanging down to the nape of her neck, like the "hats of flowers" M. Renan describes. She is difficult to judge, no doubt because to judge is to compare, and in her there is nothing that could have been seen in anyone else or anywhere else. But the whole mystery of her beauty lies in the brilliance of her highly enigmatic eyes.'[32]

Born the princesse Élisabeth de Caraman-Chimay, the comtesse Greffulhe was thirty-three, and a cousin of Montesquiou. Never had an older woman aroused such a strong flood of emotion in Proust, and he wasn't alone in feeling an adoration which scarcely fell short of worship. 'She is no easier to meet', wrote Élisabeth de Gramont,[33] 'than the Archbishop of Paris. Like Salammbo she never displays herself to the crowd except from the top of a staircase, or surrounded by kings.'

She was aware of her appeal: 'I believe there can be no pleasure in the world comparable to that of a woman who knows everyone's eyes are on her, giving her gladness and energy.' She was pleased with the sonnet Montesquiou ended: 'Fair lily, your black pistils are your eyes.' 'Only you and the sun', she told him, 'really understand me.' Her husband, comte Henri Greffulhe, heir to a Belgian banking family, was vastly rich and sixteen years her senior. He was old enough to be Proust's father, and an incarnation of the aristocratic father he'd ideally have liked – tall, arrogant, dominating. His spade-shaped blond beard made Jacques Blanche compare him to a red king on a playing card. Unfaithful but jealous, he insisted his wife always be home by 11.30.

What the comtesse inspired in Proust was a new combination of such erotic fantasies as had previously centred on his mother,

Marie de Benardaky and attractive males. Soon after the soirée he started a story about a lovely noblewoman who uses orchids to give her hair 'a Polynesian charm'.[34] The pivotal idea – one of the prettiest women in society falls for an unexceptional middle-class man – may derive from Proust's daydream that the comtesse would fall in love with him, but it is developed carefully. Profiting from the wisdom of Carmen's Habanera – if I love you, you don't love me – Madeleine de Gouvres affects indifference towards M. Lepré, but can't stop herself from inviting him to dinner on Thursday, proposing Friday when he says he's not free, and then Saturday, though this will involve her in letting down a princesse whose dinner party she'd promised to attend. She soon knows herself to be help-lessly in love. 'The reasons for her love were in her, and if they were also a little in him, it was not because of his intellectual superiority or even his physical superiority. It is precisely because she loved him that no face, no smile, no way of moving pleased her as much as his: it was not that his face, his smile, his way of moving made her love him.' Proust's analysis of hopeless heterosexual love derives from frustration he'd felt after becoming infatuated with the face, the smile, the movements of men who weren't exceptionally attractive. 'She was ready to pluck, like a bitter flower, the pleasure of finding him mediocre and absurdly out of proportion to the love she felt for him.' His indifference only inflames that love, in accord-ance with the Habanera principle. In telling the story, Proust makes frequent use of flowers. Normally her room is full of fresh flowers, but after meeting him she wants none but the wilting orchids she was wearing; meeting his white poodle alone in the Tuileries, she takes the violets from her corsage and ties them to the dog's collar.[35]

Having found a theme which touched so many of his nerve centres, Proust immediately reworked it in another story. In 'Mélancolique villégiature [Melancholy Summer] de Madame de Breyves' Françoise, who is beautiful and in demand, has no reason to fall for M. de Laléande, though he seems more interested in her than M. Lepré is in Madeleine. When Françoise sees Laléande at a reception, her first impression is that he's ugly and vulgar. Though she gives him a few flir-tatious glances, she's more frightened than pleased when, in the cloakroom, he rubs his elbow lightly against hers and, pretending to look for his cane, unceremoniously invites her to his home. But she becomes increasingly obsessed with him, though she fails in all her elaborate efforts to arrange a meeting, or perhaps because she fails. He has left Paris for Biarritz. Desire 'had been implanted in her by a thousand invisible roots which had penetrated into all her most unconscious minutes of happiness or melancholy, making a new sap run through her, without her knowing where it came from.' Though Proust isn't specific in his use of the word 'unconscious', he's focusing accurately on her helplessness, which is as irrational and inexplicable as Madeleine's. Like the frustrated Proust, both women are prone to emotions which invade them like a viral infection, and are no less arbitrary in choosing their victims. It's useless for Françoise to remind herself that Laléande is a mediocrity, a nonentity, that the love has its source in her own imagination. M. de Laléande 'would be astonished if he knew about the other existence he has in the soul of Madame de Breyves, an existence which is miraculously intense, to the point of dominating everything and annihilating everything irrelevant to it, and which is as continuous as his personal existence, translating itself with equal efficacity into actions'.[36] But since there's no reason for her obsession, there's no cure. Feeling strongly about men unaware of his reaction to them, Proust found it easy to identify with men's female victims. In both stories a picture becomes a substitute for the man. Madeleine acquires a photograph of a painting of a young man who reminds her of Lepré; after Laléande leaves for Biarritz, Françoise never sees him again, but has a huge photograph of Biarritz on her wall.

FIVE

OPTIONS

Proust had been looking forward to the long summer holidays he'd have after sitting for his law faculty examination at the end of July, but however good or bad the result was, his relaxation was going to be overshadowed by the need to decide about a career and the uncertainty about whether he'd have to go on studying. He was twenty-two, and about to receive a law diploma. He was determined not to become a lawyer: 'In my days of greatest desperation I have never conceived of anything worse than a lawyer's office.'[1] But his father – whose willpower still appeared formidable – seemed adamant that he should make some practical use of his diploma.[2] He could try to plan a career in diplomacy or in the civil service, or try to work his way towards a job in a museum, but all these would involve further study. To work for the Ministry of Foreign Affairs he'd have to sit another exam, and if he enrolled for the three-year course at the École des Chartes, he'd be twenty-five by the time he was qualified to work as a palaeontologist or archivist, but, as he told his father, 'I still believe anything I do apart from literature and philosophy is for me so much time wasted.'[3] This was as close as he could come to saying the three years of study he'd completed had been three wasted years.

But he had no intention of wasting the three weeks he was going to spend in St Moritz with Louis de la Salle, Montesquiou and Mme Meredith Howland, a close friend of Charles Haas and Edgar Degas. She was one of the few American women accepted in French society. Before leaving Paris, Proust and de la Salle made plans to collaborate with Halévy and Gregh on an epistolary novel modelled on Paul Hervieu's *Peints par eux-mêmes*, which had just been published, and on another epistolary novel *La Croix de Berny*, fruit of a quadruple collaboration in 1846 between Théophile Gautier, Mme de Girardin, Joseph Méry and Jules Sandeau. Like actors improvising, the four young friends were going to create a novel by identifying with a character and sending each other letters. Proust was going to identify with a woman, Pauline, but objected when Halévy wanted her surname to be Dreux-Dives. 'It sounds like a railway line, and I am afraid it is rather like the song in which Lavigne said if her name were Bastille, she would call her daughter Madeleine.'[4] Pauline was going to be in love with a handsome sub-lieutenant, and, as in some of his early short stories, he proceeded by translating his own experience into the feminine. As a young girl she used to stare out of the window, worrying about the weather. If it rained she wouldn't be taken to the Champs Élysées to play with the little boy she loved. She's now on holiday in St Moritz, and, like Proust, still under the spell of Wagner's *Die Walküre*, which had been staged in Paris on 12 May 1983. Writing to her priest ('mon cher petit abbé') she's unapologetic about picturing Valkyries among the trees on the Swiss mountains.[5]

In 'Présence réelle', which Proust wrote in Switzerland, as in 'Mélancolique villégiature', which he finished by the beginning of August, he was getting seriously to grips with the perverse illogicality of love and its relationship to unconscious forces. In 'Présence réelle' the narrator has never spoken to the man or woman he or she can't stop thinking about. The text specifies the sex of neither partner, and the partnership exists only in the narrator's imagination. 'But how we loved each other that time in the Engadine! Never did I have enough of you, never did I leave you at the house. You came with me on my walks, ate at my table, slept in my bed, dreamed in my soul . . . is it impossible that some sure instinct, mysterious messenger, did not tell you about this childishness in which you were so intimately implicated, in which you lived, yes, really lived, because you were so strongly present to me?' But this time the obsession is over before the narrative ends. 'Satiety came before possession. Platonic love, too, reaches saturation point.'[6] And now, instead of thinking about the other person wherever he goes, the narrator is reminded by the other's presence of the places where the obsession was so strong – Sils-Maria, Silva Plana, Crestalta, Samaden, Celerina, Juliers, Val de Viola.

One writer who may have influenced Proust was d'Annunzio, who'd been influenced by Nietzsche. Proust had read a novel by d'Annunzio translated into French as *L'Intrus*. The

hero has a multiple self not unlike that described by Proust
five years earlier. 'These contradictory crises constituted his
life, an illogical life, fragmented, incoherent. There were in
him all sorts of tendencies, the possibility of all the opposites,
and, between them, an infinity of intermediary degrees, and,
between these tendencies, an infinity of combinations . . . So
his centre of gravity was subject to displacement; his personality became another personality . . . He was *multi-souled.*'[7]

'Présence réelle' exploits scenery that contrasts strongly with
that of Paris, Auteuil and Illiers. 'Surrounding us, three lakes of
a strange green reflected the pine forests. Glaciers and mountain
peaks closed the horizon . . . Larches of a serenity so black
next to the dazzling snow held their softly, brilliantly green
branches towards the pale blue, almost mauve, water.' Proust
and de la Salle climbed in the mountains, went up the Rigi by
funicular, walked on the shores of Lake Sils-Maria, watched
pink butterflies crossing the lake and went to Alpgrün, where,
surrounded by glaciers, they looked down on mountain
streams and, beyond the wild green countryside, saw the blue
Lake of Poschiavo, the Pizzo de Verone, the Val de Viola.[8]

After three weeks in St Moritz, Montesquiou, Mme Howland, de la Salle and Proust went on to Evian, by the Lake of
Geneva. Laure Baignères was staying in her villa at Clarens,
and princesse Rachel de Brancovan was at her villa, Bassaraba,
in Amphion. Her family was of Cretan origin. She'd
befriended Fauré and Paderewski, and was herself an
accomplished pianist. She played Chopin with brilliance and a
show of reluctance. They were frequent guests in the villa, and
when Proust needed to burn powders for his asthma he used
the room of her seventeen-year-old-son, Constantin.

In September Proust went to stay with his mother in Trouville at the Hôtel des Roches Noires, which was at the end of
the promenade gossip columnists called 'Paris's summer
boulevard'. 'Trouville is very ugly,' he wrote later, 'Deauville
frightful, the countryside between Trouville and Villers
mediocre. But on the hills between Trouville and Honfleur are
the most admirable landscapes to be seen in the country, the
most beautiful, with idyllic views of the sea . . . And lost roads
admirable for horse-riding, true nests of poetry and happiness.'[9] He never forgot a night when they came back from
Honfleur – 'At each step we stumbled into pools of moonlight,
and the humidity of the valley felt like an immense pond' – or

a walk in an 'enchanted forest with rhododendrons all round you and the sea at your feet'.[10]

He was dreading his return to Paris because there would be no avoiding a confrontation with his father about his future. Of the careers open to him, the one he found least repulsive was in the Cour des Comptes, which controlled government expenditure. 'If I do not want to make my career abroad, I would be as bored in the Ministry of Foreign Affairs in Paris as I would in the Cour des Comptes.'[11] To discuss the possibility of finding a job in a museum he consulted a friend of Anatole France, Charles Grandjean, who'd been archivist of the Senate and inspector-general of historic monuments. At the end of September he wrote submissively to his father, who'd been staying in his wife's absence with a professor of forensic medicine: 'I will start to prepare seriously for the examination for the Ministry of Foreign Affairs or the École des Chartes – whichever you prefer.'[12]

But six weeks later he was still deferring the moment of decision. Though he felt attracted to the École des Chartes, Grandjean was against it. Could he ask to be attached as a volunteer to the Louvre? Then he could simultaneously prepare for the École des Chartes, or study for a degree in literature, or concentrate on his writing, though he felt insecure about his talent: 'I have written nothing but things of imagination and sensibility – and those are the two ignorant Muses who need no cultivation.'[13] He was at least half convinced his father was in the right. 'The time comes', he conceded, 'when it is no longer enough to dream one's life. One has to live it.' At the same time he knew his parents were pretending to give him more freedom of choice than he actually had. The parents in *Jean Santeuil* insist they'd never go against their son's wishes: 'We want him to be perfectly free to make his own decision, provided he settles down to a regular career such as the Law or the diplomatic service.' Reluctantly submitting to Grandjean's arguments against the École des Chartes, Proust went on thinking about the École du Louvre and the École de Rome. Would a course at either of these give him something definite to count on? And if he finally got a job in a museum, how much time would it leave for writing?[14]

He'd been thinking about a book incorporating the best of his contributions to *Le Banquet* and *La Revue blanche*, and the idea became feasible when Madeleine Lemaire agreed to provide illustrations. She was so fashionable that the book, *Les Plaisirs et les jours*, which might otherwise have been ignored, would certainly 'find its way into many of the libraries of writers, artists and people of importance in different areas of life'.[15]

Intending, simultaneously, to write a few articles for newspapers and magazines, he decided the first should be about Montesquiou. He may already have sketched out the article when they were together at Evian, but in October he diplomatically asked for the comte's help: 'I would show how much you differ from the commonplace decadent of our day, the strength of your will, the richness of your intellect and how much there is of the seventeenth century in you.'[16] Montesquiou had a reputation for being difficult, and Proust proposed to argue that, on the contrary, his work had the best kind of simplicity about it. After drafting the article, Proust gave him *carte blanche* to make any cuts or additions he liked.[17] As soon as 'La Simplicité du comte de Montesquiou' was ready, Proust was so eager to see it in print that he asked Thadée Natanson, editor of *La Revue blanche*, to use it instead of his six short pieces which were scheduled for publication in the December issue, and when Natanson demurred, he offered it to Louis Ganderax, who was on the point of resuscitating the *Revue de Paris*.

Proust also found another way of endearing himself to Montesquiou. At the salon of a dilettante composer, comte Henri de Saussine, he'd met a good-looking nineteen-year-old pianist, Léon Delafosse, who at the age of thirteen had won first prize at the Conservatoire. His fair hair and blue eyes encouraged Proust to nickname him 'the Angel' and to believe Montesquiou would be interested. Saussine had taken poems from Montesquiou's *Chauves-souris* and set them to music for vocal quartet, piano and instrumental quartet. Delafosse was going to play the piano part when they were to be performed in May at the Salle Érard, but he'd never met Montesquiou. With encouragement from Proust, Delafosse wrote three songs of his own to words from *Les Chauves-souris*, and Proust wrote on his behalf to ask Montesquiou for permission to publish them. Both young men were then invited to visit the comte, but when they arrived he said he was in no mood for music. Instead they went for a walk in the woods of Viroflay, and when they heard barrel-organ music from a distant fair, he said no music could be more romantic. But when they returned to the house, the Angel was allowed to play and sing. His singing, Montesquiou said later, sounded like that of a squashed cat, but he thought the rhythms cleverly original, and felt moved by the young man, whose face struck him as 'transfigured by superhuman beauty . . . as though godhead had suddenly descended on him'.[18]

He entered into a relationship with Delafosse which was to last for three years. Proust may have been hoping for this to happen, and hoping for gratitude. If he felt misgivings about stage-managing the liaison, he repressed them until he wrote *À la recherche*, where Morel, the unscrupulous violinist, is unmistakably based on the Angel. Brilliant but conceited, ambitious, obsequious and untrustworthy, Morel encourages Charlus to fall in love with him, and, with the baron's help, does extremely well both socially and professionally, but he abandons Charlus when he no longer needs him. The story seems rather like a speculation about what might have happened if Proust had responded more positively to Montesquiou's erratic advances.

He seems to have been more ambivalent towards Montesquiou the man than he was to the verse, which he praised lavishly, and he quoted from it in the preface to *Les Plaisirs et les jours*. But it was difficult to put up with Montesquiou's arrogant, self-indulgent and deliberately provocative behaviour. Knowing that he, like Delafosse, could benefit from the comte's connections, Proust put a good deal of ingenuity into his letters, ingratiatingly seasoning them with quotations from *Les Chauves-souris*, and he took almost as much trouble over letters to Yturri, Montesquiou's secretary-lover, who was employed as middleman when the comte wished to be more distant. Giving no sign of resentment, Proust even invited Yturri to dinner in his parents' flat. He plied Montesquiou with gifts, including cherry trees, ties from Liberty's and a plaster angel. He never took offence when he was rebuffed, and one of his conciliatory letters ends with a postscript by Anatole France: 'Dear Poet, How could it be denied that Marcel Proust has good taste when he speaks so well of your verse?'[19]

Frustrated in his efforts to publish his article, Proust sent it to Montesquiou: 'I would like to ask whether you could not, either through M. Yturri or through others, place it in a review which is sympathetic to you.' If not, Proust went on, he would end up by doing what he should have perhaps started by doing – found a review of his own. 'And if it has only a single issue, it will have lived long enough . . . if it has been able to sing your praises in its short life.' But this only irritated Montesquiou, who had no talent for concealing disappointment: 'Your conceptions invariably end in abortions.'[20] And towards the end of the month, at one of Mme Lemaire's receptions, Montesquiou cut him. Even then, Proust did not take offence.

Indefatigable though he was in efforts to make himself acceptable in high society, he was no less ambivalent about it than he'd been when he wrote 'Violante'. In his satirical 'Mondanité de Bouvard at Pécuchet', which appeared in the July-August 1893 issue of the *Revue blanche*, the two friends agree it's better to avoid talking about literature in society, but they're uncertain about bowing. Should one bow with the head only or with the whole body? Should the hands hang straight, and should one smile? Should one bow in the same way to a prince as to a locksmith? To avoid having to say 'Highness', they decide not to go into the Faubourg Saint-Germain. But the Faubourg is no longer a single area:

> you find it everywhere. It is only from a distance it appears compact and isolated . . . Besides titles are respected even more in high finance, and, as for foreign adventurers, they are innumerable. But, according to Pécuchet, you have to be inflexible with the phoney noblemen, never using their titles, even on envelopes . . . Besides, the nobility, according to Bouvard and Pécuchet, no longer existed, since it had lost its privileges. It is clerical, backward, does not read, does nothing, is as frivolous as the bourgeoisie. They thought it was absurd to respect it, and to fraternise with it was possible only if they could despise it. Bouvard said that to decide where they should go, which resorts to stay at in the summer, which habits and which vices to adopt, they should draw up an accurate plan of Parisian society. It would include, he said, the Faubourg Saint-Germain, the foreign adventurers, Protestant society, the world of arts and the theatre, and official and the academic world. The Faubourg, in Pécuchet's opinion, concealed all the libertinage of the *ancien régime* under a façade of rigidity. Every nobleman has mistresses and a sister in a convent and conspires with the clergymen. They are courageous and in debt, bankrupt and moneylenders while running them down, are inevitably the champions

of honour. They rule by elegance, invent extravagant fashions, are model sons, affectionate with the people and tough with bankers. A sword always in their hand and a woman behind them on the saddle, they dream about the restoration of the monarchy, are terribly lazy, but not arrogant with simple folk, drive out traitors, and insult cowards, deserving through a certain air of chivalry our unshakeable loyalty.[21]

In April, when Oscar Wilde came to Paris, Proust met him either at a dinner party of Mme Arman or at the house of Mme Baignères. According to Fernand Gregh, Proust and Wilde eyed each other 'with a complex curiosity',[22] and, though Wilde had brought Lord Alfred Douglas to Paris with him, it's possible he had designs on Proust. His behaviour is otherwise hard to explain. He accepted an invitation to dinner at the flat in the boulevard Haussmann and this is what happened according to two grandsons of Mme Baignères:

> On the evening of the dinner, Proust, who had been held up at Mme Lemaire's, arrived very out of breath two minutes late. He asked the servant, 'Is the English gentleman here?' 'Yes, sir, he arrived five minutes ago; he had hardly entered the drawing-room when he asked for the bathroom, and he has not come out of it.' Proust ran to the end of the passage. 'Monsieur Wilde, are you ill?' 'Ah, there you are, Monsieur Proust.' Wilde appeared majestically. 'No, I am not in the least ill. I thought I was to have the pleasure of dining with you alone, but they showed me into the drawing-room. I looked at the drawing-room and at the end of it were your parents, my courage failed me. Goodbye, dear Monsieur Proust, goodbye.'

After he'd left, Proust's parents said he'd surveyed the drawing-room and remarked: 'How ugly your house is.'[23] Proust's reaction was: 'I don't think M. Wilde has been well brought up.'[24]

In *À la recherche* there is only one reference to Wilde. Describing the plight of homosexuals, Proust mentions the 'poet who was once fêted in all the drawing-rooms and applauded in all the theatres of London, and then driven out from every lodging-house, unable to find a pillow to lie down on'.[25] But Wilde may have exerted a negative influence on Proust, who lived according to the opposite principle. Wilde prided himself on putting his genius into his life and only his talent into his work. Gide came sufficiently under his spell to declare: 'A man's life is his image,' but Proust would go to great extremes not only in declaring himself through his work but in subordinating his life to it.

SIX

MY BUNIBULS

Proust probably met Reynaldo Hahn during May 1894 at one of Madeleine Lemaire's musical evenings. Nineteen and Jewish, with a dark complexion, brown eyes, neatly chiselled features and a small moustache, he was already active as composer, pianist and singer. He became a star at these soirées, performing his song-cycle *Les Chansons gris*, based on poems by Verlaine, which he sang in his light tenor voice, accompanying himself on the piano. He was playing at one reception when his host, who was in the reserve and due to leave on manoeuvres, reappeared in his uniform. Hahn promptly modulated into La Marseillaise.

Born of French parents in Venezuela, he'd come to study at the Paris Conservatoire under Massenet and Saint-Saëns. He'd read nothing by Proust when they met but, with his combination of charm and moral seriousness, Hahn soon developed a deeper emotional relationship with him than Robert de Flers or Willie Heath. Proust could never write directly about his love for Reynaldo, but translated the relationship into Jean Santeuil's affair with the music-loving Françoise.

Jean fans the flames of his feeling for her by giving orders. Be gay, sit with your profile turned towards me. He performs small services for her and presents his life as glamorous. Seeing her every evening, he encourages her to display her fondness for him in front of other people. He enjoys refusing invitations to the soirées and dinner parties that would stop him from being with her. As part of a couple he's no longer alone in life. It's almost like having a stranger inside him, someone whose reactions can't be predicted.[1]

Proust turned down an invitation from Montesquiou – suddenly friendly again – to join him for a summer holiday in St Moritz when Madeleine Lemaire invited him and Reynaldo to spend four weeks in her country house, Reveillon. In Paris Proust did everything possible to stop his suspicious mother from discovering the true nature of their friendship; at Reveillon they could relax. The large garden was surrounded by forest; indoors, flowers from the garden augmented Mme Lemaire's flower paintings.

One day, when he and Reynaldo were walking in the garden, Proust stopped beside a bed of Bengal roses and asked to be left alone. When Reynaldo came back, he seemed to be in a trance, frowning and biting at his moustache. Reynaldo left him alone again, until Proust caught up with him and resumed the conversation as if nothing had happened.[2] It was easy for them to accept interruptions like this in their togetherness, just as they accepted differences of opinion about music. Reynaldo's taste had been influenced by teachers at the Conservatoire, while Proust, under the influence of Montesquiou, had become enthusiastic about Wagner. At a Sunday concert in January he'd heard the Flower Maiden scene from *Parsifal*, which impressed him deeply, and he argued with Reynaldo about the virtues of *Lohengrin*.[3] Proust had reservations about Saint-Saëns, but, because of Reynaldo, the main theme in the first movement of the D minor Violin Sonata became important to him, and he'd often say: 'Play me that bit I like, Reynaldo – you know, the little phrase.' And in *Jean Santeuil* Françoise plays the sonata when Jean, her lover, is questioning her about her Lesbian past, while in *À la recherche* Vinteuil's 'little phrase' is crucially important. The musical arguments between Proust and Reynaldo are amusingly refracted in the piece 'Mélomanie de Bouvard and Pécuchet' which was written (in the space of forty-five minutes) at Reveillon during August. Pécuchet, who is 'ever the friend of tradition and order', calls Wagner 'the bawler from Berlin', while Bouvard says Massenet is lacking in depth and Saint-Saëns in form.

Proust began the year 1895 'with a stronger feeling of divine grace and human freedom, with confidence in a Providence which is at least internal'.[4] Halfway through his twenty-fourth year, he'd settled into his first steady emotional relationship, and Reynaldo was accepted as his regular companion by hostesses and by Montesquiou. Proust even felt more confident about his literary potential, though his parents still believed his social life was distracting him from serious work. A friend of his was closer to the truth when he said: 'Society mattered to him, but in the way flowers matter to the botanist, rather than to the gentleman who buys a bouquet. When an invitation arrived he never said "How delightful to go to Mme de X's", but "It will be amusing at Mme X's to see whether Mme de Z will have managed to get herself invited and whether the Ys will condescend to go." '5

It would have been impossible for him to explain how minor incidents – when his emotions were involved – could serve as raw material for fiction. On the evening of 25 April, for instance, he went to the house of Alphonse Daudet for a dinner party, and, half expecting Reynaldo to arrive there, let himself be delayed by waiting to escort Madeleine Lemaire and Suzette to a ball in the avenue Montaigne. They arrived so late that people were already leaving, but, not wanting to say Reynaldo was waiting for him at the house of a marquise in the rue Cambon, Proust went in with the Lemaires. 'Wait for the little one, lose him, find him again, love him twice as much on seeing he has come back to Flavie's to find me, wait two minutes for him or make him wait five for me – that is what I call real tragedy, throbbing and profound. Perhaps I will write it one day, and in the meantime I live it.'6 He did eventually write it – in an incident about Swann, who's desperate to see Odette, and fails to meet her at the Verdurins' house. In the meantime he wrote frequently, passionately and inventively to his Bunibuls, his pet name for Reynaldo, not quite inventing a private language but sometimes writing in an eleborate pastiche of archaic French, sometimes illustrating the letter with cartoonlike drawings.

In *Les Plaisirs et les jours*, the story closest to his love affair with Reynaldo is 'La Fin de la jalousie'. Never letting two days go by without seeing each other, the lovers go on discovering new depths in their intimacy. Habituated to promiscuity, Honoré prays he'll always go on loving Françoise, and, knowing this is impossible, makes up his mind: 'I shall try, when I feel my heart detaching itself from her, to withdraw it so gently she will not notice. I shall always be as tender and as respectful.7 But his jealousy is aroused when he hears her name linked with another man's, and though she swears she never has and never would deceive him, he can't stop himself from wondering, whenever her eyes sparkle, whether other men can provoke the same reaction. Uncertainty is so uncomfortable that he tries to ease her into confessing the truth by pretending he's been unfaithful, but this distresses her so much that he's scared his suspicious nature will provoke the infidelity he dreads.

Hoping he'd be able to concentrate better on his writing when he'd solved the career problem, he was looking for a reasonably prestigious job that would satisfy his parents without occupying too much time. The salary was unimportant. Many of his father's well-placed friends had been offering advice, and it was probably the foreign minister, Gabriel Hanotaux, who suggested an unpaid job at the Mazarine Library in the Institut de France. Hanotaux, who'd been a member of the Académie Française since 1897, had combined a political career with a literary one. At the Mazarine Proust's only obligation would be to work for five hours at least twice a week. Sainte-Beuve had once been librarian there, and Anatole France had worked for fourteen years at the Senate Library in the Palais du Luxembourg. Interviews for the three vacancies were held on the day after the Daudets' dinner party. Only three candidates were being considered, and Proust, who was placed third, got the least desirable work. He was assigned to the book depository at the Bibliothèque Nationale in a job which would start at the beginning of August, but he applied for leave.

In early July he went on holiday with his mother to Kreuznach, a German spa near Bingen. They returned to Paris in the middle of the month, but two weeks later Proust left again with Reynaldo and his sister Maria to stay at a villa belonging to Clarita, their married sister, in the woods of Saint-Germainen-Laye. Here Proust worked on 'La Mort de Baldassare Silvande', and when Maria read it, she made comments in the margin. 'Your opinion is just about the *only one* that matters to me,' he told her,[8] but he still hadn't read her annotations when he left with Reynaldo to stay at Madeleine Lemaire's villa in Dieppe. Maria was instructed to post the manuscript to Mme Proust, who would forward it to the editor of *La Revue hebdomadaire*.

Dieppe was one of the most fashionable resorts. 'All Paris is there,' reported *Le Gaulois*, 'the comte and comtesse Louis de Talleyrand-Périgord, duc Josselin de Rohan, Madeleine Lemaire and MM. Marcel Proust and Reynaldo Hahn, who are guests of this eminent artist.'[9] In the intervals between socialising, they enjoyed wandering under the trees. 'On those scorching afternoons, when the light, by its very excess, escapes our gaze, let us go down into one of those Norman "depths" from which the tall, thick beeches nimbly rise, their foliage withstanding the ocean of light like a slim but impenetrable shore, admitting only a few drops, which tinkle melodiously into the black silence beneath the trees.'[10] But his health seemed precarious. 'The poor boy has had a slight touch of asthma,' Reynaldo reported to Maria on 10 August, 'and feels a bit worried.'

They were nervous his father would stop them from going on to Brittany. But after returning to Paris with Madeleine and Suzette Lemaire on the 30th, they left for Belle-Île, where they stayed at the Hôtel de Bretagne in Palais, the principal port on the island. Writing to Yturri, Proust described the apples ripening at the edge of the rocks, 'mingling the smell of cider with the perfume of seaweed,'[11] and he used the phrase in a letter to de Billy.[12]

After a week at the hotel, they returned to the mainland, opting for Begmeil on the cape of Finistère, which had been recommended by his parents' friend André Bénac, director of the Banque de Paris et des Pays Bas, and secretary of the state railways' administrative council. Staying in the small Hôtel Fermont, they spent some of their time with Bénac and his wife. Proust was planning to write about Brittany and reading a good deal, mainly Thomas Carlyle and Balzac, but *Splendeurs et misères des courtisanes* struck him as 'a stupid book'.[13]

As he said, Begmeil is 'situated at the extremity of this peninsula and to the left it looks out on the Bay of Concarneau, which washes it on the west, and to the right on the ocean, which washes it on the east . . . This peninsula is very fertile, with numerous big orchards belonging to the small, scattered farms.'[14] Eight years later he still called the bay 'the noblest, gentlest, most delicious thing I know'.[15] 'You hear nothing but the gentle ebbing of the tide in the bay or the ocean, which is equally quiet, and this one sound, or the barking of a farm dog, serves as a base for the profound silence, making it still more intense.' At the hotel 'one dines in the open air under the apple trees, which let you glimpse the sea between their branches'. After the generous hotel lunch, Jean Santeuil and his friend Henri de Reveillon take their books to the western end of the beach, where they lie down among the dunes with a wide space between them, seeing nothing but the sand, the sky and the seagulls.[16]

A lot of wishful thinking is refracted in Proust's transformation of Reynaldo into Henri, and in his account of the Reveillon family. He loved Madeleine Lemaire's house and used it,
without even disguising its name, as the family's country seat.
But, ennobling her into the duchesse de Reveillon, he invents
a benign father-figure in the duc, whose title goes back to the
ninth century, and he transforms his lover, a Jew born in
Venezuela, into the scion of this family. But alongside the
wishful thinking in the transformation is a genuine love. 'I
intend you to be ubiquitous in my novel, like a disguised god,
unrecognisable to mortals.'[17]

Whenever he went out for a walk, Proust saw artists busy
at their easels in the open air. Paint was being squeezed out on
palettes, pictures were coming to life on canvases of different
shapes and sizes. The spectacle catalysed his creativity, and
suddenly he found courage to start a large-scale project. None
of the village shops sold paper, which made him less prolific
than usual as a letter-writer, but he started writing *Jean Santeuil*
on the backs of old letters, other pieces of used paper, and
writing-paper purloined from the yacht club at Etel, a port on
the mainland. Previously his longest narrative had been the
thirty-page 'Fin de la jalousie', but during seven weeks in
Begmeil he wrote over two hundred pages of the novel – a
hundred on Jean's childhood, another hundred about the holiday at Begmeil, and eleven pages which eventually became the
fifth chapter of the seventh part. He seems to have got himself
started by developing his impressions of the town and people
he met there. He wouldn't have spent so much time writing
or have written so fast if he hadn't been enjoying himself
hugely. He never went back to writing short stories: he'd
hit on a more pleasurable way of recycling experience, with
unrestricted space for elaborating ideas, noting down insights,
describing scenery and developing minor characters. Jacques-
Émile Blanche had been right to say he had an exceptionally
good recording apparatus – an extraordinary capacity for
retaining sensations and fugitive perceptions – but it was a
capacity Proust had never fully explored or exploited. Now
he could ransack the attic of his memories, relive favourite
experiences, savouring his relish for sensations he remembered
but had never talked about, never written about. It was scarcely
less gratifying to go over experiences he regretted, but with
editorial control over the behaviour of his *alter ego* and with

godlike power to punish miscreants like the lieutenant who'd failed to return his salute.

His holiday from the library was due to end on 15 October, but he applied for an extra month, also writing to M. Bénac, asking for their railway tickets to be extended. Authorisation came in the form of a letter from the chief inspector at Orléans, and the back of the letter became part of Proust's manuscript.

One of the painters who patronised the hotel was a forty-two-year-old American, Alexander Harrison, who for the last seventeen years had spent three-quarters of his time at Begmeil, though he had a studio in Paris.[18] Proust and Reynaldo had seen one of his paintings in the Luxembourg Museum, and, pretending to be admirers of his work, sent him a note in the hotel restaurant, asking to meet him. At the end of the meal he joined them at their table.

Sharing experiences like this, alone together while planning them, and together again afterwards to look back on them and laugh, Proust and Reynaldo were happy as they could only be on holiday. In Paris they had to take precautions, or their affair would no longer be a secret. Not that this was the only reason it had to end. Proust's fiction is less autobiographical than it looks, but it was liable to influence his behaviour. Writing 'La Fin de la jalousie' and making it impossible for Honoré to go on being faithful to Françoise, Proust was not only expecting he'd be unfaithful to Reynaldo but was trying to issue some kind of warning. Perhaps to himself, perhaps to Reynaldo, perhaps both. Wanting to postpone the infidelity, he intended the story partly as an act of exorcism, partly as an apologia for what was painful but unavoidable. But it's hard to be sure whether writing the story speeded or slowed down the attrition of their feeling for each other.

Throughout his life Proust will theorise a great deal about love. The theories are based on experience, but an attractive man's experience of love depends largely on the choices he makes, while these depend partly on his theories. A man who believes he consists of several people cannot expect all of them to be faithful indefinitely to one man or woman. Proust's schoolboy formulation is consistent with the note he made in 1908: ' "Many people do not believe in a dual love." With me it is quintuple. . . .'[19] The quotation is a paraphrase from Chapter 13 of de Nerval's *Sylvie*. In *Jeunes Filles* the Narrator will be quintuply in love with the young girls; Proust hadn't fallen out of love with Reynaldo when he fell in love with Alphonse Daudet's younger son, Lucien, but the flaring of the new infatuation made both Proust and Reynaldo want to see less of each other. Six months later, in the summer of 1896, Reynaldo, who'd gone on to Cabourg after staying with his sister in Hamburg, still wanted Proust to feel impatient for his return to Paris. Though Proust writes: 'Stay there as long as you are having a good time,' the letter, without mentioning Lucien's name, offers reassurance: 'I will also be happy, oh my dear boy!, very, very happy when I can embrace you, you who are really the person I love, together with Mamma, most in the world.'[20] He was equally effusive about Reynaldo's talent: 'This sadness of yours is not only the sombre beauty of your character, it is also the lowest level of your moral and intellectual depth, the genius . . . of your music, the ballast of pleasure you must jettison in order to rise to a great height.'[21]

When he overpraised someone, he'd try to adjust the balance with trenchant criticism – confided to someone else. He praised Suzette Lemaire inordinately, but, writing about her to Reynaldo, called her the kind of person who'd turn her back to stop you from seeing her tears, but only after making sure you'd seen them in the mirror. 'You have to admit that with her what is natural is sometimes very affected.'[22]

Apart from his mother, he'd never loved anyone as much as Reynaldo, and they both suffered greatly when the honeymoon happiness ended. Even when he was being unfaithful, Proust was still possessive, still the victim of the insatiable jealous curiosity he described in 'La Fin de la jalousie'. He wanted to be told about everything happening to Reynaldo, who preferred not to know what was happening to Proust. In June Reynaldo promised to be totally open with him, and when he tried to withdraw the offer, Proust was distraught. 'That you should tell me everything has been, since 20 June, my hope, my consolation, my support, my life. To avoid hurting you, I almost never talk about it, but . . . I'm almost always thinking about it. I try to fill in the gaps in a life, which is dearer to me than anything else, but which will cause me the severest pain if I remain ignorant about any of it, even the most innocent parts.'[23] Even while still living it, Proust was developing his possessive jealousy into a work of art.

Another letter to Reynaldo starts: 'Our friendship no longer has any right to speak about this – it is not strong enough for that now.' He'd always tried to avoid causing Reynaldo pain, he says, but Reynaldo doesn't care whether he hurts Proust, who still has 'a duty not to let you perpetrate such stupid, wicked and cowardly acts without trying to reawaken your conscience'.[24] Their relationship was deteriorating fast enough to make Proust wrestle in his novel with the question of how much can survive when love sinks into the past. Surely he hadn't loved in vain, or had he? Is our love for people fundamentally different from our love for scenery or sensations? 'We say goodbye to what we have loved with a sadness which cannot last if we are to love other things and other people.'[25]

Already, at the age of twenty-five, he's asking himself whether time is irretrievably lost, but the debate is still coloured by the guilty belief he is mediocre, lazy, sterile, weak-willed. Though masturbating less, he has abused himself so much in the past he has little faith that enough strength is left for him to fulfil his artistic potential or to act in accordance with his most intense feelings. He doesn't know how much value to set on what he has made of himself. There are moments when, ignoring all invitations, he believes himself to be mediocre.

An imperious command from his father or nagging from his mother about unpunctuality is enough to make Jean Santeuil feel guilty about the daydreamy self-involvement which is inseparable from introspection in narrative that switches its searchlights on the processes of consciousness. Is there any value in memories of emotions he no longer wishes to feel? He no longer wants to fall in love with Marie Kossichef or get excited about an invitation to Reveillon, but sometimes a ray of sunlight or a gust of wind find their way to his heart, bringing back memories. Even if he never again goes sailing with Pierre or never again sits writing on the terrace and glancing at the sunlight on the red and green leaves of the vine, his yearning for these moments is proof that he still has their residue inside him. 'Within himself he felt something he had only felt during those hours still remained unchanged. And at these moments he no longer had any uncertainty, any anxiety, any sadness. And his deep calm, seemed, like the blue sky above his head and the rustling grass at his feet, to conceal a serenity, a silent joy.'[26]

SEVEN

MYSTERIOUS LAWS

When Proust asked Reynaldo to leave him alone with the rosebush at Reveillon, what happened is explained – indirectly – in a draft for an essay.[1] In a cathedral, people often linger in front of a stained-glass window, studying the complex arrangement of coloured sections; a poet may 'stand for an hour in front of a tree examining how the unconscious and infallible architectural thinking known as the double cherry tree genus has arranged, now that spring is coming, these innumerable little fluted white balls, equipped to go on spreading until they wither, a faint scent through the black and complicated branches of this tree.' But the poet isn't merely studying what's visible: he 'may be looking for something beyond the tree', as he tries to recapture his sensation at the moment of impact. 'Suddenly he feels it again, but cannot penetrate to the bottom of it, can go no further.'[2]

Proust's passionate intensity in looking at natural objects is comparable to that of poets such as Wordsworth and Hopkins, painters such as Monet and Cézanne, but behind it was a neurotic compulsiveness. With his insecure hold on his identity, he felt terrified he'd lose himself unless he could tether his reality to something in the world outside. Looking intently at roses or hawthorn bushes or trees, he's trying to take possession of something neither wholly external nor wholly internal. The reality of natural objects is undeniable, but it's of no help to you unless you firmly take hold of it. In *Jeunes Filles*, when he's taken for a drive in the carriage of his grandmother's most aristocratic friend, he sees at the edge of a driveway in Hudimesnil three trees which say as they recede: 'What you do not learn from us today, you will never know. If you let us fall back to the bottom of this road from which we were trying to rise up to you, a whole part of yourself we were bringing you will fall back for ever into nothingness.'[3] Terror and desperation were integral to his pleasure in observing.

If he came to believe in a close correspondence between the mysterious laws governing the complex architecture of the natural object and 'the mysterious laws he bears inside him',[4] this was partly a stratagem for apprehending and retaining details which could have faded quickly from his memory. Looking at the blossoming apple trees in Étreuilles (Auteuil) Jean Santeuil tells himself that each blossom, each leaf, has come in response to cravings inside him.[5] The hawthorns in *Swann* inspire a mimetic movement: looking at them on the altar of the church in Combray, and focusing on a bud which has opened, the boy tries to imitate the process of blossoming as if a human being could be capable of it. 'I imagined it as if it had been a thoughtless and rapid movement of the head, made with a flirtatious glance from contracted pupils by a girl in white, listless and lively.'[6]

It is by making the pathetic fallacy into a grappling hook that he drags natural beauty into his fiction. The indispensable premise is that nature, human and inhuman, is subject to mysterious laws, and once they make themselves felt in the poet's mind, the manifestations grow stronger, strive for expression, struggle to emerge, 'for everything that ought to last aspires to move out from what is fragile, decaying, and may perish this evening, or become incapable of generating'. The works must escape from the man before he grows too feeble to write them. 'When they are aspiring in this way to burst out of him, watch how the poet walks: he is nervous of spilling the words before he has the right receptacle into which he can pour them. If he meets a friend, or allows some pleasure to divert him, he loses his mysterious energy.' At the moment of writing he has 'exchanged his soul for the universal soul. This great transference is occurring inside him, and if you went in and forced him to become himself again, what a blow!' His mind is 'inert like the jellyfish on the shore which will die unless the tide comes to reclaim it'. He has been working on himself, dividing himself into two halves, like Dr Jekyll and Mr Hyde, and you can never see both of them. 'When you see Jekyll, no trace of Hyde is left, and when you see Hyde, no trace of Jekyll.'[7]

Intermittently Proust had been possessed by the conviction that, if only he looked carefully enough at natural objects, he might penetrate their structural secret.

Suddenly a roof, a patch of sunlight on a stone, the smell of a path would halt me by a special pleasure they gave me, and because beyond what I could see they seemed to be hiding something they were inviting me to take, but which, despite my efforts, I could never discover. Feeling this was present in them, I stood there, motionless, looking, breathing, trying to follow my thoughts beyond the appearance or the smell. And if I had to catch up with my grandfather, continue my walk, I would try to recapture them by closing my eyes; I concentrated on recalling the exact line of the roof, the detail of the stone, which, incomprehensibly, had struck me as being full, ready to open themselves to me, surrender whatever it was for which they had merely been a cover.[8]

In this way, without intentionally training himself in how to memorise visual details, the child was habituating himself to observe with precision and engrave the observation in his memory. He went on believing there was a causal principle behind what looked like architecture in organic things – a stone, a tree, the bone structure in a face – and even if he couldn't solve the mystery, he went on observing meticulously and memorising with phenomenal precision.

His later ideas about unconscious memory had their roots in this deeply ingrained habit of testing sights and smells as if they were clues. In *Jean Santeuil* the incident of the madeleine is prefigured when the white rosebush at Reveillon conjures up a childhood memory of the scent in the drawing-room of Jean's uncle after the vases had been filled on Sunday mornings with roses from the garden.

What happiness then to see, as in this flowerbed at Reveillon, all the rosebush masterpieces rising in procession, and to the heart which has been inflamed with more love than would have seemed possible for the first white rosebush, it offered another with deep purple roses, another with small pink roses like shallow bowls, and a rosebush with simple violet petals like eglantine; it was a long gallery of rosebushes, each seeming to be the most beautiful, always a rosebush recognisable by its voluptuous and grand personality, but each one enchanted by a different imagination, whether through the richness of the purple or the candour of the white petals.[9]

But it would be wrong to assume the family had nothing to do with the evolution of Proust's ideas about consciousness

and memory. Certainly he listened and probably he joined in
when his father was discussing the workings of the mind with
Robert or with colleagues invited to meals. Adrien Proust had
not only researched on the brain, made it the subject of his
agrégation thesis, and written about aphasia,[10] but had used
hypnosis on patients. He often talked to Robert about research
on memory and consciousness, and he once described a successful experiment he'd made with a patient who lost his overcoat
and couldn't afford a new one. Under hypnosis the man came
to remember where he'd left his old one.[11] Having no patients,
Marcel could interrogate only childhood recollections, but his
ideas about unconscious memory, far from being the result of
a single experience, had roots which spread right back through
his childhood. In one of his notebooks[12] he recalled a boyhood
incident in which a governess had scolded him for making a
noise with a knife or fork on the plate while trying to cut a
slice of tart, but he scarcely paid any attention to her because
the noise 'had suddenly given me an intoxicating impression
of heat, of thirst, of summer, of a stream where evening was
approaching without cooling the air, of travelling. My present
unconscious memory, fundamentally ignorant of the circumstances surrounding me . . . was sending memories in
floods.'[13]

But none of these ideas comes into *Les Plaisirs et les jours*,
which took shape around the collaboration with Madeleine
Lemaire. Though her relationship with Reynaldo was sometimes strained,[14] Proust got on well with her as she worked on
her illustrations. His favourites were the dove, the pansies, the
chrysanthemums and Violante's castle. He also got on well
with her twenty-eight-year-old daughter Suzette, who, like
her mother, painted flowers. She nursed him when he was ill
with a fever: 'if I woke I felt your dear little hands, dexterous
and cool, resting on my forehead'.[15]

After leaving Reveillon in mid-September, he spent ten days
in Trouville with his mother, again staying at the Hôtel des
Roches Noires. The Strauses were staying at their villa, and,
according to one of their irritated friends, Proust was constantly to be seen sitting on a stool at Mme Straus' feet.[16] At
the hotel he wrote 'La Mort de Baldassare Silvande', a story
about the premature death of a dignified nobleman. Proust
empathised with the dying man by using his own illness, but
the narrative is literary to the point of preciosity, and he draws

verbatim on phrases created for a story, 'Avant la nuit,'[17] which wasn't going to be included in the book. In it a young girl confesses her Lesbian past, but Proust neither dramatises it nor even explains her present attitude to it. The gratitude of the dying nobleman to the devoted Oliviane is expressed in phrases that had been used by the man who'd loved the ex-Lesbian: 'Supernatural as a madonna, gentle as a nurse, I adored you and you cradled me. I loved you with a sensitively sagacious affection, unspoiled by any hope of carnal pleasure. Did you not bring me in exchange a unique friendship, exquisite tea, naturally decorative conversation and how many bunches of fragrant roses?'[18]

'La Mort de Baldassare Silvande' was published in *La Revue blanche*, one of the little magazines that proliferated in *fin-de-siècle* Paris, but it was written for the book. By the end of the month most of the material was in the hands of Calmann-Lévy, the publisher to whom Anatole France had introduced him. He asked Montesquiou's permission to quote in the preface from one of his unpublished poems, and to accept the dedication of a story. 'I think I shall dedicate all the main stories or poems in my book to Masters whom I admire or friends whom I love.' The comte rebuked him for this 'pompous phrase',[19] but gave his consent for both the quotation and the dedication. The 'most beautiful' of the stories should be the one dedicated to him and he wanted to see it in advance. The one Proust intended for him was 'La Confession d'une jeune fille', which hints at his guilt over deceiving his mother. Here is his first fictional reference to the goodnight kiss, 'an old habit she'd abandoned because it caused me too much pleasure and too much pain – I could never go to sleep because I kept calling her back to say goodnight again.'[20]

The girl doesn't confide in her mother about her seduction at the age of fourteen by a fifteen-year-old cousin, though on leaving him she feels 'an insane need for my mother'. Nor can she talk about the sinful pleasures into which she's initiated at sixteen. The narrative is equally reticent about these, but the girl has the usual Proustian disability: 'What upset my mother was my lack of will.' And – like Proust and like Violante – she goes into society: 'Its desiccating pleasures addicted me to living permanently in other people's company and together with the taste for solitude I lost the secret of the joys which until then nature and art had given me.' While being seduced

by another man, she feels guiltily convinced lovemaking is no
less sadistically ferocious than torture.[21] The story achieves its
melodramatic climax when her mother, seeing her in the arms
of her seducer, has a fatal stroke. This is similar to the climax
of 'Avant la nuit'.

Though Proust's parents were pleased about Les Plaisirs et
les jours, they were anxious about his literature and philosophy
exam, the licence ès lettres. He was ranked twenty-third among
the competitors throughout the country.

In the spring he went to stay with Pierre Lavallée at his
parents' house in Segrez, where Proust felt intoxicated with
the beauty of the scenery and his power to describe it. A poet,
he decided, was like the sun, able to illuminate undignified
places – such as a dunghill – usually excluded from the 'realm
of art'. Peacocks parading their splendour in the barnyard
reminded him of society hostesses crossing courtyards in
resplendent gowns.[22] But his happiness was cut short by an
attack of asthma, and he disconcerted his hosts by leaving
abruptly.[23]

His relationship with Montesquiou was still unstable and
still unequal but still important to both of them. In his new
collection, Les Parcours du rêve au souvenir, which was to be
published in June, the comte dedicated a poem to Proust, who
paid him an even greater compliment by using him (together
with Baudelaire and Mallarmé) as a model when he wrote a
set of poems about Cuyp, Watteau, van Dyck and Paul Potter.
Louis Ganderax rejected these 'Portraits de peintres' when they
were submitted for the Revue de Paris, but Hahn wrote a piano
accompaniment, and with his support Proust recited them at
a soirée of Mme Lemaire on 28 May. The guests included
Montesquiou, Anatole France and Colette, who wrote to tell
Proust she and her husband found the poems 'subtle and
beautiful. . . . You mustn't undermine them as you do by
speaking them badly.'[24]

In July, when he was holidaying with his mother in Kreuznach, they were visited by Robert de Billy and his new young
wife. Fourteen years later Proust remembered 'the woods
where I walked, the blue hills which rose behind the pump-
room'. He walked in the woods and sheltered under the trees
when it rained. 'It was this town whose Gothic spire could be
seen at the bottom of the green stream; it was the little blue
mountain situated behind the pump-room which I intended to

climb when my cure was completed to see the view of the whole Palatinate.' At dinner, when his mother asked whether he'd had time to see this or that, he enjoyed the guttural German sounds in the conversation, and he felt something from the Holy Roman Empire was still reaching out toward hikers, concerts in the municipal gardens and even picnics in the mountains.[25]

On 25 October he learned he'd been transferred from the depository to the department which registered books for copyright, and the extension of his leave was cancelled. He returned to Paris on 27 October, two days before 'La Mort de Baldassare Silvande' appeared in the *Revue hebdomadaire*, earning him 150 francs. His parents were impressed, but it was hard to settle back into the domestic routine. He felt unreasonably irritated by leftovers from lunch on the dining-room table, inexplicably restless when he watched his mother working at the far end of the room, unwinding a skein of red wool.[26] Pleading ill health, he appealed to the chief librarian, Alfred Franklin, against his transfer, and, by mentioning M. Hanotaux, secured another stint of leave. He'd been thinking of going to Segrez; instead he went back to Reveillon, but without Reynaldo.

Shedding their leaves, the branches of huge chestnut trees 'looked more solid and blacker from being stripped . . . and they seemed, like a magnificent comb, to hold back the spreading golden hair of the trees'.[27] Under the heading 'Second Stay at Reveillon – The Bad Season', he writes enthusiastically about walks Jean and his friends take before dinner, passing through the village as the sun's setting and afterwards, as the moon rises, walking in single file along narrow paths between the fields. 'It was exhilarating to go out like this, without having dined, when night was already falling, and prolonging the walk by the light of the full moon, under the stars in this sleeping countryside, in this absolute silence which was almost frightening, so close did it feel, when, in the already distant villages, everyone was asleep.'[28]

Returning to Paris in November and going to look at Chardin's paintings in the Louvre, Proust started an essay which illuminates the intentions behind his novel. The domestic life he found mediocre and insipid became dazzling and appetising when he saw it reflected in Chardin's canvases. 'A bourgeois woman is pointing out mistakes in her daughter's needlework, or a cat is walking over some oysters, or a woman is carrying loaves of bread.' Looking at Chardin's view of a room with someone sewing, or a pantry, a sideboard or a kitchen, you participate in his pleasure in seeing the objects and rendering them in such 'brilliant and imperative' language.[29] Though the viewer had enjoyed looking at similar objects, he couldn't understand the pleasure without help from Chardin. 'If you can tell yourself when you look at a Chardin "This is intimate, is comfortable, is alive, like a kitchen" you will tell yourself when you walk around in a kitchen: "This is intimate, is comfortable, is alive, like a Chardin." ' Writing about everyday life, urban and rural, Proust wanted to achieve a similar effect.

But he gave Chardin no chance to reconcile him with leftovers on the kitchen table and with skeins of red wool. He was too excited about developments in his relationship with a boy of seventeen, who'd been only twelve when they first met; Alphonse Daudet's younger son, Lucien, was an art student, slim and frail, with a small moustache. Jules Renard described him as 'a handsome boy, curled and pomaded, painted and powdered, with a little squeaky voice which he takes out of his waistcoat pocket'.[30] Reynaldo, a friend of the family, had introduced Proust. They sometimes visited the Daudets together, treating Lucien like an insignificant schoolboy. The first time Proust invited him to his parents' flat, he tried to entertain him by showing him photographs of actresses and writers, and the book by Paul Bourget with photographs of Laure Hayman in it. But Lucien, who was interested in none of these things, embarrassed both of them by saying so. But he liked both Proust and the family. The two brothers struck Lucien as resembling each other only 'indirectly'. Robert 'had his father's features, but the expression on his face was that of Mme Proust. When their mother was there, you saw they were brothers.' Gradually Proust won the boy's friendship, partly by his considerateness. He never tried to solicit 'explanations and confessions which at the age of sixteen or seventeen, the age at which the demon struggles with the angel, are as scaring as they are unavoidable'.[31]

After Proust and Reynaldo had dinner with the Daudets on 14 November 1895, Proust complained about the materialism of the conversation and the habit of 'explaining character and genius in terms of physical habits or race'. He was also embarrassed by his hostess: when he thanked her for letting him come, she said Reynaldo had asked her to.[32] 'The aristocracy, though they certainly have their faults, show a real superiority in the science of good manners and easy affability. They can put on a five-minute show of the most exquisite charm and seem friendly or brotherly for an hour. And the Jews too (detested there in the name of some principle . . .) have the same quality in a different form – a sort of kindly self-regard, a cordiality devoid of pride, and this is invaluable.'[33]

Lucien's elder brother, Léon, was more rabidly anti-Semitic than the rest of the family, but nothing would have deterred Proust from going back to dine with them on 13 December, when Montesquiou was one of the guests, and another was Albert Flament, a journalist who wrote society gossip columns for several newspapers. Having heard Proust was lazy, snobbish and obsequiously dependent on Madeleine Lemaire, Flament was impressed with 'the surprising profundity of his adjectives' and with his talent as a mimic. He could reproduce Montesquiou's mannerisms with devastating accuracy. The comte, who had bad teeth, habitually put his hand to his mouth when he laughed, and he tapped his foot whenever he delivered an ultimatum or expressed enthusiasm or impatience. In the cloakroom at one o'clock in the morning, Proust 'did a virtuoso imitation of M. de Montesquiou's piercing scream', and, taking Flament home in a cab, repeated the performance.[34]

Proust's mimicry was partly an act of aggression against mannerisms that struck him as ridiculous, but he was also defending himself against the temptation to imitate people he admired. There were two others but for whom 'the manners, the diction of Marcel as a young man would no doubt have been different' – prince Edmond de Polignac and Charles Haas.[35] Proust couldn't conceal his ambivalence towards Montesquiou: though he succeeded in making his friends laugh, they noticed he was modelling his behaviour on the comte's. Jacques-Émile Blanche testifies: 'For us, talking in the manner of Montesquiou was a joke which became a habit. The wailing, the grumbling, the doleful, nettled mien, the scolding, the high-pitched yelping of "Robert" – we no longer knew whether Marcel was simulating them as a joke or had picked them up by osmosis.'[36]

Gossip about the impersonation soon reached Montesquiou's ears, but Proust said he'd only been quoting the comte, not imitating him. Montesquiou then asked why he should want to be a travelling salesman for another man's wit. Defending himself in a letter, Proust claimed he'd no longer be capable of doing this, but 'At that time, it is true, by the process which drags the body in pursuit of the soul, the voice and the accent no doubt assumed the rhythm of the alluring ideas I was borrowing.'[37] In reality he was not so much borrowing ideas as emulating intellectual strategies. The marquise de Clermont-Tonnerre describes Montesquiou as having 'a special mechanism for perception which I never saw in anyone else, and Proust exploited this for his own purposes'. Montesquiou's thinking resembled 'the reverse of a tapestry where you see a needleful of thread go right across the canvas before it is finally knotted. It is Montesquiou who inculcated in Proust the art of catching all the nuances and making ideas ricochet off each other.'[38] This may be overstating the point, but the usual mistake is to underestimate the influence.

The comte was invited to take an avuncular interest in the progress of Proust's friendship with Lucien. By now they were seeing each other every day. Lucien showed Proust his portfolio, and they went together to the Louvre. As Proust reported to Montesquiou: 'For a week Lucien and I have been unable to see each other without collapsing into the silliest, most lamentable and most irresistible fits of giggling.'[39] In spite of this warning, Montesquiou invited them to spend an evening with him and Léon Delafosse, but never forgave them for letting themselves capsize into giggling. On New Year's Eve Proust sent Lucien an eighteenth-century ivory box engraved with the words 'To friendship'.

Mme Proust was being excluded from so many of the emotional and social relationships which mattered to him that the quality of their interdependence was changing. Between bouts of irritation with Mme Santeuil, Jean feels the urge to kiss her in the old way,

but this was no longer the same woman. She had been changed by the death of her father, by Jean's laziness, by her illness, by the passing of her youth. And since she no longer wore the little coat which was too young for her, too frivolous for her eternal mourning, too tight for her widening girth, and out of fashion, she would never again look the same. And in a few years he would no longer find the woman she was today.[40]

The death of her mother had helped to age Mme Proust, while her son already had the guilty feeling which would intensify after her death – that he was accelerating her decline by causing her disappointment and anxiety.

After delaying the publication of *Les Plaisirs et les jours* by procrastinating over her illustrations, Madeleine Lemaire finally delivered them in January 1896. By the end of February the book was in galley-proofs, and J. Hubert, chief of production at Calmann-Lévy, asked Anatole France to look over the galleys and make suggestions for revisions. 'With the authority of your name, thanks to the confidence and affection he has in you and for you, he would welcome small corrections or suggestions, and I will not conceal the fact that I would consider them useful for the work whose parentage you have seen fit to accept.'[41] France had agreed to write a preface, but it wasn't ready until April, and he might have been even slower if Mme Arman hadn't put pressure on him. He didn't conceal his ambivalence. 'My young friend's book is rich in tired similes and weary attitudes which are lacking neither in beauty nor in nobility.'

The delays didn't slow Proust down in his work on *Jean Santeuil*. In March, writing in the home of Léon Yeatman, to whom he read the new material, Proust constructed an introduction in which two young men at a seaside hotel meet a novelist in the way Proust and Reynaldo met Alexander Harrison. The writer reads to them from an unpublished novel about his childhood and, when he dies with it still unpublished, one of them decides to publish the version still in his possession. This is the novel that follows. Proust ignored the inconsistency about time. By incorporating public events, such as scandals, he'd set the fiction in the period 1871–95, but, adjusting the chronology to his new scheme, he made 1859 the year of Jean's birth without adapting the narrative to the earlier period.

Les Plaisirs et les jours was due to come out in June, but on 10 May, after catching pneumonia, the eighty-year-old Louis Weil died at five o'clock in the afternoon. Proust broke the news to Laure Hayman, saying he hadn't wanted it to reach her through the newspapers,[42] but he discouraged her from attending the funeral, untruthfully telling her: 'In his religion there is no service.' The mourners would be going from Weil's flat in the boulevard Haussmann to the Père-Lachaise cemetery, 'but I fear that would be tiring for you and not many women will attend'.[43] Discreet enough not to come, she sent a large wreath. The cyclist who delivered it caught up with the flower-less Jewish funeral procession, and the courtesan's wreath was buried with the coffin.[44] Proust afterwards sent her a copy of *Les Plaisirs et les jours* inscribed: 'To Madame Laure Hayman for the infinite delicacies of her heart, her beauty and her incomparable spirit. Her friend Marcel Proust.'[45]

Proust was forced to think about Jewishness again when Zola wrote a newspaper article denying anti-Semitism had popular roots, and the anti-Semitic Montesquiou made a pro-vocative remark.[46] Proust said nothing in reply but afterwards wrote a letter: 'If I am a Catholic, like my father and my brother, my mother is Jewish. . . . If our ideas differ, or rather if I am not sufficiently detached to have those I would perhaps have on the matter, you could involuntarily have wounded me in a conversation.'[47] But when Montesquiou sent him a copy of his new collection, *Les Hortensias bleues (Blue Hydrangeas)*, Proust spent the evening reading the poems with Lucien.

In June, the month *Les Plaisirs et les jours* was published, death again struck at the family: his grandfather died at the age of seventy-nine. Proust reproached himself for feeling indiffer-ent, but after the funeral he burst into tears on entering the dead man's bedroom. Though he used the bereavement as an excuse for not attending a ceremony Montesquiou had organ-ised in Douai for the unveiling of a monument to the poet Marceline Desbordes-Valmore, Proust went out a lot during the second half of July, visiting Reynaldo in Saint-Cloud, Mme Arman, Calmann-Lévy and Madeleine Lemaire, whose name helped to secure respectful reviews for *Les Plaisirs et les jours* in *Le Gaulois, Le Figaro* and *Le Temps*. Most of the other papers ignored it, mainly because of the exorbitant price – 13 francs 50 centimes.

Léon Blum, who reviewed it for the *Revue blanche*, com-plained of 'affectation and prettiness', while Fernand Gregh was sarcastic in the *Revue de Paris*: 'he has invited all the fairies – not forgetting a single one – to the cradle of his newborn book'. In the *Revue encyclopédique* Charles Maurras predicted Proust would be a leader of the new generation. But the publi-cation of the book failed to establish him as a writer, and some friends felt it harmed him, not because of unfavourable reviews but because of its inappropriate appearance. 'It looked like one of those albums in which girls ask you to write down a thought.'[48]

Grateful for Maurras' generosity, Proust responded with flattery: 'The books you touch you find precious, without wanting to notice that it is you who have changed them into gold by touching them.'[49] In society, as in family life and love affairs, Proust indulged in emotional doublethink, entertaining positive and negative feelings at the same time. He could detach himself from any situation, giving the impression of absence while he was still present. He knew insincerity was damaging his integrity: the more you deviate from the truth, the harder it becomes to know what the truth is. Or can the truth be multiple, like the self?

In August he went with his mother to Mont-Dore, a spa in a valley surrounded by the high mountains of the Puy-de-Dôme. The waters had been famous since Roman times for treating asthma. It is thirty miles from Clermont-Ferrand. 'He detested this part of the country, found it frightful, and, though feeling oppressed, almost congratulated himself, feeling fatigued by the necessity which forces us to like things we are destined to forget quickly. Once they are over, the years we have lived most passionately are like a novel we have read to the end; once it is finished we take no pleasure in re-reading it.'[50] But the possibility of fictionalising current experience was altering the flavour of the experience: sensations and ideas could all have an autobiographical flavour.

Asthma had played its part in alerting him to the discontinuity in the existence of the self. If it had, at any moment, more than a single identity, it also differed significantly from the past self. Marcel Proust was now a different person from the healthy eight-year-old who'd had the same name but could enjoy holidays in Illiers and pick flowers with no fear of pollen. As he put it in a letter to Reynaldo, 'At every moment of our lives we are our own descendants, and the atavism which weighs on us is our past, conserved by habit. So the harvest is not entirely happy when bad seeds have been mixed among the good.'[51] The loss of his comparatively healthy eight-year-old self had created a grid he could use to measure all subsequent losses, whether of the self or of lovers. People and pleasures that make life worth living today have no necessary connection with people and pleasures of ten years ago. This insight would grow into a major theme in *À la recherche*.

Proust's weeks at Mont-Dore weren't uneventful. At the hotel he narrowly avoided fighting a duel after challenging a fellow-guest who'd accused him of cheating at cards. In *Jean Santeuil* two duels are fought: in the first Jean wounds the man who insulted him, and in the second achieves an even greater triumph when the duc de Reveillon offers to act as his second. But at Mont-Dore Proust had to battle only with the pollen diffused by the haymaking, which induced such a serious attack of hay-fever that he and his mother returned to Paris at the end of August, and when he was summoned to do national service, he evaded it by pleading ill health. He'd developed considerable expertise in the evasion of tedious jobs: he never spent any time at the Mazarine.

In September his mother left again for Dieppe, while he thought of going back to stay with Pierre Lavallée in Segrez.[52] But he stayed at home, alone with the servants, trying to fend off asthma by smoking Espic cigarettes and burning medicated powders by his bedside.[53] The attacks – each one seemed liable to suffocate him – depended partly on the weather. Rain brought relief; sunshine was dangerous. 'If the day is fine, it is in vain that my shutters exclude every breath of fresh air; my eyes may be closed, and a fierce asthma attack, caused by this good weather, this lovely golden haze I stifle in, may almost knock me unconscious, make me incapable of speaking; I can neither utter a word nor form a thought. . . . Tears of pain run down my cheeks.'[54] To send himself to sleep he was using Trional, Valerian and Amyl. Trional was a hypnotic drug consisting of an ethyl sulphone. Valerian, a herbal sedative, had been popular throughout the nineteenth century. Amyl was a tertiary amyl alcohol currently in use as a sedative.[55]

He soon recovered sufficiently to resume work on *Jean Santeuil*: within the first few days of September he'd copied the first ninety pages into an exercise book. Reading *La Cousine Bette*, he felt less hostile to Balzac, but enjoyed Sainte-Beuve's attack on him in *Port Royal*. When Proust visited the Jardin des Plantes with Mme Arman, they saw the damage inflicted by the hurricane of 26 July; it had uprooted trees from the Paris parks. The menagerie was closed, but they saw the bears, and met Anatole France, who exchanged hostile banter with

Mme Arman and invited Proust on a seaside holiday near Villers.[56]

He was unrealistic in thinking he'd be able to work for four hours every day on *Jean Santeuil* and deliver the finished book by the beginning of February 1897 to Calmann-Lévy.[57] He still didn't know how to structure it, and he'd still be working on it in 1899. Feeling unwell and finding it hard to concentrate in Paris, he moved to Fontainebleau on 19 October, though his mother, convinced it would be too damp, wanted him to stay in Cabourg.

In Fountainebleau he disliked the hotel, beautiful though it was – it had once been the duc d'Aiguillon's mansion[58] – and he especially disliked the bed he was given. It had canopies and curtains fastened to the wall. 'All the things I need, my coffee, my tisane, my candle, my pen, my matches, etc. etc. are on my right, which means I always have to lie on my bad side.'[59] He was missing his mother, who on 20 October tried to telephone him from the bakery on the opposite side of the boulevard Malesherbes. But only local calls could be made from the bakery, and she had to use the public call-box in the street. 'On the telephone her poor voice suddenly reached me, shattered, bruised, permanently altered from the voice I had always known, full of cracks and splits, and it was only when I collected from the receiver the bleeding and broken fragments that I had for the first time the appalling realisation of what was permanently broken in her.'[60] Previously he'd thought her father's death had made little difference to her, but he'd been wrong. Jean Santeuil is at Begmeil when, hearing his mother's voice over the telephone, he's stupefied by 'this little piece of broken ice where, behind the tears, seemed to flow all the griefs suffered for years, and to go on circulating in this voice, sobs and groans which she had never allowed herself to utter for fear of hurting those who were close to her, and which are hidden there nearby, like memories of the dead in the familiar appearance of her room, within reach, inside the drawers'.[61] The section in *Jean Santeuil* is based on a story Proust wrote soon after the telephone call and posted to his mother, asking her to keep it for use in the novel.

He was unwell, suffering from sneezing fits and congestion of the chest, especially at bedtime, and from intercostal pain. He was also deeply depressed, though he stopped taking the Trional, which had a depressive effect. 'Never, I believe, has any of my different kinds of anguish risen to such a pitch. I can't even try to describe it.' He had to stay in his room because none of the hotel's public rooms was in use, and he was worrying about the cost of having the fire kept up all day. When he met Léon Daudet, who was staying at the hotel, they started eating all their meals together and going for drives in the forest.[62] But Fountainebleau was noisier than Proust had expected, and he felt unsettled. After six or seven days he returned to Paris.

III

1896–1905
BREAKFAST AT NIGHT

EIGHT

FORGED EVIDENCE

In the progress of all disease, willpower plays a major part, and, despite their exceptional intelligence and good intentions, the doctor and his wife had inflicted irreparable psychological damage, undermining their son's faith in himself. In implanting the idea that he was weak-willed their intention had been to strengthen him, give him a target, encourage him to fight his weakness, but to fight effectively you need to believe in your own strength, and the only strength he'd discovered was the strength of weakness. In so far as he made a choice between the invalid life and the active life, it was based partly on what he'd learnt from his aunt Élisabeth and partly on instinct. The invalid is entitled to special care and consideration. Jealous of the attention his mother paid to her husband, Proust used illness to make her more like a nurse and less like a wife.

Throughout his life he went on exaggerating symptoms, taking inordinate precautions and unnecessary risks. Unquestionably he started life with an extremely frail constitution, and if there was a phobic edge to his anxieties and a voluntary element in his sufferings, it's hard to locate the hairline crack between the unavoidable and the theatrical. But he was making a crucial choice when he decided, at the age of twenty-five, to turn his daily routine upside down, sleeping through the day, using shutters and curtains to banish daylight and noises from the street. But at night he got up. His asthma, he said, invariably kept him awake at night, though it didn't stop him from reading and writing. He could breathe more easily at night, he said, and sleep more easily during the day.

The new scheme made it possible for him to go on living in his parents' flat while almost escaping from their control. If he went out late at night and came in during the small hours of the morning, his mother wouldn't be awake to ask where he'd been. He'd have more freedom in his sex life, but less in

his social life: he had, for instance, to sacrifice Mme Straus'
Sunday lunches, though he'd get up in time to go along afterwards and chat with the guests, even if the cigar smoke made
him cough.[1]

His new routine was to sleep from eight in the morning till
three in the afternoon, when he drank his first cup of coffee.
It became harder to spend time with friends, and easier to
devote more time to introspection. He also came to depend
more on communicating through letters. Even with his
mother, correspondence took the place of face-to-face confrontation. Later he would write about 'converts' who 'bless the
illness or misfortune which led to withdrawal from the world
and showed them the road to salvation'.[2]

It was good to have an excuse for seeing less of the eccentric
and irascible Montesquiou, who enjoyed upsetting people with
provocative and unpredictable behaviour. Proust was always
scrupulously polite when they were together, but once, invited
to dinner, he was warned the meal would be served by bats,
and once, after sending Montesquiou a pot of hydrangeas, he
was told they'd been presented to a grave which thanked him
and sent him greetings. This meant they'd been thrown out of
the window.[3] Other gestures were less unfriendly. By the
end of 1896, Montesquiou, who was preparing an anthology,
Roseaux pensants (*Thinking Reeds*), had decided to include a
story from *Les Plaisirs et les jours*. He sent Proust a four-page
letter, and after promising to provide better proof than the
length of the letter that he was taking an interest in him,
Montesquiou again complained about the mimicry. Proust's
conciliatory reply was returned with angry jottings in the
margin, like a school essay which had infuriated a teacher.
'Impertinent', 'inadmissible direct criticism', 'bitterness at not
having received a written appreciation of his book', 'frivolous',
'insolent and untrue – friendship can descend, not rise'. Montesquiou even awarded a mark: 'The top mark being 20, this
bit of epistolary homework does not deserve more than minus
fifteen.'[4]

Montesquiou's provocations he always ignored, but he
couldn't ignore a public insult thrown at him when *Le Journal*
published a belated review of *Les Plaisirs et les jours*, which had
been on sale for eight months. The review was signed Raitif
de la Bretonne, which was the *nom de plume* of Jean Lorrain,
who seldom missed an opportunity to attack Montesquiou,

and assumed Proust was one of his lovers. Seven months previously, reviewing Montesquiou's *Les Hortensias bleues*, Lorrain launched his first attack on Proust, who was mentioned in the preface, calling him 'one of those pretty little society boys who have succeeded in becoming pregnant with literature'. The second attack came in the review of 3 February 1897. Not content with denouncing Proust's prose as elegiacally sentimental, precious and pretentious, Lorrain sneered at Proust for extracting a preface from Anatole France. 'For his next book, you can be sure, M. Proust will extricate a preface from the redoubtable Alphonse Daudet, who will be unable to disoblige either Mme Lemaire or his son Lucien.'[5] The only possible response was a challenge to a duel, and Proust gained prestige by securing as one of his seconds the painter Jean Béraud, a regular at the salons of the comtesse Potocka and Mme Lemaire, and, as the other, Gustave de Borda, who'd won a reputation as a formidable swordsman and was in great demand as a second in society duels.

Through their seconds Proust and Lorrain arranged to fight with pistols on the afternoon of Saturday 6 February at the Tour de Villebon in the Bois de Meudon. Reynaldo and Robert de Flers both came along with their friend. Had the duellists been fighting with swords, they'd have been obliged to go on fighting until one of them was wounded, but the etiquette with pistols was to miss unless the grievance was exceptionally serious. Though he felt nervous, Proust behaved impeccably; he'd have shaken hands with his opponent if his seconds hadn't stopped him. Two shots were fired, but, as Sunday's *Figaro* reported, 'nobody was hurt, and the seconds declared that this meeting ended the dispute'.[6] 'Marcel was brave, frail and charming,' reported de Flers,[7] and Hahn wrote in his diary: 'During these three days Marcel's coolness and firmness, though they seemed incompatible with his nervousness, did not surprise me.'

Among those who afterwards congratulated him were Colette's husband, Willy, who wrote a letter, and Robert Dreyfus, who called to see him. He said his only anxiety had been that he might have to interrupt his habit of sleeping in the morning. But instead of being allowed to enjoy his glory, he was jerked back into his schoolboyish nightmare that friends were ganging up against him. Together with Jacques Bizet, now in his last year as a medical student, Robert Dreyfus was preparing a satirical revue to be performed in the style of the Chat Noir cabaret by shadow figures. With a mixture of amiability and envy, they were satirising the literary success of their friends. Fernand Gregh had done well with a collection of poems, *La Maison de l'enfance*, and far from being angry about their intentions, he joined in the fun by playing the piano accompaniment when the revue, *Les Lauriers sonts coupés*, was given three performances during the third week of March. The attack on Proust took the form of a conversation between silhouettes representing him and Ernest La Jeunesse, a deformed Jewish friend of Oscar Wilde's who spoke in a falsetto. Proust, whose voice was mimicked from behind the screen by Léon Yeatman, was made to argue that, in spite of the high cost, *Les Plaisirs et les jours* provided good value for money: even if his prose was worth only a franc and his verse only 50 centimes, weren't the contributions of Anatole France, Madeleine Lemaire and Reynaldo Hahn worth 4 francs each? Telling Gaston de Caillavet about it, Proust couldn't restrain his tears.[8]

Soon afterwards he was again reduced to tears in a quarrel with his parents. Told off by his mother in the presence of his father's valet, he rushed furiously out of the room, slamming the door violently enough to shatter the glass panels. Inside his bedroom, sobbing violently, he smashed a Venetian glass she'd given him. He later described this as the only real rage of his life. The quarrel had started because he wanted to wear pale-yellow gloves for a late December outing with Laure Hayman and the marquis de Modène, but his mother had bought him grey ones.[9] He relieved his injured feelings by fictionalising the incident, but Jean Santeuil smashes the Venetian glass accidentally. In other details the novel reproduces the facts of what happened, and Mme Proust wrote a forgiving – and revealing – reply to her son's apologetic letter. 'The broken glass', she said, 'will be no more than it is in the Temple – a symbol of indissoluble union.' In the synagogue wedding service, a wineglass is symbolically smashed by the bridegroom after he and his bride have drunk from it. In the novel Mme Santeuil gives Jean a kiss and whispers: 'This will be as it is in the Temple – the symbol of indestructible union.'[10]

In April, when Albert Flament accompanied him on a visit to two former servants now living in an old people's home at Issy, Proust again found a good audience for displays of skill as a mimic. Proust impersonated Mme Arman – 'If only Marcel would work!' – and some of the aristocratic ladies for whom he felt an uncomfortable mixture of admiration and contempt. He gave money to the elderly couple and promised to stay longer next time he came.[11]

He had won the right, when he gave dinner parties, to invite the cream of Paris society, and his guest list for Monday 24 May was impressive enough to make Montesquiou accept an invitation at short notice.[12] Proust's excuse for writing at the last minute was that the party was for Anatole France, who was about to leave on a long journey and hadn't been sure whether he could come. But Proust had presumably given more notice to some of his other guests – the marquis Antoine de Castellane, comte Louis de Turenne and the two seconds, Béraud and Borda. Hahn and Gaston de Caillavet were also there, the novelist Édouard Rod, who'd written a polite but unenthusiastic review of *Les Plaisirs et les jours* in *Le Gaulois*, and the playwright Marcel de Porto-Riche. The event was reported in both *Le Figaro* and *Le Gaulois*. Proust's parents had absented themselves from the flat for this all-male gathering.

In selecting his guests Proust had been careful about the way opinion was being polarised by the Dreyfus scandal. The Dreyfus affair was a litmus test for *fin-de-siècle* France as the Vietnam war was for Americans and their allies – a public event which raised such important questions that people took sides, even if they'd regarded themselves as unpolitical. After remaining detached and almost uninterested during the crisis of 1889, when General Boulanger tried to seize power, and during the Panama scandal of 1892, Proust became an ardent Dreyfusard.

Suspected of treason, Alfred Dreyfus, a Jewish captain on the general staff, had been arrested on 15 October 1894, but, long before this, anti-Semitism had become a meeting point for Catholic and bourgeois resistance to republicanism, while the left's rhetorical equation of the Jew with the capitalist had been helping the right to gain working-class support. The army, which still hadn't recovered its prestige since the defeat of 1870, had been a hotbed of anti-Semitism since the influx of Jewish officers which followed the loss of Alsace to Germany. The Dreyfus family had been among the 50,000 Jews who migrated from Alsace, motivated largely by French patriotism, only to find themselves regarded as foreigners.

The scandal had begun after a charwoman who was working in the German embassy as a counter-espionage agent found in a wastepaper basket an unsigned note offering to sell the Germans five secret documents about guns and mobilisation. First to come under suspicion were the staff officers who'd recently served in the artillery, and the handwriting looked like that of Dreyfus, who was tried by court-martial on 19 December. He was sentenced four days later to life imprisonment, and on 5 January 1895 he was publicly humiliated in the courtyard of the École Militaire. He stood to attention, surrounded by lines of soldiers, while the watching crowd shouted 'Death to the Jew!' and 'Death to Judas!' as a sergeant-major ripped off his epaulettes, tore the badges from his cap and the stripes from his trousers, finally snapping his sabre in two. The anti-Semitic Maurice Barrès, who was in the crowd, found the spectacle 'more exciting than the guillotine'.[13]

The degraded officer was shipped in February 1895 to solitary confinement on Devil's Island. As his family fought to establish his innocence, rumours of irregularities began to spread, but even in 1896, when the real traitor, an infantry officer, Major Marie Charles Esterhazy, was discovered after the same charwoman found torn pieces of a special delivery letter addressed to him, the minister of war, General Mercier, refused to reconsider the evidence against Dreyfus.

In August 1896, when Major Georges Picquart, the officer who for thirteen months had been investigating the forgeries, saw specimens of Esterhazy's handwriting, he recognised it as identical with that on the note. To prevent him from uncovering the injustice done to Dreyfus by the army, General Boisdeffre had Picquart transferred in December to Tunisia. Meanwhile Major Joseph Henry, second-in-command of counter-espionage, had been forging new evidence to confirm Dreyfus' guilt and frame Picquart as his accomplice, while Dreyfus' lawyers weren't even given access to the newly forged documents. The question of truth – was Dreyfus innocent or guilty? – was being eclipsed by the question of principle. Didn't the reputation of the French army matter more than whether injustice was being done to a Jew?

In a June 1897 letter to Montesquiou, Proust joked about the secret documents. Since September 1896 the newspapers had accepted the official view of Dreyfus' guilt, and, after Montesquiou ended his relationship with Léon Delafosse,

Proust tried to please the comte by saying he'd been uncertain whether Léon was 'This swine of a D . . .' – a phrase which occurred in one of the published letters.[14]

Though Proust was less quarrelsome than Montesquiou, his love life was scarcely less turbulent. After trying one evening to call on Lucien, Proust saw him in the street – or thought he did – and ran in pursuit until the weakness of his lungs forced him to give up the chase.[15] Besides, it was hard to be optimistic about the feelings of 'mon petit Lucien', when he ended a letter 'bien à vous' and refused to let Proust see him off at a railway station.[16]

From May to July, asthma gave Proust no reprieve. He stayed in bed till four or five in the afternoon, and friends were instructed not to ring his doorbell before three.[17] In the middle of July, when Reynaldo's father died in Saint-Cloud, the asthma was at its worst, but Proust – no one has ever taken more trouble over comforting bereaved friends – drove to their villa in a closed carriage. He was getting out when Reynaldo's English cousin, Marie Nordlinger, arrived on her bicycle. She was small, slim, sensitive, and Proust had got to know her in December, when they went to galleries together. Asking her not to tell Reynaldo he was there, he waited outside for news. He was breathing with difficulty, hay-fever exacerbating the asthma. He drove back to Paris almost as soon as she came out, but on the evening of the 16th he wrote to Reynaldo: 'Will you send me news of how you were last night and whether I can be useful in any way? Unless you tell me to, I won't come. I'm thinking of you a lot, my poor boy. I love you with all my heart.'[18]

Towards the middle of August, when his mother again wanted to take the cure at Kreuznach, he went with her. The comtesse René de Béarn was at the spa hotel. 'Thanks to this Sauce Béarnaise, which I found rather tasty,' he wrote, 'I had no trouble in swallowing the beginning of this stay.' Going back to Balzac, he was reading *Une Ténébreuse Affaire* and *Gobseck*, in which the central character is a miserly Jewish moneylender. What interested Proust most was the characterisation of the old aristocrats. He noted down character traits and remarks that seemed specially redolent of aristocratic pride, 'not in order to copy them, of course, but to inspire me'. When he told the comtesse what he was doing, she suggested he should meet Mme de Laubespin. 'But I prefer anecdotes. In five minutes a witty woman or a man of taste can give you the essence of several years' experience.'[19]

After the comtesse had left, he spent more time writing than reading; he told Léon Yeatman he'd been working so hard he hadn't had time to write any letters.[20] Yeatman was forgiven for taking part in the satirical revue, but when Proust asked for a repeat performance of the mimicry, he refused to oblige.[21] At Kreuznach Proust wrote the chapter called 'Le Salon de la duchesse de Reveillon': the first page of the manuscript is on writing paper with the spa restaurant's letterhead. He promised to show Mme de Brantes how he was characterising the duc, 'and you'll tell me whether the tics, prejudices, habits I give him are overdone'. The letter bubbles with excited curiosity about aristocrats she'd known. Did any of them offer their left hand when commoners were presented? Would they have expressed contempt in some other way? Would they feel more contempt for people who weren't well born or people who weren't in society?[22]

When he returned to Paris on 9 September, only 329 copies of *Les Plaisirs et les jours* had been sold, though it had been in the shops for fifteen months. It was too expensive. There had been talk of a cheaper edition at 3 francs 50, and when Proust left for Kreuznach, Robert de Flers, acting on his instructions, went to Calmann-Lévy's offices, only to be told they wouldn't bring out a cheaper edition until all 1,500 copies of the original edition had been sold, and that no money was due to Proust until publication costs had been recouped. 'It was a big mistake, my dear boy, not to make out a contract with such dangerously affable people.'[23]

In October, after being introduced by Reynaldo, Proust starting attending the salon of Mallarmé's friend Méry Laurent. A tall blonde, she'd been married at fifteen to a grocer, escaped to pose at the Théâtre du Châtelet, and, after a short career as an actress, worked as an artist's model. Before Mallarmé, her lovers had included Napoleon III's American dentist, Thomas Evans, and Manet. Reynaldo took Proust to her villa in the boulevard Lannes near the Bois de Boulogne. Dark walls were decorated with Turkish beads and oriental tapestries. The Japanese lantern hanging from a silk cord was lit with a gas jet, while Manet's pastel portrait of Méry stood on a plush-draped easel. One evening, when Whistler came to the salon, he denounced Ruskin as a complete ignoramus about painting.

Proust tried to defend him, and, when Whistler left his grey kid gloves behind, kept them as a souvenir.[24]

Méry Laurent's salon was becoming a meeting place for young Dreyfusards, but Mme Straus' was more important in consolidating support for the Jewish captain. In October she made her guests listen to the lawyer Joseph Reinach, who'd been secretary of the reactionary Ligue des Patriotes until 1886 and a parliamentary deputy since 1889. He said he was sure Esterhazy had written the note, and that the War Office had been aware of Dreyfus' innocence from the beginning. Gustave Schlumberger tried to defend the army, but he was shouted down and left in a huff. The other regulars to become disaffected were Jean-Louis Forain, who founded an anti-Semitic magazine, *Psst*, and Jules Lemaître, who now gave his exclusive allegiance to the reactionary salon of his mistress, the comtesse de Loynes.

During the last week in October, Hahn's 'Nuit d'amour bergamasque' was performed at the Colonne concerts, and, according to *L'Écho de Paris*, 'M. Marcel Proust and a few society ladies, who were following his example, applauded vehemently . . . the majority of the audience remaining cool.'[25] Proust described the concert in a letter to Suzette, and, perhaps forgetting how critically he'd written about her to Reynaldo, assured her he never stopped thinking about her.[26]

Almost exactly five months after Reynaldo lost his father, Lucien lost his. Alphonse Daudet died at dinner on 16 December. He was fifty-seven. 'I don't know how Marcel Proust and M. Reynaldo Hahn were informed,' Lucien wrote, 'they arrived during the evening, brotherly and in despair, and, throughout the three ensuing days, I was always supported by having them close to me.'[27] On the 20th, in the funeral procession to the Père-Lachaise cemetery, Proust and Reynaldo walked behind Zola and Anatole France. Proust stepped forwards a few times to squeeze Lucien's arm, and, in the evening, called on his bereaved friend.

He paid tribute to the dead writer in an article which, thanks to Flament's intervention, was published in *La Presse* on the 19th, the day after Flament's obituary appeared. Writing to thank him, Proust congratulated him on recreating the way Daudet had tilted his head. This 'evidences a power of physical observation which I envy you because I have always lacked it, and without it things are never fixed but left floating, as in a dream'.[28]

Towards the end of 1897, meeting Picquart at the house of Zola's publisher, Gustave Charpentier, Proust discovered the colonel was a friend of M. Darlu. From 10 January, the first day of the court-martial which Esterhazy had requested, confident the War Office would support him, Marcel and Robert Proust, the two Halévy brothers, Jacques Bizet, Léon Yeatman, Louis de la Salle and Robert de Flers met every evening in the Café des Variétés to discuss how to campaign for Dreyfus' release. For a week, Dr Proust spoke to neither of his sons.

On 12 January 1898 Esterhazy was acquitted. The next day Clemenceau's L'Aurore published Zola's 'J'accuse'. An open letter to the president of the republic, accusing the high command of an anti-Semitic conspiracy to pervert justice, it provoked a storm of protest. The militant Catholic paper La Croix, which was already crusading against Jewish army officers, took the lead in condemning Zola. Most newspapers were still hostile to Dreyfus, and in a year shadowed by industrial turmoil and prospects of a colonial war with Britain over the Sudan, many were apprehensive about the relationship between the army and the republic. Maurras said it didn't matter whether Dreyfus was innocent or guilty: France couldn't afford to undermine the army's reputation by having him acquitted. Others, remembering the army's part in the Bonapartist coup of 1851, were nervous it would forge an unholy alliance with the Church and subvert democratic republicanism.

On the 14th, when they were both having dinner with Ludovic Halévy, Proust asked Anatole France to sign a protest against Esterhazy's acquittal.[29] Among the other signatories were Louis Pasteur, Zola, Fernand Gregh and all the young friends who'd been meeting at the Café des Variétés. The petition appeared in the morning edition of L'Aurore, but the cause suffered another setback the same day, when Picquart was arrested and legal proceedings were started against Zola and L'Aurore.

For three weeks Proust went every day to the assize court. Many high-ranking officers were aristocrats – in 1899 29 per cent of the major-generals were noblemen – and with his mind still focused on the problem of characterising such men in Jean Santeuil, Proust watched the chief of general staff, General de Boisdeffre, defending the honour of the army. Threatening to

resign unless he was believed, he swore to the authenticity of
the papers Colonel Henry had forged. In *Jean Santeuil* the tall
general is seen in civilian clothes, alighting from a cab.

> You especially noticed a very high top hat, tilted at an
> angle . . . He walked slowly, with stiff legs, as if exhausted,
> sometimes coming to a complete halt. His cheeks were
> covered with a sort of fine red or violet mottling like young
> vines or certain mosses you see on garden walls in the
> autumn . . . You felt that his nervous tic, blinking eyes,
> hands which pulled his moustache, like the red embroidery
> on his cheeks, like the shabbiness of his overcoat, like the
> stiffness of the leg which had no doubt been broken often in
> falling from his horse, were the habitual particularities of this
> august thing which was called 'General Boisdeffre' and that
> they were integral to his grandeur, since it was never without
> them.[30]

Jean sees Picquart for the first time in the courtroom. Spectators are passing packages of sandwiches around when a ray
of sunlight touches the colonel's hat. He looks young, 'with a
nose slightly too curved, and his head leaning to one side . . .
His glittering hat was worn at a slight angle. He gave the
impression that his gaze floated calmly into the distance, and
that his head, though far from being stiffly mounted on his
shoulders, was immobile, even when turned to the right or
left, while his posture seemed not perpendicular but in some
fashion oblique, going from right to left, giving the idea of a
sort of lightness, which couldn't be released at this moment.'
He was 'fair-haired and clean-shaven, looking rather like an
Israelite engineer'. He stood there, 'elegant under a glistening
top hat, looking nowhere, letting his gaze float out peacefully
and as if thoughtlessly, like a slim column of smoke above a
village, rising into the blue on a sunny day like this'. When he
is cross-examined, he thinks his way into each question, acting
in involuntary obedience to an interior sincerity. One of the
expert witnesses is Paul Meyer, who, unimpressed by the
splendour of the robes and uniforms, declares his willingness
to confirm, under oath, that the handwriting isn't that of
Dreyfus. But after making a speech in defence of Dreyfus, the
socialist Jean Jaurès was physically assaulted in the Chamber
of Deputies on the 22nd, and at the end of the trial, Zola was
found guilty.

Watching the military style of the witnesses, Proust began to view etiquette in a different perspective: 'Life in society is concerned in reality with three things which constitute almost the whole of formality: snobbery, which is admiration of something in other people unconnected with the personality; backbiting, which is usually a matter of extreme attention paid (and disguised as criticism) to appearances; convention and etiquette, which erect formalism into something real and even more real than everything else.'[31]

In the flurry of committed activity – regular meetings with Dreyfusard friends in the Café des Variétés and daily visits to the court – Proust had been finding all the stamina he needed, but he couldn't sustain his new routine for long. 'I have had some choking fits,' he wrote towards the end of March, 'and it is more sensible not to speak till the end of the day . . . For several weeks I have not begun to exist until four in the afternoon, and if I want to work a bit and take the air for half an hour, it is already evening.' He was writing to Mme Daudet, trying to convince her – or himself – that in view of his illness it was better to see less of Lucien. 'Unfortunately I am not a good friend for him, excessively nervous too. He needs someone who combines similar intellectual and moral aspirations with the opposite temperament, calm instead of agitated, determined, happy.'[32] Grateful though the bereaved son had been for Proust's kindness, it had failed to produce a rapprochement. 'My dear boy,' Proust told him, 'you will never know how close to you I am. No doubt I am awkward at expressing it since letters and visits have remained unacknowledged.'[33] But sometimes Proust's breathing was so troublesome he had to stay quite still, either standing or sitting,[34] and throughout most of May he stayed in bed with a high temperature till seven in the evening.[35]

Disease was also striking at his mother, who almost died on 6 July during a three-hour operation on her cancerous pelvis. The surgeon, Dr Louis Terrier, said afterwards he wouldn't have recommended surgery if he'd known how dangerous it was going to be. She was still in danger for several days afterwards, but on the second day she said 'four or five words which with my filial prejudice I find full of wit'.[36] She was kept in the clinic for three months, and Proust spent so much of his time there he had little left for his novel or for campaigning to reinstate Dreyfus.[37]

In July, when Zola was stripped of his Légion d'honneur, Anatole France promptly resigned his. By now the Dreyfusards were making it hard for the army to go on suppressing the truth. On 7 July, trying to boost the army's credibility, the war minister, Cavaignac, damaged it. It was being generally assumed that the generals had in reserve conclusive evidence of Dreyfus' guilt. Wanting to bring this evidence out into the open, Cavaignac could produce only three documents. One was a letter Colonel Henry had forged from the Italian military attaché to a German, Schwarzkoppen, asking him to say 'we've had nothing to do with this Jew . . . nobody must ever find out what went on with him.' One was an 1896 letter in which Henry had changed the date to 1894 and the initial P to D. The last was the 'swine of a D . . .' letter, in which the D didn't refer to Dreyfus. Picquart could see all three documents were fakes, but when he said so, Cavaignac denounced him and, after being indicted, he was held in the Santé prison. But when the letter to Schwarzkoppen was inspected, it was recognisable as a forgery. On 30 August Colonel Henry was arrested; the next day, imprisoned in the fortress of Mont-Valérien, he cut his throat.

Even if Proust hadn't been so absorbed in the affair, it would have been hard, on 21 August, when Marie Benardaky married prince Michel Radziwill, to believe he'd once cared about her so passionately. When Mlle Kossichef is announced at an evening party, the adult Jean tries to avoid meeting her, though he remembers dragging his nursemaid to her house. 'Jean would feel nothing if you touched the spots which were formerly so sensitive but were now like a dead skin. We still carry it with us, but it will feel neither caresses nor pricks.'[38]

What mattered now was that Picquart was in danger. Henry's suicide was followed by several resignations, but the reactionaries were still fighting. On 25 August, Picquart's defence counsel, Maître Fernand-Gustave-Gaston Labori, submitted a complaint of fraud against Colonel du Paty de Clam, deputy chief of the Third Bureau at the Ministry of War and a cousin of Cavaignac, who resigned on 4 September, and eight days later, du Paty, who'd protected Esterhazy, had to resign. For Proust, the affair had once been Balzacian, with Esterhazy as the provincial nephew in *Les Illusions perdus* and du Paty as the Rastignac who meets Vautrin in the distant suburbs,[39] but now it had 'become Shakespearian, with its accumulation of precipitate denouements'.[40]

Picquart's trial was scheduled for the 21st, and Labori asked Anatole France to collect signatures that might impress the judges. France co-opted Proust, who co-opted Mme Straus, hoping she might get a signature from comte Othenin d'Haussonville. A member of the Jockey Club and the Académie Française, he hadn't yet declared his position. But though the petition had many famous signatories, including Sarah Bernhardt, Réjane, Edmond Rostand and comte Mathieu de Noailles, it made no impact, and on the 22nd Picquart was handed over to the military authorities and confined in the Cherche-Midi prison. From the 27th, kept in a solitary cell and allowed no contact with his lawyers, he might be shipped to Devil's Island. In the *Gazette de France* Maurras acclaimed the dead colonel's forgeries as valiant 'acts of war', while the anti-Semitic paper *Libre Parole* collected over 130,000 francs when it started a fund in aid of his widow. Among the subscribers were Barrès, Paul Valéry, the duc de la Rochefoucauld and the comte Léon de Montesquiou, comte Robert's cousin. When Maurras founded the nationalist Ligue de la Patrie Française, it soon had 15,000 members, including comte Othenin d'Haussonville, Jules Lemaître and Heredia.[41]

Though the president of the republic, Félix Faure, didn't want to admit justice had miscarried, Proust passed on to his father the story that Mme Faure shut herself up every day with the painter Alfred Rolle to read the pro-Dreyfus papers. Another Dreyfusard recruit was Constantin de Brancovan,[42] who, in early October, accompanied Proust to a meeting addressed by Jaurès. Now almost twenty-three, Constantin was old enough to become a friend, and their friendship was to become more important to Proust than any of the others which started out of the Dreyfus affair, though it brought him closer to Anatole France, who published a new novel, *L'Anneau d'améthyste (The Amethyst Ring)* in February 1899. Proust sent a congratulatory letter but still addressed him as 'Cher Maître', whereas Alphonse Daudet had been 'Cher ami'.

The affair changed Proust's view of human nature. Writing to Léon Daudet about Mercier, the villain in *Sebastien Gouves*, the novel he published in February 1899, Proust said: 'Until this past year I wouldn't have been able to believe in him because I absolutely didn't believe in evil. Now I've experienced it.'[43] Evil or immoral opportunism was still delaying the course of justice. Unwilling to risk a full revelation of the facts, the government arranged for the Court of Criminal Appeal to take over the Picquart case, and in November, at Mme Straus' flat, Proust tried to put pressure on a lawyer at the appeal court, Edmond Ployer, who was patently hostile to Dreyfus. It wasn't until 3 June that the appeal court finally quashed the sentence against him. On the 9th Picquart, after spending nearly twelve months in prison, was liberated, and Proust met him in the Charpentiers' home.

Proust had become so politically involved that he damaged *Jean Santeuil*: eager to report on developments in the case, he let it take over the narrative, using the novel almost like a diary to record events and preoccupations. At the same time he was being forced to reassess the nobility, in which anti-Semitism was more noticeable than concern for justice. Though he'd reprimanded Montesquiou for an anti-Semitic remark, Proust had listened unprotestingly to innumerable anti-Semitic conversations at salons and soirées, and he'd usually been reluctant to acknowledge the Jewish side of his heredity.

The government had procrastinated to improve its chances of survival, but it failed to survive, and on 22 June René Waldeck-Rousseau, a moderate, became the new premier. But the Dreyfus affair wasn't yet over. The new minister of war, General Marquis Gaston de Gallifet, who had to contrive a revision of the verdict without alienating the army, still believed Dreyfus was guilty. Both Mercier and Boisdeffre escaped with impunity, while the unfortunate Dreyfus, whose hair had gone white, had to face a second court-martial, which opened its proceedings in Rennes on 7 August. The long period of solitary confinement had made it hard for him to speak distinctly, and he was in no state to create a favourable impression from the witness box, while Labori, who was taking over as counsel for the defence, made the tactical mistake of attacking the army directly. At 6.20 in the morning of 14 August an assassin shot at him, but the bullet only wounded him. Proust sent a telegram acclaiming him as 'the good invincible giant' who'd demonstrated that it wasn't only soldiers who had the privilege of shedding blood.'[44]

The court-martial finally announced its verdict on 9 September. Five of the seven judges found Dreyfus guilty of high treason, but with extenuating circumstances, and he was sentenced to ten years of hard labour. Proust, who'd gone to Evian to join his parents and stayed on after they left, saw 'the shameful verdict pinned up at the Casino to the great joy of all the staff'. He went on to spend the evening with the Brancovans at Amphion, where Constantin's twenty-two-year-old sister, Anna de Noailles, who was married to a cousin of Montesquiou, comte Mathieu de Noailles, was 'in floods of tears and moaning in a half-strangled voice: "How could they do it? How could they dare to go and tell him? And in front of foreigners, the whole world? How could they?" She was weeping so violently that it was moving.'[45]

His mother shouldn't let the verdict depress her, he advised. 'It is sad for the army, for France, for the judges who have had the cruelty to make an exhausted Dreyfus find fresh reserves of courage. . . . As for the verdict, even that will soon be juridically quashed.'[46] He wrote to her every day. Though he was trying to cut down on medication, he resorted to Trional when he needed to catch up on sleep. But after two almost sleepless nights he was too weak to stop himself from giggling in front of Constantin's mother, the princesse de Brancovan, who 'consists of nervous twitches and oriental extravagance, which makes M. de Noailles smile disdainfully'.[47] In the evening at the villa, they played games with pencil and paper, and one evening, in a game of consequences, when asked for details about Alphonse Bertillon, head of the Judiciary Identification Section at the police prefecture and chief expert at Dreyfus' first trial, the princesse answered: 'I don't know. I haven't slept with him.'

Dreyfus was pardoned on 19 September 1899, but the news reached Proust some days later in a letter from his mother.[48] At the instigation of Gallifet and in opposition to the wishes of President Loubet, the cabinet had finally taken the decision Proust had predicted. The following day, Jules Guérin, editor of *L'Anti-Juif*, was arrested and sentenced to ten years' imprisonment.

NINE

AWAY FROM PARIS

Little of Proust's life was spent outside France, and none of it outside Europe. He never saw England, Germany, Spain or Greece, the only foreign countries he visited being Switzerland, Holland, Belgium and Italy – where he never went to Rome or Florence. His adult life was almost entirely divided between Paris and Cabourg, but between the autumn of 1898 and the end of 1900 he went away four times – once to Holland, once to Evian, which became his base for a motoring expedition to Switzerland, and twice to Venice.

He made the journey to Holland in October 1898, after a lot of hesitation, mainly to see a Rembrandt exhibition in Amsterdam, where he loved the canals

> and the big seagulls which pass so quickly, flapping their big wings so slowly, looking, even in the streets, in the corners to squares, as if they are seeking, scenting, feeling the sea, as if their instinct told them it was below and made something sea-like out of the whole town, where they parade, as if above waves and in the wind, their indefatigable anxiety, the joyous drunkenness of their strength and of their recognised element, swallowed and saluted by their cries.[1]

Visiting the exhibition, he noticed how Rembrandt's selection of people and places reflected his taste. A woman scrubbing a floor, or a house with the fire lit in the shadows of a dark room – these weren't just subjects. To a great artist, useful things are those which lead him to rediscover everything and attach himself to it more strongly. 'At first a man's work can resemble nature more than himself. But later, this essence of himself which is stimulated more by each favourable contact with nature, impregnates them more completely. And towards the end this essence is noticeably the only reality for him, and he struggles to reproduce it as a whole.' What he's painting in his maturity 'is in some sense the very day of his thought, the kind of particular day in which we see things at the moment of thinking in an original way.'[2] Stimulated by Rembrandt, Proust is striving after the same effect in prose, a fusion of fiction and essential truth. The literal truth, the surface, the fact matters less than the individuality of the vision, the penetration beyond a realistic reproduction of reality. Later on in the piece Proust describes the arrival of Ruskin at the exhibition. In reality Ruskin disliked Dutch painting and he was in Brantwood, in the Lake District. But Proust wanted to describe how Rembrandt's gaze, which had seemed to be staring out from the depths of his canvases, had lighted on Ruskin, in the way a king recognises another king in the crowd.[3]

From the Hague Proust made the thirty-minute journey to Scheveningen. Looking at the North Sea from the beach on a rainy day, he was reminded of happier visits to the seaside. Jean Santeuil reflects on the sadness

of recognising things we don't know, and, still worse, not being recognised by things we know, and feeling they have become unfamiliar. . . . On this Baltic beach which he didn't know, the waves he did know had the same air of not recognising him as all the strange things he'd never seen before, and the strange country under the unknown darkening sky gave the familiar voice of the little waves, whose childlike faces, delicate movements, harmonious gestures and rhythms were just the same as he'd seen in Brittany, gave even the beach the air of telling him: 'We don't know you.'[4]

Not yet thirty, Proust was inclined to look back on his past as if he were older. After receiving a Christmas card from Marie Nordlinger, he wrote to her:

While Christmas gradually loses its truth for us as an anniversary, by the gentle emanation of accumulated memories it takes on an increasingly lively actuality, where candlelight, the melancholy resistance of its snow to someone we want to arrive, the smell of tangerines drinking in warmth from the room, the brightness of the cold and the fires, the smell of tea and mimosa come back to us, smeared with the delicious honey of our personality which we've unconsciously been depositing for years while – absorbed in selfish pursuits – we didn't notice, but now, suddenly, it makes our heart beat faster.[5]

In *Jean Santeuil* Proust uses strikingly similar phrases when discussing the poetry of the vicomtesse de Reveillon, who was modelled on Anna de Noailles. Her deep sadness seems to be a point of departure for memories she savours in certain odours – 'the smell of tangerines flowing into a warm room, like the memory of all the luxurious pleasures of Christmas, where often around a bright and flower-decked table we have brought a soul full of thoughts about someone who wasn't there, who'd never come and whose absence gave to the snow outside which separated us from her, to the delivery of mail which brought us no letters from her, something not altogether empty but filled with a kind of charm'. As in the rosebush episode, the connection between smell and memory looks forward to *À la recherche*, while the faith Proust will later proclaim in literature as a means of rediscovering lost time is anticipated in the suggestion that poems are 'precisely the commemoration of our inspired moments, which are already often the commemoration of all that our being has left of itself in past moments, the intimate essence of ourselves which we exude without knowing it, but an odour smelt later, a similar light spilling into a room, brings it suddenly back to us strongly enough to intoxicate us with it and leave us indifferent to everyday life in which we never noticed it'.[6]

It was inevitable that *Jean Santeuil* would burst like a balloon when inflated with insights such as this, together with quasi-journalistic recording of developments in the Dreyfus case. What Proust needed was a form which could accommodate everything that was important to him, but, as he discovered later, there was nothing except the figure of Jean Santeuil to hold the heterogeneous elements together. Nor did Proust know how to take advantage of the contradiction between his conviction that he was mediocre and his awareness that some of his experiences were so intense that they should find their way into a novel, though he does try to dramatise Jean's attempts to deal with the same contradiction. He never penetrates more deeply into himself than at moments of questioning how much residue remains from experiences he'll never quite forget. Hadn't he given his heart to certain colours in the sky, certain movements in the sunlight, certain sensations that came from the wind? When he can make contact with the moments that mattered most and still matter most, he rises above all his negative feelings. 'And his profound calm seemed, like the blue sky above his head and the rustling grass at his feet, to conceal a serenity, a silent joy.'[7]

Proust hadn't yet found how he could draw creatively on tensions between his relationship with himself and his relationship with high society, but, partly because of the Dreyfus affair, he was beginning to take less pleasure in aristocratic salons and more in restaurants. He was especially fond of Larue's in the place de la Madeleine: many of his friendships, he said, were virtually born in the garish purple of its furnishings.[8] He also liked the gypsy orchestra, which was playing a waltz at one o'clock in the morning of 5 March, when Albert Flament and Robert de Flers were with him, discussing theatre. Proust was animated. If his asthmatic routine condemned him to nocturnal wakefulness, here was a way of passing time with friends when it was too late for him to stay on at a dinner party or a reception. At eleven o'clock on Sunday 16 April, Mme Arman's guests were already leaving when he arrived and started chatting with Anatole France. Mme Arman was talking to Flament: 'Such a pity Marcel won't work. He could write such a marvellous novel if only he didn't fritter himself away. Don't you think he's rather over-fond of society?'[9] Not wanting to be left on his own, Proust offered to take Flament home, engaged a cab in the avenue Hoche, but told the driver to follow them while they walked. Proust suggested a drive in the Bois de Boulogne, and when Flament demurred, proposed supper at Weber's in the rue Royale. After eating, they went on talking outside the door of Flament's flat.

But when Proust started planning a dinner party for 25 April, Flament was one of those invited only to the reception after the meal. A volume of sonnets by Montesquiou, *Les Perles rouges* (*The Red Beads*), was to be published in June, and at the dinner party the twenty-four-year-old actress Cora Laparcerie, who was currently at the Odéon, was to read some of these sonnets, together with verse by Anatole France and Anna de Noailles. The three writers were to be present, and Proust consulted Montesquiou about the guest list. Gabriel Fauré agreed to come, though he'd have to absent himself briefly to make an appearance at the Salle Pleyel. Proust also invited two princes, a princesse, a baronne, a comte, two comtesses, a marquis and a marquise, Mme Straus, Mme Arman, Mme Lemaire, Charles Ephrussi, the Russian-born editor of *La Gazette des beaux-arts*, and Léon Bailby, the editor of *La Presse*. This time Proust's parents came to the dinner.

Reporting the event, *Le Figaro* failed to mention either Montesquiou or the book he was keen to publicise. Its account of the 'très jolie soirée' named eight of the guests, adding 'and notabilities of the scientific, literary and artistic world'. Knowing how upset Montesquiou would be, Proust spent part of the day with Ephrussi and part with Bailby, discussing how to put pressure on *Le Figaro* to make amends. The following morning it printed a much longer piece, mentioning more of the guests by name and reporting that Montesquiou had 'scored a double triumph as author and as an exquisite speaker, having himself read, at the request of the guests, some of his poems'.[10]

Proust stayed in Paris until the beginning of September 1899, when he joined his parents in Evian, where the spa, according to his father, would be beneficial to his mother's health. During the protracted hesitation which invariably preceded any journey, Proust asked Constantin de Brancovan to recommend a quiet hotel at either Amphion or Evian.[11] The prince responded with an invitation to stay at the Villa Bassaraba, but Proust declined: he'd be delighted to pay frequent visits, especially in the evening, but needed to sleep during the morning.

The hotel, which had the name of Splendide Hôtel and Grand Hôtel des Bains, was so comfortable that he stayed on after his parents left on 9 September, the day the court-martial announced its verdict on Dreyfus. Living at the hotel, Proust was constantly short of cash, and often had to borrow from friends.[12] When the vicomte de Maugny, who owned the château of Lausenette at Thonon, three miles from Amphion, announced he was coming to dinner, Proust couldn't put him off but wished he'd chosen lunch.[13] By the middle of the month Proust was mostly staying in, because visiting friends was so expensive. At first the Brancovans were ferrying guests across the lake in their yacht, but when they were having it repaired, Proust couldn't go there without taking a carriage. 'Each time one goes to see someone, it costs ten to twenty francs.'[14] Anatole Bartholini's château was at Coudrée, near Sciez, six miles from Thonon. His wife had been lady of honour at the court of Empress Eugénie, and when Proust made friends with their beautiful daughter Kiki, they couldn't understand why he didn't visit them more often, while she grumbled jokingly about his clothes. But he was trying to economise. Prompted by his mother to buy a new straw hat, he said the old one was as good as new because the rain had straightened the straw.[15] On the 17th, when his bill for the week had come to 153 francs, he spent the evening alone, eating frugally in the restaurant instead of paying for a carriage to dine with the Bartholinis.[16] During the last week of September, when his mother sent 300 francs, he spent 236 within two days.[17]

She liked the financial nexus to strengthen the symbiosis in their relationship, while he took perverse pleasure in having his extravagance under surveillance. 'When I told you I was making calculations like this every day, I thought the hotel was not going to close until the 15th [October] and I simply wanted you to know what I was spending and to have your approbation or criticism.' His letters go into detail about his expenses, informing her about tipping a bus-driver ten francs, and asking how much to tip the hotel staff. His financial dependence was still integral to their close emotional rapport – in one letter he told her he'd been 'putting on an act of generosity with your money'.[18] The sporadic parsimony and the wish to be supervised might seem to assort oddly with his irrepressible extravagance in tipping and giving presents – in January 1900 he sent Anatole France a valuable Rubens drawing – but the common multiple was the irrational feeling that he wouldn't be liked or loved unless he paid for it, and to her the payment couldn't be made with money.

Frustrating though it was that his parents had authority over him, he still had little desire for independence. He'd earned nothing from his notional job at the Mazarine, nothing from *Les Plaisirs et les jours*, and little from his other writing. He'd been working for over four years on *Jean Santeuil*, but there was no prospect of earning money from it, and his enthusiasm for it was beginning to wane, while he was experimenting in different kinds of fiction. Collaborating with Robert de Flers again, he attempted another epistolary novel: Proust wrote letters in the character of Bernard, a lover, while de Flers impersonated his mistress, Françoise. The first of Bernard's letters appeared in *La Presse* on 19 September, followed the next day by a reply from Françoise, and on 12 October by Bernard's second letter.

The friendship with Constantin finally took root because of a motoring expedition. The motor car was still a plaything for the rich, but the twenty-six-year-old prince Alexandre de Cara-man-Chimay, husband of princesse Hélène de Brancovan, owned one, and, in his absence, Constantin invited Proust to join him and the novelist Abel Hermant in a drive to Coppet, the Swiss village where the castle had once belonged to Necker and later to Mme de Staël. Proust made the effort of getting up at seven-thirty, but it was raining, and, since the car was open, they agreed he should take the train to Geneva and meet them there. He drove with them from Geneva to Coppet, on to Pregny, and back to Geneva. Though it had become cooler and windy, they wanted him to stay with them for the drive back to Evian, but nervous that the cold air would bring on an asthma attack, he took the train.[19] Eight years later he'd describe his early impressions of motor travel in an article for *Le Figaro*, and in *À la recherche* the Narrator notices that in one bound a car can cover the distance that takes a horse twenty paces. 'Distances are only the relationship between space and time and vary with it. We express the difficulty we have in reaching a place in a system of miles, of kilometres, which becomes false as soon as the difficulty decreases.' At the turn of the century, it was decreasing rapidly and, for the motorist, scenery changed with dizzying speed. 'Gourville and Balbec-le-Vieux, Tourville and Saint-Mars-le-Vétu, prisoners as hermetically enclosed until then in the cells of separate days as Méséglise and Guermantes used to be, and which could never be seen by the same eyes in the course of an afternoon, delivered now by the giant in seven-league boots, came to gather around the hour in which we tasted their steeples and their towers and their old gardens which the neighbouring woods rushed to reveal.'[20] If the car had been commonplace by then, he might never have arrived at his perception of distance as a relationship between space and time. Bergson had said we project space into time when we juxtapose states of consciousness in such a way as to perceive them simultaneously; Proust not only appropriated this insight but dramatised it, infecting the reader with his excitement at seeing trees and steeples whirl about the sky, changing positions like dancers. Once you refuse to look at either time or space in a static perspective, they become more nearly interchangeable.

In the same way that Proust tended to arrive late at soirées and stay on after most of the other guests had left, he sometimes arrived towards the end of the season at a hotel and wanted to stay on after it closed. When he was trying to make up his mind what to do when the Evian hotel closed, Constantin again invited him to stay at the Villa Bassaraba, but it would be bad for his asthma, he said, to settle so close to the lake, and he'd have preferred the hotel at Thonon.[21] One reason for wanting to stay in the area was a new friendship with comte François d'Oncieu de la Bâtie, who had a château in the Savoy. But for a long time Proust had wanted to visit Italy, and he mentions the possibility in a letter to his mother. He wouldn't want to go alone, but if a friend came with him, he might visit the Italian lakes and Venice on the way home.[22] Three or four days earlier he'd asked her to forward his copy of de la Sizeranne's book on Ruskin, and in an early October letter, again mentioning the possibility of an Italian trip and again asking for the book, he says he wants 'to see the mountains through the eyes of this great man'.[23]

His interest in Ruskin probably began when he read part or all of Robert de la Sizeranne's *Ruskin et la religion de la beauté*, which appeared serially in *La Revue des deux mondes* between December 1895 and April 1897. Talking about Ruskin in conversations at the Café Weber during 1897, the year the book was published, Proust contended he was a better writer than Walter Pater.[24] But in the autumn of 1899 Ruskin was still virtually unknown in France, and these two letters of Proust's are the first indication of an interest that grew into a long-term preoccupation. As he'd shown in envying Abel Flament's powers of description, Proust felt particularly inadequate on this level, and, having watched painters working at Begmeil, and having looked carefully at paintings in the Louvre, he knew how different the Alps would seem if he could view them with the same attentiveness as an artist in the process of reproducing them. For Ruskin, nothing was more important than observing and describing. In *Modern Painters* he wrote 'the greatest thing a human soul ever does in this world is to *see* something, and to tell what it saw in a plain way. . . . To see clearly is poetry, philosophy and religion all in one.'[25] De la Sizeranne translated into French substantial passages from Ruskin's description of the Alps and Italy; remembering these, Proust wanted his help in looking at the Alps.

Sometimes the need for a book is all the more intense when it's inaccessible, and intuitively Proust now felt Ruskin could teach him what he needed to learn about observing and describing. If the book arrived before he left Evian, he may have started trying to view Alpine scenery through Ruskin's eyes; even if the book didn't, Proust had probably come to believe that looking at a landscape was an art he hadn't mastered and Ruskin had.

The other book Proust had read on Ruskin was J. A. Milsand's *L'Esthétique anglaise*, which came out in 1864; during the autumn of 1898, when Robert de Billy was in Paris, they discussed Ruskin when de Billy talked about visiting romanesque churches in the Auvergne and lent Proust Émile Mâle's *L'Art religieux de XIIIe siècle en France*.

After returning to Paris on 10 October, and catching cold on the journey,[26] Proust suffered from exhaustion and a pain – which he took to be rheumatism – in his foot.[27] Both may have played a part in his progressive disenchantment with the work he'd done on *Jean Santeuil*. On 5 December he told Marie Nordlinger:

> My imagination, which gave me a little happiness even if it gave none to others (for you are an exception in your taste for what I was writing, as you are in everything) seems to have suffered from the backlash of my weariness. I have been working for a very long time on a long-distance work, but without achieving anything. There are moments when I wonder whether I do not resemble the husband of Dorothea Brook in *Middlemarch*, and whether I am not collecting ruins.[28]

When George Eliot's Dorothea devotes herself to the book started by her dead husband, 'The Key to All Mythologies', she pictures 'the days, and months, and years, which she must spend in sorting what might be called shattered mummies and fragments of a tradition which was itself a mosaic wrought from crushed ruins'.[29] Proust had been collecting fragments of his own life and packing them into a framework which was roughly that of a *Bildungsroman*, but wasn't strong enough to hold them together.

In the same letter he says he's been working for a fortnight on 'a little piece of work absolutely different from what I generally do, about Ruskin and certain cathedrals'. The decision to work on Ruskin may not have been simultaneous

with a firm decision to abandon *Jean Santeuil*, but by about 20
November Louis Ganderax had commissioned an article on
Ruskin for the *Revue de Paris*. Proust's immediate concern
would be to look at some of the French Gothic cathedrals –
not mountains – Ruskin had described, but no one has
explained why Proust suddenly became so devoted to a master
whose values and vision were utterly different from those
underlying *Jean Santeuil*. Little of Ruskin's work had been
translated, and to Proust, who could scarcely read English,
most of it was inaccessible. The decision was impulsive and
intuitive, but the commitment was deep.

Sporadically working at an autobiography, *Praeterita*, Ruskin
connected the old man he'd become with his fourteen-year-
old self on the point of discovering the Alps:

> Thus in perfect health of life and fire of heart, not wanting
> to be anything but the boy I was, not wanting to have
> anything more than I had . . . and with so much of science
> mixed with feeling as to make the sight of the Alps not only
> the revelation of the beauty of the earth, but the opening of
> the first page of its volume, – I went down that evening
> from the garden-terrace of Schaffhausen with my destiny
> fixed in all that was to be sacred and useful. To that terrace,
> and the shore of the Lake of Geneva, my heart and faith
> return to this day, in every impulse that is yet nobly alive in
> them, and every thought that has in it help or peace.[30]

This passage bears on questions Proust had been asking himself
about the survival of emotional experiences and visual
impressions in the memory. At the same time he may have
believed Ruskin could train an assiduous reader – as he had
trained himself – to concentrate energy on the contemplation
of a landscape or a work of art before producing an accurate
description strongly charged with moral feeling. A fog or a
stormy sky could signify 'the cruelty of all things'. Reproducing his first impressions of Alpine clouds, Ruskin wrote: 'the
seen walls of the lost Eden could not have been more beautiful
to us; nor more awful, round heaven, the walls of sacred
Death'.[31] Nocturnal observation of the sky made Proust – who
was ill and insomniac after his return to Paris – envious of
Ruskin's power to preserve an appearance of objectivity while
projecting both malaise and morality on the universe.

But for twelve years Ruskin had been verging on madness.

His breakdown of 1878 had forced him to give up *Fors Clavigera*, his monthly letters which were issued like a magazine to keep workmen *au courant* with intellectual affairs, while he was behaving eccentrically in his dealings with Janet Leete, a governess who wanted him to write a simple book of English history her pupils could use. He agreed to the project but insisted on calling her Jessie, and his letters to her were full of crazy ardour. In 1880, when he was in France, he decided to start the book by sketching in some French history. The resultant work, *The Bible of Amiens*, invites readers to colour maps or fill them with *fleurs-de-lys*. This was the only section he completed of the book he was planning under the title *Our Fathers Have Told Us*, and, when Proust decided to translate it, he used *The Bible of Amiens* as his title. In 1889 Ruskin had another breakdown; since then he'd written nothing and seldom spoken.

A few days after Proust returned to Paris, he went with François d'Oncieu, who was now visiting him every day,[32] to the Bibliothèque Nationale, where he read the nineteen pages of Ruskin's *The Seven Lamps of Architecture* which had been translated in the *Revue générale*.[33] The book compares Gothic architecture with Greek and Byzantine. Proust then left a note for his mother, asking her to translate a page of the book; if she didn't have time, d'Oncieu could do it for him. His own English was bad enough for him to get titles wrong. At the end of November, when he wanted Ruskin's *The Queen of the Air*, which hadn't been translated, he asked Pierre Lavallée, now librarian at the École des Beaux Arts, for 'The Queen of Air', but within four months he told Marie Nordlinger he knew five of Ruskin's books by heart.[34] Knowing how little English he knew, she'd have realised the claim was absurd.

In October he started a series of Ruskinian pilgrimages to French cathedrals. First he visited Bourges, where the porch was carved with hawthorn. 'You would try to gather it forthwith,' Ruskin had written, 'but for fear of being pricked.' Proust also revisited the cathedral at Chartres before going to Amiens and using as his guide *The Bible of Amiens*, or at least his mother's translation of its fourth chapter.

Following Ruskin's advice, Proust gave money to the beggars outside the south porch and stood back to look at the Virgin who'd once been gilded and who still smiled, as Ruskin said, like a soubrette. Inside the cathedral, Proust was excited

by the cathedral choir, which had, in Ruskin's words, 'some
Flemish stolidity mixed with the playing French fire of it; but
woodcarving was Picardy's joy; and so far as I know there is
nothing else so beautiful cut out of the goodly trees of the
world. Sweet and young-grained wood it is . . . and it shoots
and wreathes itself into an enchanted glade, inextricable, imper-
ishable, fuller of leafage than any forest, and fuller of story
than any book.'[35]

The cathedral's west porch was what Ruskin had called the
Bible of Amiens: 'it is the Bible in stone'. This 'colossal and
lacelike swarming of human figures in stone which rise sky-
ward, holding their crosses in their hands' helps the viewer to
see the Bible as 'something real, belonging to the present'. If
Proust was attracted first to a book Ruskin had written mainly
for children, it was partly because the cathedral of Amiens was
the one he'd most loved and because the book gave 'the feeling
that as you leafed through it you were becoming aware that
here were things upon which Ruskin meditated continually,
those things which therefore express most profoundly his
thought; that the gift he was making to you was one of those
which are most precious to those who love, and which consist
of objects one has used a long time oneself'. While writing,
'Ruskin did not have to labour for you. He merely divulged
his recollections and opened his heart.'[36]

In a December letter to Douglas Ainslie, Proust said he had
to do something about the cathedral in Rheims and needed
help on the English language: he'd studied Latin, Greek and
German at school, but had never learnt English. He was also
being slowed down by influenza, but was already planning
more than one essay on Ruskin. A January letter to Marie
Nordlinger mentions 'some pieces of work about him'; he'd
wanted to consult her, he says, a month earlier, about 'a word,
a title, a meaning', but he'd taken advice from 'an English
friend'.[37] This may have been Ainslie, but was more likely
Charles Newton Scott, who'd written *The Foregleams of Christianity, an Essay on the Religious History of Antiquity* (1877) and
The Epoch of Marie-Antoinette (1899). Proust had been corresponding with him but could not have known him well: in
acknowledging help from him, as he does both in the note at
the head of the first chapter in the *Bible of Amiens* translation
and in the preface to *Sesame and Lilies*, Proust describes him as
'the poet and scholar to whom we are indebted for *The Church*

and Compassion for Animals and *The Epoch of Marie-Antoinette*, two books, full of learning, feeling and talent, which deserve to be better known in France'. But the first of these books was written not by Newton Scott but by Louise Amour Marie La Roche-Fontenilles, the marquise de Rambours.[38]

He was less generous in acknowledging help from his mother, but, from the moment of starting to plan Ruskin translations and essays on him, Proust was obviously counting on her inexhaustible patience. He didn't at first plan to publish the translations: according to Reynaldo, he said, 'that wicked Ruskin has forbidden anyone to translate his work into French, my poor translations will remain unpublished. But in my studies on him, I'll quote large fragments.' Why translate more than he could quote? Partly because this was the best way to make sure he'd arrived – with help from his mother's rough translations – at a complete understanding of Ruskin's English, and partly, I suspect, because he wanted a blood transfusion from Ruskin. By absorbing rhythms and syntax Proust might acquire habits of perceiving and thinking.

On 20 January 1900 the eighty-one-year-old Ruskin died of influenza at his home in the Lake District. When Proust read the news in *Le Figaro*, he felt both sad and consoled, 'for I sense what a small thing death is when I see how forcefully this dead man lives, how much I listen to him, admire him, strive to understand him and obey him, more than I do most of the living'. Grateful that Marie had sent him her annotated copy of *The Queen of the Air* – her charming notes, he said, were like dried flowers on every page – he assured her the book and her notes 'are living inside me, and not in those recesses of the self which one visits only rarely, but in that intimacy of the heart where, several times each day, one sees oneself'.[39]

He got himself commissioned to write an obituary of Ruskin for the *La Chronique des arts et de la curiosité*, a supplement to Charles Ephrussi's *Gazette des beaux-arts*, and he went to the cathedral at Rouen, mainly to look for a tiny figurine in the Porch of the Booksellers, described in *Seven Lamps*: 'The fellow is vexed and puzzled in his malice; and his hand is pressed hard on his cheek bone, and the flesh of the cheek is wrinkled under the eye by the pressure.'[40] To Proust it seemed Ruskin had done as much for the little figure as its original sculptor, and that in going to Rouen he was obeying Ruskin's dying wish.

He went with Léon Yeatman and his twenty-eight-year-old wife, Madeleine, a sculptress, who succeeded in identifying the figurine, which is only about six inches tall. 'The stone still has the hole which raises the eyeball, giving it the expression which made me recognise it.'[41]

They went on to Saint-Maclou – Ruskin had written about the desperation of the souls pursued by flames in the Last Judgment – and to Saint-Ouen, where the verger, Julien Édouard, had guided Ruskin on his visit to the church twenty years earlier. 'He claims that Ruskin told him Saint-Ouen was the most beautiful Gothic monument in the world, and in *Seven Lampes* [*sic*] Ruskin says it is a frightful monument.' This is what Proust wrote in an early March letter to Marie, which means he'd read the appendix to the book, where Ruskin called the church 'one of the basest pieces of Gothic in Europe . . . resembling, and deserving little more credit than, the burnt sugar ornaments of elaborate confectionery'.

After returning to Paris, Proust worked intensively, and by 7 or 8 February claimed: 'All my essays are finished.'[42] The obituary had appeared on 27 January, and on 13 February the new editor of *Le Figaro*, Gaston Calmette, published the first of Proust's *Pèlerinages Ruskiniens en France*.[43] And in April two more of his Ruskin pieces were published – 'Ruskin à Notre-Dame d'Amiens' in the *Mercure de France*, and the first part of a long essay, 'John Ruskin' in the *Gazette des beaux-arts*, which was to publish the second part in August. The first part is probably the one Ganderax had commissioned but never published. With two exceptions, all the quotations from Ruskin are taken – not without acknowledgment – from de la Sizeranne and Milsand, but in the essay on Notre-Dame d'Amiens and in the second part he quotes directly from *The Seven Lamps*, *The Pleasures of England*, *The Stones of Venice*, *St Mark's Rest* and *Lectures on Architecture and Painting*.

How he managed was a mystery to Constantin de Brancovan,[44] and in April 1900 Proust still thought the book Marie had sent him was called 'The Queen of Air'.[45] According to Georges de Lauris, Proust would have found it hard to order a chop in an English restaurant: 'He knew no English but Ruskin's, but he understood this in its most subtle shades of meaning.' The problem of how he coped with the language is inseparable from the problem of why Ruskin had suddenly come to fascinate him: it was as if Proust had developed a rapport with him that was more intuitive than intellectual.

More than any other writer, Ruskin encouraged his inclination to scrutinise a bush or a landscape as if it were a sacred text no one else had quite succeeded in deciphering. Ruskin passionately believed our response to the natural world should involve our whole moral being because its beauty was God's handiwork. Modern man had created industrial towns and skyscrapers, but God had created the country, and the artist would inevitably celebrate the divine soul if he told the exact truth about natural phenomena. Proust stood in roughly the same relation to the impressionists as Ruskin did to English landscape painting from Constable to Turner. The subject you chose was unimportant. Bourgeois families picnicking in a boat, a blowsy barmaid brooding, a shopkeeper asleep. Everything you saw belonged to a single system, and it was all subject to the same laws. Proust was less disposed than Ruskin to believe in a divine lawgiver, but he had no doubt there were laws. Find the principle and you understand the process. Ruskin fed his appetite for reassurance about the unity of all phenomena – natural, spiritual, aesthetic, scientific.[46] For Albert Camus, the telephone is a symbol of disjunction. When you see a man talking inside a telephone box, but don't hear what he's saying, his lips are moving meaninglessly; for Proust the telephone symbolises connectedness. The poet's mind is filled with manifestations of the same mysterious laws that govern the world outside, and the joy he takes in natural beauty depends on his recognition of the affinity between macrocosm and microcosm. When he's working creatively, he has exchanged his private soul for the universal soul, and he's 'in communication, as in a telephone or telegraphic kiosk, with the beauty of the whole world'.[47]

In Proust's struggle with the practical problems of translating from the English, Mme Proust was, according to Marie, inexhaustibly generous with her help, writing literal translations into 'several red, green and yellow school exercise books'.[48] But Proust must have found his own way to most of the quotations he picked, and even if he was a long way from knowing five of the books by heart, he acquired thirty volumes of Ruskin in English,[49] and worked prodigiously hard at familiarising himself with them. On translating *The Bible of Amiens* and writing the commentary he spent (according to his own estimate) well over a thousand hours, but he claimed the work was spread over four years, whereas it extended over little more than two. When a friend teased him – 'You don't really know English and it must be full of mistakes' – he reacted furiously: 'Not because of my talent, which is nothing, but because of my conscientiousness, which has been infinite – this will be one of the very few translations which are a veritable reconstitution.'[50]

For nearly five years his post at the Mazarine Library had been a sinecure which yielded no money; he done nothing but apply at yearly intervals for a further year's leave. But in 1899, when an inspector visited the library, his absenteeism was discovered, and on 14 February 1900 he wrote to Pol-Louis Neveu, the former librarian, now chief assistant in the government department controlling the Mazarine, asking whether there was any alternative to resigning. Could he be given indefinite leave or allowed to postpone his return indefinitely?[51] From the beginning of March he was taken to have resigned, but the news would have caused him little distress, even if he hadn't been so absorbed in Ruskin.

He was soon preparing excitedly for his first trip to Venice, planning to look at it in the way he'd looked at the cathedrals. 'My admiration for Ruskin gave so much importance to the things he had made me love that they seemed imbued with a value greater than that of life. Literally, and in circumstances that made me believe my days were numbered, I left for Venice so as to be able, before dying, to approach, touch, see Ruskin's ideas about medieval architecture embodied in palaces that were sinking but still erect and pink.'[52] He'd been planning to see Venice in the autumn, which, according to Constantin de Brancovan, was the healthiest season, but in April, when Reynaldo was in Rome with his mother, and Marie was in Florence, intending to meet her cousin in Venice, the idea of joining them both was irresistible. The Yeatmans were in Italy too, and even if they couldn't visit Venice when the others were there, Proust urged them to go, offering to lend them Ruskin's books on Italy 'so that he can guide you by dazzling you, like the column of fire that went in front of the Israelites, and can make your trip more glorious'.[53]

Proust left Paris with his mother in late April or early May. As the train carried them across the Lombardy plain, she read out the passage in *The Stones of Venice* comparing the city with a coral reef in the Indian seas and with an opal. His first glimpse of the city was therefore disappointing. 'When our gondola stopped beneath it,' Proust reported, 'it naturally could not retain the beauty it had worn in my imagination a moment earlier, because we cannot see a thing physically and imaginatively at the same time.'[54] But later he wrote: 'When I went to Venice I found my dream had turned – incredibly but quite simply – into my address.'[55]

They were staying at the Hotel Danieli, where Ruskin had stayed. It was within 200 yards of the Piazza San Marco and the Doges' Palace, and in front of it was the marble-paved Riva degli Schiavoni. On the first day, he rested after lunch and went down to look at the quays. In the evening, at Quadri's in the Piazza, he worked with Marie on *The Bible of Amiens*, and in the morning the shutters of his bedroom opened to reveal bright sunlight on the golden angel above the campanile of St Mark's. The angel 'bore me on his shining wings a promise of beauty and joy greater than he ever brought to Christian hearts when he came to announce "glory to God in the highest . . ." '.[56]

In the mornings, while his mother rested and read at the hotel, Proust went with Reynaldo and Marie in a gondola along the Grand Canal to visit the churches: 'Blessed days when with other of the master's disciples I listened to his gospel at the edge of the water, disembarking at each of the temples which seemed to rise out of the sea just to offer us the object of his descriptions and the exact image of his thoughts.'[57]

On the way back, as they passed the Salute, Proust would catch sight of his mother's shawl weighted down by a book on the alabaster balustrade, waving in the wind, 'and above it the window's rounded cusps expanded in a smile . . . and the jet of its ogival curve added the distinction of a slightly veiled glance . . .'.[58] Associated with his mother, the window lodged itself in his memories. 'Those palaces along the Grand Canal whose role it was to give me the light and the sense of morning have become so much a part of it that what the glint on the weathercock opposite makes me want to see again is no longer the sunlit church-slates flashing like black diamonds, and the market square, but only Venice, the promise that was fulfilled by the golden angel.'[59]

In the afternoons, with Marie's Venetian aunt in attendance, they'd sit in the Piazza, eating *granita* at Florian's and watching the pigeons. Sometimes he'd work on Ruskin with Marie inside the cathedral. In the evening the three young people would escape from the aunt to sit outside Quadri's, drinking coffee, or take a gondola to the Lagoon. And when Reynaldo was on his way back to Rome, Proust and Marie went to Padua, where Proust, at Ruskin's prompting, looked at Giotto's frescoes in the chapel of the Madonna dell' Arena. He'd seen reproductions of some in *Fors Clavigera*. Afterwards, in the Eremitani, they saw Mantegna's fresco depicting the life of St James, 'one of the paintings I love best in the world,' Proust said.[60]

Before leaving Venice he quarrelled with his mother. What he resented most was the restriction on his liberty. Now that Reynaldo had left, he'd have been free, if only he were alone, to pursue the sexual adventures that Venice offered. It had been his own decision to come with her, but being angry with himself made him angry with her.

> Out of spite I told her I was going away. I had gone downstairs, had changed my mind about going, but I wanted to prolong Mamma's distress at my supposed departure, and I stayed down there on the landing stage, out of sight, while a tenor in a gondola sang a serenade which the sun, on the point of vanishing behind the church of the *Salute*, had lingered to hear. I could feel Mamma's distress dragging on, waiting became unbearable and I could not bring myself to get up and go to her and say 'I am not leaving.' It seemed as if the serenade could not end and the sun could not set, as if my mental agony and the singer's notes had been fused permanently in a bitter, ambiguous and unalterable compound.[61]

Proust returned to Paris at the end of May. Since the spring they'd been looking for a new flat, partly because Mme Proust's health was deteriorating and her husband wanted to find somewhere quieter, with better air, partly because his own career was so successful he felt entitled to a more distinguished address. At the international Sanitary Conferences in 1892 and 1893 he'd played a major role in securing agreement between the European powers, and in December 1899 he'd made a tour of inspection around the Mediterranean ports. He'd lectured both at the Sorbonne and at the Académie des Sciences Morales et Politiques, and his books had consolidated his reputation.

Like his wife, he'd put on weight, and, holding his head high, he wore his spectacles low on his nose.[62]

In April they'd been hoping to move into a second-floor flat at 127, boulevard Haussmann. Since the landlord, the marquis de Réaulx, didn't want a doctor or a lawyer as a tenant, Proust asked Pierre Lavallée, a friend of the marquis' grandson, to point out 'that for several years – and increasingly each year – my father has been devoting himself almost exclusively to scientific research. He now sees so few patients that he probably receives fewer visitors than the average tenant'.[63] Lavallée tried to help, but eventually the Prousts settled on a flat less than half a mile away from their old one. It was at 45, rue de Courcelles in the fashionable quartier rue Monceau. The flat was spacious, and the street, which runs between the boulevard de Courcelles and the rue de la Boétie, was quieter than the boulevard Malesherbes. The place du Pérou is at the junction of the rue de Courcelles and the rue de Monceau, where Madeleine Lemaire was living at No. 35. Before moving to the rue de Berri, the Princesse Mathilde had lived and held her salon in the rue de Courcelles. Flaubert, Merimée, Goncourt and Sainte-Beuve used to come here every day.[64]

In June Mme Proust, suffering from rheumatism, stayed in bed[65] and in August, before they moved into the new flat, the doctor took her back to the hotel in Evian, where they joined the Duplay family – Maurice's father was a surgeon – to form what Mme Proust called 'a miniature independent republican party of our own'[66] and to avoid what, affecting to forget her ancestry, she called 'the Semitic element'.[67] The hotel was full and noisy, which was one of the reasons she discouraged her son from coming; the other was that she'd soon be in Paris again to organise the new flat.

Proust's parents made the move on 15 October, but he'd left Paris in September for Evian, and on 13 October he went back to Venice. Alone, he was free to do everything he couldn't do when his mother was there. In *La Fugitive* the Narrator jealously wanders through the humble *campi* and abandoned *rii*[68] in search of working-class girls Albertine would have loved. Proust is more likely to have been in search of working-class boys, and the Narrator seems 'to penetrate further and further into the depths of some secret thing'.[69]

But on the 19th, when Proust visited the Armenian monastery on the island of San Lazaro in the Lagoon, he found he was missing his mother, and feeling guilty about the quarrel they'd had here. He'd thought about the pointed Gothic arch of the windows as much as about anything else in Venice: 'For all its wealth of lovely design, for all its architectural renown, I remember that window as I might remember a man of genius we had met at a watering place and lived with for a month on terms of familiarity. And if, when . . . I saw it again, I wept, it was simply because the window said to me: "I remember your mother so well." '[70]

He was working on a dialogue which followed from the abortive attempt to collaborate with de Flers on an epistolary novel. The woman is again called Françoise; the man is called Henri. Proust writes better than in the collaboration, especially when dealing with jealousy. Henri speaks wistfully of places which are so beautiful they seem made for happiness, and it's impossible to be there without urgently wishing for it. Nowhere, as he says, is one more miserable.[71] Françoise realises he's distracted by the thought that his previous mistress came to this pavilion in the Bois de Boulogne with another man. In the second scene, they're in the pavilion again, and he can't help talking about jealousy. He equates it with imagining the pleasure of a woman one loves. 'To imagine the lives of other people, we lend them our own.'[72]

He returned to Paris in late October and settled into the new flat, not without trouble. He hated the smell of new paint, there was nowhere he could smoke his anti-asthma cigarettes, and the vexation exacerbated his difficulties in breathing.[73] 'I always found it as difficult to settle into a new environment,' says the Narrator, 'as it was easy to abandon an old one.'[74]

Proust started the year 1901 with a bout of influenza that kept him indoors for over five weeks. It was his mother who made the decisions about furniture and decoration. She bought a new tapestry to mask the wall dividing the large drawing-room from the smaller one. In the previous flat a room had been devoted to the display of tapestries; these and the Empire armchair were now put into the ante-room, and the painting by Govaert Flinck, *Tobias and the Angel*, into the dining-room, where the curtains were made out of tapestries.[75]

There were glass-fronted cabinets in both the doctor's bed-room and his wife's, which had blue furniture and a blue light pendant. In the room she called the smoking-room – because Proust did his fumigation in it – were the bureau and the red armchairs from his grandparents' house and the glass-fronted cabinet which had belonged to his grandmother. Parsimoniously, his mother had the carpet in this room laid reverse side up to reduce the wear and tear, knowing he'd be in and out incessantly.[76]

Not yet thirty, he looked young for his age, but the relentless tide of asthma made him feel old. 'Incessantly ill, without pleasures, objectives, activities or ambitions, with the life ahead of me finished and with an awareness of the grief I cause my parents, I have very little happiness.'[77] This was how he put it in a letter to Constantin, who was in Bucharest. 'If the soil of Rumania is favourable to your fruitfulness, stay there, dear friend, as long as necessary . . . Our only debt is to the element of eternity which is in us, and our duty is to organise ephemeral circumstances so that they contribute to it most effectively.'[78] From the depths of his depression, and with no expectation of longevity, Proust was interrogating himself about the element of eternity in himself.

He didn't feel well enough to go out till 7 February. Reynaldo, too, had been ill, and Proust thought of visiting him, but offered to stay in if Lucien felt like calling. It was a long time since he'd seen Lucien, and Proust felt 'sick of close confinement. . . . I haven't seen a living face since I saw you (except for my parents). I think about you all the time, which suits me very well.'[79]

Proust's health remained precarious throughout the winter and early spring, and one note to his mother describes an 'asthma crisis of such enormous violence, and going on for so long, and coming after three minutes of the most perfect calm I've ever had. (I hadn't smoked since four o'clock yesterday afternoon.)'[80] He could count on her insatiable appetite for details about his attacks, but he was anxiously aware of her tendency to disregard warning symptoms about her own health. Having once wanted her to pay less attention to her younger son, he now wanted her to pay more attention to him – as a doctor who could give useful advice. 'Happiness and sorrow have ripened his nature like a fruit which becomes sweet after having been a little acid. Which mean his intelligence and kindness will join forces to advise you.'[81]

In April, without any discouragement from her, he started planning another soirée with recitations by Cora Laparcerie of poems by Anna de Noailles. He arranged for the poet to rehearse the actress, and one night, arriving home from an evening with Montesquiou to find two unpublished poems had been delivered, he sat down to read the poems and write an enthusiastic letter congratulating the young poet, and quoting phrases. He said he especially liked 'the pigeons whose whiteness marches, the road of the sun without shadows or bends, the swans who dance in the wind, the low country of my tenderness, and the admirable familiarity with which you interrogate nature, calling infinity "Moon with fair cheeks" and conscience "My dear friend" '. The flattery is rooted in genuine admiration: in February 1899, when her poem 'Notre Amour' appeared in the *Revue de Paris*, he'd felt 'a new and insatiable literary passion, like the times I first saw a Gustave Moreau and first heard a melody by Fauré.'[82]

But Proust had even worse luck at this soirée than when the *Figaro* had ignored Montesquiou. This time Anna de Noailles failed to arrive. Her husband came, saying she was ill. Proust assumed she disliked Cora Laparcerie's style of reciting, but there's no hint of reproach in his letter, which describes the impact her poems had made on guests including Anatole France, and tells her illness is often 'the sagging of the body under the weight of an excessively great soul'.[83]

The poems came from her first collection, *Le Coeur innombrable* (*Unbounded Heart*), which was to be published on 7 May. Proust presented Reynaldo with a copy, which he took to Brussels and gave to Sarah Bernhardt. In his diary for 23 May he wrote: 'Sarah delighted with Mme de Noailles' book.' He wrote to Proust, who wrote to the princesse: 'She was enthusiastic, calls you the greatest of poets, a great genius etc., and immediately learned "The Offering to Pan" by heart and will recite it on Thursday at M. de Montesquiou's.' He was eager to be present, but 'I have finally, either from the Bois or from your book, caught hay-fever, for twenty-four hours I have been unable to breathe and I am very ill. I shall take all the medicines that have been invented to be able to come on Thursday, but I am no good before nine in the evening and not much good after. I would want neither the princesse de Chimay nor you to see me in one of my cacochymymic wheezing fits.'[84] Cacochymy is an unhealthy state of the body fluids.

But he recovered in time to plan a dinner party for 19 June with the de Noailles as guests of honour. If he had misgivings about her behaviour last time, he distracted himself by having the tables decorated with nosegays of wild flowers mentioned in her poems. According to Léon Daudet, Proust

> invited to his home about sixty people of differing opinions. It was possible they would start throwing crockery. I found myself sitting next to a ravishing person like a portrait by Nattier or Lagillière, and learned she was the daughter of a well-known Israelite banker. Anatole France was at the head of the neighbouring table. Deadly enemies were chewing their chaudfroid within six feet of each other. But the emanations of sympathy and goodwill Marcel exuded spread in whirlwinds and spirals across the dining-room and the drawing-room and for two hours the truest cordiality prevailed among the Atrides. I believe no one else in Paris could have brought off this *tour de force*.[85]

Proust's habit when giving a dinner party was to eat before his guests arrived and move around during the meal, changing places each time a new course was served. Most of the guests were Dreyfusards, but the marquis d'Eyragues, the marquise, who was Montesquiou's cousin, and Mme de Brantes were on the other side.

Montesquiou called it 'the dinner of the rejected' because most of the guests hadn't been invited to the soirée in May. Anatole France had brought his daughter, Suzanne, and the other guests included the prince and princesse de Polignac, the princesse de Chimay, Abel Hermant, Constantin de Brancovan, the comte de Briey, the vicomte de Maugny and Gabriel de la Rochefoucauld. Mme Proust was present, and her son made sure her name was mentioned in *Le Figaro*'s report. Though his father absented himself, his disapproval was mixed with amusement and pleasure at his son's social success. Collecting the mail and identifying one of his son's aristocratic correspondents from the envelope, he'd jovially call out: 'A letter from Madame de Noailles!' only to be reprimanded by his wife: 'Don't spoil his pleasure by telling him in advance.'[86]

TEN

NOBLE FRIENDS

If snobbery is defined as addiction to the pleasure of associating with an elite, Proust was undeniably a snob. His desperate need for love made it impossible for him not to envy the aristocrats whose birth ensured them a place at the centre of other people's attention and admiration. He could never quite forgive himself for failing to be born into the nobility; during his late teens and early twenties the best compensation was to be invited to exclusive salons, and though he felt at ease in chatting with servants, he does little in either *Jean Santeuil* or *À la recherche* to reflect working-class experience. He'll deal in passing with servants, soldiers, clients at a male brothel and working-class lovers of homosexual noblemen, but his main literary interest in servants was in picking up gossip about their masters.

In his late twenties and early thirties he enjoyed nothing more than friendships with good-looking, arrogant, stylish, charming young noblemen. The pleasure he took in their company is clear from the passage in *Guermantes* describing a visit to the barracks at Doncières. The prince de Foix belongs to a group of twelve or fifteen young aristocrats who are, by descent, sovereign princes of small territories, and though they are all heavily in debt – all hoping to regain solvency through a lucrative marriage – they take precedence over the richest dukes. Saint-Loup and the prince belong to an even more exclusive group of four, who are always invited together to country houses, where they are given communicating bedrooms, causing rumours to circulate about the extent of their intimacy, but they are above reproach.[1]

Another pleasure to be had from friendships with princes and dukes was in the impression he had of erasing his Jewishness – repeating Charles Haas' social success without living an idle life. The dark-skinned, oriental-looking Proust was irresistibly attracted to the blond good looks of young noblemen, and in

À la recherche Saint-Loup is given the blond hair and the fair skin of the dandyish marquis Boni de Castellane – he has an engaging resemblance to 'the sunniness of a golden day solidified'[2] – though most of Robert de Saint-Loup's other characteristics come from noblemen Proust knew better, while his name comes from the dark-haired sibling rival, combining the same Christian name with their mother's word of endearment, *loup*. In Proust's uncontrollable love of fair hair and fair complexions, he transforms the dark Russian Marie Benardaky into the blonde Gilberte. Towards the end of the novel the Narrator arrives at the realisation that 'the impassable abyss which I had then believed to exist between me and a certain type of little girls with golden hair was as imaginary as Pascal's abyss'.[3]

The young noblemen most likely to reciprocate Proust's interest in them were the more intelligent ones, such as Gabriel, twenty-six-year-old son of the comte Aimery de la Rochefoucauld. Proust described him as bearing his mother's bright eyes in his forehead like family jewels. Though he came from one of France's foremost ducal families, he was a Dreyfusard who'd come to feel a certain contempt for the aristocracy. Because of his fondness for late-night restaurants he was sometimes called the Rochefoucauld of Maxim's.[4] He rapidly developed much more respect for Proust and his literary potential than Proust himself had. Visiting the Yeatmans on his thirtieth birthday, 10 July, Proust said: 'I'm thirty today, and I've done nothing.' Still suffering from the conviction that he was weak-willed, he considered his father to be ' as energetic as I am lazy';[5] in reality Proust's energy, though it took a different form, was no less formidable. Even if he'd written nothing but his letters, he'd have put more words down on paper than most people do during a lifetime. But he was succeeding neither as a writer nor as a lover.

On 12 or 19 July, within six months of telling Lucien he never stopped thinking about him, Proust received a cruel snub. When they met at six in the evening, Lucien avoided mentioning the dinner party he was giving in the Bois for the comte and comtesse de Noailles and the princesse de Chimay. Proust was piqued when he found out about it later on in the day through meeting Léon Daudet, but his letter of protest to Lucien was jokey and conciliatory.[6]

He might have been able to jerk himself out of his depression if he could have gone away for a summer holiday, but he was too ill. 'Misery of miseries or mystery of mysteries?' In late August, writing to his mother, who was in Zermatt, he used this phrase of Dumas' to sum up his situation. Even when she was out of Paris, she was still his closest ally in the war against asthma. 'Yesterday after writing to you, I succumbed to relentless asthma and flux, forcing me to walk doubled over and to light a cigarette each time I came to a tobacconist's. And what is worse, I went to bed all right, at midnight, after long fumigations, and three or four hours later had the summer crisis. This is unique in my experience. It has always happened during the attacks.' Though feeling better the next day, he was worrying about being alone, 'because my attacks seem to come in the middle of the night when there is nobody to light my candle, make me something hot afterwards'. Relief at being able to share the problem mingles in the letter with anxiety about the unknown cause of the attack. It couldn't have been the pollen in the Bois, because he'd ridden only in a closed carriage. It was unlikely to be the saffron the maid used when laundering the lace to give it a delicate tinge of yellow. Nor could it be constipation. 'As for milk, I scarcely ever drink any now, and anyway I was drinking less than before, taking none in my coffee, and no soup.' Could it be the intestinal worms mentioned by Dr Brissot in his *L'Hygiène des asthmatiques*?

Anyway he still had a hearty appetite. 'All this didn't stop me from eating at about half-past two a meal consisting of two tournedos steaks – I ate every scrap – a *dish* of chips (about twenty times as much as Félicie used to make), some cream cheese, some gruyère, two croissants, a bottle of Pousset beer (I don't think beer can give one albumen?).'[7] The passionate self-absorption is founded on the luxury of knowing she devoured every detail – illness was still a means of commanding her attention – and he'd often joke about his gourmandise. 'Lunch is my favourite moment,' he told her,[8] and to Mme Daudet he wrote that Lucien had complained of being repelled by this gluttony.[9] His stomach sometimes became so distended the elastic around his underpants wasn't strong enough, and he resorted prematurely to a corset, but this, combined with the overeating, hurt his stomach so much he was soon forced to abandon both.[10]

The loss of Lucien was compensated by aristocratic friend-ships, and the one with Gabriel de la Rochefoucauld was soon eclipsed by one with the princesse Bibesco's twenty-three-year-old son, Antoine, a diplomat attached to the Rumanian legation in Paris. The first impression Proust made on him was unfavourable, but they shared an interest in Gothic architecture, and Antoine had been taking photographs of cathedrals. By the autumn Proust was writing to him almost every day. Antoine's English was good, and they were soon planning to collaborate on a translation of Thoreau, whom Proust counted as a *philosophe*.[11]

According to Ruskin, summer was the best season for visiting Abbeville and rushing down the street in time to see the church of St Wulfram while the sun was still on the towers.[12] The summer of 1901 wasn't quite over when, escaping from Paris at last, Proust revisited Amiens on 7 September, going on to Abbeville with Léon Yeatman, who was on his way to Boulogne. Left alone, Proust worked for a while in the church and bought himself dinner at six in the buffet of the railway station. During the first part of the trip he'd been feeling ill, but he recovered sufficiently to feel 'happy to see summer's reserves intact around me', though asthma was on his mind a great deal, and he hadn't overcome his anxiety about the state of his intestines.[13]

On 13 August the *Journal des débats* carried an article on the cathedral at Amiens. Though Proust wasn't mentioned, he was glad to send the author, André Michel, a copy of the *Mercure de France* with his essay in it. Michel's response, in a September sequel, was to ridicule people who visited Amiens to follow in the footsteps of Ruskin, that 'well-meaning mystical Baedeker'.

But Proust's appetite for the Gothic had been whetted again, and on 6 or 13 October, planning to revisit Illiers, he invited Antoine to accompany him as far as Chartres. At the end of the month Proust gave copies of *Les Plaisirs et les jours* to Antoine and the twenty-three-year-old comte Bertrand de Salignac-Fénelon, who'd formed a secret society with Antoine and his brother Emmanuel. They used a private language and nicknames – Fénelon was known either by the anagram Nonelef or as Blue Eyes. Fénelon is introduced into *Jean Santeuil* as Bernard de Reveillon. In one passage, by a slip of the pen, Proust wrote 'Bertrand' instead of 'Bernard'. Bernard is 'imbued with passion for intelligence, knowledge, talent, justice, progress and nobility'. Though he consciously sets little

value on his noble birth, he's one of those whose life is 'surrounded by little purple ducal coronets on their writing paper,
by footmen habitually and incessantly saying "Monsieur le
Duc", "Madame la Duchesse" as if they didn't notice they
were doing it, by ancestral portraits, by châteaux which bear
their names and by silver plate which bears their heraldic arms'.
Bernard wants nothing more than to be forgiven for being a
nobleman, but in writing about him Proust can't hide his envy
of something the middle-classes can never, in his view, achieve
– emancipation from using

> the ready-made phrase, the unpleasant little gesture in which
> a perceptive observer immediately recognises the desire to
> show that a prince is not a superior, a way of saying 'la
> Comtesse', stressing the word 'comtesse' as if one really
> should not be saying it in that way, that smallness of being
> which is reduced to almost nothing in a man who is really
> superior and which is often the legacy of honourable bour-
> geois pride from a father or a grandmother who knew how
> to 'keep their place' and understood the triviality of titles and
> ranks.

Never guilty of snobbery or condescension, Bernard is also
free from 'the calculations of ambition, the disdainfulness of
the self-made man, the bitterness of humility', and he's capable
of charmingly impulsive actions, as when, impatient to join
Jean in a crowded café, he walks with agility and grace on top
of the tables and the banquettes. This makes Jean feel that 'all
the free, alert, vigorous life of your childhood was quite wholly
present, at that moment, in your service, and you were putting
it at his service, like a generous host who gives everything he
possesses'.[14]

Studying political history at the Bibliothèque Nationale,
Fénelon had met the young comte Georges de Lauris, who
was researching there for a doctoral thesis. Fénelon tried unsuccessfully to stop de Lauris from making friends with Proust,[15]
who often invited him to midnight meetings in a restaurant.

> I can still see him, wrapped in his fur coat, even in spring-
> time, sitting at a table in Larue's restaurant, and I can still
> see the gesture of his delicate hand as he tried to make you
> let him order the most extravagant supper, accepting the
> headwaiter's biased suggestions, offering you champagne,

exotic fruits, grapes on their vine-plant, which he'd noticed on the way in . . . He told you there was no better way of proving your friendship than by accepting.

But they more often met in the Prousts' flat late at night, and de Lauris sat in the small drawing-room, not far from Dr Proust's Brazilian rosewood desk, waiting for the three rings on the bell – always three, to distinguish them from the rings of his parents – that meant Proust was ready to receive.[16] Physically attracted to both Fénelon and de Lauris, Proust was careful to give neither an unambiguous indication of what he felt. It wasn't until much later that he confessed to de Lauris:

> I had hoped at one time for a still closer friendship. But having guided you on three or four occasions, step by step, while taking you by the hand, on to the path which leads to 'the road to my heart', as soon as I left you by yourself to see whether you would take this road, you retraced your steps with a vertiginous speed . . . Obviously, from the day I decisively abandoned hope of seeing you take it, I gave up some part of you, which necessarily implies the withdrawal of some part of me.[17]

Not that the residual friendship was unimportant to Proust. He went out seldom, but it wasn't only outings that were structured around meetings with his friends. He gave a great deal of thought to them, and though, when he was with them, he usually dominated the conversation, he did it without seeming self-important. He was entertaining and informative, told so many of the latest anecdotes that no one understood how he'd picked them up, enjoyed laughing and making friends laugh. He never forced them to be serious, never asserted himself.[18] He loved being helpful, and Antoine's ambitions as a playwright gave him an opportunity to prove – after they'd quarrelled – how well disposed he still felt. It was easy, through Reynaldo, to get a copy of Antoine's play *La Lutte (The Struggle)* into Sarah Bernhardt's hands, and when she rejected it, Proust had plenty of other ideas. 'I am at your disposal for making contact with Réjane, with Franck, with Deval, with as many other producers as you like.'[19] Réjane was in her early forties and married to the director of the Théâtre du Vaudeville. Madeleine Lemaire was friendly with the wife of Alphonse

Franck, who was running the Théâtre de Gymnase, and Deval was the director of the Théâtre de l'Athenée.

Much as he enjoyed badinage and belonging to such an exalted clique, Proust still had something in him of the tortured schoolboy who couldn't feel confident his friends liked him as much as he liked them. The Bizet-Halévy pattern was repeating itself, but now there was a more developed element of masochism which made Proust side with his friends when they were being hostile. 'Don't pay me compliments,' he told Antoine. 'I have a great deal of affection for you and very little for myself. Also you give me more pleasure by saying "Your value is on the rise" than by saying things which could only appeal to my conceit if I had any.'[20] He felt a kind of collective sexual desire for the good-looking young noblemen, in rather the same way as he'd been collectively attracted, during his military service, to aristocratic young officers. Later on, in *Jeunes Filles*, when the Narrator feels excited ambition to be accepted by the girls as their friend – initially he's no more attracted to Albertine than to other members of what looks like an exclusive and self-sufficient little society – Proust was drawing on these memories of generalised sexual excitement, as well as on the experience of seeing bathing-costumed girls on the beach at Cabourg and on impressionist paintings which divide their focus between several alluring girls. But he soon began to feel more for Fénelon than he did for the others.

What attracted them to him is partly explained by Élisabeth de Clermont-Tonnerre. 'These young people feel that Marcel Proust gives them, just by his conversation and his presence, a pleasure as lively as a soirée galante.' Coming back to Paris after a stint of military manoeuvres, the young noblemen 'adore to spend an evening with Marcel, as with an inaccessible cocotte.' Invited to his parents' flat, they'd be given nothing stronger than cider to drink. They tolerated this, as they tolerated the absence of female guests and the efforts he made towards dandyishness, invariably undermined by extra layers of woollen clothing under his shirt, but they talked about him, and when Proust was invited to the Clermont-Tonnerres, he was more embarrassed than amused to find his hostess was so well informed that she gave him cider. His letter of thanks mentioned 'this vulgar and unimpeachable cider'.[21]

Reluctant though he was to sacrifice meetings with such glamorous friends, he was spending more and more of his life in bed. Though he made endless experiments, varying the time of getting up and trying to sleep, he seldom managed to average more than one outing a week during the latter half of 1901 and the first half of 1902, and often he was too ill to write.[22] He felt envious of Antoine and Fénelon, who could see each other as often as they liked, 'while the only distraction I have is to shift my position in bed. But what distances I travel in my mind and in my heart during this apparent rest.'[23] He was thinking, daydreaming and reading a great deal, but he went for over two years without publishing anything. Though he knew he'd never finish *Jean Santeuil*, he went on adding new characters to the manuscript. After meeting the baronne Deslandes, for instance, he made her into Mme Jacques de Reveillon, but most of his literary energy went into maintaining his friendships, especially the one with Antoine, by means of long and jokey letters, using the anagrammatic names as if they were passwords. Bibesco was Ocsebib, and Proust often signed himself Lecram or Lecram Stuorp.[24]

Taking enormous pleasure in the evenings he spent in fashionable restaurants such as Larue's and the Café Weber, he was aware of the impression he made on both friends and strangers. Léon Daudet never forgot what it was like to sit down with a pale young doe-eyed man sucking or fingering half of his flowing brown

moustache, wrapped in woollens like a Chinese knick-knack. He would ask for a grappe de raisin, a glass of water and declare he had just got up, that he had influenza, that he was going back to bed, that the noise was harming him, glance around him anxiously, then mockingly, finally bursting out in magical laughter and stay. Soon coming from his lips, hastily and tentatively offered, remarks of extraordinary originality and perceptions of diabolical subtlety . . . He resembled both Mercutio and Puck, pursuing several ideas at a time, adroit at excusing himself for lacking goodwill, tormented with ironical scruples, naturally complicated, throbbing, silky.[25]

Society was still split between nationalists and Dreyfusards; confrontations in restaurants could lead to duels. Daudet has described how Proust narrowly escaped one after coming into a restaurant and hearing someone say: 'Go on then, you Dreyfusard.' It was Edmond de Lagrène, a retired diplomat who was sixty but still a formidable duellist. Proust wasn't intimidated. 'I detest quarrels,' he told Daudet. 'Nevertheless I would be very grateful if you would ask M. de Lagrène whether he intended to offend me, and, if not, to apologise.' Daudet sent the tactful Robert de Flers over to Lagrène, whose response was: 'I declare on my honour I never had the least intention of offending M. Proust, whom, besides, I do not know. I would add it does not displease me at all when a young man is hot-tempered. On the contrary, this touchiness makes him sympathetic.'[26]

The evenings in restaurants were long ones, but Proust had enough energy left to work hard during the spring on the commentary for his Ruskin translation. Copying out biblical quotations in French, he found the standard translation so poor he began to look for an alternative. Mathieu de Noailles had mentioned he had a good Bible, and at the end of June Proust wrote to ask the comtesse whether he could borrow it for a few days. By then he'd almost completed his work, which he submitted to the publisher Charles Ollendorff.

Though he was trying to conceal his homosexuality from Antoine,[27] Proust took the risk of reprimanding him when he and Anna de Noailles talked openly about the overt homosexuality of the young comte Antoine de Sala. 'It's absolutely essential to stop this horrible business of being such public denouncers of Salaism,' he wrote, enclosing a draft apology for Antoine to copy out and send to the comte.[28] 'In any case,' the letter said, 'it has taught me a lesson to be more careful, and I will never again open my mouth about anything which touches on these matters either directly or remotely.'

Intolerance towards homosexual love made Proust dissimulate, and he hadn't yet discovered Fénelon was bisexual. Spending so much time alone, Proust thought a great deal about friends, distilling emotion into correspondence. In letter-writing there was no danger of being embarrassed, rebuffed or humiliated; the danger was that analysis might use up energy that could have gone into confrontation. In spite of the fondness Fénelon had shown when he clambered over tables and banquettes in the restaurant, it was too easy to assume there was no possibility the young comte might reciprocate his feelings, and instead of declaring them to him, Proust half confided in Antoine about them, but as if they added up to no more than a strong feeling of friendship:

At this moment there is in me the possibility and even the beginnings of a lively affection for Nonelef, transitory like all my partialities but which could also indeed last rather a long time. Now for me that affection, this I believe is beyond doubt, could not fail to be very unhappy. I have therefore I will not say the desire, for one never desires to fight against an affection, but the intention of trying to suppress this affection before it has taken too important a place – which so far it has not. So this is what I have been thinking. You know that no fondness, however great it is, can in my case survive absence – others much greater than mine for Nonelef so far have failed to recover from it.

If they both stay in Paris, the unreciprocated feelings will survive for twelve or eighteen months, 'the period in which affection, like disease, always recedes and disappears'. The chances of happiness are negligible: 'what you say of his character is enough to make me believe I would have nothing but sadness from it'. It would be easier to end the relationship if Fénelon 'were disagreeable, or at least cold, indifferent, etc.' But, unlike Carmen, Proust can't help responding positively to amiable behaviour, while Fénelon alternates disconcertingly between 'upswings' and 'slumps', charm and indifference. Before Antoine left for Madrid in May to attend the festivities preceding the coronation of Alfonso XIII, there had been a slump, but it was followed, at a soirée of Mme Lemaire's, by such a sharp upswing that Proust went home 'enveloped, almost imprisoned, in all this warmth of memories which undergoes no diminution and hatches nascent affection in the ensuing days'.[29]

He still hadn't picked up any signal that Fénelon might be capable of homosexual love, but Proust's feelings were too strong for him to keep silent about them, and he went on confiding in the twenty-four-year-old Antoine as if he were older, wiser, more discreet, more loyal than he actually was. Each time Antoine betrayed a secret, Proust would protest vehemently and go on trusting him. 'Oath tomb' was the code phrase he used to plead for secrecy. One letter[30] is divided into parts which are confidential and parts – contained within double brackets – which may be passed on to Fénelon. Antoine and Proust both enjoyed intrigue, and one of their schoolboyishly conspiratorial gambits was to start addressing each other informally in the second person singular and watch how Reynaldo, Constantin and Fénelon reacted.[31]

Proust was so bad at hiding his frustration over seeing little of Fénelon that his mother well-meaningly intervened, imploring the young comte to spend more time with her son. Instead of being angry at her interference, Proust merely said it had been ineffectual and asked her not to 'resume the attack',[32] while the unreciprocated love for Fénelon made him more irritable with Antoine. 'So as not to leave you in the dark about any corner in my life or your life or other people's lives or Life, I tell you what I should keep to myself, but you systematically keep to yourself everything, even what concerns me, even what could help me to understand certain things better, and to react better, in fact everything, even going so far, probably, as to conspire against me up to a point . . .'[33] But they were soon reconciled.

Even if he could see Fénelon only in the presence of Antoine and Constantin, Proust was so keen not to miss these meetings that he sometimes tried to adjust his routine by staying up all night and sleeping in the afternoon.[34] His letters to Antoine are full of elaborate warnings about when to call and when to come back if Proust is asleep when he arrives. In mid-August Proust went out on three successive nights. After going to bed at ten o'clock the next morning, he couldn't sleep or even rest. 'It would be all right if it were not for my moral worries.'[35] He got up, and – since his parents had left for Evian – made an appointment with a heart specialist, Dr Henri Vaquez, who assured him he had no cardiac disease and prescribed Trional. Nor did his palpitations have anything to do with his stomach or intestines, said the doctor, but his ennui had caused mucomembranous enteritis. He should dissolve a coffee spoon of salt in his bathwater, and avoid alcohol.

He had a short but violent asthma attack in the taxi home, and another during the night, which didn't stop him from getting up at five in the morning.[36] Constantin and Fénelon had invited him to have dinner with them, but they both let him down, and he ate alone, the only customer at Larue's, with sixty electric light bulbs burning for him. He had an another asthma attack during the meal.[37]

He soon gave up taking Trional, and, becoming ill and insomniac again, thought this might be the reason.[38] But in early September he was well enough to stay with the Daudets

at their house, Pray, in Chargé, near Amboise. He travelled
by train with Fénelon, who didn't come to the house, but after
seeing him in the railway carriage, Lucien told his mother:
'I've seen a ridiculous little creature even smaller than Marcel.'[39]
In fact Fénelon was taller than Proust, who was five foot
six, but Proust was pleased with the comment, partly because
'ridiculous' reminded him of 'mus' (rat) the term of endearment
he and Lucien had once used for each other.[40] Having sent the
Daudets a telegram asking for a hot-water bottle with spirit of
wine in it, he was puzzled to be given soup with a strange
smell: 'bouillote' had been misprinted as 'bouillon'. Lucien,
friendlier than he'd been for a long time, gave Proust a photograph of himself inscribed: 'It's two in the morning and it's
stupid that you're leaving tomorrow but I'm fond of you all
the same.'[41] But the embarrassment which started with the
bouillon was compounded when Proust found he'd left behind
a valise, his hair-brushes and a tie-pin.

After retrieving the manuscript of *Le Bible d'Amiens* from
Ollendorff, who'd kept it for five months without making a
decision, Proust offered it to Alfred Vallette, chief editor of Le
Mercure de France, the publishing house which produced a
literary review under the same name. Another publisher, Beau-
chesne, had brought out a translation of Ruskin's *Unto This
Last: Four Essays on the Principles of Political Economy*, and
announced a series of his works in translation, starting with
Sesame and Lilies. Proust wanted his *Bible of Amiens* to come
out before theirs did.

But nothing mattered so much as his relationship with Fénelon. An exhibition of early Flemish art in Bruges gave them a
pretext for leaving Paris together in October, but it is unclear
how Fénelon wanted the relationship to develop. He went on
from Bruges to Amsterdam, while Proust travelled to
Antwerp, where he felt tired but well and so eager to see his
friend again that he stayed up all night when Fénelon was on
his way to join him. Either they had at last become lovers or
at least Fénelon had been encouraging Proust's hopes. But
after arriving in Dordrecht on 11 or 12 October Proust sent
Reynaldo a sad pastiche of Verlaine beginning:

> Dordrecht, such a lovely place
> Sees the dead face

Of my dear illusions.[42]

He was only slightly consoled by the beauty of a city in which
the ivy-covered church was 'reflected in the still waters of the
interlacing canals and in the shivering, golden Meuse, where
boats gliding along in the evening disarrange the reflected lines
of the red roofs and the blue sky.'[43] He went on by boat to
Rotterdam and then to Delft, where he was excited by the
reflections of the sunlight in the canal and even more by the
reflections in a mirror outside a house. 'The prettiest thing I
have ever seen was once in the country in a mirror which was
fixed to a window, a piece of the sky and the landscape, with
a bouquet of brotherly trees.'[44]

Whatever happened or failed to happen, he hadn't had an
irreparable quarrel with Fénelon, who'd booked a room for
him in Amsterdam, where they both stayed at the 'madly
expensive' Hôtel de l'Europe, which at least had good central
heating. Together they went in a boat to Vollendamm on
Wednesday 15 October, but Fénelon left the next day, and on
Friday, after travelling alone to Haarlem, where he saw paintings by Frans Hals in the museum, Proust wrote: 'I am in such
a calamitous emotional state that I was afraid of poisoning poor
Fénelon's holiday with my sadness and I have let him distance
himself from my groaning to recover his breath.' They were
going to meet again at The Hague on Saturday, but Proust
would come back to stay in Amsterdam overnight before
returning to Paris.

If he hadn't run short of cash, he might have spent another
week in Holland or Belgium.[45] He was telling his mother the
truth when he said Fénelon had been the only possible travelling companion, though the death of Antoine's mother at the
end of the month produced a rapprochement between the two
of them. Proust couldn't have gone to such extraordinary
lengths in empathising with his bereaved friend unless he'd
been asking himself what his reactions would have been to his
mother's death. 'When I think that your poor eyes, your poor
cheeks – everything I love so much because your thoughts and
feelings inhabit them, are expressed there, come and go there
incessantly – are at this moment, will be for such a long time,
will always be filled with grief and are now full of tears, it
hurts me physically to picture you like this.'[46] He imagined
Antoine 'either weeping enough to make me desperate at the

sight, or so terrifyingly calm that I regret not seeing you find any relief in tears'.[47] Towards the end of November, hearing Antoine was intending to spend the winter in Rumania, Proust offered to stay somewhere nearby, taking work with him, 'and if I don't have asthma, I shall be able to spend February, March, if you are still there April, if there are no flowers May, close to you, not disturbing you since I should be at some distance from you, but available every day when you feel like talking to me and absent every day when you do not'.[48] But he had an ulterior motive: Fénelon was going to be in Constantinople. In spite of his youth, he'd been appointed attaché to the French embassy there and was due to leave Paris on 8 November.

But Proust's freedom of movement was restricted by his brother's impending marriage. Robert, who was twenty-nine, had qualified as a doctor in February 1902, and was already earning enough to start family life. Though Proust had always succeeded in upstaging his sibling rival, it was galling to know that his parents would have preferred him to be more like Robert. The bride-to-be, Marthe Dubois-Amiot, lived with her parents in the avenue de Messine. The wedding had to be postponed because of a death in her family, which made it harder for Proust to make plans, as did a quarrel with his mother, who was pressuring him to do more work. As if to compensate himself for the long bouts of illness, he was going to the theatre a lot, and accepting dinner invitations – from Mme Straus, from the beautiful baronne Marguerite de Pierrebourg, who was no longer living with her husband, from Anna de Noailles and her sister the princesse de Chimay. Twice at dinner parties during November he sat next to the twenty-three-year-old actress Simone La Bargy, who'd played the lead in the première of a successful comedy *Le Détour* by Antoine's friend Henri Bernstein, and was now rehearsing for another play by him, *Le Joujou*. Mme Proust was feeling neglected, as she had when he went to Holland with Fénelon. Nine years had gone by since he'd passed his law exams, and at the age of thirty-one he was still financially dependent on his parents and still living in their flat, though the amount of daily contact had effectively been curtailed by the eccentric life style he'd adopted. He wouldn't have written so many notes to her if, like her, he'd normally been awake during the day and asleep during the night, but it was easier to relegate part of his

relationship with her to letter-writing. Guilt-feelings were
active on both sides. She'd continued to keep more of a hold
on him than most mothers can on a grown-up son; he'd succeeded in evading work of the usual kind, and he was still
lavishly spending money his father had earned.

Constantly under review in conversations and correspondence with her were his finances, his diet, his medicines –
especially the use of sedatives – his mealtimes and his routine.
In theory at least there was always the possibility of reverting
to nighttime sleep and daytime wakefulness. Making plans and
negotiating involved mother and son in emotional transactions
they both enjoyed, but friction was inevitable. There was
repressed hysteria on both sides, and his relationship with her
is accurately reflected in *Sodome et Gomorrhe*, though he had no
female Albertine in his life. His life with Albertine, says the
Narrator, 'gave me calm which was destroyed when my
mother confessed the anxiety it caused her'. One day she tells
him: 'Try not to become like Charles de Sévigné, whose
mother said: "His hand is a crucible in which money melts." '[49]
Proust said these attempts at interference were counter-pro-
ductive: he couldn't stop himself from over-reacting against
them.

> I told my mother her words had just postponed for perhaps
> two months the resolution she wanted and which I would
> otherwise have taken before the end of the week. Mamma
> started to laugh (so as not to upset me) at the effect her advice
> had instantaneously produced, and promised never to talk
> about it again so as not to prevent my good intentions from
> being reborn. . . . But she did not seem convinced I was
> right. She remembered how long my grandmother and she
> had persisted in saying nothing about my work or about a
> more hygienic way of living. I used to say I was prevented
> from beginning it only by the agitation into which their
> persuasion threw me, but in spite of their obedient silence I
> had not tried to change.[50]

This echoes the point he made when he told her she 'should
have known that if I was intending to alter my life, you could
have inhibited the intention just by saying: "Alter your life or
there will be no dinner party" – and this would not be frivolous
and capricious but serious and reasonable – and that if I had
no intention of altering it, a threat or a promise would make

no difference. Otherwise, what would I look like in my own eyes or in yours?'[51] This is to apply a sophisticated intelligence to the persistent survival in adult life of his childish dependence. Proust went on living far too long in his parents' home, and, like Kafka, who made the same mistake, had no space of his own except the room he slept in.

The only advantage for a writer in having no space of his own is that it increases the emotional need for the imaginary space he creates in his fiction. But a bed makes a poor desk, and Proust had to avoid leaving books or papers in any of the other rooms. He hated having to clear up, and he must either keep enough energy in reserve to tidy all his material, or irritate his houseproud mother by leaving the smoking-room in disorder. He had to keep carrying his papers from one place to another. Sometimes he worked in the dining-room and sometimes in the smoking-room, often fighting against the cold, because the rooms were never heated overnight. Mostly he worked in bed. Marie Nordlinger has testified: 'The apparent discomfort in which he worked was quite incredible, the bed was littered with books and papers, his pillows all over the place, a bamboo table on his left piled high and more often than not, no support for whatever he was writing on (no wonder he wrote illegibly), a cheap wooden penholder or two lay where it had fallen on the floor.'[52]

He was always in danger of losing vital notebooks, and in August 1903 mislaid the proofs on which he'd noted Marie's corrections of mistakes in his translation. 'I am no longer incorporating them . . . and I do not even know whether my annoyed publisher will consent to bring out a translation by such a disorganised and tiresome author.'[53] Loose sheets of paper were easier to lose than notebooks or exercise books, but even in 1904, when he adjusted his working methods, he'd often be unable to find notes he urgently needed. Working with Marie on *Sesame and Lilies*, he lost three of the six exercise books he was using, and eventually found them again. 'By pure chance. What stopped me from finding them until now was this. I was telling everyone to look for *green* exercise books. Now the first three, the ones which we had, were green. But the next three were *yellow*. Seeing exercise books which were not green, one did not even look at them.'[54]

Working in bed was a dangerous habit. For the over-protected child, kept in bed for each cold, the main incentive to recovery is boredom with inactivity. When Proust, who loved nothing more than writing and could spread his papers nowhere else in the house, developed the habit of working in bed, he didn't realise he was issuing himself a licence to be ill.

He was also giving his mother more control over his relationships with his friends. Spending so much time in his bedroom, he liked to receive visitors there, but he often wore several old pullovers with holes in them, and she was reluctant to let aristocratic friends see him looking dishevelled. Worse still, his parents not only felt entitled to punish him but had power to, even if punishments didn't take the old form. Like Kafka's pattern of illness, Proust's may have underground connections with his domestic impotence, and while Kafka was at least earning a salary, Proust couldn't have afforded to move out of his parents' flat. Pride sometimes made him offer to pay rent,[55] but the only money he had was his allowance from his father.

Depressed and irascible in early December because of Fénelon's imminent departure, he had to put up with complaints from his mother about his 'intellectual inactivity'. He said she was being 'really quite impossible'. She should have welcomed his 'true resurrection' after so much illness, and 'admired and loved what had made it possible'.[56] But their mutual sympathy had temporarily broken down. Habitually going to bed early, she was disturbed by the noise of footsteps and closing doors if he asked the servants to do things for him when he came in late; he was disturbed during the day unless she arranged for all household affairs to be conducted very quietly. Inextricably implicated in the feuding, the large retinue of servants would sometimes be instructed not to answer his bell when he rang, sometimes not to serve him at table or to make up a fire in his room. Both mother and son could be extremely petty. She had a night-table removed from his bedroom, and he claimed to need it so badly he'd prefer to do without chairs.[57]

On Saturday 6 December, when he was expecting a visit from Fénelon, who was due to leave in two days, she complained of having been kept awake all night because servants had been carrying out his orders, and he was kept awake all day by shouting and hammering which he took to be a punishment for the 'crime' he'd committed by wanting his asthma powders and ringing for them to be brought by a maid who might not yet have finished her lunch.

When Fénelon arrived, together with Georges de Lauris, Proust was in a hyper-sensitive state. He provoked Fénelon into saying something 'very disagreeable', which provoked Proust into attacking him physically. 'No longer knowing what I was doing, I took the new hat he had just bought, I trampled on it, pulled it to pieces and ripped out the lining. In case you think I am exaggerating, I enclose a piece of the lining so you can see it is true. But do not throw it away because I want you to give it back to me in case it can still be of use to him.'[58]

Afterwards, too hot to get dressed, Proust sent to ask whether he should have dinner at home. He was given dinner in his bedroom by an embarrassed footman under orders to put the dishes down but not to serve the food. Proust provoked his mother as much as she provoked him, and the illness which made him so vulnerable also gave him power to say her actions would precipitate an attack. If she stopped the servants from lighting a fire in his room, he could catch cold, and the cold could turn into asthma. 'The truth is that as soon as I'm well, the life which makes me feel well exasperates you so much that you demolish everything until I fall ill again. . . . I have no doubt you will be nice to me again, when I am in the same state as I was this time last year. But it is sad I cannot have affection and health at the same time.'[59]

His life wasn't entirely his own, but he couldn't decide how big a share he wanted her to have. If friends mattered more than casual lovers, she mattered more than friends, but often it was easier to communicate by letter, even when they were both awake. They behaved spitefully and unreasonably towards each other, alternating between loving closeness and furious resentfulness, but her intervention in his work wasn't always counterproductive. Though he'd been losing interest in Ruskin, he went back to the translation, giving up the idea of travelling to Rumania. Alfred Vallette rejected *La Bible d'Amiens*, but wanted Proust to compile a Ruskin anthology. With his flair for intrigue, Proust involved Constantin, now editor-in-chief of the periodical *La Renaissance latine*. Invited to contribute, Proust said an excerpt from the translation might be 'more to the taste of your subscribers than my modest prose'.[60] The rival interest had the effect it was intended to have on Vallette, who reversed his decision when Proust agreed to compile the anthology on condition Mercure de France published the translation. But he was always unrealistic about the time he needed to complete a book, and on the day he wrote the long letter to his mother, he also wrote to Vallette, promising to deliver the translation by 1 February, and then to start on the anthology. His anger with his mother had hastened him into doing what she wanted him to do.

He soon realised it wasn't what he wanted to do. He was going against the grain of his talent, and the dialectic which had pulled him away from fiction was starting to push him back towards it:

> The artificial work I have resumed is causing me pain in many ways. . . . Nothing I am doing is real work, it is only documentation, translation, etc. That is enough to reactivate my thirst for creation, without of course doing anything to slake it. From the moment of looking inwards, thinking about my mind, for the first time since that long torpor, I feel all the nothingness of my life, a hundred fictional characters, a thousand ideas ask me to give them a body, like those ghosts who in the *Odyssey* ask Ulysses to let them drink a little blood to bring them to life, but the hero brushes them aside with his sword. I have awakened the sleeping bee, and I feel its cruel sting more than its feeble wings. I had enslaved my intelligence to my peace of mind. Unchaining it, I believed I was only releasing a serf, but I have given myself a master without having the physical strength to satisfy him though he would kill me if I did not resist him.[61]

À la recherche has some of its roots in his reluctant return to Ruskin.

As the year ended, he hadn't given up hope of joining Antoine in Rumania. Robert was to be married on 2 February 1903, and Proust was to be best man. He'd have to rest in bed for several days afterwards, he announced, but offered to leave France around 10 February if Antoine would like his company in Rumania or Ragusa or Egypt or wherever he wanted to go. Fénelon had left Paris on 8 December, and nineteen days later Proust had neither written nor replied to his letters, while his lingering affection for Lucien was dwindling. Having dinner with the de Noailles, Proust watched him sitting next to the twenty-three-year-old duc de Guiche. 'Which made him undergo a physical transformation and talk incessantly with a volubility I had never seen and with the joy of Madame Bovary when she cried out in front of her mirror "I have a lover, I have a lover!" For my part I was sad to see the candidate for a sickness placed so close to the bacillus [of snobbery].'[62] The qualities Proust most disliked in other people were qualities he disliked in himself.

ELEVEN

FOR *LE FIGARO*

In Proust's hands the novel became an attempt less to trap life between the pages of a book than to trap consciousness. Where Balzac and Stendhal were most concerned with action and interaction, Proust was most concerned with the world behind Marcel's eyes, and some of the novel's deepest roots were in the asthma that kept Proust in bed so much of the time, habituating him to writing letters about past and future actions and feelings. The pleasure he took in planning and analysing, at first a temporary replacement for pleasure in doing, gradually became a preferred substitute. On the face of it, many of his longer, most elaborate letters, discussing pros and cons, proposing alternative arrangements, would have been unnecessary if he'd spoken to his friends on the telephone. But this is to ignore the pleasure he took in making proposals non-committally, going on to make counter-proposals, debating more with himself than with correspondents, who had to put up with endless written dithering. 'You are too intelligent, my dear little Antoine, not to understand that the interest which propels me into continuing this debate is pleasure in discussing, love of logic and passion for investigation – not doubt, suspicions, distrust, anything like that.'[1] But doubts, suspicions, distrust were all encouraged by the habit of stopping his thoughts from proceeding in a straight line. If he couldn't find reasons for a diversion, he invented them.

At the beginning of 1903 he was hesitating about whether to go with Antoine, who said he'd visit Fénelon in Constantinople if Proust would come with him. This pretexted a series of letters, delicately piling up complications as if building a house of cards. After such a long journey, Proust wouldn't want to stay less than a month in either Constantinople or Strehaia, which made Constantinople preferable because he'd be able to spend time with Fénelon if, needing rest, he had to stay on after Antoine came back to Paris. The alternative of waiting for Antoine in Paris might seem more sensible, but Proust's parents wanted him to go away.[2] Jean Santeuil is given the same propensity for dithering: 'Normally, when he had arrived at a decision, the alternative would at once seem infinitely preferable.'[3]

Hesitations and changes of plan were enjoyable because they issued new licences for the fantasies entertained in letters. When Constantin, changing his mind about going to Rumania, said he was leaving for Bucharest on 6 February, Proust, who'd decided against Constantinople, almost changed his mind: it would have been so pleasant to have a travelling companion for part of the journey,[4] and to know Fénelon would wonder whether he or Antoine had been the main reason for the journey. Proust wasn't sure whether Fénelon would be pleased he was coming, and Antoine was instructed not to tell him about their correspondence.[5] Proust made a confidential comparison of their personalities: 'you have contrasting talents – his is to arouse suspicion and yours to assuage it. You are both sure to have enemies, but yours will be people who do not yet know you and can therefore be made into friends if you wish. While his enemies will always be old friends.'[6]

When they decided against Constantinople, Proust drafted a letter to Fénelon for Antoine to copy out. It said he'd been on the point of coming. Why had Fénelon neither written nor sent him a message through Marcel? 'We were corresponding regularly twice a week. . . . He told me he hadn't heard from you since 25 December! Is that true? But he has been told you are a great success in Constantinople. Congratulations, my dear fellow. It was no pleasure to see him again because I no longer feel any friendship for him and he is even more stupid than when I left.' It was like his schoolboy attack on himself in the letter to Robert Dreyfus; he had so much fun with the epistolary impersonation he even signed the draft 'Antoine Bibesco'.[7]

Enjoying the intrigue and intimacy, Antoine decided to raise the stakes by proposing a pact of total frankness. What happened, predictably, was that each accused the other of failing to come clean. Eventually Proust decided they should release each other from 'this impossible and cruel pact which has already done me so much harm. I am choosing to denounce it at a strange moment since I have made a thousand revelations to you, and you have not told me the slightest thing.'[8] But according to Antoine, 'Marcel, not playing the game I had proposed to him, never betrayed any confidences to me, except in a letter.'[9]

Their friendship was never more at risk than when Antoine teased him about his ignorance of English, and Constantin provoked him in the same way early in 1903 when de Lauris was with them. 'I am well aware you meant no harm, my dear Constantin. *But anyone who detested me and wanted with one word to demolish the results of my four years of hard work* conducted in the middle of sickness, someone who wanted my translation to be read by no one and to be regarded as an abortion – I ask you, *could he have done anything worse?*'[10] He knew the whole of *The Bible of Amiens* by heart, he claimed, assimilating it so deeply that it was totally transparent to him. He'd penetrated not only 'the difficulties which resist inadequate scrutiny but the irreducible obscurity of the thought'. Hadn't Antoine said: 'I would never have thought it was possible to translate anyone so well'?[11] 'If you knew there was not one ambiguous expression, not one obscure phrase on which I have not consulted at least ten English writers and on which I do not have a file of correspondence, you would not utter the word "mistakes".'[12] But he was overstating his case; there are mistakes.

If he felt especially vulnerable at the beginning of 1903, it was partly because Robert was about to get married. For the competitive and unhappy Proust, this was inevitably a moment for stocktaking. He'd been victorious in the internecine battle for their mother's love, but had it been a Pyrrhic victory? Effectively forced into the tougher arms of their father, the younger rival had successfully emulated him, and, without going into society, had become a protégé of the fashionable and powerful Dr Pozzi. Robert had grown into a healthy and attractive man, been successful with girls, established a solid professional practice, opted for the emotional security of bourgeois domesticity. To the unhealthy older brother, still frustrated professionally, still dependent financially on their parents, still without a steady lover and without any prospect of living with a man he loved, it seemed questionable whether he was better off than his defeated sibling rival.

Robert and his father were the only members of the family to survive the wedding without illness. Too unwell to attend the civil ceremony on Saturday 31 January, Mme Proust was taken in an ambulance on 2 February to the wedding in the church of Saint-Augustin.[13] It was traditional for the best man to make a collection for the poor, and though he'd dressed in white tie and tails, Proust was also wearing three overcoats, scarves and cotton wool inside his collar. Unable, in all this bulk, to move along the pews, he stood at the end of each row, embarrassing the eighteen-year-old cousin who was assisting him by explaining that he'd been ill and couldn't dress in any other way.[14] Afterwards, he was ill, as he'd expected to be. On Wednesday he thought he'd still need another week in bed,[15] and on Sunday the 14th he still wasn't getting up.[16]

But the next morning the first of two excerpts from his *Bible of Amiens* appeared in *La Renaissance latine*, and he'd accepted from Gaston Calmette a commission to write for *Le Figaro* a series of articles about hostesses and their salons. His newspaper pieces might appear unconnected with either the early stories or the two novels, but there was a continuity and an increasing finesse in his observation of social behaviour. The first article was about princesse Mathilde. Like an impresario waiting impatiently for the curtain to go up when he has royalty among the actors on stage, Proust takes undisguised pleasure in what he's offering. 'Follow me to the rue de Berri and we must hurry, for the evening does not start late . . . This is one of the few houses in Paris where one is invited to dine at half-past seven.' But most of the guests are invited after dinner.[17] Sitting next to the princesse are her lady in waiting, Mme Espinasse, the pretty comtesse Benedetti and Louis Ganderax's wife. The editor himself is sitting with a copy of the *Revue de Paris* at another table. 'A severe pince-nez masks the kindly expression in his eyes, and his long black beard is very majestic.' Among the after-dinner guests are Mme Straus, 'whose wit and beauty give her unique powers of attraction'.

Though he'd recently seen little of princesse Mathilde, Proust portrays her affectionately. Friends are encouraged to relax in her presence, to call her 'Princesse' (instead of 'Madame', as protocol demanded) and to contradict her.[18] Proust sees her as a living link between royalist tradition and modern republicanism. He signed the profile 'Dominique'.

The journalistic commission helped him to move away from Ruskin towards the novel that was beckoning, and wanting to consolidate his relationship with Calmette he was eager to invite him to a dinner party, together with Mme Lemaire, whose salon was due for treatment later in the series. It was over three months since Proust had approached his parents, who hadn't wanted another dinner party before the wedding, and now, keen to have it before Easter, he was furious when his mother kept procrastinating and implying, insultingly, that he was overplaying his role as an invalid. He didn't want to be told about friends of hers who'd said how well he was looking, and when she reprimanded him for extravagance, he said she was behaving more like a creditor than a mother.[19] There was nothing he wanted more than financial independence – for his pieces in *Le Figaro* (one and a half columns) he was paid 200 francs[20] – but he needed the dinner party to advance his career. Now that it was his father's ambition to be elected to the Académie des Sciences Morales et Politiques in the Institut de France, she willingly entertained Charles-Léon Lyon-Caen, who was one of its most influential members, and willingly entertained Robert's superiors. Why couldn't she help Marcel to entertain Calmette, Jules Cardane, the *Figaro*'s editorial secretary, and Alfred Vallette? What he really needed was a series of dinner parties. Calmette wanted to meet fashionable people, who couldn't be invited at the same time as Cardane and Vallette.

To punish her for her intractability Proust abandoned the latest in his series of programmes for reforming his routine – a triple plan for sleeping at night like everyone else, eating meals at normal times and (probably) cutting down on sedatives. The date he'd set for the changes was Friday 6 March, the day after a dinner party given by the baronne de Pierrebourg, but on Saturday the dining-room was so underheated, he said, that he caught cold, and on Saturday evening he was feverish but, intent on proving himself, worked hard at the Ruskin.[21] In some ways things had scarcely changed since the days of parental reprimands which made him promise to work harder at school.

In the end she gave in, and the dinner party was held on 1 April. The guests included the de Noailles, the Chimays, Mme de Pierrebourg, Paul Hervieu, Abel Hermant, Constantin and Antoine, who'd been in Paris since the beginning of March. After seeing him again the next day, Proust went to the Folies Bergère in the evening with de Lauris. He afterwards wrote a description of the performance and the audience, but Calmette didn't want the piece for *Le Figaro*. When Proust called in at the office about six days after the party, they discussed the tribute to Antoine which Proust was keen to interpolate into his piece about the salon of the comtesse Greffulhe.

On Good Friday, 10 April, he and Antoine went motoring in two cars with a party of friends. For Proust's sake, one of the cars was driven with its windows closed. The party included Fénelon, who was on leave, de Lauris and the vicomte François de Paris, a member of the Jockey Club. They drove to Provins, to see the partly Gothic, partly Romanesque church Saint-Loup-de-Naud, and then to Dammarie-les-Lys.

Proust saw Antoine again the next evening, when they dined with the de Noailles, and afterwards Proust went on to the offices of *Le Figaro*, where he saw Calmette and Cardane, who failed to dissuade him from incorporating a tribute to Antoine into one of his salon pieces. As he'd found in writing *Jean Santeuil*, literature could serve as a substitute for sex to give the illusion of possessing friends who attracted him. The next piece was to be about Mme Lemaire, and one objective was to thank her for the collaboration which had made his first book viable. 'Every Tuesday in May the rues Monceau, Rembrandt and Courcelles are almost impossibly congested with carriages, and a certain number of her guests inevitably stay in the garden, under the flowering lilacs, because it is impossible for everyone to be accommodated in the studio – big though it is – where the soirée is about to begin.'[22] Among the guests are Léon Bourgeois, president of the Chamber of Deputies, the Italian, German and Russian ambassadors, comtesse Greffulhe, the grande-duchesse Vladimir with comtesse Adhéaume de Chevigné, several comtes, comtesses, ducs and duchesses, Anatole France, Gaston Calmette, the baronne Gustave de Rothschild and Reynaldo Hahn, who sings at the piano when the initial hubbub has died down. The article, again signed 'Dominique', appeared in the paper on 11 May. The next day Proust dined with Mme Lemaire, and on Tuesday the 19th attended her soirée.

On the 21st, when the friends motored out to Laon, they stopped to visit the twelfth-century church at Saint-Leu-d'Es-erent, which had two Gothic towers and one Romanesque. Inside the church Antoine shocked Proust by playing a Bou-langist song on the organ, 'En revenant de la revue'. They went on to the twelfth-century cathedral at Senlis, where Emmanuel talked about church towers in the Île-de-France. In Laon they looked up at the twin towers of the cathedral, where the carved heads of eight oxen peer out from the belfry, commemorating the cattle used to drag the stones when the cathedral was built.

On the way back, stopping to see the thirteenth-century castle at Coucy, they climbed the spiral staircase of the tower, and the breathless Proust held on to Fénelon, who egged him on by singing the Good Friday motif from *Parsifal*. It was after midnight when they reached Paris, and Proust, once in bed, stayed there for a couple of days, but got up in time for Antoine's dinner party at Larue's on the day after Easter Monday.

Proust's health let him down again in May. After coming home late on the 10th, he felt extremely ill during the night. On Tuesday the 26th, when he was expected at Mme Lemaire's, he had a recrudescence of his hay-fever, and stayed in bed for a fortnight with bronchitis.

When he recovered, he struck up a friendship with the son of the duc d'Albufera. Unlike most of Proust's noble friends, the marquis Louis d'Albufera, who was called Albu, hadn't been to a university. He was a rich, good-natured, twenty-six-year-old anti-Dreyfusard, aggressive and irascible with most people, but almost as gentle with Proust as he was with his mistress, Louisa de Mornand, a beautiful nineteen-year-old actress.[23] Her real name was Louisa Montaud, and in April she'd made her début at the Théâtre des Mathurins as the maid in Tarride's *Coin du feu*. Albu had just bought her a horse and carriage. At the end of May, when she had a better part in the curtain raiser to *Rêve d'opium*, Proust, without admiring her talent, exerted himself to have her name mentioned favourably by critics he knew or could approach through friends. In June he dined several times with the couple in restaurants, and thanked Albu for a meal at Henry's by celebrating Louisa's charms in a long poem.

One evening Albu got into an argument with de Lauris about the anti-clerical prime minister, Émile Combes. He'd been in office only since 1902, but already he'd exiled many of the orders and closed nearly a third of the Catholic schools – which is to say nearly a third of the schools not run by the state. This was the easiest way to put on a show of progressive change: securing votes from workers, anti-clericalism was as convenient for the left as anti-Semitism had been for the right. Proust was upset when de Lauris defended government policy, though one of his arguments was that Catholic education tended to promote anti-Semitism and to divide France into two hostile camps. While condemning Catholics who'd accepted support from extremist anti-Semitic reactionaries such as Alphonse Humbert, a deputy who wrote for *Le Petit Parisien* and *L'Intransigeant*, Proust maintained that 'With the orders gone and Catholicism killed in France (if it could be killed, but ideas and beliefs perish not when laws are passed against them but when the truth and social usefulness in them goes rotten or dwindles) there would be just as many clerics, clerical unbelievers, and they would be a hundred times worse, more violently anti-Semitic, anti-Dreyfusard, anti-liberal.' In any case, he believed, biased teachers had less influence than the press in forming the opinion of young people. Those who never learn to think for themselves pick up ideas from newspapers; those who do learn pay more attention to literature than to men who teach them how to approach it. Proust was no admirer of the Jesuits, 'but I wish at least the anti-clericals would be a bit more subtle and at least take a closer look at the great social organisations they want to destroy. . . . In being anti-clerical the socialists are making the same mistake as the clericals did in '97 by being anti-Dreyfusard.'[24]

The disagreement did no harm to his friendship with de Lauris, who came to his dinner party on 16 July. Calmette was seated in the place of honour, and the other guests included Fénelon, Antoine, Léon Yeatman, Francis de Croisset and René Blum. Six years younger than Proust, de Croisset, whose real name was Franz Wiener, was the son of a Belgian Jewish financier and an Englishwoman. Launched into Parisian literary society by Clemenceau and Octave Mirbeau, he quickly rose to the top. René Blum, Léon's younger brother, was an editorial secretary at *Gil Blas*. Both Proust's parents were present, and Antoine, in a bout of mischief-making, provoked the doctor by questioning whether Marcel needed to protect himself quite so heavily against the cold and by saying he'd tipped a waiter sixty francs. 'I wept bitterly after this dinner,' Proust told his mother, 'seeing that one can trust no one and that the friends who seem the best have such fantastic faults. . . . Taking extreme precautions, I reminded him before the dinner: "no jokes about tipping for one thing, and for another, no silly questions to Papa such as 'Monsieur, don't you believe that if Marcel didn't wrap up quite so much'' ' etc.'[25]

His family, he said, was dearer to him than his friends, and Antoine should have known better than to provoke one of the quarrels 'which leave deep marks in Papa's mind and strengthen prejudices which cannot be dislodged by any amount of evidence'. After the doctor's repartee, which was 'so unjust', and after seeing how deeply upset Proust was, Antoine had felt contrite. 'But I refused to forgive him.'[26] This was no exaggeration: their friendship deteriorated, and their correspondence dwindled, though only three months ago Antoine had mattered enough for Proust to take the risk of annoying Calmette by insisting on having space for a tribute. He wrote: 'Everyone who says "Prince" to this young diplomat with such a great future feels like a character in a play by Racine, so strongly does he, with his mythological aspect, bring Achilles or Theseus to mind . . . His words, like the bees of Hymettus, have swift wings, elaborate delicious honey, and do not lack, in spite of that, a certain sting.'[27]

But there was an ulterior motive for refusing to forgive the latest sting. After confiding in him enough to make him the apex of triangular intrigues with Fénelon, it was easier to bypass him completely now Fénelon was on leave. He came to see Proust almost every evening, usually accompanied by de Lauris, Albu, Gabriel de la Rochefoucauld, Armand, duc de Guiche, and prince Léon Radziwill, who was nicknamed Loche. Guiche, who was twenty-three, was half-Jewish, through his Rothschild mother, the duchesse de Gramont. Proust had met him at the house of the de Noailles. Loche was twenty-two, tall, good-looking, broadly built and a distant relation of Marie Benardaky's husband. He once told Proust Ruskin's greatest talent was to make the most elevated ideas accessible to everybody. Loche was an aesthete who soon became bored when you talked to him about reality. 'After a moment the blue eyes glaze over, the anaesthetic takes effect.' But Proust found him irresistible. 'As soon as he is there, I am absent from myself, I can no longer speak, I become stupid.'[28] But of the new friendships he wanted to forge, the one with Guiche soon came to seem the most promising. The duc started his first letter 'Mon cher Proust', only to be reprimanded: Proust could understand why he didn't want to write 'Mon cher Marcel', but why not 'Mon cher ami'? It committed one to nothing, not even friendship.[29] Guiche asked his father, the duc de Gramont, to invite Proust to their estate at Vallière, but neither of them warned him that the guests would go fishing before dinner and change afterwards into their evening clothes. Proust had to go fishing in his white tie and tails.

When Fénelon fell ill during the last week of his leave, Proust, though feverish himself, visited him every day. Fénelon left Paris on 8 August, escorted to the station by Proust and Antoine, who had dinner together afterwards, but Antoine too left Paris a few days later, posted to the embassy in London.[30]

Proust took the opportunity to leave Paris at the end of the month, joining his parents again at Evian, where they'd been staying since the 18th in the Splendide. He had a high temperature when he caught the train, and, not wanting to sleep, watched the sunrise. 'It is a beautiful thing, an inversion, more charming to my taste, of the sunset. In the morning a wild desire to rape the small sleeping towns . . . the eastward ones in the dying residue of the moonlight and the westward ones in the full light of the rising sun.'

At about eleven the train reached Avallon, where he hired a carriage to visit Vézelay, 'a prodigious place in a sort of Switzerland, quite isolated on a mountain that dominates the others, visible for miles around from all directions, and harmonising most strikingly with the landscape. The church is immense and has more of a resemblance to a Turkish bath than to Notre-Dame.' He returned to Avallon in the evening with such a high temperature he couldn't undress for bed. After walking about all night, he discovered at five in the morning there was a train at six. It took him to Dijon, where he saw 'those great tombs of the ducs de Bourgogne', and he reached Evian at eleven in the evening. 'This frantic race, sleepless in spite of illness, this "race towards death" had changed me so much, I no longer recognised myself in mirrors, and people in stations asked whether there was anything I needed. . . . And since then I've spent all the time trying to recover.'[31] He stayed in bed, and at the beginning of October still wasn't getting up till two in the afternoon.[32] But he made the seventy mile journey to Chamonix to join Albu and Louisa on a mule-back excursion to Montanvert, where they went skating.[33]

Returning to Paris on the tenth, Proust broke his journey in Bourg-en-Bresse to see the church at Brou, and in Beaune to see the fifteenth-century hospital where the nurses were nuns in white habits. Afterwards he'd offer to write on either of these buildings, or on either of the churches at Vézelay or Avallon if Charles Ephrussi should ever need an article on one of these 'monuments' for the *Gazette des beaux-arts*.[34]

Proust went on making reckless efforts to spend time with Albufera and Louisa, going out when he wasn't well enough. He was with them on 17 October, when he had an attack in Larue's, and to be with them on the 29th he turned down an invitation from the de Noailles for the 28th. 'I cannot go out two days in succession, being ill for several days after each outing.' Attractive, charming, and both, in their different ways, spectacularly theatrical, 'the two Albuferas' were unlike his other friends. Louisa was passionate, demanding and extravagant, constantly forcing Albu to prove his devotion by buying presents he couldn't afford, and they quarrelled about infidelities alleged in anonymous letters he received about her. Knowing silence was the best argument, she refused to defend herself.[35] Albufera belonged to one of the most distinguished families in France; Louisa was a younger, less intelligent version of Laure Hayman, the irresistibly charismatic cocotte. She had affairs with both Proust's father and his brother, among many other men, and though Albu was unrealistic about her capacity for fidelity, it was obvious he'd never marry her. In spite of all this, their love for each other was genuine, and Proust was a fascinated spectator at their intensely theatrical displays of passion.

Never before had he been on such intimate terms with a couple, and he may have been at least half-conscious he was going to use them in his novel. He was also perhaps a little jealous of the happy-go-lucky heterosexual love from which he was excluded as an asthmatic homosexual. At thirty-two he already felt tired of a 'life in which each pleasure has to be paid for, without even being tasted'.[36] One dinner engagement with them had to be postponed four times. He was no longer presenting *Les Plaisirs et les jours* to many of his friends, but he gave them a copy at the end of the month.

On Sunday 22 November, in a political argument with his sixty-nine-year-old father, Proust said things he afterwards regretted.[37] On Monday morning the doctor worked with a sub-committee of the permanent commission on tuberculosis, and in the afternoon he saw patients. On Tuesday he went to the boulevard Saint-Germain to visit Robert, whose wife,

Marthe, was about to give birth to a baby. At one o'clock Robert walked with him to the École de Médecine, where he was due to take charge of an examination, but the doctor had a cerebral haemorrhage in a lavatory. When Robert and the cloakroom attendant broke the door in, they found him paralysed and unconscious. He was carried on a stretcher to the flat in the rue de Courcelles where Proust was sleeping. His mother tapped on the door. 'Forgive me for waking you, my dear, but your father has been taken ill in the École de Médecine.' Proust, who'd been planning to meet Lucien, sent a note telling him not to call at the flat 'because I am not leaving him, you will not see me, and it would only be complicated. . . . As soon as I can tell you anything precise about him, I will tell you. Alas, I am afraid it will only be sad news.'[38]

Without recovering consciousness, Adrien Proust died in the morning of 26 November a few hours after his granddaughter was born. While the body was lying in state before the funeral, and people were filing past to pay their respects, the widow was unfortunate enough to see a woman she didn't know laying a large bunch of Parma violets unambiguously beside the body.[39] The service at Saint-Philippe du Roule was attended by the University council and the whole Faculty and Academy of Medicine. Antoine, Albufera and Mathieu de Noailles came with Proust and Robert to the grave at Père-Lachaise, where the funeral oration was spoken by Professor Debove, a doyen of the Medical Faculty.

Before giving birth to the baby, Marthe had contracted puerperal fever and was herself in so much danger that she was told her father-in-law was recovering. She was in her mother's flat in the avenue de Messine, through which the cortège had to pass. Wanting to attend the funeral, her mother had invented a pretext for going out, and when Marthe asked what the music was, the maids told her soldiers were marching past. But she recognised it as a funeral march. 'Someone famous must have died.' They went on keeping the truth from her, and when the widow went to visit her and baby Suzy, she changed from black into a coloured dress before going into the bedroom.[40]

Proust was apprehensive about his mother's future: 'I don't even have the courage to *think* sincerely what her life will be. . . . She had given him, to an extent which would scarcely be credible to anyone who had not seen it, every minute of her life.' No one who didn't know him well could imagine how much kindness and simplicity there was in him. 'I tried, not to satisfy him – for I am aware of having always been the black spot in his life – but to show my affection for him . . . Papa had a nature so much nobler than mine.'[41]

The relationship between father and son had never quite recovered from the strained period in which the doctor tried to manoeuvre his son into a career. Proust, who'd half wanted to lose that battle, never forgave himself for winning it. The barrier between them was such that the father, who was expected to be firm, had only widened the rift when he relented. In À la recherche, the Narrator hears his father telling his mother not to worry. Their son is no longer a child: ' "He's quite capable of knowing what will make him happy in life." Unexpected kindness from him had always given me such an urge to kiss his red cheeks above his beard that if I did not give in to it, it was only from fear of displeasing him.'[42]

Proust's main source of guilt-feelings had been about not having more ambition, more definite aims in life. Instead of putting an end to this guilt, the doctor's death intensified it, making it easier for Mme Proust to manipulate her son. 'There we are. Mamma, learning that I had given up Ruskin, took it into her head that this was the one thing Father wanted, that he had been waiting from one day to the next for publication.' So Proust went reluctantly back to work on correcting the proofs.

Life would have been pleasanter if Constantin hadn't changed his mind about wanting him to write a regular column of literary criticism in La Renaissance latine. The offer had been made in September 1903 and withdrawn in December, probably because Proust seemed too unwell and disorganised to be reliable. Bitterly disappointed, he didn't try to hide his anger. 'When people are accustomed to dissolving me into gratitude, affection and tears by being nice to me, it is necessary, all the same, when one has too much of the contrary treatment, to say no, if only so as not to devalue the gratitude I show to people who are kind and good.'[43] Constantin tried to pacify his friend, inviting him to contribute as often as possible to the review, but a regular column would be too exhausting and troublesome for him.[44] Which reminded Proust of La Fontaine's line: 'Your scruples show too much delicacy.'[45] And in a letter to Anna de Noailles he called La Renaissance *latine* 'l'Indécence latine'. She sympathised: 'I know how happy it would have made me, in the dismal morning on the fifteenth of each month, to read what only you can write, that marvellous mixture of irony and sweetness, like two streams that run counter to each other but close together.'[46]

Even more upsettingly, Antoine had been saying Proust didn't seem distressed by his father's death.[47] But on 9 January the prince left for Egypt and Constantinople. 'I feel infinite sadness', Proust told Anna, 'at seeing how few people are genuinely kind, and how one only loses by giving one's heart.'[48] He took some consolation from friendships with Gabriel de la Rochefoucauld, who was contributing clever articles to *Le Figaro*, and with Marie Nordlinger, who was in Paris working as a goldsmith at Siegfried Bing's studio-gallery in the rue de Provence.

While his debilitated mother could think of little but her dead husband, Marie took over as provider of the literal Ruskin translations Proust needed. He had outbursts of resentment both against Ruskin – 'This old man is beginning to annoy me'[49] – and against his mother, who'd manipulated him into resuming the translation instead of finding his way to creative work. But while she was commemorating his father's attack, his death and his funeral every week, and later every month, there could be no question of quarrelling with her. *The Bible of Amiens* translation hadn't yet been published when he and Marie started on *Sesame and Lilies*, the three essays Ruskin published in 1865 and 1871.

In spite of continuing illness – rheumatic pains in his back were making him feverish and causing violent pain when he made certain movements[50] – Proust worked energetically. 'I have rewritten the beginning,' he told Marie at the end of January, '*changing each word*, but I have done at most ten pages. Only I believe it is in a French that is less ugly, letting fewer of the fleeing intentions of the English escape through the finer net. But if I am as scrupulous as this it will take us ten years and never has "quick and good" been so necessary.'[51] Marie was summoned frequently to the flat, sometimes by telephone, sometimes by messenger or express letter.

When I first went to the boulevard Malesherbes Mme Proust welcomed me graciously in the heavily furnished salon; though much interested in our work she always effaced her-

self and soon Félicie (alias Françoise) would take me straight
to him. I remember only a few sessions at the large oval
dining-room table with its red cover and old-fashioned oil-
lamp; he was mostly in bed, swathed in Jaeger woollens
and thermogene wadding, but invariably fastidious about his
appearance. Whatever the season, the room was oppressively
warm, Félicie would bring me an ice or 'une orangeade et
des petits fours de chez Rebattet' and boiling hot coffee for
Marcel. . . . These sessions often continued late into the
night, scrutinising or reviewing a chapter, a sentence or a
mere word, any help a dictionary could supply had been
exhausted and memorised by him before my arrival. . . .
Conversation ranged far and wide, but if anything he was
a more eloquent listener, interrogating, probing with his
strangely luminous, omnivorous eyes. Eyes I can recall alight
with fun and mimicry or suddenly suffused unaccountably,
unashamedly with tears.[52]

At the beginning of February he had to stay in bed again with
'terrible influenza, high temperature, sore throat etc.' but he
had been working 'like a nigger', revising the beginning yet
again, and writing a commentary without having decided
whether to include it as a preface or in the form of notes.
Endlessly patient with him and generous with her time, Marie
had designs on him, while he was unscrupulously flirtatious:
'As soon as I am in a state to receive you, I will write, for I
am on fire for Sesame – and for you.'[53] Temporarily, at least,
he was feeling less irritated by Ruskin, but he wasn't fulfilling
his potential as a writer. Assuming that hard work was his
best way of consoling his mother, he applied himself to the
translation with the same compulsive generosity that made him
overtip waiters. But, as he said at the beginning of March,
nothing could make up for failing to satisfy one's literary
conscience.[54] Part of his admiration for Anna de Noailles had
its roots in envy: she was succeeding creatively, as poet and
novelist, while he wasn't even putting himself to the test. He
offered to send back one of her letters 'because it seems to me
that certain phrases, formulated about me, are infinitely better
than I deserve, have a beauty which does not relate to me and
which you should publish'.[55]

She was congratulating him on The Bible of Amiens, which
had been mentioned on the front page of Le Figaro,[56] and –
thanks to Robert de Flers – in La Liberté,[57] where the title was

misprinted as *La Bible d'Amicus*. A favourable review by André
Chaumeix had already appeared in *Le Journal des débats*, and in
April Georges Richet praised the book in *Les Essais*. On 22
May, writing under a pseudonym in *L'Écho de Paris*, Albert
Flament spoke of Proust's 'rare intelligence' and his 'critical
sense which penetrates deeply into psychologies'. Six days
later, Henri Bergson, lecturing at the Académie des Sciences
Morales et Politiques, called the preface 'an important contribution to the psychology of Ruskin . . . His aesthetic is that
of a man who believes the poet and the artist limit themselves
to transcribing a divine message.' Though an idealist, 'he is a
realist too, because matter for him is only an expression of
spirit . . . Proust has translated him in a language so lively and
original that in reading this book one would not believe one
was dealing with a translation.'[58] But there was no review in
Le Figaro, though Proust more than once asked Anna de
Noailles to pressure the book reviewer, Abel Hermant, into
mentioning it, and she asked him more than once.[59]

This was galling for Proust when he'd given *Le Figaro* not
only two of his pieces about salons but also an article called
'Une Fête chez Montesquiou à Neuilly'.[60] Purporting to be an
extract from Saint-Simon's memoirs, it describes a reception
at the house, characterising him as

the wittiest man I have ever known, with a princely air
like none other, the noblest countenance, sometimes full of
smiles, sometimes most serious, at forty the appearance of a
man of twenty, the body erect, which is not saying enough,
arched and as if overturning backwards, and he truly bent it
when he had the desire, in great affability and bows of all
kinds, but it reverted somewhat swiftly to its natural posture,
which was wholly of pride, arrogance, inflexibility, of submitting to nobody and ceding ground on nothing, to the
point of walking straight forwards without considering passers-by, jostling people without appearing to notice them,
or if he wished to provoke, indicating that he did see them,
but, always surrounded by a large retinue of people of the
greatest quality and intelligence to whom he sometimes
bowed, on the right and on the left, but most often left them,
as it is said, to their own devices, without seeing them, both
eyes focused forwards, talking very loudly and well to his
familiars who laughed at all his pleasantries, and with good

reason, as I have said, for he was more witty than can be imagined.[61]

Proust signed the piece 'Horatio', but denied being Horatio when Montesquiou questioned him.[62]

He used the same pseudonym for his next piece in *Le Figaro*, which appeared on 13 May – an account of the comtesse Emmanuela Potocka's salon. She'd been important in social and literary life since the nineties: Maupassant had been one of her regulars, who now included Montesquiou, Fauré, Barrès, Forain and Gabriel de la Rochefoucauld. Proust praises her for combining antique beauty, Rumanian majesty, Florentine grace, French politeness and Parisian wit. But she'd shown her contempt for human beings and her love for animals by moving to Auteuil. If no one came so far to visit her, she'd have been able to look after the lame dogs she collected; once she was so busy nursing them that she didn't go to bed for a year.[63]

Continuing the series about salons, Proust was steadily moving towards the method he'd use in *À la recherche* of treating contemporary social history, but he was having less fun with his work than with Albu and Louisa. When they wanted to see the dress rehearsal of Feydeau's *La Main passée* at the Théâtre des Nouveautés on 29 February, he unsuccessfully asked Francis de Croisset and René Peter for tickets, and then got them from Lucien.[64] Early in April he was invited into Louisa's bedroom, and stayed there until after midnight. He may have been exaggerating when he told Gide he'd never made love to a woman, and she was certainly exaggerating when, after his death, she told the press they had a 'loving relationship which was neither a casual flirtation nor an exclusive liaison but, on Proust's side, intense passion balanced between fondness and desire, and, on mine, a deeply felt attachment which was more than friendship.'[65] It's possible he did no more than watch her read in bed, and that what she wanted was to inflame Albufera's jealousy. The verse Proust wrote is playful and ambiguous:

> On the pretext it is Sunday
> Marcel Proust stays in this heaven
> With an angel leaning out
> Till suddenly it is Monday. . . .

Nor is there anything conclusive in the poem's assertion that her two Sèvres china cupids, delicious and surprised, watch lips and hearts joining together, or in the fact that she gave him a photograph inscribed 'L'Original qui aime bien le petit Marcel'.[66] But over eight months later, at Christmas, when she sent him a gold-framed clock in a white jewel-case, his letter of thanks jokes suggestively about opening the case and being admitted to paradise after accepting an invitation to press gently at its secret button. Another reason for thinking they did make love, once, is that he wrote in *Sodome et Gomorrhe*: 'For the invert, vice begins when he takes his pleasure with women.'

Nothing in their friendship seems to have changed, but the bitterly hostile characterisation of Rachel, who is unmistakably modelled on Louisa, suggests he was suppressing a grudge against her. Maurice Duplay believed they made love,[67] and perhaps Proust's secret feelings were overwhelmingly negative. The Narrator meets Rachel in a brothel, where the madame boasts of her superior intelligence, but he never sleeps with her.[68] Becoming Saint-Loup's mistress, she treats him in the way Louisa treated Albu, exploiting his adoration to make him buy expensive presents, tormenting him by leaving letters and messages unanswered, provoking him by flirting with other men in his presence, and driving him almost insane by threatening to leave him. Louisa's coquetry may have been equally ruthless and equally calculating, but both before and after the episode in her bedroom Proust befriended her as if her beauty and charm made her behaviour acceptable; Rachel is given no redeeming qualities – she isn't even pretty. The portrait looks as though it was poisoned by resentment and memories of concealed revulsion.

If he did make love to her, it may have been because there was no other way he could make love to Albu, who fascinated him all the more because they had less in common than Proust had with any of his other aristocratic friends, though Albu was more typical of the French nobility. Proust felt an insatiable curiosity to know what it felt like to be this man, and the name Albertine may derive partly from Albufera. The lovemaking, if it happened, left no positive emotional residue. Proust fails when he tries, in the Albertine sequence, to capture the flavour of a man's happiness when making love to the woman he desires above all others, and the reader gets no vivid impression of her body. Proust is convincing when his lovers make each other jealous, but not when they give each other sensual pleasure.

The account of kissing Albertine for the first time could hardly be less erotic. It's more topographical than anatomical, as if his vision were distorted by a magnification which multiplied the face into a vast landscape:

> I would have liked, before kissing her, to have filled her once again with the mystery she had for me on the beach before I knew her. . . . But letting my gaze slide over the beautiful pink globe of her cheeks, whose gently curving surfaces came to die at the feet of the first flexures of beautiful black hair which ran in undulating chains, raising their escarped foothills and modelled the hollowing of their valleys, I had to tell myself: 'At last, not having succeeded at Balbec, I shall discover the taste of the unknown rose which is Albertine's cheek. And perhaps, since we can only cross during our lifetime a finite number of the barriers dividing us from things and people, perhaps I shall in some way be able to consider mine fulfilled when, after lifting from its remote frame the flowering face I had chosen above all others, I shall at last have knowledge of it through its lips.' I told myself that because I believed there is a knowledge through lips; I told myself I was going to know the taste of that carnal rose because I had not thought that man, apparently a less rudimentary creature than the sea-urchin or even the whale, still lacks a certain number of essential organs, and notably possesses none which serves for kissing. For this absent organ he substitutes his lips, and arrives perhaps at a result a little more satisfactory than he would have achieved had he been reduced to caressing the beloved with a tusk of horn. But the lips, made for conveying to the palate the taste of what tempts them, have to content themselves, without understanding their error or admitting their mistake, with wandering over the surface and being blocked by the barrier of the impenetrable but desired cheek. . . . At first, as my mouth began to approach cheeks my eyes had proposed it should kiss, they sighted new cheeks from their new position; the neck, seen in close-up, as through a magnifying glass, showed in its coarse grain a robustness which modified the character of the face.[69]

Proust is partly teasing the reader by fending off any erotic or emotional involvement, but the comedy is uneasy.

His dependence on the friendship with Louisa and Albu increased when he again quarrelled with Antoine, whom he now reprimanded for gossiping indiscreetly. 'In the true sense of the word,' Proust wrote, 'I am no longer your friend.' But it was always a pleasure to set eyes on him. 'Your person, your physical person itself keeps the unconscious memory of the marvellous qualities you had, and which, materialised, commanded by the fairy of your self-destructive character to be no more than glances, vocal inflections, gestures, still keep the charm of an especially touching image for the man who has known them, the image objects leave of themselves, make of themselves, an imprint which would have meaning and beauty.'[70] This is one of the central ideas to which Proust keeps returning: the imagination can come into play only when the object is no longer under observation. Consciousness can therefore apprehend the image more vividly than the reality, can get closer to the experience when it is in the past. While we're still in an emotional turmoil, our perceptions aren't accurate.

Inevitably, when Proust was writing about emotion, he was thinking about his relationships. One of his instincts, always, was to extricate himself, and already the asthma was doing for him something of what the cork-lined room would do later, but while still involved in the turbulence of friendships and loves, he was already theorising about them. For his friends, it was difficult to cope with his unreasonable demands and with his violent reactions to behaviour such as Antoine's, which was calculated to provoke offence, but not so much. Their friendship had been nourished by jokey conspiratorial intrigue and teasing, which they both enjoyed, but Antoine went too far. Or so it seemed to Proust. After the anonymous article on princesse Mathilde's salon had appeared, it was fun to discuss it in Proust's presence and watch him squirm. After realising how much he'd embarrassed his friend, and promising never to do it again, Antoine couldn't resist talking about the Montes-quiou pastiche in front of Mme Cahen, a friend of the comtesse Potocka, and in front of Lucien he talked about the piece Proust had written, but not published, on the comtesse Greffulhe's salon. Afterwards they quarrelled bitterly, Antoine accusing Proust of being too easily upset, while he accused Antoine of upsetting him deliberately.

You complain other people are often hostile to you, but it is because you are often hostile to them. . . . You are excessively touchy, you get angry about things of no importance and you are constantly doing things to other people which if they were valued on your inflated tarriff would be repaid by murder. . . . You understand that I am telling you all this in a general way because I believe that if you could change (not with me but with your future friends) it would be very valuable for you, first because you would become better, more perfect, purer and also it would be useful.[71]

TWELVE

MARIE AND LOUISA

Flirting with Marie Nordlinger, Proust treated her quite differently from Louisa. Towards the end of May, when he was staying in bed again, unable to speak, eat or sleep[1] Marie gave him a bronze urn she'd made. She was approaching the end of her employment at the studio-gallery, but was – mainly because of Proust – reluctant to leave Paris. Though he understood her reluctance better than he seemed to, he wanted her to stay, and persuaded his mother Marie would be the right sculptor to make a bust of the doctor for his tombstone. She could work from photographs.[2]

She accepted the commission, but noticed how much more energy he was putting into other friendships. Before Antoine left for the Rumanian embassy in London, Proust had forgivingly given him a letter of introduction to Douglas Ainslie, who could introduce him to George Meredith. The letter describes Antoine as having 'one of the warmest and most seductive intellects I have ever encountered.'[3] Proust also wrote to Charles Newton Scott, and to Adèle Meyer, wife of the chairman of De Beers in London, who could introduce Antoine to Sir Henry Irving and John Singer Sargent. Proust also offered a letter 'for the Royal Academy',[4] and recommended Lady de Grey, the Earl of Pembroke's sister, for her contacts with musicians. He could also meet Pinero, if he'd like to, through either Ainslie or Robert d'Humières, another friend who'd been helping Proust with his English.

Always generous, even to casual acquaintances, Proust took enormous trouble to help friends, and the one who most needed help in the summer was Louisa. Albu told Proust before he told her that he was going to marry Prince Victor d'Essling's half-Jewish daughter, Anna Masséna. Proust would do all he could to comfort Louisa, but first he wanted Albu to be reassured about the nocturnal visit to her bedroom. Couldn't she, just for once, deviate from her principle of refusing to deny charges of infidelity? 'Show him clearly, gently, kindly, tenderly, that his notions are absurd, that he is unjust, absolutely in the wrong. That is not in your character, you will tell me. Change your character for forty-eight hours, for the sake of someone who loves both of you tenderly.' He used different paper when writing to Albu, who mustn't know he'd written to her.[5]

Taken separately by each of them into their confidence, Proust tried to avoid siding with one against the other. Albu was saying everything could still be the same after the marriage, and when he was temporarily unable to communicate with the mistress he didn't intend to discard, Proust afterwards wrote to Louisa,[6] but didn't post the letter until he had Albu's permission.[7]

The engagement was announced in the papers on 5 July. 'In accordance with the tradition followed in both families,' said *Le Gaulois*, 'this marriage will unite two of the greatest names in the nobility of the empire.'[8] Proust wrote to Louisa, who was in Vichy with her mother and sister, about Albu's plans and about the princesse. 'People have been saying most favourable things about her, and I am pleased for him.'[9] It wasn't until the following week Louisa was overtaken by full realisation of what was happening. She overheard a group of people talking about her without recognising her. 'It's quite a few years they've been together and he's going to marry the little Masséna, but I don't think his mistress knows.' Then she received a letter in which Albu wrote only about his plans for the future and the need for silence about their relationship. 'I'm like a ship without sails,' she said. 'I don't know where to direct my thoughts, I could never have believed he'd lose interest in me so quickly to get interested in her. What has she got, my God? My life has just changed totally, I no longer have any wishes or desires. Do you understand me, Marcel?'[10]

Proust showed Albu this letter, but immediately regretted it, because it threw him into confusion, as Proust told her, trying to console her by saying how popular Albu was, 'and all that has the effect of doubling the admiration and sympathy people have for you, because they know he would not have gone into the marriage if you had tried to dissuade him'.[11] And he wrote to her again five days later, stressing the affection Albu still felt for her.[12] But, writing to Antoine, it was his fondness for Albu that Proust emphasised. 'Albu comes to see me more often than before, if that is possible, and he is adorable to me. . . . I like him too much to look at his marriage entirely from my own point of view.'[13]

Though the Dreyfus affair had changed Proust, making him think politically and be willing to take action, none of his newspaper articles had so far been political. But he was worried by Aristide Briand's proposal for state subsidy to be withdrawn from the Church and for cathedrals it could no longer finance to be made into museums. What if the socialists succeeded in separating Church and state?

In an article for *Le Figaro*, 'La Mort des cathédrales', Proust developed the point he'd made last year to de Lauris, asking the same question – what would France be like without Catholicism? Like a dry beach, he answered, littered with chiselled shells, empty of the life that had inhabited them. Cathedrals had a better claim than theatres or opera to state subsidy, being 'probably the highest and incontestably the most original expression of the genius of France'.[14] Though his love for them was Ruskinian and aesthetic, he made a good case for allowing worship to continue in them.

Le Figaro accepted the article but still failed to review *The Bible of Amiens*, although notices went on appearing in other papers. On 11 July, in *Le Temps*, Albert Sorel praised the flexibility and precision of Proust's translation. 'Exact, when he describes, his images, like those of his master, proceeding most often from the Scriptures, which are at once sumptuous and precise.' He called Proust the most intimately proselytised of all converts, now undertaking the most effective apostolate – that of example. 'He was ailing and troubled, he read and was cured.'[15]

An alternative cure for Proust's debility was proposed by a well-known Paris doctor, Pierre Merklen, a specialist in pulmonary and cardiac diseases. Proust's asthma, he declared, had become a nervous habit, which could be cured at a clinic in Germany, just as addiction to morphine was cured. But Proust had no desire to be treated in this way.

Another doctor whose theories struck him as ridiculous was a young Rumanian, Nicolas Vaschide, a guest at a dinner party given by the de Noailles. He was charming but almost unintelligible, speaking fast with a strong accent, and so eager to display specialist knowledge that whatever came under discussion, he'd explain it as nervous in origin. No doubt it was nervousness, later on in the evening, that made Proust knock over one of his hostess's precious Tanagra vases.[16] Ashamed, he avoided her for a year.

Though ill in bed on Monday 8 August when Marie Nordlinger arrived with a maquette of her portrait plaque for his father's tombstone, he was determined to leave the next day for a trip on a yacht belonging to Paul Mirabaud, a banker, the father-in-law of his old friend Robert de Billy, who'd invited him. Taking syrup of ether for emergency use, Proust went by train to Le Havre, where he was met at the station by the banker, who looked like a Saxon god, big and strong, with the same nose, same blue eyes, same complexion and same way of speaking as his daughter. They took a carriage to the port, where Proust immediately had an asthma attack. On board with de Billy, his wife and three other ladies, including the pretty Mme Jacques Faure, he found it was too cold and too humid to undress, and after dosing himself at about three in the morning with Trional, tried to sleep on the bunk with his clothes on. At five he went up on the bridge, and at seven they set sail for Cherbourg. After dinner he felt sure he wouldn't sleep if he went to bed, but finally undressed at about three, slept well, and woke at seven with asthma, which he attributed to the rainy weather.

M. Mirabaud had slept badly, and because he wanted to sleep all day, the yacht stayed anchored outside the harbour at Cherbourg, but a steam launch took Proust and the others to the docks. In the town, wanting to write, he asked to be left alone, but, finding no closed carriage and nowhere he could settle, wandered about and eventually went for a swim. Exhausted, he lapsed into fits of coughing when they made the windy journey back on the steam launch.

On Thursday he was intending to take the Friday morning train to Paris, stopping at Bayeux and Caen, but during the day he enjoyed himself too much. With only one fit of choking since he'd left, he hadn't used the syrup of ether, and hadn't been seasick. He was missing his mother, and worrying about her health; she was in Étretat with Robert, his wife and Suzy, now nine months old. He said he felt as if a telephone were linking him to his mother's heart, and he was impatient to tell her about everything that had happened, with constant interruptions in the narrative for kissing her, but he was so 'seduced by this yachting life' that he enquired about the cost of hiring a yacht. He didn't return to Paris till Monday the 15th, and, except on the Sunday, he was getting up as early as the others and going up on the bridge at ten. On Saturday, when he went into the country, the foliage and dust brought on an attack of hay-fever. He sent a postcard and an equally brief letter to Marie, and postcards to Louisa and de Lauris,[17] but his only long letter was to his mother, to whom he wrote again once he was back in the flat.[18]

His stamina had stood up well to the strain of staying awake through the day and adjusting to other people, but he didn't continue this routine. 'If I have to stay indoors because I am unwell, a night of that makes little difference to me because I am used to it, but in broad daylight, seeing the sun outside, being there on my own would fill me with nostalgia.' When the sun was shining, he hated to be alone in the dining-room between midday and seven in the evening.[19]

During his father's lifetime, there had been a central pillar of medical authority, and any advice he collected from books, friends and other doctors fell into perspective around his father's opinions. Since the end of 1903, with more freedom to consult other doctors and plan his own campaigns against illness, he was handicapped by his habit of cancelling and postponing, dreaming about recovery and elaborating fantasies instead of taking action. Where he did take action was in making dietary experiments. He could no longer eat a heavy meal without an asthmatic feeling which seemed more likely to be gastric or intestinal in origin, and he'd been rationing himself to one meal a day. But it was a heavy meal, usually consisting of two eggs à la crème, a wing of roast chicken, three croissants, a plate of fried potatoes, grapes, a bottle of beer, and coffee. From fear of dilating his stomach again, he drank nothing else all day except a quarter of a glass of Vichy water before going to bed.

When, after his return to Paris, he had his urine tested, he was told it contained excessive urea and uric acid, with insufficient chlorine. There were also traces of albumen and sugar in it, but these might be due to deviations from his normal diet while on the yacht.[20]

Reading Georges Linossier's book *L'Hygiène du dyspeptique*, which had been published during 1900 in a collection edited by

Dr Proust, he felt hopeful he'd at last discovered the connection
between his asthma and his indigestion.[21] Dr Linossier was
practising in Vichy, which is 220 miles from Paris, but Proust
wrote to him, hoping he could help to reverse the process in
which what had seemed to be hay-fever had developed into
asthma which had at first troubled him only in the summer
but now troubled him all through the year. The deterioration
in his health had been too gradual to panic him, but too steady
to ignore. One by one he'd given up most of the social pleasures he'd enjoyed. He'd liked going to cafés such as the Poul-
piquet in the rue de Prony, a haunt of the playwright René
Peter, who was friendly with Reynaldo and Debussy, but the
smoke-filled atmosphere was now too much of a strain on his
lungs.[22] Should he have followed Dr Merklen's advice in July?
His main question to Dr Linossier was whether to take one of
the psycho-therapeutic cures in which the treatment consisted
of isolation, controlled overfeeding and 'cure by persuasion'.
Or would the overfeeding be more likely to harm him? After
describing symptoms and campaigns against them in greater
detail than he'd intended, he decided not to burden the doctor
with such a long letter. Probably he was only partially aware
of the extent to which he was manipulating his illness as a
factor in relationships with work and people. With his mother
he was nearly always optimistic, pointing at the progress he
was making, the effectiveness of remedies and changes in his
regime, but the asthma was like a language for discussing their
mutual adoration, or a religion they shared.

Some of his habitual precautions were like rituals. What he
called letting his temperature fall was a way of preparing his
body for the transition from the warm bed to the cool room
by progressively raising the blankets to admit cool air to the
bed.[23] Knowing all this might seem absurd, he made jokey
references to Molière's *Le Malade imaginaire*[24] later in *À la
recherche*, attributing the same habit to a neurasthenic patient
of the Boulbon doctor.[25]

He went on going out, even when he was feeling unwell, if
there were people he wanted to see. He twice had dinner with
Louisa, but was remiss in dealing with Marie, whom he visited
at Auteuil in late August, but only after postponing the meeting
twice,[26] and he was disingenuous afterwards, promising that
as soon as he was well

perhaps even this Thursday evening, I will get in touch, not
for you to come and work but to come and pay me a little
visit for a chat, which is perhaps less reasonable, but still
more agreeable – for me. What gave me less pleasure than
the pretty thoughts and phrases in your letter was like a vague
allusion to some profound sadness you don't talk about, and
perhaps you were not even thinking about it when writing,
but it seemed to limit and darken your letter like an inevitable
horizon.[27]

Though he knew his indifference to her was at the root of her
depression, he procrastinated about the visit. Over two weeks
later he apologised for the delay.[28]

He was more eager to be with Albu, even wanting to join
him on military manoeuvres. On 3 September, intending to
see him off at the station and impatient at getting no news,
Proust sent a coachman with a message to Albu's concierge,
just before a telegram arrived saying Albu would be staying
the night at the Hôtel Moderne in Évreux. Deciding to catch
the 9.55 train to Évreux, Proust missed it by taking too long
to get himself ready, and when he arrived at the station, he
found the next train didn't arrive till two in the morning. He
tried to telephone Albu, but the exchange at Évreux closed at
nine o'clock. After looking forward for forty-eight hours to an
evening with Albu, Proust couldn't stop himself from weeping
with disappointment, which brought on an attack of asthma –
'I always say it is the worst I have ever had, but this time I
believe it is no exaggeration.' It lasted 'without a second's
respite' for nineteen hours. Still wheezing the following evening, he cancelled his dinner appointment with Loche, and consoled himself with the idea that experiences are less real when
you have them than when you either remember them or
imagine them. His recurrent asthma attacks, forcing him to
cancel appointments and postpone meetings, encouraged this
pattern of substituting the imaginary for the real, but it was a
two-way process in which the pattern also encouraged the
asthma. Missing the train had produced 'an intense redoubling,
an enormous growth in my friendship for you. . . . This prospect of seeing you, spending the evening with you at Évreux,
so strongly cherished, then suddenly destroyed, this enjoyable
chat with you down there, perhaps nicer and more charming
when imagined, in the smarting regret at not having had it,

all that has dealt a violent blow which reinforces the links that attach me to you'. All literary activity involves the writer in shutting himself off from contact with other people at the moment of writing; the life Proust had evolved for himself was relentlessly pushing him towards literature.

He wouldn't have written like this to Reynaldo or Lucien or Constantin or Antoine, who were all too intelligent and articulate to be used as a screen for projecting emotions. Without reciprocating Proust's obsessive feelings of attachment, Albu was sufficiently tolerant and good-natured not to raise any objections to the intensity of Proust's friendship, so long as it didn't become a nuisance. Besides, he was glad someone was befriending Louisa. Perhaps Proust could persuade her not to be in Paris at the time of the wedding – on 11 October. In fact she couldn't go away because she was playing a small part at the Vaudeville in a comedy by A. Bisson and J. Berr, *Les Trois Anabaptistes*. Proust was intending to leave Paris with his mother, but to return in time for the wedding.[29]

His relationship with Louisa went on developing as each of them found how useful the other could be. Fénelon was having an affair with her sister, and, wanting to meet him in a way that looked accidental, Proust told her to ask Fénelon to meet her one evening after the play in a restaurant or at her home. Proust would then happen to arrive. The favours he could do her made a big difference to her career: he introduced her to influential people in the theatre and secured publicity for her in the papers. Nor was it merely a matter of asking reviewers not to overlook her minuscule appearances. When Antoine idly suggested a profile of her in *Gil Blas*, she took him seriously, and Proust, failing to coax Antoine into writing it, wrote it himself.[30]

Since his father's death and his brother's marriage, he had no one to rival his claims on his mother's attention, but it seemed less of a prize now she was so weak and so depressed. Though worried about her condition, he was glad of her dependence on him, and aware she spent little money except on him.[31] Each time he came home, his first words were: 'Is Madame in?' Usually she'd appear, shy and considerate, uncertain whether she should come to him. Perhaps the outing had tired him or made him too breathless for conversation, while he felt guilty at causing her so much anxiety.[32]

There was nothing to stop them from going on a summer

holiday together, but Proust dithered like a gauche lover uncertain whether his girlfriend will really come with him. Evian was so far away, and he was undecided whether to return before 8 October, when Albu's marriage contract would be signed, or just before the ceremony, three days later. Both in Dieppe and Trouville the evenings were depressing, and Kreuznach had associations which would be painful for her. She should make the decision. But didn't she think the air at Evian was purer than the air at Trouville, and more different from the air in Paris? They should find out whether the hotel bedrooms were heated by open fires or by radiators. Perhaps Dieppe would be best if they stayed at the Hôtel Royal. Or maybe he'd feel more relaxed at Evian, and more at home. Besides, he could visit the lakes and find out how good he was at seeing landscapes with Ruskinian eyes. But was it worth going so far when they had only a fortnight? Perhaps Trouville would be better, because Mme Straus and Charles Ephrussi would both be nearby. Or if they went to Dieppe, perhaps the Chalet Bois would be quieter than the Hôtel Royal. According to Albu, the Royal was absurdly expensive, and the Roches Noires more reasonable. Would she like to ask Dr Paul Faivre, one of her husband's former colleagues, whether it was only Brest that was unhealthy? Were Quimper, La Pointe de Raz, Roskoff, Dinard and Caen any better? According to Albu, Chamonix was humid, but de Billy said it was dry. Albu said Biskra was perfect during the winter, and not too warm.[33] Soon Proust was urging her to leave for Dieppe without him. He could join her in a few days. But he was nervous of missing Albu's wedding, and the indecision, which must have been distressing for her, was so distressing for him that he fell ill, which was a way of deciding. He'd have to stay at home, hoping to recover in time for the wedding.

Marie Nordlinger, who was still in Paris, had given up neither her designs on him nor her belief she could rescue him from the invalid life he used as an excuse for sidestepping the course of true love. 'I am brimming over with health, with life, with strength, with potential for being happy.' These words, he replied evasively, were like 'an offer of a transfusion of moral blood'. And he 'understood the sadness of your solitude. But I was the last person who could cure it, not having two good hours per week, etc.etc.' He encouraged her to accept an offer of work in America and accused her of being evasive. Why didn't she want her name to appear as co-translator on the cover of *Sesame and Lilies*?[34]

While his mother was in Dieppe, he struggled against the old problem of working in unheated rooms. On Wednesday 21 September, he got up as soon as the servants had his dinner ready, not even taking time to make his temperature go down, but there was no fire in the dining-room, and when François, the barber, came to cut his hair, his throat was hurting too much for him to have it done, just as, a week later, he felt too ill to see a dentist, either in his surgery of by summoning him to the flat.[35] But he promised not to burden her with so many details about his health when she came back to Paris, though 'the consolation of the martyrs is that the God for whom they suffer sees their wounds'.[36]

He went to the jeweller's, Bourcelot, in the rue des Fontaines to see the Empire lamp she'd chosen as Albu's wedding present, and wrote to tell her it had won admiration from everybody – even the Rothschilds, the Murats, the Ephrussis and even at Versailles. 'I am full of astonishment at your extraordinary taste, which enabled you to find it, your incredible ingenuity which enabled you to make the price accessible to me, your exquisite artistry in restoring it, and above all the infinite kindness which has been the mainspring of your searching and your effort.'[37] So much of his relationship with her had been carried on through letter-writing it had come to seem natural for intimacy to mingle with polite formality.

The same evening he was 'sneezing, coughing and, worse still, full of asthma'[38] on account of 'a trifling bit of dust I inhaled'. Two days later he was feeling ill and 'very unhappy in every way, morally, physically, intellectually'.[39] He'd been invited to a rehearsal of Antoine's play *Le Jaloux*, which was to open at the Théâtre Marigny, starring Lugné-Poe, and the dress rehearsal was to be at 8.15 on the same day, Saturday, as the early evening party after the signing of the nuptial contract. If Antoine could take him to a rehearsal on Wednesday, he'd have a better chance of recovering in time for the signing of the contract on Saturday. Had he felt certain of being well enough to attend the wedding on Tuesday, he'd have sacrificed the Saturday party,[40] but, as usual, he must ration himself to a minimum of outings. When Louisa doubled her role in *Les Trois Anabaptistes* with that of an indisposed actress who'd been playing a much larger part, and sent her cook to Proust with a ticket, he used mourning as an excuse for not going to the theatre, but he'd have gone to the rehearsal of *Le Jaloux* if Antoine had taken him. Instead, wanting to be helpful, Proust interviewed him and wrote a profile, saying: 'His delicious wit is cruel,' and referring to his 'humane malevolence'.[41] Instead of publishing what he wrote, Proust gave it to Antoine, who revised it, and it was incorporated into an article by Serge Basset in *Le Figaro* on 8 October. Proust had passed no judgment on Antoine's talent, and in private he was non-committal: 'I do not know a line by him, his letters being simply telegrams (long though they are) without style, good or bad . . . indicating neither talent nor lack of it.'[42] But in *Le Journal* Catulle Mendès praised Antoine's 'very subtle sensitivity, very rare finesse in psychological observation and in sensual curiosity',[43] while reviewers in *L'Écho de Paris* and *Le Matin* were no less complimentary.[44] Proust assumed the three verdicts were well founded. Antoine's success 'has transported him into a childlike happiness which is extremely likeable'.[45]

Proust was disappointed but not surprised to be too ill for either Albu's party on the Saturday or the wedding on Tuesday; his consolation prizes were a visit from the bridal pair after the ceremony[46] and a handsome present, a cane sheathed in leather, with a gold-plated copper ring engraved with the initials M.P. and the inscription: 'L.A. 11 October 1904'. Reverberations from the wedding travelled through Paris, and it was hard for Louisa to get through the month. In the afternoon of the 21st she sent Albu a telegram which almost stopped him from leaving on his honeymoon 'BEYOND MY STRENGTH TO BEAR THIS HONEYMOON', but Proust, despite his weakness, gave both of them his support. He sent an eighty-three word telegram to Albu: 'HAVE A SINGLE THOUGHT AT EVERY INSTANT GIVE YOUR WIFE DURING HONEYMOON ALL POSSIBLE HAPPINESS GOD WILL GIVE YOU IT BACK'.[47] He promised to keep Albu informed about Louisa and not only kept the promise but befriended her with more devotion than could reasonably have been expected from someone so ill. He often had high temperatures but wrote to Louisa about tranquillisers, offering to consult a doctor on her behalf as soon as he felt well enough.[48] Knowing how low her morale was, he also knew there was no better way to raise it than by helping her career. Her good looks made this easier and, after being introduced to the playwright Henri Bataille, she was given the part of Louisa in his *Maman Colibri*, which was to open at the Vaudeville on 8 November. Not yet satisfied he'd done enough, Proust wanted to give her an expensive present, and asked Mme Catusse how much it would cost to buy a Louis XVI table with a silvered metal mirror.[49] When this turned out to be too expensive, he settled for a tapestry cushion-case.[50]

By now he had another wedding present to plan. Armand de Guiche was to be married on 14 November and when Proust asked what he'd like for a present, his answer was he already had everything, he thought, except a revolver. So Proust bought him an expensive one in a leather case painted by Reynaldo's friend Frédéric (Coco) de Madrazo. *Le Figaro*, which listed presents at society weddings, mistakenly credited the painting to Madeleine Lemaire.[51] The bride was the twenty-two-year-old daughter of the comtesse Greffulhe, who received a typically Proustian compliment on the day of the wedding, when he told her one of Guiche's objects in marrying her daughter was to gain possession of her photograph. 'She laughed so prettily I could have repeated it ten times.'[52]

Nor were Albu and Guiche the only two friends withdrawing from bachelordom into married life. Rumours were circulating that Gabriel de la Rochefoucauld was about to become engaged, and in August his mistress, the thirty-four-year-old comtesse des Garets-Quiros, who was separated from her husband, the father of her three children, shot herself in the heart. Gabriel's fiancée was Odile, the daughter of the princesse Alice de Monaco, but they didn't marry until April 1905.

While his friends were turning towards marriage, Proust was preoccupied with mortality. On the first anniversary of his father's death, a Saturday, he went with his mother to visit the grave and decorate it, but he caught cold. He was intending to see a doctor on Monday, but postponed it. The following Monday, 5 December, he was in bed, and not expecting to get up until Wednesday, when he'd see his doctors and, if he felt well enough, go on to Neuilly, where Montesquiou was holding a reception in honour of an Italian writer, Mathilde Serao.[53] 'And my outings now put me each time into such a state that I have no hope of being in a condition to get up or utter a sound on Thursday or perhaps Friday.' This outing was no exception, doing him, he said, more harm than the doctors did him good.[54] The next day he was in bed with chronic influenza,[55] and by Tuesday he was feeling no better. His temperature was still too high, and his throat was hurting.[56]

Only three days earlier, trying to plan an evening in a restaurant with Antoine and Loche, Proust had said he'd be equally happy to eat at Durand or Larue, or the Café Anglais, but on the 14th he told Antoine the air in restaurants was bad for him. He'd much prefer a private dining-room. Antoine settled it by inviting him to dinner at home on the 15th, and he went, but, unable to breathe in the warm room, withdrew into an unheated lavatory, where he had an asthma attack.

His anxiety about his health was deepening, and in December, when he went back to Brissaud's *L'Hygiène des asthmathiques*, he was disconcerted to read that asthma, like epilepsy, 'seems to choose some victims to make them pay for the invulnerability of others. Then the neurosis ceases to be protective. It impairs the organism so deeply, redoubles its attacks so relentlessly, that even the most robust have to succumb; at the least, if they do not die, they are reduced to a kind of *physiological misery*.' Asthmatics of this kind are overcome by cachexy or general debility. 'It establishes itself gradually, installs itself in them step by step, makes them thin, enfeebles them, takes away all moral support; they abandon themselves, stop eating, no longer sleep; the anasarca infiltrates them, their myocardium becomes distended, the lower area of the lung becomes congested, their extremities give in to cyanosis, become chilled, and they die.'[57] This revived the anxiety which had sent Proust to Venice in the belief he must go soon or never. 'Successive attacks', he told Lucien, 'rack the organism to pieces and hasten the final moment.'[58]

He was entitled to feel sorry for himself. Not long ago he'd complained about having to pay for each outing with two days of illness; six days before Christmas he said a fortnight of feverish temperatures could follow an unplanned outing,[59] and he had to turn down an invitation to spend Christmas Eve with Fernand Gregh and his wife in Danmarie-les-Lys, where her parents had rented a Louis XVI house.

Nor could his mother give much support. She was making only a limited effort to resume normal life. She'd moved into her husband's bedroom,[60] and left his study as it had been during his lifetime, except that she'd filled it with photographs of him.[61] On the 26th of each month she was still commemorating the day of his death, and she took little interest in other people, refusing to meet more than a few at a time, but 'near Mamma's room there is a parquet board which you cannot pass without causing a creak, and as soon as she heard this, Mamma would make the little sound with her mouth which meant "Come and kiss me." '[62] Always on the alert for sounds from her room, he was always finding pretexts to go in and kiss her.[63]

When he arranged a dinner party for Fénelon, who was briefly on leave from St Petersburg, Proust knew she'd take no part in it. The other guests were Reynaldo, Lucien, Antoine, Gabriel de la Rochefoucauld, Loche, René Peter, Fernand Gregh and Albert Flament, who may have been invited in the hope he'd chronicle the occasion in *L'Écho de Paris*, as he did, on the front page, writing under his pseudonym 'Sparklet' and celebrating the way 'art and literature make the best of social situations and aristocratic names'.[64] The intellectual conversation, he reported, had taken place 'under the sleepy-looking gaze of M. Marcel Proust, one of the best speakers of French, though he rarely consents to give written proof of this'.

Partly to cope with his guilt about the comtesse he'd driven to suicide, Gabriel had made the story into a novel, *L'Amour et le médecin*, which was due to be published on 18 January. When Proust read it in proof, he found himself portrayed as a pessimistic homosexual hypochondriac, but, as in his dealings with Montesquiou, accepted humiliation as part of the price to be paid for friendship with the aristocracy. When he started an article in praise of the novel, the editor of *Le Siècle*, Joseph Reinach, expressed interest, but Proust wanted to join the exclusive Cercle de l'Union, and, as Gabriel pointed out, publication in a left-wing paper would reduce his chances. He extricated himself by pleading ill health and the need to work on the translation of *Sesame and Lilies*.

He felt more at ease in his efforts to mediate between Albu and Louisa, and to get her a part in Brieux's dramatisation of Paul Hervieu's novel *L'Armature*, due to open in April at the Vaudeville. Proust bullied René Peter into making Hervieu intervene.[65] With help from two other intermediaries, a playwright, Henri Vaucaire, and an actress, Duluc, Peter managed to have Louisa cast in a small part.[66] Even then Proust didn't think he'd done enough. Auguste Germain, who wrote a theatrical column in *L'Écho de Paris* under the *nom de plume* Capitaine Fracasse, was anxious to please Loche and agreed to mention Louisa in his column when the play came under discussion again. Loche was asked to put more pressure on him and, when he did nothing, Proust wrote threatening to end their friendship. 'Spare me from listing my grievances. They are serious and well founded.'[67] But he never posted the letter.

THIRTEEN

SECRET PLAN

The first lecture in *Sesame and Lilies* was due to be published in *Les Arts de la vie* in March 1905, and in February Proust started work on the second lecture, 'Of Queens' Gardens', using Charles Newton Scott as his helper. 'I have spoken to you', he wrote to Marie Nordlinger, who was in America, 'about my old and charming English scholar who will act as my "Mary".'[1] On the day the first lecture appeared, three new members were elected to the Cercle de l'Union, but Proust was turned down. As he discovered later, the committee disapproved of the stand he'd taken during the Dreyfus affair.[2] He immediately offered to finish his article on Gabriel's novel. He could possibly place it in *Le Petit Parisien*, or *Le Figaro*. Alternatively he could go back to *Le Siècle* now he had nothing to lose by associating himself with it.[3]

He was hesitating about whether to take a cure at a clinic in Berne, and in mid-February he turned down an invitation for 2 March, thinking he'd be in Switzerland by then, but, after procrastinating, started to plan a dinner party on 6 March with two tables, one for his bourgeois friends such as the Yeatmans, and one for the young noblemen. He wanted Reynaldo to sing duets with the comtesse de Guerne. Deferring to his mother's wishes, he agreed to have only one table, but Reynaldo, who'd promised to play and sing at another party, refused to perform twice in one evening, even when Mme Proust sent a letter her son had secretly drafted, but he agreed to oblige his old friend at teatime. The dinner party therefore turned into a tea party, and, partly to flatter Guiche, Proust asked his advice. Would it be improper to invite the comtesse Greffulhe's sister, Mme de Tinan, when he'd been presented only once to her and her husband? Should he invite the comtesse Greffulhe herself? To justify the request for advice, he put a sentence into inverted commas – 'Dukes know better than anyone how we should live' – pretending it was a quotation from Balzac.[4] He invited the duchesse de Gramont, Mme Straus and Anatole France, who'd sent a copy of his latest book; by quoting a passage from the final chapter in his letter of thanks, Proust gave the impression he'd already got to the end.[5]

The day before the party there was a violent quarrel among the servants, and Proust's favourite maid left. At the party he wasn't at his best: 'I had not eaten for two days and I was in a kind of trance or rather nightmare which must have made me seem very odd to my guests.'[6] Reynaldo and the comtesse sang a Mozart duet, and one from *Un Coeur qui t'aime*. There were at least twenty-two guests including Albu and his wife, Gabriel and his mother, the comtesse Aimery de la Rochefoucauld, Mme Lemaire and her daughter, the princesse de Brancovan, the Guiches, the comte and comtesse de Ludre, the comtesse de Briey, the comte and comtesse Adhéaume de Chevigné and the princesse Alexandre de Chimay, the comte Ferdinand de Montesquiou, the comte Henri de Ségur, the baron Théodore de Berckheim and Francis de Croisset, who met his future mother-in-law, Mme de Chevigné. De Croisset was now collaborating with Robert de Flers on light comedies, and to complete the self-transformation which had started with the shrewd abandonment of his real name, Franz Wiener, he was dressing dandyishly in the English style. Later Proust would make his Jewish character, Bloch, take the name Jacques du Rozier, and look 'totally transformed by the English chic'.

After the party Proust was exhausted, but he went out in the evening, possibly to see Louisa in the play at the Vaudeville, and, without having recovered, went three days later to a supper party Reynaldo was giving at the Café de l'Univers with the music-hall singer Fragson. Proust stayed till asthma overcame him at 3.30 in the morning. He felt as though he'd swallowed enough smoke and dust to keep him in bed for several days.[7]

He was still going to Mme Lemaire's musical evenings, and he made an impression even on people not introduced to him. One young woman noticed the 'admirable' eyes in the very pale face. 'In all his movements was a graceful weariness; his gestures were supple, his long, thin hands sketched harmonious gestures. Sometimes one hand was folded under his chin to support it, sometimes it came in front of his mouth to conceal his laughter, and then only the sparkle in his eyes showed his gaiety.' His eyes wandered without ever settling anywhere, and his voice ranged between ringing resonance and soft confidentiality. He never failed, it seemed, to arouse the interest of people he engaged in conversation, and, when he listened to music, the eyes – so alert when he talked – seemed focused on the distance; slightly thrown back, his immobile head appeared 'overburdened by the mass of black hair. His limbs were as flexible as a child's, his wrists were double jointed, and his legs coiled about each other like tropical creepers.'[8]

Going out so little, he rarely saw Montesquiou, who hadn't been invited to the tea party, and wrote an offended note enquiring about Proust's resurrection. In reply he pretended to think the comte had been away, and to be distressed at 'watching the escape of the big turbot one could have served up to one's guests, seeing it too late as it swims across the front of the aquarium'. Anyway it hadn't been a resurrection but a farewell to social life before taking a rest cure. 'To stop it from being said I had gone mad and been interned, I invited people to show them I will be leaving in possession of my mental faculties (if I ever have been) and of my own free will (in so far as such things are ever done willingly).'[9]

But he went on procrastinating about the clinic, though March was a bad month. Unable to sleep during a prolonged attack of breathlessness, he went on smoking anti-asthma cigarettes, and thought of using a sedative based on heroin, but he decided against it.[10] One night, when he wanted to go out for half an hour, the short outing 'made my attacks so much worse that I do not know when I shall get up'.[11] At the end of the month he mustered the energy to thank the comtesse de Guerne by writing an article about her for Le Figaro. He called her 'one of the two or three greatest living singers'. Her voice was 'not only pure but so spiritualised that she seems rather a sort of natural harmony, I will not even say the sighs of a flute, but of a reed in the wind'.[12] Though he stayed indoors for three weeks, he was eager to go on being helpful, not only to Louisa but also to Mme Straus, who was recuperating from her neurasthenic illness at Territet, by Lake Geneva. 'If there happen to be any commissions you want carried out in Paris, or any information you need, or indeed anything at all, if you do not wish to trouble or disturb M. Straus, I would be only too happy for you to make use of me.'[13] He was using his uncomplaining mother to run errands for him,[14] not knowing how weak she was.

Having to pay such a high price in malaise for each outing, he decided – at the risk of offending Montesquiou – not to attend his lecture on 21 April about 'The End of Satan'. Not content with reproaching Proust for failing to appear, the comte threatened to call on him at the beginning of June and give a fifteen-minute lecture to celebrate the publication of his new book, *Professionelles Beautés*. Proust was instructed to invite 'two or three of our friends, and we can discuss which ones'.[15] Politely he tried to dissuade Montesquiou from taking so much trouble, but preparations for this lecture – correspondence about date, time and guests – were going to sap a good deal of Proust's energy during April and May, though he was behind schedule in preparing *Sesame and Lilies* for the publisher, and on 23 April, in spite of feeling ill, he worked from midnight till nine in the morning.[16] Reading and writing, recklessly, with an unshaded electric light bulb, he was straining his eyes, though his once-perfect vision had begun to deteriorate. By the beginning of May he had difficulty in reading his own handwriting,[17] but despite the pressure of work, the persistent malaise and a series of chronic asthma attacks, he found a good way of resolving the tension created by giving so much time to translating instead of working more creatively. 'Sur la lecture', the long introduction he wrote for *Sesame and Lilies* (promising it for preliminary publication in *La Renaissance latine* during June) is actually an original piece of work – a bridge from Ruskin to *À la recherche*. In the same way that he'd mix critical and creative writing in *Contre Sainte-Beuve*, he started writing *against* Ruskin, opposing his own ideas to those of his master.

Working as a translator had made him think about writing as a process of translating substance into words.

> Between the ideas in one of his books and between the books there are connections he does not show but allows to appear for a moment and which he has perhaps woven retrospectively, but these are never artificial because they are always drawn from the substance of his thinking, which is identical with itself. The multiple but constant preoccupations of this thinking guarantee to these books a more authentic unity than the unity of composition, which is often absent, it must be said.[18]

Ruskin hadn't come closely enough to grips with the life of

the mind. When you're lying in bed unwell, a book is your natural companion, and from hours of reading that extended over days and weeks, Proust knew that sentences on a page are more valuable when taken not as a substitute for the experiences they describe but as a stimulus to related mental experiences. Ruskin was guilty of 'idolatry' because he wrote as if truth were a material object that could be inserted by the writer into a book and taken out intact by the reader.

Like Ruskin, who tended to leave work unfinished, to revise compulsively, and to go back, unsatisfied, over ground already covered, Proust struggled to bring consciousness of experience closer to the experience itself and literature closer to consciousness. An adult who'd lived like a child in his parents' home, he reacted to the work of other writers as to rooms he'd played no part in furnishing. He was used to rooms which reflected neither his taste nor his consciousness, rooms 'where my imagination is excitingly plunged into the womb of the non-ego'. He was also familiar with hotel rooms where noises help the silence to reassert itself and where other people's dreams seem to have left their imprint on the shape of the andirons and the pattern of the curtains.[19]

His dissatisfaction with himself and his continuing belief he lacked willpower are evident when he writes about nervous diseases which engulf the sufferer so deeply in inertia that he needs help. 'He is not really unable to work, walk, eat, expose himself to the cold, but he is incapable of propelling himself towards these actions.'[20] He needs a doctor to re-educate his willpower. Proust had bought several books on psychoneurosis including one by Théodule Ribot, who discussed the consistent failure of the highly gifted Coleridge to realise the gigantic projects floating through his mind. Implicitly Proust compared himself not only with Coleridge but also with the nobleman who'd lived so long among highwaymen that he'd almost forgotten his name. The passage is reminiscent of 'Violante', his 1893 story about the girl who lost her self-control. Twelve years later, Proust is still using his writing as a means of merging the admonitory parental voice with the voice inside his head.

The introduction moves on to an attempt at mixing recollected fact with improvised fiction. Giving an accurate description of Dordrecht, as he remembered it from his 1902 visit, and assuming – without checking – that one stopped there on the way to Utrecht, he transposed his experience of travelling in a canal boat at Vollendam among the weeds, and, together with nuns he saw in the hospital at Beaune during 1903, a channel he saw in Delft is transported to Utrecht and described lovingly: 'the seventeenth-century chimes startle so tenderly the naive water of the canal which is dazzled by the pale sunshine between the double row of trees, which have been bare since the end of summer and which brush the mirrors fixed to the gabled houses on both banks.'[21] Working on this page of the introduction, Proust consulted Francis de Croisset, who knew Holland well: it was a passage 'which does not need to take pains about being exact, but which is true (impressions felt and names changed). I would not want, all the same, to perpetrate topographical heresies which (for those who know the country) would get in the way of what is called "evocation".'[22]

Without consciously preparing himself for a return to fiction, Proust was characterising individuals and social contexts by quoting selectively in his long letters from overheard conversations. 'My dear, it's a question of what you want, Madeleine takes pride in well-cooked food, me I prefer to give people good music. She pays her cook two thousand francs, I'd rather pay good money to my artists. It's always the same amount. Madeleine likes guests to put her into their mouth, me I prefer to be put into their ears. It's a matter of taste, my dear, it's a free country, I presume.'[23] This was written mainly to vent his irritation at the marquise de Saint-Paul, who'd been talking loudly on her way out of a concert, but residual anger, a good memory and a good ear for the rhythms of the spoken language are leading Proust towards satirical fiction.

Throughout the four weeks of corresponding with Montesquiou, who'd decided to read from his book instead of lecturing, Proust gave no sign of impatience. Since his mother was still avoiding all social gatherings, she'd have to be 'exiled' from the flat for the occasion, but, as if to compensate for not being more enthusiastic, Proust offered to write about the book.[24] On 25 May, he'd promised to attend a concert featuring Reynaldo's suite for wind instruments, two harps and a piano, but the reading could be on the 23rd, the 29th or the 30th. 'You put so much sauce around the fish,' objected Montesquiou, 'that it disappears rather,' but he opted for the 23rd. Since he wanted to read the chapter about Mme Aubernon, it would be appropriate to invite people who knew her, and he suggested several, including Madeleine Lamaire, who said she had no free evening until after 30 May and expressed a preference for 2 June. Nervous she might feel sleepy after so many engagements, Montesquiou proposed the 3rd, but this didn't suit her, and he settled for the 2nd.[25] In the second half of May, Proust had a prolonged attack of asthma, and he was worried that if Lucien called to find out how he was, he'd see the overcoats in the ante-room and be offended at not having been invited. When the evening came, Proust was too ill and exhausted to shave, but all went well, and it was, according to *Le Gaulois*, 'a great literary success for comte Robert de Montesquiou-Fezensac, who was paying a surprise visit to give a reading of fragments from his new book and from unpublished art criticism'.[26]

Proust still hadn't recovered when Marie Nordlinger arrived in Paris. 'I found him in bed, his eyes glowing, his pale face framed by a strong black beard. . . . Only his voice could smile: "Give me a kiss, Mary. I still think about you a lot. Tell me, what have you seen? Have you seen beautiful things in America?" But *Sesame* was waiting. We had to make haste. We worked till dawn.'[27] Her visit cheered him up, but 'I had very little to ask her.'[28] As soon as she'd left Paris, he realised he should have questioned her on many other points. 'You arrived in Paris like the Messiah, but you left like a demon and were gone like a dream.'[29]

By June he was thinking about his promise to write on Montesquiou. Without mentioning his name, the notes to *Sesame and Lilies* refer to him as a great contemporary idolater the translator has often compared with Ruskin, but in the new critique, which Proust titled 'Un Professeur de beauté', he accoladed the art criticism in the new book: 'there is perhaps more truth of artistic judgment, of justice in taste, in each of these short essays than in Ruskin's big books', Montesquiou's talent consists 'above all of being able to see distinctly where others can see only indistinctly', and each of the essays was 'an original creation, carefully thought out . . . and with what marvellous richness, what strength and what originality!'[30]

In June Anna de Noailles broke the long silence by sending Proust a copy of her new novel *La Domination*. To the adulation he spread over two long letters, full of quotations to show

how carefully he'd read it,[31] she responded by inviting him to dinner on 10 June. He felt too weak to accept:[32] he was coughing a lot and his throat was sore, but after surviving the first ten days of June without a real attack, he hired a closed carriage. Extravagantly keeping it from 6.30 in the evening till 1.15 in the morning, he dined alone at Larue's and went on to the de Noailles' house, where he made peace not only with them but with Barrès.[33] Five days later, when 'Sur la lecture' appeared in *La Renaissance latine*, Anna was at last able to reward him for his unstinting generosity towards her work. 'My dear friend, I see nobody who is not dazzled, moved, touched, made morally better by the dear, divine pages you have written. . . . I thank you for each line of these pages as for a perfect and tender happiness.'[34] Her enthusiasm encouraged the critic André Beaunier, who wrote such a long and encomiastic review in *Le Figaro* that Proust almost had the impression he'd been writing at Anna's dictation.[35] He called the essay 'charming, moving, in several passages marvellous', and went on to describe the style: 'These long phrases, weighed down with all the details and all the circumstances, have a strange and distinctive charm: it is meticulous veracity which gives it to them, and they are disturbing because the smallest truth which is wholly true has something frightening in it.'[36]

The next day, Anna called at his flat, left without seeing him, but wrote another letter about his essay: 'I swear to you it has made a *great*, deep impression on Paris. Everybody, I mean the people who matter, because I do not know whether the others exist, everybody, then, has read these unique pages.'[37] He'd been asleep when she called, he told her, dreaming 'that the greatest poet of all time writes to me that I am marvellous, that I have talent, I wake up, I am already irked at not having the letter from this sublime poet. But I do not have two seconds to wait, for I ring and her letter is immediately brought in.'[38]

Reynaldo was less impressed by the Proustian syntax. Invited to comment on the proofs of *Sesame and Lilies*, he objected to a sentence which went on for fifty-five lines, and he made several suggestions, but apart from rewording a sentence which had the word 'avoir' too close to the word 'avait', Proust ignored the advice. But the experience of correcting the proofs led him to an important insight, which he wrote down in the form of a note on Ruskin's epigraph, a quotation from Lucian:

'You shall each have a cake of sesame, – and ten pounds.' For Proust this sentence projected 'like an additional ray of light that not only touches the last sentences of the lecture but retrospectively illuminates all that preceded'. Reading could open the door of treasuries which contained wisdom, just as the word 'Sesame' opened the door of the thieves' cave. But, by insisting on the grain of sesame, the epigraph pointed to the primordial meaning of the word, while its meaning in Ruskin's title is at two removes from this. The third meaning is what Proust calls 'an allegory of an allegory'.

> From the beginning Ruskin exposes in this way his three themes and at the end of the lecture he will combine them inextricably in the final sentence, where the final chord will recall the tonality of the beginning. . . . He moves apparently at random from one idea to the next. But in reality the imagination which leads him follows his deep inclinations, which impose a superior logic on him in spite of himself. So much so that at the end he finds he has obeyed a sort of secret plan which, finally unveiled, retrospectively imposes a kind of order on the whole and makes it appear magnificently organised to culminate in this apotheosis.[39]

This was Proust's principle in his long sentences. Mistrusting the intellect, he believed he was more likely to be steered by deep inclinations if he tried to abdicate from conscious control over his material, preserving as long as possible his ignorance of where each sentence would carry him. Once he'd begun a sentence, he tried to let the middle float freely. He wrote very fast, trying to reclaim solid possessions from the waters of Lethe and to catch almost unawares the self he equated with the past, seeing his existence as indistinguishable from his memories. He didn't move at random from one idea to the next, but he did believe a superior logic would impose itself if he gave it a chance. At a risk of confusing the reader, he lets the narrative flow from one time to another, one place to another. As in dreams, the dead are revived; he lets one place, one phase of his life melt into another without signposting the transition. The underlying idea is close to Freud's principle of free association; say whatever comes into your mind and more significant patterns will emerge than the ones you'd have imposed by planning or structuring. Perhaps Proust had already glimpsed a possibility of using Ruskin's idea, letting his imagination follow his deep inclinations not just in long sentences but in a book as long as any of Ruskin's.

FOURTEEN

CATASTROPHE

Of the marriages that were putting paid to so many bachelor friendships, Loche's was the only one in which Proust was humiliated. As he'd indicated in his portrait of the prince, their relationship was precarious. Like Albu's, Loche's personality had almost nothing in common with his, but Loche was less good-natured. In spite of the unposted letter telling him their friendship was at an end, Proust had invited him to the tea party, and he sent a thoughtfully chosen wedding present – a twelfth-century alabaster figure of Christ engraved on its pedestal with a quotation from Ruskin. The present he received in return was ambiguous – a gold tie-pin in the shape of a hunting horn – the Radziwill family crest. It was believed that tie-pins brought bad luck, and when no invitation arrived for the wedding on 27 June, Proust consulted his mother about whether to send the tie-pin back. She advised him not to. 'It is the only thing I can do,' he told her, 'which, so far as the others are concerned, shows that I do not accept a line of action whose motive I do not understand, although there evidently is one.'[1] But it looked more as if the tie-pin had brought bad luck on the giver: a week after marrying his nineteen-year-old cousin, he left her, and their divorce (in July 1906) was followed by Papal annulment of the marriage.

The one rapprochement in Proust's life was with Montesquiou – a rapprochement caused by neither the reading in Proust's flat nor the encomiastic article on his art criticism but by the death of his faithful valet Yturri. There was still no cure for diabetes, and in April Yturri had been sent to recuperate in a Frankfurt clinic, but had insisted on returning for his master's lecture on 21 April. He was extremely feeble, and the June heatwave, coming suddenly after a long spell of cold weather, exacerbated his condition. Unaware that his mother was too ill to be sent on errands, Proust twice sent her to enquire about Yturri, and the second time she arrived in Neuilly too late. Instead of telling her son the bad news immediately, she prepared him for it by saying Yturri was in a very bad state; it was only in the evening she admitted he was dead.[2] As he'd shown after the death of Reynaldo's father, Antoine's mother and Lucien's father, Proust was at his best when consoling a bereaved friend. Montesquiou didn't find it easy to be emotionally direct, but in his responses to Proust's understanding letters he took the unprecedented risk of writing to him with neither irony nor formality.

Proust had been living ever since his father's death with the fear that his mother, though only fifty-four when she was widowed, would have little incentive to stay alive. 'Mamma, who loves us so much, does not understand how cruel it is not to want to get better.'[3] Having failed to go on holiday with her in the summer, he was again too ill. The heatwave which had been lethal for Yturri had been beneficial to Proust, but the revitalisation had been brief. When he wrote to Louisa in mid-July, he hadn't been outside the flat for three weeks. 'I have a beard which no longer even looks dirty because it is so long.'[4]

Imprudently, he got up to attend the duchesse de Gramont's funeral at eleven in the morning of 28 July, and went on afterwards to consult Dr Brissaud, who recommended treatment in the sanatorium of the neurologist Paul-Auguste Sollier in Boulogne (Billancourt). 'But one can only see doctors during the day. And I pay for each daytime outing with a month of high temperatures.' The additional cost of this outing was an attack of bronchitis,[5] while his eyes were hurting more than ever. His handwriting changed during the summer, the letters becoming larger.[6] Nothing was done to give him a better electric lamp. 'I am not writing to you at great length,' he told Louisa in August, 'because my eyesight is permanently tired by the lighting of the household or rather the menagerie in which I work, with crude light falling on me from above as on the face of poor dazed lions.'[7]

He was still unwell in September, when he left for Evian with his mother. He arrived in a state of collapse, but her state was still worse. Like many people close to death, she'd been siding with the forces of destruction and weakening her body by adamantly refusing to eat. The train journey brought on a severe attack of nephritis. 'Two hours after our arrival Mamma had a fit of vomiting and giddiness and became gravely ill.'[8]

As usual, she tried to ignore symptoms, doing her best to carry on as if she were quite well, except that she went on refusing to take any food. 'When the giddiness was at its worst, I had the ordeal of watching her, in spite of everything I could tell her, go down in the morning into the lounge, so that she had to hold on to two people to stop herself from falling over. In such a feeble state that only the fact of her having eaten nothing for two weeks can give you any idea of it, she goes on forcing herself to get up, wash, put all her clothes on, which is horrible for her. And impossible to make her take any medicine.'[9] She went on refusing to admit she was ill, and when Mme Catusse, who lived nearby, arrived in response to Proust's telephone call, all his mother seemed to want was to have her photograph taken. 'She was torn between the wish to leave me a final image of herself and anxiety it might be an unbearably grim one.'[10] In À la recherche it is the dying grandmother who hesitates about whether her grandson ought to have a picture of her to keep, or whether she'd changed so much that it would be worse than not having one.[11]

Since Proust was too ill to travel back with her to Paris, Robert came to Evian, and her reluctance to leave was neutralised by her feeling of uselessness: 'Like this I can no longer be of any help to you when you're ill.'[12] Though the journey made her worse, she was still resistant when Robert insisted on her seeing a doctor. Her uraemia was so bad she should never have left Paris. By the time Proust arrived back at the flat, she seemed slightly better, and the doctor said that if she survived the crisis, her health would be no worse than before. But 'I am sure she is convinced the opposite is true and that morally she is suffering terribly. I had always wanted to survive her, to spare her the grief of losing me. But I do not know whether her present anxiety is at thinking she may be on the point of departing from us, leaving me so incapable of being alone in life, or whether the fear that she may go on living incompletely, damaged, is torturing her still more.'[13]

Literary to the end, the dying woman communicated with her heartbroken son through quotations. 'I never saw a better-timed departure' came from Molière's Le Misanthrope, and, more indistinctly, she repeated the Corneille line she'd so often used in his childhood when he was tearful about an impending separation: 'If you are a Roman, then deserve to be one.' In her final coma she trembled whenever she heard the bell ringing. On 26 September 'she died at the age of fifty-six, looking thirty, because the illness had thinned her and above all because death has restored her youth of the period before her sufferings, when she had no grey hairs'.[14] Helplessly he went on kissing the dead face.[15] 'To me,' said Anna de Noailles, 'the unhappiness of other people seems less shattering than yours.'[16]

The funeral was on the 28th. No prayers were said, but there were flowers on the hearse, which left the rue de Courcelles at noon. The report in *Le Figaro* mentioned the wreaths from the marquis d'Albufera and Mme Félix Faure[17] but not 'that immense crown of admirable flowers'[18] Louisa had sent. Many of Dr Proust's most distinguished colleagues came to the funeral, as did Albu and his wife, Anna and her husband, the comte and comtesse Adhéaume de Chevigné, the vicomte and vicomtesse de Grouchy, the baron Robert de Rothschild, Reynaldo, Lucien, Henri Bergson, Abel Hermant and Francis de Croisset.

In the flat Proust was left alone with the servants, who moved silently about in the way she'd trained them. He couldn't sleep, but they were reminding him constantly of the efforts she'd made to protect him from being disturbed. He knew he couldn't go on living in this flat, which would endlessly remind him of her. 'I have gone into certain rooms which chance ordains I had not revisited, and I have explored unknown areas of my grief, which spreads ever more widely as I go further into it.'[19] To Montesquiou, who hadn't recovered from Yturri's death, Proust wrote: 'From now on my life has lost its one aim, its one sweetness, its one love, its one consolation. . . . I have been drenched with all the sorrows, I have lost her, I have seen her suffer, I can believe she knew she was leaving me and was unable to give me any advice, but it may have been agony for her to remain silent, and I have the feeling that because of my poor health I was the sorrow and the anxiety of her life.'[20]

For several days he stayed in bed, weeping, grieving, not eating, and writing only brief notes to close friends, telling them not to come.[21] The one welcome visitor was his uncle Georges. Proust had often gone with his mother to have dinner at her brother's flat in the boulevard Haussmann, and it was

surprisingly comforting to have long conversations with him
about her: never before had he heard so much about her from
another viewpoint. His uncle called almost every evening until
his health – he too was suffering from uraemia – stopped him
from coming.[22]

All through November Proust could do nothing except take
the elementary actions to keep himself alive. Depressively
browsing through his parents' papers, he had moments of
feeling almost happy – transported into the past when they
were still alive, and still further into the past when a photograph or letter offered a link. They'd often dined, for instance,
with M. d'Osmond, the nephew of Mme de Boigne, who'd
written her memoirs for him. His photograph therefore
reminded Proust of balls at which Marie-Antoinette had
danced.[23]

He thought a great deal about his mother's hesitation over
whether to have her photograph taken for him. She had left
him many images of herself, but one he'd never lose was that
of her newly dead face. In the novel he draws on his father's
death in making the grandmother have her final stroke in a
public lavatory, and on his mother's in making the dead face
look suddenly young.

As my lips touched her, my grandmother's hands quivered,
a long shudder ran right through her whole body, possibly
a reflex, or possibly certain forms of tenderness have a hyper-
aesthesia which recognises through the veil of unconsciousness what they can cherish almost without needing to sense
it. Suddenly my grandmother half sat up, made a violent
effort like someone defending her life. . . . My grandmother
was dead.

A few hours later Françoise could for the last time, and
without causing any pain, comb that beautiful hair which
was only beginning to grey and which had seemed younger
than she was. But now, on the contrary, it was alone in
setting the crown of age on the rejuvenated face from which
the lines had vanished together with the wrinkles, swellings,
strains, sagging, added over so many years by suffering. As
in the distant time when her parents had chosen a spouse for
her, she had features delicately traced by purity and submiss-
iveness, cheeks glowing with chaste hopefulness, a dream of
happiness, even with an innocent gaiety, which the years had
little by little destroyed. Life in withdrawing had just

removed the disillusionments of life. A smile seemed to have settled on my grandmother's lips. On this last resting place, death, like a medieval sculptor, had put her down in the form of a young girl.[24]

IV

1905–9
FREEDOM TO WRITE

FIFTEEN

NUMBED

The loss of his mother was the biggest challenge Proust ever had to face. Death had smashed the looking glass he'd been using for thirty-four years – two-thirds of his life. The face it reflected had been the face of a child, little Marcel, and all his fiercest battles had been against his parents. Defeated in his first attempt at a relationship with a girl, when his mother's jealousy separated him from Marie, he'd been victorious in his evasion of jobs, but defeated in the battle over Ruskin, had gone on working as a translator.

The question now was what kind of maturity he'd achieve. For Baudelaire genius was 'childhood clearly formulated' and childhood rediscovered at will (*l'enfance retrouvée à volonté*). Proust will substitute involuntary memory for Baudelaire's will, but the lost time he'll search for is mainly childhood. The genius, says Baudelaire, will combine adult articulacy with the analytical mind that can bring order into accumulated experience. Proust's powers of observation and recall had been strengthened by the training he'd given himself. Already he was an adult version of Baudelaire's child, staring with animal curiosity when confronted with anything new.[1] But will his search for the past be escapist? Will he merely try to resurrect the dead mother, grandmother and father as if memories of them are more accurate and more real than the people were when alive? Will he stare at the outside world with childlike stubbornness or shut his eyes to recall memories as if they were more precise than they actually are?

As a lover he'll never again feel inhibited by interrogation from his mother, or by her unvoiced suspicions, but as an invalid he'll be alone. Doctors will prescribe, friends will sympathise, servants will carry out orders and make tentative suggestions, but no one will enter into partnership as she and his grandmother did. In *Jeunes Filles*, wanting to keep the

Narrator's mother alive, Proust uses the dead grandmother as a receptacle for memories of his mother.

> I knew, when I was with my grandmother, however much pain I was in, it would be received with sympathy still greater; that everything which was mine, my cares, my desires, would be supported in my grandmother by a desire far stronger than I had myself to preserve and enhance my own life; and my thoughts extended undeviatingly into her because they moved from my mind into hers without any change of milieu or personality. . . . When I had my mouth glued to her cheeks, to her forehead, I was drawing from her something so beneficial, so nourishing that I was as motionless, as serious, as calmly greedy as a baby at the breast.[2]

His asthma will never relax its grip, but for twenty-seven years daily negotiations with his mother have been integral to the disease. Unable to make her into a Jocasta, he made her into a nurse, addicting himself to a need no one else could satisfy. No lover will ever share his home except male employees, and he'll make unrealistic demands on the feminine side of their nature. With the most important of these, Alfred Agostinelli, he'll succeed in establishing a goodnight-kiss routine, and though he'll fail, in reality, to make Alfred into a woman, he'll pull off a greater fictional coup than the translation of Reynaldo into Françoise when he makes Alfred into Albertine.

From now on Proust will have a home of his own and money of his own. After thirty-four years of financial dependence, after living twice as long as most people do in his parents' home, waited on by their servants, he's now in control of funds and living space, with unrivalled authority over servants. Never again will a footman be instructed not to light a fire in his room or not to serve his food. But can he move confidently into the future, or will he live parasitically on the past? His main achievement, packed into the last fifteen of his fifty-two years, will be a massive novel about repossessing the past, and his ambivalence will surface in such sequences as one in which he resents the presence of the woman he loves, Albertine, because she distracts him from memories of his grandmother.

Again and again he comes back to this question of whether past pleasures and pains remain in our possession. Even if they do, they are inaccessible most of the time, and we're no longer the same person who experienced them. It was his mother's death that convinced him we never fully experience anything except retrospectively. The presence of the beloved person or object or landscape activates the senses; the imagination functions only in their absence. When his mother was alive, he couldn't have written about the free passage of thoughts from his mind to hers or the feeling of being nourished when he kissed her. He often felt unsure whether he could get through the next hour or day or week without her, but impatience for her presence had always yielded to impatience with it: only after losing her permanently could he know what he'd lost. This loss was the starting point for all his best work.

It was work that could be done only in isolation. He'd taken a crucial step towards cutting himself off from other people in 1897 when he started staying awake at night and sleeping through the day, but for eight years deterioration in his health had progressively been attenuating his connections with the outside world. Sometimes he'd spend six hours a day on fumigations which produced an atmosphere almost unbreathable to other people. The fumes lingered stubbornly in the room, helping him to breathe but making everyone else cough and bringing tears to their eyes.

Sooner or later he must carry out his intention of going into a clinic. He booked a room at Dr Déjérine's clinic in the rue Blomet for three months, but on the day he should have moved in, he asked Dr Sollier to call, hoping he could arrange to be treated in his own bed. This was out of the question, said the doctor, but instead of going to Déjérine's clinic, he went to Sollier's in Boulogne-sur-Seine (or Billancourt). There the doctor failed to win his confidence, though an argument they had about Bergson can hardly have been as crucial as Proust made it out to be. Probably Dr Déjérine was making a major tactical mistake in forbidding his patient to write. Letters had served as a safety valve for feelings that had to be contained when he was confined to bed. He defied the veto in a letter to Louisa[3] and a brief note to Marie Nordlinger,[4] but before mid-December he'd decided 'my treatment is doing me the greatest harm and I think I shall break it off without waiting for more'.[5] But he did wait.

One stratagem for coping with isolation was his loquacious letter-writing. Deprived by the doctor's veto of this vicarious contact with friends, he rapidly lost faith in the future, becoming unhappy and pessimistic. Lucien came to see him twice, but they quarrelled both times.[6] If Proust had still been hopeful when he moved in, he soon understood the disease was incurable, though he was unrealistic about the speed at which it would kill him. He felt glad his mother had died without realising how bleak his prospects were.[7] Breaking the rules in January 1906 to write a letter of condolence to Francis de Croisset, who'd lost his mother, Proust admitted to envy 'at your having by your talent and your glory given such great pleasure to your Mother that you should be able to think of the past with a satisfaction that has been denied to me'.[8]

He moved out of the clinic in the last week of January 1906, feeling worse than when he moved in, but he'd have been feeling worse still if he'd stayed in the flat. The six weeks of supervised rest had got him over the worst of the pain. Back in the flat, alone with the servants, he stayed in bed, and Dr Sollier called twice to examine him, but in February he started getting up at five in the afternoon. Albu called every day, and Proust soon resumed the helpful role he liked to play in his friends' lives. Antoine, who wanted his new play to be read by Alphonse Franck, director of the Théâtre du Gymnase, was advised to congratulate Madeleine Lemaire, a friend of Franck, on being awarded the Légion d'honneur. By March Proust could usually count on having five good hours, from five o'clock onwards, when friends could call. He was thirsting for more conversation with Mme Catusse about his mother. She'd find him in a pullover – he could scarcely ever bear tight-fitting clothes – and she was instructed to tell no one else he was well enough to receive visitors.[9] Apart from her, Albu and Lucien, he received Mme Straus and Mme Lemaire, who promised to approach Franck as soon as Antoine's play was ready.[10]

His first venture into the open air was planned carefully. If he went for a walk by himself, he could avoid opening his mouth and letting cold air in.[11] Making therapeutic plans in isolation was less fun than making them with his mother, but at least he could chat to friends in letters. In the second week of March he felt worse than he had in three years,[12] but while reading Antoine's play, he got so absorbed he forgot he was warming up a medicine, and the overheated bottle exploded, staining the walls, the cover of the script and the notes he was

making.[13] Though it was an effort to write, these notes grew
to eleven pages. He didn't get up the next day,[14] and after
catching influenza on an Easter Sunday outing to meet Guiche,
he had to stay in bed for two weeks,[15] and indoors for three.
As Reynaldo said, he obviously needed a doctor, but, not
wanting to go on using Sollier, he called in Maurice Bize,
who'd been his first choice in August 1903, during his father's
absence, when he saw Dr Vaquez only because Bize was
unavailable. Bize, who'd been at medical school with Robert,
was a small man, affable, calm, serious, polite.[16] But Proust
didn't take the 'thousand medicines' he prescribed. 'This is
only the hour of consultation. The hour of obedience is yet to
come.'[17] It never did come: he went on for the rest of his life
calling Bize in and discussing symptoms but ignoring advice.
It was almost as if Proust were intent on demonstrating
allegiance to the mother who'd trusted her sickroom instincts
more than any doctor's prescriptions. Only two kinds of tablets
now had a place on Proust's bedside table – Veronal for use as
a sedative and caffeine for use as a stimulant.[18]

He hadn't been in touch with Montesquiou since his period in
the clinic, and in May, when the comte wrote, Proust invited
him to call after nine in the evening 'if a very warm room
does not alarm you'.[19] Two weeks later, when Montesquiou
lectured on Gustave Moreau to open an exhibition of his work
at a gallery in the rue de Sèze, Proust said he'd been planning
to come but had been stopped by a high temperature. He was
so eager to see the exhibition, which was on from 9 to 28
May, that he tried to get himself admitted late one evening.
An old schoolfriend of Antoine's was working for the gallery
– Jacques Copeau, who was later to make his name in the
theatre – but he was unable, he said, to make any special
arrangement for Proust.[20]

Waiting for the translation of *Sesame and Lilies* to be published in early June, Proust felt depressively envious of Lucien,
who seemed so creative, so talented. 'It would be so satisfying
before I die to do something which would have pleased
Mamma. So when I hear you saying you feel discouraged and
that you would like to smash the frames of your paintings, I
tell myself what an ungrateful little fellow he is, towards life
and towards God.'[21] Proust still hadn't got used to having no
mother. 'I do not stop thinking about her for a moment, even

while sleeping, I see her near me all the time, do not stop interrogating her about everything I do, and believe I hear her answering me.'[22] 'I dream about her as soon as I fall asleep, and as I sleep several times, I dream of her several times each day. But almost invariably she is in so much pain and so sad that it hurts me infinitely, and in contrast to what most people experience it is almost a relief to learn on waking that this is false, that she is not sad, that she is no longer in pain.'

Depression and illness interpenetrated. 'My strength is being sapped by so many months without any air.'[23] Still too ill to go out or dress,[24] or even get out of bed until after dinner, he decided to send out the presentation copies of Sesame and Lilies himself, because the publisher, Mercure de France, had been so inefficient over sending out The Bible of Amiens. 'For several days I have been working like a grocer with balls of string and wrapping paper and Paris directories.'[25] Once again he was promising himself to start going for walks, even if he dressed only by throwing an overcoat over what he'd been wearing in bed. But plans were fantasies; he cheered himself up by deciding next year he'd go out every day.[26]

He wrote to Gaston Calmette, asking whether Sesame and Lilies could be reviewed or at least mentioned in Le Figaro, and offering to write about it. The ideal reviewer would be Anna de Noailles, but Calmette shouldn't tell her he'd suggested her, and shouldn't approach Beaunier, 'who has already been so kind to me (that it would be better not to importune him)'.[27] On 5 June a profile appeared on the front page of the paper. 'M. Marcel Proust. One of our most subtle, most refined writers. Prose writer and poet. . . . His translations are very faithful and of such quality that they add to the beautiful Ruskinian work a beautiful French work. . . . A man of scholarship with the skills of an essayist – what is rarer, more valuable?' The piece was unsigned. Delighted, Proust immediately wrote to thank Calmette,[28] and discovering Beaunier had written it, thanked him profusely, insisting he wasn't scholarly or subtle or refined, 'or anything of what you say in your inconceivable goodness'.[29]

But Calmette and Beaunier hadn't finished. Prominent on the front page of the 14 June issue was a long review calling the translation

a masterpiece of intelligent tractability, an astonishing

success. . . . He reads Ruskin rather in the way Montaigne read Plutarch: he tests his own thinking through contact with that of another; he questions himself on how much he believes in this or that opinion of a man he respects; he has doubts, he sees the multiple differences between the affirmation of the other and that which he would have liked to formulate; and by slow degrees he arrives at giving an account of himself. This is the strategy of a delicate moralist, irresolute because he has the spirit of finesse and sees the different aspects of things.[30]

It was hard to accept so much praise. Like maternal love, it was almost intolerable, because of the pain he'd endure if it were withdrawn. 'I am afraid Beaunier will take a dislike to me, and I like him so much that it would hurt me enormously. I shall never publish another line (alas that is quite probable in any case) without first demanding a written promise that he will not discuss it.'[31] Proust thanked Calmette with a painting by Madeleine Lemaire. 'I wanted flowers to convey my message to you and my grateful thoughts. And for them to last as long as what they express, and not to fade, I asked Mme Madeleine Lemaire to paint them, knowing a bouquet would be more welcome if it bore her signature, which you value.'[32]

His happiness at the profile and review was mixed with incredulity when he found they'd been read by none of the friends who'd been visiting him. Reynaldo had somehow missed both, while Albu, after saying it was strange *Le Figaro* had ignored the book, told Proust he must be mistaken about the two pieces. 'My wife reads *Le Figaro* every morning from cover to cover, and there has been absolutely nothing about you in it.' Lucien, who also read *Le Figaro* every morning, missed both pieces, and asked Proust to send them.[33]

In spite of Beaunier's review, Proust felt sure he wasn't writing as well as he had in *Les Plaisirs et les jours*. 'As for the notes, they are pure chit-chat, and I would prefer to work seriously. But a minimum of physical well-being is necessary not just for working but even for receiving poetic impressions from the external world. And when one feels better for a second and they are there, one enjoys them as a convalescent pleasure, but one's strength, constantly engaged in repairing the ravages of the disease, cannot be diverted into availability for incarnating what one has felt.'[34] Half aware his plans for the future were too much like daydreams, he made sporadic efforts to translate them into reality, but on 18 June, when he went out for a fifteen-minute walk without getting properly dressed, asthma attacked him so fiercely that he went back, defeated, to his old habit of rising at ten in the evening.[35]

Despite his debility, his sexuality was reasserting itself. After living too close to his parents for so long, he at last had as much freedom as he'd had in 1894 on holiday with Reynaldo or in Venice without his mother during 1900. Most of his friendships with handsome young noblemen had been Platonic; now he was free to be sexually intimate with social inferiors. A June letter to Reynaldo asks about a young man called Bardac. Is 'this guinea-pig in pink coral' currently in Paris? 'What is his Christian name? I would write to him. . . .'[36]

In July Lucien is asked to find out the name of a young employee of the Swedish legation.[37] In August the thirty-one-year-old nephew of Proust's cook, Félicie Fitau, Robert Ulrich, returned via a friend of Reynaldo's a thousand francs Proust had either loaned him or tried to give him.[38] After about twelve years of service in the Republican Guard, Ulrich was a corporal, and in November Proust reasked de Billy whether he could pull strings to get him a job in the office of the Ministry of War, or find a job for another young man, a twenty-five-year-old, 'very distinguished and good in appearance, writing well, quite good at book-keeping, very nice manners, very serious but not educated beyond a certain point'.[39] And in December Proust tried through Reynaldo to get two theatre tickets for Ulrich.[40]

The favour Proust asked Lucien in July was to find out the identity of the *Gaulois* reviewer who'd signed himself 'Pepper and Salt' and written: 'M. Marcel Proust is right to popularise among us the curious works of this poet–philosopher who speaks sometimes with the ardent voice of inspiration, sometimes with the prickly accent of the pedagogue, who utters righteous shouts and devious explanations, who is good at feeling and not so good at reasoning. . . .'[41] The reviewer was Léon Daudet, but it wasn't from his brother that Proust found out. He concluded that Léon had been motivated more by goodness than by taste, 'that Ruskin and I set his teeth on edge, and that he went at it like a dog being whipped, or rather whipping himself'.[42]

The July issue of *Le Mouvement* carried a favourable review written by Marcel Cruppi, a distant relation, his mother being the granddaughter of Mme Proust's great uncle. Thanking Cruppi, Proust objected to his differentiation between writers who excite blind love and those who provoke long commentaries. 'I think they are the same, but taken at a different stage in our admiration for them. What I believe is that they are fruitful only in the first period, when we admire them blindly, because then they act on our sensibility. Later they excite only our critical sense. . . .' Sometimes, he said, he shared a writer's opinions without admiring him, but had infinite admiration for Ruskin, while seldom agreeing with him.[43]

Another review appeared in the new review *Les Lettres*: 'M. Marcel Proust's translation is written in excellent French. . . . A translation of this kind is a veritable collaboration. One must congratulate the charming author of *Les Plaisirs et les jours*'. Fernand Gregh was one of the principal contributors to *Les Lettres*, and since the review was signed Henry Chalgrain, a pseudonym he'd used in *Le Banquet*, Proust assumed Gregh was the reviewer,[44] but it was his wife.

Still trying to help Louisa, Proust received a visit from her on 12 July. Réjane was forming a company for a new theatre she was opening in December, and Louisa was hoping to work there. Proust asked Reynaldo to 'advise Réjane to say something friendly to Mornand',[45] but it led to nothing.

The day she visited Proust was the day the appeal court quashed the verdict passed at Rennes seven years earlier, when Dreyfus had been found 'guilty with extenuating circumstances'. It was obvious the court's deliberations had been unreasonably protracted, and on 14 July, when the Chamber of Deputies voted to rehabilitate Dreyfus and Picquart, this was only an opportunistic manoeuvre, consequent on the electoral success in May of the radicals and united socialists, who were out to damage the army and the Church. Six days later, in a ceremony at the École Militaire, Dreyfus, elevated to the rank of commandant, was made a *chevalier* in the Légion d'honneur. Picquart, who'd been forced into retirement during 1898, became a general, and, later in the year, minister of war. Nor was Zola forgotten. On 13 July the deputies voted for his remains to be moved to the Panthéon. But Reinach was ignored, though, as Proust said, 'he did much more than Zola'.[46]

Proust knew the rehabilitation of Dreyfus and Picquart had nothing to do with justice. Without forgetting what General Mercier had done, Proust felt sorry for this seventy-five-year-old man when he was insulted in the Chamber by men who'd been Dreyfusards for only a few weeks,[47] and was savaged by the press as if he alone had been responsible for the miscarriage of justice. 'It is horrible to read,' wrote Proust, 'because in the most wicked man there is a poor innocent horse which suffers, a heart, a liver, arteries, where there is no malice and which are in pain. And the beautiful hour of triumph is spoilt because there is always someone who suffers.'[48] For the two principal victims of the affair, life had been 'like a fairy story or a romantic novel'. But this was exceptional. 'Alas, for ten years, we have all had plenty of griefs, plenty of disappointments and plenty of torments in our life. And for none of us is the hour going to strike when grief changes into ecstasy, disappointment into unexpected fulfilment and torment into delicious triumphs. My illness will become worse, the people I have lost I will miss more and more, and everything I have dreamed of getting from life will become increasingly inaccessible.'[49]

The only therapy he could offer himself was another bout of planning for a holiday he'd never take. His first idea was to hire a boat and sail round the coast of Normandy and Brittany, sleeping on board, but he couldn't afford a large yacht, and maybe the smaller ones were unsafe. Why not rent a villa near Cabourg with Albu and his wife? Perhaps, once he knew their address, Mme Straus could find out whether the area would be healthy for him. Or he could rent a chalet in Trouville, taking Félicie with him. Did Mme Straus know whether the Chalet d'Harcourt was available, and if so was it draughty? Or he might rent a two-room suite at the Hôtel des Roches Noirs, unless the walls were too thin. Besides, the sea air and the evening mist from the valley would be bad for him. 'Nevertheless, if I could find a well-built property, not humid, not dusty, modern and sparse in style, not crowded behind the houses but either on the beach or on the hills and not costing more than a thousand francs for the month of August, I would perhaps take it.' At a hotel, of course, he'd be prepared to pay more, but then the price would include food. But even if he implemented one of these plans, he might be ill and have to leave after two days.[50] He was partially aware of the fantasy element in his preparations. 'In this time of "holidays" my consumption of timetables is frightening (and Platonic) and I mug up a thousand "circular voyages" which I make between two o'clock and six o'clock in the morning on my chaise longue.'[51] In *À la recherche*, Swann, when Odette leaves him, will 'plunge into the most intoxicating of romantic novels, the railway timetable which taught him means of rejoining her'.[52]

Two days later Proust doubled the amount he was willing to offer for a villa in Trouville, provided it was 'really dry, *not among the trees*, high but not overlooking the valley where there is mist (high, I mean not in the town, but on the beach would suit me well), electricity if possible, built fairly recently, neither dusty (the modern style is the type I need for breathing easily – what a style –) nor humid; I need only my master bedroom, two servants' rooms, a dining-room, a kitchen. A bathroom is not essential, though very agreeable. A drawing-room useless. The more WCs the better.'[53]

Three days later he was still hesitating, though the possibility of sharing a villa with the Albuferas had almost vanished. Albu had left for Germany, where his brother-in-law, Prince Eugène Murat, had been killed on 26 July in a motoring accident. Still unable to choose between a villa and a hotel, Proust was sharing hesitations with Mme Straus as he once had with his mother. Would it be ridiculous to take his old cook to a hotel? 'Wherever it is, I would like gas not to be indispensable; because if there is gas, I cannot make use of it because it makes me ill.'[54]

Five days later, on Monday 6 August, he moved into the Hôtel des Réservoirs in Versailles, only fifteen miles from the centre of Paris. Knowing his uncle Georges was seriously ill, he'd decided he couldn't go further afield: 'I felt the force of my will to leave wear away.'[55] Once he'd settled into the hotel, which Reynaldo sometimes used when trying to concentrate on work, Proust felt ill himself. 'I believe that as soon as I am in a state to leave Versailles,' he told Mme Straus, 'I will do so. But even if I should go to Trouville, it would not be immediately, because I am too exhausted.' The hotel, an eighteenth-century mansion, had been built for Mme de Pompadour, and Proust had 'an immense and admirable suite (which is certainly going to cost me much more than Trouville!) but so depressing, black and glazed with pictures, tapestries and looking glasses. . . . I do not know how it has been arranged for the sun never to penetrate it at any hour.' But he had two pianos, with a bust on one of them.[56]

He wrote to ask Reynaldo how much to tip the maid, the valet de chambre, the telephonist, the hall porter with theatrically powdered hair and the head waiter, Hector, who'd opened an antiquarian business as a sideline. One of the guests was a painter who knew Reynaldo – Hans Schlesinger. He told Proust his beard suited him: 'they always look good on an old or ageing face'.[57]

Thinking about his uncle's uraemia, Proust was thinking about his mother's. Georges Weil's illness had taken the form of muscular paralysis, and for two months almost every movement had made him cry out in pain, but physical pain had played such a small part in Mme Proust's suffering that no one could have known how difficult it was for her to cope with the progress of the disease. 'Since her death I have never gone for an hour without trying to relive what she must have thought and suffered after her return from Evian and, when I succeed in imagining such sufferings, I would far prefer her to have had physical pain, which I know she could have tolerated.'[58] His own life, he had to recognise, was less troubled without her. 'I no longer tremble constantly for her. So much so that since she is no longer there, I feel a frightful peacefulness, an agonising serenity. A great love is an agony at every moment.'[59]

Though Proust was also worrying about his uncle, the dying man didn't benefit from the proximity of his nephew, who made himself ill by forcing himself to get up and go out. 'Everything seems black and impossible when I have an asthma attack.'[60] On 22 August, when his uncle was in great pain, Proust threw a mackintosh over his nightshirt and travelled to Paris, but arrived too late for the dying man to recognise him.[61] Taken ill on the way back, he stayed for two hours at the Gare Saint-Lazare, where he tried to revive himself with coffee. The shaming accident he had (and refused to describe) was presumably due to coffee's diuretic effects, and he was helped by a likeable young railwayman. But, much as he wanted to attend his uncle's funeral on the 26th, he didn't trust himself to make another journey.[62]

The lease on the flat in the rue de Courcelles was going to run out in September, which prompted another orgy of abortive planning: de Lauris, de Billy and René Peter were mobilised into looking at flats for him. Peter was asked to inspect the empty mezzanine floor of the house in the boulevard Haussmann where uncle Georges had lived, and look at properties in the place Louvois, the rue de Prony and the rue Lapérouse.[63] De Lauris was briefed to find out about flats in new buildings with lifts in such streets as the rue Cambracères, rue de la Ville l'Évêque, rue Chateaubriand, rue Lord Byron, rue Washington and rue d'Artois, taking comfort, noise and dustiness into account.[64] He was generous with the time he spent. 'This tremendous list of flats in your handwriting, when one realised you had visited them all, became almost epic, heroic, and I felt quite small in face of your goodness.'[65] De Billy was told his goodness in inspecting flats had reduced Proust to tears, but the letter went on to ask another favour: would he without spending more than a hundred francs buy porcelain plates as a wedding present for Lucien's sister Edmée?[66] This mission was accomplished, but the hours de Billy, Peter and de Lauris spent on flat-hunting were all wasted. Wanting a familiar space, he opted for his dead uncle's flat:

> I could not make up my mind to go and live in a house which Mamma would not have known and for this year, as a transition, I have sub-leased a flat in our house in the boulevard Haussmann, where I often came to dinner with Mamma, where we sat together, watching my old uncle [his great-uncle, Louis Weil] dying in the room I shall occupy. So, you see, I shall have everything! The terrible dust, the trees under my window, almost touching it, the noise of the boulevard. . . .[67]

The boulevard even had a tramway in it.

A year after complaining in 'Sur la lecture' about living in rooms which reflected neither his taste nor his consciousness, rooms he'd played no part in furnishing, he couldn't take advantage of the chance to impose his own style on his surroundings. The house, which had belonged to Louis Weil, had been left jointly to his son Georges and his daughter. Her share was now divided between Proust and Robert, while Uncle Georges' share belonged to his widow, Émilie. When Peter, de Billy and de Lauris had been flat-hunting for him, Proust had meticulously stipulated his requirements, but he exempted himself from any obligation to respect them. 'With its gilt decorations on flesh-coloured walls, with the dust of the *quart-ier*, with incessant noise, and with trees leaning against the window, the flat obviously fails to correspond to the flat I was looking for.' Few men – especially invalids – would want to sleep in a room they associate with a deathbed, but Proust, believing it would bring him closer to his dead mother, willingly risked avoidable asthma attacks. 'If I cannot stay there I will leave,' he added.

It was a large flat on the first floor of No. 102 in the boulevard, with two drawing-rooms, an ante-chamber, a dining-room, a smoking-room and two bedrooms, plus rooms for servants, and it would be too expensive, he said, to be his permanent home, but it would be cheap for the first year because the rent was still being paid by someone else.[68]

Since his mother's death his friends had become less important to him. What he mainly wanted was contact with people who'd been close to her, and since the death of Uncle Georges, the best conversations he could have about her were with Mme Catusse. He was keen for her to visit him in Versailles though he was fending off other people with variations on the formula he used to Antoine – 'It is impossible to see me before eight o'clock in the evening and difficult after that.'[69] Reynaldo kept telephoning[70] and, ignoring discouragement, paid at least one visit, bringing books. The only invitation Proust issued was to M. and Mme Catusse: she should telephone him one day at five to find out whether he was well enough to give them dinner at the hotel. But she must mention the invitation to no one, to 'make sure you have no imitators, since it is so dangerously exhausting for me'. 'I have a small drawing-room where you will shut your eyes to my nightshirt and my pullovers.'[71]

It was with her that he indulged in his next elaborate game of planning. Since Robert and Marthe wanted none of the furniture from the rue de Courcelles, Proust had to make decisions about what should go where, and he wanted to have as much of the furniture as his new flat would hold.[72] Some of his grandparents' red furniture would have to go into the linen room and some into the bathroom. In his bedroom he'd have either the furniture from his father's bedroom or the blue furniture from his mother's, but not the black glass-fronted cabinet from her room – he preferred one that had been in the lumber room[73] – and not the oil painting done of her in 1880 by Mme Beauvais. It wasn't much good and 'I am afraid its vague resemblance to her, which was accurate only when Mamma was so incredibly rejuvenated by death, would be painful for me.' He would put it up, but in the large drawing-room, where he'd see it less often.[74] He was intending to keep all the old photographs, 'because I want my grandparents and even their parents, whom I did not know but whom Mamma loved, to be close to me'.[75]

He was sentimental about possessions and even carpets. The one from the dining-room 'is also an old servant. Could it not have an honourable retreat in some room?' But he was prepared to give away some of the bronze ornaments 'to people whose aesthetics are not on the same level as their goodness of heart'.[76] The room which, apart from his bedroom, would be in use most was the small drawing-room, and here he could use the furniture from the small drawing-room in the rue de Courcelles. If the noise of the trams and the other boulevard traffic made the large bedroom insufferable, he'd move into the small one, which adjoined the dining-room and overlooked the courtyard. The glass-fronted cabinet from the smoking-room could go into this room. If he decided to sleep in it, the large bedroom could become a third drawing-room, and most of the blue furniture would go into a store. His plan for coping with the problems of noise and dust was to have carpets and rugs in every room, and to buy one of the new vacuum cleaners, which were such a novelty that he was unsure about the spelling. In addition, the carpets in his room would have to be taken up and beaten regularly, so they shouldn't be nailed down.[77] Like his aunt Élisabeth, who controlled other people's lives from her bed in Illiers, Proust, bedridden in Versailles, wrote detailed instructions to Mme Catusse, who took on the unpaid role of interior decorator, arranging furniture, carpets, curtains and tapestries.

In October he started paying rent on the flat,[78] but a month later he still couldn't move in, because Robert and Émilie Weil had decided to let the empty flat on the mezzanine floor, and builders were noisily making alterations for the new tenant, a doctor.[79] 'That will force me to stay on indefinitely, freezing and paying out a great deal of money at Versailles, where, from my bed, I have not seen so much as a dead leaf or a jet of water.'[80] Neither the windows nor the doors of his rooms at the hotel would close properly, while, spending most of his time in bed, and the whole of it indoors, he saw neither the château nor the Trianon,[81] nor visited Yturri's grave, where Montesquiou had erected an imposing tombstone.[82] Life was deeply depressing. 'I do not open my eyes until darkness has fallen, and I often ask myself whether the hermetically sealed room lit with electricity is situated elsewhere than in Versailles, where I have not seen a single dead leaf floating on any of the lakes. Such is my splendid youth and my enviable life.'[83]

Nor did he catch more than a glimpse of the famous beauty, Gladys Deacon, who was staying in the room above his, though he suspected Robert Dreyfus of starting the rumour he was on good terms with her. He did muster the courage, one evening, to go up and knock on the door of her suite, but she was in bed, and he spoke only to her mother. Proust was in bed on the one occasion he saw her: wearing a thick veil, she was getting into a car.[84]

Throughout most of his life, Proust's campaign to monopolise his mother had involved him in carrying on as if his younger brother didn't exist. If she had at first tried to improve their relationship, she must have given up when they were still young, and in the rivalry for her attention Robert had no weapon to use against Marcel's illness. The younger son's only hope of winning back her love was by battling through to success as a doctor. No doubt both parents took pride in his achievements. The contrast between the brothers could hardly have been greater, and they both still tried to avoid direct confrontation, though they did so in different ways. Robert's strategy was to leave all decisions about furniture and tapestries to Marcel, who was told repeatedly: 'Whatever you decide is all right with me.' His strategy was to deal with Robert through intermediaries. Mme Catusse was asked to negotiate with him about tapestries. 'Your idea of talking to Robert is admirable. Because he will probably tell you more frankly what his wishes are, and whatever he wishes is what I wish.' She should meet him at the boulevard Haussmann flat, show him what she'd done, tell him Marcel wanted him to have half the carpets and tapestries, but she must go on to say they wouldn't look good in the boulevard Saint-Germain. 'But if he looks disappointed, give him everything he wants.' And she must not pay too much attention to Robert's protestations that Marcel should do whatever he wishes, because these 'can only be half sincere'. If Robert suggests his aunt should help in arranging the flat,

Mme Catusse should refuse, and she must be careful when talking to Robert and Mme Weil not to sound enthusiastic about the flat 'because they are my landlords, and, should I stay on, I would want them to give me substantial reductions'.[85]

There were big disadvantages in having them as his landlords. The sibling rivalry, so long concealed, was forced out into the open. They argued about marquetry furniture Proust said their mother had given him as a present, and to Robert it seemed absurd that Proust refused to have any of the other furniture sold, while to him it seemed extraordinary that Robert should refuse to accommodate any of it, except for the bureau from their father's study and half the carpets and tapestries. He couldn't have taken more without discarding furniture he'd already bought, but Proust convinced himself that Robert was forcing him to rent a bigger and more expensive flat than he really wanted. Even this one wasn't big enough to absorb all the inherited furniture. 'All right,' said Robert, 'fill the boulevard Haussmann as full as you can, stuff it so full that nobody can get in, and later on we'll see.'[86] Proust knew he was being 'sentimental', but he couldn't sell these objects which embodied his past. Wanting to sleep in his mother's bed, he was at first reluctant to have it remade. 'I would not allow anything to be touched in order to keep everything as it was in the last days.'[87] Something of her presence seemed to linger in the small pink marble table with gilded feet shaped like a goat's, and in the little chest of drawers he took to be Ceylonese or Japanese, with appliqué metal facing on the drawers.[88] But he was worried about the residual talcum powder in her furniture, and wondered whether to have his bedroom disinfected. Could he be sure the disinfectant left no smell?

Strain soon developed in his relations with Marthe, now the only Mme Proust in the family. Before he moved into the flat he was already thinking about moving out, since it was almost intolerable she should be one of his landlords. 'I shall no doubt take something a bit larger in the area of rue du Cherche-Midi or perhaps Neuilly.'[89] He had his furniture moved into the mezzanine flat in the boulevard Haussmann, hoping to leave it there until his carpets had been laid, but they made him move it all out.[90] Hostility towards them mingled with hostility towards himself: thanks to Mme Catusse, he came to realise the double danger of accumulating dust and living with furniture he wanted to keep but not to use. Since he needed constant warmth and slept during the day, the flat would have to be cleaned without opening windows and without making noise, except possibly at night. Ideally his home would be as barely furnished as a hospital; besides, William Morris had said: 'Have nothing in your houses that you do not know to be useful or believe to be beautiful.'[91] Not wanting to be the one who chose what to keep and what to store, Proust asked Mme Catusse to pick out the 'most exquisite' furniture and store everything else. Perhaps he'd eventually have to live in the country, and perhaps he'd use more of it then. For the moment, he didn't know whether he needed a desk. Would he ever write again except in bed? He decided to keep his great-uncle's bureau in its original place near the window in the small drawing-room. Here perhaps it would resume 'something of the inaesthetic but moving life it had preserved in my imagination, the only setting in which places remain the same'.[92]

The need to take decisions about furniture had helped to stop him from working. Since September he'd been wanting to collaborate on a play with the friendly René Peter, who'd harnessed his unexceptional talent into winning enviable success in boulevard theatre. Why shouldn't Proust, instead of envying, share a theatrical success? His plot idea was that a husband who adores his wife should use prostitutes to indulge sadistic inclinations and to devalue his feelings towards her. Talking about her to them, he becomes more compulsive in his need to degrade her, though he's soon disgusted with himself. One day, coming into the room unexpectedly, she over-hears what he's saying. After leaving him, she ignores all his entreaties to return. The prostitutes pursue him, but sadism would now be too painful for him, and he commits suicide.[93] The mixture of tough psychological realism with soft-centred boulevard melodrama was unpromising, but they completed the play, and Proust contributed two acts. In the middle of November he sent a copy to Reynaldo, wanting his reaction.[94]

But Proust was doing more reading than writing, and he enjoyed one of the books Reynaldo had brought – *Le Chevalier d'Hermental* by Alexandre Dumas. As he complained, 'it is very badly written', but the hero rents a room from a family which struck Proust as 'worthy of both Balzac and Paul de Cocke [*sic*]'.[95] Some critics had compared Paul de Kock with

Dostoevsky, and the family lives in a street called the rue des Temps-Perdu.

SIXTEEN

HOME OF HIS OWN

A t the end of 1906 no one could have predicted the thirty-five-year-old Proust would become a great novelist. He'd begun to escape from the thrall of Ruskin,[1] but the invalid life had conditioned him to inaction, and when it came to making plans, he was more unrealistic than ever. Either he'd dither endlessly, converting daydreams into double-entry book-keeping, involving friends in calculations of pros and cons as if their participation could solidify castles in the air, or else, desperate to stop himself from hesitating, act with foolhardy impulsiveness. His decision to move into the flat was even more precipitate than his decision about moving to Versailles. After a solitary Christmas in the hotel, he made up his mind in less than an hour.[2]

Far from feeling better, he thought he'd have to stay in bed indefinitely, and, expecting to be less uncomfortable in his own flat, he moved on 27 December, without giving Antoine, the concierge, and Jean Blanc, Dr Proust's former manservant, any chance to get the flat ready. (Of his parents' servants, the only other one he'd kept was Félicie, the cook, who'd been with him in Versailles.) He simply arrived, feverish and incapable of doing anything but collapse into bed. When, three days later, he contacted Mme Catusse, he told her to keep his arrival a secret.

Knowing he'd have to put up with noise and dust from the street, he'd moved at a time when he'd have to put up with extra noise and dust from the builders working on the floor underneath. He was hoping to stop the persistent hammering by protesting to Dr Gagey, the new tenant,[3] but on New Year's Eve he was awakened at dawn by a cabinet-maker who'd been sent to work on his furniture; if a workman had been seen arriving at his flat, how could he say his illness obliged him to sleep through the morning? The hammering resumed on the floor below,[4] and in mid-January his condition

1 'With his enormous eyes, his big white collar and flying cravat,' said a school friend, he looked like 'a sort of disturbed and disturbing archangel.' (page 28)

2 'I should like to greet her with special words,
words made specially for her, words like none that exist,
words which would alone be enough to make soothing
tears flow.' The 18–year–old soldier quotes Loti
in a letter to his mother. (page 53)

3 'He often wore his greatcoat unbuttoned
and the shako looked strange on him, while his hair
and his oval face assorted oddly with his uniform.'
(page 53)

4 Standing L. with his
hand on his hip is
Charles Haas, Proust's
model for Swann, and
seated R. Genevieve
Straus.

5 Anatole France.
The 45-year-old writer
turned out to be 'a small
man with a red nose like
a snail's shell and
a pointed black beard'.
(page 48)

6 Luncheon party in the
country – Proust is in
the centre of the people standing.

7 Lucien Daudet, 'a handsome boy, curled and pomaded,
painted and powdered, with a little squeaky voice
which he takes out of his waistcoat pocket'.
(page 104)

8 Jacques-Emile Blanche so disliked this portrait
that he tore up the canvas, and all Proust could salvage
was his head and shoulders.

9 In one of Madeleine Lemaire's illustrations
for Proust's first book, *Les Plaisirs et les jours*,
the author is depicted at table. (pages 107–8)

10 Marie Nordlinger.

11 Alphonse Daudet.

12 Reynaldo Hahn.

13 The actress
Louisa de Mornand.

14 *above left*
Gaston Calmette,
the editor of *Le Figaro*.

15 *above*
Bertrand de Fenelon,
close friend and
principal model for
Saint-Loup.

16 *left* 'A tall, rouged
woman with false hair
and arching eyebrows,
Mme Lemaire was
fashionable as a painter
of flower-pieces . . .
"No one except God,"
said Dumas *fils*,
"has created more roses." '
(page 73)

17 Laure Hayman. At 37 she was the mistress of Proust's 70-year-old uncle, Louis Weil, and she gave the young Marcel a book by one of her other lovers, Paul Bourget, bound in silk from one of her petticoats. (pages 35–6)

18 The Grand Hotel, Cabourg. 'The hotel was bustling with waiters, porters, pageboys and lift attendants, who knew one infallible way of securing a generous tip.' (page 266)

19 Alfred Agostinelli,
'a young man whom I probably loved more
than all my friends'. (page 394)

felt 'a thousand times worse than ever before, truly atrocious'.[5] 'For the first time in my life I have (four times already) had attacks which last thirty-six, forty, fifty hours! And during that time . . . death! . . . I go for three days without eating.'

The deterioration may have been due partly to panic at realising he was on his own. In the clinic and in Versailles, with nurses and hotel staff in constant attendance, he could forget that from now on he'd never have anyone to look after him except Félicie and other paid servants. Even now he couldn't quite face a future of living here, alone. He discussed with Dr Bize the idea of settling in Versailles[6] or in the south of France – perhaps at Nice.[7] Unless his health improved, the doctor agreed, he shouldn't stay in Paris. But gradually he established himself in the big flat.

He urgently needed a manservant. In Versailles the ageing Félicie had waited on him, doing everything he didn't want the hotel staff to do, and she helped him to move into the flat. But he was going to live mainly in bed, and he needed a valet who could both take care of his everyday needs and mediate more competently than she could between him and the world outside the bedroom. The thirty-three-year-old Nicolas Cottin, who'd worked for his parents, had left the job to become a croupier at a fashionable club, the Cercle Anglais. A shrewd judge of servants, Mme Proust had predicted he'd sooner or later want to come back into domestic service, but she'd warned her son not to give him a job. He'd no longer be the same man. Félicie, who disliked him, reminded Proust about this warning, threatening to leave if Nicolas came, but he still seemed the same – pleasant, discreet, intelligent, deferential, never saying 'you', always using the third person, and it was natural for him to go on saying 'Monsieur Marcel', like the family servants in the old flat, not 'Monsieur Proust'. Above all, he'd been trained by Mme Proust to provide service and attention of the kind Monsieur expected. Like the furniture, he was a link with the past. Proust's only misgiving was that Nicolas looked so ill. He might even have something contagious. Dr Bize was called in to examine him. He had a tired heart, said the doctor, and must avoid strain, but there was nothing else to worry about.

More than any friend or lover, Nicolas Cottin was going to be at the centre of Proust's life. By the bed there were three pear-shaped switches – one for the bedside lamp, one for the electric kettle and one for the bell which summoned Nicolas. Tidying the bed was one of his main jobs. Always surrounded by newspapers, letters, notebooks and pages of manuscript, Proust made little effort to keep them under control. Nicolas also had to cook, make the coffee, clean the flat, go out to buy groceries and other household necessities, deliver letters, make telephone calls, light the log-fire in the bedroom, change the bed linen, warm the sheets and towels, heat the water for Monsieur Marcel's footbath.

Proust required rigid adherence to a routine. Deprived of the mother who'd organised the household around his eccentric needs, he now had to establish his own routine, depending on a valet who couldn't possibly fill the empty space. But there was no question of shedding habits which had been established over thirty-four years: he'd inevitably approximate to the life style he'd evolved in his parents' two flats.

Partly because he was lying still most of the time, and partly because he wasn't eating much, Proust suffered acutely from feeling cold. People who shook hands with him were slightly surprised by the coldness of the hand he held out, but the only covers on his bed were a woollen blanket and a quilt. Wearing long woollen underpants and a thick soft woollen jumper under his white pyjama jacket, he relied for warmth mainly on hot-water bottles and pullovers. His head was propped up by two pillows. The armchair was piled with pullovers, and when he felt cold, he'd ring for one and put it round his shoulders like a cloak. When it fell off, he'd ring for another, and often he'd have four or five jumpers wedged between him and the pillows.[8]

The five-panelled Chinese screen behind the big brass bed was exquisite, but some of the furniture was contrastingly simple, including the three tables he kept within reach. Books, handkerchiefs and hot-water bottles were piled on the lower shelf of the carved bamboo table, while the old rosewood table he called 'the rowing-boat'[9] accommodated manuscripts, notebooks, inkwell, penholder and watch. The third table was for his coffee tray. The room was oriented to the one activity which mattered – writing. But when Horace Finaly sent him a beautiful antique writing-box, he only had it put away. Nor did he have any interest in the fountain pens which were becoming fashionable. He was a victim of habit, and his writing habits were already formed. He kept about fifteen penholders within reach because if he dropped one, it couldn't be picked up without disturbing the dust on the floor, which could only be done in his absence. In the pens he used plain, pointed nibs, and the inkwell was a simple one – a glass cube with four grooves, a round opening and a stopper. He could write very fast, though he was in an uncomfortable position, leaning on one elbow. 'After ten pages I am shattered.'[10] Bed-tables were already available, but the residue of guilt from masturbation and parental accusations about weakness of will had left him with a strain of masochism. During his mother's lifetime, work had been partly a peace-offering to her. After going one day in 1896 without working, he promised: 'From now on I shall not miss a single day.'[11] Ten years later he was still keeping the promise, and if writing was acutely uncomfortable, so much the better. He was undeniably making a sacrifice.

Outside the bedroom's two large double windows the shutters were kept closed, while, inside, the heavy felt-lined blue satin curtains were drawn, giving four layers of protection against noise and dust, but also excluding sunlight. In the large, high-ceilinged room, he lived by lamplight, but the big chandelier was never switched on except when visitors came; nor were the two blue-globe candelabra next to the matching bronze clock on the thick white marble mantelpiece. The only light in regular use was the small, long-stemmed bedside lamp which had a weak bulb masked by a green gathered shade lined with white silk. Visitors were surprised he did so much writing with so little light. In his parents' flat he'd complained about the 'menagerie' in which he had to work, with crude light falling from above on the poor dazed lions, but now he was having to take adult responsibility for his own lighting, he was equally cruel to himself, working under inadequate, one-sided illumination, and refusing to make any change, even when friends made practical suggestions or when his eyes protested by giving him pain.

On the bare oak parquet floor an oriental carpet served as a bedside rug. The room was full of heavy furniture. In the space between the windows was an imposing rosewood mirror-wardrobe with bronze trimmings, a bracket lamp and a door which could never be opened: it was too close to the grand piano which had been his mother's. Next to it was a massive oak desk, piled with books. The wall to the right of the win-

dows had at both ends double doors opening into the main
drawing-room. The doors next to the window were used as
the entrance to the bedroom, but they were covered with a
curtain. The other double door was blocked with two revolv-
ing bookcases, and in front of these was his mother's old work-
table, carved with her initials. He kept his cash and banknotes
in the little Chinese cabinet which had, on top of it, photographs of himself and Robert as children. Next to it was a large
rosewood chest matching the wardrobe. The photographs and
souvenirs he'd accumulated were in the drawers and on the
white marble top two white bowls with scalloped edges flanked
a white statuette of the infant Jesus crowned with bunches of
grapes. Above it was a ceiling-high mirror. But among all this
furniture there was only one seat apart from the piano stool –
the velvet armchair from his father's study.

A small door opened into a corridor leading to another large
bedroom, which he converted into his dressing-room, and to
the lavatory. The two salons, large and small, were both
usable, but the large one was never used. Nor was the dining-
room, except as a store-room for furniture.

When he dressed, but not for going out, he wore a shirt
with a pullover underneath it, a smoking jacket, trousers and
slippers.[12] An overcoat with a sealskin collar and a mink lining
was left hanging at the end of his bed for use indoors. He
never used soap but washed meticulously by dabbing at his
face with damp towels. He never shaved himself, and always
let his beard grow unless he was going out. The barber, who
came from the boulevard Malesherbes whenever he wanted a
shave or a haircut, left a complete set of equipment in the flat
– shaving brushes, razors, scissors, etc. – but Proust did curl
his own moustache with a curling iron.[13]

He didn't expect Nicolas to stay awake all night: before
going to bed at about midnight he had to remove the silver
tray and bring in Evian water, a small cup, a bowl of sugar
and lime blossom on a lacquer tray in case Proust wanted to
make tea during the night. In fact the electric kettle was rarely
switched on, except accidentally, when he pressed the wrong
button and realised his mistake as the smell of burning metal
reached his sensitive nostrils.

Félicie didn't immediately carry out her threat to leave, but
she didn't do much cooking. If he wanted a meal, it would
normally be at about five or six in the evening, and he'd

occasionally ask her for a sole, but, increasingly irritated by the smell of cooking, he more often sent out for food from Larue's, while hot food for the servants was fetched from the restaurant Louis XVI on the boulevard.[14] His main needs were for silence and coffee, which had to be very strong, made from a tightly packed filter of finely ground, freshly roasted coffee, always bought from the same shop, and in the morning he drank it in two stages. When he woke up, he rang for café au lait and a croissant. The coffee was served in a silver pot with his initials on it, with boiling hot milk in a lidded porcelain jug, sugar in a gold-rimmed bowl with the family monogram. The croissant always came from the same baker, in the rue Pépinière. When the bell rang, Nicolas had to go in without knocking or speaking and put down the tray on the bedside table. Proust would never begin to pour the coffee until he was alone. If he drank a second cup, it would be with freshly boiled milk, and a second croissant had to be ready, but he didn't always want it.

Because of his sensitivity to dust, neither the bedroom nor any of the other rooms could be cleaned except when he was out, and, because of his sensitivity to smells, this was the only time the parquet could be polished. Instead of having a 'smoking-room', he now did his fumigations in bed after starting the day with coffee, and the brass of the bedstead was soon stained with the fumes of the Legras powders. He had several cartons of these ordered at a time from Leclerc, the chemist in rue Vignon. To avoid the smell of sulphur he never used matches, but two candles, one of them lighted, were always kept on the small table in the corridor. He poured powder into a saucer, lit a small square of white paper from the candle, lit the powder and made the room thick with fumes which could afterwards be dispelled with smoke from a wood fire. Not wanting to speak after a fumigation, he waved his hand for it to be lit.[15]

He may have been aware the powders were addictive – sometimes he made efforts to stop 'smoking' – but he didn't realise that in a bedroom ventilated only by the draught from the chimney, the carbon monoxide produced from burning the powders and the wood could have helped to cause the malaise he progressively suffered – headaches, nausea, exhaustion, weakness of vision and changes in the functioning of his central nervous system. The powders contained atropine and hyoscy-

amine, which relieved the asthma by dilating and drying the
bronchial tree, but also tended to blur the vision by dilating
the pupils, and it could have contributed to the weakness,
giddiness, cardiac palpitation and the disturbance of speech and
gait he was later to suffer. Caffeine is a methylated xanthine
which relaxes the constricted muscles of the bronchi, but the
strong coffee could also have helped to cause insomnia and
palpitations.[16] He was doing himself more harm in the bedroom than the smell of cooking could have done him from the
kitchen.

Throughout the first phase of mourning for his mother, he'd
been identifying with both parents, trying to emulate actions
they might have taken. 'The letters I write now are mostly ones
I believe they would have written,' and in the early summer of
1906, he wrote to a man he'd occasionally met at dinner parties,
Henri van Blarenberghe, who'd just lost his father, an acquaintance of Proust's parents. In condoling with victims of bereavement, no one has ever matched Proust's ability to empathise,
and this letter made the grieving son feel he'd received a
'posthumous message' from Proust's parents.[17] Van Blarenberghe was chairman of the Chemins de Fer de l'Est, and,
hoping to trace the young railwayman who'd befriended him
at the Gare Saint-Lazare, Proust wrote to ask whether he could
help. He couldn't, but he expressed fellow-feeling for the
bereaved Proust and an understanding of the connection
between mourning and lowered resistance to illness. Forwarded from the hotel in Versailles, his letter arrived on 17
January, and eight days later Proust read in Le Figaro that van
Blarenberghe had murdered his eighty-year-old mother, tried
to cut his throat and finished himself off with a bullet in the
head.

   Trying to remember the young man, Proust found 'the
image which seems to remain clearest is always a smiling face,
smiling with his particularly fine eyes, the mouth still half open
after making a good repartee'.[18] Hearing Proust had been in
correspondence with the matricide, Calmette wrote to commission an article for Le Figaro. The letter arrived on Wednesday 30 January, but Proust didn't read it until ten in the
evening. He rested till two in the morning, got up and started
work at three.[19] Thinking about the son's love for the mother
he'd killed, Proust was thinking about himself. Especially

when copying out van Blarenberghe's letters to him, 'I wanted to be able to convey the extreme delicacy, or rather the incredible steadiness of the hand which had traced those letters, so clean and fine. . . .' Perhaps the two sons hadn't been so different in their relationship with their mother. The dying words of the eighty-year-old woman had been: 'What have you done to me?' But 'perhaps there is no really loving mother who could not, on her last day, and often previously, address this reproach to her son. The truth is that as we grow older, we kill all those who love us by the cares we give them, by the anxious tenderness we inspire in them and incessantly activate.' Proust was picturing not the deterioration in an octogenarian body but in a much younger one: he described 'the gradual work of destruction wrought by the grieving tenderness which animates her, the fading eyesight, the hairs which had remained indomitably black finally defeated, like the rest of her, and whitening, the hardening arteries, the blocked kidneys, the strained heart, the courage to face life finally exhausted, the pace slowing down, becoming heavy, the mind which knows there is no hope left . . .'.[20]

This sense of being responsible for his mother's death is present in the novel. After Albertine's death the Narrator at first feels pity, combined with

> shame at surviving her. Indeed it seemed to me in the hours when I suffered least that I was benefiting in some way from her death because a woman is of greater usefulness to our life if she is not an element of happiness but an instrument of grief and there is not a single woman who is as precious when we possess her as the truths she reveals by making us suffer. In these moments, connecting the death of my grandmother with that of Albertine, I felt my life had been corroded by a double murder for which only the world's cowardice could pardon me.[21]

Proust was used to discomfort in his right hand when working in bed, but, writing the article for *Le Figaro*, he was suffering so much – especially in the little finger – that by eight o'clock he felt unable to go on. He went back to sleep, after asking to be called in time to finish the article. But at 8.30, when builders started work on the floor below, he felt so ill and dispirited that he sent the unfinished article to *Le Figaro* without even reading what he'd written. Proofs arrived at eleven in the

evening, but instead of correcting them he wrote a final paragraph. In classical times, he said, no altar was accorded more
veneration 'than the tomb of Oedipus at Colonus and the tomb
of Orestes at Sparta, this Orestes whom the Furies had driven
right to the feet of Apollo and Athene saying: "Far from the
altars do we chase the patricidal son." '[22] At midnight he sent
the article back with a message that not a word in the new
ending must be altered, though anything else could be cut. In
the morning paper the whole final paragraph was missing. The
night editor, Cardane, had found it came too close to condon-
ing the act of patricide.[23] Protesting to Calmette, Proust said
the Greeks had always punished patricides, but 'to re-establish
a higher justice, since they had been criminals involuntarily,
their memory was honoured, sacred'. Hadn't the oracles predicted that only Oedipus and Orestes could guarantee the greatness of the city?[24] Proust wasn't familiar with Freud's theory
of the Oedipus complex; matricide had driven him independently to the Greeks.

The article brought him more feedback – all of it favourable
– than any previous contribution to Le Figaro,[25] but it failed to
boost his flagging self-esteem. It was the first writing he'd
done since the translation of Sesame and Lilies, and, feeling
guilty – as if what had stopped him from making better use
of his time were lack of willpower – he was more than usually
prone to overestimate his friends' talent and underestimate his
own. He suspected Robert Dreyfus' congratulatory letter of
being 'a charitable lie to an invalid',[26] and when Lucien, who
was still painting prolifically, praised the article, he responded:
'I swear to you that when I receive a letter from you about
something I have done, I have the feeling – I can even say the
certainty – the letter is superior to what I have done.'

But he did have inklings of the power latent inside him. 'If
I find that I have no talent, that I have been unable, for many
reasons, to develop my gifts into talent, that my style has
rotted without ripening, I know on the other hand that there
are in what I do more true ideas and more feelings than in
nearly all the articles which get published. . . . I want to tell
you that while believing you to be very superior to me, I
believe you still more superior to many people who are very
well regarded.' The modesty is genuine, but when the phrase
'temps perdu' comes into the letter, Proust is talking mainly
to himself: however much time had been lost, it still wasn't

too late. 'It is a mistake always to consider oneself *inside time*. The valuable part of ourselves, at the moments it is valuable, is outside time. . . . Your sadness will vanish if you think of yourself only as an instrument capable of making experiences of truth and beauty.' Besides, Lafontaine hadn't started to work till he was forty, and Franz Hals had been over forty-eight when he did his best work, and Corot over sixty. So although Lucien shouldn't waste time, he shouldn't regret time that was already lost.[27]

Proust had been losing time since his mother's death. He was now getting up once a week, but not putting his clothes on,[28] and it had been harder than ever to keep in touch with friends – even with Mme Catusse, who'd spent so much time getting the flat ready for him.[29] At the beginning of the year, Louisa, whose photographs had been appearing in the papers, had sent him a little bell he could keep by his bedside and ring to summon servants.[30] Wanting to buy something for Albu, Proust asked her what would please him most – a car or a jewel.[31] Later on, when he was ill with typhoid fever, Proust visited him, only to find afterwards that his insomnia was punctuated with sleep ruined by dreams of his friend's suffering.[32]

In the middle of March, to resume contact with another friend, he offered to review Anna de Noailles' new collection, *Les Éblouissements*. As if she were a genius, worthy of comparison with Voltaire and Claude Monet, he hailed the book as 'one of the most astonishing successes – perhaps the masterpiece of literary *impressionism*',[33] but each of his many excerpts contains deplorably banal writing. Quoting her description of a bird detaching itself from an invisible leaf and shooting to the summit of the world, he asks: 'Do you know an image more splendid and more perfect than this one?'[34] Any reader of poetry or even prose could answer 'Thousands.' But in his uncritical enthusiasm he wrote a piece that was going to be far too long for *Le Figaro*. He stayed up all night cutting and counting letters. He calculated that the review contained 16,900 characters, and that four columns of *Le Figaro* would contain 18,000. He asked Anna de Noailles to intercede with Calmette for four columns on the front page, but Proust was asked to cut two-thirds of what he'd written.[35] Relegated to the supplement, the review finally appeared in the middle of June. Proust tried to keep Montesquiou in ignorance of the attention he was paying to Anna de Noailles, but the jealous comte found out.

Two years had passed since they'd seen each other, and the copy of *Sesame and Lilies* Proust had sent hadn't been acknowledged. In a January letter to Reynaldo, he said he felt more embarrassed with the comte than with anyone else. Nothing would induce him to invite Montesquiou to call, because he'd be furious if, incapacitated by an attack, Proust couldn't receive him, whereas other friends made allowances.[36] Tactlessly, Reynaldo showed this letter to the comte,[37] who didn't know Proust had left Versailles. On 23 March Montesquiou wrote to him at the hotel, suggesting they should visit Yturri's grave together.[38] But he discovered his mistake before posting the letter, and wrote another, enclosing the first. Telephoning to thank him, Proust didn't suggest they should meet, and received a third letter: 'Do not be too grateful but always be affectionate.' On 19 April Montesquiou promised to associate their names, and three weeks later Proust found out what he meant. In his new book, *Altesses Sérénissimes* he'd reprinted the whole of Proust's 1905 essay on him, 'Un Professeur de beauté', without asking for permission, or giving Proust an opportunity to revise it.[39]

Just as a recently cured drug addict may feel most at home with others who have experienced both addiction and cure, Proust felt most rapport with people who'd just been bereaved or were just about to be. Yturri's death had led to a rapprochement between his master and Proust, but the effect had worn off, and Georges de Lauris, whose mother was dying, now had the strongest claim on Proust's affection. 'My heart splits into two or rather into three as soon as I stop thinking of you, I think of your mother's anxiety, and then of your poor father.'[40] When the dowager marquise, who was only fifty-three, died on 15 February, Proust wrote: 'It seems to me I am losing Mamma for the second time.'[41] The next day he sent flowers and felt too upset to start working on the obituary due to appear in *Le Figaro* on the morning of the funeral, but to console Georges he wrote: 'When you had your mother you thought a lot about the present time in which you no longer have her. Now you will think a lot about the past in which you had her. . . . It is a comfort to know one will never love less, will never be consoled, will remember more and more.'[42] Proust's search for lost time was partly the search for a dead mother. His fourth letter to Georges in just over four days said: 'The eyes of memory end up by seeing nothing when one focuses them too hard. At this moment try simply to live, to survive, letting all that go on in you without the collabor-ation of your willpower, and the soft images will by themselves be reborn in you, never to leave you again.' If Proust was moving towards formulations he'd make about involuntary memory, it was with exemplary absent-mindedness. 'You must know, Georges, I no longer think about anything else, and my need to see you at this moment is above all a need to hear you talk about her.' He'd sleep better if Georges could call on him about nine or nine-thirty in the evening.[43] He was at the same time sharing his friend's grief, reliving his own mother's death, and laying foundations for *À la recherche*.

But praise from Georges was no more acceptable than from anyone else. The article 'Journées de lecture' – the second to be given this title – appeared in *Le Figaro* on 20 March. It makes a show of failing to engage with the subject he'd wanted to discuss:

Alas! Here I am in the third column of this paper and I have not even begun my article. It should have been called 'Snobbery and Posterity', I shall not be able to use this title since I have filled the whole space which had been reserved for me without yet saying a single word to you about either Snobbery or Posterity. . . . It will have to wait till next time. And then, if any of the ghosts which incessantly thrust themselves between my thinking and its object, as happens in dreams, still come to importune my attention and sidetrack it from what I have to tell you, I shall drive them away in the same way Ulysses used his sword to drive away the shades which crowded round him begging to be given a human shape or to be buried.[44]

Here, in what purports to be an apology, Proust is focusing on his own act of writing to spotlight the way consciousness works. Without any help from Freud, he's free-associating while writing as entertainingly as any journalist. Yet when de Lauris congratulated him, comparing him to Francis Jammes, Proust complained: 'your infallible critical sense is so kindly and so completely mistaken when it comes to me. . . . The friendship which finds in me as much talent as in Jammes is a great friendship.'[45]

In February he reported to Reynaldo: 'My nose has become such a fountain etc. etc. that I literally cannot open eyes [sic].' While writing the letter he has wiped his nose, he says, eighty-three times.[46] Each time he tries to write, the pain in his little finger begins to affect his handwriting.[47] Since moving into the flat, he's been suffering incessant asthma attacks from which the only relief is in sleep – a luxury put out of reach by noise. There was now silence in the flat underneath, where Dr Gagey had moved in, but the adjoining flat in the house next door had been rented to a Mme Katz, who was having new lavatories installed within yards of Proust's bed. 'The workmen (both those working for her and the landlord's) arrive at seven in the morning, insist on showing what a good humour they are in at this time of the day with a fearful banging and by using their saws to make a scratching noise behind my bed.' Various noises persisted through the morning, receding into the distance at midday, and there was silence from two o'clock, unless carpets were being nailed down.[48] Proust had rearranged his routine, staying awake during the day, but the afternoon, the only time he could have slept, was also the only time he could concentrate on writing or reading. His life was being disrupted as badly as it had been by the builders underneath.

Discovering Mme Katz's son was a judge who knew Émile Straus, he approached Mme Straus: would her husband speak to the son about his mother? Proust offered to reimburse the cost of paying the men to work in the afternoons, so that the job could be finished more quickly. M. Straus should explain that Proust badly needed fresh air, but outings were a strain he could risk only if he could count on uninterrupted sleep the next day.

The few people invited to visit him were asked not to smoke or wear scent or a flower in their buttonhole.[49] His one regular visitor was Reynaldo, who sometimes had to come back four times, at intervals of an hour, if Proust was fumigating, and if he was in no state to talk, he carried on his side of the conservation by writing on slips of paper. Nor was it easy to reach him by telephone, for he often left the telephone downstairs with the concierge, who could be asked to go up with a message, but might find Proust was asleep or fumigating. One friend who visited him occasionally was Illan, the marquis de Casa-Fuerte, a fellow asthmatic, son of the Empress Eugénie's niece, Flavie Lefebre de Balsorano. Lucien had introduced them in 1899 at the Grand-Guignol, but it was only now that Proust felt the 'sharp, sweet march' of his affection for a man whom some of their friends called an incarnation of Wilde's Dorian Gray. Proust was also seeing Georges de Lauris, but Robert Proust was too busy to gamble time on visits which might be abortive, and Albu had neither called since the end of the year nor – in spite of Proust's efforts to persuade him – read the *Bible of Amiens*.

Dr Bize said it would be better to move out of the flat than to go on losing sleep. Proust felt sure that, even after Mme Katz moved in, 'she will go on for months while she settles in having things she considers beautiful or luxurious nailed to the wall, which will drive me into my grave'.[50] The Strauses invited her son to lunch, but throughout March the workmen went on banging between seven and ten in the morning 'as frantically as if they were building something as majestic as the Pyramid of Cheops'. According to Proust, the hammering was doubling the ferocity of each asthma attack and shortening his life. When work was suspended for a few days while the paint was drying, he felt so much better that he went out on the balcony and for short walks in the street.[51] But in early May, when he was shortening his review of Anna de Noailles' book, the hammering climaxed in the collapse of his fireplace, leaving a big space which admitted dust from where the builders were working. 'In spite of the fearful attacks I had yesterday, I had to call in builders, and, being in no state to get out of my bed, had the fireplace rebuilt under my nose, with everything that entails of plaster, bricks and dust.'[52]

When Montesquiou wanted him to review *Altesses Sérénissimes* in *Le Figaro*, he was in no mood to say yes, and he spoiled his diplomatically couched refusal by adding: 'I have still other reasons to give you, deriving from the subject itself (not *the book*, but *you*) which would make that especially exhausting.'[53]

In late May he had a series of violent asthma attacks, but afterwards met Montesquiou at a soirée of Mme Lemaire's, and on 11 June he rashly undertook to give a dinner party, prompted by gratitude to Calmette and embarrassment over being taken up promptly on what was intended only as a vague invitation. Chatting to Calmette late one night in his office at *Le Figaro*, Proust said he'd like one day to give him dinner, and the editor immediately took out his diary.[54]

Proust booked the petit salon in the Ritz for 1 July, and

invited guests Calmette would be glad to meet – the marquis and marquise de Clermont-Tonnerre and Madame d'Hausson-ville, Aimery de la Rochefoucauld and the princesse de Monaco, and Jean Béraud, but not Reinach because Clermont-Tonnerre was strongly anti-Dreyfusard. The comtesse de Chevigné promised to come, changed her mind, and finally consented to arrive after dinner. Since Reynaldo was going to be in London, Proust hired Gabriel Fauré to play the piano. The other guests included Guiche, who agreed to select the menu and the wine, Albu, Emmanuel Bibesco, Jacques-Émile Blanche and Beaunier, the comtesse de Brantes, the marquise de Ludre and Anna de Noailles.

Though he made Ulrich do most of the inviting by telephone, Proust had three exhausting weeks of preparations for the party. Mme Straus wasn't going to come, but he asked her advice on how to seat the bourgeois guests, including Fauré, and, since it would be too exhausting for him to play solo, booked Marguerite Hasselmans, the harpist and pianist who'd play duets with him and accompany the violinist Maurice Hayot. But Fauré fell ill. Proust didn't find out until the evening of the day before the party,[55] but managed to book Édouard Risler, a well-known concert pianist.

Proust kept his fur coat on throughout the evening, as did Anna de Noailles, perhaps as a gesture of solidarity, but they both struck Elisabeth de Clermont-Tonnerre as looking like eskimos.[56] Guests invited after dinner, but in time to hear the music, were Illan de Casa-Fuerte and his marquise, the vicomte and vicomtesse d'Humières, the princesse de Polignac, Robert Proust, Robert Dreyfus, Maurice Barrès and his wife, Albert Henraux and Joseph Primoli. Proust would have liked music by Reynaldo, Schumann's *Scènes de carnival* and Liszt's *Les Soirées de Vienne*, but refusing to play anything he didn't know by heart, Risler performed music by Schumann, Beethoven, Chopin, Chabrier, Couperin, Fauré and (at Proust's request) arrangements of the *Liebestod* from *Tristan und Isolde* and the overture to *Die Meistersinger*. Hayot played two pieces by Fauré. The evening cost Proust 2,300 francs, a thousand of which went to Risler. For the same price, he said, he could have engaged the Society of Wind Instruments.[57] But the evening was a success, and he was too exhilarated to feel exhausted or depressed by the departure – on the day of the party – of his 'pseudo-secretary', Ulrich, and his old cook, Félicie, who belatedly carried out her threat to leave.[58] But the next day, still in bed, he started a cold.[59]

July brought warm weather, and he not only got up more often than during the months before the party but, with encouragement from Dr Bize, started making plans for a holiday. This of course precipitated an avalanche of fantasies, including one about taking a boat-trip with his brother.[60]

Robert de Flers hadn't been invited to the dinner party, but when he lost his grandmother, Mme de Rozière, Proust started his letter of condolence: 'I can scarcely write to you because tears are blinding me,'[61] and on the day of the funeral, 23 July, *Le Figaro* published an article by Proust – 'La Vie de Paris: une grand-mère'. Like him she'd been an invalid: 'So frail, so thin, she always kept afloat above the most fearful surges of illness, and when it looked as though she had been laid low, there she was again, going strong, at her best.'[62] Adapting what Mme de Sévigné had said about her seventeen-year-old grandson who read no books – 'His youth makes too much noise for him to hear' – Proust, thinking as much of himself as of Mme de Rozière, said it was true of many people who were bedridden that, although silence is recommended to them, 'their thinking makes too much noise'. Discussing the relationship between grandmother and grandson in the most revealing part of the article, Proust repeats the empathic gambit he'd used when writing about the van Blarenberghe case. 'Such perfect friendships', he says, should

> never come to an end. What? Two beings so totally compatible that nothing existed in either without finding in the other its *raison d'être*, its objective, its satisfaction, its explanation, its tender commentary, two beings who each seemed the translation of the other, though each had great originality – do we really have to think of these two beings as meeting each other only by chance, for an instant, in the infinity of time, where they will no longer be anything to each other, nothing more particular than they are to billions of other beings? All the letters in the witty and passionate book which was Mme de Rozière – have they suddenly become meaningless, illegible?[63]

Proust's refusal to believe his mother has become illegible will be one of his principal reasons for depicting lost time as redeemable.

His hesitations about the holiday were as protracted as usual. In mid-July he was almost on the point of leaving for Lozère in the Cévennes, but felt too ill and would probably have come back to Paris anyway for the funeral.[64] On 1 August he didn't know whether to stay in Paris or leave for Brittany, Cabourg, Touraine or Germany.[65] The indecision ended, as so often, in impulsive action, and on the 4th or 5th he left for Cabourg, after hearing the Grand Hôtel was more comfortable than any other hotel on the coast,[66] but the decision was prompted partly by posthumous devotion to his mother, who in 1903 had suggested he should go there. He'd considered Cabourg last summer, but hadn't been there since September 1891, when he was overtaken suddenly by accesses of grief for the grandmother who'd been dead for nearly two years. She'd been his companion on childhood holidays there. Perhaps the decision to go now also derived partly from empathy with the bereaved de Flers, and from emotional confusion of both dead grandmothers with Proust's dead mother.

SEVENTEEN

SEASIDE RESURRECTION

Cabourg had come into existence as a seaside resort during the Second Empire, but in 1907, when it hadn't yet become fashionable, the appearance of a well-known face, such as François de Croisset's, caused quite a stir, whereas Proust's presence went unnoticed.[1]

The train-journey from the Gare Saint-Lazare took five and a half hours. On the Cherbourg express he travelled with a fashionable surgeon, Eugène-Louis Doyen, who spoke rapturously about the comtesse de Greffulhe,[2] and at Mézidon Proust changed to the Trouville train, which stopped at almost each village and each small seaside resort.

The hotel and adjoining casino form the point on which a fan-shaped network of roads converges, while the superb promenade, over two miles long, is almost unequalled on French beaches. The hotel had 200 bedrooms, palatial lounges and a sumptuous, chandeliered dining-room with enormous windows opening out on the promenade, where holidaymakers took their daily walk *en famille*, more interested in being looked at than looking at the view. From bedrooms facing the sea you hear the endless sound of the waves, and there was a bandstand immediately below the hotel. Together with cheerful music, laughter and loud conversation from swimmers and sunbathers intruded on Proust's wistful memories of seaside holidays with his mother and grandmother.

On 6 August he was still feeling ill and exhausted from the journey,[3] and two days later he was undecided whether he should retreat to Paris,[4] but something happened to make him step vigorously out of his invalid routine. In the hotel he had the same opportunities of sexual adventure as he had when he went back to Venice in 1900, taking a brief holiday from the unspoken maternal veto on homosexual activities. Since her death there had been the episode with Félicie's nephew, Ulrich, the pseudo-secretary, but mostly he'd been restrained by illness and the invalid life which imprisoned him in his flat.

The hotel was bustling with waiters, porters, pageboys and lift attendants, who made more money from tips than from salaries and who knew one infallible way of securing a generous tip. The fastidious Proust could feel more at home in a hotel bedroom – his for the duration of the stay – than he ever could in a male brothel, and, as if basing the observation on someone else, he'd later describe the way a predatory homosexual looks for potential partners in a hotel.

> He spoke only to his wife, the rest of the hotel seemed not to exist for him, but when a waiter took an order, was quite close, he rapidly raised his blue eyes and threw at him a glance which did not last more than two seconds but in its limpid clairvoyance seemed to indicate an entirely different level of curiosity and scrutiny from that which might have motivated any ordinary customer in giving more than a glance at a pageboy or a waiter in order to make humorous or other remarks about him to friends.[5]

In the schoolboy letter written nineteen years earlier about 'the different gentlemen of whom I consist', Proust had seized gleefully on the possibility of writing about himself – and reviling himself – as if he were someone else. 'For my part I rather dislike him.' His fiction provided another way of writing gleefully about himself and reviling himself as if he were someone else. While he took every precaution to keep his homosexuality secret, he could write extensively about the habits and techniques of homosexuals.

We know nothing about his liaisons in Cabourg, but he soon felt sufficiently rejuvenated to lead a more active life, and he enjoyed the view from his bedroom window. In the novel the Narrator is so excited by it that after washing his face in the morning, he keeps putting down the starched hotel towel to gaze out at the placid violence of the emerald waves with their toppling slopes. Afterwards he often takes up his position at the window to watch the dancing hills of sea, which sometimes withdraw so far that the undulations are visible only at the end of a long sandy plain.

Proust enjoyed the theatricality of hotel life, and the luxury of having a battalion of obliging, smartly uniformed servants to carry out his orders. It was like living in a restaurant, with the added luxuries of sleeping under the same roof as the other diners and gossiping with waiters, porters, pageboys and liftboys about the people under observation. He'd add a twenty-franc tip to the ten-franc bill for a meal, and when he went to his room about midnight, he'd invite one of the staff in to play draughts with him and chat about the guests. If there was a hierarchy in the staff, there was a less obvious one among the guests: some were favoured with window tables and more attentive service. He enjoyed watching all this, though he found most of the other guests tiresome and vulgar – especially the manager of a large shop and an old croupier.[6]

One guest he liked was the art dealer René Gimpel, who'd noticed him – as everyone did – because he never took off his old twill overcoat, which had several heavy linings in it and was so faded it looked stained. His big eyes and his dark, slightly curly beard made Gimpel think of men in African deserts. He talked disparagingly about doctors, including his father, who'd said salty sea air would be bad for him; obviously it was doing him good. One friend who visited Proust at the hotel was the playwright Henri Bernstein, who was an amusing companion, but Gimpel never saw him in conversation with any of the other hotel guests, though he knew a lot about them, having collected a great deal of facts and rumours from the staff.[7]

The casino contained a theatre and a concert hall, but, more interested in the entertainment to be had from sightseeing, the revitalised Proust wrote for advice to Émile Mâle, author of *Art religieux du XIIe siècle en France*, which Robert de Billy had loaned to him in 1899. Apart from cathedrals and monuments, what should he see in Normandy? From his 1903 trip to Evian he remembered glimpsing from the train a little medieval village, Semur. Were there interesting old towns near Cabourg? What about Fougères, Vitry, Saint-Malo and Guérande? Were they worth a visit? And if he took taxi-rides into Brittany, what sightseeing would Mâle recommend for the sake of the art or scenery, or from the viewpoints of history and legend?[8] He also wrote asking Emmanuel Bibesco to recommend landscapes or monuments.[9]

The first friend he saw was Georges de Lauris, who was staying with his father at Houlgate, only two miles away, and Proust was energetic enough for a twelve-mile walk with

Georges to Trouville, stopping on the way at Houlgate, where Proust met the marquis, Georges' father. At Bénerville Proust and Georges visited Guiche and his duchesse in the villa they'd rented, and at Trouville the two friends visited Louisa de Mornand and the Strauses. Before saying goodbye to Georges, Proust borrowed a photograph of the dead marquise. 'Forgive me for being so demanding: I needed to see her alone, and the emotion she gave me so surpassed my expectations that I did not regret depriving you of it.' Together with the marquis' face, the marquise's enabled Proust to 'rediscover the genealogy and, one after the other, all the *titles* of your intellectual, moral and physical nobility'.[10]

Proust also paid a late-evening visit to the Clermont-Tonnerres in their château at Glisolles, near Évreux, and when his hostess invited him to come back in the morning to see the roses, he said: 'Show them to me tonight,' and got Agostinelli to use the car's headlamps as spotlights. 'The roses', she wrote, 'looked like beauties woken up from their slumber.'[11] He invited the Clermont-Tonnerres to dinner, hiring a tenor and a private drawing-room for their after-dinner entertainment.[12]

It seems as if a bizarre tug-of-war was going on inside Proust. Impressed by the aristocracy's façade of dignity and upright behaviour, he also enjoyed betraying its ideals and standards of behaviour – just as aristocrats betrayed them – in intimacies with hotel staff and footmen. There is a continuity between his early story 'La Confession d'une jeune fille' and the unconfirmed rumour that he later showed photographs of his mother to casual acquaintances in a male brothel. Needing to violate the image of the little Marcel she'd believed in, he felt stimulated and excited when he could function like a double agent between the low life and the high life. His ambivalence was complicated by an almost morbid involvement in bereavement and by feelings towards Georges which still didn't fall far short of love. He was the unavailable aristocratic alternative to the working-class lover, and Proust enjoyed Georges' physical way of expressing affection: 'your beautiful hands so gently seeking mine in a movement of persuasive eloquence when sometimes they express a doubt about your friendship'. Proust was delighted by 'this mental spontaneity which is *you*'.[13]

Strenuous exertion in the fresh air must have been a shock to lungs and muscles unaccustomed to outdoor exercise, but he had enough stamina to get up and go out every day. He was ambitious in explorations of the neighbourhood, but instead of going for long walks, he travelled in a taxi, hiring one which belonged to Taximètres Unic de Monaco, a company owned by Jacques Bizet, who'd studied medicine, but had turned into a businessman. 'To my right, to my left, in front of me,' wrote Proust, 'the windows of the automobile, which I kept closed, placed the beautiful September day, so to speak, under glass, and, even in the fresh air, one saw it only through a kind of transparency.'[14] Eight years had elapsed since his drive to Coppet with Constantin de Brancovan and Abel Hermant in prince Alexandre's car, but he'd had so little experience of motoring that he was still excited by the whirling changes of perspective. In 1899 he'd enthused about the 'giant in seven-league boots' who delivered steeples and towers and old gardens which previously could never have been tasted during the same afternoon; now, driving to Caen, he was happy to observe the slow dance performed by the steeples.

> Alone, rising from the uniform level of the plain and as if lost in open country, the two steeples of Saint-Étienne were climbing towards the sky. Soon we saw three of them, the steeple of Saint-Pierre had joined them. . . . The minutes were passing, we were moving fast, but the three steeples were still alone ahead of us, like three birds perched on the plain, immobile, visible in the sunlight. Then, distance tearing itself to pieces like a fog which lifts to reveal in all its detail a form still invisible a moment earlier, the towers of the Trinité appeared, or rather just one tower, so precisely was the other concealed behind it. But it stepped aside, the other came forward, and they stood together. Finally a procrastinating tower (that of Saint-Sauveur, I suppose) came with a bold leap to place itself opposite them.[15]

Afterwards, when he was driving away from Caen, the two steeples of Saint-Étienne and the steeple of Saint-Pierre, still visible on the horizon long after the town had disappeared, 'waved their sunlit apexes once more in farewell. Sometimes one would stand aside to let the two others go on seeing us a moment longer; soon I saw only two of them.' As when he was writing about the gondola journey in Venice back towards his mother, the conceit depends on transposition between observer and observed. 'Then they swerved a last time like two golden pivots and disappeared.' On subsequent outings with the same chauffeur, Alfred Agostinelli, Proust often saw the steeples again, but from such a distance that they looked like 'flowers painted on the sky above the fields'.

When they motored to Lisieux, they were late in leaving Cabourg, and the sun was setting as they drove down a steep hill

> at the end of which, in the bloodstained bowl of sunlight we were approaching rapidly, I saw Lisieux, which had got there first, hastily raising and arranging its wounded houses, its high, purple-tinted chimneys; in an instant everything was in place, and when we stopped some seconds after at the corner of the rue aux Fèvres, the old houses, whose fine branches of ribbed wood spread to support intersections with the heads of saints or demons, seemed to have made no movement since the fifteenth century.

The taxi broke down there, and it was dark by the time they got to the cathedral of Saint-Pierre, but Proust wanted to study the leafwork on the façade, which Ruskin had described.

> I was going forward, however, wanting at least to touch with my hand the illustrious stone forest planted on the porch. Passing through it, perhaps the nuptial procession of Henry II of England and Eleanor of Guyenne would have passed between the two lines of trees which had been so nobly hewn. But just when I was groping my way towards it, it was flooded with a sudden brightness; trunk by trunk the trees emerged from the night, vividly detaching in bright light on a background of darkness the large model of their stone leaves. This was my mechanic, the ingenious Agostinelli, who, conveying to the old sculptures a greeting from the present whose light could not be better used than in reading the lessons of the past, successively directed the headlights of his motor at all the parts of the porch as I wanted to inspect them.[16]

Agostinelli was repeating the trick he'd learnt from the midnight inspection of the roses.

Now that Proust's invalid life had come to seem natural, the active life seemed artificial, hyper-active, 'the life of a cannonball in its trajectory'.[17] To be capable of it, he pepped himself up with caffeine, sometimes drinking over a dozen cups of coffee. 'You would be astonished to see me on the road every day,' he told Emmanuel Bibesco, but the caffeine made him feverish. 'I do not know what I think or feel,'[18] and sometimes, during the drives, he could see nothing of the scenery.[19] When he finally got out of the taxi, 'a sort of shaking, like that of the engine, goes on whirring inside me, and the trembling stops my hand from settling or obeying me'. He slept well, but memories of his mother intruded on nearly all his waking thoughts, and he wished she could have seen him being so active, but the persistent trembling made it difficult for him to write. 'I have never been so agitated, so sterile, so unhappy,' he said, comparing himself enviously with Antoine, and hoping he was 'well, calm, industrious, happy. Everything which I am not!'[20]

He visited the cathedral at Bayeux, which he much preferred to the churches of Caen.[21] He especially liked the oriental figures in the nave and the statues on the ridges of the roof.[22] The painter Paul Helleu, a protégé of Montesquiou, who'd introduced him to Proust, was staying at Deauville, which is contiguous with Trouville and only twelve miles from Cabourg. Proust didn't remember the harbour from his holiday with his grandmother, but after visiting Helleu and looking at the harbour, 'which looked like a pearly vestibule of infinity',[23] Proust never again forgot it. The two men also went to Balleroy together to look at the Bouchers owned by the comte who had the same name as the village.

Across the river from Cabourg is Dives, where the tower of the fourteenth/fifteenth-century church has an oriental look. He also visited the château of Norrey at Bretteville-l'Orgueilleuse, attended a concert at the hotel and visited the painter Édouard Vuillard, a friend of the Bibescos. Robert Dreyfus was with the Strauses, and they got into an argument about the imperial German court. Proust also went to watch polo, and played baccarat every evening in the casino, usually losing.[24] Francis de Croisset was also in Cabourg with his mistress, the actress for whom he'd soon fight a duel with her other lover, Alfred Edwards, and though Proust saw little of them he offered to charter a boat if they'd like to sail back to Paris with him. 'It would have cost me no more than the taxis and the baccarat.'[25]

A month after his arrival in Cabourg, he was still persisting in his exhausting new routine, half appalled, half cheered to find himself in the grip of new habits. 'I have the feeling of no longer having a mind or a heart, except a physical heart, more weary each day, palpitating and mournful. But habit is dragging me along, as it did in bed. And I feel I am using and squandering the last of my strength.'[26] But he stayed on until the hotel was about to close in the third week of September. The Clermont-Tonnerres had invited him to stay in their château at Glisolles, but he decided to stay in Évreux and visit them from there.

On the way to Évreux, the driver took him into a misty valley, where he inhaled enough damp air to bring on a chronic asthma attack. After almost suffocating in the car, he tried to minimise the noise he'd have to suffer at the Hôtel Moderne by reserving the room above the one he was going to sleep in. He went to see the late-fifteenth-century bishop's palace adjacent to the cathedral at Évreux, and visited the eleventh-century Roman abbey of Saint-Taurin. He also drove to the church at Conches, where he liked the sixteenth-century stained glass, but his asthma got worse, and on the fourth day, travelling by taxi to the château, he dosed himself with seventeen cups of coffee on the way.[27] He enjoyed the château, especially when the marquis, to help him down a dark, unbanistered staircase, led him, like a child, by the hand.[28]

He'd intended to visit Claude Monet's garden at Giverny,[29] but his asthma was so bad that he made the whole journey back to Paris in a taxi, driven by Agostinelli. Feeling constantly breathless, Proust knew he was in for a bout of illness when he arrived. He stayed in bed for six days and got up on 7 October to hear Mayol sing. With his fat body, his curly wig, his eloquent gestures and a sprig of lily of the valley eternally in his buttonhole, he was the most popular of all the café-concert singers.[30]

When the Bibesco brothers invited Proust to join them for a motoring holiday in England, he was still too ill to accept,[31] and during his first three weeks in Paris he got up only twice.[32] Climbing stairs he became breathless sooner than ever before,[33] and felt convinced it would be unwise to go on living in Paris.[34]

On 8 November his, Robert's and his aunt's shares in the house were auctioned, but, when he got up, it was to attend a lecture on Versailles by Montesquiou at his house. Afterwards Proust regretted not going to the auction, where his aunt bid her way into sole ownership of the property, reducing his income without increasing his capital enough to satisfy him.[35]

He tried to celebrate the end of the year by visiting his parents' grave, but felt so ill that he turned back before reaching the cemetery.

EIGHTEEN

MAN OF LETTERS

For thirty-six years, the preparation for writing *À la recherche* had mostly been unconscious, but in 1908 determination began to harden. On 2 February, when Proust said he wanted to 'start a rather long work',[1] he'd already started in one of the five elegant notebooks Mme Straus had given him for New Year's Day. Slim enough to fit into a pocket, they were used for preliminary jottings.[2] The first two pages of these show how intimately the enterprise was connected with his mother. A quotation from Thomas Carlyle's confession to his mother – 'I am not so ill as I tell you' – is followed by notes on a dream in which Mme Proust comes back, groaning, and pleads with her sons not to prolong her suffering by making her undergo an operation.[3]

It wasn't Proust's original intention to exclude Robert from the fictional family. In early January, when the *Chronique des arts* was advertising cheap engravings, he wrote asking the editor to send '*on approval* some of your English engravings, especially those in which an animal is depicted next to the character(s) being portrayed'.[4] His plan was to start the novel with a chapter called 'Robert and the Goat: Mamma leaves on her travels'.[5] Describing his brother as he kisses the goat on its innocent nose, Proust refers to 'English painters who have often painted groups including a child caressing an animal'.[6]

He got sidetracked from the book when he started a series of pastiches, but he wasn't wasting his time. He later called the pastiches 'literary criticism in action'; the novel started as criticism of Sainte-Beuve in action. The pastiches were prompted by daily reports in the newspapers about the biggest scandal since the Dreyfus affair. Claiming he could manufacture diamonds out of carbon, an electrical engineer, Lemoine, had duped Sir Julius Wernher, a governor of De Beers, into giving him more than £64,000. Proust, who held shares in De Beers, was worried they'd go down in value, but he was soon taking a more literary interest in the scandal. It had struck him in 1898, after Colonel Henry killed himself and Cavaignac resigned, that the Dreyfus affair, which had once been Balzacian, had 'become Shakespearian, with its accumulation of precipitate denouements'.[7] He now saw how to exploit the way in which public events often seem to mimic literature: why not write a series of parodies showing how Balzac, Flaubert, the Goncourts and other writers might have dealt with the Lemoine scandal?

Pastiche had been particularly important during the stylistically self-conscious 1890s, the decade in which Proust came of age, and it was a form which came to him almost effortlessly. For years he'd been writing to Reynaldo in a style which mimicked the spelling and syntax of Montaigne and Pascal; in 1906 he'd even tried, in a series of thirty drawings for him, to parody different schools of painting.[8]

From dressing the reported facts of the Lemoine affair in an assortment of literary disguises he could learn a great deal. Information relayed to a reader is always dependent on a writer's way of choosing viewpoints and incidents, while comedy, which must predominate in parodies, had been almost entirely absent from *Jean Santeuil*. Though Proust had understood that style invariably implies an attitude, he hadn't realised how much it says about social background.

Wanting – before he plunged into the novel – to caution himself against the dangers of eclecticism, he intended his pastiches to have the same immunising effect on his prose that mimicry had once had on his behaviour, countering the temptation to emulate people he admired. Temperamentally rebellious writers – Rimbaud, Sartre, Brecht, Beckett, for instance – are less prone to eclecticism, but Proust, still believing Anatole France, Montesquiou, Anna de Noailles and even Lucien Daudet to be his superiors, needed to flex his literary muscles. As he wrote, 'I am the enemy of all pastiche, except when it is voluntary.'[9] Later he said: 'Not trying to be "brilliant", I pour generously into these pastiches things a better administrator of his own goods would prefer to have for his personal honour and signature.' And later still: 'The whole thing for me was above all a matter of hygiene; one must purge oneself of the natural vice of idolatry and imitation. And instead of slyly doing Michelet or doing Goncourt while signing [one's own name], doing it openly in the form of pastiche, in order to go back to being no more than Marcel Proust when I write my novels.' When he started on critical studies of the writers he was parodying,[10] he was effectively combining his critical and creative powers in a campaign to crystallise his literary identity.

In the Balzac pastiche he indulged (without much subtlety) in satire on aristocratic manners: 'While pressing the princess's hand, she kept the impenetrable calm possessed by the ladies of high society at the very moment when they plunge a dagger into your heart.' And he makes fun of Balzacian social detail: 'Mme Firmiani was sweating in her slippers, one of the master-pieces of Polish industry.'[11]

The Goncourt parody comprises two days of the brothers' diary. On the first, believing Lemoine's invention to be genu-ine, they see the scandal as a possible subject for 'a play in which one could have strong things about the power of today's high industry, a power which at bottom controls government and justice, and sets itself against anything that would be disas-trous for it in a new invention'. They hear Marcel Proust has committed suicide after losing part of his fortune when dia-mond shares went down in value, and Lucien Daudet tells them this Proust is a strange fellow 'who would live entirely in fits of enthusiasm, in *blessing* certain landscapes, certain books, a fellow who could for instance be captivated by Léon's novels'. (As in the schoolboy letter about multiplicity of per-sonality, he enjoys writing disparagingly about himself.) But on the second day they hear he hasn't committed suicide and Lemoine hasn't invented anything.[12]

After the Balzac pastiche had been published, together with the Goncourt, the Michelet and the Faguet, in the literary supplement of *Le Figaro* on 22 February, Proust responded to Anna de Noailles' congratulations by calling the enterprise 'a facile and vulgar exercise', but claiming 'these are good "copies" as they say about paintings'.[13]

Whatever Proust meant when he called himself a strange fellow, he was lavish in giving but strangely resistant when receiving. He got into a friendly argument with Helleu after visiting his studio towards the end of February and admiring a painting called *Autumn in Versailles*. Helleu sent it to him, and Proust wanted it, but not as a gift. Couldn't he buy it? Helleu refused, and, when it was returned, sent it back to Proust with an inscription.[14] Wanting to give something in return, Proust asked Mme Catusse to find out the cost of an old Dutch caravel made in silver plate.[15]

He wrote more pastiches in the intervals between asthma attacks, but these were becoming more severe, lasting over twenty-four hours. They were 'not like death, because there is nothing calm about them, but like agony'.[16] Two of the new pastiches appeared in the supplement on 14 March – one of Flaubert, together with a critique, ostensibly by Sainte-Beuve, of Flaubert's novel on the Lemoine affair. The Flaubert passage starts with a courtroom scene painted in the exotic colours of *Salammbô*: 'The heat became suffocating, a bell tolled, some turtle-doves took flight, and, the windows having been closed at the order of the president, the smell of dust was diffused. He was old, a clown's face, a robe too narrow for his corpulence, pretensions to wit. . . .'And within a few sentences, the narrative has focused on a Negro who draws attention to himself by producing an orange from his pocket and offering segments of the fruit to his neighbours, starting with a priest, who claims 'never to have tasted such a good one; it is an excellent fruit, refreshing'. Nearby is a woman with a parrot on her hat. Lemoine's lawyer 'had a southern accent, appealed to the feelings of generosity, kept taking off his pince-nez'. In French the rapid succession of three verbs in the imperfect tense incisively reproduces the Flaubertian combination of brusque summary with random selection of detail as in a leisurely conversation.

By parodying Sainte-Beuve Proust drives home many of the points he often made in his explicit criticism of the critic. Loftily condescending towards an 'author who belongs to the school that never sees anything noble or admirable in humanity', Proust's Sainte-Beuve complains about the clown's face, 'which is enough to make the reader lose interest'; at the narrow robe – 'a rather clumsy feature which tells us nothing'[17] – and at the Negro with the orange. In spite of his pretensions to objectivity and impersonality, Flaubert has superimposed on his picture colourful details imported from the Carthage of *Salammbô* – a Negro, an orange, a parrot. Underneath the fun Proust is having at the expense of both Flaubert and Sainte-Beuve is a serious criticism of the way subjectivity invades realism.

The last and longest pastiche – of Ernest Renan, who wrote *La Vie de Jésus* – appeared on 21 March. Lemoine had claimed to be manufacturing the diamonds at a factory in Lille, and

Renan is made to procrastinate in a loving description of the surrounding countryside. 'Even in our days, after all the deforestation it has undergone, it is a veritable garden, planted with poplars and willows, sprinkled with fountains and flowers. . . . An Englishman who lived in this epoch, John Ruskin, whom we read unfortunately only in the pitifully platitudinous translation which Marcel Proust has left to us, lavishes praise on the grace of these poplars, the glossy freshness of these springs.'[18]

Writing pastiche is like acting in a mask, and in his Renan comedy Proust is at last able to make fun of Anna de Noailles. After praising her work as a hundred times better than the book of Ecclesiastes, Renan is made to believe she 'led in the country, perhaps not without a certain quantity of boredom, a completely simple and isolated life, in the little orchard which usually serves as her interlocutor'.[19]

Proust enjoyed himself with this pastiche. 'It came to me in such torrents that I added whole pages by glueing them into the proofs, and at the last minute there were quotations from Mme de Noailles that I could not check. I had adjusted my interior metronome to his rhythm, and I could have written ten volumes like that.'[20] But he was unsure whether it was worth while. 'I shall do no more. What an idiotic exercise!'[21] To another correspondent, who'd praised the pastiches, he responded: 'In more skilful hands than mine I think it could become like an indirect, more discreet, economic and elegant form of literary criticism'.[22] But he wasn't too modest to want the pastiches to appear as a book, and he was willing to pay publishing costs.[23] After Mercure de France and Fasquelle rejected the idea, he offered it to Calmann-Lévy.[24]

The friends who wrote to congratulate him included Anna de Noailles[25] and Mme Léon Fould, wife of a prominent banker. He was specially pleased to hear from her because she could possibly introduce him to the comte de Goyon's twenty-year-old daughter, Oriane, who reminded him of Gladys Deacon. She also had a surname mentioned in Chateaubriand's *Mémoires d'Outre-Tombe*.[26] The comte was the younger brother of the duc de Feltre, and with his interest in genealogy sharpened by his plans for the novel, Proust was studying the *Almanach de Gotha*, which contained in close proximity entries about the Essling, Feltre and Fezensac families,[27] but he didn't know Oriane's aunt, the duchesse de Feltre, was the sister of Albu's mother. In March Proust asked Mme Fould whether her daughter Elisabeth knew Oriane, who was going to be at a musical soirée given by the comtesse de Saussine on 30 March. He tried to get himself invited, but it wasn't until mid-April that he approached Albu about her.[28]

Albu might be useful, too, in arranging another meeting Proust wanted. Hadn't he once had some letters delivered by a young man, a telegraph messenger related to one of his servants? 'In which case you could help me for I need to meet a telegraph messenger because of something I am writing.'[29] But he didn't want Albu to call. He was planning to move away from Paris in July, he said, and of all the friendships he'd have to sacrifice, he'd miss the one with Albu most.[30] They could correspond, but Albu was a careless letter-writer: once he'd written 'boulevard Haussmann' on an envelope without any house number.[31]

Recently Proust had been seeing more of Georges de Lauris, who'd been a frequent visitor during the winter, but fell ill in the spring.[32] Proust's health remained poor, and when he needed to go out, he fortified himself with caffeine, which usually put his breathing on an even keel for a few hours,[33] at the cost of making his gait unsteady. When he called on Albu and met the 'ravishing' marquise, he felt sure he was 'tottering like a mad beggar'.[34]

After staying in bed for a week at the end of March with bronchitis and a high temperature,[35] he was harassed throughout most of April by noise: this time the tenant of the flat above him, M. Pernolet, was moving out, and the disturbance often lasted all through the morning.[36]

His health was better in May, but when he joined the Polo Club, thanks to Guiche, who proposed him, there was little chance he'd put in many appearances there. If he was still interested in high society, it was mainly because he wanted to feature it in the novel. By now, as notebook jottings show, he'd sketched out the Narrator's main relationship. 'In the second part of the novel the girl will be ruined, I will keep her without trying to possess her by incapacity for happiness.' This phrase picks up from a sentence on the first page: 'I do not love you, if I see you I will love you; trick. Not trying to possess by incapacity for pleasing and giving happiness. Chartres.' His original intention was to call the girl Maria (after Marie Benardaky) and to make the Narrator imagine, before he met her, that the wind was carrying messages of love to her in Chartres.[37]

He took a decisive step when he bought exercise books of the kind used at the Condorcet.[38] So long as he wrote on loose sheets of paper, which could easily get lost, he felt less committed to writing something of substantial length. In choosing school exercise books he was emotionally going back to a period during his mother's life when he had specified tasks to fulfil. He subsequently destroyed many of the exercise books, but the seventh page of the notebook lists the chapters he'd drafted by about July:

> Robert and the goat. Mamma leaves on a journey.
> The Villebon Way and the Méséglise Way.
> The mark of vice and openness of the face. Disappointment which is a possession, kissing the face.
> My grandmother in the garden, M. de Bretteville's dinner party, I go upstairs, Mamma's face then and since in my dreams, I cannot sleep, compromises, etc.
> The Castellanes, hydrangeas in Normandy, English land-owners, German; Louis-Philippe's granddaughter, Fantaisie, the mother's face in a debauched boy.
> What the Villebon and Méséglise walks taught me.

Bretteville was his original name for Swann, and the dinner party was going to lead into the episode of the goodnight kiss. This is the first mention of the two walks which were going to evolve into Swann's Way and the Guermantes' Way, one associated with the bourgeoisie, the other with the aristocracy. He was planning the novel as a *Bildungsroman*: the Narrator will learn from his experiences. Boni de Castellane, a fair-haired, fair-skinned dandy, epitomied the aristocratic life, but the family, like the hydrangeas, has been transplanted. The splendid château of Villebon is near Illiers, and Fantaisie is another château Proust considered 'as aristocratic as certain families'. The theme of the innocent mother and the child who turns vicious will be resumed à propos the baron de Charlus, and the cryptic note about the mark of vice and openness of the face shows Proust was already wrestling with a problem which will be crucial. After the Narrator has misread a face, disappointment precedes the enlightenment which is like an asset. Proust is at an early stage in the thinking that will lead to the development of what he'll call 'prepared characters' –

characters who at first seem different from what they are.
Charlus doesn't immediately appear to be homosexual. Legrandin seems in his first scene to love the simple life and despise
the nobility; but he soon turns out to be a snob and will
eventually be ennobled. This educational disillusionment with
individuals becomes part of a larger theme; the Narrator will
discover it was naive to place so much faith in the power of
love and in the aristocracy.

Behind the jottings that record these new insights is a
vocational pull towards creative didacticism: Proust, like
Darlu, will invite others to share the fruits of enlightenment,
and something of this original formulation about vice will
survive in one of the key passages which combine the theme
of appearance and reality with the theme of ageing. Mme
Sazerat's name remains unchanged, but the woman does not:

> However, in the same way as I would have done with the
> idea of royalty or vice, which loses no time in giving a new
> face to a stranger, with whom one could so easily, if one's
> eyes were still blindfolded, have made the blunder of being
> insolent or respectful, and in the same features in which
> one now sees something distinguished or suspicious, I made
> myself interpolate in the stranger's face the idea that she
> was Mme Sazerat, and in the end I rehabilitated the former
> meaning of this face which would have remained really alien-
> ated for me, wholly that of another person no less devoid of
> all the human attributes I had known than a man changed
> into a monkey, if her name and the affirmation of her identity
> had not set me, despite the complexity of the problem, on
> the track of the solution.[39]

There's no mention of Sainte-Beuve in the early notes, but in
a May letter Proust had listed eight projects:

a study of the nobility
a Parisian novel
an essay on Sainte-Beuve and Flaubert
an essay on women
an essay on pederasty (not easy to publish)
a study of stained-glass windows,
a study of tombstones
a study of the novel.

The list, made when he was hoping Albu would let him see

albums of old family photographs and a genealogy showing the two lines of his ancestry,[40] should not be taken to mean that the novel, the four studies and the three essays were being planned as eight separate pieces of writing. The criticism of the critic was going to be dovetailed with the criticism of the novelist, while the study of the nobility wouldn't necessarily be separate from the Parisian novel. He could accumulate material and, at the same time, start commenting on it by manipulating it. Much of the best modern art has been born from a negative reaction against other works of art – Duchamp's readymades, for instance, or the first plays by Beckett and Ionesco; a letter to Robert Dreyfus shows Proust's plan for the novel was evolving out of hostility to narrative that merely presents the surface of incidents: 'my reason for thinking the importance and suprasensible reality of art prevent certain anecdotal novels, however pleasing they are, from deserving quite the rank you award them (art being something too superior to content itself with counterfeiting life, as we judge it with our intelligence and depict it in our conversation) – this same reason does not allow me to make the realisation of an artistic dream depend on factors which are themselves anecdotal and drawn too directly from life not to participate in its contingency and irreality.'[41] Hostility to this kind of narrative would coalesce with hostility to Sainte-Beuve.

Mme Straus' brother, Ludovic Halévy, died on 8 May, and Proust started an obituary, but abandoned it in deference to Dreyfus, who was writing an article on him. Concerned about Mme Straus, Proust wrote to her on 10 May, and six days later, when Robert de Billy's wife lost her father, again showed how good he was at comforting bereaved friends: 'I entreat you to believe that you are never out of my sad thoughts and that I never stop praying for him.'[42] And in June, when Pierre Lavallée's mother died, 'All the tenderness of the old days springs back to my heart to weep with you at the loss of this admirable mother, so beautiful, so intelligent, so good, so steadfast, so gentle. . . .'[43]

But at the end of May Proust was still planning to live in the country, separated from all his friends. To Albu, about to move into the avenue Hoche, Proust wrote enviously about the balls he was going to miss: 'in all my dreams of young girls I think only about the balls. . . . And when you are giving them, I shall no longer be in Paris, alas, and shall be living in some hole.'[44] For the moment, he was contributing to the social column of *Le Figaro*, but, unable to go out much, he depended on information Albu supplied, listing the most distinguished guests at the parties he attended. Proust wanted to reward him with either a beautiful chandelier or a piece of furniture. 'Tell me frankly and quickly what would give you most pleasure, and if you do not let me give you something of importance I shall conclude you do not want your home to contain something beautiful which reminds you of me.'[45]

Albu still hadn't arranged for him to meet Oriane de Goyon, and when he heard she'd be at a ball given by the princesse de Polignac at the Washington Palace in the rue Magellan, he asked the princesse de Caraman-Chimay to procure an invitation for him: 'for something I am writing, for sentimental reasons too, I would like to go to a ball'.[46] It's hard to be sure – Proust may himself have been unsure – whether he wanted to use Oriane as a model, or whether he was pursuing her to contradict rumours about his homosexuality. Anyway, the princesse obliged, and *Le Figaro* praised the occasion as 'truly marvellous and of a supreme elegance. . . . In the garden, magically illuminated with coloured lanterns, hunting horns were sounded at intervals.'[47] But the evening was disastrous for Proust, whose motives were misinterpreted when he complimented the vicomte de Paris on his looks. Proust left miserably, without even waiting to be presented to Mlle de Goyon.[48]

He met her on 22 June, at a soirée given by the princesse de Murat, but his excitement was mixed with embarrassment caused by the Lemaires and by André de Fouquières, who introduced him to her. 'Suzette,' said Madeleine Lemaire, 'show me the girl Marcel's talking about,' and, after staring at her, 'She's very ugly and she looks as if she needs a wash.' Suzette made matters worse still by laughing loudly and drawing Proust aside to look at the unfortunate girl from a different angle. Fouquières, who was drunk, asked audibly: 'What do you say to those little cheeks? You'd like to pinch them, eh? And what would you say to a little kiss? . . . Just as well you've trimmed your beard. You're looking good.' 'The expression about wishing to be swallowed by a hole in the ground is inadequate to describe my feelings or those of the young girl or those of her fiancé, who was standing there.'[49] 'I thought I was going to fall over, but it was also rather a big disappointment, because she looks better at a distance and she is slightly irritating as soon as she speaks, and more flirtatious than likeable. I am going to think about her again more quietly, all my ideas are a little confused.'[50] He left without waiting to be presented to her father. 'I had lost my head. Besides, he might have hit me because it was my fault his daughter had become everybody's target.'[51] Proust wouldn't have been able to sleep if he hadn't distanced himself from what had happened by telling the story in letters to Albu, Reynaldo and Mme Straus, to whom he described Oriane as 'a girl I love'.[52] Albu was asked whether he knew where she'd be spending the summer.

Proust's own plans were still uncertain. Perhaps he'd settle near Paris and near Albu; perhaps he'd 'buy a little house above Florence and try to tell some poor Italian woman how I am inspired by this and that and especially Mlle de Goyon'.[53] An alternative, recommended by Fouquières, was to stay at Dinard,[54] but at the end of June he was still undecided. Either before leaving or on his way into the country, he was keen to see the vicomte de Paris. Part of Proust's interest in him depended on the name Guermantes, which had lingered in his mind from an old song a nursemaid had once sung to him.[55] The Château de Guermantes, which is near Lagny, twenty-one miles from Paris, belonged to the vicomte's grandmother, the baronne de Lareinty, and to his parents, the comte and comtesse; though it cost Proust a great effort to go out during the day, he offered to visit the vicomte there.[56] Wishing to see it was wishing to start some kind of dialectic between the real château and the vague plans he had for the way he'd use it: 'château of Guermantes, kind of forbidden paradise – fantasy place to satisfy erotic dreams of Narrator. First it is a medieval castle, then monastery sheltering remains of Saint Hilaire.'[57]

Impatience to make headway with the book was a factor in his decision to stay in Paris. His health might suffer, but he was becoming firmer in his intention to sacrifice his life to his art, and if he uprooted himself it might be a long time before he felt sufficiently settled to concentrate seriously on the work which had already been postponed so long. At the beginning of July he renewed his lease on the flat.

On Sunday 12 July, he got up during the day for the first time that year. It was to visit Robert at Louveciennes, near Bougival, where he often stayed with his wife and daughter,

Suzy, in a small villa they rented from an actress. But Proust's arrangements went wrong, and at the end of an exhausting journey he failed to find his brother. The decision to eliminate Robert from the novel must have been taken around this time. Proust still brooded enviously about his brother's success in measuring up to the standard of success their father had set. In July Proust made these notes on a dream: 'Papa near us. Robert speaks to him, makes him smile, makes him give exact answers to everything. Absolute illusion of life. So you see that dead one is almost alive. Perhaps he would be mistaken over the answers but still, a semblance of life. Perhaps he is not dead.'[58]

Perhaps his mother wasn't, either. She still appeared in his dreams. 'Rapidly following people along a cliff, at sunset, overtaking them, not quite recognising them, here is Mamma, but she remains indifferent to my life, she says good morning to me, I feel I shall not see her again for months. Would she understand my book? No. Yet the power of the spirit does not depend on the body, Robert says I should find out her address in case I am called for her death, but I do not know the district or the name of the person who is looking after her.'[59] This sense of failing in his duty towards his dead mother is echoed in a dream of the Narrator's about his dead grandmother, but here there is no brother to remind him of his responsibilities. Tall forms approach and glide away, leaving him in tears. He searches unsuccessfully for his grandmother, knowing she still exists, though with diminished vitality. For weeks he has not written to her. Alone with the nurse who is looking after her in a small room, fit for an old servant, she must think he has forgotten her. He must go there straight away. How can he have forgotten the address?[60]

Three or four days before the abortive visit to Louveciennes, Proust had got up at midnight to meet Henri Bernstein, who'd promised to take him to a brothel – perhaps he was planning a brothel episode in the novel – but Bernstein thought he looked too scruffy. 'I keep this memory in reserve,' Proust wrote, 'for the times I would be tempted to admire you excessively. For in this respect you are inferior to François de Paris and to many others.'[61]

Though Proust's clothes often created a bad impression – it was hard for him to look elegant when he needed to wear so many layers of wool – clothes were important to him. Ordering an overcoat with a bright violet lining, he said 'I shall always take it off in the cloakroom because if, for my part, I do not mind mockery, I do not want to inflict it on my friends. This coat, if I unbutton it in a carriage, will make anyone who sees it think I am a bishop on his round.'[62] And to Bernstein Proust wrote: 'I have ordered at the Carnaval de Venise a collection of carnavalesque and Venetian clothes with which I shall try to repair my irreparable lack of chic when we are seen together.'[63] In fact he bought all his clothes from the Carnaval de Venise, a shop near the Opéra, which sent an elderly English cutter to his flat for fittings. Everything was made to measure. Apart from his tails and his dinner jacket, he had a black jacket with piping and several jackets he wore with striped trousers.[64]

By the middle of July he was trying to decide whether he should spend the summer in Cabourg, though the Grand Hôtel was under new management, and it would cost at least 9,000 francs to stay for two months.[65] He makes the Narrator say:

> I had come the first time to look for the unknown; I now came looking for what was known to me. I had come in search of an eternal mist, etc; I came back in search of memories of dining behind the blue windows in the sun's rays on the shutter. . . . I had come to look for a Persian church; I was coming in search of what Elstir had told me about the church and the seas he had painted and what I will find in spite of myself (that will explain without my saying so the descriptions of the Turneresque seas). I had come for an unknown society; I was coming now above all because I knew everybody.

The Persian church was the oriental-looking one at Dives.

Taking Nicolas with him, he travelled on Saturday the 18th, and arrived with a high temperature, which kept him in bed for several days. He'd expected the sea air and the hotel's various amenities to resuscitate him as they had last summer, but he was disappointed: this time, as in Paris, he didn't get up till the evening.

The hotel was full, and the guests irritated him even more than last year: 'What a crowd! Nobody whose name you would know. Some Israelite wholesale dealers are the aristocracy of the place, and proud of it too.'[66] If pro-Jewish feelings had predominated during the Dreyfus affair, he'd now reverted to an anti-Semitism like that of his Jewish mother. He didn't even mind contributing to an anti-Semitic paper, provided he could do it anonymously. Before leaving Paris he'd written an enthusiastic review of Lucien's novel, *Le Chemin mort*. 'In the exquisite and powerful book with which he makes his brilliant début, one indubitably rediscovers the qualities of Alphonse Daudet – the inexhaustible intelligence, the inspirational observation, a sensitivity which makes people funnier and things sadder. . . .'[67] But when Proust went to the offices of *Le Figaro*, Calmette was in Switzerland, and it was so hard to place the review that, after taking it with him to Cabourg, he posted it to Lucien, inviting him to pass it on to *Le Gaulois*, *L'Intransigeant* or *Libre Parole*. 'In which case I would prefer it not to be under my name, because I would be afraid it might look disrespectful towards Mamma that I should write for a paper whose objective, whose policy is nothing but anti-Semitism.'[68]

At the hotel, he met the president of the local golf club, the vicomte d'Alton, with his wife and their two daughters; the vicomtesse was responsive to questions about the language and customs of the nobility.[69]

Shortly before they left Paris, Proust and Nicolas had both been called up for fifteen days' military service. Proust got himself exempted, but failed to secure exemption for Nicolas, though he asked Reynaldo to use his contacts at the War Office. On the day after Nicolas left him alone in Cabourg, Proust succumbed to asthma and, not wanting to look after himself if he became ill, sent for Ulrich, for whom he booked a room at another hotel.[70] But he benefited so little from having him there that he sent Ulrich away again.

Before the end of July Proust gave a dinner party at the hotel for seven guests including Louisa, her sister, Loche Radziwill and his mistress, Christiane Lorin.[71] Robert de Billy wanted to come, but, discouraged by Proust from staying at the hotel,[72] he stayed in Trouville with the Finalys at 'Les Frémonts', where Proust visited him. On the way back to Cabourg he'd intended to visit Louisa and her new lover, Robert Gangnat, who were renting a villa in Bénerville, but he felt too ill to call. Gangnat was a forty-year-old lawyer, agent for the Société des Auteurs Dramatiques. He'd been supporting her since February 1906, while she'd been keeping him in ignorance of the allowance she was still receiving from Albu.

Proust spent most of his holiday in bed, but he risked a chill

one evening by standing still for a long time on the promenade
when he saw the actress Lucy Gérard. 'Her dress was pink and
from a great distance added to the orange sky the complemen-
tary colour of the twilight. I stayed for quite a long time,
looking at the fine pink blob, and returned, with a cold, after
I had seen her blend into the horizon at the edge of which she
was gliding like an enchanted sail.'[73] This was how he described
her to Reynaldo, but his notebook entry runs: 'I do not know
about respectable society, but that of the riff-raff is delicious.
She was less indifferent to my gaze than the others. She often
walked alone in the evening, and I looked at her as she passed,
she looked at me. I told myself: tomorrow this woman will
perhaps be my friend etc., perhaps tomorrow she will remain
(and always) a stranger.' He'd liked her at first because he'd
mistaken her for another woman, but after watching her go
into a house, he felt sure she was full of regret at not knowing
him. It's hard to be sure whether he was teasing himself with
the idea of a liaison or rehearsing for the Narrator's feeling of
generalised love for the group of 'jeunes filles en fleur'. Certainly she made him think of Laure Hayman: he goes on to
use the phrase 'lost time' in relation to his uncle Louis, who
'spends his life on linking himself with the small world of the
woman he loves'. In the novel Swann does this, and, looking
at Lucy Gérard, Proust may have been empathising with the
way Swann would look at Odette. He may also have been
comparing the actress with Mlle de Goyon and blending the
two images in a premonition of the way he was going to end
the novel by uniting the bourgeoisie with the aristocracy in
the beautiful person of a young girl who mingles the good
looks of Gilberte and Saint-Loup. But he was thinking mainly
about the absurdity of unreciprocated love, the longing felt for
someone who may be indifferent: 'We would do anything at
all to go where they are, they go there out of some meaningless
obligation and not for one moment would they entertain the
idea of altering their plans for us.' He also sketches out the
principle he'll explain in *Le Temps retrouvé* about cutting across
the subjectivity of a lover's fond beliefs, never writing 'She
was so sweet' but always 'I enjoyed embracing her.'[74]

He let about four weeks go by without calling on Louisa,
'though each day I tell myself tomorrow I shall be able to'.[75]
He was still hoping to mediate between her and Albu, who
wasn't entirely cured of his addiction. By trying to keep in

touch, he was still giving her power to provoke him with protracted silence, making him alternate between anxiety and anger. After ten of his letters went unanswered, Proust intervened: 'His friendship is quite genuine, perfectly disinterested . . . why do you refuse him the one thing he asks of you – to know how you are, to give him your news?'[76]

When Proust finally called on her and Gangnat at the Chalet Russe, they were receiving a visit from the son of a neighbour, Mme Gallimard, who owned the Manoir de Bénerville. The twenty-seven-year-old Gaston was surprised by Proust's battered straw hat, his threadbare black suit and his long velvet-lined cape. He looked so dusty and exhausted that when he talked about stopping at farmhouses on the way to rest and ask for coffee, Gaston Gallimard assumed he'd walked all the way from Cabourg.

He invited all three of them to dinner at the hotel, where his other guests included Louisa's sister, Loche Radziwill and Christiane, together with an old marquis who suffered from *locomotor ataxia*: Proust not only helped him to move about but steered the conversation into subjects on which he could shine.[77]

At Trouville Proust went to see the Strauses, who had Hervieu and Mme de Pierrebourg with them, and he met a couple called Daireaux, who'd rented a villa at Cabourg, and their twenty-four-year-old son Max, the youngest of four brothers. Proust had known the older brothers during his friendship with Gaston de Caillavet and Jeanne Pouquet.

Of the young men Proust met in Cabourg, his favourite was the nineteen-year-old Marcel Plantevignes, who was introduced to him in the casino by the vicomtesse d'Alton. Marcel Plantevignes was holidaying with his parents; his father was a rich manufacturer of neckties. The young Marcel was soon visiting the older one every evening at the hotel, where he read to the boy from his work in progress, but one day on the promenade, meeting a lady who often teased Proust about his indifference to women, Marcel was warned that Proust was a homosexual. Cutting the woman short, he made his escape, but next time she met Proust she made a joke about his young friend, and soon afterwards he wrote to accuse Marcel Plantevignes of stabbing him in the back and 'clumsily spoiling a friendship which could have been very beautiful'.[78] The boy couldn't understand how he'd offended Proust, and when his father called at the hotel, wanting to find out, Proust not only refused to explain but challenged him to a duel. When the uncomprehending Camille Plantevignes paid him a second visit, Proust merely told him to find seconds as soon as possible. Reluctantly he approached the vicomte d'Alton, only to be told he'd already agreed to act as Proust's second, but he and the marquis de Pontcharra, who was to be Proust's other second, promised to see whether the dispute could be settled amicably. Though Proust was adamant, his intention was to fire into the air if they fought with pistols, and several days passed before he hinted to d'Alton that his grievance stemmed from a conversation between Marcel and a woman. By paying a third visit to Proust at the hotel, Camille Plantevignes persuaded him to meet Marcel and listen to the boy's explanation.

In cutting the woman short, Marcel had used the words 'I know, I know,' which Proust took to mean Marcel knew he was a homosexual, when all the boy had meant was 'I know what you're going to tell me.' 'But how did you know?' Proust demanded, and Marcel had to answer: 'Because that's what they all say on the promenade.' 'Proust's face, already ivory-coloured, seemed to become even paler, taking on the tint of polished marble.' Sorrowfully and sarcastically he said: 'How charming to arrive somewhere preceded by one's reputation!' He then asked the boy what he believed and what his parents believed. Told none of them believed a word of it, he was conciliatory, but warned Marcel to be more discreet: 'Our friendships, our loves, are made in order to be mocked and vilified. Don't tell anyone you come to see me. Better still, say you aren't seeing me any more.'[79]

Proust would have liked to stay on and write in the hotel after it closed, but he was told this would be impossible, and he left when he heard on 25 September that Georges de Lauris had been injured in a motoring accident, fracturing his thigh-bone. But instead of going back to his flat, Proust booked a room in the Hôtel des Réservoirs at Versailles, and on 26 or 27 September made the journey in a taxi driven by Agostinelli, stopping en route to look at the Merovingian crypt and the abbots' tombs in the ruined abbey of Jumièges.[80] He arrived at the hotel in an exhausted state. 'Staircase to go to the bath at the Réservoir[s], white flowers of the carpet answering the sweet white flowers on the wall, silent staircase waiting, you speak in low voices the smell of the house sweats, cinerary urns when you arrive.'[81]

At Versailles he formulated ideas basic to the novel. Some of the notebook jottings are about what he'd later call involuntary memory and about illness as an incentive towards writing the novel:

> We believe the past to be mediocre because we are *thinking* it, but the past is not that, it is so much unevenness in the paving stones of St Mark's Baptistry (photograph of the St Mark's Bap about which we'd no longer been thinking), making the sun blinding for us on the canal.
>
> Perhaps I should bless my poor health, which has, through the ballast of fatigue, taught me immobility, silence, the possibility of working. Premonitions of death. Soon you will no longer be able to say all that. Laziness or doubt or impotence fleeing in uncertainty on the art form. Should it be made into a novel, a philosophical study, am I a novelist?[82]

He will develop the idea of involuntary memory in such a way that stimulus from a photograph will be inadmissible. In *Le Temps retrouvé* the Narrator trips on an uneven paving stone, and the sensation is what jogs his memory, but Proust himself had obviously been reminded of the Baptistry by a photograph. He'd already been feeling premonitions of death in Cabourg, where he'd often quoted to Marcel Plantevignes Baudelaire's line: 'Brief spell of duty, the tomb awaits, she is greedy.'

He made notes in Versailles about the use of literature as a substitute for direct contact with friends; he was becoming more aware of the function his letter-writing had been serving. In one 1908 letter he claimed: 'It is the privilege of those who always live alone to fashion in their mind substitutes for real people and be able to like them without ever seeing them.'[83] Correspondence gives the illusion of direct contact without confrontation. In a sense, the whole novel is an extension of his correspondence: he wanted to 'say all that' to his friends before it was too late. One of the characters was to be a 'man of letters' who makes contact with his friends through literature. 'Man of letters near Cabourg working in the hope of seeing friends from time to time, of appearing to them through what he does, then the thought of his friends becomes a substitute for them, he never sees them.' The model for the man of letters was to be Alexander Harrison, and Marcel –

the note is ambiguous: Marcel may be either the Narrator or Plantevignes – was going to approach him in the way Jean Santeuil and Henri had approached the novelist C. by sending a note to him in a restaurant, except that Marcel would go to see the writer without having read any of his work.[84]

Some of these ideas will crystallise around the painter Elstir when the Narrator and Saint-Loup send a note to him in a restaurant. When they visit him in his studio, the genuine generosity of a great artist makes aristocratic charm look artificial. 'And no doubt, at the beginning, he had thought with pleasure, even in his solitude, that by means of his work he would address himself at a distance, would give a more elevated idea of himself to those who had misunderstood him or hurt his feelings. So perhaps he lived alone not from indifference but from love of other people.'[85] This passage occurs in *Jeunes Filles*, which was mostly written in 1912, but the key points don't deviate from the notebook formulation of 1908.

When Reynaldo came to the hotel, he saw no signs of the progress Proust was making. He was usually to be found playing dominoes with Agostinelli or Nicolas. And though he'd come back from Cabourg because of the motoring accident, Georges de Lauris was immobilised in a bedroom on the second floor of his parents' house in the rue Washington, where the asthmatic Proust had enormous difficulty in climbing the two flights of stairs. On 28 September he paid his first visit to Georges, and stayed on in Paris to take Marcel Plantevignes and four other young friends from Cabourg to a comedy, *Le Roi* by Caillavet, Robert de Flers and Emmanuel Arène. It had opened at the Variétés in April and was now reopening after the summer recess.

Proust came back to see Georges in Paris on 2 or 3 October but felt much worse at the end of the journey. Though he dosed himself with strong coffee, he still couldn't face the climb up the staircase. Apologising to Georges by letter, he attributed the sudden malaise to the change of altitude – Versailles is eighty-three metres higher than Paris.[86]

In Versailles he felt well, sometimes almost euphoric: 'day of sun and cold where the sun at moments puts an enchantment in the bare, reddish brown trees if there are certain colours in the houses (Versailles), carriage taken at the station, going towards the château. Or on foot, happy at each footstep on the stone.'[87] But in Paris the energy drained out of him. He tried to arrange a dinner party for Marcel Plantevignes to meet Albu, Loche and Gabriel de la Rochefoucauld, and wanting to see Marcel, who was due to leave Paris in ten days, Proust sent Agostinelli to him with a note suggesting he should either come to the boulevard Haussmann or meet for a chat in the car.[88] On 7 October he made a third visit to Paris but again baulked at the stairs in the rue Washington.

October was the worst month he'd ever had. At Cabourg the asthma attacks had stopped, but now they resumed savagely, hitting him especially hard after the three trips to Paris. In Versailles he seldom felt well enough to write in bed and was liable, when he did, to lose what he'd written.[89] Nor could he be sure, when he made the effort to write letters, that they were posted: he gave them to a waiter who didn't always ask for a stamp, and at least one letter failed to arrive.[90]

'I am very very ill my dear Robert,' he told de Flers, 'scarcely ever get up any more, and frightful attacks incessantly, I no longer even have a brain.'[91] 'My life consists of affliction.'[92] 'For a month I have been unable to get up for a single day, more tortured by incessant suffocation than ever before.'[93] He was 'in a state of malaise caused by the medicines I take all the time with no result. But I think it would be worse if I didn't take them.'[94] In previous bouts of illness he'd always let Reynaldo visit him, but not even he was allowed to call,[95] nor was Robert Proust.[96] He thought about Albu, he said, much more often than once a day, but scarcely saw him more than once a year.[97] And he told Mme Straus: 'Since the last evening I saw you I have seldom gone for four or five hours without thinking of you.'[98]

Unable to update memories of friends by keeping in touch, he felt more than ever driven to get something down on paper. 'In my less bad times I have started (twice for twenty minutes) to work. It is so tiresome to think so many things and feel that the mind where they are coming into play will soon perish and nobody will know them.'[99] He felt like a pregnant woman unsure whether she'd live long enough to give birth.

Everything is fictional laboriously, because I have no imagination but everything is filled with a sense I have long carried inside me, too long, because my thought has forgotten it, and my heart has grown cold. . . . Work makes us a little like mothers. Sometimes, feeling close to my end I said to

myself, feeling the child which was forming in my stomach,
and not knowing whether I could collect the strength to give
birth to it, I said to him with a sad and gentle smile: 'I would
never see you.'[100]

At the end of October he was 'worse than ever, unable to get
up or talk or eat or breathe or sleep' and, as so often in his
Paris flat, he was disturbed by persistent noise. In the street,
workmen were laying new paving stones, 'and it is atrocious'.[101] Though he was verging on bronchitis,[102] he decided
to have himself moved back to his flat, and he left Versailles
on 3 or 4 November.

NINETEEN

INVISIBLE SUBSTANCE

'An illness can be as absorbing, as demanding, as tiring, as ageing as the hardest of jobs, even manual. Whatever the origin and the nature of the commitments which relentlessly fill my life, it is always true that I have no leisure, that it is hard for me to find a few hours for working.'[1] It was particularly hard when he arrived back in Paris. Builders were at work in the dentist's flat on the second floor, and Proust felt 'asphyxiated by a radiator which is not working properly. As soon as I can get up, I will escape, but I do not know where.' He was 'coughing incessantly, with a high temperature, but keeping three windows open until one in the morning to fight against the radiator'.[2]

His discomfort was often severe enough to make him forget that his condition could worsen but, once the radiator had been repaired, his shutters remained permanently closed and his curtains drawn.[3] 'I hesitate before making the slightest movement, stretching out my arm, etc. . . . . I have eaten nothing for four days, gone without sleep for ten, been in pain every minute.'[4] Previously he'd dosed himself with caffeine only in preparation for an outing, but now he started using it when he wanted to write, and sometimes he had to end a letter abruptly when an attack was coming on.[5] But he kept himself informed about the stock exchange, corresponding about shares with Albu and with Lionel Hauser, Paris representative of the Hamburg bankers Warburg and the New York company Kuhn-Loeb. Nor did Proust feel too ill to resume his contributions of social gossip to *Le Figaro*, but when he asked Emmanuel Bibesco to help in the way Albu had by listing the most distinguished guests at parties he attended, the prince refused.[6]

Proust was provoked into thinking about literature again when Bizet's collected letters were reviewed by Louis Ganderax, whose pompous pleonasms provoked angry formulations about the need for linguistic innovation.

> It is nonsensical to believe there is a French language, existing outside writers and in need of protection. . . . Each writer has to make his own language just as each violinist has to make his own *sound*. . . . Correctness, stylistic perfection exist, but only on the far side of originality. . . . The only way of defending the language is to attack it. Yes, Madame Straus. Because its unity consists only of neutralised opposites, of an apparent immobility which conceals a vertiginous and incessant life.[7]

He was still undecided about staying in Paris. At least twice a week he had severe attacks – some lasted over forty hours – making it impossible for him to write or eat, and almost impossible to move or breathe. In two months he got up once,[8] let his brother call twice, and received few other visits,[9] but had frequent letters from Reynaldo.[10] Eating, on average, once in forty-eight hours,[11] he sometimes fasted for three days,[12] but he didn't abstain from nocturnal outings,[13] and, far from being unbalanced by his physical state, he was thinking soberly about the book. In his 1905 preface to *Sesame and Lilies* he'd argued: 'Sainte-Beuve misunderstood all the most important writers of his time.' But was Proust going to correct him in a straightforward critique or blend criticism with fiction? Perhaps he'd write 'a story about the morning, about waking up, Mamma comes to my bedside to see me, I tell her I have had the idea for a study of Sainte-Beuve, I submit it to her and develop it for her.'

He asked Anna de Noailles and Georges de Lauris for advice.[14] Georges was in favour of a straightforward essay, but Proust was already gravitating towards the fictional alternative, partly because his memories of Sainte-Beuve were fading,[15] but mainly because he wanted to resurrect his mother by merging autobiography with fiction. The compulsion to re-enact experiences of frustration coalesced with guilt about all the vengeful fantasies he'd aimed against her. Still mourning her death and blaming himself for overloading her with anxiety about his health, he was trying to stabilise his thoughts and dreams about her through a literary recreation of their relationship. Quotations and literary allusions had, since early childhood, bulked so large in their conversations that it was natural to do part of his critical thinking in terms of an imaginary dialogue, as if he were submitting ideas to her.

By the end of the year he'd completed one more pastiche – of Chateaubriand[16] – but still hadn't decided between the alternatives of essay and story. 'If I were capable of moving,' he wrote towards the end of December, 'I would leave in a few days to isolate myself somewhere to write the book. But since I see nobody, I am isolated here.'[17]

He could no longer afford to tell himself he didn't feel well enough to write. He hardly ever felt well enough, and if he used that as an excuse for procrastinating, the book would never be written. At the beginning of 1909 he couldn't write ten lines without bringing on a headache that would last for several days, accompanied by insomnia,[18] while his asthma attacks were becoming more painful, more frightening and more prolonged. 'I have just been through some days which – since I could no longer feel any pity for other people – are, I believe, the worst in my life, since for the first time I was totally demoralised, life is impossible with such incessant attacks.'[19] In early February he complained of 'ten lethal attacks of asphyxiation every day'.[20]

If he ever managed to finish the book, he'd be able to make the same claim as Joubert had – 'Underneath the strength of many men was weakness; underneath my weakness was strength.'[21] But after Nicolas had fetched seven volumes of Sainte-Beuve's *Port-Royal* for him, he couldn't settle down to read. His life was not only too disrupted by malaise but too disorganised. He wanted Georges to read his pastiches of Régnier and Chateaubriand, but couldn't find them and thought they'd be illegible even if he did.[22] Notes and jottings would often disappear, while he was liable to lose both letters he wrote and letters he received.[23] 'As I listlessly open my correspondence, it sometimes happens if the letter has fallen from my bed without my being able to find it again that I no longer know whether I have dreamed about reading the letter or whether it really arrived.'[24] But the chaos was useful in spurring him on to create a novel which, better than any filing system, would organise memories, insights and dreams into a coherent structure. He'd taken a decisive step when he bought the school exercise books.

He could have let himself be distracted from the book when

the Lemoine scandal again became headline news. On 1 February the swindler was sentenced in his absence to ten years' imprisonment. Later in the month, when Proust, on one of his rare outings, went to see the Daudets, he found Montesquiou and Jules Lemaître with them. Lemaître was enthusiastic about the pastiches. 'As soon as the mechanism can be dismantled like this and reassembled, it is enough to stop one from daring to write . . . it is not just extraordinary but *terrifying*.' Proust should go on to write pastiches of Merimée and Voltaire, he said, and Maurice Barrès sent an encouraging letter: this 'delicious' form of literary criticism proved there was no difference between substance and style – 'to write in a certain manner is to think and feel in a certain manner'.[25] After Proust found the manuscript of the Régnier, it was published – with a few of the spicier passages cut – in *Le Figaro*'s literary supplement of 6 March, where it impressed Montesquiou: 'What an *astonishing* thing your last pastiche is!'[26] But he had no time to write any more.

Reading was now as dangerous as writing, causing long-lasting headaches. His bookcases were a long way from his bed, but at night he was reluctant to ring for Nicolas, even when he felt too weak to get up.[27] He read whatever was within reach, and one of the papers he took was *Cahiers de la quinzaine*, which on 16 and 23 February published the second volume of Romain Rolland's novel *Jean Christophe à Paris*. Like Ganderax's review, it irritated Proust intensely but fruitfully: 'When we see a writer, on each page, in each situation where he finds his character, failing to deepen the characterisation or reconsider it, and using ready-made expressions . . . we find such a book, even if on each page it condemns mannered art, immoral art, materialistic art, much more materialistic itself.'[28]

Intending to formulate his critical ideas à propos Sainte-Beuve, he'd been mulling over them for so long that each literary provocation helped to galvanise him. In March he wrote: 'What has the best chance of appearing one day is Sainte-Beuve (not the second pastiche, but the study) because it is troublesome to have this bulging suitcase in the middle of my brain, and I must make up my mind whether to leave or unpack it. But I have already forgotten a lot, and though I should not read at all, I read a lot, and in quite a different way. Nevertheless, if I am still alive this autumn, there are chances that *Sainte-Beuve* will have appeared.'[29]

A passage, mainly on Sainte-Beuve, in one of the notebooks shows how Proust forced himself to write. He'd been preoccupied since boyhood with anxiety about whether he was weak-willed. Was he wasting his talent? Proceeding as if he were writing a leisurely article like the second 'Journées de lecture' and as if it wouldn't matter if he never got to the main point, he said that, though he was only thirty-eight, he might soon be dead.

> I have reached a time, or, if you like, I find myself in circum-stances that make one afraid the things one most wanted to say . . . can suddenly no longer be said. One no longer considers oneself to be more than the trustee, who can vanish at any moment, of intellectual secrets, which will vanish too, and one would like to check the inertia that proceeds from one's previous lethargy by obeying Christ's beautiful com-mandment in St John: 'Work while ye have the light.'

Much of what he wanted to say would be 'in connection with' Sainte-Beuve but not 'about' him. Proust was concerned with 'things which perhaps have their importance, and in showing how he erred, in my view, as writer and as critic, I would perhaps arrive at making some points that have often occurred to me about what criticism ought to be and what art is. In passing, and in connection with him, I will do what he so often did – use him as the pretext for talking about certain forms of life. . . .'[30]

This resolution to work while he had the light almost coincided with an experience which formed a watershed in all his ponderings about involuntary memory.

> The other evening, having come in chilled, by the snow, and not being able to get warm, as I had started to read in my room under the lamp, my old cook offered to make tea, which I never drink. And chance had it that she brought me some slices of toast. I dipped the toast into the cup of tea and at the moment of putting the toast into my mouth and having the sensation against my palate of its sogginess permeated with the taste of tea, I felt a disturbance, scents of geranium and orange trees, a feeling of extraordinary light, of happiness; I stayed motionless, fearing a single movement could interrupt what was happening in me, which I did not understand, but still concentrating on this taste of dunked

bread which seemed to produce such wonders, when suddenly the shaken partitions of my memory caved in, and it
was the summers I spent in the country house I mentioned
which burst into my consciousness, with their mornings and
drawing with them the procession, the non-stop charge of
happy hours. Then I remembered: every day when I was
dressed, I went down into the room of my grandfather who
had just awakened me and was drinking his tea. He used to
dunk a rusk and give it to me. And when these summers
were over, the taste of rusk dunked in tea was one of the
hidey-holes where the dead hours – dead to the intellect –
went to tuck themselves up.[31]

This was the seminal moment of insight, and in several drafts
for the episode in *Swann*, Proust kept the rusk (*biscotte*), before
substituting the madeleine.[32] His decision had been variously
explained: the word 'madeleine' has religious associations,
while his description of 'the little shellfish of pastry, so fattily
sensual, under its severe and pious folds',[33] suggests the female
orifice, and, for Serge Doubrovsky, Proust's emphasis on the
'little drop' of limeflower scent which carries the 'enormous
edifice of memory' insistently recalls the drop of sperm mentioned in the earlier account of masturbation, which is associated with repressed desire for the mother.[34]

Sainte-Beuve may have been an innovator in carrying the
methods of natural history into moral history,[35] but he ignores
the discontinuity between a writer's work and his everyday
life, and this infuriates Proust, for whom the writer has two
selves. 'A book is the product of a different self from the one
we manifest in our habits, our social life and our vices.' The
act of writing should be a matter of making contact with 'the
deep self which is rediscovered only by abstracting oneself
from other people and the self which knows other people, the
self which has been waiting while one was with other people,
the self one feels is the only real self, and artists end up by
living for this alone, like a god whom they cease to ignore and
to whom they have sacrificed a life which serves only to honour
him'.[36] Writing emerges from an underground stream of deep
reflectiveness; the everyday transactions are as superficial as
everybody else's.

This use of the religious words 'god' and 'sacrifice' is far
from casual, and it helps to explain how Proust managed to

work so hard when reading and writing were both painful. 'If I have no faith as you say,' he wrote, 'on the other hand the religious preoccupation is never absent for a single day from my life.'[37] He'd inherited from his father something of the capacity for dedication that had inspired his early belief in a calling to the priesthood and his later devotion to public hygiene. His son was as far from being a materialist as he was from being a Christian. 'I have a clear view of life as far as the horizon,' he wrote in an unpublished note, 'but I am interested only in portraying what lies beyond.'[38] Sainte-Beuve was helpful negatively: his complacent preoccupation with mundane materiality was so repulsive that Proust rebounded towards the alternative way of living through literature – sacrificing his life to the inner self as if it were a god.

Ignoring the inner self, Sainte-Beuve refused to think of literature as distinct or separable from the rest of the man and his nature, maintaining that to understand an author you need answers to certain questions. 'What were his religious views? How was he affected by the sight of Nature? How did he behave with women, and with money? Was he rich, poor? What was his routine, the style of his daily life? What were his vices, weaknesses? None of the answers to these questions is irrelevant in judging the author of a book and the book itself. . . .'[39]

Proust's hostility to this view was inflamed by keen ambition to make his unwritten book add up to more than his unsatisfactory life. He'd never had an adequate literary receptacle for the memories, images and ideas that swirled through his mind when he was in bed, but now, blending criticism experimentally with autobiography in his attack on Sainte-Beuve, he was taking the first steps towards the autobiographical fiction which would resurrect his past while putting his literary principles into practice.

His equation of the self with the past, his theory of involuntary memory, his notions about the way consciousness works were ideas he could either explain or demonstrate: explanation would require illustration, while demonstration would require theoretical interpolations. Like Nietzsche and Freud, he proceeded from scrutinising his own consciousness towards generalising about human consciousness. Modelling himself partly on Darlu, who interpolated moralising generalisations into his lessons, Proust let his theorising intellect enjoy itself with fragmentary memories from the time that had been 'lost', interweaving philosophy, psychology, criticism, fiction and autobiography, while he developed momentum out of his excitement at having finally made a start on a major work.

Even Sainte-Beuve had changed his life style when he started on *Les Causeries de lundi*, realising 'that a life of forced labour, such as he was leading, is fundamentally more fruitful, and necessary to certain temperaments which are indolent by inclination, for without it they would not yield their resources.' Proust had reached a turning point. In all those years of feeling guilty about failing to make more effort, he never felt so attracted by the idea of commitment to hard work. From now on he'll go all out to fulfil his potential before death steps in to extinguish his consciousness. He wants the world – he thinks of it as consisting of readers, primarily friends – to know his life no longer consists merely of *Les Plaisirs et les jours* together with the Ruskin translations and the journalism. He must trap these shifting memories and ideas in a work of art. He was thinking of himself when he wrote about the disparity between the two selves of a great writer. 'The man who lives in the same body as a great genius has little affinity with him, but this is the man his friends know. So it is absurd to do what Sainte-Beuve did and judge the poet by the man or by what his friends said about him.'[40] The secretions of his innermost self can be communicated only to the reader imaginative enough – creative enough during the act of reading – to reproduce them inside himself.

Like the involvement with Ruskin, the work on Sainte-Beuve used the earlier writer as a ladder towards self-discovery. Proust had apprenticed himself to Ruskin so long and so devotedly that the moment had to come when he could be himself only by rejecting his mentor. The involvement with Sainte-Beuve was briefer and less intimate, but in rejecting him Proust was again discarding an earlier Proust. It was like a conversion, and he might have been incapable of it had he not felt so close to death. While he spent so much of his life in bed, his waking thoughts were often like dreams, merging past and present. As memories, desires and regrets interpenetrated, his mother and the feelings she aroused were almost as potent as they'd been during childhood moments of separation from her. Cut loose from its moorings in space and time, the floating consciousness is ignorant of its relationships with places, objects,

people. It is no accident *À la recherche* begins by evoking bedrooms he used to sleep in and childhood transitions from wakefulness to sleep. The tentative consciousness drifts now, as it
drifted then, between solid objects.

> Everything revolved around me in the darkness, things,
> countries, years. My body, too sleepy to move, tried, follow-
> ing the pattern of its tiredness, to locate its limbs, so as to
> deduce the position of the wall, the arrangement of the furni-
> ture, to reconstruct and identify the house it was in. Its
> memory, the memory of its ribs, its knees, its shoulders,
> presented it successively with several rooms where it had
> slept, while around it the invisible walls, shifting with the
> shape of the imagined room, whirled around in the dark-
> ness.[41]

Proust had been experimenting in new ways of working.
Buying the exercise books had been crucial. Six which survive
from 1909 show he tended to start simultaneously from his
sense of place and character. They contain sketches of Combray
(his name for Illiers), Balbec (his name for Cabourg), Doncières
(mainly Évreux, the garrison town), Paris, Padua and Venice;
and of Swann, the Verdurins, the Guermantes and the marquis
de Guercy (his original name for baron Charlus), together with
a rough draft of the fancy-dress ball sequence he was already
intending to use at the end.

For many writers, drafting, revising, rewriting and restruc-
turing are activities which overlap, but Proust wrote down
fragments of text without knowing where he'd place them. Of
the exercise books which survived – he ordered his housekeeper
to destroy thirty-two of them – each one contains a disconnected series of passages, and before trying to arrange them in
order he'd use the phenomenal energy he salvaged from his
malaise to rewrite passages again and again, still untroubled
about where he'd place them, but probing more deeply each
time into memories and insights. Often he'd follow the impulse
of the moment, whether it was ordering him to start or to
break off. Sometimes writing in direct speech, sometimes in
oratio obliqua, he'd use the verso and recto pages of the exercise
book independently, as if wanting the right-hand page to know
not what the left-hand page was doing. Sometimes he'd turn
an exercise book upside down and start again from the other
end. One book contains sixteen versions of the sequence about

movements of consciousness between sleep and wakefulness. Sometimes he'd rewrite a passage thirty times.

Noting down ideas that would help to characterise, he hadn't yet decided which character would be the receptacle for them. One jotting in the second notebook starts: 'For Bloch or Guercy or someone else', and one in the fourth notebook starts: 'Important for Mme de Guermantes or for Albertine or for Saint-Loup.'[42] Drafting a description of a pink satin dress, he hasn't yet decided who will wear it: 'If I do not use this passage for Mme de Guermantes, I will use it for Mme Swann.'[43]

His method corresponded to his habits of thinking. Going out so seldom and staying in bed so much, he had fewer experiences outside his own home than most people, but reflected on them more. Chewing the cud of impressions, thinking and theorising about sensations, finding words and phrases for them, whether he wrote these down or not, he'd incessantly been preparing himself for *À la recherche*. Indelible but blurred memories of car journeys that made tree-tops dance in the sky mingled with memories of steeples rearranging themselves, and each memory changed slightly each time he thought about it. Lying in bed and redrafting the same passage again and again was like lying in bed and re-enacting the same experience again and again.

Except that now he was creating a permanent record. His work on the pastiches – especially the Flaubert pastiche – had taught him that in writing nothing matters more than the arrangement of the words. Sainte-Beuve had failed to notice what was most innovative in Flaubert's work. 'He took such pains over his syntax that he lodged his originality in it once and for all.' Flaubert's syntax gave more prominence to appearance than to dramatic conflicts of willpower. 'In his great sentences things do not exist as accessories of a story but in the reality of their appearance. . . . Even when the object represented is human, since it is recognised as an object, what appears of it is described as appearing, and not as produced by the will.' This form, discovered by Flaubert, is 'more innovative than anything else in the whole history of French literature'.[44]

Proust's originality is built on top of Flaubert's, and achieved in the same way – by taking immense trouble over syntax. But this is not the only form of continuity between the Lemoine pastiches and the novel. Much of the dialogue is pastiche of his friends' conversation. Charlus talks like Montesquiou, and, describing his use of Mme Straus not only as the source of the 'Guermantes' wit' but as a model for the duchesse, Proust wrote: 'Not only the quotations are from her (she did not want me to mention her name in the novel) but I have made a pastiche of her conversation.'[45]

Far from feeling confident, though, Proust still considered his friends more talented than he was. But this made him want to give them readable proof there was more to him than had been apparent. The more he thought about unconscious memory, the clearer it became that his previous writing was inadequate to express whatever it was that came to him during periods of intense observation, like the one of studying rose-bushes at Reveillon. When unconscious memory took over, looking at the past could be almost like looking at a rosebush. It was almost as if consciousness could be opaque and trans-parent at the same time. Aware of himself seeing, but concen-trating on what he saw, he could identify with the object in all its complications, remembering as if he were perceiving, and moving from one detail to another with the painterly passion Ruskin had helped him to cultivate.

He was tentative in blending criticism with autobiographical fiction, which is advantageous, especially in passages where his distrust of intellect and his faith in involuntary memory persuade him to let the prose reflect the actual movement of his consciousness. By writing long sentences, he stops himself from interrupting the momentum of thinking that has more to do with reconstituting visual memories than with intellec-tion. As one visual detail recalls another, the association drags the narrative like a balloon in its wake, abolishing frontiers of time and space, as in a dream. Sunshine in the Paris street during a conversation with Mamma[46] makes him look at the 'tawny gold enamelling' on the iron weathercock of the house opposite, which makes him think about Illiers – already he's fictionalising it into Combray – where perhaps, at this moment, because of the heat, the awning has been let down above the draper's shop, which is about to close for high mass, which reminds him of eggs and poultry sellers in the marketplace, and his thoughts fly to ten o'clock sunlight enamelling the golden angel on the campanile of St Mark's in Venice and then return to the draper's awning and the barber's pole in Combray. The rapid, unexplained movement may confuse the reader, but he was still writing for himself: he'd never have wanted to publish this passage without rewriting it many times. What we have is only fragments of a draft. He was testing his memory and technique, finding how rich his memory was in details which could be unloaded evocatively into meandering sentences as he climbed beyond narrative chronology towards a conjunction of three periods. Over thirty years have gone by since his boyhood holidays in Illiers; nine since he was in Venice, while the reminiscent consciousness is situated in a present detached from both past tenses. Proust is rejecting the static perspective in time as he did in space. It is in this – limited – sense that his work is Einsteinian. Like your view of trees or steeples when you pass them at speed, your impression of any incident in your past depends on your present situation. The present has always turned into the past before you can make any statement about it, even to yourself, and the French language is better equipped than English to deal with this gap between sensation and formulation. The imperfect, while reproducing an impression, registers that it was already sinking into the sand. Something which was happening is no longer happening. *Mes yeux se fermaient si vite que je n'avais pas le temps de me dire: 'Je m'endors.'* We can say either 'My eyes used to close so fast I had no time to tell myself "I'm going to sleep" ' or 'My eyes closed', but not 'My eyes were closing . . .' because that would suggest it happened only once. Following Flaubert, Proust made such abundant use of the imperfect that any English translation is severely handicapped by the difficulty of rendering past continuity.

Even in his earliest sketches the quality of the writing depends partly on his sensitive approximation to precision in examining visual memories, as if they were still physically available, like old photographs. One of the ways he uses them is to explore the discomfort he'd always felt at being tugged between two classes. The career of his anti-socialite father had in the end depended partly on social and professional connections; without competing consciously against his father, Proust had proved he could succeed brilliantly as a social climber, and, greatly though he enjoyed having princes and dukes among his friends, he was constantly under stress, and was badly upset when neither Loche nor Georges invited him to their wedding, while his ambivalence about salons, bourgeois and aristocratic, is reflected first in Swann's behaviour and then in the Narrator's. Swann resembles Charles Haas in being the son of a Jewish stockbroker and in being welcome, despite both disadvantages, in the most exclusive salons. Unlike Haas, he drops his duchesses in favour of the homely salon run by Mme Verdurin because it's here he can meet the beautiful Odette de Crécy. Though Mme Verdurin's vulgarity, pretentiousness and insincerity are satirised, they don't detract from the force of the comment: 'usually the intellectual merits of a salon and its elegance are inversely proportional'.[47]

After the Narrator has replaced Swann as the central figure, the narrative becomes more like a *Bildungsroman* in which the sensitive hero's innocence and ignorance are progressively eroded. The realisation that came to Proust with the death of his mother comes to the Narrator with the death of his grandmother. After believing he couldn't live without her, he finds the diseases of old age ravage her appearance, and when she's dying it looks as if a beast is crouching among her bed-clothes, wearing her hair.[48] Confronting life without his princi-pal protector, he hasn't yet lost faith in romantic love or in human greatness as institutionalised in the aristocracy. Whereas Swann, in the first volume, had achieved social success before we met him, the Narrator is seen rising in society, and gradu-ally accumulating insights into its worthlessness. Incredulous at being invited to a ball given by the prince and princesse de Guermantes, the Narrator finds himself behind the duc de Chatellerault in the queue of guests waiting for the footman to announce their names. The duc is a homosexual who spent the previous night with the footman, but it is only now that the man discovers the name of his lover. Later the prince himself is revealed to be predominantly homosexual, and in the final sequence he's so senile as to be almost unrecognisable. The Narrator has known from the outset that the prince was anti-Semitic and strongly anti-Dreyfusard, but this, unlike homosexuality and old age, plays no part in discrediting him. The Narrator's education comes through a series of disillusion-ing experiences, but Proust's handling of them is mainly comic. If the comedy is least prominent in the sequences dealing with Albertine's death, this is because they were written too soon after the death of Agostinelli.

In the early summer of 1909 Proust still hadn't decided about the name 'Guermantes', and in May he again interrogated

friends. Did this name currently belong to the Paris family, or
was it 'extinct and available for a writer'? Did Georges de
Lauris know any 'other nice names of châteaux or people'?[49] 'I
do not want to offend anyone except unknown people who
are not related to the people I know, and I do not have the
impudence of Balzac. . . . But I do not want my château to
belong to the family whose name it bears.' Georges guessed
he was embarking on a fiction, but he denied it: 'I am not
working on a novel, it is too complicated to explain. . . . First
of all I am not working on anything. But I would like to
work.'[50]

His nocturnal day had been starting later and later: in the
second half of March he was waking up at two in the morning,[51] and breakfasting at three, but only on alternate days,
taking no food, he said, for forty-eight hours at a stretch.[52]
Asthma attacks could now last fifty-four hours.[53] He called in
a variety of specialists, eventually settling on Paul Dubois, the
Swiss neurologist he'd thought of consulting in 1904 after
Gregh had recommended him.[54] Proust was saying he got up,
on average, only once in two months,[55] and on 8 May, when
he tried to see Monet's *Nymphéas* paintings at the Durand-Ruel
gallery, the exertion brought on a fit of paralysis.[56] He got up
again on the evening of the 9th and tried unsuccessfully to
telephone Reynaldo.[57]

On 18 June, wanting to attend Montesquiou's afternoon
reception, Proust got up at eleven in the morning and took a
bath. 'And then I have never been so ill. What a day, what a
night!'[58] He was becoming increasingly isolated: he couldn't
even contact friends by telephone. 'I have neither enough voice
nor enough breath.'[59] In desperation he launched himself in
mid-June into work as if single-handedly besieging an impreg-
nable fortress. In the long battle waged in his exercise books
between criticism and fiction, fiction decisively got the upper
hand, but when he mentioned the book in letters to friends,
he called it '*Sainte-Beuve*': 'Georges, I am so exhausted after
having started *Sainte-Beuve* (*I am hard at work*, and the results
are detestable) that I do not know what I am writing to you.
I literally cannot write.'[60]

But the desperation which made everything seem difficult
made nothing seem impossible. 'Georges, if I leave Paris it will
perhaps be with a woman. Is this rather ridiculous!'[61] 'Woman'
may be a euphemism for 'man', or he may have wanted to

counter rumours about his homosexuality. It's hard to see how a relationship could have started when he was so ill, so exhausted and so busy. Though he'd certainly made a start on the novel, he stopped again in late June, hoping to resume early in July. But Georges, who'd drafted a novel, *Ginette Chatenay*, was eager he should read it. 'If it is urgent,' Proust replied, 'to hell with *Sainte-Beuve*.'[62]

The other distraction was renewal of interest in the Lemoine affair. Five months after being sentenced *in absentia*, the swindler appeared before the tenth Chambre du Tribunal Correctionnel between 16 June and 5 July, and Proust promised to have some new parodies ready by 2 July. But he was also working on the novel. 'Writing I had started at the same time made it impossible for me to do my pastiches.'[63] His energy came in fits and starts, while, unable to sleep, he exploited his wakefulness, reading as well as writing not only the novel and pastiches but also letters. 'If you could see my body while I am writing to you, it is . . . courageous! More than sixty hours have gone by since I last – I will not even say slept but switched off my electricity.'[64] He completed a Ruskin parody, 'La Bénédiction du sanglier' ('The Blessing of the Wild Boar') and sketched out pastiches of Maeterlinck and Chateaubriand. Though still ambivalent about their usefulness, he was becoming tired of parodies, even if he said so by parodying Taine:

> Good, you say, there is a writer who understands the strengths and the weaknesses of other writers, who makes a game out of reproducing the same stylistic gestures alongside the general appearance of their thinking. He knows that in illuminating a character or giving information about a period, nothing is negligible; he ignores none of the syntactical peculiarities which give away the movement of the imagination, the current manners, the received ideas, the inherited temperament, the fundamental powers. . . . But one soon becomes tired of caricature.[65]

Working less enthusiastically on the pastiches than he was on the novel, he had none of them ready in time for *Le Figaro*, which had published nothing by him for over fifteen months apart from the Régnier parody on 6 March. None of the new pastiches was to appear during his lifetime.

What he'd enjoyed most when writing the earlier ones was the opportunity to combine in a single text so many critical and creative ideas, but the book, combining critical and creative elements more fruitfully, had already begun to satisfy him more deeply. Nothing that happened in his sleeping or waking life was irrelevant. Dreams, memories, passing fancies could all be woven into the fabric, as could a good meal cooked by Nicolas' wife, Céline, who found it enviably easy to complete her jobs. 'I send you warm compliments and thanks for the marvellous *boeuf mode*. I would very much like to achieve the same success with what I am going to do tonight. I hope my style will be as brilliant, as clear, as solid as your jelly, my ideas will have as much flavour as your carrots, and be as nourishing and fresh as your meat. Not yet having finished my work, I congratulate you on yours.'[66]

He waged his battle against Sainte-Beuve as vigorously in the new fiction as in the abandoned critical essay, demonstrating that the critic's view of character was old-fashioned. Interpolated into Proust's narrative are critical comments and generalising pronouncements:

> Even in the most insignificant things, we are not a materially constituted whole, identical for everybody and accessible to anyone like an account-book or a testament; our social personality is created by other people's thinking. Even such a simple act as the one we call 'seeing a person we know' is partly an intellectual act. We fill the personal appearance of the person we see with all the notions we have about him, and in the total impression we form, these notions certainly play the major part. They end up by swelling his cheeks so perfectly, following the contours of his nose so exactly, they merge so well into the timbre of his voice, as if it were no more than a transparent envelope, that each time we see this face and listen to this voice, it is these notions that we are recognising and hearing.[67]

Here Proust is at the epicentre of modernism's quarrel with the nineteenth century.

At the same time, his preoccupation with inner reality made it easier for him to write about himself while ostensibly writing about people very different from him. There is a continuity between his 1888 schoolboy insight about 'the various gentlemen of whom I consist' and his 1921 remark to Gide about the possibility of saying anything about yourself so long as you don't use the first person. His approach to his own story in *Swann* is even more oblique than in the volumes which have the Narrator as their central figure: at first Proust needs a thicker mask than he will use later, but Swann's age usually remains so vague and his appearance so unfocused that his baldness is nearly always a surprise when it's mentioned – the first reference to his toupée comes on page 348 – but, picturing someone physically so different from himself, Proust was fabricating a persona through which he could safely talk about himself.

Throughout much of his life, Swann resembles Violante: he has been steered by vanity 'towards this fashionable life where he had squandered his intellectual gifts on frivolous pleasures and used his artistic erudition to advise society ladies on what pictures to buy and how to furnish their houses'.[68] Proust had spent a lot of time in conversation with society ladies, but there's also a connection with the Marie Benardaky episode. Almost as soon as he sees Gilberte, the Narrator longs for an invitation to the Swanns' house. When the ambassador, M. de Norpois, promises to speak about him to Mme Swann, he feels miserably certain the promise won't be kept – Mme Swann will know nothing about his longing. Much later, after his decision to stop seeing Gilberte, he goes on seeing her mother, glad to be on visiting terms, although, as a former courtesan, she has only a precarious position in society.

Writing *Jean Santeuil*, Proust had incorporated memories of Marie almost without changing them, but, by transforming her into Gilberte, he's altering her social position. The Benardakys had been more exalted than the Prousts, but Gilberte is the daughter of a marriage which had lowered a man who could have moved upwards. In portraying Swann's obsession with Odette and the Narrator's with their daughter, Proust is drawing on a rich mixture of past ambivalences and experiences, including early meetings with Laure Hayman and the knowledge that his parents had tried to stop him from meeting the glamorous young mistresses of his uncle Georges. The Narrator and his parents visit his uncle Adolphe 'only on certain days because on other days came the ladies whom his family could not have met'.[69] At the same time, writing about Swann's wastefulness in giving himself to the inferior Odette, Proust must have thought about his own feelings when taking servants as lovers.

It's more obvious he's using homosexual love affairs as his

model when Swann's promiscuity is described. Though he
could plausibly be promiscuous, it seems out of character for
him to have an affair with a friend's cook,[70] but Proust seems
to have had a lot of affairs with male servants. What's remarkable is that he so seldom strikes false notes when translating
homosexual experience into fiction about heterosexuality.
Swann's proprietorial jealousy is convincing. He hates being
excluded from so much of Odette's life, but the torture streng-
thens his love for her, and in the end he marries her partly in
order to introduce her to the duchesse de Guermantes. It's one
of the novel's ironies that he never succeeds in effecting the
introduction but that the two women become friendly after
his death.

Unhealthier but busier than ever, Proust was in this first furore
of activity on the novel when he was approached by the comtesse Greffulhe, who'd refused to let him write about her in
his series on salons, but now wanted him to report on the fête
organised at Bagatelle by the Société des Grandes Auditions
de France. When he excused himself, pleading illness, she not
only sent him a vine teeming with magnificent bunches of
grapes, but offered to visit him.[71] There was nobody (not even
Montesquiou) whose presence in his bedroom would have
embarrassed him more, but his ideas for the end of the novel
– from writing the beginning he went straight on to sketch
out the end – may have been influenced by the friendliness of
this formerly remote beauty who was one of his principal
models for the duchesse de Guermantes.

Proust was putting himself under so much strain that in early
August he was forced to suspend work, which exacerbated
his bitterness about 'the infinite impotence of my life'. His
temperature was regularly 102 degrees, and his asthma attacks
sometimes lasted until three in the morning. He also had a
painful abscess caused by the hollow tooth which the dentist
had refused to work on in June, finding him too exhausted.
Knowing he needed a change of air, he was thinking of going
to Cabourg, but thinking more about finding a publisher.

He didn't want to risk a second rebuff from Mercure de
France, and he'd have approached Calmann-Lévy 'if my book
were not obscene'.[72] What he meant by this was explained
when he offered it to Alfred Vallette: 'I am finishing a book
which in spite of its provisional title, *Contre Sainte-Beuve,*

Souvenir d'une matinée, is a veritable novel and an extremely indecent novel in certain places. One of the principal characters is a homosexual.'[73] Were it not for these obscene passages, he said, he could have published the book in *Le Figaro*, with two instalments appearing each week. 'But first of all the suppression of the obscene parts would be extremely hurtful to me, and then it is a book of events and the reflections of one event on another, with years passing, and it could not be serialised except in big instalments.' He asked Vallette to ear-mark thirty or more pages of the *Mercure* from 1 or 15 October until January – enough space to accommodate 250 to 300 pages. 'The novel part would then have appeared.' When he'd begun working on the novel in 1908, he'd intended to begin with the Narrator's memories of childhood. What he intended now was to follow 'the novel part' with a long conversation between the Narrator and his mother about Sainte-Beuve and about aesthetics. The whole volume would be roughly as long as Régnier's *La Double Maîtresse*, which Mercure had published in 1900 – 425 pages. And Proust offered to pay printing costs if Vallette would like to publish the book, choose the paper and organise the publicity.[74] But Vallette said no, and Proust, taking one of his abrupt decisions – eight hours before leaving he was still uncertain of whether he'd go[75] – left for Cabourg with Nicolas.

Travelling by train, he found himself in the same compart-ment as Camille Plantevignes, and they talked for two hours.[76] Ill when he left Paris, Proust was disappointed when the Cabourg air failed to make him feel better. 'I could not do a thousandth of what I could still do a year ago.'[77] He was afraid (as he had been in 1907) that illness might cut the holiday short.[78] The bedroom he was given had sinister stains all over the wallpaper, and it was so humid that each sheet of paper soon began to feel damp.[79] This time, disturbed by music and noisy hotel guests, he didn't enjoy seeing the sea, and he was sometimes feverish. Getting up between half-past nine and ten in the evening, he could go to the casino without going out of doors. Two weeks later, he still hadn't been outside the building.[80]

In a mid-August letter to Mme Straus he claimed to have just finished 'quite a long book' which needed a great many revisions. What he meant by 'finished' was that he'd written the end, though not the middle. Depressed by the rejection from Vallette, he doubted whether the book would ever be published: he promised to read it to Georges, whom he now considered his closest friend.[81] He also wanted a reaction from Mme Straus,[82] and planned to visit her in Trouville as soon as he felt well enough. He invited Georges to stay at the hotel, promising to find a better bedroom than the one he'd been given after complaining about the humidity. Insecure though he felt about what he'd written, he'd actually fixed a firm framework for the novel by writing the beginning and end. Though the work would become much longer than he now envisaged, he never deviated from the pattern he'd established.

The fragments he wrote for the end are designed to expose the world of the Guermantes as less heavenly than it had seemed, while revealing the nature of time by focusing on the way its passage has marked the people who once seemed so noble and enviable. After a long absence from Paris, the Narrator attends another ball given by the prince and princesse de Guermantes, which reminds him of one they gave when he was still in his youth. Time is a magician, and one of his tricks is to 'make a statue of Mme de Forcheville jut out in the body of her daughter, deforming it and making it enormous'.[83] Comparing present experience with memories of the earlier ball, the Narrator giddily realises how many years have passed.

> I suddenly felt underneath me those twenty-three years, one going down from the other, deeper and deeper into invisibility and all that was still myself, lived by me, what I was seeing at a distance of twenty-three years, it was still myself, twenty-three years away from me, and I felt almost fearful of not having the strength to stay for long at such a height of life already used, which I always had to keep under me, always tied to me, me with the feeling of my continuity into this immense depth, already of twenty-three years, a whole continuity, a lived and living thing, going down into the darkness.[84]

Later on, writing about his intentions, Proust would say: 'This invisible substance of time, I have tried to isolate it, but to do that, the experience needed to be one which could last. I hope that at the end of my book some small and insignificant social fact, some marriage between two people who in the first volume belonged to quite different worlds, will show that time has passed and will take on the beauty of leadwork at Versailles with a patina which time has encased in an emerald sheath.'[85]

He was now on the top floor of the hotel, overlooking a small courtyard. The room was small and airless, but he took it because of the fireplace. 'Nicolas, on the other hand, has a superb room with a bathroom for which I am his tributary.'[86] The other friend Proust missed was Reynaldo. Eating in the big empty restaurant one evening, he asked the gypsy musicians whether they knew anything by Hahn, and when they played *Rêverie*, Proust, to the consternation of the waiters, began to weep.[87]

Calmette was staying nearby and, when he heard about the novel, he offered to serialise it in *Le Figaro*'s literary supplement. Proust hesitated. Impatient to validate his life by bringing the book into existence, he'd have been glad to see it in print immediately and have it read by his friends. On the other hand, as he'd surmised before talking to Calmette, publication in *Le Figaro* would involve cutting passages which could be considered 'obscene'. In any case the book ought to make its first appearance as a book. Besides, Beaunier, who wanted to write a critical essay on Sainte-Beuve, might think Proust was invading territory he intended to cover. But even when Proust demurred, he knew he might change his mind.[88]

In late August he again moved to a new bedroom, but this one was humid with noisy guests on either side. He'd have preferred a suite or a flat, with nobody in the neighbouring rooms except Nicolas and Ulrich, who'd been summoned to provide secretarial help.[89] Towards the end of September Proust still needed an undisturbed month to finish the novel, but cracks had appeared in the walls of the hotel, necessitating building work. He felt nervous of returning to Paris: the central heating, the dentist and the prospect of severe asthma attacks were powerful deterrents. 'I am afraid. I anticipate something worse than my Calvary of last winter. How can I live like that – without being able to work, to see anyone, to eat, to breathe. I am too exhausted to try new places if they do not let me stay here.'[90] But he was again refused permission to stay on in the hotel, and, not relishing a return to Versailles, he settled back into his Paris flat in late September or early October.[91]

TWENTY

MACHINERY OF FRIENDSHIP

If letter-writing had once been a substitute for personal relationships, that function had now been taken over by the novel. The act of thinking about them had become inseparable from using them as models. 'My solitary life has enabled me to recreate through thinking those whom I liked.'[1]

Fénelon had become the model for a character, Saint-Loup, who comes to Balbec on a visit to his aunt, the comtesse de Marsantes. Though handsome and dashingly elegant, he at first seems cold and arrogant. As soon as he befriends the Narrator, he makes quite a different impression. Like Fénelon, he has an egalitarian contempt for the privileges bestowed on rank, and he sides with the Dreyfusards. His indulgent treatment of his mistress, Rachel, derives from Albu, whose warm generosity he combines with Fénelon's thoughtful solicitude. Saint-Loup is described as characteristically French in the way he combines physical gracefulness with openness of mind and heart. His complexion is attractive, while the curves of his nostrils are designed as delicately as a butterfly's wings.

When Fénelon was due back in Paris, Proust naturally wanted to see him again, but the fact of having brought Saint-Loup into existence made the need for personal contact less urgent. Fénelon now mattered less than Georges de Lauris, who was told: 'If he had on your friendship for me as bad an influence as you once had on his for me, I would feel the same kind of resentment against him as I used to feel against you.' One of the reasons Georges mattered so much was that Proust was impatient for his reactions to what he'd written. 'I will have a copy made from my rough sketches for the first paragraph (it is almost a book, this first paragraph!). . . . Even if I can scarcely speak, what I have written will speak to you.'[2]

His other friends wouldn't yet have access to it, but already, besides evoking their presence, it enabled him to confront everything he disliked about them. After repressing all his reservations about Montesquiou for sixteen years, he could at last express them by making him into the baron de Charlus. Truthfully, but with no risk of being understood, Proust told him: 'I am thinking about you so much, I re-read you and remind myself of your sayings and gestures.'[3]

He was also thinking about the novel's other function as a cog in the machinery of friendship. In emotional negotiations and transactions with friends he'd always enjoyed intrigue, plotting his life as if it were a novel. Now, living in greater isolation, he enjoyed unilateral control over an elaborate mechanism securely screwed into his relationships. He could express appreciation or resentment in portraits of friends and acquaintances who might or might not recognise themselves; he could tease friends, along with other readers, by revealing one side of a character who'd later emerge as quite different. 'The little Saint-Loup whom you find so nice is going to make you shudder.'[4] Underneath this pleasure in springing surprises on friends and in constructing a variation on Ruskin's idea of the secret plan which wouldn't be revealed until the end, something more sinister was lurking – a dim memory of thinking about the way his mother would have shuddered on discovering the truth about her little Marcel. His abundant experience of dissimulation had been an excellent preparation for writing a novel in which the characters would nearly all turn out to be radically different from what they first appear to be.

The same memory of deceiving his mother is refracted in his treatment of the Lesbianism which parallels his homosexuality. Concealed under the reactions of the composer, Vinteuil, to his daughter's Lesbianism are speculations about whether Mme Proust would have withdrawn her love if she'd discovered the truth about her son. 'Facts do not penetrate into the world inhabited by our beliefs, persistently without weakening them, and a continuing avalanche of disasters or illnesses in a family will not make it doubt the goodness of God or the competence of the doctor.' But when M. Vinteuil tries to think about himself and his daughter from the viewpoint of other people, his judgment is no less hostile than that of those who condemn them most vehemently.[5]

Generally, as André Gide noticed, it's only the unattractive aspects of homosexual love that are represented directly in Proust's novel, and Lesbianism is always treated with even more disapproval than male homosexuality. When Odette confesses 'two or three' experiences of Lesbian love to Swann, we are told he had 'rarely imagined anything so evil'.[6] The two most squalid and sadistic sequences in the novel are the one in which the Narrator watches Mlle Vinteuil encouraging her girlfriend to spit on her father's photograph, and the one in which the baron de Charlus is beaten in the male brothel. The men who turn out to be bisexual or homosexual after seeming initially to be heterosexual – Saint-Loup, Charlus, Morel, Legrandin, the prince de Guermantes and many others – are all made to seem less sympathetic than they did at first, while 'inverts' are generally treated as a 'race on whom a curse has been laid'. Apart from the childhood romance with Gilberte, nearly all the happy moments of sexuality derive from homosexual experiences translated into heterosexual terms, while the homosexual episodes are nearly all tinged with condemnation. The most sordid relationship in the novel is the one between Charlus and Morel. It isn't surprising most readers failed to guess Proust was a homosexual.

He didn't, of course, want them to guess, and this is one reason for being so negative in his portrayal of homosexual love. The habit of dissimulation was deeply ingrained, but he wanted friends to know more about him than they did. He confided in Anna de Noailles about his 'wish finally to put enough of myself into something for you to know me a little and value me'. Though he wanted – or said he did – to see her again, it was more urgent to finish the book: 'I do not want to risk the slightest exhaustion, which, in my condition, which has become so precarious, is a great danger.'[7] He'd have to 'live in a glass case' until the book was ready.[8] Then, he promised, 'before leaving this earth I will dedicate myself to seeing some of "the companions that have given all the best joy of my life on the Earth" '.

Impatience for other people to read his work finally overrode his resistance to serialisation. Eager to publish the novel, Calmette offered to deviate from normal practice: he'd publish instalments whenever Proust delivered them – even after the book had appeared in the shops. Told he'd probably receive the first episode in November, Calmette promised to have it in print within a week.[9]

Proust was making rapid headway, in spite of a setback in early November when the central heating was switched on. The radiator next to his bed brought on attacks of orthopnoea, making it hard for him to breathe without sitting upright.[10] But the novel was growing so fast that by the middle of the month he thought it would run to three volumes.[11]

He wasn't well enough to work every day, but again, as in June, the combination of exertion with the fact of writing fiction – the validation of fantasy – revived his desire to settle down with a partner, though he was at least half aware of how unrealistic he was being. He asked Georges for advice: 'To make a delicious young girl share my frightful life, even if it does not scare her, would this not be criminal?'[12] If it was really a girl he had in mind, it was probably either Estie or Anita Nahmias, but it may have been their twenty-three-year-old brother, Albert, who was good-looking but lacking in self-confidence, affectionate but shy. Their father, a financier, had a house in Cabourg, and Proust met them through a friend, Constantin Ullmann. Proust did his best to dissuade Albert from undermining his future happiness by settling down to live with the girl he intended to marry,[13] and, according to Antoine Bibesco, Albert and his sisters all served as models for Albertine. 'There were several of us,' confirmed Albert when asked whether Albertine was based on him.[14]

It was characteristic of Proust that the question to Georges about the delicious young girl was posed inside a parenthesis, the main purpose of the sentence being to arrange an outing. He chose the evening of Saturday 27 November. Any plans he made were liable to be cancelled if he succumbed to an attack at the last minute, but at Cabourg he'd been getting up every day, if only in the evening. Wanting to meet Marcel Plantevignes and some of the other young men he'd seen there, including Pierre Parent – no Salaism involved, he insisted – he invited them to the theatre in a party with Georges, Reynaldo, Louisa de Mornand, Emmanuel Bibesco, Fénelon, François de Paris, Loche Radziwill and Christiane.[15]

He was working steadily and rapidly. By now he'd drafted about 200 pages – the section called 'Combray'. More than in any of his previous writing he was benefiting from the training he'd given himself in committing visual detail to memory. What he'd done when he stared at a rosebush or a landscape was what his Narrator does when gazing at the hawthorns: assuming natural laws are involved in the intricate pattern, he exerts himself to solve the mystery behind it, trying at the

same time – it is part of the same effort – to fix the visual
details in his mind.

> It was in vain that I lingered in front of the hawthorns to
> inhale their invisible and unchanging odour, to parade it in
> front of my mind, which did not know how it should handle
> it, to lose it, to find it again, to join myself with the rhythm
> the blossoms threw out, here and there, with a youthful
> frivolity and with unexpected gaps, like certain musical inter-
> vals, they went on ceaselessly offering me the same charm
> with inexhaustible profusion, but without letting me pen-
> etrate into it any more deeply, like those melodies you can
> play a hundred times without coming any closer to sharing
> their secret. . . . It was in vain that I made a screen with my
> hands, to have nothing but them in view, the feeling they
> were rousing in me remained obscure and vague, trying in
> vain to detach itself, to join itself with the blossoms.[16]

The tacit assumption is that he has inside him something which
belongs with what he's looking at but has been separated from
it, like the lovers in Plato's *Symposium* who are two halves of
the same self, struggling to reunite their bodies. Proust's faith
in the oneness of nature had been fortified by Ruskin, but the
habit of loving observation had already been formed. Much of
the writing in *À la recherche* owes its vitality to his genius for
reproducing visual details which he'd have forgotten if he'd
been less attentive, less disciplined, in moments of scrutinising.
In spite of – or because of – his invalid routine, he still had a
keen appetite for the visual pleasures stored in the larder of his
memory.

He projects his invalid self into Tante Léonie, modelling her
on his aunt Élisabeth, who'd set the pattern he was following,
progressively isolating herself from the outside world, receiving fewer visitors, spending more time in bed, becoming less
of a hypochondriac, more genuinely ill. If he'd previously been
unaware of the extent to which he was repeating this pattern,
he must have discovered this by blending himself into the
character:

> What had begun in her – earlier than is usual – was this great
> renunciation of old age which is preparing itself for death,
> enveloping itself in its chrysalis, and which can be observed
> at the end of lives which are prolonged, even in people who

have loved each other most, and in friends who have been united by the closest intellectual bonds but, at a certain age, stop making journeys or even going out in order to see each other, stop corresponding and know they will have no more contact in this world. . . . This reclusion was forced on her by the diminution she could feel each day in her strength, making each action, each movement, exhausting, if not painful, which gave passivity, isolation and silence the restorative and blessed sweetness of rest.[17]

To characterise her he's paraphrasing letters he'd written to friends about his own condition.

Later on, inspired perhaps by Monet's water-plants, he compares the hypochondriac's neurasthenic habits with the water-lily's tangled roots, which drag it back to the same bank after the current has thrust it towards the other. On each walk by the river, the Vivonne, the Narrator finds the water-lily helpless in the same place, 'reminding one of certain neurasthenics, among whom my grandfather included my aunt Léonie, who present over the years the unchanging spectacle of bizarre habits which they always believe themselves to be on the point of shaking off and which they always keep; caught in the net of their maladies and phobias, they make futile efforts to escape, which only tighten it and trigger the mechanism of their strange, inescapable and deadly dietetics.'[18] At least he could see the comic side of his own predicament, and he may even have been hoping a precise formulation like this one would help to liberate him.

He also uses the invalid routine as an image for abdication of control over one's own life: one puts oneself into the hands of people who seem more competent and knowledgeable. But are they? His point is about the importance of fidelity to one's own judgment. Sainte-Beuve is condemned for focusing on received wisdom, on the social personality, the cliché; the artist with originality is praised for penetrating underneath the crust of consensus – rejecting the stereotypes which have been assimilated by the public.[19]

No less important was another kind of rejection which was basic to Proust's way of thinking. Seeing himself as consisting of various gentlemen, he could like some and dislike others. Freud, in an 1896 paper on the neuropsychoses of defence, started his enquiries into the process by which paranoiacs –

and not only paranoiacs – deal with unpleasurable experiences by projecting intolerable ideas outwards. The experiences and ideas may derive from desires, feelings or qualities; refusing to recognise these as internal, the neurotic repudiates them by locating them in other people. The novelist can use a parallel process, projecting them on characters.

Of the gentlemen who add up to Proust, the ones he seems to dislike most are the Jew and the homosexual. Vain about his appearance, Proust had let Jean Santeuil take pride in being just as handsome as the young Duke of Richmond in van Dyck's painting. But Proust's dark good looks were unmistakably inherited from the Jewish side of his ancestry, and he nowhere shows any pride in being half-Jewish. The Dreyfus affair had given only a temporary boost to the positive side of his Jewish self-consciousness. When the Narrator brings home Jewish schoolfriends, his grandfather disapprovingly hums 'Oh, God of our fathers' from La Juive,[20] and the Narrator says Swann, 'like certain other Jews', could be accused of having contrived to illustrate all the stages through which his race had passed – from naive snobbery and crude vulgarity to exquisite good manners.[21] Two of the most unsympathetic characters in the novel, Bloch and Rachel, are Jewish, and though Bloch is ridiculed for affecting anti-Semitism,[22] Proust seems half-hearted in condemning the anti-Semitism displayed by Albertine and Charlus in disparaging Bloch and his family.[23]

Many of the attractive aristocrats, first presented in a favourable light as heterosexual, will turn out to be homosexual and less admirable than they seemed. In one passage Jews are compared with homosexuals: members of both minorities shun each other and seek out the company of dissimilar people, forgiving rebuffs, dazzled by condescension.[24] Implicitly and sometimes explicitly, Proust pours scorn on Jews who condemn Jews and on homosexuals who affect disgust at homosexuality, but he comes close to committing both sins.

On the whole, though, Proust's homosexuality was advantageous to the novel. Like Freud, he assumed there was no such thing as normality, no clear-cut difference between heterosexuality and deviations from it. 'It appears that no healthy person', said Freud, 'can fail to make some addition that might be called perverse to the normal sexual aim: and the universality of this finding is in itself enough to show how inappropriate it is to use the word perversion as a term of reproach.' 'If there is something of perversion or aberration in all our loves,' wrote Proust, 'perversions in the narrower sense are like loves in which the germ of the disease has spread victoriously to every part.' As an asthmatic, he was inclined to view love as an incurable disease whose symptoms need close scrutiny.

No one could have reacted more strongly against the romantic idea that sexual desire is a consequence of falling in love. With no help from Freud, Proust became convinced there was no emotional connection between the sexual drive and its object: 'When we are in love, the love is too big for us to contain it within ourselves. It radiates towards the person we love, finds a surface which stops it, and it is this ricochet of our own feelings which we mistake for the other person's feelings, and which charms us more than on its outward journey because we no longer recognise it as having emanated from us.'

When sexual relationships in the novel support this idea, we can't say facts are being tailored to fit the theory because the facts are mostly – or at least partly – fiction, but it wasn't a matter of waiting for the story to precipitate the theories. Proust's theories and his fiction derive from his life, but the theories had begun to evolve before the fiction did. Men fall in love with women suitable as opponents in sado-masochistic power games but unsuitable in every other way. The coquettish Odette and Rachel are made of coarser material than the sensitive Swann and the considerate Saint-Loup. Swann is clever, perceptive and witty, but, like Saint-Loup, helplessly in the grip of a passion fuelled by agonising uncertainty about whether his mistress is unfaithful. Absence makes the heart distrustful. 'That is how a woman, by every fresh torture she inflicts on us, often quite unknowingly, tightens her hold on us and heightens our demands on her. With each injury she inflicts, she encircles us more completely, redoubling our chains but also the ones we had previously thought adequate to bind her and give us peace of mind.' But when he uses the word 'torture', the implication of sadistic malice is unintentional. He'd used the word to describe reactions to his mother's attacks of malaise: 'Each time I see her looking unwell, I feel a complex emotion for Mamma. I torture myself about her. She puts me in the position of the victim in relation to his torturer. Except that the victim adores the torturer, and detests him precisely because he adores him.'[25]

No one has written more powerfully than Proust about jealousy and insecurity as necessary ingredients in passionate love. 'Surely in the whole of literature,' wrote Samuel Beckett, 'there is no study of that desert of loneliness and recrimination that men can call love posed and developed with such diabolical unscrupulousness.' 'There can be no peace of mind in love,' says Proust, 'since what one has obtained is never anything but a starting point for further desires.' 'Desire, reaching out always to what is most opposite to oneself, forces one to love what will make one suffer. . . . It is a mistake to speak of a bad choice in love: as soon as there is a choice it can only be a bad one.' Thanks mainly to observation of Albu and Louisa, he could write knowingly about attraction and titillation, about possessive jealousy and the torture lovers inflict on each other, but he wouldn't have observed them in the way he did if his feelings for his mother hadn't already taught him that a great love is non-stop agony.

With his asthma worse than it had ever been, he was desperate to fight back. Still expecting an early death, he was no longer demoralised by the idea. During his 1907 holiday at Cabourg he'd been testing himself by leading a strenuous life; now, exerting himself both mentally and physically by writing so much, he projected his situation into the Narrator's childhood: after long periods of reading he'd go out for a brisk walk and 'my body, which had been obliged to stay motionless for a long time but had been charging itself on the spot with energy and accumulated speed, then needed, like a top which has been whipped, to discharge the accumulation in all directions'.[26]

The extra energy increased his impatience for reactions from his friends. He read what he'd written to Reynaldo, who reacted enthusiastically.[27] The manuscript consisted of three exercise books, and the typists he employed had difficulties in deciphering his handwriting. Though he'd promised to deliver the complete typescript for this section to *Le Figaro* by 24 November, they were still at work on the 25th.[28] They promised to deliver it by 2 December. He lent the three exercise books to Georges, who was deeply impressed and read some of the novel to his father. This pleased Proust, who asked Georges to make sure at least this section found its way into print, even if sudden death stopped him from completing the book.[29]

V

1910–14
Reclusion

TWENTY-ONE

VIEW FROM THE ARK

In 1897 Proust had taken his first big step towards isolating himself when he started getting up at night and staying in bed during the day; he took the second in 1910. This was the year, according to Robert Proust, he withdrew from society. 'It was from then on a life of renunciation, a genuinely ascetic life in which, cloistered at his home, surrounded by his exercise books, scarcely going out any more, he brought his formidable work into existence.'[1]

It was less a matter of physical debility or subordinating the present to the past or trying to escape from time, than reluctance to commit any of the shrinking future to experiences that would leave no trace. In January he made a note about Musset: 'One senses in his life, in his letters, as in a mineral where it is scarcely recognisable, some lineaments of his work, which is the only *raison d'être* of his life, his love affairs which exist only to the extent that they are the materials, which reach towards it and will remain only in it. . . . He was a lover and, when in love, was in a state of delirium, gave an account of his feverishness to God. All that, poured off, passed into his poetry and into *On ne badine pas avec l'amour*.'[2]

Proust's talent for companionship depended largely on the qualities that had got him into high society; none of these was going to vanish suddenly, but he'd begun to set a lower value on friendship. Loyal, generous, considerate, lively, Saint-Loup has been the best of companions, but in *Jeunes Filles*, when he speaks reverently about 'our friendship', the Narrator finds it hard to answer, knowing he's happier when alone than when they're together.[3] And, as if to prove he's right to devalue their friendship, the narrative makes Saint-Loup behave badly. ' "You know I told Bloch," Saint Loup said, "you don't like him all that much, that you found him vulgar. That's what I'm like. I like clear-cut situations." '[4] Saint-Loup's character goes on deteriorating as he turns into a homosexual. 'It was only when he was still a lover of women that he was genuinely capable of friendship.'[5] But Proust goes on in *Le Temps retrouvé* to an abrasive condemnation of all friendship, comparing social pleasures to indigestible food which causes discomfort. Friendship is 'a pretence, since, for whatever moral reasons he does it, the artist who gives up an hour of work for an hour of chatter with a friend knows he is sacrificing a reality for something which does not exist (friends not being friends except in that amiable delusion to which we succumb throughout our lives but which in the depths of our mind we know to be the mistake of a madman who believes the furniture is alive and talks to it)'.[6]

With his incurable habit of setting a lower value on himself than other people set on him, Proust had never been able to venture out into society without great expenditure of his energy to overcome his reticence. He now felt committed to reserving most of his energy for work, concentrating more on what was going on inside himself and on interaction between self and environment. 'On certain fine days it was so cold, one was in such close contact with the street it seemed as if the walls of the house had been dismantled and each time a tram passed, its bell reverberated like a silver knife tapping against a house of glass.' Instead of going out with Albertine, the Narrator prefers to stay in bed.

> This ideal morning filled my mind with a permanent reality, identical with all similar mornings, and gave me a vivacity which my physical weakness did not diminish: since well-being results for us much less from our good health than from unused surplus of our energy, what is no less effective than increasing our strength is restricting our activity. That with which I was overflowing, and which I powerfully sustained in bed, made me throb, jump inwardly, like a machine which, prevented from moving, turns on itself.[7]

Turning in on himself, turning away from this particular morning towards the thought of what it had in common with other mornings, he was turning away from the world outside the window, if only half voluntarily. He wasn't only caught up in the invalid routine, but also in the conflict between the Decadents' rejection of nature and the impressionists' celebration of sea, sky, open air. At one stage Proust had modelled himself on

the man who'd been the original for Huysmans' des Esseintes.
'Nature has had her day,' said Huysmans. 'The disgusting
monotony of her landscapes and skyscapes has finally proved
too much for refined and sensitive temperaments.' Proust
wouldn't have said this, but his life had shaped itself as if he
were, in spite of himself, in agreement. A critic who analysed
4,578 of the images in *À la recherche* found 944 had their source
in nature (326 of these derived from water and the sea), 203
from painting and 171 from music,[8] but as he grew older he
drew increasingly on the images stored in his mind. This
involved him in deepening commitment to the Romantic idea
that the imagination offers access to an alternative mode of
being and that this, once perceived, can be rendered as art.
When he's concentrating on the words in front of him, every
writer is cutting himself momentarily off from the sights and
sounds and people of the world outside, but Proust had a
different kind of interest from most novelists in the interaction
between world and work.

This isn't a new development but an intensification of an
old one. In the four notebooks he started using in 1908 one of
his jottings runs:

What presents itself so darkly at the bottom of consciousness,
it is necessary, before realising it in daylight, before bringing
it out, to make it traverse an intermediary region between
our obscure self and the exterior, our intelligence, but how
to get it as far as that? You can go on for two hours trying
to repeat the first impression, the unseizable sign which was
on it and which says 'Deepen me' without approaching it,
without making it come to itself. But that is the whole of
art, the only art. Nothing deserves to be expressed except
what has appeared in the depths and habitually, except in the
illumination of a flash of lightning or in periods which are
exceptionally lucid, loving. These depths are dark. This darkness, this need for ourselves is the only mark of value, so
perhaps of a certain joy. It matters very little what the subject
is. A hair, if it is out of reach for days, has more value than
a complete theory of the world.[9]

Many of his most important passages of narrative are concerned with extricating involuntary memories of specific
experiences, but the design of the novel is idealistic. 'In the
same way that I shall present as an illumination in the manner

of *Parsifal* the discovery of time regained in the sensations spoon, tea, etc., this will be a second illumination, dominating the composition of this chapter, but subordinate to the first, and perhaps when I ask myself what will assure the material of the book which will make me perceive that all the episodes in my life have been a lesson in idealism.'[10] With these priorities, he felt he was gaining more than he was losing by staying in his room. In the same way that blindness permits a greater concentration on sounds, he was insulated from the distraction of new impressions. At one stage, he said, he'd felt sorry for Noah, who had to stay shut up in the ark for forty days, but he realised later 'that Noah could never have seen the world as well as he did from the ark, in spite of the fact that it was enclosed and that darkness was covering the earth'.[11]

Not that he'd ever been interested in descriptive writing except as a means of reaching towards the mysterious laws secreted behind surfaces.

> For, moved by the instinct within himself, the writer, long before he was expecting to become one, invariably failed to look at so many of the things other people notice, which made them accuse him of inattentiveness, and made him accuse himself of being unable to hear or see, but all the while he was commanding his eyes and his ears to retain for ever what to other people seemed like puerile nothings, the tone in which a phrase had been spoken, the expression and the shrugging shoulders of someone about whom he perhaps knows nothing else at the time, which all happened many years ago, and then because he had already heard that tone, or thought he might hear it again, that it was something recurrent; it is this feeling for the general which, in the future writer, chooses for itself that which is general and can enter into the work of art.

This implies a sense of vocation which could hardly fail to isolate him.

For the moment, not cutting himself off from other people but using a different strategy to impose his will on them, Proust was sinking deeper into the invalid routine. The development was in line with his childish success in getting a goodnight kiss by insisting he couldn't manage without one. What he'd discovered at the age of seven was how to snatch strength out of weakness. The family myth about his lack of willpower had taught him to make weakness into a weapon. When he wanted alcohol, he exaggerated the asthmatic symptoms till they dosed him with it. He'd now use the same tactic against the rest of the world.

Unfortunately, though, the routine which was cutting him off from the world was making him increasingly dependent on narcotics which worked against his intention of keeping his mind clear for his work. This was the reason he gave for eating so little, but he'd started using opium-based anti-asthma powders,[12] while he was still using caffeine as a stimulant and had started using a new sedative, Veronal – a proprietary name for barbital, which was used as a soporific, the normal dose never exceeding half a gram,[13] but Proust speaks of taking several grams. As a friend told him, 'You're putting your foot on the brakes and the accelerator at the same time.'[14] But he was caught in a vicious circle. With no fresh air and no exercise, he was giving his body no chance to establish its own rhythms. He couldn't sleep without the Veronal, couldn't wake up without the caffeine.

His few social outings were likely to have ulterior motives: concerned with collecting new facts and tightening his grasp on memories of people he was using as models, he gladly spent time with acquaintances he no longer liked. Basing the bossy, self-satisfied Mme Verdurin mainly on Mme Lemaire, he went to see her in mid-January,[15] though he made himself ill by doing so. He was keen, too, to meet Gaston de Caillavet's fifteen-year-old daughter, Simone, who was about the same age as Gilberte when the Narrator meets her. When Mme Arman died, Proust wrote not only to Gaston, to Jeanne and to the bereaved lover, Anatole France, but also to Simone, the only one of the four who didn't reply. Answering her mother's answer, he wrote: 'I hope Mlle Simone had my letter but that above all she does not trouble to reply.'[16] Which forced her to reply, and by corresponding with her he prepared the ground for a meeting.

The sixty-five-year-old Anatole France promised to go on feeling grateful for Proust's letter 'throughout the small number of excessively long days which remain for me to live'.[17] With only thirty-eight years behind him, Proust had better reasons for believing he had few ahead of him. Discussing debentures which wouldn't be convertible till 1912, he said: 'I have little chance of being alive then.'[18]

Life in Paris was suddenly disrupted by floods. After persistently heavy rainfall the Seine burst its banks, and on the night
of 22 January all the pneumatic clocks stopped at 11.10. Flooding in cellars at the Popp factory on the quai National had
stopped the circulation of compressed air. The express post
was crippled, and within two days the electricity supply was
cut off and telephone communication broke down.[19] The
Métro was flooded, some theatres closed, and at others the
stage was lit by acetylene lamps. From the Trinité to the Gare
Saint-Lazare, streets looked like canals. After a sewer burst in
the rue du Havre, swarms of rats were seen, and rumours
spread about the danger of cholera. Fifty thousand refugees
were housed in public buildings, and soup kitchens were set
up.

On 29 January the flooding reached the rue de l'Arcade, and
cement barriers were built to keep the water out of the boulevard Haussmann. The rue de Rome was like a river, and in
front of the Hôtel Terminus the tide was rising at the rate of
a centimetre an hour. Proust made jokes about the danger of
drowning.[20]

The water finally began to subside on the 30th, and while
most Parisians were better off, his ordeal got worse. In mid-
February, when the cellars were being pumped dry, carbolic
fumes from the disinfectants brought on a series of asthma
attacks 'from which nothing gives me any relief'. Nor could
he recover by resting: workmen were removing rotten parquet
from the basement flats, and hammering new parquet into
place. The lift, damaged by flooding, had to be repaired, while
Dr Gagey was having new mains drainage installed, and the
plumbers started work in the early morning.[21] Suffering now
from albumen in his urine, Proust exacerbated the trouble with
Veronal and anti-asthma powders.[22]

On 13 February he got up to watch the dress rehearsal of
Reynaldo's ballet, Fête chez Thérèse, which had been created in
collaboration with the writer Catulle Mendès, but was too ill
to attend the première on the 16th,[23] though he went on writing
and reading. Thomas Hardy's novel The Well-Beloved, which
had come out in a French translation, reminded him of his
own work, though he judged the English novel to be 'a thousand times better'. Seeking perfection of form in both life and
art, Hardy's sculptor hero falls successively in love with a
beautiful woman, her daughter and her granddaughter. They

all have the same name, Avice, but, marrying none of them, he ends up with an elderly widow when, like the stone on the island, the lovers have both been eroded by time. Proust was already committed to the pattern in which the Narrator, in his love for Gilberte, runs up against the same frustration her father, Swann, has encountered in wooing Odette. What may derive from Hardy is the idea of making Odette offer the Narrator an introduction to her daughter.

'It is curious', wrote Proust, 'that in all the contrasted kinds of writing from George Eliot to Hardy, from Stevenson to Emerson, there is no literature which exerts on me a power comparable to that of English and American literature. Germany, Italy and quite often France leave me indifferent. But two pages of *Mill on the Floss* make me weep.'[24] He asked Robert de Billy, who knew a high-ranking official at the British embassy, to enquire 'whether he knows Thomas Hardy and Barrie, what sort of men they are, in society, collectors of women, etc.'[25] Forgetting his principle about the irrelevance of biographical facts, Proust was lapsing into Sainte-Beuvian curiosity.

In mid-February, Montesquiou, who hadn't seen him since 1905, when he came to give a reading in the flat, decided to visit him. The comte had given up his Pavilion des Muses in 1909 and settled in Vésény, a suburb ten miles to the north-west of Paris. As so often before, Proust tried and failed to dissuade him from coming. Arriving on 7 or 8 March, Montesquiou talked about Reynaldo's ballet, which he'd reviewed in *Gil Blas*, describing Carlotta Zambelli's legs as 'admirable pillars, animated and witty'.[26] Proust said the review was 'delicious', but gently reprimanded Montesquiou for the way 'in which you speak of my dearest friend'. It 'would be delicious if it were not also malicious'.[27]

He was still seeing Reynaldo, who was more persistent than any of his other friends in calling at midnight, and more tolerant if he was turned away five times out of six, but Proust was still involved in the offstage dramas of Louisa's life. Over-estimating her capacity for monogamy and underestimating her duplicity, Robert Gangnat was now suffering in the same way Albu had. Convinced she was being unfaithful, he complained to Albu, who passed the news on to Proust, counting on him to intervene tactfully. He did, without disclosing the source of his information. 'In two words, my dear little Louisa, it appears that R believes – wrongly I imagine – that you are on very good terms with a very well-known artist.' Praising Gangnat's 'noble nature', he warns her how unhappy she'll be if she provokes a separation.[28] But he deals more perceptively with her talent for arousing and exploiting jealousy in the fiction he was writing at this time, depicting Swann's accumulating rage as Odette, living at his expense, progressively gives him less time, less opportunities to sleep with her and more evidence to suggest she's sleeping with other men.

Apart from using them as models, Proust could rarely afford to have any dealings with his friends except by letter. During the third week in April, wanting to discuss investments with Lionel Hauser, he got up after preparing himself for the outing in his usual way with large doses of strong coffee. The result was a series of chronic attacks with symptoms that seemed to indicate cardiac trouble and angina pectoris. From now on he'd have to cut down on coffee, and on the day after the outing, trying to recuperate, he was disturbed by a noise in the wall. He called Nicolas and Céline, who thought he was imagining it, but a large pigeon had flown into the chimney and got itself trapped. 'Such things happen to no one but me.'[29]

He still didn't know whether the novel was going to be serialised in Le Figaro. Nervous though he was about the protracted silence, he'd been too embarrassed to break it. Though Calmette had promised to give the serialisation priority over everything else, over four months had gone by, several other serialisations had been started, and there was no word from Calmette about the episodes Proust had sent to Beaunier. On 24 April, the day of the legislative elections, Proust hadn't entirely recovered from his last bout of illness, but at eleven in the evening he got up and went to the newspaper offices, where he found everyone involved in the election results. Calmette, who was too busy to see him, had obviously lost interest in the novel.

In approaching Louisa about her relationships with men, Proust was invariably diplomatic, but, less skilful in handling his own affairs, he'd made a major mistake in sending the typescript to Beaunier. Not wanting him to think all the arrangements had been made without consulting him or that the novel overlapped with anything he might write about Sainte-Beuve, Proust had ignored the risk of upsetting Calmette. Beaunier was comparatively unimportant. Even if he didn't like the book, he wouldn't have been able to make Calmette reverse his decision. Proust knew that, but he didn't know how insecure Calmette felt. Already jealous of Beaunier's reputation in the literary world, he resented the implication that he'd need advice from someone who knew more than he did about literature. Finally understanding what had happened, Proust asked Beaunier not to say another word about the novel to Calmette, but this was misunderstood too – it looked as if he thought Beaunier had been trying to dissuade Calmette from going ahead.[30]

If Proust hadn't made this tactical mistake, *À la recherche* would have been shaped quite differently from the novel we know. When he gave up hope of serial publication, he shifted into a slower rhythm. While he was excited by the prospect of immediate feedback from friends he seldom saw, his tempo had quickened. Soon his friends would have more respect for his taste, his temperament, the workings of his consciousness, his past. He was going to show he was a serious writer, not a dilettante. Even when he was using incidents which had occurred and remarks which had been made in his presence, he'd been remodelling them, he believed, in such a way as to draw from 'the depths of myself'.[31] He was enormously disappointed when he could no longer count on being put in touch with his readers immediately; the consolation was that the book would be better if he geared himself to write it without deadline pressure. Since starting on it two years ago, he'd done a tremendous amount of rewriting, but in the material he'd handed to Beaunier, he'd structured highly polished fragments hastily into a coherent narrative. Now he could take more time on structuring and even more on rewriting. He went over the same passages again and again, penetrating more deeply into his memories. Calmette had never exerted more influence on French literature than he did by changing his mind about the serialisation. Proust would have grown into a different kind of novelist if it had gone ahead. He now asked Beaunier for comments and revised slowly, taking them into account. In mid-April he'd been saying it would take him several months to finish the novel;[32] by the end of the month he was taking a different view of the amount of time he needed.[33]

It was because of the novel that he called on the Caillavets towards the end of April, more eager to see the young Simone than he'd been to see any woman since Oriane de Goyon and

Lucy Gérard, the actress at Cabourg. Though it was almost midnight when he arrived, he persuaded Jeanne to wake her daughter up and bring her downstairs. Afterwards he said Simone's smile had made him fall in love with her, but he had no designs on her except as a model. If Oriane and Lucy Gérard had helped to give him a way of bringing the bourgeoisie and the aristocracy together in the body of a sixteen-year-old girl, Simone's resemblance to the young Jeanne Pouquet put Proust in touch with his past. There had never been any realistic possibility he'd marry Jeanne, or that he'd ever have a child, but if they'd had a child together, she'd have looked something like this; at the end of the novel, seventeen years after Saint-Loup's marriage to Gilberte, the Narrator will say their daughter resembles his youth.

The physical strain of the outing combined with the emotional strain of the bad news about the serialisation to make Proust ill again: he succumbed to 'severe bronchitis, redoubling my emphysema'.[34] Just after King Edward VII died of bronchitis, Proust said: 'I really believed I was going to do what the King of England had done.'[35] 'For nearly two weeks I have been shaking with fever and coughing enough to split my soul.'[36] But when Antoine Bibesco, hearing his play was going to be staged at the Théâtre Réjane, asked Proust to write about it, he promised an anonymous article and asked for authorisation to attend a rehearsal.[37] And in early June he went to see Diaghilev's Ballets Russes in *Scheherezade, Carnaval, Le Festin* and *Prince Igor*. He didn't share the general enthusiasm for Nijinsky, but he accepted an invitation from the comtesse Greffulhe to join her in her box to see *Les Sylphides, Cléopâtre* and, once again, *Scheherezade*.[38] Seventeen years ago, seeing the comtesse with mauve orchids falling to the nape of her neck, he'd thought she was the most beautiful woman he'd ever seen; his evening with her at the ballet is refracted through the Narrator's evening at the theatre with the Guermantes. He realises he's overrated their importance and underrated his importance to them. 'Now I knew that these were not goddesses but women less poetic than any others, that their life had no delights or mystery in it, that there was nothing in it which could not be found elsewhere, and no such thing as this delicious life I had pictured them as experiencing.'[39] Now their friendship was available, Proust no longer valued it, but he was glad he'd accepted the invitation.

Generally he had as little interest in going out as in receiving visitors. The only regular caller was Reynaldo, who came to see him in July, and played Wagner on the piano. Proust thanked him with a series of small, captioned, cartoon-style drawings laid out like panes of stained glass in a Gothic window. In the first, Proust is lying in bed, listening to music. In the second, Reynaldo is playing the overture to *Die Meistersinger* on the other side of the door. In the next Céline is cooking a sole in the kitchen. Reynaldo, annoyed he let himself be persuaded to play, leaves in a hurry, but Proust weeps with gratitude. Nicolas and Ulrich are shown knocking at a door, and in one cartoon Proust speaks to his brother over the telephone. He studies the score of a march Reynaldo has written for the wedding of his niece, Olga, in August. At sunrise Proust draws the curtains of his room and goes back to bed. The thirteenth cartoon is captioned: 'The image of Bunibuls [his nickname for Reynaldo] appears to the grateful soul of Buncht [Reynaldo's for him] who clasps his hands to God in thanks for possessing such a friend.' A spectacled doctor tells Proust he's going to die, and he does. The last cartoon shows a tomb piled with flowers and hawthorn trees. A top-hatted Reynaldo is taking leave of his friend.[40]

Proust's summer holidays were invariably taken after a crisis of indecision about whether he was well enough to leave Paris. If he went to Cabourg this year, he said early in July 1910, it would be to work on the novel, which would soon be finished,[41] but he was also convinced he needed a change of air.[42] Besides, it would be convenient to hand the flat over to builders. Ever since he'd moved in, he'd suffered so much from noise that he decided to have the bedroom walls lined with cork. The idea derived from a literary joke. Two years ago he'd written in the Flaubert pastiche about people with cork lining in their bedrooms to protect them against noisy neighbours. Why not translate the conceit into reality?

Without telling Reynaldo he was leaving Paris,[43] he went to Cabourg on the 17th, after packing in such a hurry he needed help not only from the concierge, Antoine, but also from his wife and son. He took Nicolas with him, but not Céline, who was left in charge of the flat, though she was liable to invite friends in.[44] He was scarcely well enough to travel, and, reaching the hotel at about midnight, was devastated to find the luggage had gone astray. Antoine must have made a mistake in labelling it. Proust had his own suitcase and the hatboxes of an unknown lady, who'd taken all his trunks with her to Brittany.[45] None of the things he needed for the night had been packed in the suitcase. 'I could neither lie down, nor get undressed, nor anything. That I had to spend the night, then the morning, then the day and the evening like this will make you feel sorry for me.'[46]

Agitation and exhaustion brought on a mild heart attack, which he ignored, but he thought about cutting his holiday short because Albu's life might be in danger after an operation for acute appendicitis. Another reason for returning to Paris was toothache, which made Proust want to see his dentist, but a reassuring letter arrived from Albu's doctor, and, once the toothache had receded, Proust started to feel better than usual, though not well enough to work on the novel more than one day in ten.

It was disappointing that Cabourg was doing so little to boost his health. Only three years ago he'd gone out every day in a closed car, and two years ago he could still go on the beach. Even last year, though he hadn't ventured out of doors, he'd got up at nine in the evening to gamble in the casino; the most he could manage this time was to spend an hour or two there once every two or three days.[47] But he was doing enough work to believe the end was in sight. He'd have liked an excerpt to appear in the *Grande Revue*, but the whole novel should be ready so soon he thought it was already too late to approach the editor of a review, who'd inevitably ask for a long interval between the appearance of the excerpt and the publication of the book.[48]

It would still be dedicated to Calmette, 'because I was not dedicating it to him opportunistically',[49] and when the two men met at the seaside the editor was full of praise for what he'd read. He was staying at Houlgate, and one evening, when they went for a walk arm in arm with Proust's cousin, Valentine Thomson, who was staying in Cabourg, Calmette said her cousin was a genius who'd written something solid and magnificent. Watching him in the casino, she thought 'Marcel looked like an oriental sorcerer with his black beard and his black-rimmed eyes. But his only magic was to produce twenty-franc gold coins from his pocket and give them to girls who happily staked them on the gaming tables.'[50]

Needing a typist, he'd have liked Ulrich to come, but the young man was in hiding from his parents after a troublesome love affair, and Proust didn't want to give the impression he was sheltering a fugitive.[51]

Though he hadn't been seeing Georges, he was doing his best to continue the relationship. Reviewing a collection of four stories by Lucien Daudet, *Le Prince des cravates*, in *L'Intransigeant*, he compared the description of a road at Carenton with 'the Norman roads of Georges de Lauris in his beautiful and profound *Ginette Chatenay*'. He continues the digression to praise Georges' 'delicious talent as psychologist and writer'.[52] And in Cabourg Proust received a letter from Georges, announcing his impending marriage to the beautiful Madeleine de Pierrebourg, who'd been unhappily married to Louis de la Salle. 'I am happy', wrote Proust 'that this delicious and slightly bruised creature will be with the man I consider the most intelligent, the best looking, the best even in this sense that in regrafting his sensitivity on his mind, he has brought to maturity a gentle goodness which was perhaps not congenital.'[53]

Proust returned to Paris in late September, making the 140–mile journey in a taxi. He'd been looking forward to a quieter life, but instead of profiting from the cork lining on his walls, he succumbed to a series of asthma attacks and suspected the cork of causing them.

But, reading *Le Figaro* on 4 October, he was delighted to find himself mentioned in an article on the cathedral in Strasbourg. The writer, who signed himself Louis Chevreuse, referred to Ruskin's *The Bible of Amiens* – 'so magnificently and delicately translated and annotated, several years ago, by M. Marcel Proust'. Eager to find out whether Chevreuse was a *nom de plume*, Proust asked Robert Dreyfus, who was still writing regularly for *Le Figaro*, signing himself D, to find out.[54] Dreyfus admitted he was Chevreuse and offered to pay Proust a nocturnal visit 'at the hour when your receive your friends'. 'Dear trinity,' Proust wrote, 'my threefold blessing on you – I am full of gratitude to D, to Chevreuse, and my favourite of the three is Robert Dreyfus.' Dreyfus could telephone him on 292 05, 'but it is so seldom that I have an evening without an attack', and 'except for Reynaldo and you, no one is allowed to come, and no one does'.[55]

But he was still liable to be deeply upset by rebuffs. After all the trouble he'd taken to befriend Georges, he was incredulous at not being invited to the wedding on 26 October. 'Your silence felt so much like that alibi-silence, that scrambled silence which is preserved before a situation in which one is neither invited nor told that one is not going to be invited.' But Proust was still conciliatory. He was glad, he said, to learn that Fénelon had been one of the witnesses at the ceremony, and Georges would be welcome to call with his new comtesse. 'Of course, if you come, do not say a word in front of Nicolas etc. or on the telephone about my reproaches over the wedding. It would be too wounding to my *amour propre*.'[56]

He received a deeper wound when Robert Gangnat died at the age of forty-four. 'I did not think I would be able to weep so much for someone I knew so little.'[57] 'I have witnessed the death of everything which was good, noble, generous, capable of loving, worthy of living. And those who remain I shall have to see stricken, wounded, in tears always at new tombstones.'[58] The day-to-day activities of his friends touched only rarely on what he called 'an existence with so little resemblance to life', but their deaths struck at him with exceptional ferocity, partly because his whole life was perched so close to death, and partly because his mother's death had marked him so deeply. Fondness for Albu had stopped him from liking Gangnat as much as he might have done otherwise, but awareness of this made the blow harder. 'Oh, you whom I have loved so much, Louisa, I pity you from all my heart. I know what you have lost. You can however be proud and bless God because you have inspired first in Louis and in Gangnat . . . perhaps the two purest, most chivalrous, greatest examples of devotion a woman has ever inspired.'[59] The compliment assorts oddly with the way he was writing about her in the novel.

Though it's hard to be sure how rapidly he was progressing with it, one clue is provided by his wish to re-read his 1893 story 'L'Indifférent', which had been published, over two years after he wrote it, in *La Vie contemporaine*.[60] Having no copy, he wrote to Robert de Flers: 'I happen to need it, and you would be doing me a service in sending me this issue.'[61] Proust had excluded the story from *Les Plaisirs et les jours* because it was too much like a first draft for 'Mélancolique villégiature'. Both stories had been written in the aftermath of seeing the comtesse Greffulhe, and the idea which had excited him then was still important, though the homosexual theme is now developed into the opposite heterosexual variation. In both stories a highly desirable woman is infected with incurable love for an unexceptional man; in 'L'Indifférent' Madeleine de Gouvres had been willing to pluck like a bitter flower the pleasure of finding M. de Lepré mediocre and unworthy of the feelings he's aroused in her. Proust has no difficulty in making his readers feel Odette, despite her beauty, is unworthy of the feelings she's aroused in Swann, but while both stories deal only briefly and laconically with the lack of rapport between the lovers, Proust charts the development of Swann's ill-fated passion in great detail. Handling possessive love and passionate jealousy with a strategy that depends partly on an invisible metaphor linking fixation to disease, he's no longer asking the reader to accept his summarised judgments about the worthiness of one lover and the mediocrity of the other. We see for ourselves, suffering with Swann, witnessing Odette's ruthlessness. The intensity of the man's emotion is unconnected with the qualities of the woman who seems to be inspiring it.

On Monday 7 November Proust went out in the evening, hoping to find Robert Dreyfus at the offices of *Le Figaro*. He wasn't there, and, after going on to Larue's, Proust found, as so often, he had to pay a high price in malaise for the outing. In the morning he felt so ill he didn't even read the newspapers. If he had, he'd have discovered the reason for Dreyfus' absence: his brother had died earlier in the day at the age of fifty-three. Proust was late in writing a letter of condolence,[62] but he wrote a second letter ten days later,[63] and sent flowers on 7 December, explaining it was 'the first seventh of a month since that frightful day'.[64]

Unable to plan ahead, because he never knew how ill he was going to be the next day, he went on giving priority to the novel, which meant procrastinating even more than formerly over everything else. In theory the time would come when the book would be finished, leaving him free to catch up with all the tasks which had been accumulating.[65] But the end, which had seemed to be in sight, kept vanishing like a mirage. 'The novel is lengthening ahead of me,' he wrote in November, 'and my strength is dwindling.'

On 13 December he got up at two in the morning to write, and at nine, exhausted, he was torn between the need to sleep and a sudden desire to visit Montesquiou in Vésény. Never opening his shutters, Proust depended on Céline and Nicolas for information about the weather. After a long spell of rain and cloudiness, the sun was shining brightly. In Paris he hadn't gone out in the morning for about ten years, but, trusting his impulse, he ordered a taxi and started out for Vésény. On the way he noticed bouquets of sweet peas in the window of a florist's shop. Unthinkingly, he stopped the taxi and bought them for Montesquiou, but the aroma of the flowers brought on such a severe asthma attack that he was forced to go home, where he felt too ill to lie down.[66]

Another friendship had begun in March when he met the twenty-year-old Jean Cocteau at one of Mme Straus' dinner parties. He'd achieved fame by the age of nineteen, when he recited his poems from the stage of the Théâtre Fémina. By the end of 1910 Proust was addressing the young poet by his Christian name, but they quarrelled so violently that Cocteau returned one of Proust's letters, accompanied by a letter full of angry eloquence, which touched Proust, but 'not by its beauties: for each of us eloquence is a defensive weapon which camouflages defects of character'. It moved him because it reminded him of an angry letter he'd once written to his mother, and to make sure he'd one day regret writing it, she kept it intact.[67] Cocteau's gesture no doubt originated the episode in the novel where Swann returns a letter to the Narrator. Proust's next letter to Cocteau starts: 'Your silent lines are addressed to me with the friendly and distant brilliance of a star which has filled me with tenderness and dreaminess. I thank you.'[68]

When Cocteau wanted to make friends with Anna de Noailles, he secured Proust as his ally in persuading her to write out some of her poems for him. She was glad to oblige,[69] and, advising him how to thank her, Proust told him not to be too restrained. 'She is at once divinely simple and sublimely proud.'[70]

Cocteau was also friendly with Reynaldo and with Lucien, who never called on Proust. But on 9 January 1911, when Le Figaro published an enthusiastic article on him by the critic Marcel Ballot, Proust felt a strong desire to see him again and congratulate him on the article. 'Though suspended between caffeine, aspirin, asthma, angina pectoris, and, altogether, between life and death every six days out of seven, I wanted to tell you how delighted I was.' He made an effort to get up, but he was too ill, and when he wrote to Lucien the next day, he felt doubtful whether he'd ever be able to finish the novel 'even in a botched and approximate form'.[71]

Soon after this he found a new way to relieve the monotony of spending so much time in bed. Today television is a constant source of distraction to bedridden invalids; the closest approximation available in 1911 was the Théâtrophone. By paying the telephone company a monthly subscription of sixty francs, you could listen in to performances at the Opéra, the Opéra-Comique, the Comédie Française, the Concerts Colonne, the Variétés, the Nouveautés, the Châtelet or the Scala.[72] Though the quality of the sound was poor, and it was a strain to keep holding the receiver to his ear, Proust enjoyed it when he was too weak to work. 'I no longer sleep, no longer eat, no longer work, there are still many other things I no longer do, but those have long been missing from my life.'[73]

On the Théâtrophone he listened more to opera than to drama, concerts or variety. After hearing an act of *Die Meistersinger*, he felt convinced Reynaldo was overestimating it;[74] after listening to Debussy's *Pelléas et Mélisande*, he became addicted to it. Each evening it was staged, he asked the operator to connect him with the performance. 'And all the rest of the time there is not a word that does not come back to me.'[75] On evenings when another opera was being staged, he rehearsed it mentally, often singing the part of Pelléas aloud. He liked the orchestral passages best of all, and, though it struck him as plagiarised from *Fidelio*, he loved the moment when Pelléas emerged into the daylight with the words 'Ah, I breathe at last.' 'There are some phrases truly impregnated with the freshness of the sea and the smell of roses carried by the breeze.'[76] In March, after receiving from Reynaldo such an affectionate letter that it made him weep, Proust sent him a pastiche of the plot with Reynaldo as Pelléas and himself as Markel (a combination of Marcel with Arkel, Golaud's father). Markel tells Pelléas he has 'the sad and tearful face of those who have had a long-lasting cold'. Pelléas, who has lost his hat, laments: 'One could say my head has begun to be cold for ever.'[77]

Though Proust had no desire to stay in bed for the rest of his life, he didn't want to be Antoine Bibesco's guest in London. 'Alas I am not well, and work is as impossible for me as travel.' But, uncertain whether he'd ever go back to Cabourg, he enquired about the Travellers' Club in London:

did it stay open late in the evening, serve meals, provide accommodation, was the membership exclusive?[78]

He made another effort to get up in the last week of March. After hearing on the 23rd that Mme Fould had died, he set out on the 24th for her funeral, but had a fit of giddiness and a cardiac spasm on the way. He was forced to stop, and his doctor advised him to rest his eyes, but he disobeyed. Profoundly depressed, partly because he was making so little headway with the novel, he saw the last fourteen years of his life as a period in which 'I have lost everyone I cared about, my health has been irreparably ruined and I have been bedridden for about ten years, getting up for a few hours about once a month, seeing nobody, not even my brother, never opening a window or a shutter, not eating.'[79]

This was how he summed it up when he decided to get in touch with Louis de Robert, a writer he hadn't seen since the Zola trial. In 1909 de Robert had won the Prix Fémina for his psychological novel *Le Roman d'un malade*, which presumably inspired the attempt at rapprochement. Writing to Antoine, Proust reported he never slept for a moment.[80] He thought frequently about the happy past, and, in an effort to encourage involuntary memories of his first meetings with Mme Straus, ordered from a stationer folded mauve writing-paper and envelopes with mauve lining, such as she'd used when she first wrote to him. But the stationer produced only a poor approximation.[81]

After so many abortive attempts to get up, he succeeded during the second week of May – lured partly by the knowledge that Fénelon was going to be there – in attending a ball arranged by *L'Intransigeant* at the Hôtel Carlton. There he saw the princesse Marthe Bibesco, the twenty-four-year-old cousin of the brothers and of Anna de Noailles. At the age of nineteen she'd married another cousin, prince Georges Bibesco, and she'd written a book, *Huit Paradis*, which Proust had admired. He was eager for a conversation with her, but she tried to avoid him. 'What did he want here, this strange man who was shivering inwardly?' Wearing his fur coat with the collar turned up, he seemed to be exuding cold air. 'With his body a captive in the fur coat which was too big, he looked as if he had come from his coffin.' She was dancing at the other end of the room, and seeing him beyond the dancing couples she thought his face looked anaemic, and his black beard made her think of an

Armenian Christ in his tomb. Proust sent Fénelon to fetch her and, reluctantly, she joined him. He asked her whether she was going to write another book, and 'he started to explain at length something which sounded, so far as the music and the conjoined feet of the dancers allowed me to hear, like a eulogy of defeat, of what could have been and has not been. All his investments were bad ones, he said: he wanted to explain that in gambling what matters is to lose.' She listened impatiently, wanting to go on dancing.[82]

Eleven days later, already feeling fit for another outing, he went to the Théâtre du Châtelet for the dress rehearsal of d'Annunzio's *Le Martyre de Saint-Sébastien*, which had music by Debussy, décor by Léon Bakst and choreography by Fokine. Proust found nothing to admire except the legs of Ida Rubinstein, who played the saint. He found the play boring, the music insubstantial, and both 'the publicity and the orchestra quite enormous for these few farts'.[83] He saw Montesquiou in the audience, and in the interval went to sit next to him. Hearing afterwards that the comte was writing in praise of the play, Proust sent him a disingenuous letter: 'I was so happy I could listen to you during the intervals, and be so close to you while listening to the last act, in which, linked to your enthusiasm by the cuff of your coat, as if by a metal electrode, I was as convulsively aroused as if my seat had been electrified.'[84]

TWENTY-TWO

REJECTION

'It is truly odious', Proust complained, 'to subordinate the whole of one's life to the confection of a book',[1] but the process of subordinating experience to literature had begun long before he started on the book. The pleasure he took in elaborating his plot had been prefigured by the elaborate plotting and intrigue in his relationship with Fénelon and the Bibescos; doing so much of it in his letters to them, he'd already been on the way to making it a literary affair. Progressively withdrawing from society and depending mainly on correspondence for contact with his friends, he'd been inserting in his life the thin end of the literary wedge he designed partly to give permanence to moments which would otherwise have left no residue. Letters couldn't be monumental; a book had a better chance of surviving, but he'd have been incapable of bringing his book into existence if he hadn't enjoyed the process. The experience of remembering, researching and planning was gratifying in the same way as writing letters – and often it involved writing letters – because it increased his imaginative intimacy with experiences and people he cared about. The deeper he sank into the invalid routine, the more his relationships with external reality depended on the complex machinery in which the two principal cogs were correspondence and the book.

His main problem was structural. He had faith in the quality of the ingredients that were going into the book, but the chaos of memories and ideas in his mind had to be assembled in a form that would make them communicable. The need to write such long sentences and to rewrite each of them so many times reflected the need to find a syntactical correlative to the complexity of what had to be said. Nothing must be simplified in the process of imposing order on it. The difficulty was reflected by the chaos of books, newspapers, notebooks, loose sheets of paper on his bed. He'd never been good at putting things away and, as his physical condition deteriorated, he made less effort to keep his papers tidy, and it's altogether remarkable that so much good writing emerged from the chaos of papers on the bed. He was even liable to muddle letters. When the duc de Gramont died, Proust wrote letters of condolence to both his son, Guiche, and his daughter, the marquise de Clermont-Tonnerre. The letter to him had a postscript about his 'admirable' sister, the letter to her praised the excellent qualities of her brother. He then put the two letters in the wrong envelopes.[2]

Since the room could be aired and cleaned only when he went out, it had become stuffier, dirtier and untidier now he was going out so rarely. When Cocteau called, he was aghast at its disorderliness, with cloth covers everywhere, the gas-lamp wrapped in cotton cloth, the Théâtrophone sharing space on the table with medicine bottles and exercise books, the rest of the furniture permanently coated with dust, including the ebony table in the shadows crowded with photographs of great beauties, aristocrats and footmen from palaces. There was a false mirror on the mantelpiece, and the room smelt of anti-asthma powders.

Thin and cadaverous, Proust looked like a caliph, Cocteau says, when he was bearded, and like an egg when he was clean-shaven. He received visitors lying on the bed, fully dressed, wearing not only a starched collar and tie but gloves. He was constantly in terror of perfume. 'Dear Jean, you didn't hold the hand of a lady who might have touched a rose?' And he'd explain, half-jokingly, that Debussy's orchestral mimicry of wind on the sea in *Pelléas* could bring on an asthma attack. He'd often read from *Swann*, choosing a passage at random, skipping a page, interrupting himself to explain how a gesture in the first volume would be illuminated in the last, laughing behind his gloved hand, stopping and apologising for reading so badly. He should never have begun. 'This is too stupid. No, I won't read any more. It's too stupid.' But he liked being persuaded to go on. Sometimes he'd get up, take off his jacket, run a hand through his dark hair, go into his dressing-room and stand in his shirt-sleeves, holding a plate of spaghetti in one hand and eating from it with a fork.[3]

With his health at such a low ebb, it was absurd that he was still liable for military service, but he couldn't get himself permanently exempted from military duties until he discovered

Calmette's brother, Henri, was director of the army's health service. Never averse to asking influential friends to help, Proust approached Calmette. During the second half of May 1911 an army doctor called at nine in the morning, and within four months his name was removed from the list.

It was during this month that Alfred Agostinelli, the chauffeur, reappeared. Though he was good-looking, and Proust liked him, it had never seemed likely this man would have an important role to play in Proust's life, and it still didn't. What he wanted was help in finding a menial job in the Théâtre des Variétés for his girlfriend, Anna, who'd been working as a cleaner at the Théâtre Réjane. Within a fortnight Proust had written two letters to Francis de Croisset, asking him to use his influence,[4] and soon a letter arrived from the secretary-general of the theatre, offering the young woman a job. 'I was so impressed by the headed writing paper of the Variétés, the signature of Brasseur, the speed of the arrangements and the number of luminaries involved that suddenly the unfortunate Agostinellis struck me as quite insignificant, totally unworthy of triggering this august and dizzying machinery.'[5] And, once again, the insignificant Agostinellis disappeared from Proust's life.

It may not have been coincidental that after this meeting Proust again began to feel the need for a male secretary. Though he was averaging only one day of work on the novel each month,[6] he persuaded himself he might finish it more quickly if he had secretarial help for two or three months. Towards the end of June he sat down at four o'clock in the morning to write a long letter to a young man he'd met with Constantin. Working conditions, Proust warned, would be appalling: 'A room full of smoke from my fumigations, impossible hours, the impossibility of planning from one day to the next because of the suddenness of the attacks – these are the smallest horrors of this life.' He described the work as 'a novel or book of essays'. He already had a fair copy of the Combray section, and wanted to dictate the rest to a secretary who'd take it down in shorthand and type it out in his absence. But instead of finding out whether the young man knew short-hand before offering him the job, Proust offered to read it out, if necessary, at dictation speed. The young man would be free during the morning and after lunch; they'd work together in the early evening or after dinner, going on until late.[7]

No answer had arrived by 11 July, when Proust made one of his abrupt decisions to leave for Cabourg. The day was his fortieth birthday, but there was no question of celebrating, and the seaside failed to make him feel better. 'I am dying of asthma here this year.'[8] 'I am having incessant and terrible asthma attacks, so bad that if they go on I shall have to have an isolation cure at La Colline with Dr Widmer (on Lake Geneva).'

When he discovered the hotel employed a shorthand-typist who was available to work for visitors, he felt ambivalent about extricating himself from his commitment to the young man. Always generous, always liable to dither, he offered 300 francs – as much as he'd been earning in a month – 'as a compensation for the trouble you have had in writing to me and in receiving such arid letters from me'.[9] But if the young man felt brave enough to arrive in Cabourg, despite the chronic asthma and the danger Proust might leave the town within a few days, he'd receive 400 francs a month, plus 250, or, if necessary, 300 for his meals. To Robert de Billy Proust wrote: 'Do not come to Cabourg without warning me because I am very ill and do not believe I shall be able to stay',[10] but to the young stranger he suggested: 'If you do not smoke and are not in the habit of sleeping with the windows open (two things I dread) it would be best for you to sleep at the hotel in my suite, where you would have a pleasant room.'[11]

The young man probably realised what risks he'd be running if he slept in the suite, and he never materialised, but Proust consoled himself by intensifying his friendship with twenty-five-year-old Albert Nahmias, who didn't quite accept the secretarial job Proust offered, but helped with financial affairs and generally supervised the typing of the novel by the hotel's shorthand-typist, who turned out to be an Englishwoman with limited French, Cecilia Hayward. But Proust dictated to her on the days – an average of one in four – he felt well enough to get up. 'My novel is getting itself written in an intermediary language.'[12]

Dictating a fiction designed partly to resurrect a happier past, partly to give him a new perspective on it, he couldn't help brooding on pleasures that had vanished from his life. 'Alas, dear Antoine, there were some months at the rue de Courcelles when I was really ill, suffered more than today, but happiness still existed for me then. . . . That year was more beautiful for me because it had the charm of your first visits, of your friendship in which I then believed, in which I had faith. How distant all that is.'[13] And to the one friend who'd remained loyal he wrote: 'Just imagine, my Bunibuls, how every evening as the sun sets and I have not yet switched on the electricity, I think of you in my little bed with a bit of sadness, and at that moment, in the distance on the beach, stout women come to play waltzes with hunting horns and cornets until nightfall. This makes one throw oneself into the sea of melancholy.'[14]

He took some comfort from believing time need not be wholly lost; besides, any conversation could be recycled into dialogue. 'I think I have already pointed out to you', he told Reynaldo, 'that the noun most often attached to *eternal* was *cigarette* . . . Another phrase often said (comparable to "I have no success with my tea") "That looks good, what are you eating there." '[15] He used these sentences to characterise Odette's conversation in the first part of *Jeunes Filles*.[16]

Calmette was in Cabourg, but Proust didn't see him till mid-August, when they talked about Reynaldo, who'd been omitted from the July nominations for the Légion d'honneur. Calmette offered Proust a drink. 'I said rather vulgarly that it was I who would have wished to buy him one, and then, in that tone which is familiar to you, he said: "That is of no importance so long as we are together." I believe on the contrary that he detests meeting me.'[17]

During eleven weeks in Cabourg the only major social event he attended was a ball given at the Golf Club by its president, the vicomte d'Alton. There Proust saw François de Paris, Anna de Noailles and her husband, and Calmette. Here was an opportunity to broach the question about the name Guermantes with François de Paris, who soon made it obvious Georges had never broached the question. 'I have no confidence in your commissions,' Proust told him.[18] But from now on he could feel free to use the name.

Though Maggie Teyte, the soprano who'd sung Mélisande, was giving regular concerts in the casino, Proust didn't go.[19] He went there only once, in September, hoping to find Calmette, and to thank him for the intervention which had led to the removal of Proust's name from the list of army reserve officers.[20]

Cecilia Hayward left for Paris during September, but, using Albert Nahmias as his intermediary, Proust, who stayed on in Cabourg till almost the end of the month, went on employing her, at the same time dictating to another shorthand-typist. Between a fifth and a quarter of his book was typed by the end of the summer. Towards the end of the month he had a series of bad asthma attacks, which finally drove him back to Paris, but this time he didn't make the journey in a taxi. Going to the railway station, he was going out into the air for the first time since arriving in Cabourg eleven weeks ago. He arrived in Paris at six in the morning of 1 October, feeling feeble, exhausted and as if his body consisted more of bone than flesh.[21]

Seeing no one except Nicolas and Céline, he thought frequently about Reynaldo and his new dog, who was named after Voltaire's Zadig. Proust, who'd have enjoyed thinking of the dog as his present to his best friend, wanted to pay for it, but, like Proust, Reynaldo hated receiving presents. Jealous of Zadig, who was going to spend so much more time than he could with Reynaldo, Proust addressed a letter to the dog:

> When I was small and felt miserable about parting from Mamma, or going on a journey, or going to bed, or about a little girl I loved, I was unhappier than today, first of all because, like you, I was not free as I now am to go and distract myself from my grief, and I shut myself up with it, but also because I was tethered up in my mind, where I could not escape into ideas or memories of reading or plans for the future . . . But this intelligence does nothing for us except replace impressions which make you love and suffer with enfeebled facsimiles which cause less pain and less affection . . . And that seems to me so much better than the rest, that it is only when I have gone back to being a dog, a poor Zadig like you, that I start writing, and it is only books written in this way that I like.[22]

The final sentence is written partly in reaction to a book review in the *Nouvelle Revue française* describing an ideal novel diametrically different from what he was writing. The predominant taste of the French reading public, it said, wasn't for novels of the kind Flaubert and Balzac had written but for 'stories usually short, strongly constructed, and going straight to the point, while the characters, with features which may be strongly

delineated or delicately nuanced, but are always precise,
develop their personality logically, illuminating some moral
problem into the bargain. In these works life is observed not
in its details nor in its complexity, but in its broad outlines.'[23]
Always willing to compare his own achievements unfavour-
ably with those of others, Proust found the review depressing.
Was this really what the French public wanted? 'One wonders
for whom one is writing.'[24]

Throughout the winter he spent little time out of bed, and
though he'd promised to make contact with Lucien Daudet,
Georges de Lauris and Montesquiou as soon as he was better,
he felt incapable of the effort.[25] He no longer even wanted
Nicolas or Céline to bring food into his bedroom. They were
ordered to leave milk and eggs outside the door: if he felt
hungry, he said, he'd get up and cook them himself.[26] His
orders were obeyed, and none of the eggs was ever cooked.

But on 5 December he got up in time to go at 1.30 with the
Bibescos' friend Lucien Henraux to the opening of an exhibition at the Durand-Ruel gallery of ancient Chinese paintings
and lacquered screens. Proust was sufficiently enthusiastic to
think of buying some of the screens if he made enough profit
on his latest investments. They met Georges Rodier, a rich
dilettante who'd been a regular at Mme Lemaire's. He looked
'much older, unrecognisable under the hat . . . weatherbeaten,
hardened and rusty, like a blob of honey which would have
melted unsymmetrically, almost scowling (until he saw us)
and then very well, much improved'.[27] This was one of many
encounters which contributed to Proust's revision of the sketch
he'd made for the sequence in Le Temps retrouvé about the way
time has changed everyone he knows.

Rodier, who was one of Proust's models for the snobbish
Legrandin, a provincial scholar, also talked about Cocteau.
' "But what worries me for him", said Rodier, "is the world.
He spends too much time in society. If he spends time in
society he is lost." But I saw he was saying this not as a
fashionable man deploring the grounds of his own weakness,
but as a recluse giving the recipe for his virtues.'[28]

Far from making enough profit on his new investments to
buy a Chinese screen, Proust incurred heavy losses in consequence of taking Albert's advice instead of Lionel Hauser's. 'I
have done well', he told Reynaldo, 'not to involve you in my
vast speculation, because what is vast about it is the enormous

losses it entails.'[29] But he took great pleasure in thinking about the impact the novel would make on Reynaldo. 'I have just been chatting with you all night, asking you "Is this nice? Do you like it?" '[30] Proust also relished the impact it would make on other friends. Nor was this the only way they could go on being important to him without ever seeing him. Once the novel had grown too big for one volume, he approached them for advice. Should the two volumes have different titles? Should they be published simultaneously or separately? Was the publisher likely to say 300 pages was the maximum length for a volume? In which case two wouldn't be enough.[31]

He was still using Albert as his intermediary in having the manuscript typed, and paying him for his time. The handwriting was difficult to decipher, and they alternated between two methods of working. Sometimes Proust would dictate to him, and sometimes hand over the exercise books for him to transcribe into new exercise books. In either case the typist worked from Albert's manuscript. At the beginning of 1912, when Cecilia Hayward, the typist from Cabourg, arrived in Paris, Proust told him to use her, making sure she worked intensively.[32] At the beginning of the year he sent Albert two exercise books, one red and one blue, containing the description of Tante Léonie's room, accounts of a visit to the theatre, an episode about a letter from Odette to her lover, Forcheville, and fragments of other episodes in *Swann*. He wanted the first page of the typescript to be numbered 560.[33]

Knowing the novel was being typed, he had an extra incentive to go on producing raw material for the process.[34] By the end of February he had what he called 'a real volume' ready for the typist, and, by the end of March, he thought the novel would run to eight or nine hundred pages.[35] Most of his work now consisted of rewriting fragments written in exercise books, but, adding phrases, sentences, incidents each time he rewrote, he kept revising his forecast about the total number of pages. In an April or May letter, after saying the first volume would be 650 pages, and the second perhaps 500, he crossed out the 650 to substitute 700, and changed the 500 to 600.[36]

But he wasn't neglecting his finances. He read newspaper reports on companies that interested him and asked financially informed friends for advice. The price of gold had been falling and, rashly, in December 1911, he'd gambled nearly 300,000 francs on the assumption it would soon go up, buying shares he'd have to pay for in the future at a price already fixed. But their value went down, and to pay the differential on 31 January and 29 February, he had to dip heavily into his capital. It's possible that Robert de Billy, though he knew Proust tended to exaggerate his financial difficulties, may have helped him by buying some of the shares from him.[37] In one letter to de Billy, Proust compared his passion for investment with his passion for baccarat.[38]

Late in January 1912, he tried to give up Veronal, which seemed to be making him ill, but though he resolved never to use it again,[39] he didn't keep to this decision. He was eating only one meal a day, often postponing it until four or five o'clock in the morning.[40] As usual, his only regular visitor was Reynaldo;[41] he hadn't been seeing either his doctor or his brother. He was seldom getting up,[42] and seldom going out, except to the offices of Le Figaro. In April he claimed to have gone nowhere else since the previous summer.[43] Calmette had apologetically offered to publish an extract from the novel, and on 11 March Proust forgivingly gave him a passage about the hawthorns. Ten days later it appeared on the front page, but Proust's title, 'Épines rouges, épines blancs', was replaced with 'Au Seuil du printemps' ('On the Threshold of Spring'), and a sub-editor had interpolated the phrase 'which finishes today' after Proust's phrase 'this relatively mild winter'. He was furious,[44] but Calmette promised he'd recommend the novel to Eugène Fasquelle, publisher of Flaubert, Zola and the Goncourts.

In April Albert sent Miss Hayward a new consignment, consisting of the stay at Criquebec (later Balbec) and the meetings with Montargis (Saint-Loup) and Fleurus (Charlus). Albert took his responsibilities seriously, conscientiously writing to question Proust about anything doubtful, and struggling patiently with problems of legibility. Montesquiou, who had exquisite handwriting, said most people manage to write either legibly or attractively; 'only Marcel finds a way to combine in his handwriting ugliness and illegibility'.[45] 'Are you still trying to compete with Oedipus,' Proust asked Albert, 'in decoding the sphinx-like riddles of my handwriting?'[46] But when the young man sent him a present, it was rejected. 'And, since I would have sent it back to you even if it had been something of a sentimental character, I am almost happy that it should be something electrical, which you will be less angry to receive back.'[47]

In May he accepted from the comtesse Greffulhe another invitation to the theatre, and in her box he was presented to her sixty-five-year-old cousin, the once-beautiful Mme Henry Standish, who'd been mistress to General Gallifet and to Edward VII before he became King of England. At one time Queen Alexandra had imitated her French chic, but now it looked as if she was still dressing in the style of the queen. 'I thought her (making all allowances for her age, etc.) astonishing for her sea-damaged elegance and her artificial simplicity.' Though Proust had little opportunity to chat with her, he knew he was going to write about her style of dressing, and wished he could have discussed this with Mme Straus, who knew her. 'You could have said things which would be precious for my book.'[48] He still believed she was better at using words than he was. 'My letters are not like yours,' he told her. 'They lack charm.'[49] He went on thinking about the contrast between the two styles of elegance, and he asked Jeanne Caillavet, who knew both ladies, whether she'd ever seen them in clothes such as they might wear to the opera. She mustn't tell them he was enquiring about them, he said, or they'd assume they'd been models for characters he wanted to dress in their clothes.[50]

What he claimed to find 'still better dressed than Mme Standish' were three blossoming apple trees he saw at six in the evening on a muddy road.[51] He drove back several times in a closed car to see 'the furbelows of the three apple trees in their ball gowns under a grey sky', and when he saw real ball gowns, he compared the colours with those of the trees. 'Once an impression has been made on me, I would need precise words to explain it. And I do not know them. Then I leaf through botanical books or architectural books or fashion magazines. And of course the words are never there.'[52]

The comtesse followed the invitation with yet another – to see Chaliapin as Don Basilio in Rossini's *Barber of Seville* – but didn't invite Proust until the day of the performance. He was resting when the message arrived, and didn't receive it till the following day.[53]

Among the articles he'd sent *Le Figaro* in March was 'Rayon de soleil sur le balcon', which mentioned his boyhood passion for Marie Benardaky, and before the piece was published on

4 June he told Jeanne Caillavet about it, explaining he'd met
Marie before he met her.[54] He also wrote to Anna de Noailles
after reading some of her verse in the *Revue de Paris*. He told
her about his feelings after finding an exercise book in which
his mother had made hour-by-hour reports on the final illnesses
of his grandfather, his grandmother and his father – 'narratives
which, without having the least intention of suggesting anything at all, are so distressing it is hard to go on living after
having read them'.[55] It was in this mood that he made final
revisions to *Le Temps retrouvé* before sending it to the typist at
the end of June.

In July, after catching a cold, he was coughing and feeling
rheumatic, but casually, in the postscript to a letter about his
health, he invited Reynaldo to move in. His mother had died
in March, and Reynaldo lost his flat when the lease expired at
the end of June. 'I could make my dining-room, which is very
big . . . into a bedroom for you. I would have double doors
put on the small drawing-room, which would be yours, and
you would be able to make music in it as loudly as you
liked. . . . Céline would cook for you, and you would be
spared the bother of having to keep accounts, housekeeping
etc. And if you do not like the house, I will move and we will
go where you like.'[56] The offer was seriously intended, and
the idea of living together, which might have been feasible
eighteen years ago if all four parents had been dead, belonged
to the same level of fantasy as Proust's plans for moving out
of Paris. Reynaldo knew him too well to take the offer seriously or even accept the invitation to use his empty flat while
he was in Cabourg.[57]

He'd been vacillating since the spring about whether to spend
the summer there. 'Life is so short I would like to see other
places. But it has many attractions for me.'[58] With his usual
abruptness he decided on 7 August to leave the same day,
asking Albert to come with him, and inviting Vaudoyer to be
his guest later on at the hotel, where, to minimise disturbance,
he took five adjacent rooms on the top floor. Though Vaudoyer didn't accept the invitation, they met later in Cabourg,
where he was staying with friends,[59] and Proust had many
other friends within reach. Reynaldo's friend Henri Bardac
was at Cabourg, the Guiches at Bénerville and the Strauses at
Trouville. Calmette, who was staying with friends at Houlgate, often went to the casino at the Grand Hôtel in Cabourg,

and one evening in September he took Marie Scheikévitch, the twenty-eight-year-old daughter of a Russian aristocrat and mistress of Adrien Hébrard, editor of *Le Temps*. She knew Reynaldo and had met Proust at Mme Lemaire's. 'I was surprised to see Marcel Proust,' she writes, 'wandering, lost, tottering under the lights, dressed in spite of the heat in a heavy overcoat half open above a loosely hanging dinner jacket which revealed several woollen waistcoats. He had a beard which lengthened his face, made it look like an El Greco. In his hand he was carrying an astonishing straw hat.' Impatient to play baccarat, Calmette promised Proust more space in the literary supplement and left them alone together. After spending the rest of the evening in conversation, they went on to see a good deal of each other.

> He pronounced Swann's name in quite a bland way, *Suane*, as if something confidential were sliding from his lips. He expounded the guiding ideas of the book which was planned and partly written, digressing at length to describe its composition, stopped abruptly to explain an important detail, all that with parentheses, making comparisons with the lives of people we both knew. It felt like looking at the wrong side of a tapestry. . . . There was a very curious contrast between his obstinate modesty about himself, or even humility, and his sarcasm, his ruthless remarks when portraying some of our contemporaries with stinging comments, but almost immediately it seemed as if he wanted to cancel these with others which were more benevolent, sometimes even excessively indulgent.[60]

He even danced with her. 'I dance a little every other day,' he told Reynaldo, 'to get the rust out of my joints.'[61] And on 20 August he attended the Golf Club dinner. But after hearing about two accidents he was nervous of motoring expeditions. On the day before the dinner, he'd arranged that Albert would drive him to Trouville, where he wanted to visit Mme Straus. They were to meet on the promenade at Cabourg between six and seven, and Proust was so furious when the young man failed to turn up that he wrote to say there was no question of continuing the friendship. After feeling extremely fond of him, Proust said, he felt uncertain whether he wanted to hit him, to weep or to drown himself.[62] On his way to Deauville Albert's car had hit a young girl who had rushed out in front of it. She died two days later, and at Houlgate on the same day the chauffeur Proust had intended to hire, Marius Mendès, knocked over a ten-year-old girl, who died instantly. 'I have not left the hotel once since I arrived,' Proust wrote on 22 August to Mme Straus, who then offered to lend him her car or visit him in Cabourg, but he found he could hire the hotel omnibus, which was big and inelegant but safe. 'It would enable me perhaps to come on my own,' he told her.[63] He didn't go until mid-September, two days before he left for Paris.

The revised typescript was now ready, and he embarked on a long series of abortive negotiations with publishers. He loved indirect approaches, hated talking on the telephone, loved writing letters, loved involving friends and loved the conspiratorial intrigue that had complicated his friendships with Bibesco and Fénelon. In spite of his sensitivity and capacity for empathy, he was gauche in using friends as intermediaries, as he was when he contacted Louis de Robert. Though they hadn't met for fifteen years, the warmth of their correspondence made Proust feel entitled to enlist his help. But when Robert recommended the book to Fasquelle, he was entreated to keep silent about his intervention so that Calmette could go on thinking he was the only one to have approached Fasquelle.[64]

Proust was equally maladroit with publishers, using indirect approaches and alienating people by taking excessive precautions not to alienate them, as he had when he sent the typescript to Beaunier. By offering to pay the printing costs, Proust made himself look like a rich dilettante eager to buy social prestige through getting a book into print.

At the end of October, with no news from Fasquelle, he was wondering whether to approach a 'purely literary publisher'.[65] Antoine, who'd shown his *Figaro* articles to Jacques Copeau, said Copeau thought them 'too good for a newspaper', which made Proust gravitate towards the *Nouvelle Revue française*. After founding the review in 1909, André Gide, Jacques Copeau and Jean Schlumberger had set up their own publishing house two years later under the direction of Gaston Gallimard, who'd been working as their art critic. Proust soon convinced himself the NRF could provide a 'better milieu' than Fasquelle 'for the ripening and the dissemination of the ideas contained in my book', but instead of speaking to Copeau or Gallimard, he asked Antoine to find out whether they'd be interested in publishing the novel at his expense.[66]

He was still worrying about its length. Writing to Antoine, he said 1,300 very full pages, but crossed out the 1,300 to substitute 1,250. He'd prefer to have 700 pages in the first volume and 550 in the second; alternatively 600 pages in each, or three volumes of 400 pages. There are three postscripts to the letter, and the third asks Antoine not to approach the NRF yet. Proust was dithering even more than usual. He told Mme Straus he'd gone for four days without an hour's sleep, suffering from fever, asthma and insomnia. When he'd tried to stand up, he couldn't, and he'd probably be in bed for several days. How could he make plans for the novel when he didn't know how long he could stay alive? But he wanted her to prod Calmette: 'There is nothing to ask him, it is only a matter of reminding him not to forget he made the offer to me.' If she preferred not to intervene, he could approach Calmette through Madame Lemaire or Reynaldo, but, to encourage Mme Straus, he said her red dress and red shoes were going to be worn in the second volume by the duchesse de Guermantes, who'd make only a fleeting appearance in the first.[67]

Referring to friends in the narrative was one way of carrying on relationships with them. Instead of writing to them, he was writing to himself about them, though this didn't stop him from writing to them about the references, while it could be said that all his letters had been written mainly to himself. Like his newspaper articles, they'd won him a rich harvest of admiration and affection, but he was still finding it hard to believe in his own talent, or even in his identity. 'I have not written a thing,' he said, 'on which I have not received letters from her [Anna de Noailles] so superior to the prose which has occasioned them.'[68] '*I am totally unknown*,' he complained. 'When readers write to me at *Le Figaro* after an article, which happens rarely, the letters are forwarded to Marcel Prévost, for whom my name seems to be no more than a misprint.'[69]

Nor was he sure whether the book was a novel. 'I call it a novel because it does not have the contingency of memoirs (there is nothing contingent in it except what is meant to stand for the element of contingency in life) and the construction is very severe, though elusive, because complex; I could not say what its genre is.'[70] Intending to call the first volume 'Le Temps perdu' and the third 'Le Temps retrouvé', he was writing under the influence of physiologists such as Pierre-Henri Roeser, who argued in *Vieillesse et longévité*[71] that age was a malady, and Proust assured Mme Straus, who'd been looking healthier when he saw her at Trouville, 'It is certain that this summer you made "a conquest of the past". . . . Philosophers have done well to convince us that time is a process of enumeration which corresponds to nothing in reality.'[72] He may be thinking of Bergson, who makes a distinction in *L'Évolution créatrice* between real time and abstract time, describing real time as a flux in which 'the very mobility of being' eludes the grip of scientific knowledge.[73]

There was an unmistakable element of procrastination in Proust's elaborate, self-frustrating game of oblique approaches and stammering letters which effectively cancelled the requests they were making, but Antoine hurried things forward by ignoring the third postscript and approaching Copeau. Proust immediately sent him a long and embarrassed letter, explaining the prince must have failed to read the postscript. Copeau then met Proust and suggested he should approach Gallimard. Meanwhile Calmette had written to Fasquelle,[74] asking him to meet Proust one day in the late afternoon, and wrote, two days later, to Mme Straus[75] saying Fasquelle had written to Proust, asking him to send the manuscript. According to Calmette, Fasquelle had promised to publish the first volume. 'As for the two other volumes, he will discuss them after the publication of the first.'[76]

Eager though he was to see the first volume in print, Proust was nervous the publisher might then want to abandon the novel. Writing to Fasquelle, he said it was the last book he'd write. 'I have tried to put all my philosophy into it, to make all my "music" resonate, and if, after the first volume, you break my work in two, like a vase which is smashed, by stopping the publication there . . .' He left the sentence unfinished as if the idea were unthinkable. The danger seemed all the greater because the second volume explored homosexual territory uncharted in the first.[77] The second part was already in existence, he said, but only in manuscript. The typescript of the first part, which Proust enclosed with the letter, was 'except for some rare passages, very chaste', but in the second part 'an old gentleman from a great family will find himself to be a pederast, which will be described in a comic fashion but which, without a single coarse word, shows him seducing a concierge and keeping a pianist'. But the character was rather original, a virile pederast, disillusioned with 'effeminate young men who deceive him about the quality of the goods on offer, being only women'. He asked Fasquelle to treat all this information as confidential, and without waiting for a reply, wrote again, a few days later: could Fasquelle publish the volume in February and send proofs straight away?[78]

In early November, though he still hadn't heard from Fasquelle, Proust was half expecting proofs to arrive.[79] But, acting with the same abruptness as when he went on holiday, he made a determined attempt to set up a meeting with Gallimard, writing three letters to him, trying to reach him by telephone and enlisting Antoine, too, to telephone him. Eventually he received a letter in reply, and immediately wrote a fourth letter full of premature questions. Could the volumes each have 550 pages with thirty-five lines on each page and forty-five characters on each line? Could the price be kept down to 3.50 francs for each volume? When could the second volume be put on sale?[80] All this before Gallimard had seen the typescript. This time he got an answer, and in his next letter to Gallimard he suggested 'Les Intermittences du coeur' ('Irregularities of the Heart') as an overall title for the novel. The first volume, he suggested, should come out in February, the second, which could be called 'L'Adoration perpetuelle' or perhaps 'À l'ombre des jeunes filles en fleur', should follow in November, and the third, 'Le Temps retrouvé', in February 1914. To warn Gallimard about the homosexuality in the second volume, he summed up the story of the old pederast, using almost the same words as in the letter to Fasquelle. Hesitating about whether to enclose the exercise books containing the manuscript text, he wrote a postscript saying he would, but he changed his mind.

He was at least half aware he was working against his own interests. 'I am coming almost to hope you do not like my work and do not want it, in order to spare myself in this way from current anxieties and the regret I would feel if I received proofs tomorrow from Fasquelle, now that I have glimpsed the possibility of working with you. And I am like those travellers who, unable to abandon a journey which tempts them, try to make themselves late, to miss the train, to be prevented from going.' In the penultimate paragraph of the letter he flatteringly incorporates a phrase from a review Galli-

mard had contributed to the *NRF*, and, a day or two later, he
sent Copeau some excerpts from the book for publication in
the review.[81] But these were rejected, and when, wanting to
thank Calmette for his help, he went to the offices of *Le Figaro*,
the editor refused to see him.[82]

After this he felt too ill to get up, 'and the last dead leaves
have fallen without my being able to see them, and there goes
another autumn in which I have not known the colour of
the season'.[83] He consoled himself with the memory of the
blossoming apple trees. 'Last year, for the first time in twenty
years, I could go to see apple trees in bloom. I am simultaneously making progress and in decline.'[84]

By mid-November he was well enough to accept an invitation from Mme Straus to a play by Robert de Flers and
Armand Caillavet at the Théâtre des Variétés, and in December
he went with her to the dress rehearsal of Edward Knoblauch's
Kismet. But he arrived wearing a morning-coat over his white
waistcoat. The other guests in her box included Calmette, Paul
Hervieu and Jacques Bizet. Almost as soon as they'd arrived,
Bizet quarrelled with another man, comte Hubert de Pierredon, slapped his face, and, despite his friends' efforts at concili-
ation, accepted a challenge to a duel.[85] When Proust got home,
and Nicolas asked whether he'd kept his fur coat on in the
theatre, he realised what he was wearing. 'What must Hervieu
and Calmette have thought; above all what must Jacques have
thought! It is nice of him not to have punished me with a slap,
especially as I am less burly than M. de Pierredon.'[86]

After the outing Proust had to stay in bed for nearly a
fortnight,[87] and for several days he was ill with 'something
astounding which I at first thought was angina but is only a
little weariness and a cold'.[88] He was waiting impatiently for
news from Fasquelle and Gallimard until, just before Christmas, he was rejected by them both. Fasquelle returned the
typescript on Christmas Eve, the day after Gallimard had
rejected it. Christmas had often been an unhappy time for
Proust, but he'd never felt more depressed.

TWENTY-THREE

DOING A DEAL

After the double rebuff from Fasquelle and Gallimard, Proust was dejected and restless. For five years he'd been trespassing courageously on the threshold of pain to work on the novel, giving it priority over everything else and believing it would stand as the one unchallengeable achievement in an undistinguished, unsatisfying life. Now it seemed he'd never find a publisher, even if he paid for publication. He had no lover, no friend he could turn to for consolation. Instead of telling Mme Straus the truth, he said he'd refused to make the revisions Fasquelle wanted, and had withdrawn the book from Gallimard because it was dedicated to Calmette, who wouldn't have liked it to be published by the NRF.[1]

But he told Louis de Robert the truth, wanting to go on using him as a middleman, and Proust wasted no time. Robert, who'd already suggested Paul Ollendorff, was told to approach him, asking for the first volume of 650 pages to be published in the spring and the second about ten months later. Towards Fasquelle Proust felt no bitterness, he said. 'I think he is wrong, but one can make mistakes in an intelligent way.'[2] And he offered Fasquelle a collection of essays and pastiches.[3]

Robert said he shouldn't mention Fasquelle to Ollendorff, and shouldn't offer to pay for publication. But in early January, sending the typescript to Alfred Humblot, Ollendorff's managing director, Proust couldn't stop himself from offering to subsidise printing costs. Nervous that Robert would be upset, he explained the offer had been made in a postscript to his letter, and the postscript, written sideways on the edge of the paper, wasn't very legible. 'But you must authorise me, in the event of his refusing to pay for publication, to suggest then that he does it at my expense.'[4]

If Robert thought he was eccentric, he made an even stranger impression on a twenty-one-year-old who was eager to meet him. Maurice Rostand, whose father had written *Cyrano de Bergerac*, sent a letter which Proust thought 'delicious and very beautiful',[5] but in reply he proposed a rendezvous in front of Notre-Dame at six in the morning. Still under the influence of Émile Mâle's book on thirteenth-century religious art,[6] he wanted to make an expedition to the Sainte-Chapelle in the Palais de Justice, where he was keen to look at the stained-glass windows and the twelve columns, each with the statue of an apostle. He also wanted to visit Notre-Dame, to look at the Sainte-Anne gate, 'where for eight centuries there has been a humanity much more charming than the one we are keeping company with'.[7] But he'd have to wait till he was feeling well enough to go out during daylight, and this occurred so seldom he was eager to do two or three things at the same time. It didn't occur to him Rostand might think the proposal unreasonable.

In late January, wearing a fur coat over his nightshirt, Proust set off by himself to look at the Sainte-Chapelle and spend a couple of hours studying the Sainte-Anne portal of Notre-Dame. Some of the detail in the Sainte-Chapelle went into his description of the chapel, while the porch of the church in Balbec derives partly from the portal. When Elstir talks about it to the Narrator, Proust is borrowing from Mâle's book, as well as drawing on the idea behind Ruskin's *Bible of Amiens*. Elstir says 'the most beautiful illustrated Bible the people have ever been able to read' is the porch at Balbec with its Virgin and the bas-reliefs telling the story of her life. The anonymous medieval wood-carver had profound thoughts and created 'delicious poetry . . . a gigantic theological and symbolical poem'. 'It's mad, it's divine, it's a thousand times better than anything you'll see in Italy or anywhere else. . . . The chap who sculpted the façade, believe me, was just as interesting, had ideas just as profound as the men alive today you most admire.'[8]

Proust gained so much from the outing that he wished he could muster the energy more often to go out into the world by daylight, but the expedition left him so exhausted that he once again resigned himself to a routine with no space in it for watching people in the street or for visiting cathedrals and museums. 'In fifteen years I think I have been able to go twice to the Louvre.'[9] This morose, matter-of-fact statement says nothing about the ideas which teemed so richly through his mind when he looked at a masterpiece. He was as responsive to painting and sculpture as he was to literature, and he'd learnt to look at a landscape or a townscape as caringly and as creatively as a painter, but his routine had virtually banished him from the daylight world.

When he did go out, it was in a taxi, with the windows closed, driven by his favourite cab-driver, Odilon Albaret. Seeing almost no one but Nicolas, Céline and Albaret, Proust found he was rather 'developing the mentality of elderly female invalids and distrusting the people who immediately surround me. When I need to have specially personal letters delivered or commissions performed, I wait for a messenger I can trust.'[10]

His first evening expedition of 1913 was to the offices of *Le Figaro*. In spite of the rejection from Fasquelle, he felt indebted to Calmette for the overtures he'd made and, wanting to thank him with a present, Proust had bought a cigarette case bound in black moiré with artificial diamonds. It came from Tiffany's, and had cost 350 francs.[11] 'Calmette is not only unappreciative of presents: they make him less pleasant. But I did it for me.'[12] The cigarette case was packed in the Tiffany's box.

'I wanted to come on New Year's Eve', Proust told him, 'with the simplest of little cigarette cases.' Calmette 'shrugged his shoulders affectionately without saying anything, I looked at the box as if to say "Open it," he looked at the box vaguely, not opening it. He said: "I hope Poincaré will get in," and led me to the door.'[13]

Raymond Poincaré did get in at the elections on 17 January, and, though Proust never received a letter of thanks from Calmette, he was at least spared the humiliation of having the present returned. But he went on worrying. Knowing he'd forgotten to take out a slip of paper with pencil marks on it, he thought this might be either a bill or, worse still, a note containing a much higher figure, which Calmette might mistake for the price.[14] As it was, Proust took the editor's continuing silence to confirm the suspicion that Fasquelle had never made any promise about publishing the novel.

The more Proust worked at the novel, the more he came to believe that the truth he had to tell about the external world was identical with truth about the inner self. What he valued more than skill in constructing a narrative was capacity for penetrating deeply and accurately into private experience – as

Francis Jammes could. 'The cell itself, the atom, that is to say
the epithet and the image, are of a profundity and a rightness
achieved by no one else. At bottom we feel things are like this,
but we lack the strength to reach the extreme depths where
truth is situated, the real universe, our authentic impression.'
This attitude set Proust at odds with prevailing literary
fashions. The NRF was by far the best of the literary reviews,
but its editors published and presumably admired the prose
poems of Charles Péguy, who failed to rise above 'a sort of
laziness in which one word leads you to think of another'.[15]

Proust's dissatisfaction with contemporary French culture
was one of the forces which made him create imaginary artists.
The writing, painting and music prominent in the novel derive
partly from contemporary work, and partly from work better
than any that was currently being produced. The flow of
imaginary art in his mind had its main sources in previous
periods. In 1912 he'd seen neither the June impressionist exhibition at the Manzi gallery of the Hôtel des Arts, nor the
collection of Degas' friend Henri Rouart.[16] At the beginning
of 1913, getting up, on average, only once a week, and only
for an hour or two,[17] he felt hungry to hear Beethoven's late
quartets. He was too ill for concert-going, 'but, fortunately,
nature was benevolent enough to give me something worth
more than health – illusion.'[18] The faculty which often made
him over-optimistic about prospects of rallying strength for an
outing was inseparable from the imagination which conjured
up works of art to substitute for the ones he couldn't enjoy.
And without comparing his talent to Beethoven's, he claimed
to be enjoying nature like the deaf Beethoven, who conjured
up sounds he could no longer hear in his Pastoral Symphony.
Proust described landscapes he could no longer see.[19]

The inadequacies of the NRF didn't deter him from wanting
to publish excerpts in it, and he corresponded energetically
with Jacques Copeau. In one angry letter Proust offered to
fight a duel with him over the question of whether editorial
preference was given to subscribers.[20] But eventually the hostility modulated into epistolary friendship.

Though Fasquelle had given no sign of interest in a collection
of his essays and pastiches, Proust tried to find copies of his
essays. He had no filing system, even for his own work,
only his untidy bedroom 'where everything piles up and gets
muddled'.[21] When he approached Le Figaro, he was told they

kept no archive – 'After four years, everything is destroyed' – and in February, while he was checking whether Anna de Noailles still had his review of her *Éblouissements* or his essay 'Sur la lecture',[22] the novel had its third rejection.

Humblot's letter to Robert was so rudely dismissive that he wrote back, asking for a politer letter he could pass on to Proust.[23] The reader at Ollendorff had been Georges Boyer, the drama critic on the *Petit Journal* who'd been secretary-general at the Opéra for eighteen years, but it was Humblot who signed both letters to Robert. The second started: 'Dear Friend, Perhaps I am narrow-minded, but I cannot understand how a man can take thirty pages to describe how he keeps shifting his position in bed before falling asleep.' This was the letter Robert showed Proust, who called it 'a little vulgar, and more lacking than I would have believed possible in even the most superficial knowledge of literature'. But when Robert said he intended to find a new publisher for his own books, Proust persuaded him not to leave Ollendorff.[24] The friendship between the two men was strengthened by the episode, and three months later, when Robert's mistress abandoned him, Proust, wanting to act once again as a conciliator between lovers, offered himself as a friend who could talk to her about him in such a way as to make her nervous she'd already lost his love irretrievably.[25]

Determined to lose no more time over getting *Swann* into print, Proust proved himself capable of acting swiftly. He tried to telephone Léon Blum's brother, René, who was friendly with Bernard Grasset, the young publisher who'd brought out Georges de Lauris' novel *Ginette Chatenay*, and, failing to reach Blum by telephone, Proust wrote to him. Ten years earlier, Blum had been a habitué of the Café Weber and, as general secretary of the newspaper *Gil Blas*, had recently used Antoine as his intermediary to approach Proust about publishing an extract from the novel. This made it easier to ask whether he was willing to approach Grasset, and, ignoring Robert's caveat, Proust offered to pay for both printing and publicity. If Grasset refused, he'd approach *Vers et prose*, a quarterly review edited by the poet Paul Fort, and if Fort refused, he'd ask Robert to look for 'a printer who specialised in printing the books of people who cannot find a publisher'.[26]

'I am very ill,' Proust told Blum, 'I need certainty and rest. . . . I want you to tell me within a week the *business* is settled, your book will appear at such and such a date. And that is possible only if I pay for the publication.' No one else should know he was paying for it, and to justify this demand he pretended 'a very famous publisher had wanted to publish this book at his expense and on conditions which were very favourable to me.' The friends he'd told about this, Proust said, would think he'd been lying if it now emerged that the book was being published at his own expense. Without knowing whether Blum would be his intermediary or whether Grasset would be interested, Proust was already introducing conspiratorial intrigue. He asked Blum to use sealing wax on any letters and, if he telephoned, not to tell Nicolas what it was about.[27]

The day after writing to Blum, Proust thought it had probably been a bad idea.[28] But Grasset's response was positive: he'd publish the book – at Proust's expense. After ten months of frustration, Proust could do a deal. Soon he was explaining his structure. The characters are ' "built up" in this first volume, that is to say they will do in the second exactly the opposite of what would be expected from the first'. The first volume had, unfortunately for the publisher, less narrative than the second, while the composition was so complex it wasn't at first apparent that all the themes were coming together.[29]

The next day, 24 February, Proust sent the typescript of the first volume to Grasset. Nothing was missing except the dedication to Calmette, 'which will perhaps occupy a few pages', and Proust made suggestions about typeface.[30] Aiming for 'the penetration of my thought into the greatest possible number of brains susceptible of receiving it', he baulked when Grasset wanted to price the two volumes of Le Temps perdu (as Proust intended to call it) at ten francs each. After his experience with the expensive first – and only – edition of Les Plaisirs et les jours, Proust insisted these books should cost no more than 3 francs 50. But, wanting to give Grasset a good deal, he accepted only 1 franc 50 (instead of the 50 per cent he was offered) on each copy sold. Twelve hundred were to be printed.[31] Grasset later admitted he did the deal without reading the book. After signing the contract, Proust paid 1,750 francs on 11 March.[32]

Worried about format, he again made stipulations about the number of lines and the number of characters in each line,[33] and consulted Jean-Louis Vaudoyer about the idea of having a red frame around each page – an idea Vaudoyer discouraged.[34]

As soon as he was confident the deal wasn't going to fall through, Proust became restless. Feeling 'an irresistible desire to see Florence', he thought of acclimatising himself to getting up during the day by staying in a sanatorium at Valmont, and going on from Switzerland to Italy. But it was already too late: hay-fever would have forced a retreat from Florence in early April.[35] By now he was staying awake more during the day, but, unable to make up for it by sleeping at night, felt exhausted.[36] In April, when Robert de Billy was in Rome, Proust thought of joining him there, but was again deterred by fear of hay-fever.[37]

At least he satisfied his urge to hear Beethoven, going with Georges de Lauris to the Salle Pleyel for a performance by the Capet quartet of two late quartets and the *Grosse Fuge*. Proust had been trying to imagine the music of his fictional composer, Vinteuil, and the chamber music recital laid the foundations for listening to César Franck's violin sonata, 'which I love so much', played by Paul Goldschmidt and Georges Enesco on 19 April at a hall in the rue de Rocher. 'Now I found it *admirable*, the doleful chirping of his violin, and the moaning appeals in response at the piano, as if from a tree, from mysterious foliage.'[38]

By then the first galley-proofs had come from the printer, Charles Colin. For Proust, reading proofs was more a matter of making additions than correcting misprints, and he now introduced Vindeuil (later Vinteuil) by merging two characters – Vington, the naturalist father of the Lesbian, and Berget, the composer. When Vinteuil's violin sonata is played at a soirée, 'at first the solitary piano complained like a bird abandoned by its mate; the violin heard it, answered it as from a neighbouring tree. Is this a bird, is this the still incomplete soul of the little phrase, is this a fairy, this invisible and moaning creature whose plaint is then tenderly echoed by the piano?'[39]

In April Proust met Odilon Albaret's shy young wife. In March, when Odilon said he was going away for a few weeks to get married, Proust asked when and where the wedding was going to be. Before bride and groom set out for the church, they were surprised to receive a telegram conveying M. Proust's congratulations.[40] He was also a determining factor in Odilon's decision about where to make his new home. Previously Proust had summoned him by leaving a message at the café run by his sister, but the messages invariably came so late at night, and there were so many of them that Odilon now looked for another café which had a telephone, stayed open late and was situated near a garage that could service his taxi. After settling on Levallois, he took his wife with him when he went to tell Nicolas how M. Proust should get in touch with him from now on. Nicolas insisted on telling Proust they were there.

Céleste Albaret, who was twenty-one, had never left her native village – Auxillac in the Lozère – until she married. When Proust came into the kitchen, she was especially impressed by the elegance of this 'great gentleman', his fine skin, his white teeth, the curl on his forehead, and the impression he gave of husbanding energy and breath.[41]

Nearly all his energy, in fact, had been going into his first bout of correcting proofs. In the middle of May he returned the first forty-five galley sheets, aware he'd made an abnormal number of corrections. 'I am ashamed of sending them back in this condition. . . . I have gummed on pieces of paper which could easily be torn, which would create endless complications.'[42] Much as he'd liked the title 'Les Intermittences du coeur', he now abandoned it, giving as his reason the appearance of a novel with the title Le Coeur en désordre, though it had already been published six months ago, when Proust was proposing 'Les Intermittences du coeur', and anyway there isn't much similarity between the two titles.

He seized every opportunity to explain the intentions behind the novel to friends and acquaintances. Carrying on so many of his friendships by letter, he was generous in giving friends the benefit of the doubt when they possibly had an ulterior motive for taking an interest in him, as Jacques Copeau did when raising funds for a new theatre by selling shares in the Société du Théâtre du Vieux-Colombier. Two hundred shares were to be sold at 1,000 francs each, and Proust bought three of them, not because he needed Copeau's help but mainly because he was enjoying the correspondence and the opportunity to confide in the ex-editor about involuntary memory. This was something quite different from the 'contingent and accidental' pressures which had embedded the front door of the old moneylender's house in the memory of Dostoevsky's Raskolnikov.

Proust was less interested in building a drama than in explaining how consciousness works by moving from observation to general laws.

> When all the material elements which constituted the anterior impression find themselves modified, the memory takes on, from the viewpoint of the unconscious, the same generality, the same force of superior reality as *the law* does in physics by variation in the circumstances. It is an *action* and not a passive pleasure. Besides, the notion of pleasure does not exist for me. . . . I never look for it. It is only the concomitant of the ardent love I feel for things and which is perhaps rather over-excited by deprivation.[43]

Trapped for so much of the time in the same bed, focusing on the same blankets, the same walls, the same litter of papers on the bed, his eyes pounced delightedly on anything they saw outside his flat.

After another long period of deprivation, he felt well enough to go out more often during the second half of May. On the 15th he went to the Ballets Russes at the Théâtre des Champs-Élysées, where he saw Marie Scheikévitch, looking, he thought, like 'a dove who has been stabbed'. Later on, 'Colombes poignardées' would be one of the titles he'd consider for his novel instead of 'Les Intermittences du coeur'.[44] Two nights later, going back to the Ballets Russes, he saw Nijinsky in *L'Après-midi d'un faune*, afterwards dining with him and Maurice Rostand at Larue's.[45]

One night he had dinner at the home of Marie Scheikévitch, who afterwards sent him an enormous bouquet of lilacs. He responded by cutting four passages about lilacs from the galley-proofs, pasting them rather clumsily on sheets of paper and sending them to her. No one else had seen these, he said.[46]

On the 22nd he went to the first night of *Boris Godunov* with Fyodor Chaliapin at the Théâtre des Champs-Élysées, where he saw Copeau and Anna de Noailles, and a week later he went to the first night of *Le Sacre du printemps*, dining afterwards at Larue's with Stravinsky and Cocteau.

This exceptional fortnight of activity coincided with a period of intensive work on the proofs. At the end of May he felt

'crushed by proof-correcting and unable to make an end of it.
I am changing everything, the printer will be totally at sea,
my publisher is checking on my progress every day.'[47] After
sending back the first galley-sheets, he had to pay 595 francs
for the extra printing costs.[48]

TWENTY-FOUR

RITUALS OF PROFANE LOVE

Suddenly Proust's life was turned upside down by the reappearance of Alfred Agostinelli, who called at the flat, asking to be taken on as a chauffeur. Proust didn't want a chauffeur – Albaret's taxi was all he needed – but he didn't want to turn Agostinelli away. He was good-looking and had shown, both in conversation and in letters, that he had a flair for words. Though Proust thought of him as a mechanic, and of the typewriter as a machine, there was no reason to think he'd be either competent or happy as a typist, but Proust was tired of living alone with Nicolas and Céline, as he'd indicated when he invited Reynaldo to move in. Now, taking one of the abrupt decisions which cut through his habitual dithering, he asked Agostinelli to be his secretary and to live in.

Needing urgently to convert a manuscript into an accurate typescript – the printer was waiting for it – any other writer would have hesitated before employing a new secretary with no experience of typing. Agostinelli would have to cope with difficult handwriting and extremely long sentences, while Proust would have to cope with the presence of a man liable to distract him from the work they should both be concentrating on.

Agostinelli said he and Anna had married. They hadn't, but they spoke of each other as 'my husband' and 'my wife', and Proust didn't find out the truth until long after they'd moved in. She was surprisingly ugly, and he never liked her, but she and Agostinelli adored each other, though he was regularly unfaithful.[1] Proust, while jealous of their relationship, could learn from them, as he had from watching Albu and Louisa.

From now on he was not only surrounded by the drama of a feuding couple but was involved in it. Instead of searching for lost time, he defended himself against the present by diverting it into his fiction. Fragments of Agostinelli's life with Anna, and Proust's with Agostinelli, could immediately be incorporated into the additions he made while ostensibly correcting proofs.

The tempo of life had suddenly changed. After a long adagio, he'd been pitched into a dizzying presto agitato. There was no one he could confide in, except by letter, and he didn't want to discuss the new relationship with Reynaldo. Writing to Robert, who'd replaced Georges as his principal confidante, he concealed more than he revealed.

> What things I would like to tell you; I am so unhappy as to be in serious need of your sweetness; things are going *very badly* with me, and what is more, I have a great deal of misery. But perhaps it is better like this; because I do not have the strength necessary to cope with happiness. (You understand that I am speaking of sentimental happiness and misery. You do not suppose, I imagine, that I am speaking about my *career*. That has always been a matter of indifference to me, and now!)[2]

But he was closer to happiness than ever before in his adult life. Though he'd been fond of Reynaldo, incredulous and delighted to have his feelings reciprocated, their youthful love for each other had lacked the passionate, desperate intensity of Proust's one-sided feelings for Agostinelli. For the first time, he was living with the man he loved, and, knowing he didn't have long to live, he was willing to pay any price for happiness. Since the end of the affair with Lucien there had been no happiness without paying a price. Most of his previous relationships with working-class lovers had been fairly casual, but he'd never been less casual than he was with Agostinelli.

They had hours of ecstatic happiness, even if these were brief in comparison with Proust's bouts of agonised jealousy. He says a lot about his reactions to Agostinelli's presence in his flat through the Narrator's account of his relationship with Albertine, who's living in his flat like a prisoner. If her behaviour is patterned mainly on Agostinelli's and Anna's, they were much noisier than Nicolas and Céline, less respectful, less considerate about disturbing him. They had to adapt themselves immediately to an eccentric routine which was even more awkward for them than it had been for the servants in his parents' flat. It's a fair guess that, like Albertine, Agostinelli never closed doors and never hesitated about entering a room when the door was open. That he hummed incessantly and had bad taste in music. That Proust at last had a replacement – and a satisfyingly sacrilegious one – for the ritual of the goodnight kiss. Before the two men separated at night, Agostinelli's tongue would slide into his mouth like a slice of bread. No previous lover, bourgeois or working-class, had ever constituted such a threat to the memory of Proust's mother. The son of a woman who'd never shake hands with a footman, he was living with a chauffeur, and sexually he was mostly feeling inferior and struggling for equality. He found it intensely pleasurable to do what he could never do when his mother was alive, and the rejection of her values wasn't incidental. He was profaning her memory and enjoying it.

The bathroom Agostinelli used was so close to Proust's that they could carry on a conversation while they washed in 'double privacy'.[3] Proust did everything in his power to keep Agostinelli happy, make his situation agreeable, pamper him with expensive presents – scared of losing him, but aware of him as a permanent danger. This is what he means when he says, à propos Albertine, that his suffering is less unbearable than the idea that it could stop. Proust was gladly sacrificing his peace of mind, losing sleep, losing weight. 'Once Albertine had gone out of the flat, I felt how exhausting this perpetual presence was for me, insatiable in restless vitality, disturbing my sleep with its movements. . . . There are in life certain situations . . . in which the problem of whether to continue a shared life or return to the separate life of the past becomes almost a medical one: to which of the two kinds of rest must we sacrifice ourselves (by continuing the daily tension, or returning to the agony of absence) – to that of the mind or that of the heart?'[4] Agostinelli was unpossessable. When he was present, Proust couldn't know whether his feelings coincided with what he was expressing; when he was absent, Proust couldn't know what he was saying or doing. There were so many different ways in which he could betray the man who was obsessed by him, and no way in which Proust could liberate himself. Nor was his jealousy confined to the present: he was in love with Agostinelli at every moment of the past and future. 'A being scattered through space and time is no longer a person but a series of events we cannot illuminate, a series of problems we cannot solve, a sea which, like Xerxes, we thrash with rods in the ridiculous desire to punish it for having engulfed our treasure.'

Proust didn't want visitors to meet Agostinelli or suspect that he was living in the flat. He'd tactfully refrain from coming into the room when Proust had a visitor with him. In agonies of jealousy, Proust cross-questioned him about his past and about his movements whenever he went out, and this produced a noticeable change in his personality.

> Everything she would have told me casually and willingly when we were just friends had stopped flowing as soon as she thought I loved her, or, without perhaps naming love to herself, had recognised an inquisitorial sentiment which wants knowledge but suffers from it, and presses for more knowledge. Since that day she had concealed everything . . . My ignorance collaborated with her in accentuating the inoffensiveness of the character she gave to the parts of her life that were unfamiliar to me.[5]

Proust's generosity was never going to do him more harm. Intoxicated by happiness and willing to loosen all his moorings, he was plunging more deeply than ever into the lifelong habit of trying to buy goodwill. Even when making love or when having love made to him, he couldn't believe he was lovable. Even if Agostinelli had been in possession of a less limited repertoire of words and actions for indicating affection to a man, he wouldn't have wanted to discourage Proust's conviction that he needed to buy goodwill with magnanimous tips and expensive presents. There was nothing he wanted more than to keep Agostinelli dependent, but there was no quicker way of making him independent than by giving him large sums of money. At first it seemed to be just a matter of indulging his extravagance, and Anna's. 'When they have fifty francs they spend twenty on peaches, twenty on taxis, and the next day, they have nothing.'[6] But Proust was so over-generous that Agostinelli could save even more than he was spending.

The placid and reclusive existence Robert Proust characterised as 'a life of renunciation, a genuinely ascetic life' had unpredictably blossomed into a climax of profane sensuality. Since 1910 Proust had consistently been living in accordance with his principle that the artist who gives up an hour of work for conversation with a friend is sacrificing something real for something illusory. But now he was happily sacrificing hours of work for lovemaking and chatting, gladly letting his life be disrupted at the worst possible time, when, after six years of intensive, painful work, he was on the point of getting the novel into print.

Even more unsure of himself that he would have been in Agostinelli's absence, he asked advice from friends. Should he make cuts? Should some of the less interesting passages be printed in the form of footnotes? Was it right to have the dialogue printed without starting a new paragraph for each speech?[7] He also checked some of his similes by putting semi-scientific questions to Max Daireaux.[8] But Agostinelli, who was typing the second part of the book, must have needed more assistance than an experienced typist would have, and Proust must have taken much more time on answering questions than he would have if he hadn't been in love with his typist. He knew he was being irresponsibly slow over correcting the proofs, but there was nothing he could do to speed himself up.

In July, sending Grasset 595 francs for extra printing costs on the first forty-five galleys, he said he'd 'almost finished correcting the second proofs', meaning the galleys which started with the one numbered 96.[9] The reason he hadn't returned the first proofs, he said (meaning galleys 46–95), was that to accommodate all ninety-five galleys, the first volume would have to go above 700 pages. About ten galleys would need to be held over for the second, which meant finding a different ending for the first. 'That calls for reflection and arrangement.' He promised to solve the problem and send back both sets of proofs within a few days,[10] but he didn't keep this promise: he hadn't even started correcting the second set.[11]

It was harder than ever to decide about taking a holiday in Cabourg, as he regularly had for the last five summers. If he went on his own, he'd be racked with jealous anxiety about what was happening to Agostinelli in Paris, but if he took Agostinelli, he also had to take Anna, and what impression would they make on his Cabourg friends and acquaintances? Perhaps it would be better not to go away. Telephoning Mme Bizet in an effort to find employment as a chauffeur for Robert Ulrich, who was out of work and starving, Proust said he'd no doubt stay in Paris all through the summer. An hour later he left for Cabourg, taking not only Agostinelli and Anna but also Nicolas. They went by car but, after getting lost, arrived at five in the morning. Before he went to bed, Proust wrote to Reynaldo, but without mentioning Agostinelli.[12]

It might have been more sensible to go somewhere else. Agostinelli, who'd worked as a taxi-driver in Cabourg, was known both to the porters and to the waiters at the hotel. Proust was intending to spend most of the time correcting proofs, but if he and Agostinelli ate all their meals in the bedroom, Agostinelli would grow restive, while it was impossible to take him into the dining-room or the casino or on the promenade without meeting people Proust knew. He didn't even get in touch with the vicomte d'Alton.

Within less than a week he'd made up his mind not to stay much longer, but his decision to leave was taken as abruptly as his decision to come. On 3 August he and Agostinelli were in the car, on their way to Houlgate, when either they quarrelled or Agostinelli showed how impatient he was to go home. Like a father giving in to a spoilt child, Proust made him stop at a café, where he telephoned the hotel, instructing Nicolas and Anna to pack their suitcases, inform the management of their departure, and follow. He and Agostinelli then went straight to the station at Trouville and caught the first train to Paris.[13]

Because the vicomte d'Alton must by now have heard he was in Cabourg, Proust wrote to apologise for his abrupt departure, inventing an elaborate pretext for asking him not to mention Agostinelli to any of their friends.[14] He made the same request to Albert Nahmias: 'People are so stupid that they might see something pederastic in it (as they did in our friendship).'[15] To Georges, Proust explained his sudden return by saying he'd been missing a 'person' who was in Paris.[16]

He was intending to go away again within a few days, but he was so weak that another journey might kill him – or so he told Albert and Georges.[17] He was prone to exaggeration, but even before Agostinelli's arrival he'd been in an extremely debilitated state. In the seven years since he'd moved into the flat, he'd been eating with increasing irregularity, especially since Félicie left. Nicolas had sometimes been asked to cook a sole or to fetch a hot dish from Larue's, but Proust had grown noticeably thinner, and the emotional relationship was causing so much stress that it looked as if he'd either have to get rid of Agostinelli or move out himself if he wanted to survive. Staying in the flat, he had only one weapon of defence – the novel, which 'refers to things which have made me suffer so much that it seems impossible that my prose has not drunk some of my tears and retained the bitter taste'.[18] Later he'd translate Agostinelli into Albertine, but already, correcting the proofs of *Swann*, he made elaborate additions, putting in 'some very important little details which tighten the knots of jealousy around poor Swann'.

He still hadn't had time to devise a new ending for the first volume,[19] but beyond the 'moral troubles, material anxieties, physical suffering and literary problems',[20] he took some comfort from knowing that friends would soon read the book and see unsuspected depths in him. One friendship which had failed to fulfil its potential was with Lucien, who wasn't someone Proust felt free to question when checking facts for his fiction, and he'd been upset to receive no invitation to the wedding of Lucien's sister, Edmée. But when Proust offered to let him read the first volume,[21] Lucien, after asking to see proofs as soon as possible, responded so enthusiastically Proust was incredulous. As soon as the proofs arrived, Lucien spent the whole day on them and part of the night.[22] Rapturous, he sent Proust a ten-page letter praising the book, making minor constructive criticisms, and offering to review it when it came out. Delighted, Proust suggested he should do it for *Le Figaro*,[23] and later consulted him on alternative endings for the first volume.[24]

This was due to come out on 14 November, but instead of enjoying the run-up to publication, he was suffering at the hands of the friend 'who, with my mother and father, is the person I loved the most'. Agostinelli, while failing to reciprocate this passion, benefited from Proust's phenomenal generosity and enjoyed the complex negotiations they had about presents. But Proust, getting little in return for the money and the emotional energy he unstintingly invested, was 'too unhappy to enjoy the pleasure I could perhaps otherwise have taken in seeing the book finished and read by the people for whom it is destined'.[25] Though he felt he had 'put all my thought, my whole heart, my very life' into the book,[26] and attached 'infinitely more importance to it than to everything else I have done until now',[27] what mattered more urgently was his day-to-day relationship with Agostinelli, who hadn't settled down since they returned from Cabourg. He was too ambitious and adventurous to be content with a secretarial job. During his career as a chauffeur, cars had been a novelty; what he now wanted was to learn how to fly.

It was obvious the relationship could never settle into a permanent one, and Proust was thinking of escaping from it by leaving Paris, but he was too ill for the journey, and, at the beginning of December, Agostinelli took the initiative by leaving him. According to Céleste, who'd just moved in to work as housekeeper, the main reason was that Anna hated Paris.[28]

Reconstituting the experience in terms of the Narrator's loss of Albertine, Proust said the news 'produced in my heart so much pain that I felt I could not endure it for much longer', a pain he found incomprehensible when he compared 'the mediocrity of the pleasure Albertine gave me to the richness of the desires she prevented me from realising'.[29]

Promising himself nothing would stop him from finding the missing man, and wondering whether to employ a private detective,[30] Proust received a letter saying Agostinelli had joined his father in Monaco. The ever-willing Albert was despatched as emissary and briefed in lengthy telegrams – unsigned or conspiratorially signed with a false name – about strategy to use in negotiating with the father, Eugenio Agostinelli. Albert's mission was to bring Agostinelli back to Paris with him.[31] Proust told Nicolas to wake him at any time if Albert telephoned from Monaco, but when he did, the line was so bad they could barely understand each other. Proust's telegrams to Albert pass on addresses and such detailed information about the movements of father and son that he must have been using a detective. 'I imagined Albertine starting a life she had wanted, separated from me, perhaps for a long time, perhaps for ever, realising that unknown something which already had so often worried me, although I then had the happiness of possessing and caressing what was outside it, that sweet face, impenetrable and captive. It was this unknown element that was the base of my love.'[32]

As so often when under pressure, Proust fell back on money and intrigue. Albert was told to offer Eugenio Agostinelli a regular monthly allowance if he could make his son return to Paris and stay until April, but Agostinelli must not know about this financial arrangement,[33] and Albert must offer him no money 'BECAUSE HE DOES NOT DESERVE ANY'. The negotiations, of course, failed, and on 7 December Albert was summoned back to Paris.[34] Proust called December 'the most painful period of my life since the death of my mother'.[35]

He was too depressed to write or work on the galleys which hadn't been accommodated in the first volume.[36] And when the book was published and a congratulatory letter arrived from Montesquiou, comparing it 'with its rich crop of words and ideas' to the hawthorns, 'pullulating with pointed petals', Proust replied that for twelve months his life had been so overwhelmed with misery that publication had given him no pleasure.[37]

He took some comfort from listening to music, and when he felt well enough to get up he went to recitals of Beethoven's quartets.[38] He also bought a pianola, but there was no piano-roll transcription of the music he most hungered for – Beethoven's C sharp minor quartet, Opus 131.[39] As usual, pleasure wasn't separate from work on the novel. Under the heading 'For Vinteuil', his current notebook contains jottings on Beethoven, César Franck, Schumann, Wagner and Schubert.

Only the beginning of the next volume was in proof and only part of the remainder had been typed by Agostinelli before his departure, which had made Proust feel incapable – as he still did – of re-reading the typescript.[40] Nor had he filled the hole left by the episode he'd taken from the second volume to end the first.[41]

At five o'clock in the afternoon of 30 May 1914, the twenty-six-year-old Agostinelli crashed his plane into the sea. A pupil at the Garbero school of aviation, he'd been making a practice flight between Antibes and Cagnes. The pilot's wife, reported the *New York Herald*, was among the horrified spectators who could see the machine hadn't sunk completely, and some seconds later they saw the pilot clinging to the fuselage. Shouting for help, he went on waving frantically until the plane was sucked into the sea.[42]

Proust hadn't been totally unprepared for the possibility he'd be killed in a plane crash. Knowing he was using the money he'd saved to pay for flying lessons, Proust had written to warn him: 'If ever misfortune involved you in an aeroplane crash, make it clear to your wife she will find in me neither a

protector nor a friend, nor will she ever have so much as a sou
from me.'[43]

Anna had encouraged him to train as a pilot, believing he'd
earn a lot of money,[44] and in March he enrolled at a school
near Antibes, using the name Marcel Swann. But Proust hadn't
given up hope of enticing him back, and there was a large
element of bribery in the decision to buy him two extravagant
presents – one was an aeroplane, the other probably a Rolls-
Royce. In spite of his financial difficulties, Proust was willing
to spend money on long-distance lovemaking as lavishly as he
spent time on letter-writing.

In correspondence with Agostinelli, Proust had tried unsuccessfully to dissuade him from becoming a pilot,[45] and now,
giving him a plane, Proust was slipping back into the role of
over-indulgent parent, in directly apologising to the uncontrollable child for having once tried to control him. But the tactics
were no less subtle than those used by the Narrator: though
he wants Albertine more than anything else in life, he has come
to believe, almost religiously, in hiding his emotion and taking
nothing at its face value. Instead of trusting her letter saying
she'd have been only too delighted to come back if only he'd
written to her instead of sending a friend as ambassador to her
aunt, he replies deviously. Confident he will again possess her,
but not wanting to seem impatient, he writes as if he approved
of her decision to leave him. Life had driven them apart, he
says. When intending to marry her, he'd planned to give her
a yacht and a car, but not to spend time with her in either.
Next, knowing she'd accept neither gift, and having no use
for them himself, he'd wanted her to cancel the orders – which
had been placed, in her name, with a middleman – but now
although the two expensive toys are completely useless to him,
he prefers to keep them himself.

In writing so deviously, he's trying to capitalise on her
perversity: she'd always given him the opposite response from
the one he wanted. But this time she replies by offering any
help he wants in cancelling the gifts. 'I am very touched you
have kept a pleasant memory of our last walk. Believe me, I
shall never forget that doubly crepuscular walk (since night
was falling and we were going to separate) and it will vanish
from my mind only when darkness falls completely.'[46] The
last sentences are taken from Agostinelli's letter: thanking him
for it, Proust writes: 'one phrase was *ravishing* (crepuscular,

etc.)'. And when Proust goes on to write that it would be indelicate to accept 'a service of this kind', he's presumably turning down Agostinelli's offer to cancel orders which have been placed in his name, for he goes on to say that M. Collin, the intermediary through whom the order has been placed, is being so generous in allowing him to extricate himself from his commitment that he cannot possibly avail himself of such generosity. Finally, Proust asked Agostinelli to return his letter. This may have been a discreet precaution, or may mean he was already thinking of incorporating the episode – and perhaps the wording – into the novel.

Though he was recycling all these events, he was simultaneously developing Albertine's character through background and metaphor. In one note he tells himself: 'Extremely important. For what I think I possess' – he means for what the Narrator thinks he possesses – 'in Albertine there must be some of the loveliest images of Balbec, for instance the blue mountains of the sea (which can perhaps be made to reappear when I hear music in the morning) so that Albertine reminding me of the music reminds me of the blue mountains. . . . In any case solid metaphors and the same ones, linked together well.'[47]

He'd already started work in 1913 on the story of a second stay in Balbec, but he now amalgamated the two episodes – introducing Albertine as one of the flower-like girls who go around in a group – and he started a second Balbec sequence in which the Narrator is alone with her.[48] The apparent self-sufficiency of the girls helps to make them provocative and appealing: as an outsider he wants nothing more than to be accepted as a member of the group. The subsequent relationship with Albertine is primarily a reconstruction of his tantalising experiences with Agostinelli.

Proust had already spent 27,000 francs on the aeroplane, wanting it to be a surprise, and in Paris a Rolls would have cost about the same amount of money. But behind his generosity was the realisation there was nothing in life he wanted more than Agostinelli, and if he was still for sale, there could be no better way of spending money. Proust had been acting in accordance with the view of love he was adumbrating in the novel, but all these ironies were trumped when Agostinelli was killed on the day he wrote the letter.

Anna broke the news in a telegram, and when Agostinelli's

twin brother, Émile, arrived in Paris from Antibes, Proust wept in his arms.[49] Jean was asking for 5,000 francs to pay for divers to search for the body of Agostinelli, who'd been carrying all his money on him. Proust was inconsolable, even blaming himself for the death. 'If he had never met me and had not earned so much money from me, he could never have afforded to study aviation.'[50] When Anna arrived in Paris, Proust let her move in with him, and attempted to 'give her the courage I lack myself', but she tried more than once to kill herself.[51]

Agostinelli's body was found on 7 June. It was buried in the cemetery at Nice, and Proust spent 400 francs on a wreath for the funeral, but the family was disappointed he hadn't bought artificial flowers.[52]

TWENTY-FIVE

ENTER SWANN

Nervous that people would assume the book was only a collection of articles which had appeared in newspapers, Proust tried to secure advance publicity by writing to journalist friends such as Robert de Flers.[1] Apart from *Le Figaro*, most of the important newspapers had announced by 12 November the book was about to be published and, after writing to Calmette,[2] Proust found himself described on the front page of the paper as having 'an artistic soul and a literary talent truly without any equal'.[3]

Granted an interview during the week before publication, the journalist Élie-Joseph Bois was allowed to read the long statement Proust had written a year earlier when submitting his typescript to the NRF. In his article for *Le Temps*, Bois describes Proust lying down in a bedroom with shutters almost permanently closed. 'Electric light accentuates the pallor of his complexion, but underneath the hair falling over his forehead two admirable eyes gleam with feverish vitality.' He said the book could be seen as a series of 'novels of the unconscious', and compared its structure to solid geometry, with time as the third dimension. He dissociated himself from the Narrator – 'who is not me' – but claimed to have found all the elements of his book deep inside himself and to have had as much trouble in extricating them 'as if they were no less strange to the world of intelligence than . . . a musical theme'.[4]

Approached by the paper *Excelsior* to suggest a writer to profile him, Proust proposed Cocteau, who responded with an article describing the book as 'a giant miniature, full of mirages, of gardens laid on top of each other, of games in space and time, of great fresh touches in the style of Manet',[5] and on 27 November Lucien's article appeared on the front page of *Le Figaro*. 'Never, I believe, has analysis of everything that constitutes our experience been pushed so far. . . . knowing the unknowable, explaining the inexplicable, M. Proust's analysis is so clear that it reminds one of the clear blue ether on certain summer days.'[6] Nor was this all: a review followed in *Le Figaro* on 8 December, written by Chevassu.

Proust took a lot of trouble over inscribing presentation copies for friends. Hearing Céleste Albaret was bored and unhappy when left alone all day in the flat at Levallois, he told Odilon she could have the job of delivering the books. Following Proust's instructions, Nicolas wrapped them meticulously in pink or blue paper, according to the sex of the recipient. Céleste, almost invariably choosing a horse-drawn cab – 'they were so pretty' – in preference to a taxi, delivered them, afterwards recovering the fare from Nicolas. Proust, generously concerned to make life less boring for her, arranged for her to go on calling at his flat every day in case there were letters to be delivered.[7]

He was already beginning to prefer Céleste to the bossy Céline, who cooked well but tried to impose her ideas about how the flat should be run. When she had to go into hospital, Proust arranged for Robert, now Dr Pozzi's assistant, to take her as his patient in the Hôpital Broca. Nicolas was given permission to visit her every afternoon, and Céleste was employed to take over his work between two and about four-thirty. It was Nicolas who told her what to do. By two Proust would normally be awake and would have drunk his first cup of coffee and eaten his croissant. But in case he wanted a second croissant, one always had to be ready on a saucer that matched the coffee cup. She was to sit in the kitchen waiting for the bell to ring twice. If it did, she was to go along the corridor, across the hall, through the big drawing-room and go – without knocking – into the bedroom, where she was to put the croissant down on the silver tray on the table by the bed and to go out of the room again without speaking unless Proust spoke.

For days there was no ring, and the first time she went into the big, cork-lined bedroom, it was hard to see through the thick cloud of fumes from the Legras powders. The only light was a green glow from the shaded lamp by the bed, and it was thanks to the gleam from the silver of the tray and coffee-pot that she found her way to the bedside table. Sitting with the upper part of his body propped against two pillows, M. Proust was wearing a white shirt and a thick sweater. Two intimidating eyes stared at her through the fumes, but he didn't speak. When she bowed, he thanked her by waving his hand.[8]

He was so depressed[9] and had lost so much weight that Dr Bize had forbidden him to do any writing.[10] Grasset was submitting the book for the Goncourt prize, but usually, Proust was told, preference was given to writers under the age of thirty-five and in unfavourable financial circumstances.

If anything could have distracted him from his grief at losing Agostinelli, he'd have been intensely happy with the letter he received on 9 December from Francis Jammes, who liked the unpredictability of the characters, and praised the novel for being 'so logical in its apparent illogicality'. After paying tribute to 'phrasing in the style of Tacitus – knowing, subtle, balanced', Jammes went on to put Proust on the same level as Shakespeare, Cervantes, Molière and Balzac.[11] But his pleasure was punctured by a hostile review published on the same day in *Le Temps* by the influential Paul Souday. Instead of having the proofs checked after Proust corrected them, Grasset had sent them straight to the printer, with the result that the book had come out with hundreds of misprints in it; Souday uncharitably interpreted these as grammatical and syntactical mistakes.[12]

Fortunately, this review was read by Gabriel Astruc, who'd been running the Théâtre des Champs-Élysées and had once worked for Ollendorff. After buying the book, he wrote about it in *Gil Blas*, calling it 'adorable'.[13] Habituated to reading with pencil in hand, he'd marked the misprints, and Proust was afterwards able to borrow his corrected copy and have the mistakes eliminated from the new edition Grasset wanted to put in hand immediately.[14]

But Proust was annoyed by Grasset's campaign to promote the book as a 'philosophical' novel. 'Such a work', said one of the advertisements, 'is the most thrilling illustration of Bergson's famous theories. It is the novel of intuition and M. Marcel Proust is the realist of the soul.'[15]

There were many favourable reviews, but some of the most enthusiastic were almost as upsetting as the hostile ones. Writing in *Comoedia* on 26 December, Maurice Rostand said Proust 'comes to us speaking the language he alone speaks and which he has created himself to express his soul . . . and this masterpiece, at once so lucid and so mysterious, in which he has found the means to express what seemed inexpressible, say what seemed unsayable – it is a soul under guise of a book'. The review goes on to rank Proust with Pascal, Shelley, Leonardo da Vinci, Goethe, Plato, Nietzsche, Dostoevsky and Shakespeare. This didn't please Proust. 'Of all the people who have written about the book, this is perhaps the one, or one of the two or three in which the ridiculous exaggeration shocks me the most.'[16]

He was equally displeased with the review in the *NRF* by Gide's close friend, the playwright Henri Ghéon, who accused Proust of having too much time on his hands and indiscriminately trying to reproduce each experience he'd enjoyed, together with each individual who'd impressed him.[17] This provoked a twelve-page letter in which Proust – not writing the apologia for publication but addressing Ghéon personally – explained how he'd tried to forge connections between scattered memories of 'passionate and clairvoyant hours' spent looking at nature and works of art. What he was searching for was 'the profound laws of life and nature'.[18] Ghéon had hurt him because there was no truth in what he said. The book was a hold-all (in default of a filing-system) for everything Proust didn't want to lose. 'Forgetting myself entirely, and thinking only of the *object* I wish to know . . . I do not surround this little bit of truth with lyricism. But when I have found other little bits of truth, I put them end to end in an attempt to reconstitute, to restore the object, as if in a stained-glass window.'[19] Ghéon's friendly reply made Proust happier, he said, 'than the most flattering article could have done'.[20]

The other main source of gratification was Gide's volte-face. 'My dear Proust, For some days I have not put your book down. . . . The rejection of this book will remain the most serious mistake of the NRF – and (because, to my shame, I was largely responsible) I feel bitterly regretful and remorseful. . . . I believed you were – shall I admit it? – "du côté de chez Verdurin"; a snob, a socialite amateur. . . . I cannot go on. I feel too much remorse, too much pain.'[21] Proust told him the pleasure of receiving his letter 'infinitely surpasses that which I would have felt in being published by the NRF',[22] but he was discouraging when Gide offered to call on him,[23] though he was well enough to receive visitors and wanted to see Lucien.[24] But he discouraged another old friend, Henry Bordeaux: 'I remember so well those short moments we spent together, I prolong them, and I have always interrupted in this way the prescriptions of friendship.'[25] It was as if, nervous of direct confrontations, he preferred the literary alternative – correspondence and fiction.

Besides giving Agostinelli more money than he could afford, he'd been losing heavily on the stock exchange, but he didn't stop speculating. In January he sold his shares in Royal Dutch,[26] and, shortly afterwards, invited Albert to go fifty-fifty with him in a new gamble. He thought they'd make a profit of 6,000 francs with no risk,[27] but the result was a loss, and in May, forgetting he'd sold his Royal Dutch, he asked Hauser to raise 10,000 francs by selling them.[28] Proust's financial embarrassment didn't make him any less magnanimous to Grasset, who brought out four editions of *Swann* within two months: on each occasion Proust accepted only half the money he was offered.[29]

The book was making an impact on a wide variety of readers. Edith Wharton, who was living in France, has described in her memoirs how she found herself trembling with the emotion only genius can produce, and how she sent the book to Henry James, who 'recognised a new mastery, a new vision and a structural design as yet unintelligible to him but as surely there as the hard bone under the soft flesh in a living organism'.[30] In Germany Rilke advised the publisher Anton Kippenberg to secure a translation of this 'incomparably remarkable' book, which was written in a 'most original' style.[31]

Some of Proust's friends reacted disappointingly. Jeanne de Caillavet said she kept re-reading the passage about Swann's first communion because she'd experienced the same angüish and the same disillusion.[32] There's nothing about first communion in the book, and Proust's telephone conversation with Albu was still more absurd:

'Read your book? You've written a book?'

'Yes, Louis, I even sent you a copy.'

'Ah! My dear Marcel, if you sent it to me, I've certainly read it. Only I wasn't sure I'd received it.'[33]

But while old friends failed to respond, enthusiastic responses led to new friendships. Fifteen years younger than Proust, Jacques Rivière had married the sister of Alain-Fournier, and since 1910 had been secretary of the NRF. His first letter to Proust has been lost, but it prompted the reply:

'At last I find a reader who can *make out* that my book is a dogmatic work and a construct!'[34] Later, describing his first reaction to *Swann*, Rivière said: 'I shall never forget the amazement, the profound emotion into which I was immediately plunged.'[35] In another letter, written about ten days later, Proust again insists on the 'essentially dogmatic' nature of his novel.[36] Meaning that it makes a case for idealism.

He enjoyed discussing the book in letters. In correspondence with Gide, Proust was congratulatory about Lafcadio in *Les Caves du Vatican*. 'No one has been so objectively perverse since Balzac and *Splendeurs et misères*. But what helped Balzac, I think, in the creation of Lucien de Rubempré was a certain personal vulgarity. There is a certain "feel of skin" in Lucien's dialogue.'[37] The allusion is to Mallarmé's comment on Zola's 'unique sense of life, his crowd movements, the grain of Nana's skin, which we have all caressed'.[38] What Proust didn't like in *Les Caves du Vatican* was the 'thousand material details; for my part I cannot, whether through weariness or laziness or boredom, describe, when I write, anything which has not produced an impression of poetic enchantment or made me believe I am seizing on a general truth. My characters never change their ties, or even buy new ones.'[39]

In the middle of March, just as he was beginning to recover his equilibrium after losing Agostinelli, Calmette was murdered. He'd been campaigning in *Le Figaro* against the unpopular left-wing finance minister, Joseph Caillaux, who'd been trying to raise the level of income tax to pay for rearmament necessitated by Germany's build-up of military strength. The French government had legislated in August 1913 for three years of compulsory military service, followed by seven years in the territorial army and seven in the reserve. Proust had intensely disliked Calmette's tactics. On 13 March his front-page article had been captioned 'PROOF OF M. CAILLAUX'S SECRET MACHINATIONS – THE THINKING REVEALED IN HIS HANDWRITING – THE SHATTERING DOCUMENT'. The article was illustrated by a facsimile reproduction of an old letter from Caillaux to his first wife, boasting of his success in winning support from centre and right by cutting down income tax. 'I was sorry', said Proust, 'that politics and even patriotism inclined such a good man as Calmette to harshness.'[40] But Nemesis was even harsher. Caillaux's second wife arrived at the *Figaro* offices on the evening of the 16th. After sending her card in to Calmette, she was shown into his office. She seemed calm, but both her hands were concealed in a muff and, as soon as they were alone together, five shots rang out. The next day, Proust, deeply upset by the news, went to the *Figaro* offices, where he met Robert Dreyfus, Jacques Bizet and his wife. The Bizets dissuaded him from writing a letter of condolence to Calmette's mistress, Henriette Ballot, who was still married to the *Figaro*'s literary critic, Henri Ballot.[41]

Proust hadn't recovered from the shock when he had to decide about a tempting offer from Gide, who wanted the NRF to publish the second and third volumes, paying all the costs, and to reprint the first volume as soon as Grasset's stock was sold out.[42] Instead of writing 'Mon cher Gide', Proust began his reply 'Mon cher ami', and went on to say: 'This is the honour I have most coveted, as you know, and you will convey my thanks to your friends for bestowing it on me. But the desire I have to say yes must not make me behave badly to Grasset. . . . (In any case, if I accept, and I do not believe I will, one absolute condition is that the costs of publication *would be met in their entirety by me*.)' Before ending the letter he spoke more encouragingly about the possibility of meeting for a chat.[43]

In his next letter Gide admitted to being in deep personal trouble. After reading an instalment of *Les Caves du Vatican* in the March issue of the *NRF*, Claudel, who'd never realised Gide was a homosexual, had written: 'Must I quite decide, as I never wished to, that you yourself participate in these horrendous practices?'[44] Without knowing why Gide was so upset, Proust offered his help.

I have been endowed (and it is certainly my only gift) with the power of procuring happiness for others and saving them pain, quite often. I have reconciled not only enemies but lovers, I have cured the sick, though I can only make my own condition worse, I have made lazy people work without ceasing to be lazy myself. . . . If you think I can intervene in any way in the affairs which are distressing you, I am ready to go wherever you like, to travel if necessary and within 24 hours. Let my state of health give you no anxiety. . . . When I was writing my book, I felt that if Swann had known me and could have made use of me, I could have made Odette fall in love with him.[45]

Apart from the return of Agostinelli, nothing could have given Proust more pleasure than Gide's offer. On 24 March he asked Émile Straus whether the contract with Grasset prevented him from using a different publisher for the second and third volumes, but, before Straus had replied, a letter arrived from Grasset. Realising he was in danger of losing Proust, he offered to launch the second volume in late May or early June. By 'launch' he may only have meant start the advance publicity, but the suggestion was still unrealistic when the volume was so far from being ready.

Proust was upset that Grasset, without consulting him, had been canvassing for subscriptions to all three volumes,[46] but, in the negotiations which ensued, it was goodwill and generosity that stopped Proust from transferring his allegiance to Gide and the NRF. Writing to Grasset, Proust said he was sure he owned the copyright of his work and had the right to bring out other editions,[47] but Grasset's reply was disarmingly generous. 'Do not consider yourself to be under any obligation, since I gladly release you from anything in our first agreement that could put you under any shade of an obligation, and you can make decisions in all the plenitude of your independence.'[48] This was well judged to disarm Proust. 'I could do nothing but abdicate the freedom he was giving me.' All he could offer Gide was excerpts for the NRF.[49]

Encomiastic reviews were still appearing in the press. In the *Écho de Paris* on 15 April Jacques-Émile Blanche praised 'a rare banquet, a gust of air which blows away the soporific vapours of the current output. . . . It reveals itself, like every exceptional work, to be original and beautiful.'[50] Proust paid for an excerpt from this review to be reprinted as an advertisement in *Le Figaro*; meanwhile the *Criterium*, a horse-racing daily, published an article by Henri Bernstein, who called the novel 'admirable . . . a great book among the greatest'.

It was even more gratifying to learn, later in the month, that Rivière wanted to print not an excerpt from the new volume in the *NRF* but the whole of it. 'If you really want to publish the whole of my second volume (with some cuts), I consent willingly, but it seems to me a terrible burden on your review.'[51] In the end only a series of excerpts was published. When Rivière, wanting to meet Proust, offered to deliver the proofs of the first excerpt personally, he was invited to find out by telephone whether Proust was well enough to receive him. 'The nuisance is that often the atmosphere in my room is made rather disagreeable by the fumigations I am obliged to have. But I will endeavour to abstain during the hours preceding your visit.'[52] But before they met, they got into a chivalrous argument about who should pay for any alterations Proust made to the proofs.[53]

His reputation had improved so greatly that he should no longer have any difficulty in finding a publisher for a collection of pastiches and essays. He first offered them to Grasset,[54] who thought the NRF would be a more suitable publisher for them.[55]

Nicolas' wife, Céline, had moved out. When she'd come out of hospital in January, she'd gone to convalesce in the country, and, no longer needing to go out every afternoon, Nicolas had resumed his normal duties, while Céleste had taken care of the household linen. When Céline returned, she seemed jealous of Céleste and asserted herself even more than usual, criticising Proust's extravagance. Saying he didn't need her advice, he sent her away for another rest, but when she came back, she again started interfering, and he sacked her. Given the choice of leaving with her or staying without her, Nicolas stayed, and Céleste came every day to help him.

In July Proust was using Émile as a typist, but was in no state to work on correcting proofs. They arrived each day in bulky envelopes, and he let them pile up, unopened.[56] But he couldn't leave his financial affairs in abeyance. Share values were still sliding downwards, and at the end of each month, having to pay the external brokers a differential corresponding to the depreciation in value of the shares he'd bought, Proust had to deplete his capital by paying over thirty or forty thousand francs.[57] His difficulties had been exacerbated by his extravagance over the two presents. Writing to Robert de Flers, who'd taken over as editor of *Le Figaro*, he said he was 'more or less bankrupt' and asked to be considered if a vacancy ever occurred for a regular columnist. He could write about the weather, or high society, or the stock exchange, or music, or the theatre, or even dogs killed in accidents. 'And you will see I can abstain from literature, can be brief and matter-of-fact.'[58] De Flers rang up to make him an offer, but Proust had already changed his mind,[59] partly because it was easier than he expected to borrow. In July he opened an account with Crédit

Industriel, which gave him an overdraft facility of 200,000 francs.[60]

Meanwhile the flow of congratulation continued. 'I am full of admiration,' wrote Gide after the Balbec episode with the grandmother had been excerpted in the *NRF* on 1 June. 'Thanks to the powerful and extraordinary flexibility of your style, these are my own memories I seem to be reading here, and the most private of my own sensations. I see everything again; I live through it all again. . . . As for the characterisation of Charlus, it is really marvellous.'[61]

Replying to Gide, Proust said he'd tried 'to portray the homosexual enamoured with virility because, without knowing it, he is a Woman. I am far from claiming this is the only kind of homosexual. But it is a very interesting one which, I believe, has never been described. . . . In the same way that it can be said "There is a connection between the arthritic or nervous temperament of someone and his gifts of sensitivity, etc." I am convinced that it is to his homosexuality that M. de Charlus owes his understanding of so many things which are incomprehensible to his brother, the duc de Guermantes.'

Proust confided in Gide about 'the death of a young man whom I probably loved more than all my friends because it makes me so unhappy', and he went on to say: 'I have had from him letters which are those of a great writer. . . . But he died without really knowing what he was, and before quite being it.'[62]

Once again Proust was reaching, through correspondence, towards intimacy. In his next letter, written from Cuverville par Criquetot, Gide reproached himself for not coming to knock on Proust's door when he was in Paris. 'I curse this extreme discretion which constantly paralyses me and makes my whole life stiff-jointed.'[63]

VI

1914–22
Rehearsals for Dying

TWENTY-SIX

WAR

On 28 June 1914 the Archduke Ferdinand and his wife were assassinated at Sarajevo by a Bosnian nationalist. When the Austrians accused the Serbian government of instigating the plot, it was hard to believe war could be averted. Proust had been selling shares to pay the brokers at the end of each month, but he hadn't sold enough by the middle of July to save himself from heavy losses as news of troop movements sent share prices sharply downwards. With Austrian troops collecting on the Russian frontier, Proust was still hoping for an improvement on the stock exchange,[1] but on 1 August, three days after Austria declared war on Serbia, Germany declared war on Russia. The French started mobilising, and two days later Germany declared war on France. 'In these terrible days,' Proust told Lionel Hauser, 'you have other things to do than write letters and concern yourself with my poor affairs, which, I swear to you, seem quite unimportant when I think that millions of men are going to be massacred in a *War of the Worlds* comparable to that of [H. G.] Wells because it is advantageous to the Austrian emperor to have an outlet on the Black Sea.' But he was still hoping for 'a supreme miracle which will stop the omni-murderous machine from being set off at the last second'.[2]

His brother was called up as a medical officer, and Proust went with him to the Gare de l'Est, where he had to catch the midnight train to Verdun.[3] The advancing German army occupied Brussels on 20 August, and Lille a week later. People were expecting Paris would soon be under siege, and, feeling he must protect his sister-in-law and niece, Proust hesitated even more than usual about whether to holiday in Cabourg.[4]

When Odilon Albaret was called up, Céleste was left alone in their flat at Levallois. Proust asked whether she'd like to move into the boulevard Haussmann flat and work for him full time, but she preferred to go on coming in every day from

Levallois. Nicolas was in the reserves and, when he was called up, Proust again spoke to Céleste, offering her the empty room and asking her to look after him until he replaced Nicolas. It would be improper, he said, for a young woman to wait on a man who spent most of his time in bed, but she'd have little to do except make the coffee. She was inadequate anyway, he told her. She knew nothing – not even how to address people in the third person. She didn't even know what the third person was. Amused, he let her go on saying 'vous', but, rejecting her invitation to call her 'Céleste', he addressed her as 'madame'.

She noticed that whenever she went into his bedroom, only his eyes moved. Never starting to sit up, or even reaching to take a piece of sugar for his coffee, he'd always lie motionless with the sheets drawn up around him, waiting for her to go.[5]

He took on a tubercular-looking young manservant recommended by Coco de Madrazo, but lost him almost immediately to the army.[6] By advertising for a valet de chambre, he found a good-looking young Swede. Ernest Forssgren was nineteen, blond and six foot three. Hoping to study French and Latin at the Sorbonne and eventually to teach languages, he'd come to Paris in 1913 and been taken on as a valet by prince Orloff, but lost the job when war broke out and the prince left for his country villa. Intrigued by Ernest's looks and his interest in languages, Proust thought he might be able to work as a typist. As soon as Marthe Proust left for Pau with Suzy, Proust decided he'd take both Ernest and Céleste to Cabourg.[7]

The German army, which had taken Amiens on 30 August, was advancing towards the Marne, while the panic-stricken French government was hastily planning its withdrawal to Bordeaux. One night before he left for Cabourg, Proust wandered out into 'moonlight which was clear, dazzling, reproachful, serene, ironic and maternal, and seeing this immense Paris which I had never been able to love so much, waiting in its useless beauty for the onslaught which appeared to be unavoidable, I could not stop myself from weeping'.[8]

Ernest was sent to the Gare du Nord to buy three first-class tickets, while Céleste packed under Proust's supervision. The manuscripts went into a battered old valise made of tough cardboard covered with beige canvas. His trunk was big enough to hold two vicuña overcoats, which had been made for the seaside, his jackets, trousers, shirts, a big enough supply of underwear for him to change vest and pants every day, and his own blankets. The hotel's, he said, smelt of mothballs.[9] But when they left on the evening of Thursday 3 September, they couldn't get a taxi to the station – most of the taxis in Paris had been commandeered for the war – and the trunk had to be left behind. They could take only three suitcases: Ernest carried Proust's and his own, while Céleste carried hers.

Frighteningly overcrowded, the train took thirteen or fourteen hours to reach Mézidon, where they had to change. Céleste had brought a thermos flask of hot milk for Proust, but they had nothing else to eat or drink, and when they got off the train, he was so weak that Ernest carried him into the waiting-room. Two of the English soldiers on their way to the front gave up their seats, and Ernest booked rooms for Proust and Céleste to stay overnight at the neighbouring hotel, while he spent the night in the station, waiting for news about when there'd be another train to Cabourg.[10]

The next one left at four in the afternoon, and, when they finally arrived at the hotel, Proust was too exhausted to appreciate the welcome from the staff, who remembered how well he tipped.[11] The dining-room and the first two of the three floors had been converted into an extension hospital for wounded soldiers, but Proust, Céleste and Ernest were settled into three rooms on the top floor. Knowing Proust wouldn't have enough work for him to fill the day, Ernest offered to help nurse the wounded soldiers, and Proust encouraged him: 'Of course you can. You're a charming young man.'[12]

Proust followed a regular routine, waking earlier than in Paris and knocking on the wall when he wanted Céleste to prepare coffee in the pantry used by floor-waiters and chambermaids. He seldom went out and did little writing. Mostly, wearing a thick woollen dressing-gown, he stayed in his room, where he ate his meals, which she served. At ten in the morning she made his bed, aired his room and cleaned it, while he waited in Ernest's. From eight till twelve each day Ernest worked in the hospital, and he spent an hour each day with Proust, reading to him from newspapers and books. Occasionally Proust would interrupt to correct his pronunciation, and he seemed to enjoy explaining subtleties of the French language. They also spent a lot of time playing draughts and chess. Proust was always scrupulously polite: if Céleste interrupted a game to bring in a letter, he'd apologise as if Ernest were a friend. He complained that chess put too much of a strain on the mind, and Ernest taught him some new card games, as well as performing for him conjuring tricks he'd learnt from his father, an amateur magician.[13]

According to Céleste, Ernest was 'as pleased with himself as if he were the King of Sweden, if not God Almighty'.[14] But he liked her: she and Proust, he decided, were the nicest people he'd ever met, but he was sometimes unnerved by Proust's behaviour. One evening when they were playing chess, Céleste came in with a letter, and Proust, after reading it, handed it to Ernest. When Céleste knocked again, Ernest threw it on to the bed before she came in, afterwards explaining he hadn't thought it was *comme il faut* for a servant to be seen reading his master's correspondence. Insisting he wasn't a servant but a private secretary and confidant, Proust wanted to reward him for his tact with a present of 500 francs. Ernest hesitated. 'As you know, sir, we made a pact which prevents you from tempting me in this way.' But Proust persuaded him to pocket the money. 'It is of no importance to me and a great deal to you. It can help you to forge the brilliant future you want.' When he handed over the cash, Ernest thought he saw 'a kind of disappointment in his expression'. Ernest tried to cheer him up by performing a conjuring trick and teaching him how to do it. ' "Ernest, you're a tonic," he said, holding out his arms to embrace me. "I've never known anyone like you." '[15]

Ernest used the money to buy presents for the wounded soldiers, saying when he handed them over that they were from Proust. The hospital was being run by a comtesse, who came to Proust's room with three other ladies to thank him for his generosity. Confused at first, he soon realised what had happened.[16]

Though Montesquiou, the Greffulhes, the Clermont-Tonnerres and the Strauses were all nearby, he didn't contact them. Montesquiou called once at the hotel, and Greffulhe twice, but they were told M. Proust wasn't well enough to receive them, though here he had the curtains drawn back in the afternoons, and he relaxed sufficiently to start saying 'Céleste' instead of 'madame'. One talent they had in common was for mimicry, and in the absence of the solemn Ernest, they had fun together at his expense.[17]

Proust sometimes worked at the novel in the afternoon or evening, writing in his exercise books, and sometimes went downstairs, but ate no dinner. The wounded soldiers included blacks from Senegal and Morocco; after the confusion over the presents, he took to visiting them every day, taking packs of cards and games of draughts for them.[18] He told Lucien he spent nearly all his money on them.[19]

Proust stayed in Cabourg about six weeks. Before he left, he went to Trouville, where Mme Straus had the actress Réjane staying with her. Though Réjane had met Proust before, she took him for a German and called him a boche.[20] Her son, Jacques Porel, who'd seen him walking in his mauve-lined overcoat on the golf-course at Cabourg, and who'd become a devotee of *Swann*, was much friendlier.

On the journey back to Paris, Proust had a bad choking fit just after the train left Mézidon. His medicines and Legras powders were inside a suitcase in the luggage van, and the guard refused to give Ernest acccess. But Céleste, afraid her master was dying, fought her way into the van when the train stopped at Évreux, and triumphantly returned to the carriage with the powders.[21] When they arrived in Paris, cleaners were at work on the flat with huge hoovers. He sent them away and collapsed into bed with several hot-water bottles. Sweating and choking as he bent forward to inhale the fumes from the powders, he ordered Céleste out of the room. She felt uncertain whether he'd survive.[22]

He was ill for several days, but said he felt 'glad at being able in this way not to be the only one who is not suffering while the whole world is dying or seeing relations die'.[23] The German army, which had occupied Rheims at the beginning of September, had been driven back by the allies, while in Poland the Germans were getting the worst of fierce fighting with the Russians.

In Cabourg, finding he could go for hours without thinking about Agostinelli, Proust had guiltily felt he'd reached 'the first stage of detachment from my grief',[24] but after returning to Paris, he soon found he hadn't. 'In spite of the distance which alas I sometimes feel momentarily, I would not hesitate, even in those moments, to leap at the chance of having an arm or a leg cut off if that could bring him back to life.'[25] And later he wrote 'Nobody has lived more than I do with incurable nostalgia for two or three people, or rather, I am not really living but dying from it.'[26]

He now went a lot further towards cutting himself off from

social life. He'd never again go to Cabourg, he said, or anywhere else.[27] Towards the end of the year, he had his telephone
cut off, pleading poverty as an excuse. When he told Albu he
was ruined, he offered money, but Proust refused.[28] His financial problems were less serious than he made them out to be;
he never had the telephone reconnected, even when he was
spending lavishly on meals at the Ritz. His intention was to
be disturbed less and to concentrate more on the novel.

This didn't stop him from trying to help his friends.
Together with Robert Dreyfus and Fernand Gregh, Reynaldo
had been posted to a regimental depot in Provence. When he
tried to get himself sent to the front, Proust intervened, writing
to his medical officer, and telling Reynaldo it would be criminal
to keep his commanding officer in ignorance about his bronchial condition and his fainting fits.[29] But the authorities were
in such a state of panic that ill health counted for little. Gabriel
de la Rochefoucauld escaped enlistment because he'd gone
blind,[30] but it seemed possible Proust would be called up. 'I
am going to see an army medical board, and I will probably
be accepted, because they are accepting everybody.'[31]

The main practical difference the war made to him was that
it interrupted publication of the novel. Grasset was called up,
and his company closed down. Proust went on writing, but
working without the prospect of immediate publication was
quite different. Like Calmette's volte-face over serialisation
four years ago, the interruption had far-reaching effects on the
overall construction. The novel became three times as long,
and incomparably better. What makes it different from any
novel previously written is that the narrative gives us so many
different views of each character at so many different stages of
his development.

When a ray of sunshine on the balcony had prompted him
to connect the present moment in Paris with both Venice and
Illiers, he'd found himself making a triangular comparison
that extended through time as well as space. The device had
methodological implications. Constantly hoping to deduce
general laws from particular circumstances, he saw that metaphor, simile and other figures of speech could lift experience
away from time and contingency. 'Truth will begin only at
the moment the writer . . . dealing with a quality common to
two sensations extrapolates their common essence by making

a connection between them to withdraw them from contingencies of time in a metaphor.'

This helps to explain his aversion to photographic naturalism. The camera can only reproduce surfaces at one moment. Because it never compares two sets of surfaces or circumstances, it can't offer access to the truth which comes into focus when you penetrate beyond the contingent, though you can do this by comparing two photographs – or memories – of a person in different circumstances.

> People never stop changing position in relation to us. In the imperceptible but incessant movement of the world, we regard them as immobile in an instant of vision too brief for us to notice the movement which is propelling them. But we have only to select from our memories two pictures of them taken at different times, but similar enough for them not to have changed in themselves, at least not perceptibly, and the difference between the two pictures is a gauge of the displacement they have undergone in relation to us.

This is how the novel had traditionally used this device to focus development in characters, but no previous novelist had been so systematic and so persistent in taking a multiplicity of vantage points scattered through time.

Charlus, for instance, is already a mature man when we first meet him, a gentleman in a linen suit, staring with popping eyes at the Narrator, whose opinion of him changes slightly when he turns out to be the brother of the duc de Guermantes, and changes again when his nephew, Saint-Loup, talks about his reputation for womanising. The Narrator sees him again outside the casino, again with his aunt, Mme de Villeparisis, again when Charlus invites him to tea, and again when the baron comes to his bedroom to lend him a book. At each encounter, all previous impressions are modified, but although we see a good deal of him all through *Jeunes Filles* and *Guermantes*, it's not until the beginning of *Sodome et Gomorrhe* that the Narrator, overhearing a conversation between him and Jupien, the tailor who's said to be an ex-convict, realises Charlus is a homosexual. He seems different again when observed at a station trying to start a liaison with Morel, the young violinist, and from having moved on more exalted levels of society he takes to frequenting Mme Verdurin's salon, at first being treated like a star, later being humiliated. During the war further modulations in the characterisation reveal him as an addict of flagellation and as a sympathiser with the Germans. He's arrested at Morel's instigation, and later released. At the end of the narrative his beard and snowy hair make him look like King Lear. Diminished by illness, he's scrupulously polite to a woman he'd always despised, and Jupien says he's 'just a big baby now'.[32] His character could hardly have undergone more sea-changes, but if it hadn't been for the war there wouldn't have been so many.

On the other hand, the objection could be raised that because work on the novel was spread over fifteen years, the book is a collaboration between different Prousts. The thirty-seven-year-old who wrote *Swann* is recognisably different from the fifty-one-year-old who put in the final additions. Though sketched out immediately after *Swann*, *Le Temps retrouvé* was substantially altered by these, and the preoccupation with death, disease, disintegration make the texture quite different from that of *Swann*. Ideally, a novelist would never try to incorporate new material into a draft without asking himself whether the rest of it needs to be adjusted. Every part needs a relationship with every other part. Certainly Proust's additions do much more good than harm, adding to the multiplicity of viewpoints from which all the major characters are observed, but, alert though he was to discontinuity in their development, he failed to make allowances for the discontinuity in his own which produces shifts of interest and emphasis in the narrative viewpoint. The sense of decay at the end of the book spreads powerfully from individual characters to the whole society, but this effect could have been even more telling, if it had been possible, by revising the earlier parts of the story, to make them build up to it. Nor was he using the novel in the same way at the end as he was at the beginning. It was always an extension of his life, but by 1914 it had less to do with the machinery of friendship, and though he did not allow the war to dominate the novel in the way the Dreyfus affair had taken over *Jean Santeuil*, he used *À la recherche* like a pair of binoculars through which he could view the war: it was always there between him and what he observed. Each raid on Paris, each encounter with a soldier on leave offered itself as raw material.

Generally the war made more difference than might have been

expected to the routine of Proust's life, and he was annoyed
to hear he was being quoted as saying: 'The war? I don't have
time to think about it.' He suspected Cocteau of originating
the story. It would be less misleading, he objected, to say he
never thought about anything else. 'Even if one thinks about
other things, even if one is asleep, this discomfort does not
stop, like the neuralgia which makes itself felt during sleep.'[33]
Though he never called the Germans 'the boche', and never
indulged in mindless jingoism, he read seven newspapers every
day, checking military action against the maps he had all over
his bed, and scanning the deaths column nervously. But he
found the papers 'quite inferior to the big things they discuss'.[34]

Fénelon had volunteered for military action. Though the
government would have preferred him to go on working at
the embassy in Christiania, he fought as a sub-lieutenant at
Artois in December 1914 and, on the 17th, disappeared during
fighting at Mametz. It was possible he'd been taken prisoner,
and Proust oscillated between pessimism and optimism until
the middle of March, when the newspapers reported he'd been
killed by a bullet in the head.[35]

Meanwhile, on 13 January, Gaston de Caillavet died after
months of battling against uraemia. The next day Proust, writing to Jeanne, said he'd adored Gaston, and could neither stop
weeping nor believe he'd never see him again. 'Oh, Madame,
if only we could weep together.'[36]

Absurd though it would have been to conscript an invalid,
he seemed to be in genuine danger. At the end of January he
hadn't stepped outside the flat for nearly three months;[37] he
was eating almost nothing and dosing himself almost hourly
with medicine,[38] but he was summoned to appear before an
army medical board at the Hôtel de Ville at 3.30 in the morning
on 13 April, and the notice ended with the admonition that
anyone who failed to appear would be deemed fit for military
service.[39] He sent Céleste to Dr Bize, who certified: 'M. Proust
Marcel is afflicted with chronic daily asthma attacks, with
generalised emphysema. These episodes have caused cardiac
dilatation. In addition, symptoms of renal inadequacy necessi-
tate a strict lacto-vegetarian diet. For many years, M. Proust
has been confined to bed and in such a state of physical disability that it will be impossible for him to appear before the
medical board.'[40]

He knew it would kill him if he had to go back into the

army.[41] 'Undoubtedly the life I lead is devoid of gratifications and while knowing I cannot be of any use to the army, it would be useful to me if I could be finished off. But I badly want to complete the work I have started and to incorporate truths on which I know much depends and which will otherwise be destroyed with me.'[42]

It was almost true that his life was devoid of gratifications. Food, once a source of so much pleasure, had progressively come to matter less. The main turning points had been the death of his mother, the departure of Félicie, and the arrival of Céleste, who'd never been taught how to cook. But his progressive loss of interest in food was part of a reorientation in which he came to take an almost sensual pleasure in remembering the past and to care less about other sensual pleasures in the present. By 1914 he was asking for a cooked meal only once or twice a month, usually to strengthen himself for an outing, and Céleste noticed that when he felt a sudden craving for a particular dish, his appetite had been momentarily stimulated by a memory of Félicie's *boeuf à la mode* or some other favourite dish. His eyes would gleam with pleasure, and he'd say he could eat some of it right now, but if she offered to go out and fetch some, he'd invariably tell her not to.[43] Eager to go on remembering a combination of flavours with the same precision as he remembered visual details, he didn't want to eat an inadequate approximation to the dish he remembered. She formed the impression that he ate little even when he went out to restaurants with friends, but she was wrong. According to the maître d'hôtel at the Ritz, who was aware he ate little at home, he dined at the Ritz with an appetite that was astonishing, always ordering two kinds of meat, always asking for second helpings, and washing them down with the best wine.[44] But he didn't eat out often enough to keep himself properly nourished, and when a guest came to his home for a meal, Céleste had to clear the bedside table and set a place for one. The food was usually fillets of sole, chicken, and an ice from Poire-Blanche. Occasionally she'd be asked to fry potatoes in the middle of the night for someone he'd brought back with him. But when she remonstrated with him about untouched food on the trays she brought him, she was told he needed to be alert, couldn't afford to make his mind torpid with heavy meals. He was unimpressed by the argument that he needed nourishment to keep up his strength for his work. Once he asked for redcurrant syrup from Tanrade's in the rue de Sèze, where his mother used to buy it, but complained he remembered it as tasting better.[45]

In the middle of April, Céleste's mother died. She came into his room 'screaming with pain'[46] and, when he sent her back to her family in Auxillac, she left her sister-in-law to look after him until she returned. The substitute housekeeper 'does not know the flat, can hardly find her way to my room when I ring, would be unable to make my bed if I got up'. Nor could he send her to deliver messages, which had become more important now that he was without a telephone.[47]

One new friendship that developed at this time was with comte Louis Gautier-Vignal, who'd once taken flying lessons from Raymond Garros, and the acquaintance began when Proust telephoned him at eleven o'clock in the evening, hoping for background information about Agostinelli's last weeks. When Gautier-Vignal came to Proust's room, the furniture looked as if Proust had only just moved in and the cork walls were blackened by dust. Proust had intended to have the cork covered with wallpaper or fabric but had never got round to it. He complained about being uncomfortable in bed and about being unable to read his own handwriting but demurred when Gautier-Vignal offered to type from his dictation. To other friends he reported that Gautier-Vignal threw himself at people like a big insect,[48] but they saw each other once or twice a week, and he was glad to let Gautier-Vignal chauffeur him in a closed car. They drove to the Bois de Boulogne, the banks of the Seine, Notre-Dame, the Louvre, the Tuileries, Versailles, none of which Proust had seen recently, even from outside, though he'd been writing about them in the novel. It struck Gautier-Vignal, whom he interrogated about Velasquez, Goya and El Greco, that he was also referring to painters whose work he didn't know. Though he told Maurice Duplay that he had a very good museum inside himself and told Gautier-Vignal he was like one of those people who live in the country and generate their own electricity,[49] he was depending heavily on second-hand information and stale memories, as well as on gossip from servants. Not that he lacked the genius to turn all this dross into good writing.

One old friend he wanted to see was Jeanne Caillavet, who'd written, asking to meet him because Gaston, before he died, had made her promise to pass on some information. On one of the rare evenings he was well enough to get up, he tried to telephone her from the café, got no answer, but took a taxi to her flat. It was a quarter to eleven when he arrived, but no lights were on, and in case she was sleeping, he went away without ringing the bell. 'Perhaps it is better like this. For me the dead are alive. For me that applies to love, but also to friendship. . . . When the whole of my *Swann* has appeared, if you ever read it, you will understand me.'[50] But she came to see him, and the blonde hair he remembered – she'd once worn it in plaits – had turned white. What she'd promised to tell him was that Gaston had fallen in love with another woman and broken off the affair for her sake, but had never got over it.[51]

Another death which deeply saddened Proust was that of Robert d'Humières, who'd helped him with his Ruskin translations. As a lieutenant in the Zouave regiment, d'Humières was shot in May while leading his company in a charge. Though Proust had recently been seeing little of Fénelon, and had never seen much of d'Humières, 'I am weeping night and day for Fénelon and d'Humières, as if I had only parted from them yesterday.'[52]

To commemorate the anniversary of Agostinelli's death on 30 May, he arranged to have a wreath put on the grave in the cemetery at Nice. Mme Catusse was enlisted to buy the wreath from a florist and have it delivered to Agostinelli's sister. But this time, instead of spending 400 francs, he was spending 30.[53]

In June, feeling well enough to go out more often, he spent an evening with Georges de Lauris and his marquise, and another at Larue's, where he saw Georges de Porto-Riche. Before the end of the month he visited the comtesse de la Beraudière, who was a mistress of the comte de Greffulhe and was helping Jacques-Émile Blanche to get an article into print, and called on his old friend Henri Bardac, believing him to be on the point of leaving for the front.

Early in July Proust went in a taxi to Auteuil to see Blanche and promised to help in correcting the proofs of his book *Cahiers d'un artiste*, a series of letters on the war, featuring many of his friends under disguised names. Though Blanche was studiously considerate, lending Proust a cloak when he complained of the draught from the window, he noticed the absence of 'the affectionate smile which used to seem happy at seeing me again'.[54] Worse still, Proust caught cold, and afterwards had to stay in bed with a high temperature, which seemed to be caused partly by a kidney infection.[55]

Montesquiou, who'd finished a new collection of poems, *Les Offrande blessées, élégies guerrières*, which was due to be published in July, autographed an advance copy for Proust, sending it him early in June, and insisted on visiting him when Proust made excuses for not attending the reading the count was giving for his friends. After promising not to tire the invalid and to stay for only five minutes, Montesquiou paid the threatened visit on 13 July and stayed so long that Proust remembered the visit as lasting for seven hours.[56] Another visitor in July was Grasset, who was on leave. Proust had now had the proofs for over a year.

At the end of June he'd received a warning he was to be examined by an army medical officer. He was expecting the officer on 7 July, but he didn't materialise until early August, and when Proust was ausculted, his lungs produced such a sinister rhonchus that he was reprieved for six months.[57] The suspense had been oppressive, and he was suffering from noise while the house next door was being demolished. He was getting only about fifteen minutes' sleep each night, he said, because his asthma attacks lasted until about seven in the morning, and the demolition men arrived at seven-thirty, and he was resorting to 'terrible – and useless – doses of drugs'.[58] He then had another, unexpected, visit from army medical officers, who were under the impression he was an architect, but he was so unmistakably ill that they proposed him for exemption.[59]

He was now writing more often to Lionel Hauser than to anyone else, sometimes discussing not only his financial affairs but his beliefs. 'The more religious one is, the less one dares to affirm anything beyond one's beliefs. While I deny nothing, and believe in the possibility of everything, I think the objections based on the existence of evil etc. are ridiculous, since it is only suffering that seems to have made and go on making man better than a brute. But from there to certainty, or even to hope, is a long journey I have not yet made. Will I ever make it?'[60] Which raised the question of whether there was a religious element in all his speculations – a desire to put himself at the mercy of powers beyond his control, and to be penalised if he deserved to be. For five years he'd been writing long letters to Hauser about individual purchases, but he'd almost deliberately kept himself in the dark about his overall position, politely refusing when friends offered to have his portfolio monitored.[61] Dealings on the French stock exchange had been suspended at the end of July 1914, but when a new account day was announced for 20 September 1915, he was aghast to find he'd been debited with 8 per cent per month in addition to the ordinary interest on his outstanding account.[62] One share, which had yielded no interest and decreased in value to less than half what he paid for it, cost him 18,000 francs in annual interest.[63] He was 150,000 francs in debt, and though he had ten months to pay, it meant finding 15,000 francs each month. The differential between the current value of his shares and the price he'd paid for them didn't need to be settled so long as the moratorium lasted, but it might soon end.[64]

During the second half of October he met Hauser to discuss the situation, and Hauser offered – for a fee of 150 francs – to look through his portfolio while his cashier checked his accounts. This work hadn't been completed when Proust wrote for advice about whether to buy some shares in United States Steel.[65] 'I have no advice to give you,' Hauser answered, 'but if you do decide to buy these shares, you are taking the risk of losing the little you still have.' He went on, in spite of himself, to give advice.

> You imagine, as so many others do, that the profit you make on the stock exchange depends mainly on which shares you buy. Well, paradoxical though it may seem, I can tell you it depends mainly on the person who is speculating. Some people I know have made a lot of money on the stock exchange by buying tenth-rate shares, and others have gone bankrupt with blue-chip shares. This is a highly personal matter. Some people are born to do deals of this kind, and others are born to burn their fingers when they try. I do not think I am exaggerating when I say you belong to the latter kind, but if you are not convinced, you are free to continue the experiment.[66]

Instead of taking umbrage, Proust was apologetic for giving him so much work on the basis of such exiguous assets, and they went on exchanging long letters. Hauser, who was literary and cultured, was glad to cultivate the kind of epistolary friend-ship he was being offered, while Proust appreciated the *homo duplex*, not restricted exclusively to work but able to keep what Montaigne too modestly called the rear workroom because it looked out on infinity. Proust tried to persuade some of his noble friends, including Guiche, to become clients of Hauser.[67]

Though he and Proust wrote to each other in the second person singular, the financier had issued no warning when Proust had most needed one, and it was only now that he admitted: 'the interests of the banker who runs an account for a client are generally in inverse proportion to the client's interests'.[68] After going through the figures, he calculated that once Proust's liabilities were paid off, he'd be left with an annual income of only 27,390 francs. Proust was appalled, but not too dejected to make a literary allusion: 'But how did such pure gold turn coarsely into lead?'[69]

He'd have liked to spend another summer in Cabourg, but, not wanting to stay at the hotel, he asked Albert to find out whether his father would be willing to rent his villa. After a long delay, the answer was that Nahmias would gladly lend it to Proust, but wouldn't accept any rent. To Proust, who always insisted on paying his way, this was tantamount to a refusal.[70]

On most days he was spending less than fifteen minutes out of bed and, before making any of his rare outings, he had to calculate how much exertion would be involved. Wanting to see Mme Catusse, he wrote to check whether there was a lift in the block of flats.[71] In August and at the beginning of October he paid two visits to the elderly comte Clary, who'd been gentleman-in-waiting to the exiled empress Eugénie. Now paralysed and almost blind, he must have reminded Proust of the decrepit prince de Sagan, and it may have been partly to map the deterioration of Charlus that he spent so much time with the old count and put so many questions to his Japanese valet, Mineguishi. Afterwards Proust sent the valet an autographed copy of *Swann*, 'because I kept him up till the most unearthly hours'.[72]

Since the comte Adhéaume de Chevigné had died in 1911, the countess had been living in the rue d'Anjou house of Cocteau's family, and Proust went there twice in October. During the second visit, tirelessly researching to get the social background right, he questioned her about clothes and about cooking.

Like his recreation of his childhood, the process of transforming Alfred into Albertine and their relationship into a heterosexual one helped him to gain control over experiences which had been uncontrollable at the time he was having them. Now they had no existence except in his memory, and recollections which could have tormented him were being made into material he could mould. Except when working on the novel, he thought less about Alfred, dwelling more, during moments of inaction, on friends he'd lost during the war. 'I think about nothing else.'[73]

He fought against depression by working, and hugely enjoyed other people's reactions to his novel, as Marie Scheikévitch noticed when he visited her.

> There was often an obstinate modesty in his way of speaking about himself, especially at the beginning of a visit, but when he was certain the compliments paid to him were based on a profound familiarity with his work, his distrust changed excitingly into bursts of warmth and sincerity. At moments such as these, no one revealed joy more pure, or a nature nobler than his. He forgot his illness, his routine, his sadness, abandoning himself to childlike gaiety.[74]

She was probably thinking of herself when she asked what Odette was like as she aged. She became more beautiful, he said, but he was more interested in telling her about Albertine. He had, he said, 'a strong desire to unveil to you the part of myself you know least, and which is contained in germ in the first *Swann*, but it is invisible there.'[75] Writing on the blank pages in her copy of *Swann*, he gave her a detailed summary of the Albertine episodes, copying passages from his exercise books.[76]

The desire to reach outwards through his writing was at odds with the growing tendency to reclusion, and during late October and early November persistent fog, rain and snow encouraged this tendency. Dr Bize warned him that weather like this could be fatal to people suffering, as he was, from emphysema.[77] Certainly it had its effect, and in the middle of November, when Reynaldo came home on leave for the first time, daily asthma attacks stopped Proust from going to more than one of the parties at which Reynaldo was playing music he'd written at the front. On the day before he had to leave, he called on Proust, 'but I could hardly see him through the clouds of fumes'.[78] Two weeks later, still unable to go out, Proust asked Henri Bardac to discuss his affairs with Lionel Hauser.

No solipsist, Proust knew what he was doing in giving the book priority over everything else. He particularly regretted having to waste his talent for friendship. 'No one would like to like friendship more than I, and I believe no one would be better at it,' if only fate hadn't made him 'unable to draw profit from anyone but myself'. His life was unjustifiable, absurd.

> Instead of ennobling me, this kind of solitude smothers me, I can never work in it, and everything I have done has been done at other times. But I am myself only when alone, and I profit from other people only to the extent that they lead me to discoveries in myself, whether by making me suffer (more often through love than through friendship) or by their absurdities, which I dislike watching in a friend, and which I never mock, but they make me understand the characters.

During the last ten years he'd spent scarcely any time with his friends, and, during the last fifteen, had made only three attempts to see Anna de Noailles, though 'I admire her more than any other writer, feel profound friendship for her and recognise there are things in her conversation you do not find in her books.' While he still regretted seeing so little of her, it was 'salutary regret, since it makes me wonder whether I would not have "profited" from being with her (since we are speaking here only of intellectual profit)'.[79] The novel was written out of asking himself questions such as this one about friends who were no longer companions, while for companionship he depended increasingly on Céleste.

Sometimes their conversations would go on for hours. She was warm but simple. He had to explain to her that Napoleon and Bonaparte were the same man, and when she told him she'd seen a big black woman walking aimlessly up and down in the rue Tronchet with her handbag over her arm, he laughed delightedly and said she was one of those women who earned their living by walking up and down. But Céleste was devoted, conscientious, discreet and good at looking after him. No one could have done what his mother had, but Céleste was a better replacement than any manservant, and she was a good listener. When he was too unwell or too tired to write about the past, he reconstituted it by reminiscing. When he came home from an outing, he chatted about people he'd met, and she was a good audience for his mimicry. He was fond of asking for advice, and Céleste, because she was always there, was often consulted. After following a suggestion from his barber (or someone else), he came home one day with a Charlie Chaplin moustache. Did she think he looked foolish with this little toothbrush under his nose? On the contrary, she said, it made him look younger. He was almost equally delighted when she told him that he worked like a ploughman. He could never collect enough evidence to satisfy himself his parents had been wrong about his willpower.

He rarely displayed any emotion in her presence, and seldom let her assist him when dressing or undressing, except occasionally to help him with his shirt front if the buttonholes were stiff. One evening, about to go out, he asked her to hand him his boots and, when he put them on, she knelt down to button them up. Protesting, he almost jumped backwards, but he also said: 'Céleste, I love you.'[80] She'd just done something his mother used to do.

Of the friends he was no longer seeing, Fénelon was the most important. Modulating slowly into certainty, uncertainty about his death had been painful. 'What made it bearable was that I had not seen Bertrand for ten years, that the memory nourishes the heart, and they weaken together. . . . In spite of that, since Bertrand disappeared, I have been unable to stay in bed without quantities of Veronal, because I am so violently upset not by the uncertainty but by the confrontation between memory and the reality which contradicts it.' In fact it was less than five years since they'd met at the ball in the Hôtel Carlton, but it felt like more, and felt as if Proust had neither expected nor wanted to see him again, 'preferring to preserve the memory of a life in which we were together all through the day and all through the evening'.[81] All the same, he felt deep grief at the loss: 'This death, if you add up all the pain caused to three people out of four by the death of their best friend and even their parents, you do not arrive at the pain it caused me.'[82]

In February he received a long letter from Albu, who, after acting as chauffeur to the commander-in-chief, was serving as

a sub-lieutenant in the heavy artillery.[83] He still hadn't read
any of Proust's writing,[84] and they hadn't seen each other for
eight years, but he was still a friend, which could scarcely be
said of Guiche or Radziwill. Though it had once seemed highly
desirable that Guiche should propose him as a member of the
Polo Club, he had never once been there, or even found out
where it was.[85]

But friendship can still be felt in his letters; some of them
are warmed by the same childlike enthusiasm he displayed
when talking to Marie Scheikévitch about his novel. Asking
Maria de Madrazo for information about the influence of Carpaccio on the Venetian couturier Fortuny, he said he didn't
want to discuss artists 'in the continuation of my *Swann*,
because it's not a critical book, but about life'. In the third
volume, though, when Albertine was engaged to him – he
always said 'I' or 'me', never 'the Narrator' – she was going
to talk about Fortuny dresses, and he was going to surprise
her by giving her one. Imaginatively he was still involved in
the Alfred relationship as if it had a future, but whereas the
Narrator's mother never dies, he was incorporating Alfred's
death into the fantasy. 'The novel follows its course, she leaves
me, she dies. A long time afterwards, after great suffering
followed by comparative oblivion, I go to Venice but in the
pictures of XXX (let's say Carpaccio) I find a dress like the
one I have given her.'

Mme Straus offered to lend him her Fortuny coat, but a
book on the couturier would have been more useful. What he
needed was to have 'the right' to mention him. 'The result will
be a line here and there, but even to say one word about
something, and sometimes even not to mention it at all, I need
to saturate myself with it indefinitely. . . . There is not a single
day when I do not look at reproductions of Carpaccio.'[86]

Letters to friends often served as rough drafts for passages
in the novel. In another March letter to Maria de Madrazo, he
described Carpaccio's *Patriarch of Grado Exorcising a Demoniac*.
'There is quite a flowering of bell-mouthed chimneys, as
beautiful as a flowering of tulips, and I would not be surprised
if it had helped to inspire some of Whistler's little Venice
pictures.'[87] In *La Prisonnière* he wrote: 'I looked at the admirable
rose and violet sky with, silhouetted against it, tall encrusted
chimneys, tulip-like in their bell-mouthed shape and their red

flowering, and reminiscent of so many Venice paintings by Whistler.'[88]

Even when he decided to 'make peace' with Gide, it would have been impossible to start a real friendship with him. Proust sent Céleste in a taxi with a letter inviting him to call, and afterwards asked her to describe him. 'He looks like a fake monk, monsieur. You know, the ones who look at you all the more piously to hide their insincerity.'

Gide came on the evening of 24 February, wearing his home-spun cape. They talked about homosexuality and about Rivi-ère, who was now a prisoner-of-war and had been enthusiasti-cally re-reading *Swann* in the camp. Gide said his rejection of the novel was the biggest mistake he'd ever made, and they discussed the question of transferring it to the NRF, which, unlike Bernard Grasset, was still active as a publishing house. Though he'd been upset when publication was interrupted, Proust now had no desire for the remainder of the novel to appear before the war ended. But, knowing he didn't have long to live, and thinking that if preparations were started well in advance, the NRF could bring out all three volumes simultaneously, he felt less bound by his obligations to Grasset than he had two years ago.

Since the spring of 1915 his eyesight had been deteriorating, and by March 1916 it was painful to do more than a little writing, but he procrastinated about consulting an oculist, saying he never felt well enough during the day to visit one.[89] Another reason for staying in bed was that he was expecting another visit from an army medical officer and didn't want it to look as if he'd recovered his health.[90]

His financial experiences of 1915 and his correspondence with Hauser had made him more cautious about income and outgoings. His revenue from shares during 1915 had been 32,778 francs, while interest had amounted to 22,000. He was paying an annual rent of 7,000 francs for the flat, so how was he going to make the income tax authorities believe he was living on an income of 10,000? Not that he'd go on having to. By the end of March he'd paid off 80 per cent of his liabilities to the brokers, and, once he'd settled the remainder, he was expecting his annual income to be in the region of 30,000. Far from feeling sorry for himself, he felt sorry his mother couldn't have known how well things would turn out for him, as this 'would have relieved her of so many anxieties'.[91]

As he went on working at the novel, Vinteuil's imaginary music began to bulk larger. In the afternoon on 14 April he went to hear Fauré's chamber music performed at the Odéon by the composer, Lucien Capet, André Hekking and Raymond Pétain. The programme included the first quartet for piano and strings, and, wanting to hear it again, Proust decided to organise a performance in his flat. He got Fauré to introduce him to the other musicians. Proust needed to get his piano tuned and, though he went out in the afternoon, he was at first unable to find a piano-tuner. But he paid Gaston Poulet, Louis Ruyssen, Victor Gentil and Amable Massis 250 francs to play him Beethoven's Opus 130 quartet in B flat major and César Franck's quartet. Afterwards he wrote to Pétain, inviting him to call '(*on condition that you allow me to offer you an indemnity for this inconvenience*)' so that they could discuss further private performances.[92]

At the committee meeting of the NRF on 14 April Gide won support for the idea of taking over publication of the novel, and when René Blum arrived in Paris on leave, he offered to act as intermediary between the NRF and Grasset. Meanwhile Gallimard wrote to Proust, who needed reassurance. What if he lost Grasset and then found the NRF wanted to abandon the book or demand major changes? He felt no resentment, he said, about the rejection three years ago, and didn't want the NRF to publish it now if the only motive was to make amends. He said the book was liable to shock both reviewers and readers, especially homosexuals, who'd find the characterisation of Charlus uncompromising, and he asked whether the NRF would be prepared to pay Grasset an indemnity.[93]

He wasn't sure whether he'd signed a new contract with Grasset after the discussions in 1913 about leaving him – Veronal and other medicines were affecting his memory, or so he believed – and in briefing Blum for the negotiations he was less magnanimous than he'd been three years ago, making out that only a small proportion of the second volume had gone into proofs, and that these proofs were so full of mistakes the printer would have to start all over again. He also wanted Blum to give Grasset the impression that he urgently needed to earn money and that the NRF was going to publish the book before the war ended.[94]

In mid-May, by selling about 100,000 francs worth of shares, he reduced his debt to the Crédit Industriel, and Lionel Hauser found another bank to take over the outstanding balance at an interest rate of only 5.5 per cent. But this wasn't the end of Proust's dealings with the Crédit Industriel. In June Hauser calculated his annual income would be roughly 24,000 francs.[95] But at the beginning of July, when he heard Nicolas had died of pleurisy in a military hospital, he was less generous to Céline than he usually was on such occasions. Though he liked her much better than Anna, it was impossible – because she and Céleste hated each other – to offer her a home.[96] Six weeks later she was still uncertain whether she'd get a pension from the army.

It was hard to contact Grasset, who was convalescing in Switzerland after catching typhoid fever in the army. He'd been given extended sick leave, followed by a temporary discharge, while at his offices in the rue des Saints-Pères the skeleton staff had been cut down to two women. Still enjoying intrigue, Proust asked Blum to write to Grasset. Proust would take the letter to the offices and try, by bribing the concierge, to have it forwarded by registered mail.[97] Scrupulous though he was on some matters, Proust was now so desperate to have the book published by the NRF that he distorted some of the facts. Grasset had been paid for printing 749 pages, he said, but had incurred a printer's bill for only the 525 pages in the first volume plus a few pages of the second, which hadn't been printed till May 1916.[98] This doesn't tally with what Proust told Gallimard, who was going to have all the galleys for the second volume forwarded to him.[99] Blum's letter to Grasset was written on 11 July, and the reply, dated 1 August, shows how upset he was at the prospect of losing Proust, 'one of the authors who matter most to me'. He said he'd incurred heavy expenses through Proust's reworking of the second volume, but that he had 'too much pride to hold on to an author who no longer has confidence in me, and I will arrange to free him completely from any commitments. But first I want you to pass my letter on to him. . . .'[100]

Anxiety over the delay helped to screw up the tension which produced a heart attack, more painful than dangerous, in early August, and for several days even the slightest movement felt

like a precarious undertaking.[101] Suffering for over ten days
with neuralgia and a high temperature, he couldn't even digest
his usual milk.[102] His eyes were still painful, which made writing difficult, and he was having trouble with his teeth. He
could make little headway with the novel, though he was
thinking about the episodes involving the young girls and
planning to quiz Albert about girls he'd known in Cabourg
and what preparations they'd have made for going out to
dinner.[103]

Still ill, and weak from being unable to digest any food,
Proust was nervous Grasset might campaign in the press
against the second volume and make out he'd 'refused to publish such filth'.[104] Writing to him, Proust started the letter
'Cher Monsieur', and said he found the letter to Blum 'most
offensive'. Two years ago, when Grasset had offered him complete freedom, Proust, though he'd been under no legal con-
straint, had remained loyal to him. But Grasset should
acknowledge that the war had changed everything. To a publisher who had so many authors, the work of one could be
'only a negligible grain of sand', but if Grasset would like
compensation, all he had to do was name the figure, so long
as it was a modest one. After writing a fifteen-page letter,
Proust apologised for starting the last page on a sheet of paper
that already had the words 'Madame la duchesse' written on
the other side.[105] He crossed them out.

By the last week in August, he was feeling better, but fragile,
and his eyes were still painful.[106] Lionel Hauser now recommended an oculist and did his best to persuade Proust not
to go on procrastinating. He'd gone out during the afternoon
when he was looking for a piano-tuner, and even if he couldn't
get up during the day, and an oculist couldn't bring all the
necessary apparatus to the flat, it would be easy to arrange an
evening consultation.[107] Replying twelve days later, Proust said
Dr Bize was arranging for an oculist to call at the flat.[108]

Grasset's answer, abandoning his claims on the second
volume, is dated the 29th. After this Proust went back to
addressing him as 'Cher ami', but said he was asking for too
much money, which was unfair to the NRF. After all, Proust
had financed the printing costs and remained proprietor of the
novel.[109] In October he sent the manuscript of *Jeunes Filles* to
Gallimard, together with the first twenty pages of *Guermantes*
and notes about the two remaining volumes.

In October, when the comtesse Greffulhe repeated the mistake of sending an invitation too late,[110] she offered, by way of compensation, to call on him one evening between five and six, giving him the opportunity to cancel the rendezvous by telephone if he wasn't well enough to see her,[111] but he elegantly rejected the overture: 'It is of course impossible that you should venture into my trench among the asphyxiating gases which are my anti-asthma fumigations.'[112]

His brother Robert, who'd joined the army with the rank of sub-lieutenant, had come back as a major. He'd been commended by his commanding officer for bravery, but had made himself ill by working day and night.[113] Now, after seeing almost nothing of him ever since Robert had left home, Proust made inordinate efforts to call on him, and paid for them with another period of illness.[114] He was averaging less than one outing a week,[115] but to celebrate the end of the year he went to a party Mme Daudet gave on 27 December for Francis Jammes. The other guests included Paul Claudel and Misia Edwards. Songs by Darius Milhaud with words by Claudel and Jammes were performed.[116]

TWENTY-SEVEN

FINAL FLING

With all great writers it's easy – though dangerous – to assume that the life, like the piano accompaniment of a great song, was the best imaginable backing for the voice as we hear it in the work. It would be simplistic to say *À la recherche* could have been written only by an invalid, but it couldn't have been written by anyone who didn't oscillate between invalid isolation and exuberant partying.

While his mother was alive, a crucial biographical question was how much he exaggerated symptoms to gain her love. After her death, as his illness progressed, and his self-knowledge deepened, interplay between voluntary and involuntary elements became more complex. More aware of how important the voluntary elements were, he became more self-critical, which was dangerous, because it led him to ignore symptoms, trying to override with adult willpower tendencies that had been launched in boyhood. Unconsciously, perhaps, he was trying to punish himself; consciously he took enormous risks, as if what remained of his health were so exiguous that he couldn't lose much, even if he staked everything he still had.

Besides, he was bored. It was good to win plaudits from writers he admired, but ever since childhood he'd been bombarded with the same demoralising symptoms, increasing in severity but tedious in their lack of variation – asthma, like the most self-indulgent writers, was boringly repetitious – and it was frustrating to have Céleste as the only audience for his reminiscences and his mimicry. At the beginning of 1917 he decided to enjoy what was left of his life.

Obviously, choices he'd previously made had exacerbated his sufferings. His mother, giving her hunches priority over prescriptions and professional advice when she lovingly nursed him, had implanted the idea that instincts about illness are the best possible guide. But his resistance to common sense was overdeveloped. For nearly two years pain in his eyes had been

disrupting his work, but though he'd got up in the afternoon
to look for a piano-tuner, he'd resisted all advice and refused
to get up for an oculist. He'd also been suffering from toothache, but hadn't been to see a dentist. Obviously he'd been
making the wrong decisions. Therefore it was time to do the
opposite of what he'd been doing.

Like most new years, 1917 started badly for him. In early
January he went for over two days without resting, but hyper-
activity became almost euphoric when he harnessed it to his
work on the novel. 'I have neither sat down (one cannot sit
when a long time has gone by without going to bed) nor
stopped speaking.'[1] Like Flaubert, he tested what he'd written
by reading it out out loud. Being out of bed was so enjoyable
he decided to be more active. Even heart attacks could be
regarded as misleading messages designed to keep him in bed.
No, why should he let them keep him indoors? During the
first week of March he suffered 'terrible cardiac crises which
put me between life and death',[2] but he'd felt suspended
between life and death for so long that nothing was going to
stop him from changing his routine. The ultimate penalty was
death, which no longer scared him. By mid-March his weight
was down to forty-five kilos, but, despite insomnia, he was
enjoying himself – inviting friends to his flat and dining out at
Larue's. He'd made enough progress with the novel – the
revised manuscript of *Jeunes Filles* was being typed at the offices
of the NRF – to feel entitled to reward himself. Nearly ten
years had passed since the dinner for Calmette at the Ritz, but
his memories of the hotel were so pleasant that he longed to
have dinner there again 'if it is still under the same management'. Since abandoning his summer holidays in Cabourg,
he'd had nothing of the hotel luxury he loved except at the
Ritz, and he even thought about settling in as a resident.[3]

Colette saw him there one night, receiving four or five
friends. He was wearing his fur coat over his evening suit, and
his cambric tie was half unknotted.

He never stopped talking, trying to be gay. Because of the
cold, and making excuses, he kept his top hat on, tilted
backwards, and the fan-like lock of hair covered his eyebrows. Full-dress uniform, but disarranged by a furious
wind, which, pouring over the nape of his hat, rumpling the
calico and the free ends of his cravat, filling in with a grey

ash the furrows of his cheeks, the hollows of his eye-sockets and the breathless mouth, had hunted this tottering young man of fifty to death.[4]

After one of Proust's dinner parties at the Ritz the head waiter, Olivier Dabescat, would sometimes be given a tip of 300 francs, which aroused protests from Proust's friends at the bad example he was setting.[5] But he succeeded in getting preferential treatment. When he went to the Ritz to write, he insisted on a room with a constant temperature of 86 degrees, and he sat in front of the enormous fire, wearing his overcoat. Here he used Olivier in the way he'd used the staff at the hotel in Cabourg, collecting gossip about his illustrious clientele. Olivier felt uncomfortable in the overheated room, but couldn't protest when Proust asked him to stay and questioned him. He said he was going to put Olivier into the novel exactly as he was. The head waiter also went to Proust's flat, arriving about midnight and staying till three or four in the morning, distracted by Proust's charm into forgetting that time was passing, despite the stuffiness of the room.[6]

Proust was also making new friendships. Hearing that a friend of Henri Bardac and Cocteau, the twenty-eight-year-old Paul Morand, a young diplomat, had loved *Swann*, Proust called on him at eleven-thirty one evening. Morand was in his pyjamas.

'You will find, quite rightly – do please go back to bed, you'll catch cold, you'll no doubt find it unseemly that someone wakes you up at this time of night, but I scarcely ever go out, I got up late – and besides it's a mistake to get up because I pay for it the next day with atrocious suffering and with far too many ridiculous and exorbitant attentions, which are however a necessity, because chronic illness is an old lady who adores it when one shows regard for her (you would be entitled to complain, you too – although you're a young man and not an old lady – that I'm lacking in regard for you when I ring your doorbell at midnight) if I've taken this liberty it's because I had the strongest desire to meet someone (this is you) who has expressed about me – so I've been told – (I don't yet know you well enough for anyone to tell me about anything you've said which wouldn't be agreeable and even delicious for me to hear) who has expressed about me, or to be more exact about my book – I wouldn't dare to say

"the most apposite" opinions . . . but the most delicate . . .'
The sentence was only beginning. It wouldn't finish before
the middle of the night. This singsong cavilling, reasoning
sentence, responding to objections one wouldn't have
dreamed of making, raising unforeseen difficulties, subtle in
its triggers and its quibbling, with astonishing parentheses
which suspended it in the air like balloons, dizzying in its
length, surprising in the assurance concealed under the deference, and well constructed in spite of its disjointedness, it
plunged you into a mesh of such confused difficulties that
you would have let yourself be numbed by its music if
you hadn't suddenly been tugged by some thought about
unheard-of depths or dazzling comedy.[7]

Morand was at Proust's flat one evening in late January when
Antoine Bibesco arrived. He was still based in London, but he
was on leave. He asked Proust whether he'd changed.
'You're less.'
'Less what? Less intelligent? Less beautiful?'
'Less, that's all.'
Which made Antoine anxious.[8] Clément de Maugny, who
was on leave from the army, was another visitor during February, and on the 14th Antoine came back with Morand. The
next day, hearing Cocteau was ill, Proust went to see him.
The temperature in Paris was seven degrees below freezing,
and, coming home, Proust found his 'heart was in great pain
(physical)'.[9]

His friendship with Morand started to develop more rapidly
when the young diplomat bought a copy of Swann and sent it
to him with an inscription. Proust interpreted the joke to mean
this was a book Morand might have written had he not had
better uses for his time. When he was dining at Larue's on 22
February with Henri Bardac's brother, Jacques, Proust heard
Morand was dining at Viel's, in the boulevard de le Madeleine,
with a beautiful woman, and sent a note saying he didn't dare
to intrude but would like to see him soon.[10]

The woman was the thirty-eight-year-old princesse Soutzo.
Born in Rumania of Greek and Rumanian parents, she'd married prince Dimitri Soutzo-Doudesco. Formerly an attaché in
Paris, he was now at the Rumanian front[11] while she was living
in the Ritz. When Proust dined with her and Morand at Larue's
on 4 March, he studied her black wrap and ermine muff 'like
an entomologist absorbed in the nervures of a firefly's wing'.[12]

Afterwards he was mortified to discover he'd been wearing an old waistcoat and a shirt stained with shaving soap. 'What must the marvellous lady have thought of me?'[13] Making Antoine Bibesco arrange a dinner for all four of them at Ciro's, he appeared in a starched shirt with a very high tight collar. It was partly that he was falling in love with another couple, as he had with Albu and Louisa, and partly that he was, as Morand saw, helplessly in love with youth. 'In his eyes the brilliant start made by an adolescent took on an incomparable beauty; he followed it with curiosity, despair and envy of the purest, noblest quality. On his weak, withered and ardent personality, a creature in flower projected a shadow that didn't make him take offence.' The irresistible allure of youth tempted him to spend more of his limited time out of bed with new young friends than with old ones.[14] He tried to compensate for this in his letter-writing. Hearing Mary Finaly was dead he told her mother: 'I think of you with a tenderness, a grief you cannot imagine. Nothing from the past is lost to me.' And he told Mme de Chevigné: 'I shall never forget you. Besides, do your eyes not tell all of us not to forget them? They are two forget-me-nots.'[15]

He caught cold after an evening out on 22 or 23 March, 'which, pushing my asthma up to its highest degree, meant that the neighbours, hearing a continuous growling and spasmodic barking, believe I have bought a church organ or a dog, or at least that by impure (and purely imaginary) relations with a lady I have had a child which has whooping cough'.[16] He recovered in time for the princesse's dinner party at the Ritz on 30 March. She promised to send a car for him, but forgot, which made him very late, but another guest, the princesse Lucien Murat, was equally late, and it was nine-thirty when they sat down to eat. Lucien Daudet was one of the guests, but Antoine Bibesco, who'd been expected, was in bed with flu.[17] Afterwards both princesses and Morand accepted an invitation to dine at the Ritz again on 3 April as Proust's guests, but at dinner parties he now spoke less than he used to. His voice was no longer strong enough to override interruptions.[18]

On 6 April Emmanuel Bibesco arrived in Paris. Three years ago, returning from Japan, he was already in the grip of general paralysis, and by now, one side of his face was paralysed. Antoine had never mentioned this to Proust, who was taken by surprise when Antoine rang his bell one evening in late

April. 'You know, Emmanuel is downstairs, but he's waiting in the cab because he doesn't want anyone to see him.' Morand was with Proust, and when they went down to the cab, the prince offered to sit in the tip-up seat, but Antoine, to protect him from showing the paralysed side of his face, made him stay where he was by sitting down next to him: 'The two Bibesco brothers are staying in the back.' With a laugh, Emmanuel told the driver to drive backwards. 'Then Marcel Proust and Paul Morand can see where they are going.' Proust started worrying about how long Emmanuel would want to survive, but after he went back to London, news about him was reassuring.[19]

He went on dining at the Ritz whenever he felt well enough for an outing. Afterwards he went up to the princesse Soutzo's drawing-room – the liftboy had been instructed to take him up without announcing him. When they ate together, as they often did, he insisted on contributing at least half the cost of the meal.[20] The friendship caused a quarrel on 23 April, when he was at one of her dinner parties with Morand, the comtesse de Chevigné, Cocteau, the marquise de Ludre and the abbé Mugnier. The comtesse, who'd been under the impression Proust never went out, failed to conceal her rage when the princesse revealed the truth, and Proust, who'd scarcely slept for six days, was too exhausted to be tactful. Starting an apologetic letter to her the same evening, he assured her that she was 'prettier than ever'.[21]

Emancipated by his drastic change of routine, Proust could celebrate his new freedom on both the highest and lowest social levels. He invested money in a male brothel. He'd known Albert Le Cuziat since 1911, when he was a thirty-year-old footman working for the comte Orloff.[22] Finding him infallibly well informed about genealogy and etiquette, Proust called him a walking *Almanach de Gotha*, and consulted him on such questions as whether a bishop would be given precedence over a general at a duchess's dinner party. Proust sometimes asked questions by letter and sometimes sent a taxi to fetch Le Cuziat.

He often sent taxis to pick up people who could provide useful information. Studying criminal psychology and anthropology in Italy, Sylvain Bonmariage had collected about 700 case-histories in a card index. After arousing Proust's interest in a conversation, he was taxied to the flat and asked to copy out his notes on the case-history of a homosexual count who enjoyed flagellation and tried to strangle a young lover who was about to get married. Proust seems to have used this case-history in developing the relationship between Charlus and Morel.[23] The baron's character had been sketched out in 1908-9, but Proust hadn't arrived at the name Charlus, which he took from a vaudeville singer who worked as a male prostitute. According to Maurice Duplay, the real Charlus had the body of a circus strong man and the head of an old woman. 'You never saw so many scars on one face.'[24] Ennobling his name was a joke which only a few friends would share, but Proust took perverse pleasure in giving the name of a male prostitute to a character who had Montesquiou's voice and the body of the effete and elderly baron Albert-Agapit Doazan,[25] whom Proust had first met in 1892, at the salon of Mme Aubernon de Nerville. He was fat, with a bloated face and a moustache dyed black. He hated Montesquiou, who'd taken Yturri from him.

Proust took pride in the need to find squalid details for the novel. 'The writer, you see, is a strange bee who indiscriminately sucks his honey from flowers and from excrement. What matters is the quality of the honey.'[26] Often the instincts of the researcher were tied up inextricably with sexual desire, as they were when he helped Le Cuziat to open the brothel, contributing both furniture and money. The house was conveniently close – in the rue de l'Arcade, a turning off the boulevard Haussmann. Proust spent a good deal of time there, and it was soon after the brothel opened in 1917 that Charlus was made to share the Italian count's taste for flagellation. To Céleste, who hated Le Cuziat, Proust talked about visiting the brothel to watch through a small window while an industrialist from the north of France was chained to a wall and whipped 'till the blood spurted out all over everything'. Proust told her he hated having to witness such sadistic scenes. He did it, he said, only for the sake of his book. This is unlikely to be true, but he never wanted to be beaten.

What he did in the brothel has been described by Marcel Jouhandeau, who, when he was about thirty, worked there and kept a notebook. In the spring of 1917, according to him, Proust used to come in and pick up a partner by watching through a window while boys played a card game. When Jouhandeau was chosen, he had to go to the upstairs room where Proust would be lying in bed with the sheet drawn up to his chin. The boy had to take all his clothes off and masturbate. Watching him, Proust did the same and, if he achieved a climax, the boy would smile at him and leave the room without touching him. If he failed to come, he'd give a signal which meant Le Cuziat was to bring in two cages, each containing a rat which hadn't been fed for three days. The cages were positioned on the bed, end to end, and the flap-doors were lifted. 'Immediately the two starving animals threw themselves at each other, emitting heart-rending cries and tearing at each other with their claws and teeth.'[27] Once, Gide records, 'Proust explained to me his preoccupation with combining, for the sake of orgasm, the most heterogeneous sensations and emotions. This is how his pursuit of rats, among other methods, is to be understood; in any case this is how Proust was inviting me to understand it.'[28]

The furniture he provided for the brothel had been in store, and Proust afterwards said that in giving it away he'd contributed to the happiness of other people. But in the novel, when the Narrator presents some pieces of furniture inherited from his aunt Léonie to the madame of a female brothel, he afterwards feels guilty. 'As soon as I saw them again in the house where these women were putting them to their own uses, all the virtues that had pervaded my aunt's room at Combray at once appeared to me, tortured by the cruel contact to which I had abandoned them in their defencelessness! Had I outraged the dead, I would not have suffered such remorse.'

Perhaps Proust wanted to make himself feel remorseful by outraging the dead through the furniture, and there may – in spite of Céleste's testimony that the photographs of his mother left the chest in his room only when he showed them to her – be some truth in the story that he took them with him to the brothel and showed them to clients, who were expected to react with some such question as 'Who the hell's this little tart?' This would tie in with the compulsion registered in the early fiction to degrade someone who is also adored. In the story 'La Confession d'une jeune fille', the mother dies of an apoplectic stroke after seeing her daughter in the arms of a young man, while, for the girl, the sensual pleasure is insepar-able from pleasure in 'causing my mother's soul, the soul of my guardian angel, the soul of God, to weep. I have never been able to read without shuddering with horror stories of

those beasts who torture animals, their own wives, their own
children; I now felt that in every sensual and sinful act there is
just as much ferocity on the part of the body in the throes of
pleasure, and that in us so many good intentions, so many
pure angels are martyred and weep.'

From the mother who is totally adorable but impossibly
demanding there are many escape routes, but they all lead into
blind alleys. Proust developed a taste for physical gratification
from partners who, being almost mindless, made no demands
of any kind. Among servants, workmen, peasants, sailors, he
could find partners who were willing, on payment, to let
themselves be used. Having once taken great pleasure in food,
he liked to compare sex with eating. An early draft of *Sodome
et Gomorrhe* contains a passage he later cut: 'You love a woman
the way you love the chicken whose neck you happily wring
to eat it at dinner, except that with women you want to kill
them not so much for the pleasure as to deprive them of
pleasure with other people.' Alongside the sadistic dehumanis-
ation of the sexual object is the fear of possessive jealousy. He
despaired of finding anything between the two positions.
Either you reduce the person to object status or else resign
yourself to endless frustration at being unable to claim undivided attention.

At the same time, he seems to have felt friendship, respect
and even admiration for some of the young soldiers he met at
the brothel when they were on leave. Unlike him, they were
being useful in the war, risking their lives. 'I admire soldiers
more than churches, which were only the solidification of a
heroic gesture, which is today being repeated every second.'[29]
To the soldiers he liked best he went on sending weekly parcels
when they were back at the front – tobacco, cakes and chocolate.[30]

Certainly the men he met in the brothel had an effect on the
language he used in the novel. It is only in late additions to
the text that we find such slang expressions as 'fout' le camp'
and 'zigouiller' (murder). Probably it's also to the brothel that
Proust is indebted for the way Albertine's vocabulary changes
in *Guermantes*. The Narrator takes her slang to be an indication
of sexual availability.[31]

If the novel was Proust's thoughtful distillation of his life, it
was upsetting to find other people could write about him by

regurgitating shared experiences and reproducing superficial impressions. At Larue's on 22 February Léon Daudet mentioned a book of his that was about to appear, *Salons et journaux*. When, after finding a description of the figure he'd cut in the days of going regularly to Larue's, Proust read that his *Swann* was 'often breathtaking and full of promise',[32] he was deeply hurt by the patronising praise, but he wrote to congratulate Léon on looking 'so young, so handsome (and even improved), so agreeable, so unaffected'. Proust was 'swimming in joy', he said, at the evidence of the friendship Léon felt or might be able to feel for him, but the letter culminates in a statement about literary truth: 'it is like a physical *law*. One either finds it or fails to find it.' He again attacks Péguy – this time for approximating to a point three times instead of stating it once accurately. Léon, he obviously feels, is open to the same charge.[33]

Proust's principle was at the opposite extreme. Like some of the impressionist painters, he maintained that, in a work of art, the subject didn't matter.[34] If the writer is capable of apprehending the truth, it will make itself felt. In the novel the painter Elstir is the mouthpiece for the view that 'regattas, race meetings where well-dressed women are bathed in the glaucous light of a seaside race-course could be, for a modern artist, a motif as interesting as the festivities Veronese or Carpaccio so loved to portray were to them'.[35]

The commonsensical friends who'd have advised Proust against resuming such an active social life would have predicted he wouldn't be able to sustain it, but in May he was still going out a lot, in spite of the uncured trouble with his eyes and the springtime hay-fever which exacerbated his asthma. For forty-eight hours he felt as though he was going to suffocate.[36] But he recovered in time to dine with Guiche in mid-May. Proust wanted to say goodbye before he left for the United States. The US had declared war on Germany at the beginning of April, and Guiche was on a mission to advise the Americans about manufacturing aeroplanes for military purposes.

On another evening outing Proust was dining at Larue's when the *patron* said: 'That gentleman opposite you is the King of England's son.' Proust didn't know whether to believe him, but 'if it is true, he is charming and has done a certain number of extremely kind things which princes never do'.[37] It was the Prince of Wales, later, briefly, Edward VIII.

About six days after dining with the Guiches, Proust went to the Théâtre du Châtelet to see Cocteau's new ballet, *Parade*, with music by Satie, choreography by Massine and décor by Picasso. On Saturday 25 May Morand received a telephone call from Céleste, inviting him to dine with M. Proust, but without any ladies, because M. Proust was still unshaven. Morand wasn't free, but they met two days later, which may have caused what Proust described as 'a long and terrible attack'.[38] But it failed to make him more cautious.

Another new friendship with a young man was with Jacques Truelle – a diplomat who'd lost a leg at the beginning of the war. After they'd dined together in March and begun to correspond, Proust encouraged him in his literary ambitions, and in May, when Truelle lost his father, sent him a warm letter of condolence.[39] And before the end of the month he went back to the Robert de Rothschilds' home, where the old butler remembered him.

When Marie Scheikévitch gently reproached him for neglecting his old friends,[40] he tried to fix a meeting with her,[41] but paid no heed to her caveat. One evening at the Ritz, the Ballets Russes designer, Léon Bakst, complimented him on *Swann*, saying several times it was 'superior to some famous works . . . to which I know it is infinitely inferior'.[42]

The Ritz was a meeting point for aristocratic refugees from salons and châteaux which had been closed down by the war, and Proust often found himself face to face with people he hadn't seen for years, such as the Clermont-Tonnerres.[43] The main inconvenience was that, since the hotel was opposite the Ministry of Justice, wartime austerity regulations couldn't be ignored, and it was impossible to linger over dinner when lights in the restaurant were turned out at nine-thirty or sometimes nine o'clock. At Ciro's and the Crillon, the lights weren't switched off till two in then morning, and Proust could stay on after dinner, correcting proofs, observed only by Americans he didn't know. But he disliked the waiters at the Crillon[44] and felt more at home at the Ritz, thanks mainly to Olivier, who was always willing, if Proust arrived after the restaurant closed, to have a table laid for him under the staircase leading up to the first floor.[45]

It was so long since he'd seen Louisa de Mornand that one day in a restaurant he mistook another woman for her, but she wrote to him after her brother was killed at the front in April, and he wrote back affectionately, condoling and saying how much he'd wanted to meet her brother. 'I have always been curious about the way a liked or loved face could be transposed from the masculine sex into the feminine, and vice versa.'[46]

Believing he had little to lose, Proust went on squandering his health and his money, risking and surviving heart attacks, eating at the Ritz, extravagantly entertaining friends there, taking endless taxis and tipping with reckless generosity, though he'd soon start selling his furniture to raise cash. July was full of social activity, though he paid for each outing with exhaustion that made it difficult for him to wake up in the evenings and start his fumigations,[47] and at the beginning of the month it was hard to travel around Paris in the evening because the taxi-drivers stopped working at seven in protest at the surtax imposed by the Prefecture of Police on drivers who bought more than two cans of petrol.

On the 5th, Proust was one of the princesse Soutzo's nine guests at a Ritz dinner party. The others included Morand, the comtesse Étienne de Beaumont, Walter Berry and the abbé Mugnier, the priest who'd converted Joris-Karl Huysmans in 1892. He was the vicar of an aristocratic parish, Sainte-Clothilde, and had been attending society dinners for thirty years. Proust afterwards sent some of his pastiches to the abbé. On the 14th he saw the de Beaumonts again, giving a dinner party at the Ritz for them, the princesse and Morand. Afterwards the de Beaumonts invited him on the 17th and again on the 21st. On the 27th he went to another of the princesse Soutzo's dinner parties at the Ritz. This time Cocteau was among the guests, and so was Joseph Reinach, whose hair had whitened. Proust's admiration for him had turned to violent disapproval: 'The majesty of age seemed to have reached this inferior brother, and at moments his eyes looked almost human.'[48]

The comte de Beaumont talked during the meal about an amateur hypnotist from Compiègne, unintelligent but effective, and telephoning him after they'd finished eating, they engaged him to come along. He soon put the comte to sleep, but when he prodded his victim's cheeks with pins and scissors, the comtesse screamed.[49] Proust was sceptical about the hypnotist's powers: when the princesse Murat was regaining consciousness, he had to speed up his gestures to make it look as though he was in control, and he seemed nonchalantly ignorant of anatomy. Inviting the spectators to stick pins into a victim who was in a trance, he said: 'Try not to prick him in an artery.'[50]

The demonstration was interrupted by an air-raid. There had been Zeppelin raids in 1916, but this was the first in which the Germans used their large bombers, the Gothas. The lights went out, and in the moving beams of searchlights, French planes slid into action. When the sirens sounded from the Tour Eiffel, Cocteau said: 'That's somebody else treading on the Tour Eiffel's toe: she's crying.' 'Proust, perfectly calm, carries on with the conversation: he says people in trances ask to be told about the future in order to evade their past.'[51] Then he went out on the balcony and stayed for over an hour watching 'that admirable Apocalypse in which planes, climbing and diving, were forming constellations or pulling them to pieces'.[52]

While the sky was full of brilliant activity, the interior of the Ritz was like a hotel in a Feydeau farce: 'ladies in night-dresses and even in bath-robes roamed through the vaulted lounge, clutching their pearl necklaces to their heart'.[53] The action on two levels reminded him of El Greco's *Burial of Count Orgaz*, in which the apocalyptic action in the sky parallels the action on the ground. He makes the point in *Le Temps retrouvé*, when the Narrator discusses air-raids with Saint-Loup, who says that in the large hotels American Jewesses would have been seen in their nightdresses, hugging to their ravaged bosoms the pearl necklaces which will enable them to marry a ruined duke.[54]

Though Proust was consciously being spendthrift with his energy, he was forced into planning his outings more carefully at the beginning of August, when the lift in his house broke down, adding two flights of stairs to each journey. Wanting to attend a soirée to be given by Valentine Gross, a friend of Cocteau's, on 20 August, he was planning to climb the stairs slowly and in silence.[55]

On 22 August, Emmanuel Bibesco killed himself in London at the age of thirty-five. A telegram from Antoine revealed the bare fact of his death; the details emerged later. He hanged himself in a hotel. Trying to console their sister, the princesse Alexandre, Proust argued that someone so intelligent and so well informed about toxins would never have chosen 'a form of death so pointlessly painful, so atrocious in the memory of other people, and so precarious' if he'd been in full possession of his willpower and his reason.[56] And, in a letter to princesse Marthe Bibesco, Proust made a mistake which may have been significant – referring to 'Antoine's death'.[57] A month later he still hadn't got used to the idea he'd never see Emmanuel again. He told Antoine Céleste had been in tears after the suicide,[58] but in her book she says he was prone to exaggeration about weeping.

It was twenty-four years since Gide had come to see him, but in correspondence Proust was pressing explicitly for a greater degree of familiarity. Why was Gide still addressing him as 'Mon cher Proust', instead of 'Cher ami'? With his failing eyesight, he said, he'd been making Céleste read to him from *Nourritures terrestres*, and she'd been referring to it ever since in conversation. Inviting Gide to pay another visit, he said he liked Gide's face, and remembered a smile on it which revealed moral beauty. Applying his strategy of quoting from or alluding to the work of almost every writer to whom he sent a letter, he claimed to have been following Gide's precept: 'That which someone else would have written equally well, do not write it.'[59] Proust was quoting from memory; what Gide says in the book is: 'That which someone else would have done equally well, do not do it. That which someone else would have said equally well, do not say it – or written equally well, do not write it.'[60] But Gide was only reiterating a dictum of Rémy de Gourmont. The only excuse a man has for writing, he says, is to unveil for others the sort of world reflected in his individual mirror. He should say things no one else has said in a form never previously formulated.[61] Staying on good terms with Gide was easier than fulfilling his obligations to the NRF. On 13 October 5,000 pages of proofs arrived. Correcting them would have been laborious even if his eyesight had been normal, but 'it will mean 15,000 since I shall have to correct them three times. Without glasses and without much eyesight. It will be a frightful job.'[62] But even this failed to scare him into arranging a prescription for the spectacles he knew he needed. Four days later a publisher's advertisement in *Excelsior* announced the continuation of his novel in five volumes: *À l'ombre des jeunes filles en fleurs*, *Le Côté de Guermantes*, *Sodome et Gomorrhe* in two parts and *Le Temps retrouvé*.

Though he'd been deeply upset by Emmanuel's suicide, it had

made no practical difference to his daily routine, but in late October he was about to lose the young man who'd rapidly become his best friend: Paul Morand was being promoted and posted to Rome as secretary to the embassy there. Told before the news became public, Proust wrote: 'I am very touched you have taken the trouble to inform me of your appointment and my misfortune.'[63]

Since meeting Morand and the princesse, he'd tasted pleasure and elation unequalled since he'd been the third point of the triangle involving Albu and Louisa, and surpassed in intensity only by the brief and unhappy affair with Alfred. But now he was to lose Morand, and at the beginning of November his depression was exacerbated by heart attacks and by fog. 'I have little time left before my death (but there is nothing sad about this, since for some years I have been no good for anything, even correcting my proofs).'[64] And in the last week of November he wrote: 'Princesse, my cardiac condition is so bad this evening I am afraid my heart may suddenly go to pieces.'[65]

But he went on with his busy social life. Getting up in the evening on 7 November, he was unsure whether he'd be well enough the next day for the dinner party with the princesse and the de Beaumonts, but he was, and he'd have gone on afterwards to see comte Louis Gautier-Vignal if it hadn't taken the night-porter at the Ritz over an hour to find a taxi for him.[66] Gautier-Vignal was an extremely rich friend of Lucien Daudet whom Proust had known for two years. Before he died in 1982, he admitted to having had an intimate relationship with Proust.

When Proust went out on the 9th to meet Robert de Billy, he caught a cold while waiting for a taxi to bring him home. On the 14th he dined alone at the Ritz, but he'd invited Truelle and four other friends to join him there afterwards. They arrived late. Unable to find a taxi, they'd had to walk, which was hard for the one-legged Truelle, and Proust was embarrassed at being unable to take them into the restaurant, which had closed at nine-thirty.[67] The next evening he dined at the Crillon with the princesse and Walter Berry, afterwards making himself ill by walking a long way in the fog.[68] But he dined there again with her and Marie Scheikévitch on the 21st, when seven or eight other friends joined them at the table after the meal. The princesse, who was due to have an appendectomy, wasn't well enough to join him when he dined with Berry again on the 23rd, or on the 25th, when he had dinner at the Crillon with Berry and Guiche, who afterwards took him to meet Mme Hennessy, daughter of the Catholic socialist leader, Le Cuziat Hennessy. In the evening he again dined at the Crillon with the princesse, Morand, Truelle and Mme Catussa, and on both the 27th and the 29th he saw Guiche at Mme Hennessy's. All this was precarious: one of his invitations to Berry was phrased: 'I intend, dead or alive, to invite you for dinner . . .'[69] And he complained to Marie Scheikévitch that Guiche, who was in Paris only briefly, 'is making me ill without realising it because he does not know I am incapable of going out so much'.[70]

He calculated he was now spending almost ten times as much as before he started going out so often, and his first idea for raising money was to sell excerpts of the forthcoming volumes to newspapers and magazines.[71] When he decided to sell some of his furniture, it wasn't merely to solve his own financial problems. Marie Scheikévitch had talked frankly about losing her fortune in the Russian Revolution, and there was another old friend he wanted to help, an artist who could no longer sell her work – perhaps Madeleine Lemaire or perhaps Laure Hayman.[72] Feeling himself to be under a 'moral obligation',[73] he remembered Mme Catusse had once mentioned, when he was worrying about income tax, that his four Louis XVI armchairs and sofa would fetch a good price. Unused in the flat, they were being eaten by moths. He could also sell some tapestries, but wanted to keep the arras. He could sell the two carpets which were in store and the leather chairs in the dining-room where he'd never once eaten a meal. Mme Catusse, who'd given up so much time to help him when he moved, was one of the friends he enlisted to help; the others were Walter Berry and the Strauses. Marie Scheikévitch was moved when he offered to share the proceeds with her, and though she said she couldn't accept,[74] he went ahead with the sale. Berry came to view the objects in the flat, and Mme Catusse sent along two female antique dealers, for whom the shutters were opened at two o'clock in the afternoon – 'the only time this has happened since I have been living in the boulevard Haussmann'.[75] But it was through Émile Straus that the sale was effected. By keeping the carpets and the Louis

XVI furniture in his home and showing them to dealers, he got 10,000 francs for the furniture and 4,000 for the carpets.

Proust didn't go out any less when Guiche left. He started December by going to the princesse's dinner party in the Ritz. He left early, feeling ill, but, though he failed to find a taxi until nearly all the other guests had left,[76] he wrote a long letter to her before going to sleep. The last ten days before Morand left were going to be so tantalising, he said, that it would be better to take a large dose of Veronal and not wake up till he was in Rome. But the pain of the separation would be almost eclipsed by the pain of knowing one always recovered from grief. Meanwhile the princesse should be careful not to get overtired. 'Think of your body, which is more alive than any other body I know.'[77] And in another letter he advised her to have the operation before Morand left: from seeing his mother after her operation, he remembered 'the extraordinary bonus of beauty' that comes on the day after an operation. 'I am suffering in advance at thinking of this marvellous pallor that ensues on anaesthesia . . . you will have no other opportunity (let us hope) of showing yourself transformed into the most transparent and most sublime alabaster.'[78]

Wanting Morand to know he'd be missed, Proust could do no better than refer him to a passage in *Guermantes* which had already appeared in the *NRF*.

> A memory, a grief, are mobile things . . . There were days when I no longer thought about Mme de Guermantes. But on certain evenings, crossing the town towards the restaurant where Saint-Loup was dining, I could scarcely walk, it would have been said a part of my chest had been cut into sections by a skilful anatomist, removed and replaced by an equal quantity of intangible suffering, by a coefficient of nostalgia and love. And it makes no difference that the stitching was well done, life is rather uncomfortable when the viscera have been replaced by homesickness for someone, it feels as though this person is taking up more room than they are, can constantly be felt, and then, how complicated it is, being forced to *think* a part of one's body.[79]

He dined at Robert de Billy's house on 2 December. On the 4th he had dinner at the Ritz with Truelle and some other friends, and went out again on the 6th. On the 9th, the evening Morand was leaving, he turned down an invitation from the princesse Edmond de Polignac, but saw her a few evenings later, and on the 16th went to her house for a dinner party followed by a recital of organ music. He was making little headway with correcting the proofs he'd received in mid-October, and by mid-December the NRF was putting pressure on him.[80]

He'd lost his certificate of exemption from military service and, if a policeman asked to see his papers, he was in danger of being arrested as a deserter.[81] His depression exacerbated his recklessness, and his cardiac condition was so bad he knew he was risking his life by going out so much. 'It cannot go on like this for long,' he wrote on 29 December.[82] And to Dr Bize he wrote: 'I have to take more care than an old man of eighty if I want to finish this book.'[83]

TWENTY-EIGHT

EJECTED

At the beginning of 1918 there was deep snow in Paris and 'the rays of the moon were lying as if they had been poured out over the snow in the boulevard Haussmann, now untouched by the broom of any sweeper',[1] and though Proust would have liked to visit the princesse Soutzo, who was still unwell, he scarcely had the nerve to walk the hundred yards to the Ritz.[2] When a New Year's Day letter arrived from the overtipped Olivier, it felt rather like being given a reference by a servant, but Proust welcomed it as 'a magnificent example to hold up against the bad manners of the others'.[3] He was corresponding with Walter Berry and sent him a box of cigars 'as an ironic reminder of the clouds you could not send up to the firmament on the ceiling at the Beaumonts''.[4]

At the end of January, when sirens sounded to signal another air-raid, Proust had just left Gabriel de la Rochefoucauld's house after a private performance of a Borodin string quartet. Instead of going back indoors, he got into a taxi, but it broke down in the avenue de Messine, where he got out and stood in the street, listening to the gunfire and falling bombs. When the taxi arrived in the boulevard Haussmann, Proust invited the elderly driver to sleep in the small drawing-room if he was scared of driving back, but he must have been deaf. 'Oh no, I'm going to Grenelle. It's only a false alarm and they haven't dropped anything at all on Paris.' He was still speaking when a bomb exploded not far away.[5]

As Proust told Morand, the war was like a substance interposed between him and everything else, but he was too moribund to be scared of raids.[6] Céleste, on the other hand, though generally brave, was frightened of bombs and guns. Whenever the sirens sounded, she went down to the shelter, and Proust, underestimating the depth of her commitment to him, was nervous she might want to leave Paris.[7]

On 3 February, attending a reception at Mme Daudet's house

in honour of Francis Jammes, he met François Mauriac, who decided he was rather small and round-shouldered, with bulging eyes. Stuffed into a very high collar, said Mauriac, his starched shirt bulged 'like a breastbone'.[8] He went to dine with the Daudets again two nights later, and had dinner with the princesse Soutzo twice in February.

Memories of Emmanuel Bibesco's last visit made Proust all the more alarmed when his illness entered a new phase in early April with partial loss of control over his speech, and facial paralysis. 'It is hard for me to interpret certain symptoms. The doctors are aggravating in refusing to tell the truth. Unfortunately I have the art of extorting it from them, which does not by any means amount to the same thing as if they told me, because they say nothing, and only their embarrassment betrays them, and one is left threatened but not forewarned.'[9] Taking the new symptoms to mean he might not have much time left for revising the novel, he introduced them, together with his uncertainty, into the action. Walking through the Champs-Élysées, the Narrator remembers the stroke which had finished off his grandmother one afternoon she was taking him for a walk. Her blithe unsuspectingness is compared with that of a clock's hands, ignorant of when their movement is going to make the hour strike.

> Perhaps the fear of having already traversed almost the whole of the minute which precedes the first chime, when this is already preparing itself, perhaps this fear of the blow about to ring through my brain, this fear, was it like an obscure knowledge of what was going to happen, like a reflection in consciousness of the precarious state of the brain whose arteries are about to collapse, which is no more impossible than this sudden acceptance of death that comes to wounded men who, although the doctor and the will to live both try to deceive them, see what is going to happen and say: 'I am going to die, I am ready,' and write their farewell to their wife.[10]

Dr Bize advised him to rest and do no writing, but he couldn't resist the inclination to do more.[11]

In April he was approached by a man who asked him to inscribe the copy of *Swann* he owned – one of the five printed in 1913 on Japanese vellum. Jacques de Lacretelle had already questioned him about the sources of his fiction, and now, on three blank vellum pages, he wrote a three-page statement: 'there are no models for the characters of this book; or rather there are eight or ten for each one'. In a pigeon-shooting sequence he thought of Odette as looking like the courtesan Closmesnil, but only at that moment. Similarly, some of the stained windows in the church of Combray came from Évreux, some from the Sainte-Chapelle, some from Pont-Audemer. Discussing the sources of Vinteuil's music, Proust pointed to 'the charming but really mediocre phrase in a sonata for violin and piano by Saint-Saëns, a musician I do not like', and he'd drawn also on César Franck, Schubert and Wagner.[12]

Working at this time on the preface for Blanche's book, he incorporated some of the unused Sainte-Beuve material, including the point about his confusion of the artist's inner self, which does the creative work, with his outer self, which other people meet. Describing Auteuil as it had been during his boyhood, and his long stays at his uncle's house during spring and early summer, Proust used the description he'd written of his uncle's dining-room and the garden, which had since been cut in two when the road was built.[13]

One of the painters Blanche discussed was Fantin-Latour, who rooted himself in to the sedentary stability of bourgeois life. Proust connects this with the life style of his grandfather, who never left Auteuil except when Paris was under siege.[14] In a passage which was going to annoy Blanche, Proust went back to his old theme of the tug of war between serious work and social distractions. Blanche, he said, was a witty and elegant man who might have spent too much time in society, but, fortunately, his 'reputation for scandal-mongering quickly alienated the people who could have stopped him from painting'.[15] 'Nature invents protective neuroses when they are needed, or tutelary misfortunes to stop the necessary talent from lying fallow.'[16]

He was thinking mainly of himself. He'd fought audaciously against the protective illness which had stopped him from going out, but it appeared to be counter-attacking fiercely in late May, making it look as if he might have to stop seeing friends.[17] As the recent symptoms became more pronounced, he lost control over his speech and part of his face was paralysed. He felt so convinced his brain was affected that he asked a brain surgeon, Dr Joseph Babinski, to operate on him, but the doctor refused; Proust was deluding himself.[18]

By mid-June, he was recovering, but he was depressed to hear that a demented patient had killed Dr Pozzi. A regular dinner guest at the boulevard Malesherbes, the charismatic doctor had been the first to invite Proust into society, had helped Robert throughout his career and had testified Proust was unfit for military service. Writing fancifully to Pozzi's former mistress, Mme Straus, Proust said the murder reminded him of Calmette's: both victims had been innocent, and it looked as if they'd been 'sacrificed mystically' – Calmette to usher in the war, and Pozzi, perhaps, to foreshadow peace. Perhaps the two men were 'the two bleeding pillars which stand at either end of the war.'[19]

But on the western front the German army was advancing. Soissons and Rheims had fallen at the end of May, and Paris appeared to be in danger. Princesse Soutzo went back to Biarritz, and Proust thought of joining her there, but he'd always been good at finding reasons to postpone a journey, and Céleste was ill. It was fortunate he was in Paris during June, when Gaston Gallimard, who was living in the United States, came back on a visit and arranged to buy from Grasset the unsold copies of *Swann*, which now appeared in the bookshops in a new wrapper, with an NRF label pasted on the title page over the name Grasset. Gallimard also agreed to bring out the pastiches and essays which for ten years Proust had wanted to see in print as a collection. He wrote to Lucien and Robert Dreyfus,[20] asking for help in finding texts of his newspaper pieces, and in the summer he rewrote the Saint-Simon parody, making it six or seven times as long. Luxuriating in his mimicry of the style and his identification with the eminent courtier, he mingles current events with history, and friends with characters from the early eighteenth century.

He introduces the capture of Château-Thierry by the advancing German army on 31 May, and mentions Albu, Guiche and Mme Straus, who'd be pleased to find herself at the court of Louis XIV.[21] In the pastiche she receives the princesses of the Blood, but fails to return their visits. There was nothing Proust enjoyed more than letting literary energy filter into his friendships while he stayed in bed; in his additions to the pastiche he also mentions the Hinnisdals, Mme Standish, the princesses Soutzo and Murat, and even Olivier, who becomes the king's head butler. Proust asked Mme Straus' permission, but – fearing a veto – not princesse Murat's.[22] The parody centres on the claims of the Murats to the rank of sovereign princes.

It was in about July, over four years after Agostinelli's departure, that Proust lost his heart to another young man who'd eventually be appointed as secretary and would live in. Henri Rochat, who'd been working under Olivier at the Ritz, was Swiss, silent and self-effacing. He had beautiful handwriting and ambitions as a painter. Proust sometimes took him out to look at paintings, but Henri had a liaison with a girl who lived not far away, and Proust had little happiness from the relationship. In October he said it was poisoning every minute of his existence, and would certainly be the cause of his death.[23] Six weeks later the situation hadn't improved. Mme Straus was told he'd 'embarked on emotional things without any outcome or any pleasure, constantly producing weariness, suffering, ridiculous expenditure'. The liaison even lowered his self-esteem. 'I scarcely like myself,' he said.[24] When Reynaldo was on leave, Proust invited Jean-Louis Vaudoyer to dine in his bedroom at ten-thirty with them and 'a boy I have been sheltering for several months but who will not disturb us because he says nothing'.[25] Céleste, who inevitably disliked the young man, thought he was trying, like Ernest, to affect airs of superiority and to rise above his station. Proust dictated to him, but found it more exhausting than helpful, she says.[26]

He still hadn't received any royalties for copies of *Swann* sold during the war, and complained to Grasset, who refused to pay until his negotiations with Gallimard were completed. Proust's letter to him was written on 18 July, the day the Allies launched their great counter-attack, and they crossed the Marne four days later. With Mme Straus at Trouville, Proust thought of going to Cabourg, but again he used Céleste, who'd gone home to her family and wouldn't come back till the second week in August, as a pretext for staying where he was.[27] He still drank coffee in bed, but had stopped eating there.[28] He dined alone at the Ritz several times, and once with Mme de Chevigné. He also dined in town a few times, and found he was still trying to think of the Castellanes as young, though their son was in the war, while the duc de Gramont had become 'massive, venerable and white'.[29]

But it wasn't long after this that the war ended. The armistice with Austria-Hungary was signed on 3 November, and with Germany on the 11th. 'What a marvellous allegro-presto in this finale after the infinite slowness of the beginning and everything that followed.'[30] But he didn't approve of the victory celebrations: 'We are mourning so many dead that such gaiety is not the form of celebration one would prefer.'[31] 'It is only in the plays of Shakespeare that one sees all the events precipitated in a single scene and hears in a single scene: Wilhelm II: "I abdicate." The King of Bavaria: "I am the heir of the most ancient race in the world, I abdicate." The Crown Prince weeps, sighs, his soldiers assassinate him . . . But for my part, I am such a lover of peace, because I resent human suffering, I believe all the same that since one has been wanting total victory and a secure peace . . . I would have liked conditions to be more rigorous.'[32]

Odilon Albaret returned from the war with his health apparently ruined. Proust not only resigned himself to having him live in the flat – 'he is to be hospitalised here', he complained to Lucien – but helped him to recuperate, prescribing tea made from cherry stalks, which seemed to work therapeutically.

High society was never quite the same after the war, which had both a levelling and a demoralising effect. The Narrator looks at the social changes through the eyes of a charming American woman, a friend of Bloch and of the duchesse de Guermantes. Though the people she talks about form the core of the new society, their names are unfamiliar to the Narrator, while the stories he tells her about the society of the past are full of names which mean nothing to her.[33]

Much had disappeared which Proust was sorry to lose, but there was some social compensation in the flurry of diplomatic activity which brought bright young men to Paris. He made friends with a twenty-year-old Englishman, a diplomat who'd arrived during 1917. In his introduction to the published version of Henry (Chips) Channon's diaries, Robert Rhodes James cautiously reveals that Proust 'took an interest' in Chips, who was charming and attractive. The interest was sufficient – and sufficiently reciprocated – to make Proust write about six hundred *billets doux* and postcards. Before destroying these, Channon consulted a friend, who suggested he should give them to the British Museum with a 'restriction' lasting for thirty years or longer, but in January 1944 Channon wrote: 'Gone are all the Proust letters which in my youth and folly I burnt.'[34]

Shortly after the Armistice Channon sat between Proust and Cocteau at a dinner party. Cocteau, he noticed, was already haggard at twenty-seven.

> They seemed to compete as to which could be the more engaging. Proust is quieter, longer winded and more meticulous. His blood-shot eyes shine feverishly, as he pours out ceaseless spite and venom about the great. His foibles are Ruskin, genealogy and heraldry. He knows the arms and quarterings of every duke in Europe. His black hair was tidily arranged, but his linen was grubby, and the rich studs and links had been clumsily put in by dirty fingers. Proust has always been kind to me. . . . Does the world know that he tips with thousand franc notes, and that he has prolonged evening gossips with the Figaro coiffeur at the Ritz? With questionable taste, I asked him if it was true at dinner, and he nodded.[35]

On one of these evenings at the Ritz Proust met the writer Sydney Schiff, who used the *nom de plume* Stephen Hudson, and his wife Violet. Having read *Swann* during the war and corresponded with Proust, they'd arranged to meet him after dinner at the Ritz, but didn't know him by sight. When they'd finished their meal, Olivier told them M. Proust was in the restaurant and was expecting them. Sitting at his table wearing white kid gloves and a fur coat which was open, revealing a coloured waistcoat buttoned high up to the neck, he was eating asparagus. He struck Violet Schiff as looking about thirty-five, and after his death it seemed to her remarkable that he'd written so well about old age in *Le Temps retrouvé* without living beyond the age of fifty-two. He took them to his flat in Odilon's taxi. 'The entrance hall looked sordid, the staircase was in darkness, and those not using the lift had to hurry from one floor to the next in order to reach the switch before the light went out.'[36]

With the war over and with the novel finished, Proust should have been able to relax, but, already suffering from insomnia and from severe pain around the heart, he was plunged into anxiety when his aunt told him she'd sold the building to a banker, who was going to convert it into a bank. Since Proust had no lease, he might have to move out with only a few days' notice. He'd stopped paying rent in 1916, saying he'd resume when the war ended and he could cash his 30,000 franc Warburg cheque for German shares he'd surrendered in 1914. This might mean the new landlord could demand arrears of rent – about 25,000 francs.[37] The panic exacerbated Proust's aphasia, and he developed laryngitis, which gave him a temperature of 102 degrees and kept coming back each time he got up.[38]

It would cost a great deal to move, and he wasn't yet earning any money from the novel, though in late November the printer completed his work on *Jeunes Filles*, which came to 433 pages. Proust had been adding so much to the later volumes, from *Sodome et Gomorrhe* onwards, that by December he was expecting the novel to fill six volumes (not just five).[39] To raise money he could think of no alternative to selling more furniture. He still had a carpet the Shah of Persia had given his father, as well as a Smyrna carpet. He'd once tried to make the Strauses accept both as a present,[40] but they'd refused, and now got him 3,000 francs for the Smyrna, while Walter Berry arranged for his tapestries and furniture to be moved into the cellars of the American Chamber of Commerce, where anyone could view them. Proust also had a lot of silver he never used.

Céleste was the only woman who was allowed to see Proust in bed, but after Antoine Bibesco got engaged to Elizabeth Asquith, he brought her to the flat, and, by a trick, into the bedroom. Apparently intending to leave her on the landing, he asked Céleste whether he could go into the bedroom alone. When she went in to ask Proust, Antoine picked up his fiancée like a doll and marched in after Céleste, throwing Proust into a paroxysm of embarrassment. But once he felt more relaxed with the new princesse, he liked her so much that he made an addition to the Saint-Simon pastiche, which was already in proof.[41] She is described as probably the most intelligent woman in any country and as 'looking like one of those beautiful figures painted in the frescoes one sees in Italy'.[42]

Albu, ranked by Proust's Saint-Simon as 'greatest of my friends', sent a press-clipping which said landlords couldn't evict civilian tenants who gave notice they wanted to stay on for two years. On the other hand, since Proust couldn't have stopped the new owner from covering over the inner courtyard and converting the house into a bank, there was no point in trying to stay on when he'd have found the builders' noise insufferable. It was Guiche who turned out to be the most helpful of his friends, negotiating with the banker, who not only waived arrears of rent but paid a handsome indemnity. Guiche also arranged the sale of the cork from his walls to a manufacturer of corks for bottles. Or so Proust told Walter Berry,[43] but Céleste denies this: according to her, the sheets of cork were stored in a garage.[44]

The helpfulness of Proust's friends was matched by his to them. Marie Sheikévitch, who was still in financial trouble, was hoping to earn money by painting, and, gently warning her this was unrealistic, Proust made an equally unrealistic suggestion. Since she had connections with *Le Temps*, why didn't she offer to write a daily column? To save her from the drudgery of writing the piece, he'd ghost it for her, sending Céleste over with the copy every day. It was as unlikely she'd accept such an offer as that his health – which was even worse than it had been five years ago, when he'd proposed himself as a regular columnist for *Le Figaro* – would allow him to write a daily column, but he was sincere both in making the offer and in saying he wanted her to keep the whole of the proceeds, not share them with him fifty-fifty.[45]

The same compulsive generosity towards friends made him start planning a second Saint-Simon pastiche, though he was ill at the end of January for several days, with a sore throat and a high temperature.[46] What friends – especially rich ones – appreciated more than any present he could give them was the literary tribute he paid by working in references to them in what he was writing. He wanted to say more about the princesse Soutzo, whom his Saint-Simon had already mentioned as 'the only woman who, unfortunately for me, has been able to prise me out of the withdrawal in which I had been living since the deaths of the Dauphin and the Dauphine'.[47]

At one of her Ritz dinner parties he met the young Harold Nicolson, a member of the British delegation negotiating the peace settlement at the government buildings in the quai d'Orsay. Nicolson has described the 'white, unshaven, grubby' diner who questioned him eagerly on English etiquette and, when they met again at the end of April, talked about homosexuality. When Nicolson said it was 'a matter of glands or nerves', Proust, whose relationship with Rochat was coming to an end, contradicted him: it was 'a matter of habit', he said, but withdrew, when challenged, into calling it 'a matter of delicacy'.[48] He asked questions about the behaviour of upper-class English ladies towards social inferiors they found unsympathetic, and when Nicolson assured him they remained polite, Proust thought he was joking. As he revealed when he mentioned Nicolson in a letter, Proust assumed the name Harold started with an A.[49]

Proust's last meeting with Montesquiou took place in the middle of the night, when the comte almost forced his way into the flat and stayed for two hours, reciting his verse and tapping the rhythm with his foot, indifferent to the risk of waking neighbours. He was going to live in the south of France, he said, and promised to send gilded chocolates from Nice. They were likely to be poisoned, Proust told Céleste.[50]

When Gallimard had committed himself to the novel, he'd underestimated the trouble that would be caused by additions to proofs, though he'd been with Copeau when he looked at the proofs Proust had corrected for Grasset. 'But it's a new book!' Copeau said.[51] By 1919 Gallimard had forgotten this, and Proust had to argue: 'Since you have the goodness to find in my books something fairly rich which you like, understand that it is precisely due to this overnourishment, which I reinject into the books while living what materially translates itself into these additions.'[52]

In mid-March, when he sent Gallimard the text for the collection he called *Pastiches et mélanges*, he dedicated it to Walter Berry. The reason, he told Antoine, was that Berry had won the war by persuading the United States to join in.[53] Helpful though Berry had been in letting him put his furniture on show in the basement of the American Chamber of Commerce, buyers were unresponsive, and the prices realised in the saleroom were pathetically disappointing. A handsome sofa, almost new, fetched forty francs; the chandelier from his parents' dining-room thirty-eight.[54]

He was also frustrated by delays over publication. The NRF's monthly review, which had been suspended in 1914, was to be relaunched on 1 June, and Jacques Rivière approached Proust about excerpting the new volumes of the novel in the first issue. Gallimard promised to hold back publication for only a few days after publication of the review, but the books wouldn't appear in the shops until the end of June.

It would have been nightmarish anyway for Proust to make

arrangements about moving out of his flat. His two main reasons for moving in had been that his uncle had lived there, and that the house belonged to the family. Now, at the age of forty-eight, he was being forced for the first time in his life to inhabit unfamiliar territory. Besides, he was too ill to look at properties. He was suffering from aphasia, which grew worse when he was under stress. He wanted to believe what the doctors told him – that he'd brought it on himself by taking too much Veronal; by now he was using about 1½ grammes a day – but his fear was that the aphasia which had overtaken his mother before her death would overtake him before he'd got the rest of the novel into print.[55]

For the time being, at least, he could go on enjoying his outings, and one attraction of a fifth-floor flat he found in the rue de Rivoli was its proximity to the Ritz. The writer Jean-Louis Vaudoyer, who'd helped to get him interested in the Ballets Russes, went to look at the flat for him, but he was too slow in making up his mind. He had to move out of the boulevard Haussmann flat by the end of May, and in the final weeks neither he nor Céleste got much sleep. Sharing the strain with him, she became tetchy and unmanageable.[56] On 29 May, with only two days in hand, he still had nowhere to go. What saved him from his predicament was an offer from Réjane's son, Jacques Porel, who was living with his wife and baby at his mother's house in the rue Laurent-Pichat, a small street off the avenue Foch. Réjane lived on the second floor, the Porels on the third, and on the fourth was a large furnished flat she'd been keeping for her daughter. She rented it to Proust for a month, but he had to dispose of all the furniture which had filled his flat for over thirteen years. The grand piano, the huge mirrored wardrobe, the big chest and some other pieces were sent into store, but the dining-room suite and most of the inherited furniture was auctioned. He didn't attend the auction, but sent Céleste, who couldn't bear to see the crystal chandelier knocked down for five francs and brought it back for him.

In the panic-stricken days of emptying the flat, one of the minor problems which looked like major problems was what to do with four dresses which had belonged to his mother. He sent Céleste out to deliver three of them to members of the family, and the fourth to Mme Catusse. This was the dress his mother had worn only once, at Robert's wedding. When Marthe had asked for it, he'd refused to part with it.[57]

After he moved into the new flat, his temperature remained for days on end at 104, and he wasn't expecting to feel any better until he moved into a permanent home.[58] The proximity of the Bois de Boulogne, which was higher in altitude than the flat, made his asthma worse, while the walls were so thin that, deprived of his cork-lining, he was tormented by a variety of noises. He told Mme Straus he was 'in a house where you hear every word the neighbours say, where you know each time a window is opened, where I have not slept for twenty days'.[59] On the other side of the courtyard the Comédie Française actor Le Bargy could be seen through uncurtained windows, declaiming lines, going into his bathroom, quarrelling with his wife and emitting loud howls.[60] At first Proust was amused, later enervated.

But when June was nearing its end, he'd still found no alternative accommodation. He was thinking of moving to Nice, though Dr Bize was against it. Even if he travelled with a nurse, and even if she gave him injections on the journey, it was doubtful whether he'd be well enough to stay there or well enough to travel back. But could he possibly face a winter in Réjane's house? Could he accustom himself to the central heating?[61]

He confided his address to Mme Catusse, but to almost none of his other friends – not even Lucien – and, because of delays in forwarding mail from the boulevard Haussmann, his contacts with them were even more tenuous than usual. Nor was he in any state to prepare literary Paris for the long-delayed publication of his second volume. Instead of writing round, as he had before *Swann* came out, to secure advance publicity in various newspapers, he approached only Robert de Flers, asking for a front-page review in *Le Figaro*. Gide, Léon Blum and Louis de Robert were among the reviewers he suggested, but after *Jeunes Filles*, a new edition of *Swann* and *Pastiches et mélanges* had all been published during the last week in June, *Le Figaro* was silent until 7 July, when a front-page news item appeared in print that struck Proust as too small.[62]

As in 1914, when the first edition of *Swann* came out, it was worrying that the public would have no notion of the overall structure. 'I see readers imagining I am writing the story of my life, trusting myself to arbitrary and fortuitous associations of ideas.'[63] In fact the architecture of the vast novel owes something to his deep-seated interest in cathedral architecture, and at one stage he'd considered giving the volumes such titles as 'Porch One: Stained-Glass Windows in the Apse'.

During his first two months at the new flat, he rarely got up, and couldn't settle down to correcting proofs.[64] He dined three or four times at the Ritz, but not until ten-thirty in the evening.[65] His most urgent task was to find a new home, and he could do little from his bed. He didn't want the new flat to overlook a courtyard or a garden, and he couldn't decide whether to rent temporary accommodation and go on searching until he found a flat on the top floor in the rue de Rivoli or the rue de Castiglione – 'at least in the part where the proximity of the Seine dilutes the dust'.[66] The advantage of the top floor was there would be no overhead footsteps. When a fourth-floor flat became available in the boulevard Malesherbes, he liked the idea of moving back into familiar territory. He'd have preferred to be higher up and farther away from the dust and the noise of the trams, but he was less irritated by street noise than by neighbours, and he'd be next door to Robert Dreyfus, whom he questioned about humidity, and the thickness of the walls, and smoke from the nearby railway, and whether any building work was imminent in neighbouring houses.[67] But he hesitated too long, and the agent let the flat to someone else.[68]

The first impression of *Jeunes Filles* was quickly sold out and reprinted, which gave him less pleasure than distress, because he wanted to send inscribed copies to his friends, and though he protested when Gallimard sent only copies of the second impression, a book club had bought up all available copies of the first.[69] Proust couldn't even send Céleste out to search in the shops because he'd given her leave of absence for a niece's wedding. It was small consolation that a third impression followed quickly on the second. Failing to find copies even for Mme Straus, Anna de Noailles and Maurice Barrès, he could scarcely sleep for three weeks. It wasn't until the end of the year that he got hold of a few copies.[70]

In the summer there had been talk of launching a new political party led by the intelligentsia. Advocating 'an intellectual federation of Europe and the world under the aegis of victorious France, the guardian of all civilisation', a manifesto appeared on 19 July in *Le Figaro*'s literary supplement. Among the fifty-four signatories were Francis Jammes, Henri Ghéon, Jacques

Maritain, Paul Bourget and Daniel Halévy. Though Proust was less sceptical about the value of intelligence than he'd been when he started work on Sainte-Beuve, he thought the idea of intellectual federation was stupid,[71] and told Jacques Rivière: 'I do not even believe intelligence is *primary* to us . . . before it I posit unconsciousness, which it is intended to clarify – but which determines the reality, the originality of a work.'[72]

His asthma was troublesome in July:[73] 'The rattling in my throat drowns the noises of my pen and of someone taking a bath on the floor below.'[74] Odilon went in his taxi to the Ritz every day and often at night to buy the ice-creams Proust found soothing to his throat, though he would swallow little else, and he was in so much discomfort he could see no point in staying alive except to finish the novel. His aphasia seemed to be getting worse, but he was confident it wasn't a symptom of general paralysis. 'I am afraid the day will come when I can no longer articulate any words. Then I shall have only one thing to do – not see a single living person, shut myself up in the dumbness the illness is imposing on me.'[75]

When Jacques-Émile Blanche called on Réjane, not knowing Proust was in the house, he found out from the butler, and, going up to see him, thought he looked about twenty-nine – no older than he did in the 1891 portrait, which was on the wall, 'but his cheeks were paler, blanched by the furnace in which he fused the metal of his book'.[76]

In August Proust was planning to stay in Cabourg, leaving on the 15th, but he changed his mind after dining at the Ritz with Berry on the 14th. He'd briefed an estate agent in the place Victor-Hugo to look for a flat, and during September, while Réjane and the Porels were in Venice, he was told about a fourth-floor flat in the rue Hamelin, a residential street close to the avenue Kléber. The building, which had a lift in it, had just been bought by a woman, Mme Boulet, who wanted to rent furnished flats. Proust sent Céleste to look at it and, without even seeing it, decided to take it. He wasn't intending it to be his permanent home, but he felt ill at ease in Réjane's house, and here he could make himself more comfortable.

TWENTY-NINE

A SMALLER SPACE

Though Proust was paying for a furnished flat, he had Mme Boulet's furniture moved out. To minimise the noise, he wanted fitted carpets everywhere, and Céleste went along to supervise the carpet-layers. As at the boulevard Haussmann, he had three switches installed above his bed, one for the bell, one for the lamp and one for the kettle. The layout was similar to that of the old flat, but the rooms were smaller.

He moved in on 1 October 1919. His bedroom was at one end of the flat and Rochat's at the other. Céleste's opened on to the hall. There were two salons, one large and one small, and a fourth bedroom, which was soon filled with books and unused silver. With the screen behind it, Proust's big brass bed, badly tarnished by his fumigations, was positioned as close as possible to the fireplace, but now there was barely enough room at the foot of the bed to open the door. The little Chinese cabinet was put in the same position as before, and so were the three tables for exercise books and writing papers, handkerchiefs, papers for lighting the Legras powders, and watch.

A row of books stood on the mantelpiece. On the windows he had blue satin curtains. The pictures he kept included portraits of his parents, Blanche's portrait of him, and the painting by Helleu. If his previous bedroom had struck visitors as over-furnished, this one seemed almost bare. There was only one window, while the woodwork, which hadn't been repainted, had big scratches in it,[1] and, worst of all, it was difficult to heat without using the central heating, which he couldn't bear. The fireplaces were small and smoke drifted back into the room, making him feel ill. So no fires were lit.[2] Relentlessly, almost religiously, he worked in the unheated room, never complaining of the cold, asking only for more sweaters, but never letting Céleste help him into them, and never putting them on. As before, he put them on his shoulders, like a cloak, and, as before, they slipped off, piling up behind him.

In November he was so ill that for several days he was 'incapable of the slightest movement'.[3] In spite of being told it was bad for his aphasia, he'd become more dependent on Veronal.[4] But he wasn't sufficiently ill to ignore an essay by Albert Thibaudet in the November issue of the *NRF*. Titled 'Une Querelle littéraire sur le style de Flaubert', it argued: 'Flaubert was not a great thoroughbred writer . . . complete verbal mastery was not one of his natural gifts.' With his books stored in a warehouse, Proust would have to quote from memory, as he did in his letters, but he defended Flaubert in a fifteen-page essay, 'À propos du "style" de Flaubert'. 'By the entirely new and personal use he made of the past definite, the past indefinite, of the present participle, of certain pronouns and certain prepositions,' Flaubert 'has renewed our vision of things almost as much as Kant, with his Categories, renewed our theories of Cognition and the Reality of the external world.' As Thibaudet later objected, La Fontaine had already been using the same form of narrative imperfect in the seventeenth century, but Flaubert used it more systematically.[5]

Not that it was Flaubert's style which made Proust admire him: 'I believe only metaphor can give a style some kind of immortality, and perhaps there is not a single beautiful metaphor in the whole of Flaubert. Moreover, his images are generally so feeble that they scarcely rise above those his most insignificant characters could have found for themselves.'[6]

Proust's view of Flaubert had changed. If he'd asked himself when he was writing his pastiche 'whether the tune I heard inside me depended on the repetition of imperfects or present participles', he'd have been incapable of mimicking it. Pastiche may be a form of literary criticism, but to write one is the opposite of writing the other, satisfying though it is to move between the two activities. 'Our mind is never content unless it has been able to give a clear analysis of what it had already produced unconsciously, or a living recreation of what it had patiently analysed.'[7]

Proust can't resist the opportunity to advertise his novel in the essay. His structure, he says, though concealed, has been carefully planned, while the 'phenomenon of memory', on which his whole 'theory of art' is based, was so important to Gérard de Nerval that almost any of his works could have had the title Proust had thought of using – 'Intermittences du coeur'.[8]

The essay was delivered to the *NRF* on 10 December, the day the judges met to award the Prix Goncourt. In September Proust had told de Robert he was intending to apply, and no instinct could have been more inspired. When Reynaldo had gone to stay with the Daudets in their country house near Tours, it was clear Léon would go all out to support Proust, and both Robert de Flers and Louis de Robert had been well placed to exert influence. Daudet arrived in the afternoon of 10 December with the news Proust had won, and was still with them when Gallimard, Rivière and their editorial manager, M. Tronche, arrived. But Proust could hardly believe his good fortune, especially when he saw advertisements in the newspapers proclaiming: 'Prix Goncourt: Raymond Dorgelès. *Les Croix de bois.*' The words '4 votes out of 10' followed in smaller print.[9] Six of the judges had voted for Proust.

Suddenly, at the age of forty-nine, he was famous. In the morning, twenty-seven newspapers carried articles about him. The most discerning was in *Excelsior*, where Rivière welcomed the novel as the largest 'psychological monument' since Saint-Simon's memoirs, and praised Proust for penetrating so scrupulously and patiently into his characters' feelings. 'He is an anatomist. He is as innocent of laziness as a scholar. He also recoils like a scholar from any word which is too big, any immoderation in attitude. He is profoundly, seriously, anti-romantic.'[10]

By the end of the month he'd received 870 letters of congratulation.[11] When Réjane wanted to give him a present, he asked for a photograph of her as the prince de Sagan. When it came, he admired her elegance in top hat and monocle, but objected to the ear-rings she was still wearing.[12]

The prize consisted of 5,000 francs, much of which was spent at the Ritz, but, as with most literary prizes, the main remuneration came through the boost to sales. Stocks of *Jeunes Filles* in the bookshops were soon exhausted, but a new impression was ready by 21 December, and, with a 'Prix Goncourt' wrapper around it, sold rapidly.

Proust was lionised. In the evening, writes Harold Nicolson, 'he would put on his elaborate evening clothes (those white kid gloves clasping an opera hat) and attend the receptions given to members of the Peace Conference. He appeared there

like Beethoven at the Congress of Vienna . . . He would flit
from Mr Balfour to M. Venizelos, from Marshal Foch to Mr.
Berthelot. He was very friendly, and ill, and amusing. He
enjoyed hearing stories about the Conference. He seemed quite
unaware of the early and enduring monument of his own
impending fame.' At one of these receptions Proust insisted on
introducing Nicolson to a man he already knew, the marquis
de Chaumont. Surely Nicolson must understand how much
pleasure it would give him to take an Englishman by the
arm, propel him across the room and say: 'Mon cher Jacques,
permettez . . .' Nicolson hesitated. 'Don't you see? It's so
simple! Let's go. Don't be unintelligent.' And when Nicolson
submitted, he 'purred like a small Siamese cat'. But when he
wrote to de Chaumont, asking for permission to mention him
by name in the Saint-Simon parody, the anti-Semitic marquis
refused, nervous it might prejudice his chances of being elected
to the Jockey Club.[13]

Though the Goncourt improved Proust's financial position,
the problem of the Warburg cheque was as complicated as
ever. In October, when Robert de Billy heard about it, he
offered to cash it through his bank, which would accept it only
as security for an advance he'd have to guarantee. But he did
this, and gave the money to Proust, who no longer needed it,
thanks mainly to his Royal Dutch shares. He'd intended to sell
them but forgotten how many he had, and three were still in
his possession. Because of a bonus issue, the three had become
eleven, and because of post-war inflation in oil prices, they
were worth 375,000 francs.[14]

Of all the admirers he gained by winning the prize, the one
who came to matter most was Jacques Boulenger, editor of
L'Opinion, who published in it a discerning appraisal of the
novel[15] and wrote a letter appointing himself as Proust's 'champion'. What Proust didn't yet know was that after years of
developing and maintaining friendly relationships with a minimum of face-to-face confrontations, he'd found a man with
the same inclination to make friends through writing and shy
away from personal encounters. Eager to meet his champion,
Proust invited Boulenger to a small dinner party in his bedroom on 4 January and to a dinner party at the Ritz. Boulenger
parried the invitations but remained friendly in his letters and
even friendlier in his published comments. In the next few
months, Proust, who seldom met his match as an evader of

confrontations, went on trying unsuccessfully to meet Boulenger.

Warming to the epistolary intimacy, Proust presented himself rather as if answering questions once again in a confession album. He was a man who never even tried to sleep during the night and slept only for a few minutes during the day. His regular intake of Veronal had doubled, and he'd given up trying to correct his proofs. His greatest exertion was playing draughts with Henri Rochat. He met his best friends once every ten years, and his only ambition was to be a source of enlightenment.[16] He was still doubtful whether he had any talent.[17]

His other champion was Jacques Rivière, whose essay, 'Marcel Proust et la tradition classique' appeared in the February issue of the *NRF*. Since Stendhal, it contended, the only psychological insights in literature had been impressionistic, but in bringing consciousness back into focus Proust was in the tradition of Racine. This was a powerful argument against the reviewers who'd found the novel too innovative or too self-indulgent.

Proust didn't know how long it was since he'd been to the Louvre. Twenty-six years, he told Boulenger, but to Vaudoyer he said it was 'more than 15'.[18] The question came up when Daniel Halévy circulated a questionnaire to fashionable writers asking which eight paintings should be exhibited if the Louvre were to mount a selection of French masterpieces. In a long letter to Vaudoyer, explaining illness had stopped him from replying to Halévy, Proust said he'd have opted for three paintings by Chardin – a self-portrait, a portrait of his wife and *Nature Morte;* Millet's *Le Printemps;* Manet's *Olympia;* a Renoir or Corot's *La Barque du Dante* or his *La Cathédrale de Chartres;* and *L'Indifférent* or *L'Embarquement* by Watteau.[19]

Renoir had occurred to Proust because of the spectacles he'd finally bought after so many years of procrastinating. In the painter as in the writer, he said, originality is the power to make connections between things not normally connected, and at first the public has difficulty in responding. The artist proceeds like an oculist, he said (connecting two things not usually connected), and the public's resistance is finally overcome when it's made to look. 'And suddenly the world, which has not been created once and for all, but is recreated each time a new artist emerges, appears to us – so different from the old

458 REHEARSALS FOR DYING

world – perfectly clear.'[20] After years of allowing himself to be impeded painfully in his reading and his writing, Proust could suddenly see clearly again, and in the novel the Narrator makes the same point about the way an optician gives his customers a new vision of the world. But Proust was still too vain to wear the glasses outside his bedroom.

He was always on the look-out for opportunities to help needy friends, and in March, when Pierre de Polignac married the prince de Monaco's adopted daughter, Charlotte Grimaldi, duchesse de Valentinois, Proust thought he might be able to arrange a series of lectures in Monaco for the impecunious Rivière, whose wife had just had a baby.[21] It wouldn't be until later in the year that Proust could come financially to his friend's aid, and though he had misgivings about the way Rivière was editing the NRF,[22] their friendship was a factor in arrangements at the NRF as Rivière acted as intermediary between Proust and Gallimard.

Proust was finding it so hard to make headway with his proof-correcting that he asked for help, and the twenty-four-year-old Dadaist André Breton was chosen for the task, which he performed inefficiently, though he infected his follow Dada-ists with enthusiasm for the book.[23] In order to get another volume into the shops without inordinate delay, Gallimard enlisted Rivière's help in persuading Proust to publish *Guerm-antes* in two parts. Once Proust had agreed, he was forced to hurry with the proofs for the first part, which he delivered in mid-May.[24]

By then the NRF had published fifty copies of *Jeunes Filles* in a luxury edition priced at 300 francs and containing autograph material. The extensively corrected galleys of the proofs for the 1914 Grasset edition had been cut up and bound into fifty copies. The princesse Soutzo bought one, and Berry bought three,[25] but Sydney Schiff didn't want to subscribe, saying it would annoy him to think anyone else could buy a copy for the same price.[26]

Proust didn't let the work on proof-correcting restrict his outings, and, without trying to, he went on collecting more material for the fancy-dress ball episode. Going to a perform-ance by the Ballets Russes in late April, he found nothing on stage interested him so much as the seventy-seven-year-old comte d'Haussonville in the audience. 'The years had given his head, without modifying its contours, a greater degree of majesty than it had previously had,' he told Mme Straus.[27] He uses the same word in his description of the ageing duc de Guermantes: 'His face . . . kept the style, the contours I had always admired.'[28]

Though he was so ill in late May that he could write letters only by dictating them, he felt sufficiently fortified by his Goncourt to hope for admission to the Académie Française. Rivière received a letter in Rochat's beautiful handwriting, asking whether it would be 'agreeable to the NRF, advantageous or disadvantageous for my books if I presented myself (with a chance of success for without that I would not do it) to the Academy'.[29] Rivière knew it was hopeless. 'You are too richly textured, too positive, too truthful for those people. As a group they cannot understand you: they are too deeply asleep.'[30]

By mid-June he was well enough to accept the princesse Soutzo's invitation to watch the dress rehearsal of *Antony and Cleopatra* in Gide's translation from her box at the Opéra. Another guest of hers was Henri Bardac, who complained Proust never stopped talking,[31] but when, during the interval, the news reached him that Réjane was dead, he hurried to the house where he'd so recently lived.

At the end of June, Rivière read the proofs. 'You are a great writer, and in this beginning of your new book, which is still more poetic than psychological, or at least contains more extended passages of exterior description than any of the earlier volumes . . . you develop still more astonishing stylistic qualities than those you had already demonstrated.'[32] After a condescending article by Pierre Lasserre, 'Marcel Proust humoriste et moraliste', appeared in the July issue of *La Revue universelle*, Proust drafted about ten lines of refutation to be included in the 'Revue des Revues', which was a regular feature in the *NRF*. Sometimes it was anonymous, but, if it was signed, he wanted it to look as if the signatory had written the ten lines which would actually be written by him.[33] Rivière agreed, offering to sign the article and write the rest of it.[34]

Rivière, who was no less deeply committed than Boulenger to championing Proust, was in a key position. 'I consider it to be an important part of my task as editor to clear a path towards your writings. . . . If I am capable of anything, I undertake to create, little by little, in people's minds a slope which will lead to an increasingly profound and increasingly passionate understanding of your work. . . . I want to strive towards a renaissance of psychology. And, inevitably, you appear to be not only its precursor but its essential protagonist.'[35]

Proust then sent Rivière a passage much longer than ten lines, and centring on a lengthy quotation from Émile Blanche's article. As everyone at the NRF knew, Proust detested the title À la recherche du temps perdu. He'd wanted to call the book Le Temps perdu, but had abandoned the title when he heard Francis Carco was about use it for the review he was going to edit.[36] Unwilling to cite Blanche, who'd often been his adversary in controversies, and reluctant to publicise Proust's reservations about the title that had been established, Rivière wrote his own spirited defence of Proust, but conceded that Lasserre was right to accuse him of having too many 'vivid, personal, original, colourful impressions which are worth the trouble of writing down'. Proust, said Rivière, had to struggle constantly against the flood of impressions: 'his whole art perhaps confines itself to confronting, holding up its head against his memory – one of the most copious that has ever been known'.[37] After reprimanding Rivière for obstinacy in refusing to quote Blanche, Proust told Boulenger: 'Jacques Rivière is gentle and good like the infant Jesus, but stubborn as a she-ass.'[38]

But Proust wasn't too annoyed to sponsor him for a literary prize worth 12,000 francs. A rich American woman, Mrs George Blumenthal, had started a fund to help a young French writer, and recruited Proust for the jury, which included Bergson, Gide, Valéry, Robert de Flers, Anna de Noailles, René Boylesve and Edmond Jaloux. When they met at the end of September, Proust got up during the day, but arrived late. According to Boylesve, he was looking like a female palmist,[39] and he was not only in pain – his earplugs were causing recurrent otitis – but he had great difficulty both in speaking and in standing erect. But he secured a unanimous vote for Rivière.

Bergson was now sixty-one and suffering from insomnia. Discussing this malady and what they both did to counteract it, he and Proust looked, according to Jaloux, like 'two black nightbirds used to seeing clearly in the darkness, marvellous prospectors of the treasures of the mind and of unconscious thought.' They made 'insomnia seem almost like a blessing' as they drew inferences about the operation of mysterious laws.[40]

It was mainly to extricate and formulate these laws that Proust had evolved his idiosyncratic prose style. Praising Paul Morand for having 'a singular style', Proust was thinking of his own writing and of the way he'd characterised originality as a talent for making unexpected connections. 'The beauty of a style is the infallible sign that thought is moving higher, that it has discovered and secured the necessary links between objects which had been left separate by their contingency.'[41] 'This new writer is generally rather tiring to read and hard to understand because he unifies things by making new connections.'[42] The point is also reminiscent of the one he'd made à propos Renoir and the oculist.

When this eleven-page essay was published in *La Revue de Paris*, Calmann-Lévy sent him only 200 francs – the amount Calmette used to pay for a short article – and Proust asked Boulenger whether he was being underpaid.[43] He wasn't, but he could economise by recycling his reflections about death in *La Prisonnière* and *Le Temps retrouvé*. They had nothing to do with Morand's stories, but, ever since his *Figaro* journalism Proust had been liable to digress about personal preoccupations.

Though going less often to the Ritz, he spent one evening there with Berry, Marthe Bibesco and her husband. At first she failed to recognise him. Without a beard he looked 'supernaturally young, wearing only a small black moustache. . . . Proust looked at me with his big eyes which did not seem to me sadder, but animated with an extraordinary life. He scrutinised my face with no pretence of propriety, with a quiet and grave curiosity. Then, talking to Walter Berry, he started talking about the design of the wings of my nose, as if I were an inanimate figure. "It's that line," he said, "I remembered. That's what I was looking for." '[44]

On 8 September, when he had a dinner party at the Ritz, one of his guests was Paul Souday, who'd discussed him in an article which appeared the next day in *Paris-Midi*.[45] Later in the month Proust became a *chevalier* of the Légion d'honneur, but it mattered to him less than his malaise. Deprived of the cork lining on his walls, he constantly had to choose between noise and the earplugs which caused otitis. At the end of the month he was again suffering from this,[46] and for ten days in the middle of October his temperature often went above 104 degrees.[47]

During the long period of rising temperatures, failing eyesight and dwindling energy, the disorder in his bedroom had worsened. Though Céleste did her best to keep the bedroom tidy, storing his letters in boxes,[48] Rochat was too lazy to be good at filing papers. Caring more about good looks than efficiency when he selected his male secretaries, Proust was expecting to go on being surrounded by a chaos of papers. Because of his sensitivity to dust, Céleste wasn't allowed to tidy the papers on the bed when he was in the room,[49] – often she aired and cleaned the room at midnight when he was out – and, as always, letters he wrote or dictated were liable to get mislaid, reappearing twelve months later.[50] Nor did he always receive letters sent to him, because the concierge used a four-year-old granddaughter to take them upstairs and sometimes she found it was more fun to tear them up.[51] Proust also lost copies of his own books. The printer finished work on the first volume of *Guermantes* in mid-August, but half the copies sent to Proust disappeared.[52]

The NRF proved to be no more punctual than Grasset at paying royalties,[53] but the first part of *Guermantes* was on sale from the end of October. Each time a new volume came out, he had to sign 150 copies, because it was NRF policy to send out review copies signed by the author.[54] He also inscribed copies for friends. Writing in one for Vaudoyer, Proust invited him to a bedside performance of Beethoven's Opus 132 quartet.[55] The November issue of the *NRF* contained an unsigned paragraph on 'this third volume of his immense and magnificent novel. . . . Once again, and with more reason than ever, the great psychologist, Marcel Proust, will be admired for his mastery over the progressive and detailed manner, the art of constructing from the interior, of creating characters through analysing only their manias, their tics, their language.'[56] It was obviously Rivière who'd written this.[57] Both his champions were serving him well, but some of the reviewers were more critical, and Paul Souday, writing in *Le Temps*, accused him of begin snobbish and 'feminine'.[58] 'How,' Proust objected, 'knowing in all probability that I have known duchesses de Guermantes throughout my life, have you failed to notice how much effort I had to make to put myself in the place of someone who would not know any of them but wished he could?'[59]

On 3 December he had an attack at five in the afternoon; at seven he was still too ill to be told Gallimard and Rivière had called. They left without seeing him,[60] but in the morning he read the critique by Boulenger in *L'Opinion*. 'There are passages of a really surprising profundity, and an astonishing felicity of expression for things which are almost inexpressible.' In his gratitude, Proust bought two of the deluxe editions of *Guermantes*, one for Boulenger and one for his novelist brother, Marcel.

In addition to asthma, insomnia and pains in his eyes, he caught bronchitis in January 1921, and, coughing constantly, he felt 'shaken about as if I were on a boat'.[61] For over two weeks his temperature was high and his voice so painful and hoarse he couldn't dictate,[62] but the novel by now had an independent life. On 1 January the account of the grandmother's death appeared in the *NRF*, and three weeks later, under the title 'Soirée de brouillard', the *Revue hebdomadaire* published an episode in which the Narrator dines at a restaurant with Saint-Loup on a foggy evening. Then on 1 February 'Un Baiser' was printed in the *NRF* – Albertine's first visit and their first kiss.

All Proust's plans for the future of the novel had to be tentative – subject to survival. Writing to Gallimard on 11 January, he envisaged that the second volume of *Guermantes* and the two volumes of the first part of *Sodome et Gomorrhe* would be followed 'at rather long intervals (if God lends me life)' by three more parts of *Sodome* and by *Le Temps retrouvé*, all four of which would be long.[63] He'd finally given up hope of simultaneous publication. By the end of the month he'd received an advance of 7,500 francs on *Guermantes*, but the rest of the novel still existed only in manuscript.[64]

Afraid Montesquiou would recognise himself as Charlus in the second *Guermantes* volume, which was due out on 2 May, Proust wrote to him on 9 March, promising to send both volumes and to confide in him about 'the only two false keys in the whole work, which unlock only two chapters'. Montesquiou's reply showed he'd been speculating about models. In *Swann* he recognised Charles Ephrussi and in Saint-Loup a mixture of Albu and Guiche, while he took the comte and comtesse Greffulhe to be the originals for the duc and duchesse de Guermantes. He assumed Charlus was based on Balzac's master-criminal, Vautrin.[65] In reply Proust identified the Saint-

Loup of the restaurant sequence as Fénelon, and the Charlus of the casino sequence in Balbec as 'the late baron Doazan, a habitué of Mme Aubernon's salon, and rather like this', but Charlus, he said, was constructed on a much bigger scale and 'entirely invented'.[66]

Wanting to salve his conscience and win gratitude by doing Montesquiou a favour, Proust recommended him as an art critic to Jacques Boulenger, who was now running the *Revue de la semaine* as well as *L'Opinion*. Proust claimed to have written: 'What a shame that no art criticism of importance is entrusted to the greatest art critic of our age, M. de Montesquiou.'[67] Proust did describe Montesquiou as 'the best art critic of our epoch',[68] and himself as 'one of the only people with whom he has never quarrelled'.[69] But, isolated in his old age, without the fame he'd expected, Montesquiou was jealous of Proust's success, and angrily rebuffed Boulenger's overtures.[70]

Since the winter, Proust had been suffering from uraemia,[71] and in early April he caught a rheumatic fever: once again it was painful and difficult to make the slightest movement.[72] Before he'd recovered, he caught a chill, which brought on fits of breathlessness and choking that went on day and night.[73] But, fighting doggedly against the discomfort, the fever and the exhaustion, he wrote for the *NRF* a long essay on Baudelaire in the form of a letter to Rivière, quoting extensively from the poetry – and from Victor Hugo's. But, too ill to check the quotations, Proust relied entirely on his excellent but fallible memory. His verdict is that on love, Hugo had written more accurately than Baudelaire, presenting it as conflict:

> Elle me regarda de ce regard suprême
> Qui reste à la beauté quand nous en triomphons

> (She looked at me with that supreme look
> Which beauty keeps when we triumph over it)

This is better, according to Proust, than Baudelaire's

> cette gratitude infinie et sublime
> Qui sort de la paupière ainsi qu'un long soupir

> (that gratitude infinite and sublime
> Which comes from the eyelid like a long sigh)

But Baudelaire, better than any other nineteenth-century poet, had manipulated the rhythms of the language to explore gaps between the jagged edges of emotional experience and the smooth surfaces of proprieties imposed by Christianity and decorum. His original title for *Les Fleurs du mal* had been 'Les Lesbiennes', and, as Proust saw it, the connection he made between Sodom and Gomorrah prefigured the statement Proust was making through Morel, the bisexual violinist modelled on Léon Delafosse. But Morel is vulgar and brutish, while Baudelaire, having no character to use as intermediary, could only use himself, and Proust failed to understand why he should want to.[74]

All the same, admiring Baudelaire for exposing the sordid underside of city life, Proust holds him up as an example to

> our elegant ladies of the last twenty years, who would not admit the slightest bad taste into their home. They should remember that in contrast to the apparent purity of style they strove for, it was possible 'to be the greatest and most artistic of writers while depicting only beds with curtains that could be closed, entrance halls like hothouses, beds full of faint odours, divans as deep as a tomb, shelves with flowers, lamps that did not burn for very long, so that the fire gave out the only continuing light'.[75]

Proust was thinking of his attempt to bring the contemporary Sodoms and Gomorrahs into the same focus as affectations of elegance in the salons.

But his affinity with Baudelaire goes deeper than this. Nietzsche had shown how illness could goad the mind into speculation about whether suffering had any purpose, and about the relation between pain and consciousness, consciousness and self. In April, writing about Baudelaire, Proust cites him and Dostoevsky as writers who 'between their attacks of epilepsy etc.' did what could never have been done by 'an army of a thousand artists who just have normal health'.[76]

Proust could himself be described in the way T. S. Eliot described Baudelaire – as 'one of those who have great strength, but strength merely to *suffer*. He could not escape suffering and could not transcend it, so he attracted pain to himself. But what he could do, with that immense passive strength and sensibilities which no pain could impair, was to study his suffering.'[77] Looking from a Christian viewpoint at a counter-romantic poet, Eliot praises Baudelaire for concerning himself with the real problem of good and evil, and perceiving 'that what really matters is Sin and Redemption'.[78] In 'a world of electoral reform, plebiscites, sex reform and dress reform', damnation is 'an immediate form of salvation – of salvation from the ennui of modern life, because it at last gives some significance to living'.[79]

In his attempt to assimilate the cities of the plain to the perspective of the salons, Proust was closer to Baudelaire than to Eliot, but like Eliot he wanted to see the invisible substance of time. *Four Quartets* gets off to a Proustian start, asserting that time present and time past are both perhaps present in time future, and time future contained in time past. If all time is eternally present, says Eliot, all time is unredeemable. Reviewing the second poem in the sequence, 'The Dry Salvages', when it appeared in 1942, Dr Leavis characterised the technique of Eliot's poetry from *Ash Wednesday* onwards as 'a technique for sincerity – for giving "sincerity" a meaning. The preoccupation is with establishing from among the illusions, evanescences and unrealities of life in time an apprehension of assured reality – a reality that, though necessarily apprehended in time, is not of it.' In 'Burnt Norton' Eliot conducts a radical and useful enquiry into his own methods of exploring concepts and experiences, but the achievement of 'Little Gidding' isn't on the same level, partly because Eliot fails to recognise the personal roots of his need for impersonality, and partly because the quest for spirituality rests on generalised and unbacked assertions, such as 'To be conscious is not to be in time.' There's no poetic substantiation of the space outside time for which the poet yearns.

Proust was no less preoccupied with establishing an apprehension of assured reality from among the illusions, evanescences and unrealities of life in time, but he did recognise the personal roots of his need to penetrate beyond the contingency of personal experience, and although, before Eliot, he used the same notion of situation somewhere 'outside time' for realisation of 'the essence of things' at moments when memory is working involuntarily, the extratemporal existence of these moments is only a diagram which established a perspective for all the solidly realised experiences the narrative presents.

Using personal experience, Proust is telling the story of what is simultaneously the rediscovery of the past and the discovery of the vocation which will control the future. When the book ends, the Narrator has found his way to the point at which he can begin to tell his story, but the story has been told by the book we've just finished reading. Dramatising what Eliot would later assert about the eternal presence of all time, Proust was trying to demonstrate the opposite of what Eliot contended. All time is redeemable. The work of art can rescue the artist's life from discontinuity, giving it a solidity which cures his vertigo. Ending the novel with an explanation of why the Narrator sacrificed everything else in his life to writing a book, Proust's completion – or near-completion – of the novel represents the culmination of a life in which he consciously sacrificed his health and social pleasures in asserting the primacy of art. Without trying to eliminate himself from the picture, as Eliot did, Proust had evolved a technique for giving sincerity a meaning.

Looking at Baudelaire's preoccupation with the sordid flowers of evil in comparison with Dostoevsky's, Proust recognised the novelist's as more 'sincere',[80] but when Rivière wanted him to write on Dostoevsky for the *NRF*, Proust preferred to introduce everything he wanted to say about him into a conversation with Albertine. The Narrator claims to find the immersion in squalor as far removed from himself as it could be, 'unless there is something in me of which I know nothing, for self-realisation comes only gradually. In Dostoevsky I find the penetration is exceedingly deep, but only into some isolated points of the human soul.'[81] Comparing Dostoevsky's world with Rembrandt's *Night Watch* – the characters are really quite ordinary but the lighting and the costume make them look fantastic – the Narrator praises the novels for being 'full of truths, profound and unique, which belong only to Dostoevsky. . . . It could be said that for him love and the most desperate hatred, goodness and treachery, timidity and insolence are only two sides of a single nature.'[82]

Letting the Narrator lecture Albertine on literature, Proust didn't need to be scholarly, and, snatching his insights from moments of lucidity between turbulent accesses of pain, it was easier to write like this. Since he still had a secretary on his payroll, it's hard to explain why he sent off the Baudelaire essay to the *NRF* with quotations and paraphrases still unchecked, unless Rochat was incapable of checking them.[83]

While there was no risk of upsetting a dead poet by misquoting him, Jacques Boulenger was upset when he read the essay. Proust had called him 'by far the best critic of his generation, and much more than a critic', but had reprimanded him for daring 'to tell us that Baudelaire's poetry is devoid of ideas'.[84] Boulenger had complained about the dandyism in *Journaux intimes* but had never said his poetry was devoid of ideas. Far from wanting to alienate Boulenger, Proust felt so well disposed he offered him an introduction to Gide,[85] and tried to find out whether the *NRF* had given a favourable review to Boulenger's collection of critical essays *Mais l'art est difficile*. The reviewer was Louis Martin-Chauffier, but, after glancing too hastily through his typescript when Proust enquired, Rivière said it was favourable. This was the news Proust passed on to Boulenger, who was furious, when the review was published, to find he was accused of including an essay on René Boylesve in the hope of winning his vote for the Académie.[86]

It was after this that Boulenger finally went to see Proust.[87] Well-meaningly, he suggested Boulenger should send a reply to the *NRF* – advice he followed but Proust, forgetting what he'd said, told Boulenger he'd have done better to ignore the accusation. Boulenger's reply was published in the next issue of the *NRF*, followed by a letter from Rivière, who sided with Martin-Chauffier.[88] Boulenger went on championing Proust, but never again went to see him.[89]

THIRTY

STRANGER IN MY BRAIN

It was atrocious, complained Proust, 'to be dying incessantly without achieving death'.[1] 'Lamartine was right to say it is unpleasant to die more than once.' The ultimate death was 'the good one, which gives us courage "to walk into the evening" '.[2] His relationship with the death awaiting him had changed in 1917 when he started ignoring the minor heart attacks and going out recklessly; in the autumn of 1920, it changed again, as did the intimations of impending death. Every day, he said in September, death encroached further on his strength.[3] He'd started using 'death' and 'dying' almost synonymously with illness: in one attack he'd been 'very particularly and frightfully dying'.[4] He was exaggerating when he said he'd gone for seven months during the summer without getting up,[5] but he'd almost abandoned the Ritz and, to avoid the crowd in the dining-room when he did go, he usually booked a room for a few hours.[6]

He didn't have enough strength to correct his proofs, he said;[7] he was in 'a state of half-death, in which for weeks on end I cannot open my eyes or hold a pen'.[8] In an article on Paul Morand's short stories, *Tendres Stocks*, he wrote: 'A female stranger has settled in my brain. She went, she came; soon, from the way she carried on, I got to know her habits. Besides, as a considerate lodger, she was keen to have direct dealings with me. I was surprised to see she was not beautiful. I had always thought she was, or how would she get the better of us?'[9]

The relationship with death had as much urgency as a love affair. In the novel 'the idea of death installed itself definitively' in the Narrator's mind, making him incapable of giving his attention to anything else unless 'that thing first traversed the idea of death, and even if nothing occupied my attention and I relaxed completely, the idea of death kept me company as incessantly as the idea of myself'. The idea did not seem to have derived from the symptoms – inability to walk downstairs, to remember names, to get up – but to have arrived simultaneously with them.[10]

Always a considerate host, Proust welcomed his guest by eating less. For breakfast he took nothing but café au lait; it was partly that the drugs were affecting his appetite, but he knew he was keeping himself undernourished. Sometimes he asked for stewed fruit or hot milk, but invariably left both nearly untouched. Céleste did her best to coax him into building up resistance to the chilliness of the room, but his intake of food had dwindled to almost nothing. All he ever seemed to fancy – in spite of the coldness – was iced beer, which had to be fetched from the Ritz. He thought Ritz beer was different from the beer that could have been bought from the brasserie on the corner. When he talked about dying, she did her best to convince him he'd live on indefinitely, but his bronchial tubes were like old elastic, he said, his heart worn out by years of gasping for air. He was a very old man, he said.[11] He was forty-nine.

Ignoring her advice with the same stubbornness as he ignored Dr Bize's, he was unquestionably shortening his life. A little light is thrown on his self-destructiveness by remarks to Lionel Hauser about never letting a day go by without religious thoughts, and to Marthe Bibesco about staking everything on a game of 'loser wins'. He wanted to sacrifice his life to art, and the jackpot was immortality that didn't consist merely of posthumous fame. What he wrote about Bergotte shows how open his mind was to the possibility of life after death.

Seriously ill, Bergotte is convinced neither that death will be the end nor that he could prolong his life by following commonsensical advice. Nature seems capable of giving us only rather short illnesses, 'but medicine has taken over the art of prolonging them. Medicines, the relief they bring, the discomfort provoked by discontinuity in taking them, create a simulacrum of illness which is eventually stabilised by the patient's habituation. . . . Then the medicines have less effect, doses are increased, they do no more good, but they have begun to do harm thanks to this continuing indisposition.' Like Proust, Bergotte had stopped going out, had never cared much for society, or had come to despise it, not because it was out of his reach, but because it wasn't. He lived so simply that people who knew how rich he was took him to be a miser, but he was exceptionally generous, especially to girls, 'knowing he could never produce such good work as in an atmosphere of believing himself to be in love. . . . We do not achieve happiness, but we gain more insight into what stops us from being happy than we could have done without these brief passages of disappointment.'

Swathed in travelling rugs, Bergotte jokes apologetically to the few visitors he receives: life, as Anaxagoras said, is a journey. 'In this way he went on growing progressively colder, a small planet prefiguring the last days of the greater one, with heat and then life withdrawing gradually from the earth.' His nightmares are harder to bear than his insomnia. It feels as if a damp cloth is being rubbed over his face by an evil woman, or as if a crazy taxi-driver is assaulting him, gnawing at his fingers. The doctors blame his condition on overwork, though for twenty years he has done nothing. They recommend sunshine, though his few years of comparative health were due to staying indoors. They advise him to eat more, though food makes him thinner, nourishing only his nightmares. When he obeys the doctors, his condition deteriorates. He feels better when taking unprescribed drugs, but he gives himself excessive doses.[12] After he dies, the narrative asks:

Dead for ever? Who can say? Neither spiritualism nor religion have proved the soul survives death, but everything happens in our life as if we came into it with an onus of obligations contracted in a previous life; nothing in the conditions of life on this earth made us believe ourselves required to do good, to be considerate, or even polite, or to make the atheistic artist believe he was obliged to make twenty fresh starts on a piece of work that may excite admiration which will be of little importance to his body when worms are eating it. . . . All these obligations which do not have their sanction in our present life seem to belong to a different world, founded on goodness, scrupulousness, sacrifice, a world entirely different from this one, which we leave to be born on this earth, before perhaps going back to live again under those unknown laws which we have been obeying because we were carrying their doctrines in us without knowing who implanted them, those laws to which all profound intellectual work approximates and which are invisible only – if at all – to fools. So the idea Bergotte was not dead for ever is not improbable.[13]

In the May 1921 issue of the *NRF*, which was published a day before the second part of *Guermantes*, Gide welcomed the new book with a rejoinder to objections which had been raised. The length of Proust's sentences was balanced by their composition, he contended, and the hidden pattern in the structure of the novel brought it in line with the work of Balzac and Montaigne.[14] This made Proust want to see Gide again, and on four successive evenings he sent Albaret's taxi to collect him, failing three times and succeeding on 13 May. But when he arrived, he was received by Céleste, who said M. Proust would be unable to see him but added: 'Monsieur asks M. Gide to be assured that he thinks of him incessantly.' But then Proust appeared, dressed to go out. After staying in bed for a long time, he'd arranged to meet a friend, and had sent the car without really expecting Gide, who'd said he probably wouldn't be free.

They sat down together in an uncomfortably warm room, but Proust, whose bedroom was still warmer, shivered incessantly. Gide drank only mineral water,[15] but they went on talking for an hour. Discussing homosexuality, Proust interrupted himself, complaining his life was nothing but a slow agony, and asking Gide to explain the teachings of the Gospel: he was hoping to derive comfort from them, and had heard Gide spoke about them particularly well. Previously Gide had suspected his illness was only a charade to protect his work, but now there could be no doubt it was genuine. He seemed bloated, and spoke of lying in bed for hours without even being able to move his head. 'Sometimes he moves along the wings of his nose the edge of a hand which seems dead, with fingers bizarrely stiff and spread, and nothing is more striking than this maniacal and clumsy gesture, which looks like the gesture of an animal or a madman.'

Gide lent him a copy of *Corydon*, and talked about writing his memoirs. Proust said: 'You can tell everything, but on condition you never say "I".' Far from hiding his homosexuality, he seemed to pride himself on it, and claimed he'd never made love to a woman, but Gide didn't believe this. Proust said Baudelaire was a homosexual: 'The way he talks about Lesbos, and, besides, his need to talk about it would alone be enough to convince me.' And, when Gide demurred, Proust seemed to think he was disparaging Baudelaire by doubting it.

Four days later, Gide was on the point of going to bed when

the doorbell rang. Albaret had come to return the copy of *Corydon* and to fetch him if he'd like to pay another visit: M. Proust was well enough to receive him if it was convenient for him to come. This time the whole conversation was about homosexuality, and Proust blamed himself for the 'indecisiveness' which had made him

> nourish the heterosexual side of his book by transposing 'à l'ombre des jeunes filles' everything his homosexual memories suggest to him of what is gracious, tender and charming, in such a way that nothing is left over for *Sodome* except what is grotesque and abject. But he seems to be deeply touched when I tell him he appears to have intended to stigmatise homosexuality; he protests; and I finally understand that what we find ignoble, ridiculous or disgusting, does not, to him, seem so repulsive. When I ask him whether he will never present this Eros to us in its young and beautiful aspects, he says that first of all what attracts is almost never beauty, and he thinks it has little to do with desire – and that, as for youth, it was what he could most easily transpose (what lent itself best to transposition).[16]

Meanwhile Rivière, still assuming Proust, like his narrator, was heterosexual, took him to be avenging himself on 'the race of Sodomites. . . . Without being in the least shaken by it, I had too often heard the notion of love being falsified in my presence not to experience a delicious relief at hearing it discussed by someone as healthy, as happily balanced as you.'[17] And later, when Roger Allard wrote in the *NRF* about Proust and homosexuality, his article was based on the same assumption: he praised the new volume for breaking 'the aesthetic spell of sexual inversion' which had been so damaging to both literature and the arts.[18] Inadvertently, both critics were confirming Gide's complaint that Proust was projecting only negative feelings about homosexuality.

Gide wasn't the only witness to form the impression parts of Proust's body were already dead. When François Mauriac was invited to a bedside dinner during March, he described the bedroom as 'a black den' and Proust's face as a waxy mask: 'only the hair was alive'.[19] Later on in the year, when he went to visit the American writer Natalie Clifford Barney, she thought he looked 'like a corpse laid out in a coffin', his eyes 'ringed with black by the vampires of solitude'.[20]

Aware death was encroaching on parts of his living body, he used this idea in late additions to the novel. Odette in old age is described as having the look of 'a sterilised rose'; her hair and her stiff face are like those of a mechanical doll.[21] One of the strips of paper glued on the typescript of *Sodome et Gomorrhe* described Morel, when he knows Charlus is spying on him in the Maineville brothel, as 'Morel enbalmed, not even Morel resuscitated like Lazarus, a ghost of Morel'. He had 'lost all colour, as happens after death'.[22] And the sleeping Albertine is described in another late addition as looking like a corpse. 'Her sheets, wound like a shroud around her body, had assumed, with their beautiful folds, the rigidity of stone. One would have said, as in certain medieval Last Judgments, that only the head rose out of the tomb, asleep while waiting for the Archangel's trumpet.'[23]

Another visitor he received not long after Gide was Bernard Fay, a young man who knew Lucien, the de Beaumonts and a soldier Proust had met in the brothel. At the risk of waking his family, Fay arranged to be picked up by Odilon in time to arrive in Proust's room at half-past three in the morning. 'Proust's face, pale and bloated, seemed greyish because of the unbarbered beard which was sprouting; his voice seemed greyish too.' A bottle of champagne and plates of food were waiting among the medicines on the bedside table. The bed was covered with half-corrected proofs. 'I couldn't understand how the pale light of such a feeble lamp sufficed him for this exhausting and delicate work. Nor could I understand how it was possible to live in this overheated, smelly, fume-filled atmosphere.'

Fay noticed how Proust wanted to know what his feelings were towards the friends they had in common. 'I quickly found in Proust a habit I knew in myself: never get to know anyone without clearly marking the point at which friendship, trust, liking must stop.' Proust spoke affectionately of Reynaldo and Léon Daudet, but seemed cooler towards 'little Lucien'. He talked disparagingly about Gide – 'in spite of his ingenuity, he cannot write fiction' – and described their recent meetings as if there had been only one of them and as if they'd parted on bad terms. Several times during the conversation Fay went into an adjoining room, where he opened a window, and filled his lungs with fresh air before going back into Proust's room.[24]

Proust had the fire in his room lit in summer as in winter,

and he kept seven woollen blankets and his fur coat on the bed, as well as three hot-water bottles inside it.[25] Unmistakably, though, his health was deteriorating. His aphasia had worsened, and in a restaurant one day, asking for mineral water, he had to say 'Contrexéville' nearly ten times before the waiter understood.[26] But he was going out less often, spending less time out of bed and eating less, sometimes going for ten days without food,[27] or living for several weeks at a stretch on nothing but ice-cream.[28]

Going from one room to another, he was liable to fall over,[29] but his passion for Vermeer would have made it intolerable for him to miss the exhibition of Dutch paintings at the Jeu de Paume. At this time there was no adequate electric lighting in galleries, and, wanting to see the exhibition by daylight, but not wanting to get up in the morning, he sat in the armchair all night and ate boiled potatoes in the morning to give himself strength.[30] In the last week of May, at 9.15 in the morning, he sent Albaret to fetch Vaudoyer, and, refusing to be deterred by a fit of giddiness as he left the house, let Vaudoyer support him by the arm as he stumbled towards what he'd remembered since his 1902 visit to The Hague with Fénelon as the most beautiful picture in the world, Vermeer's *View of Delft*. His niece Suzy, when she talked enthusiastically about the exhibition, was asked whether she'd noticed 'the pink sand and the little characters and the roofs so meticulously painted you'd think they'd been lacquered'.[31] He later wrote to Vaudoyer about keeping the 'luminous memory' of the morning when 'you affectionately guided my exceedingly unsteady footsteps towards this Ver Meer where the gables of the houses "are like precious Chinese objects" '.[32]

Afterwards, rallying, Proust made Vaudoyer take him on to the Ingres exhibition in the rue de la Ville-l'Évêque, where he stared lovingly at Rome as depicted in the background of a portrait. He lunched with Vaudoyer at the Ritz, but when they arrived back at the rue Hamelin he told Céleste he didn't know whether he'd ever go out again.[33]

The novel was putting some of his friendships in jeopardy. There was no protest from Montesquiou about the new book, but it remained to be seen whether he'd recognise himself in *Sodome et Gomorrhe*. The friend Proust now lost was Albu. For nineteen years he'd read none of his friend's work, and when he read the second part of *Guermantes*, he never forgave Proust for recycling his quarrels with Louisa as Saint-Loup's with Rachel.[34]

A different kind of friendship ended in June, when Proust lost Rochat, who was in trouble after breaking his promise to marry a concierge's daughter. Hoping to find a job for him abroad, Proust wrote to various friends, without hiding the facts that Rochat was lazy and no good at figures. Eventually, thanks to Horace Finaly, the young man was exported into a banking job in the United States.

Meanwhile Proust was still trying to promote his novel. He got Boulenger to publish in *L'Opinion* an extract from Gide's *NRF* note,[35] and, showing no more compunction about negotiating with *L'Action française* than he did about befriending one of its co-founders, Léon Daudet – without whose help he wouldn't have won the Goncourt – he arranged for the anti-Semitic paper to publish an extract from an article by Fernand Vandérem which had appeared in *La Revue de France*.[36] When *L'Action française* refused to mention the name of the 'dirty Jew' who'd written the article, Proust accepted the phrase 'dirty Jew' as 'a Homeric epithet in the household', and agreed – provided Vandérem had no objection – to the amended text, which also omitted the title *Sodome et Gomorrhe*, which the editor found offensive.[37]

In the middle of June, attending a dinner party given by Mme Hennessy to celebrate Gladys Deacon's engagement to the Duke of Marlborough, who'd finally secured a divorce from his first duchess, Proust found himself invited to England, and, hearing he was bedridden, the Duke promised to put him in a sleeper at the Gare du Nord. 'I'll tuck you up in a cabin on the boat, and you can stay in bed at Blenheim.' Meanwhile, the Duke suggested, Proust should keep telling himself he felt marvellous. 'If you believe you're well, you'll be well.'[38] But the dinner party was to be his last outing for about three months.[39]

Guiche was one of the other guests, and the conversation touched dangerously on whether his mother-in-law, comtesse Greffulhe, had been the model for the duchesse de Guermantes, who's portrayed unsympathetically in the second part of *Guermantes*. In *Swann* she was the glamorous object of the Narrator's daydreams, and in the first part of *Guermantes* he was 'genuinely in love' with her.[40] But in the second part he recognises her perversity, the extent to which she's been corrupted by life in high society, and the speed at which she vacillates between infatuation and disgust.[41] No, said Proust, Mme Greffulhe was the princesse de Guermantes, but a few days later he wrote to Guiche, insisting that the duchesse was virtuous, except for a slight resemblance to Mme de Chevigné, 'the little tough hen whom I long ago took for a bird of paradise, and who could only repeat like a parrot: "Fitzjames is expecting me." '[42] Not long after this, Mme de Chevigné asked him for a copy of the book, but threatened not to read it. Proust complained about this to Cocteau, saying all the best parts of the duchesse derived from her. Fabre had written a book about insects, said Cocteau, but didn't expect them to read it.[43] She could hardly have been expected to like the way she'd been treated in the book, but he felt rejected, just as he had twenty-nine years ago, when he accosted her in the street. He told Guiche her injustice to him was 'one of the only great sorrows that can affect a man at the end of his life after he has renounced everything'.[44]

In September he hurt himself by falling over in his bedroom, and soon afterwards took seven tablets of opium, Veronal and another narcotic, Dial, thinking each contained only a tenth of a gram, when it was actually a gram. He was told his stomach would have to be washed out. It wasn't, but his temperature remained high for several weeks, and it was hard for him to turn over in bed.[45] Like his mother, when she was dying, he was half-consciously accelerating the process by refusing to eat, but seldom confronting his situation squarely, unless forced to, as he was by a phrase in a letter from Sydney Schiff.

A part of your letter threw me into a profound despair, it was the admirable sentence about friendship which should not be realised materially (the sentence which finished with the harrowing words, worthy of something more important: 'To avoid having to put up with the end'). You cannot imagine the grief this sentence caused me. You must indeed realise that going for years without even seeing my family, being able neither to read nor to write, nor eat, nor get up, with, from time to time and very rarely, an outing like the one I had one day to see you, I can continue with such a frightful existence only thanks to the illusion, which is dispelled every day, and renewed the next, that all this is going to change. I have been living for fifteen years in a day-to-

day optimism. And your letter compelled me, in a vertigo
of sadness, to confront for several minutes the reality I do
not wish to see. Do not regret this, truth is always salutary,
and then I soon regained my courage and resumed my work
in order not to think.[46]

He'd started making additions to the second half of *Sodome*,
but he could work only sporadically. In September he thought
it would be impossible for him to go on working.[47] In October
an extract appeared in the *NRF* under the title 'Intermittences
du coeur', but, still eager to make up to Boulenger for the
embarrassment over the review in the *NRF*, and to punish
Rivière for siding with Martin-Chauffier, Proust responded
favourably when Boulenger acted as intermediary for Henri
Duvernois, editor of *Les Oeuvres libres*, who was eager to secure
an extract of the novel. Afrer Gallimard had reluctantly agreed,
Proust gave Duvernois 150 pages, which appeared in his
November issue. It was misleadingly announced as a complete
unpublished novel, but Proust was paid 10,000 francs, and he
insisted on dedicating to Boulenger the extract which was
published in the December issue of the *NRF*.

Wounded by these extracts from *Sodome*, Montesquiou filled
a notebook with acid comments. At first he'd seen no resemblance between himself and the repulsive old baron, a failed
artist who became involved with such vulgar people in such
sordid situations, but he was soon in no doubt that he'd served
as Proust's model and that readers who recognised him would
believe the portrait to be accurate. 'Will I be reduced to calling
myself Montesproust?'[48] Ill in bed, he wrote to announce his
imminent death to Proust, who replied: 'It is with a note from
a man of twenty-five that you announce this sad news to
your friend, who is himself over a hundred.'[49] But he said the
publication of the novel had prostrated him,[50] and he died
on 11 December. Two months later Proust, uncomfortably
playful, still pretended to doubt whether he was really dead.
'Once again I have every reason to believe in a last trick magi-
sterially performed by this marvellous man of the theatre.'[51]

Proust can't be accused of killing him, and the baron de
Charlus is one of the greatest comic creations in literature, but
Proust knew he'd poisoned the last weeks in his old friend's
life. Montesquiou had influenced his thinking and helped him
when he was going into society; it was as if he'd decided the

time had come to settle accounts and had presented the sick old man with an extortionate bill for the introduction to Delafosse and for flattery supplied when it would have been too risky to show both sides of his ambivalence. With Charlus, as with homosexuality, it is mainly the negative side that goes into the narrative. Undeniably, Montesquiou had been shamelessly arrogant and grotesquely affected: Proust had done what all good writers of comedy do, focusing sharply on absurdities they couldn't have invented. Filled with bitterly impotent rage on his deathbed, Montesquiou reproached himself for being so tolerant after he heard Proust was mimicking him. The comparatively innocuous private performance had been erected into a monument from which his posthumous reputation would never recover.

In November Proust sent back corrected proofs for the second part of *Sodome*, asking for bigger print. Gallimard protested, but capitulated when Proust offered to let any additional cost be deducted from his earnings. The first part then had to be reset.[52] By now Proust had got into the habit of refusing requests for interviews, but at the end of the year he made a statement by letter in reply to questions from André Lang, who was assembling a collection of interviews. Were there still such things as literary schools? Could any meaningful distinction be made between the analytical novel and the novel of adventure? Self-analysis, said Proust, interested him less than laws of general validity, which were as likely to surface in the novel of adventure as in the introspective novel. 'Everything is equally valuable which can help to reveal laws, to illuminate the unknown, to yield a deeper understanding of life.' His mind still worked in the same way as that of the *lycée* botanist trying to deduce general laws from observations. The analytical novel, he said, should not merely involve the intelligence.

> It is a matter of drawing something out of the unconscious to make it enter the domain of consciousness, while trying to preserve its life, [not to] mutilate it, to keep leakage to a minimum – a reality which could apparently be destroyed by exposure to the light of mere intelligence. To succeed in this work of salvage, the whole strength of the body and the mind is not too much. Something like the same kind of effort

– careful, gentle, daring – is necessary to someone who while
still asleep would like to examine his sleep with his intelligence, without letting this interference wake him up.[53]

He disliked the term analytical novel. 'I like working with the
telescope rather than the microscope.' And a few months later
he said the best image for what he was doing was a telescope
pointed at time. 'For the telescope reveals stars invisible to the
naked eye, and I have tried (I do not correspond at all to
my image) to reveal to consciousness unconscious phenomena
which, completely forgotten, are sometimes situated very far
away in the past.'[54]

He knew the length of his novel made enormous demands
on his readers, requiring them to give up other activities in its
favour. He couldn't have written it without giving up most of
his social life, and they were expected to find in it encouragement for taking at least a step or two in the same anti-social
direction. 'If you read my book,' he told Sydney Schiff, 'you
will see the infatuations and the bad moods of the fashionable
society from which I withdrew at the age of twenty. . . . But
you are not reading my book because, like all the fashionable
people who do not like it, you are too excitable in Paris, too
busy in London and too hospitable in the country.'[55] Proust
needed readers who reacted more like Mme Straus: 'I take the
book, cut the pages and tell myself: I am going to read for a
quarter of an hour, and then the quarter of an hour goes by . . .
I am reading . . . I keep on reading. They tell me dinner is
ready, I say "I'm coming" . . . and then I go on reading.'
Her husband is infuriated. 'It's abominable, this woman who's
always reading – morning, day, evening, night, she reads and
reads and does nothing but read!'[56]

But with Gallimard's dilatory approach to paying royalties,
the sales, though substantial, did little to ease the financial
pressures on Proust and at the beginning of 1922, when Walter
Berry mentioned the high fees paid by American magazines,
guilt feelings about Montesquiou didn't stop Proust from wondering whether to propose an anecdotal article about the
comte's life in high society.[57]

Proust started 1922 by staying all night at the de Beaumonts'
ball, and he went, two weeks later, to another ball at the Ritz,
where he saw Morand.[58] But he rejected Antoine Bibesco's

invitations to dine either at his home or anywhere else and with any other guests he wanted. Nor was he sending Antoine his books.[59] Giving preference to Sydney and Violet Schiff, Proust was seeing them each time they were in Paris and, when they weren't, writing letters that approximated to conversation, discussing whether he should sell corrected proofs to collectors, paying elaborate compliments to Violet – 'elusive flower, fragrant and marvellous' – and envying Sydney's ability to work. 'Me, I can do nothing, not even read.'[60] Sometimes he felt suicidal: his health, he told Gallimard, had reached the point at which he regretted not having any cyanide.[61]

On 7 February, at a soirée given by princesse Soutzo, he met Roger Martin du Gard, editor of *Les Écrits nouveaux*, which had published a hostile review of the second *Guermantes* volume. The critic, André Germain, said Proust was like 'an elderly governess who had become the family footman's mistress'.[62] Still priding himself on his willingness to fight duels, Proust hadn't given up the idea of challenging Germain, though he might have wanted, as Morand said, to fight in his overcoat.[63] He let himself be dissuaded, and obviously enjoyed his conversation with Martin du Gard, declaring himself to be not just a novelist but a 'moral poet'. He also questioned the editor about his beliefs, and sent him home in Albaret's taxi.[64]

Since Rochat had left, Céleste had often had to take dictation, but Proust was better served when her sister, Marie-Gineste, moved into the flat with her daughter, Yvonne, a typist, who dealt with correspondence and typed what Proust was still calling the third and fourth parts of *Sodome* – later they'd be *La Prisonnière* and *Albertine disparue*. He announced the new title, *La Prisonnière*, in a mid-May letter to Jacques Boulenger.[65]

In February an article by the German critic Ernst Robert Curtius appeared in the *Neue Merkur*. Quoting Stendhal's description of the novel as a mirror you take along the road, Curtius praised the 'beautiful disorder' of Proust's fiction, compared him with Monet, and said he'd subsumed symbolism and subjective idealism.[66] Proust was delighted, as he was when he heard from the mathematician Camille Vettard. After reading *Swann*, *Jeunes Filles* and *Guermantes*, Vettard wrote an admiring letter and, in a dedicatory preface to an unpublished novel, praised him as a literary counterpart to Einstein. Failing at first to interest Rivière in publishing this preface as an article, Proust succeeded in interesting Boulenger, but Vettard refused to have it published in the *Revue de la semaine*, and eventually it appeared in the *NRF*.[67]

It was at the beginning of the spring that Proust wrote the words 'The End' and, apparently, gave himself permission to die. He'd kept Céleste talking all night, and it was nine in the morning when she left him. At about four in the afternoon he rang once – two rings meant she was to bring a tray in – and she went in empty-handed. He looked tired but radiant, she thought. He seldom spoke before drinking his first cup of coffee, but he said good morning, told her a great thing had happened during the night, and asked her to guess what. She tried, but failed, and, laughing like a small boy, 'Last night I wrote "Fin". Now I can die.' She protested, and he went on laughing. 'Now my work can be published. I shall not have given my life in vain.'[68]

His relationship with her had changed. Inevitably, having much greater importance than anyone else in his daily life, she'd become more like a mother. He often felt incapable of taking minor decisions without her advice. Was it too late to telephone the princesse Soutzo? He'd started accepting help from Céleste in getting dressed, and she intervened to stop visitors from staying too long. If she thought he was being exhausted, she half-opened the bedroom door and signalled to them.[69] Her willpower was quite strong, and often he capitulated. One evening he was grumbling about lukewarm tea, but when she made an impatient gesture he gave in. Of course she was right to serve it like this. He could see on reflection it would be better for him if he drank it like this.[70]

Often he fought her as he'd fought his mother, using illness as a weapon. This is apparent from some of the notes he wrote when he wanted to rest his voice. 'You have torn my whole chest by forcing me to speak in the morning air.' 'Never again do what you are unfortunately doing now. Come in when I did not ring (this time an appearance for the pullover). Never come in again unless I have rung. You do not know how much harm you are doing me for the whole day. Now I cannot stay in bed and I must start fumigating again already.'

Most of the time she was his ally, as his mother had been, never happier than when discussing his elaborate campaigns against the illness. Nervous of the concierge's granddaughter, who had measles and whooping cough, he wanted all the mail to be soaked in a bowl of formol for two hours before he opened it. She complied but, when he did open it, he was often in a drowsy state. Which may have been why he got caught on 28 April in another of the misunderstandings which seemed to lie in wait for him. Reading a letter from Sydney Schiff which said 'We are here,' he assumed they were staying at the Ritz. Determined, in spite of a high temperature, to get up, he started giving himself injections. Not feeling well enough to change into evening dress, he booked a room at the Ritz, though the only one he could get was one he'd have to vacate before seven in the morning because it was needed for new arrivals. At least he could see the Schiffs in it, he thought, and go back to sleep in his own flat. Arriving at the Ritz, he found they were at Foyot's. Disconsolately, he went home to rest and recuperate.

His next attempt to see them was equally unsuccessful: he gave himself an overdose of adrenalin, which had replaced caffeine as the stimulant he used. He'd recommended Sydney Schiff to take an ampoule if ever he was feeling exhausted. 'It will give you more stimulus than champagne.'[71] Getting ready for the Schiffs' party on 2 May, the publication day of *Sodome*, Proust forgot to dilute the dose he was giving himself, and burned his digestive tube, suffering so much pain that he lost consciousness.[72] But he succeeded in seeing them on 18 May at the supper party they were giving at the Ritz after the première of Stravinsky's ballet *Le Renard* – a party for Stravinsky, Diaghilev, the dancers, Picasso, Proust and James Joyce, who'd arrived in Paris. Choosing the wrong moment to ask Stravinsky whether he liked Beethoven, Proust was told that he detested him and that the last quartets were the worst things he ever wrote.

It's hard to choose between conflicting versions of his conversation with Joyce. Joyce, who arrived late, didn't possess a dinner jacket; Proust was wearing his fur coat. They sat down together and, according to one account, Joyce said: 'I've headaches every day. My eyes are terrible.' Proust answered: 'My poor stomach. What am I going to do? It's killing me. In fact, I must leave at once.' 'I'm in the same situation,' Joyce replied, 'if I can find someone to take me by the arm. Goodbye.' 'Charmé,' said Proust, 'oh, my stomach.' Joyce afterwards told one friend that Proust asked whether he liked truffles and, when he said he did, commented: 'Here are the two greatest literary figures of our time meeting and asking each other whether they like truffles.' But Joyce told another friend: 'Proust would only talk about duchesses, while I was more concerned with their chambermaids.' A third friend, Frank Budgen, was told: 'Our talk consisted solely of the word "No". Proust asked me if I knew the duc de so-and-so. I said, "No." Our hostess asked Proust if he had read such and such a piece of *Ulysses*. Proust said, "No." And so on.'[73]

The next day Proust tried to soothe the offended Laure Hayman, who'd come to believe she was the model for Odette. Assuring her Odette couldn't have been more unlike her, he called her a cruel correspondent who wrote only to cause him pain, 'but in my memories you were really remarkable'.[74] Like the comtesse de Chevigné, she was one of the women he'd most admired, and it was painful to know the novel had made them both so hostile. Writing about Edmond de Goncourt in an article for *Le Gaulois*[75] (27 May 1922), Proust wryly recalled how guests at princesse Mathilde's salon had gone out of their way to avoid telling Goncourt which day they were 'at home'. 'He listens, he repeats, he bases his memoirs on us.'[76] Now it was Proust who was under fire for making public use of private experiences, and he deeply resented 'the cruelty of a woman I loved thirty years ago. . . . Such letters, and having to answer them, finish off all work, quite apart from pleasure, which I gave up long ago.'[77]

Violet Schiff remembered Proust as a man whose 'first impulse was always to try and make everyone who came near him happier than they had been before, to help them in any way . . .'.[78] With the time approaching for a new Blumenthal award, he wanted to help Rivière's assistant, Jean Paulhan, but there was an age limit of thirty-five, and Paulhan was thirty-seven. Proust tried to persuade Mme Blumenthal to make an exception in view of Paulhan's war record – 'I have written 20 pages of irrefutable arguments'[79] – but she refused, and when the jury met on 13 June the prize was awarded to Benjamin Crémieux.

Three days earlier, eating ice-cream and iced beer in his overheated room, Proust caught a chill,[80] and though he got up to attend a party at Mme Hennessy's on the evening of the 12th, he missed the meeting. At the party he met Marcel Prévost, and they discussed the possibility of serialising *La Prisonnière* in the *Revue de France*. Writing to Rivière, Proust said he'd probably give it to Prévost, but changed his mind after a strong protest from Rivière and a visit from Gide, who accused him of being abysmally ungrateful to the NRF.[81]

Also at the party was Jeanne de Caillavet, who'd married again. He offered her a lift home in his taxi, and, when she refused, told her they'd never see each other again.[82] When Lucien Daudet called, he didn't need to be told. Diffident and sad, he said little, and when he talked about the memento Proust had given him twenty-six years ago, a little carved ivory box with the words 'To Friendship', Proust offered him anything in the room as a keepsake. When he was leaving, scarcely able to restrain his tears, Lucien wanted to embrace Proust, who pulled away, saying he hadn't shaved or washed. Lucien kissed his left hand and hurried away.[83] But he was always inconsistent in his assumptions about how much life he had ahead of him: in a letter to Tronche on 24 or 25 June he said: 'The reworking of this typescript where I am making additions everywhere and changing everything, has hardly begun.'[84]

In June he agreed to meet a protégé of Curtius at the Ritz. Jacques Benoist-Méchin was received in a room lit only by a small lamp with pink shade. Lying on a divan, Proust was wearing a starched shirt under his evening suit, but his legs were covered in a tartan rug. 'His cheeks, though shaved, had a charcoaly colour, and the hand he held out was in a grey cotton glove.' He looked like 'an Assyrian magus with heavy eyelids'. But Benoist-Méchin never forgot the 'dark velvet eyes, deep and penetrating . . . luminous, soft, resplendent with intelligence'.[85]

During the third week of June Proust succumbed to a rheumatic fever which kept his temperature steadily at 102 degrees,[86] but by the middle of July he felt well enough to go out with Edmond Jaloux, Paul Brach and some other friends to the Boeuf sur le toit, the cabaret Cocteau had made fashionable. The evening started quietly, but after Jaloux left for a party, a drunken brawl developed between a group of Brach's friends, including the comte de Maleissye-Melleville, and a group which Proust described as consisting of pimps and queers.[87] He had the impression the patron, Moyse, and the waiters were supporting this group. Insulted by a drunken stranger, Proust promptly challenged him to a duel, and they exchanged names and addresses, but the man, Jacques Delgado, sent a charming letter of apology.[88]

Feeling capable of working, he felt inclined to postpone publication of the next volume. 'On both parts there is still work to be done. . . . It is better to let my world breathe and appetite return.'[89] Hearing the title 'La Fugitive' was to be used for a Tagore translation, he wanted to give it up, but let himself be persuaded to keep it. In correspondence with Gallimard, he philosophised about ends and means. 'Make it an objective, and happiness destroys itself totally. It gives itself totally to people who do not look for satisfaction and live altruistically for an idea.'[90] There is also some moralising about generosity in late additions to the novel, as if he were wanting to incorporate a valedictory message to mankind. The more emphasis there is on vocation, the less there is on self-assertion, and the more on altruism.

In July and August he made two last contributions to newspapers. On 22 July *La Renaissance* published his reply to a questionnaire about the continuity of style. Writers should not concern themselves with originality of form, he said. 'The eyes of the mind are turned inwards, one must render the interior model with the greatest possible fidelity.'[91] In mid-August, he was one of the writers to answer a question posed by *L'Intransigeant*: what would you do if the world were about to come suddenly to an end? 'I believe life would quickly seem delicious, if we were suddenly threatened with death, as you suggest. Indeed, think how many projects, journeys, love affairs, periods of study it – our life – holds in solution, invisible to our laziness which, confident of the future, incessantly postpones them.'[92]

The typist, Yvonne, had been dismissed in June, but at the end of August he re-engaged her to retype *La Prisonnière*, only to find he was too ill to say what he wanted her to do. In early September he had some of the worst asthma attacks of his life, followed by giddiness, falling over whenever he tried to stand up.[93] Nor did he have control over his speech or his memory. 'I have been deprived successively of speech, sight and movement,' he told Curtius, 'at least I fall over at each step I take.' But he went on in the letter to assert that true literature 'familiarises people with parts of the soul which are still unknown. We must never be afraid to go too far, for truth lies beyond.'[94]

Domestic problems had always presented themselves to him in the cruellest possible form at the worst possible moment; now he became convinced there were cracks in his chimney, letting fumes of carbon monoxide into his room. 'The effect is a despair worse than death. And, obliged to work without a single day of remission, I do not like to complain.'[95] A letter written by Céleste on 20 or 21 September told Rivière that for three days Proust had been having chronic asthma attacks.[96] But, when he was able to go out to the Ritz, he felt better, and took this as a confirmation that carbon monoxide fumes were making him worse. He stopped having his fire lit, and, depending on pullovers and hot-water bottles, the body he'd accustomed to an overheated atmosphere continued its progress towards death in an unheated room.[97]

He was more ambivalent than ever about wanting to live on. In so far as he did, his hopes were fed by a new asthma remedy called Évadmine, which had become available. A mixture of adrenalin and hypophysial extract, it had to be administered by subcutaneous injections, and Proust was being injected with a mixture of Évadmine and Kola.[98] Though the immediate effect was stimulating, he felt more exhausted after an hour or so.[99] But he was still struggling to work, and three times he made radical changes to the opening of *La Prisonnière*.[100]

His unhappiness at this time was compounded by what Sydney Schiff told him about Scott-Moncrieff's English translation. The title, taken from a Shakespeare sonnet, is triply inept since the three key words, 'remembrance', 'things' and 'past', fail to correspond with 'recherche', 'temps' and 'perdu', while, as Proust explained in a letter to the stubborn Scott-Moncrieff, he was destroying the balance between the overall title and the title of the final volume. The English title for the first volume, 'Swann's Way', so annoyed Proust that he told Schiff: 'I certainly shall not allow *Du côté de chez Swann* to appear under the title you tell me.'[101]

He still had financial problems and still dithered over ways of resolving them. Serge André, proprietor of the reviews Jacques Boulenger edited, was offering 10,000 francs for the corrected proofs and the manuscript of *Sodome* Part Two, and though Proust had no objection to selling them, he felt unable to accept money from a friend, and, feeling that André liked him, refused to sell them to him. In order to make the same amount of money, 10,000 francs, he agreed to condense the whole of *La Prisonnière* into 127 pages for *Les Oeuvres libres*. One reason he needed the money was that he'd lent 5,000 francs to friends he described as 'overwhelmingly needy'.[102] As

Dr Bize told him, he was in no state to work, and at the beginning of the autumn, thanks mainly to the unheated room, he caught influenza, and then refused to collaborate with Dr Bize's attempts to cure it. Because of his phobia about germs, he was fanatically careful about disinfecting letters, but he refused to rest, and, even when he asked for stewed fruit or fresh fruit, ate almost none of it. Apart from the milk in his coffee, he was taking no nourishment, saying you could cure a fever only by starving it. All he fancied was iced beer, which he constantly demanded, and Albaret was despatched to the Ritz. When Dr Bize prescribed medicines, Proust invariably sent Céleste out to buy them, but they were nearly always thrown away unused. He said he was a better doctor than the doctors. To relieve the congestion of the bronchial tubes and lungs, Dr Bize prescribed injections of camphorated oil. 'Maître,' said the doctor, 'this influenza is nothing, I assure you. If you'll agree to look after yourself as I suggest, it will be cured inside a week.' In what Céleste calls his 'gentle, gasping voice', Proust answered: 'My dear doctor, I must and shall go on correcting the proofs. Gallimard is waiting for them.'[103]

He not only made extensive alterations to the proofs but, with secretarial help from Yvonne, prepared a new and much shorter ending to the Albertine story, using the title *Albertine disparue*, instead of *La Fugitive*, and cutting about two-thirds of the book. There's an unequivocal note indicating a cut from the end of the first chapter on page 648 to the beginning of the Venice episode on page 898. *Albertine disparue* is a very short volume, but in August 1922 he wrote to Gallimard: 'it is certain short books sell better'. When Robert Proust and Jacques Rivière edited his final volumes for publication, they knew about his changes to the Albertine story. The typescript of *Albertine disparue* has notes on it in Rivière's handwriting, but although Proust undoubtedly regarded it as definitive, and although he was saying, only three months before he died, that he was dissatisfied with *La Fugitive*,[104] this was what they published in 1925, and it has always been accepted as the sixth of the seven volumes in the novel. After the death of Robert Proust, his daughter, Suzy Mante-Proust, joined the conspiracy of silence, and it was only after her death that *Albertine disparue* was published in 1987.

It would seem that Robert Proust and Rivière had two

reasons for suppressing it. One was that they couldn't simply have substituted it for *La Fugitive* since it doesn't lead straight into *Le Temps retrouvé*. The other is that they thought Proust's interests would be better served if they gave the impression he'd died with his work on the novel more or less complete – that the text they were publishing was definitive. This was misleading. Proust's correspondence with Gallimard, which was published in 1989, leaves us in no doubt that, even if he'd already written the word 'Fin', Proust was still intending to make a lot of additions to the novel. In February 1922 he told Gallimard he'd have 'more books to offer you' if only he lived. It is clear that what he had in mind was whole volumes to be interpolated between *Albertine disparue* and *Le Temps retrouvé*. '*À la recherche du temps perdu* is scarcely beginning,' he said.[105]

What remains unclear is how much he'd have salvaged of the material discarded from *La Fugitive*. Though it would have been obvious to anyone else that he didn't have much time left, it was only intermittently obvious to him, and, working with a temperature that never fell below 102 degrees,[106] he was in no state to be consistent in the changes he made. In *La Fugitive* Albertine is killed in a riding accident in Touraine, and Aimé, the head waiter modelled on Olivier, is sent there to make posthumous enquiries about her sexual activities. The Narrator's jealousy has outlived her. In *Albertine disparue* she dies on the banks of the River Vivonne, and the question of her bisexuality is resolved much more quickly by indicating that she ran away to rejoin Mlle Vinteuil and her girlfriend. But not all the references to Touraine are cut, though Proust obviously intended to cut them.

In 1921 he'd told Gallimard the death of Albertine and the process of forgetting her were better than anything else he'd written, which makes it seem likely that in one of the new volumes he'd have salvaged quite a lot of this material. In all the rewriting he'd done since 1914, his habit had been to add, not subtract. Just before the 250–page cut, the Narrator is reminding himself that it shouldn't be impossible to believe in one's own death: death is in action every day of our lives. The final sentence of the chapter affirms that Albertine had been an obstacle between him and the demi-goddesses who fill us with a longing to penetrate their mythological existence. She stood between him and his vocation. The sequence after the massive cut deals with the trip to Venice. We now have an effective jump-cut from the demi-goddesses to the glittering golden angel on the campanile of St Mark's, promising with its out-stretched arms certain joy in the future.

With at least part of his mind Proust still believed he had ahead of him the joy of fulfilling his vocation. Perhaps, with his high temperature, he even half believed that, if he threatened to scrap some of the best sequences he'd ever written, he'd be spared for long enough to work them back into the texture of the narrative. Could God want him to waste those 250 pages containing the memories of a sweetly innocent Albertine, the exploratory conversations with Albertine's friend Andrée, the incredulous discovery that the article he sent to *Le Figaro* has been published, the conversation which reveals how much the duchesse de Guermantes' attitude to Swann has changed since his death, the part Gilberte plays in helping the Narrator to forget Albertine, and the discovery of Saint-Loup's homosexu-ality? A good reason for thinking Proust didn't intend to scrap this revelation is that he hasn't cut the first of the incidents building up to it – an overheard conversation which shows Saint-Loup to be on friendly terms with a footman.

But we now have to admit there will never be a definitive version of *À la recherche du temps perdu*.

THIRTY-ONE

EXIT NARRATOR

In mid-September he ignored his influenza in an abortive attempt to see Ernest Forssgren, who was about to sail for New York and was briefly in Paris, staying at the Riviera Hôtel in the rue Papillon. Finding the boulevard Haussmann building had been made into a bank, he went to see Robert Proust's concierge, who refused to give him the address but promised to forward a letter if Ernest wrote one. He did, expecting it would take two or three days to reach Proust, but two days later, returning to his hotel at three in the morning, Ernest found a note from Proust, who'd just left. According to the hotelier, he'd called in the afternoon to ask what time M. Forssgren usually came back in the evening. Yesterday, said the hotelier, he'd come back at eleven o'clock. Arriving before midnight, Proust waited about three hours. He was wearing a heavy fur coat, but soon started shivering. The note said: 'Sorry to miss you. You did not come back! Do not call at my flat now, but let me know when you are leaving. Write to me at the Ritz, place Vendôme, please forward.'[1]

It was presumably Céleste's hostility to Ernest that made Proust want to meet him at the hotel, but, two days later, he received a letter asking him to call at the flat.[2] Céleste opened the door, 'stiff, pale, like a ghost. "It's you, Ernest. You see, I am still here." '[3] She led him into the drawing-room, told him how famous M. Proust had become, but didn't allow Ernest into the bedroom. M. Proust had made himself ill, she said, by going out at night.

But in early October he again went out. This time it was to test an episode he'd already written: at the comte and comtesse de Beaumont's soirée he'd see nearly all the survivors of Parisian high society. It was a foggy night, and on the way home he caught another chill. According to Céleste, the only witness, this was a turning point. In his last seven weeks he scarcely slept.

When he wasn't shaken with coughing or struggling for breath, he was working, in dread of failing to finish correcting the proofs of *La Prisonnière* in time for the NRF. He was always ringing the bell, for a hot-water bottle or a pullover, a book, an exercise book or a slip of paper to glue in. Later there were telephone calls to be made to Dr Bize and Professor Robert Proust. . . . I went to and fro. I made hot milk and coffee. He wanted some stewed fruit immediately. He wanted some iced beer; I sent Odilon. . . . Those last weeks are a sort of long tunnel, more than ever without days or nights – a long darkness with no light but the gleam of the little green lamp.[4]

He coughed incessantly, but never coughed anything up. 'I can't,' he told her. 'I haven't the strength. And it's choking me.'[5] On 19 October he tried to go out in the late afternoon, but came back almost immediately, shuddering, coughing and sneezing.[6] He stayed in close touch with Rivière, who'd submitted a novel, *Aimée*, for the Prix Balzac. Proust tried, unsuccessfully, to secure it for him, and, through him, obtained information about streptococci from his brother, Dr Marc Rivière, who wrote to Proust on 25 October. Proust, who wanted the information partly for his novel and partly to understand his own condition, described the doctor's answers as 'graceful Bordelaisian pastorals in which each microbe is a sign of health'. He also asked Rivière not to let Robert Proust know he'd been in touch with another doctor.[7]

It was Dr Bize who, nervous his uncontrollable patient would die of pneumonia, asked Robert to intervene. Arriving unexpectedly at the flat, Robert tried to persuade his brother to take better care of himself, if only for the sake of his work. The unheated room was dangerous, and around the corner, in the rue Puccini, was a well-run clinic with heated rooms, doctors and nurses. When Proust insisted that Céleste was the only one who understood him, Robert said he could have her admitted with him. But Proust adamantly refused to be moved, and when Robert cautiously hinted at the possibility of forcing him, he was told to go away and not to come back, if it was with the idea of using force. Before leaving, he told Céleste to let him know if Proust got any worse, but Proust told her not to admit either Robert or Dr Bize. 'I don't want anyone here but you.'

Afterwards Robert regretted he hadn't thought of suggesting

his brother should move into the Ritz.[8] He asked Reynaldo to intervene, and, though he knew how resistant Proust would be, Reynaldo wrote a long letter, telling him what Robert had said. 'Marcel doesn't have anything *serious*. It's a matter of pneumococcia, that's to say something which gets better and can easily be cured.' In the last paragraph of the letter, Reynaldo said how much he regretted not having the least influence on Proust, and 'it pains me to think you didn't even try to eat a little purée, as you'd promised, and that you went on observing a regimen of fasting, which can't be good at this time'.[9]

But Proust, not wanting to get better, assumed he couldn't have got better, even if he'd wanted to. Talking to Céleste, he said it was awful to think doctors could torture dying people by injecting serums to give them ten more minutes or perhaps twelve more hours of a wretched life. He made her promise never to let them give him any injections.[10]

A few days later, he asked her to telephone Robert, who saw he was welcome to come as often as he liked, on condition he didn't try to intervene. Reynaldo was another regular caller, but mostly left without being able to see him. Morand called, but failed to camouflage his sadness at seeing how changed he was.[11] For a long time he'd been trying to economise with energy, funnelling it all into his work and, towards the end, he tried to use his voice as little as possible. Mostly Céleste could understand what he wanted from a sign or a look; sometimes he'd write on little squares of paper, and she was so familiar with his handwriting she could read it upside down. 'I'm so hot from coughing I will probably try to drink a hot tisane.' 'I have just coughed more than three thousand times, my back and stomach are finished, everything.' 'Céleste, I want an empty teacup and some sugar.' 'Can someone run and get me a peach or an apricot from the Ritz?' 'I need very hot sheets and pullovers. Remember, all your sheets have a smell that makes me cough uselessly.' 'I hope you'll pay strict attention to my orders, or I shall be very cross.' But when he wrote the word 'cross' he'd look up and smile to show it was a joke.[12]

In the second week of November he asked her to have a bunch of flowers sent to Dr Bize, and to take one to Léon Daudet, who'd just written another long article on him. She saw Daudet, who kept her talking on the stairs and tearfully told her she could send for him at any hour of the day or night if he could be of any help.[13] And as a final gesture of reconciliation to Marie Scheikévitch, he instructed Céleste that after his death she should return the cigarette lighter she'd given him.[14] He also told Céleste he was going to leave a letter for her in the little Chinese cabinet. Half jokingly he tried to make her promise not to open it until he was dead, and half jokingly she refused to promise.

On Friday 17 November he rang for her in the evening and, before she went out of the room, told her to turn her back on him. 'I want to try to sit up on the edge of the bed.' When he gave her permission to turn round, he was back in bed, covered up. 'My poor Céleste, what is going to happen if I cannot manage by myself any more?' She told him it was just a passing weakness, but by then he had pneumonia and an abscess on the lung.[15]

In the evening of the same day, saying he felt better, he asked her to cook him a sole. Sole was what his mother had given him to eat during childhood illnesses. Céleste was preparing it when Robert arrived. While the brothers were together, Proust called her in and said he didn't want the sole after all. Before leaving, Robert explained that after examining him he'd advised against eating it because his heart was rather tired. At midnight Proust rang for her, wanting her to do some work with him. He seemed almost cheerful. If he got through the night, he said, he'd have proved he knew better than the doctors did. After chatting with her for a while, he started adding material to the proofs and correcting them, dictating until he said it was more tiring to dictate than to write. He took his pen and worked for over an hour. When he said he was too tired to go on, it was half-past three. What had probably happened was that the abscess had burst and septicaemia set in. He told her where to paste in the strips, refused a warm drink, and kept telling her how kind she was. He was breathing with difficulty, and sometimes his eyelids would flutter.

At about seven in the morning he asked for coffee. Moving like a sleepwalker, she went to the kitchen, where she told her sister she wouldn't be able to hold out much longer. When she took the coffee in, he seemed so weak that she offered to hold the saucer. After drinking a little, he signalled that he wanted to be left alone. Trying to hold her breath, she stood behind the door beside the bed, and, when he rang, went in by the other door. He knew where she'd been, and told her not to switch the light off. Pulling at the sheet and trying to pick up the papers on the bed, he said there was a big woman in the room, a horrible big fat woman in black, and he wanted to be able to see. When Céleste offered to chase the woman away, she was told not to touch her. When he seemed to be resting, she sent Albaret to fetch Dr Bize, and went down to the baker's shop to telephone Robert. She'd been scared by the movements of his fingers: it had been said in the village that dying people try to gather things.

Before the doctor arrived, Proust asked for cold beer, and as soon as Albaret came back he went out again to fetch it. When the doctor arrived at about ten, Céleste told him Proust was too weak to resist an injection. Dr Bize wanted to give it to him in the thigh, and, lifting the sheet, she tried not to offend the dying man's modesty. He was on the edge of the bed, with a slightly swollen arm hanging down over the side. She put the arm back under the covers and held the sheet while Dr Bize bent forwards. With his other arm Proust pinched the skin on her wrist. 'Oh Céleste,' he cried out. 'Oh Céleste!' It was worse than accusing her of breaking her promise. As soon as Dr Bize had left, Robert arrived. He'd seen Bize go in and had waited outside in his car. When he said: 'I'm going to give you adrenalin, do you know what that is?' Proust responded by quoting from a schoolboy essay of Robert's.[16] He didn't stay long, but came back an hour later. He told Odilon to bring cupping glasses and told Céleste to fetch an eiderdown and more pillows. He lifted Proust gently up in bed, and, as his breathing became more laboured, sent Odilon out for oxygen cylinders. Later he sent for Dr Bize, and they agreed to call in Dr Babinski, who arrived at about four. When Robert suggested an intravenous injection of camphor, Babinski said there was no point in making Proust suffer. Babinski and Bize left before he died, alone with Céleste and Robert, who closed his eyes. It was half-past four.

Together they laid him out. Robert dressed him in a clean nightshirt, and they changed the sheets and pillows. Robert told her to cut off a lock of hair for him, and one for herself. She forgot Proust's request that she should entwine his fingers with a rosary Lucie Faure had brought back from Jerusalem; she remembered his wish for the abbé Mugnier to come and pray at his deathbed, but the abbé was too ill to come.[17]

Reynaldo arrived later, and telephoned the news to Proust's friends. The first to arrive was Léon Daudet, who wept. He stayed all night, sometimes chatting with Céleste, sometimes staying by the body. Robert decided that, because Proust looked so 'well', the funeral should be delayed until Wednesday 22 November, so that friends could come and pay their respects.

To Edmond Jaloux, he looked 'more dead than other corpses. He was totally absent. His thin, hollowed mask, blackened by a sick man's beard, was bathed in a greenish shadow, half-mysterious. A big bunch of violets was resting on his chest. . . . In the same way that he hadn't been alive like other people, he wasn't dead like others, and the grief of his friends was taking part in something of the inexpressible majesty which emanated from his immobile face.'[18]

But when Paul Morand came on Sunday, he told Céleste that sometimes Proust, closing his eyes out of weariness, had told him to go on talking. 'And he'd shut his eyes but leave one eye just slightly open to watch. . . . He's doing that still, even now: one lid is just slightly raised.'[19]

REFERENCE NOTES

Though I've translated all the passages of quotation from the French, I've given references, wherever possible, to existing English translations, since most readers will be referring to these rather than to the French texts. See Bibliography for details of the editions used. There are two translations, both incomplete, of *Contre Sainte-Beuve*. The reader will therefore find some notes referring to the French text, some to *Against Sainte-Beuve* and some to *By Way of Sainte-Beuve*.

Abbreviations

Bulletin = *Bulletin de la Société des Amis de Marcel Proust*
NRF = *Nouvelle Revue française*
CG = *Correspondance générale*

Chapter 1

1 Francis and Gontier, p. 57
2 Gregh, p. 32
3 Letter to Mme Straus, shortly after 21.5.11
4 March, p. 20
5 Albaret, p. 135
6 Adrien Proust, *Traité d'hygiène* (Paris, 1881), *Éléments d'hygiène* (Paris, 1883)
7 *Contre Sainte-Beuve*, p. 575
8 Ibid., p. 573
9 *Remembrance of Things Past* 1, pp. 123–4
10 Ibid., p.125
11 Duplay, p. 42
12 Letter to Montesquiou, 28.9.05
13 *By Way of Sainte-Beuve*, p. 46
14 Ibid., p. 68
15 Ibid., p. 186
16 Ibid., p. 190
17 Francis and Gontier, p. 66
18 *Remembrance of Things Past*, 1, p. 12

19 Ibid., 1, p. 40
20 Letter to Pauline Neuberger, undated
21 *Remembrance of Things Past*, 1, p. 125
22 Maurois, p. 22
23 *Remembrance of Things Past*, 1, p. 45
24 Ibid., p. 43
25 *Jean Santeuil*, pp. 377–8
26 Ibid., pp. 404–5
27 *Remembrance of Things Past*, 1, p. 519
28 Ibid., p. 39
29 Ibid., pp. 31–2
30 Freud letter to Marthe Bernays,19.10.85.
31 Maurois, p. 23
32 *Remembrance of Things Past*, 1, p. 36
33 Ibid., p. 38
34 *By Way of Sainte-Beuve*, p. 23
35 *Remembrance of Things Past*, 1, p. 81
36 Ibid., p. 79
37 Ibid.
38 *L'Indifférent*, pp. 42–3

Chapter 2

1   Louis Veuillot, *Les Odeurs de Paris* (Paris, 1867), p. 22
2   *Remembrance of Things Past*, 1, p. 637
3   Bibliothèque National Cahier 20, fol. 294
4   *Jean Santeuil*, pp. 67–8
5   Ibid., pp. 69–70
6   Ibid., p. 85
7   Albaret, p. 162
8   Francis and Gontier, p. 146
9   *Jean Santeuil*, p. 66
10 Letter to Léon Daudet, 7.21. *Lettres retrouvées*
11 *By Way of Sainte-Beuve*, p. 24
12 I owe this to Elizabeth Russell Taylor
13 *Remembrance of Things Past*, 1, p. 13
14 Ibid., p. 172
15 Ferré, pp. 90–9
16 Ibid., pp. 110–11
17 Ibid., p.115
18 *Jean Santeuil*, p. 65
19 Ibid., p. 66
20 Dreyfus, pp. 16–17
21 Albaret, p. 134
22 *Contre Sainte-Beuve*, pp. 112–13

23 Bulletin 7, p. 272
24 Ferré, p. 132
25 *Remembrance of Things Past*, 1, p. 724
26 Letter to Mme Catusse, undated
27 Catusse, p. 132
28 Dreyfus, p. 12
29 Francis and Gontier, p. 114
30 Halévy, pp. 132-3
31 *Remembrance of Things Past*, 2, pp. 646-7
32 Halévy, p. 122, and Dreyfus, p. 152
33 *Jean Santeuil*, p. 534
34 Letter to Robert Dreyfus, 28.?8.88
35 Ferré, pp. 142-4
36 Halévy, pp. 122-3
37 Dreyfus, *Cahiers Marcel Proust*, 1, p. 23
38 Ibid., p. 21
39 Letter to Antoinette Faure, 15.7.87
40 *Jean Santeuil*, p. 604
41 Ibid., pp. 605-6
42 *By Way of Sainte-Beuve*, p. 58
43 Letter to Antoinette Faure, 15.7.87.
44 Ibid.
45 *By Way of Sainte-Beuve*, pp. 184-5
46 Letter to his mother, 24.9.87
47 Letter to Robert Dreyfus, 28.8.88
48 CG, 4, p. 3
49 Letter from Robert Dreyfus, undated
50 Dreyfus, p. 30
51 Letter to Robert Dreyfus, 28.?8.88
52 Ibid.
53 Ibid.
54 Ibid.
55 Ibid.
56 Ferré, p. 198
57 Letter to Robert Dreyfus, 7.9.88
58 Story told by Gregh, Ferré, p. 170
59 Halévy, cited by Ferré, pp. 166-8
60 *Remembrance of Things Past*, 1, pp. 81-5
61 *Contre Sainte-Beuve*, p. 257
62 Adams, p. 48
63 Letter to Robert Dreyfus, 25.9.88
64 Letter to his mother, 5.9.88
65 Ibid.
66 Letter to Robert Dreyfus, 10.9.88
67 *Jean Santeuil*, pp. 159-60

68 Gregh, pp. 141–3
69 Ibid.
70 Manuscript in University of Illinois collection
71 *Jean Santeuil*, p. 232
72 Prize-giving speech, 8.90
73 Ferré, p. 244
74 Pierre-Quint, p. 30
75 Letter to Halévy, undated
76 Sigmund Freud, *Leonardo da Vinci and a Memory of His Childhood*
    (1910). Reprinted in *The Standard Edition of the Complete
    Psychological Works of Sigmund Freud*, ed. James Strachey (London,
    1953–74)
77 Duplay, p. 14
78 Letter to Mme Straus, shortly after 21.5.11
79 Letter from his mother, 7.9.89 & ?9.89

Chapter 3

1   Theodore Zeldin, *France 1848–1945* (Oxford, 1977–80), vol. 1,
    p. 405
2   Letter to Mme Straus, 17 or 18.2.03
3   Élisabeth de Clermont-Tonnerre, *Mémoires*, vol. 1 (Paris, 1928),
    p. 4
4   Fernand Gregh, *L'Age d'or* (Paris, 1947), p. 179
5   Morand, *Journal*, p. 224
6   Letter to Anatole France, *ca* 15.6.89
7   Gregh, *L'Age d'or*, pp. 175–6
8   Letter to his father, 23.9.90
9   Colette, pp. 84–5
10 Duplay, pp. 24–5
11 Clarac and Ferré, pp. 104–6
12 *Pleasures and Regrets*, pp. 150–1
13 Letter to Jeanne de Caillavet, 19.4.22
14 *Pleasure and Regrets*, pp. 150–1
15 *Cahiers Marcel Proust*, 1, p. 38
16 *Pleasures and Regrets*, pp. 150–1 p.
17 *Remembrance of Things Past*, 2, p. 131
18 Albaret, p. 148
19 *Jean Santeuil*, p. 435
20 Ibid., p. 531
21 Ibid., pp. 531–2
22 Ibid., p. 533
23 Letter from his mother, 14.2.89
24 *Cahiers Marcel Proust*, 1, pp. 46–7
25 Ibid., pp. 25–7

26 Letter from his mother, 23.4.90
27 Letter from his mother, 28.4.90
28 Letter from his mother, 26.6.90
29 *Remembrance of Things Past*, 2, p. 796
30 Pouquet, pp. 16–21
31 Maurois, pp. 53–4
32 Letter to his father, 23.9.90
33 *Jean Santeuil*, p. 191
34 Ibid., p. 504
35 Ibid., p. 260
36 Letter to Mme Straus, 22.11.90
37 *Cahiers Marcel Proust*, 1, p. 49
38 Clermont-Tonnerre, *Robert de Montesquiou et Marcel Proust*, pp. 9–10
39 Robert de Billy, NRF, XX, 1923
40 *Contre Sainte-Beuve*, p. 643
41 15–20.3.91.
42 Albaret, pp. 154–5
43 De Billy, pp. 69–70
44 22.11.90
45 Letter to Mme Straus, 1891
46 Letter to Mme Straus, 13.11.91
47 Gregh, *Cahiers Marcel Proust*, 1, pp. 35–6
48 *Remembrance of Things Past*, 1, pp. 584–5
49 'Journées de lecture', *Le Figaro*, 3.07
50 Letter to Robert de Billy, 10.1.93
51 *Pleasures and Regrets*, p. 73
52 Footnote on p. 196 in vol. 1 of Kolb's edition of the letters
53 'Les Maîtresses de Fabrice', *Le Banquet*, 2, 4.82
54 Letter to Mme Straus, 12.92 or early 93
55 Pierre-Quint, p. 46

Chapter 4

1 Kolb, *Correspondance*, 1, p. 62
2 Adrien Proust, *L'Hygiène du neurasthénique* (Paris 1897), p. 147
3 Ibid., pp. 27–31
4 *Pleasures and Regrets*, pp. 87–99
5 Ibid.
6 Ibid.
7 Ibid.
8 *Cahiers Marcel Proust*, 1, p. 51
9 Ibid., pp. 47–9
10 Gregh, *L'Âge d'or*, p. 166
11 Letter to Robert de Billy, 19.8.92

12 *Pleasures and Regrets*, pp. 193–7
13 Ibid., p. 168
14 *Textes retrouvées*, p. 59
15 Ibid., p. 72
16 *Jean Santeuil*, p. 302
17 Duplay, p. 60
18 Letter to Robert de Billy, 26.1.93
19 Letter to Robert de Billy, 10.1.93
20 *Contre Sainte-Beuve*, p. 547
21 CG, 4, p. 4
22 *Journal des débats*, 14.4.93
23 Clermont-Tonnerre, *Robert de Montesquiou et Marcel Proust*, pp. 136–7
24 Huysmans, *À Rebours* (Paris, 1884), p. 15
25 *Journal des Goncourts* (Paris, 1956–9), 7.7.81
26 Letter to Montesquiou, 29.4.92
27 3.7.93
28 *Remembrance of Things Past*, 1, pp. 154–5
29 Ibid., 2, pp. 295–301
30 *Contre Sainte-Beuve*, pp. 572–6
31 Ibid., pp. 574–6
32 Letter to Montesquiou, 2.7.93
33 Adams, p.63
34 *L'Indifférent*, p. 39
35 Ibid., pp. 51–7
36 *Pleasures and Regrets*, pp. 172–91

Chapter 5

1   Letter to his father, 28.9.93
2   Ibid.
3   Ibid.
4   Letter to Daniel Halévy, 21.7.93
5   Excerpts from unpublished material, *Le Monde*, 26.7.85
6   *Pleasures and Regrets*, pp. 156–60
7   P. 30 of French translation: *L'Intrus*
8   *Pleasures and Regrets*, pp. 156–60
9   Letter to Louisa de Mornand, 21.5.05
10 Letter to Louisa de Mornand, 14.7.05
11 Letter to Robert de Billy, 6–16.9.93
12 Letter to his father, 28.9.93
13 Letter to Grandjean, 13.11.93
14 Letter to Grandjean, 19.11.93
15 Letter to Robert de Billy, 5.11.93
16 Letter to Montesquiou, 10.93

17 Letter to Montesquiou, *ca* 11.93
18 Quoted by Jullian, p. 165
19 Letter to Montesquiou, 6.8.94
20 Letter from Montesquiou, 18.6.94
21 *Pleasures and Regrets*, pp. 100–8
22 Gregh, *L'Âge d'or*, pp. 191–2
23 Philippe Jullian, *Oscar Wilde* (Paris, 1967), p. 246
24 Painter, 1, p. 159
25 *Remembrance of Things Past*, 2, p. 638

Chapter 6

1 *Jean Santeuil*, pp. 583–4
2 Painter, 1, p. 161
3 Letter to Reynaldo Hahn, 16.9.94
4 Letter to Montesquiou, 3.1.95
5 Daudet, p. 22
6 Letter to Reynaldo Hahn, 26.4.95
7 *Pleasures and Regrets*, p. 197
8 Letter to Maria Hahn, 8.95
9 *Le Gaulois*, 24.8.95
10 *Pleasures and Regrets*, pp. 165–6
11 Letter to Yturri, 9.95
12 Letter to Robert de Billy, 9.95
13 Ibid.
14 *Jean Santeuil*, p. 371
15 Letter to Georges de Lauris, 20.8.03
16 *Jean Santeuil*, pp. 371–6
17 Letter to Reynaldo Hahn, 3.96
18 Letter from Reynaldo Hahn to Maria Hahn, 27.9.96
19 *Carnets de 1908*, p. 66
20 Letter to Reynaldo Hahn, ?3.8.96
21 Letter to Reynldo Hahn, 28 or 29.8.96
22 Letter to Reynaldo Hahn, 18 or 20.8.96
23 Letter to Reynaldo Hahn, between middle of 7.96 and 8.8.96
24 Ibid.
25 *Jean Santeuil*, p. 399
26 Ibid., p. 400

Chapter 7

1 *Contre Sainte-Beuve*, p. 417
2 Ibid., pp. 417–18
3 *Remembrance of Things Past*, 1, p. 773
4 *Contre Sainte-Beuve*, p. 418

5   *Jean Santeuil*, p. 85
6   Ibid., p. 121
7   *Contre Sainte-Beuve*, p. 420
8   *Remembrance of Things Past*, 1, p. 194
9   *Jean Santeuil*, pp. 264–5
10 *De la Paralysie labio-glosso-laryngée* (1870), *De l'Aphasie* (1871), *Aphasie et trépannation: localisations cérébrales* (1894)
11 Francis and Gontier, pp. 92–3
12 Cahier, 20
13 Cahier, 20, p. 9
14 Letter to Suzette Lemaire, 25 or 26.9.94
15 Ibid.
16 Gustave Schlumberger, *Mes Souvenirs*, vol. 1 (Paris 1934), pp. 305 ff
17 December 1893 in the *Revue blanche*
18 *Les Plaisirs et les jours*, p. 34, and *Textes retrouvées*, p. 64
19 Letter to Montesquiou, 18.9.94, and letter from Montesquiou to Proust, 1.10.94
20 *Pleasures and Regrets*, pp. 31–47
21 Ibid.
22 Ibid., pp. 117–19
23 Letter to Pierre Lavallée, 7 or 8.4.95
24 Letter from Colette, spring 95
25 *Textes retrouvées*, pp. 209–10
26 *Against Sainte-Beuve*, p. 122
27 *Pleasures and Regrets*, p. 167
28 *Jean Santeuil*, p. 417
29 *Against Sainte-Beuve*, p. 123
30 Jules Renard, *Journal* (Paris, 1948), 2.3.95
31 Lucien Daudet, pp. 13–18
32 Letter to Reynaldo Hahn, 15.11.95
33 Letter to Pierre Lavallée, 7 or 8.4.95, and letters to Reynaldo Hahn, 15.11.95
34 Albert Flament, *Le Bal du Pré Catalan* (Paris, 1946)
35 Blanche, *Cahiers Marcel Proust*, 1, pp. 49–50
36 Ibid., p. 50
37 Letter to Montesquiou, 13.12.95
38 Clermont-Tonnerre, *Robert de Montesquiou et Marcel Proust*
39 Letter to Montesquiou, 12.95
40 *Jean Santeuil*, p. 215
41 Letter from J. Hubert to Anatole France, 28.2.96
42 Letter to Laure Hayman, 11.5.96
43 Letter to Laure Hayman, 12.5.96
44 Letter to Lionel Hauser, shortly after 12.5.99

45 Catalogue G. Andrieux sale of 24.11.28, Kolb, *Correspondance*, 2, p. 123
46 *Le Figaro*, 16.5.96
47 Letter to Montesquiou, 19.5.96
48 Duc de Gramont, Bulletin
49 Letter to Charles Maurras, 28.8.96
50 *Jean Santeuil*, p. 395
51 Letter to Reynaldo Hahn, *ca* 18–20.8.96
52 Letters to Pierre Lavallée, 29.8 and 1.9.96
53 Letter to his mother, 2.9.96
54 *By Way of Sainte-Beuve*, p. 33
55 Straus, pp. 104–5
56 Letter to Reynaldo Hahn, 3 or 4.9.96
57 Letter to Montesquiou, 9.96
58 Letter to Montesquiou, 22.10.96
59 Letter to Montesquiou, 21.10.96
60 Letter to Antoine Bibesco, 4.12.02
61 *Jean Santeuil*, p. 369
62 Letter to Montesquiou, 22.10

Chapter 8

1 Flament, *Le Bal du Pré Catalan*, pp. 155–9
2 *Remembrance of Things Past*, 2, p. 972
3 Letter to Jacques-Émile Blanche, 9.02
4 Letter from Montesquiou, early 1.97
5 *Le Journal*, 3.2.97
6 *Le Figaro*, 7.2.97
7 Letter to Gaston de Caillavet, undated
8 Pouquet, p. 24
9 Albaret, p. 139
10 *Jean Santeuil*, p. 218
11 Flament, *Le Bal du Pré Catalan*, pp. 109–13
12 Letter to Montesquiou, 21.5.97
13 Jean-Denis Bredin, *The Case of Alfred Dreyfus* (London, 1987), passim
14 Letter to Montesquiou, 29.6.97
15 Letter to Lucien Daudet, 6.97
16 Lucien Daudet, p. 202
17 Letter to Lucien Muhlfeld, 7 or early 8.97
18 Letter to Reynaldo Hahn, 16.7.97
19 Letter to Mme de Brantes, 1.9.97
20 Letter to Léon Yeatman, 1.9.97
21 Letter to Mme Léon Yeatman, 4.01
22 Ibid.

23   Letter from Robert de Flers, 20.9.97
24   Letters to Marie Nordlinger, 1st week of 2.04 and 9 or 10.2.05
25   *L'Écho de Paris*, 26.10.97
26   Letter to Suzette Lemaire, 24.10.97
27   *Cahiers Marcel Proust*, 5, p. 34
28   Letter to Anatole France, after 18.12
29   A. Silvera, *Daniel Halévy and His Times* (Ithaca, NY, 1966) p. 96
30   *Jean Santeuil*, pp. 324–5
31   Ibid., pp. 328–49
32   Letter to Mme Daudet, after 22.3.98
33   Letter to Lucien Daudet, 1.1.98
34   Letter to Abel Desjardins, 98
35   Letter to Jean Helleu, soon after 2.6.98
36   Letter to Mme Catusse, 7.98
37   Letter to Constantin de Brancovan, end of 9.98
38   *Jean Santeuil*, pp. 495–6
39   Kolb, *Correspondance*, 2, pp. 252–4
40   Letter to Mme Straus, 9.98
41   List published in *Le Temps*, 1 January 1899
42   Letter to Constantin de Brancovan, towards the end of 9.98
43   Letter to Léon Daudet, soon after 25.2.99
44   Telegram to Labori, 11.8.99
45   Letter to his mother, 10.9.99
46   Ibid.
47   Letter to his mother, 12.9.99.
48   Letter to his mother, 22.9.99

Chapter 9

1   *Textes retrouvées*, p. 99
2   *Contre Sainte-Beuve*, p. 660
3   Ibid., p. 664
4   *Jean Santeuil*, p. 402
5   Letter to Marie Nordlinger, soon after 25.12.98
6   *Jean Santeuil*, p. 722
7   Ibid., p. 400
8   Letter to Louis d'Albufera and Louisa de Mornand, 30.10.03
9   Flament, *Le Bal du Pré Catalan*, pp. 217–19
10   *Le Figaro*, 26.4.99
11   Letter to Constantin de Brancovan, 15.8.99
12   Letter to his mother, 28 or 29.9.99
13   Letter to his mother, 12.9.99
14   Letter to his mother, 15.9.99
15   Ibid.
16   Letter to his mother, 17.9.99

17 Letter to his mother, 28 or 29.9.99
18 Letter to his mother, 2.10.99
19 Letter to his mother, 22.9.99
20 *Remembrance of Things Past*, 2, p. 1047
21 Letter to his mother, 28 or 9.9.99
22 Ibid.
23 Letter to his mother, 2.10.99
24 According to Douglas Ainslie
25 *The Works of John Ruskin*, ed. E.T. Cook and Alexander Wedderburn (London, 1903–12), vol. 5, p. 333
26 Letter to Pierre de Chevilly, 13.10.99
27 Letter to Montesquiou, 10.99
28 Letter to his mother, 2.10.99
29 Chapter 48
30 *The Works of John Ruskin*, vol. 35, p. 116
31 Ibid., p. 115
32 Letter to Chevilly, 14 or 21.10.99
33 *Revue générale*, 57, 10.95, pp. 481–99
34 Letter to Marie Nordlinger, 7 or 8.2.00
35 *On Reading Ruskin*, p. 18
36 Ibid., p. 14
37 Letter to Marie Nordlinger, soon after 21.1.00
38 Tim Hilton, 'Ruskin Retrouvé', *New York Review of Books*, 22.10.87
39 Letter to Marie Nordlinger, soon after 21.1.00
40 Ruskin, *Collected Works*, 8, p. 217
41 *On Reading Ruskin*, p. 45
42 Letter to Marie Nordlinger, 7 or 8.2.00
43 *Le Figaro*, 13.2.00
44 Painter, 1, p. 258
45 Letter to Marie Nordlinger, 25 or 6.4.00
46 *On Reading Ruskin*, p. 14
47 *Against Sainte-Beuve*, p. 150
48 *Lettres à une amie*, p. 14
49 Letter to Antoine Bibesco, 20.12.02
50 Letter to Constantin de Brancovan, 2nd half of 1.03
51 Letter to Pol-Louis Neveu, 14.2.00
52 Preface to *The Bible of Amiens*, p. 91
53 Letter to Léon Yeatman, soon before 3.5.00
54 *By Way of Sainte Beuve*, p. 66
55 Letter to Mme Straus, CG, 6, p. 123
56 Painter, 1, p. 253
57 Footnote to *Le Bible d'Amiens*
58 *By Way of Sainte-Beuve*, p. 66
59 Ibid., p. 67

60 Letter to Montesquiou, CG, 1, p. 12
61 *By Way of Sainte-Beuve*, p. 67
62 Obituary by Maurice de Fleury, *Le Figaro*, 27.11.03
63 Letter to Pierre Lavallée, shortly before 29.4.00
64 *Contre Sainte-Beuve*, p. 449
65 Letter to Lucien Daudet, 6.00
66 Letter from his mother, 14 or 15.8.00
67 Letter from his mother, 17.8.00
68 *Remembrance of Things Past*, 3, pp. 641–67
69 Ibid.
70 *By Way of Sainte-Beuve*, pp. 66–7
71 *Textes retrouvées*, p. 105
72 Ibid., p. 107
73 Letter to his mother, 24.1.01
74 *Remembrance of Things Past*, 2, p. 3
75 Letter to Mme Straus shortly after 21.5.11 and to Reynaldo Hahn shortly after 24.12.11
76 Letters to Mme Catusse, 16.9.06, 10.06 and soon after 26.10.06
77 Letter to Constantin de Brancovan, 31.1.01
78 Ibid.
79 Letter to Lucien Daudet, 7.2.01
80 Letter to his mother, undated, Kolb, *Correspondance*, 2, p. 419
81 Letter to his mother, 11.8.04
82 Letter to Anna de Noailles, 1.5.01
83 Letter to Anna de Noailles, 7.5.01
84 Letter to Anna de Noailles, 27.5.01
85 Léon Daudet, *Souvenirs des milieux littéraires et politiques* (Paris, 1920), p. 641
86 Letter to Anna de Noailles, 8.1.04

Chapter 10

1 *Remembrance of Things Past*, 2, pp. 419–20
2 Ibid., p. 722
3 Ibid., p. 714
4 Montesquiou, 'Cahiers secrets', *Mercure de France*, 15.4.29, p. 313
5 Letter to Anna de Noailles, 8.1.04
6 Letter to Lucien Daudet, 13 or 20.7.04
7 Letter to his mother, 31.8.04
8 Ibid.
9 Letter to Mme Daudet, 18.5.04
10 Letter to Dr Georges Linossier, 9.04
11 Letter to Antoine Bibesco, 6, 7 or 8.1.03
12 *Praeterita*, 1, ch. 9, section 181
13 Letter to his mother, 8.9.04

14 *Jean Santeuil*, pp. 290–7
15 Letter to Georges de Lauris, early 10.09
16 Georges de Lauris, *Cahiers Marcel Proust*, 1, pp. 38–9
17 Letter to Georges de Lauris, 9.04
18 Georges de Lauris, 1st cahier
19 Letter to Antoine Bibesco, 12.04
20 Letter to Antoine Bibesco, 11.04
21 Clermont-Tonnerre, *Robert de Montesquiou et Marcel Proust*, p. 11
22 Letter to Éduard Rod, summer 02
23 Letter to Antoine Bibesco soon after 6.6.02
24 Various letters around 6.02
25 Léon Daudet, *Salons et journaux*, (Paris, 1917), pp. 298–9
26 Daudet, *Souvenirs*, pp. 639–40, and *Paris Vécu*, 1st series (1929), p. 184
27 Letter to Antoine Bibesco, 9.9.02
28 Letter to Antoine Bibesco, 6 or 7.02
29 Letter to Antoine Bibesco, 10.8.02
30 17.8.02
31 Letter to Antoine Bibesco, 10.8.02
32 Letter to his mother, 14.8.02
33 Letter to Antoine Bibesco, 8–9.02
34 Letter to Antoine Bibesco, *ca* 6 or 7.02
35 Letter to his mother, 14.8.02
36 Letter to his mother, 15.8.02
37 Letter to his mother, evening of 15.8.02
38 Letter to his mother, 1.9.02
39 Letter to Lucien Daudet, 5.9.02
40 Cp. *CG*, 2, p.211, and 3, p. 398
41 Inscription dated 6.9.02 on photograph
42 Letter to Reynaldo Hahn, 10.02
43 *On Reading Ruskin*, pp. 118–19. Preface to *Sesame and Lilies*
44 Letter to Marie Nordlinger, *ca* 8.04
45 Letter to his mother, 17.10.02
46 Letter to Antoine Bibesco, 3.11.02
47 Letter to Antoine Bibesco, 10.11.02
48 Letter to Antoine Bibesco, 23.11.02
49 Inaccurate quotation from Mme de Sévigné's letter of 27.5.1680 about her son
50 *Remembrance of Things Past*, 2, pp. 815–16
51 Letter to his mother, 9.3.03
52 Wildenstein Gallery Catalogue, *Marcel Proust and His Time* (London, 1955)
53 Letter to Marie Nordlinger, early 8.03
54 Letter to Marie Nordlinger, 27.5.04
55 Letter to Antoine Bibesco, 6 or 7.4.03

56 Letter to his mother, 9.3.03
57 Letter to his mother, 6.12.02
58 Ibid.
59 Ibid.
60 Letter to Constantin de Brancovan, soon before 24.11.03
61 Letter to Antoine Bibesco, 20.12.02
62 Letter to Antoine Bibesco, 22, 23 or 24.12.02

Chapter 11

1 Letter to Antoine Bibesco, 16.2.03
2 Letter to Antoine Bibesco, 19.1.03
3 *Jean Santeuil*, p. 206
4 Letter to Antoine Bibesco, 28.1.03
5 Letter to Antoine Bibesco, 16.2.03
6 Letter to Antoine Bibesco, 5.2.03
7 Letter to Antoine Bibesco, 10 or 11.3.03
8 Letter to Antoine Bibesco, between 25 and 30.3.03
9 Antoine Bibesco, p. 120
10 Letter to Constantin de Brancovan, 2nd half of 1.03
11 Ibid.
12 Ibid.
13 Letter to Constantin de Brancovan, 1.2.03
14 Valentine Thomson, 'My Cousin Marcel Proust', *Harper's Magazine*, 5.32
15 Letter to Louisa de Mornand, 4.2.03
16 Letter to Lucien Daudet, 14.2.03
17 *Contre Sainte-Beuve*, p. 446
18 Ibid., pp. 447–51
19 Letter to his mother, spring 03
20 Letter to Jacques Boulenger, 23.11.20
21 Letter to his mother, 9.3.03
22 *Contre Sainte-Beuve*, p. 459
23 Letter to Lionel Hauser, 27.5.16
24 Letter to Georges de Lauris, 29.7.03
25 Letter to his mother, 16.7.03
26 Ibid.
27 *Contre Sainte-Beuve*, p. 461
28 Ibid., pp.476–8
29 Gramont in Bulletin
30 Letter to Georges de Lauris, 20.8.03
31 Letter to Georges de Lauris, *ca* 8 or 9.09
32 Letter to Robert de Billy, 2 or 3.10
33 Letter to Robert de Billy, 17, 18 or 19.8.06
34 Letter to Auguste Marguiller, 20.10.03

35 Kolb, *Correspondance*, 4, p. xiii
36 Letter to Anna de Noailles, 26.10.03
37 Letter to Anna de Noailles, 3.12.03
38 Letter to Lucien Daudet, 25.11.03
39 Albaret, p. 141
40 Ibid.
41 Letter to Anna de Noailles, 3.12.03
42 *Remembrance of Things Past*, 1, pp. 500–4
43 Letter to Anna de Noailles, 8.1.04
44 Letter from Constantin de Brancovan, 12.1.04
45 Letter to Anna de Noailles, 13.1.04
46 Letter from Anna de Noailles, 14.1.04
47 Letter to Antoine Bibesco, 1st week of 1.04
48 Letter to Anna de Noailles, 15.1.04
49 Letter to Marie Nordlinger, 24–5.1.04
50 Letter to Anna de Noailles, 8.1.04
51 Letter to Marie Nordlinger, 30.1.04
52 Wildenstein Gallery Catalogue
53 Letter to Marie Nordlinger, 6.2.04
54 Letter to Mme Daudet, early 3.04
55 Letter to Anna de Noailles, 12.3.04
56 3.3.04
57 Letter to Robert de Flers, 2nd half of 4.04
58 *Séances et travaux de l'Académie des Sciences Morales et Politiques*,
    vol. CLXII (Paris, 1904), pp. 491–2
59 Letter from Anna de Noailles, 25.4.04
60 *Le Figaro*, 18.1.04
61 *Contre Sainte-Beuve*, pp. 710–11
62 Ibid., pp. 710–12
63 Ibid., p. 470–4
64 Letters to François de Croisset, René Peter and Lucien Daudet,
    29.2.04
65 *Candide*, 1.11.28
66 Wildenstein Gallery Catalogue
67 Duplay, p. 138
68 *Remembrance of Things Past*, 1, pp. 620–1
69 Ibid., 2, pp. 377–8
70 Letter to Antoine Bibesco, *ca* 28.3.04
71 Letter to Antoine Bibesco, 1–19.9.04

Chapter 12

1 Letter to Marie Nordlinger, *ca* 25 or 6.5.04
2 Letter to Marie Nordlinger, 27.5.04
3 Letter to Douglas Ainslie, 6.04

4   Letter to Antoine Bibesco, 6.04
5   Letter to Louisa de Mornand, 26.6.04
6   Letter to Louisa de Mornand, 3.7.04
7   Letter to Albufera, 4.7.04
8   *Le Gaulois*, 5.7.04
9   Letter to Louisa de Mornand, 3.7.04
10   Letter from Louisa de Mornand, 13.7.04
11   Letter to Louisa de Mornand, 13.7.04
12   Letter to Louisa de Mornand, 18.7.04
13   Letter to Antoine Bibesco, soon after 17.7.04
14   *Contre Sainte-Beuve*, p. 772
15   *Le Temps*, 11.7.04
16   Letter to Antoine Bibesco, 17.7.04
17   Letter to Albufera, 4.7.04
18   Letters to his mother, 11 and 15.8.04
19   Letter to his mother, 21.9.04
20   Letter to Dr Linossier, 9.04
21   Ibid.
22   Letter to René Peter, 25.10.04
23   Letters to his mother, 21 and 23.9.04
24   Letter to his mother, 21.9.04
25   *Remembrance of Things Past*, 2, pp. 315–16
26   Letter to Marie Nordlinger, 22.8.04; letter to Louisa de Mornand, 24.8.04
27   Letter to Marie Nordlinger, 31.8.04
28   Letter to Marie Nordlinger, 17.9.04
29   Letter to Albufera, 4.9.04
30   Letters to Antoine Bibesco and Louisa de Mornand, 14 and 17.9.04
31   Letter to Gabriel Mourey, 1st half of 11.05
32   Letter to Mme Straus, 8 or 9.11.05
33   Letters to his mother, 16–17 and 17.9.04
34   Letter to Marie Nordlinger, 17.9.04
35   Letter to his mother, 29.9.04
36   Letter to his mother, 21.9.04
37   Letter to his mother, 3.10.04
38   Ibid.
39   Letter to Antoine Bibesco, 5.10.04
40   Ibid.
41   *Contre Sainte-Beuve*, p. 499
42   Letter to Lucien Daudet, middle of 10.04
43   11.10.04
44   Both 11.10.04
45   Letter to Lucien Daudet, middle of 10.04
46   Letter to Georges de Lauris, 1.11.10

47 Telegram to Albufera, 23.10.04
48 Letter to Louisa de Mornand, *ca* 11.04
49 Letter to Mme Catusse, 11.04
50 Letter to Louisa de Mornand, 5 or 12.12.04
51 *Le Figaro*, 15.11.04
52 Letter to Guiche, 23.11.04
53 Letter to Montesquiou, 7.12.04
54 Letter to Louisa de Mornand, 5.12.04
55 Letter to Francis de Croisset, 8 or 9.12.04
56 Letter to Antoine Bibesco, 13.12.04
57 Published 1896, pp. 197–9
58 Letter to Lucien Daudet, 16.12.04
59 Letter to Montesquiou, 19.12.04
60 Letter to Mme Catusse, 10.06
61 Letter to Laure Hayman, 9.06
62 Letter to Anna de Noailles, 28.9.05
63 Letter to Louisa de Mornand, early 10.05
64 *L'Écho de Paris*, 8.1.05
65 Letters to René Peter, 1 or 2.05
66 Letters to Lucien Dudet, 1 or 2.05 and 2–3.05
67 Letter to Radziwill, 28.2.05

Chapter 13

1 Letter to Marie Nordlinger, 9 or 10.2.05
2 Letter from Jean Béraud, first months of 08
3 Letter to Gabriel de la Rochefoucauld, 16.3.05
4 Letter to Guiche, 2.3.05
5 Letter to Anatole France, 4.3.05
6 Letter to Francis de Croisset, 8.3.05
7 Letter to Louisa de Mornand, 10.3.05
8 Scheikévitch, pp. 125–6
9 Letter to Montesquiou, 6.3.05
10 Letter to his mother, undatable
11 Letter to Georges de Lauris, *ca* 3.05
12 *Le Figaro*, 7.5.05, and *Contre Sainte-Beuve*, pp. 503–4
13 Letter to Mme Straus, 9.4.05
14 Letter to his mother, shortly before 21.4.05
15 Letter from Montesquiou, 3.5.05
16 Letter to Louisa de Mornand, 23.4.05
17 Letter to Mme Straus, 7.5.05
18 *Sésame et les lys*, footnote to p. 61
19 *On Reading Ruskin*, pp. 106–7
20 Ibid., p. 116
21 Ibid., p. 119

22 Letter to François de Croisset, after the middle of 5.05
23 Letter to Mme Straus, 28.4.05
24 Letter to Montesquiou, 4.5.05
25 Letter from Montesquiou, 17.5; letter to Montesquiou, 21 or
    22.5.05; letter from Montesquiou, 22.5.05; letter to
    Montesquiou, 23.5.05 and letter from Montesquiou, 23.5.05
26 *Le Gaulois*, 4.6.05
27 *Lettres à une amie*, p. x
28 Letter to his mother, 2.6.05
29 Letter to Marie Nordlinger, 24.6.05
30 *Contre Sainte-Beuve*, pp. 512–14
31 Letters to Marie Nordlinger, 3–4.6 and 4–5.6.05
32 Letter to Marie Nordlinger, 6, 7 or 8.6.05
33 Letter to his mother, 10.6.05
34 Letter from Anna de Noailles, 19.6.05
35 Letter to Anna de Noailles, 19.6.05
36 *Le Figaro*, 19.6.05
37 Letter from Anna de Noailles, 20.6.05
38 Letter to Anna de Noailles, 20.6.05
39 Proust's note to epigraph

Chapter 14

1   Letter to his mother, shortly before 27.6.05
2   Letter to Montesquiou, 9.7.05
3   Letter to Mme Straus, shortly before 26.9.05
4   Letter to Louisa de Mornand, 14.7.05
5   Letter to Anna de Noailles, early 8.05
6   Letter to Antoine Bibesco, 7 or 8.05
7   Letter to Louisa de Mornand, 25.8.05
8   Letter to Mme Straus, shortly before 26.9.05
9   Ibid.
10 Letter to Mme Catusse, in 1910
11 *Remembrance of Things Past*, 2, p. 804
12 Letter to Georges de Lauris, 7.10.08
13 Letter to Mme Straus, shortly before 26.9.05
14 Letter to Anna de Noailles, 27.9.05
15 Letter to Louisa de Mornand, early 10.05
16 Letter from Anna de Noailles, early 10.05
17 *Le Figaro*, 29.9.05
18 Letter to Louisa de Mornand, early 10.05
19 Letter to Anna de Noailles, evening of 28.9.05 or soon afterwards
20 Letter to Montesquiou, shortly after 28.9.05
21 Letter to Anna de Noailles, evening of 28.9.05 or soon afterwards
22 Letter to Reynaldo Hahn, 26.8.06

23 'Journées de lecture', *Le Figaro*, 3.07
24 *Remembrance of Things Past*, 2, p. 357

Chapter 15

1 Baudelaire, *Selected Writings on Art and Artists*, Penguin edition (Harmondsworth, 1972), p. 398
2 *Remembrance of Things Past*, 1, p. 718
3 Letter to Louisa de Mornand, first days of 12.05
4 Letter to Marie Nordlinger, 6.12.05
5 Letter to Francis de Croisset, first half of 12.05
6 Letter to Lucien Daudet, *ca* 3.06
7 Letter to Robert de Billy, late 1.06
8 Letter to Francis de Croisset, 6.1.06
9 Letter to Mme Catusse, *ca* 3.06
10 Letter to Antoine Bibesco, 14.3.06
11 Letter to Lucien Daudet, *ca* 3.06
12 Letter to Antoine Bibesco, 9.3.06
13 Letter to Antoine Bibesco, 14.3.06
14 Letter Éduard Rod, shortly after 16.3.06
15 Letter to Elaine de Guiche, 10.04
16 Albaret, p. 60
17 Letter to Reynaldo Hahn, 21.4.06
18 Albaret, p. 61
19 Letter to Montesquiou, 11.5.06
20 Letter to Reynaldo Hahn, 28.5.06
21 Letter to Lucien Daudet, early 6.06
22 Letter to Ladislas Landowski, shortly after 8.6.06
23 Letter to Lucien Daudet, 17.6.06
24 Letter to Beaunier, 5.6.06
25 Letter to Mme Catusse, shortly after 8.6.06
26 Letter to Robert Dreyfus, 12 or 13.6.06
27 Letter to Gaston Calmette, *ca* 1.6.
28 *Le Figaro*, 5.6.06
29 Letter to Beaunier, 5.6.06
30 *Le Figaro*, 14.6.06
31 Letter to Robert Dreyfus, 20.6.06
32 Letter to Calmette, 7.06
33 Letter to Robert Dreyfus, 20.6.06
34 Letter to Robert Dreyfus, 12 or 13.6.06
35 Letter to Robert Dreyfus, 20.6.06
36 Letter to Reynaldo Hahn, 6.06
37 Letter to Lucien Daudet, 5.7.06
38 Letter from Robert Ulrich to René Peter, 20.8.06
39 Letter to Robert de Billy, 1st days of 11.06

40 Letter to Reynaldo Hahn, *ca* 14.12.06
41 *Le Gaulois*, 4.7.06
42 Letter to Lucien Daudet, shortly after 5.7.06
43 Letter to Marcel Cruppi, 7.06
44 Letter to Fernand Gregh, 10.7.06
45 Letter to Reynaldo Hahn, shortly after 12.7.06
46 Letter to Mme Straus, 21.7.06
47 Ibid.
48 Letter to Anna de Noailles, 16.7.06
49 Letter to Mme Straus, 21.7.06
50 Ibid.
51 Letter to Georges de Lauris, 26.7.06
52 *Remembrance of Things Past*, 1, p. 319
53 Letter to Mme Straus, 28.7.06
54 Letter to Mme Straus, 1.8.06
55 Letter to Robert de Billy, *ca* 17, 18 or 19.8.06
56 Letter to Mme Straus, 8.8.06
57 Letter to Reynaldo Hahn, between 14 and 20.8.06
58 Letter to Mme Catusse, early 9.06
59 Duplay, p. 79
60 Letter to Georges de Lauris, 21.8.06
61 Letter to Mme Catusse, early 9.06
62 Letter to Reynaldo Hahn, 26.8.06
63 Letters to René Peter, 9.06
64 Letters to Georges de Lauris, 9.06
65 Letter to Georges de Lauris, 27.9.06
66 Letter to Robert de Billy, late 9 or early 10.06
67 Letter to Mme Straus, 9.10.06
68 Letter to Mme Catusse, 10.06
69 Letter to Antoine Bibesco, towards end of 11.06
70 Letter to Mme Catusse, 12.12.06
71 Letter to Mme Catusse, 10.06
72 Ibid.
73 Letter to Mme Catusse, 5.11.06
74 Letter to Mme Catusse, 10.06
75 Letter to Mme Catusse, 5.11.06
76 Ibid.
77 Letters to Mme Catusse, 10.06 and 5.11.06
78 Letter to Mme Catusse, 1st days of 11.06
79 Letter to Robert de Billy, 1st days of 11.06
80 Letter to Mme Straus, shortly after 26.10.06
81 Letters to Mme Catusse, 10 and 26.10.06
82 Letter to Reynaldo Hahn 7.1.07
83 Letter to Mme Gaston de Caillavet, 8.12
84 Letter to Mme Straus, shortly after 26.10.06

85 Letter to Mme Catusse, 1st days of 11.06
86 Letter to Mme Catusse, *ca* beginning of 12.06
87 Ibid.
88 Letter to Mme Catusse, 4.12.06
89 Letter to Mme Catusse, *ca* beginning of 12.06
90 Letter to Mme Catusse, 4.12.06
91 *Hopes and Fears for Art* (London, 1882), p. 108; letter to Mme Catusse, *ca* 12.12.06
92 Letter to Mme Catusse, *ca* 10.12.06
93 Letter to Reynaldo Hahn, 18 or 19.9.06
94 Letter to Reynaldo Hahn, 15 or 16.11.06
95 Letter to Reynaldo Hahn, 13.12.06

Chapter 16

1 Letter to Jacques Hébertot, 3.1.07
2 Letter to Mme Catusse, 30.12.06
3 Letter to Mme Straus, middle of 3.07
4 Letter to Mme Catusse, 31.12.06
5 Letter to Robert de Flers, 14.1.07
6 Letter to René Peter, 14.1.07
7 Letter to Mme Catusse, shortly after 21.1.07
8 Albaret, pp. 64–5
9 Francis and Gontier, p. 165
10 Gautier-Vignal, p. 23
11 Letter to his mother, 9.96
12 Albaret, pp. 34 and 86
13 Ibid., p. 83
14 Ibid., p. 72
15 Ibid., pp. 46–63
16 Straus, pp. 38 and 103
17 Letter from Henri van Blarenberghe, 24.9.06
18 *Contre Sainte-Beuve*, p. 151
19 Letter to Robert Dreyfus, 3.2.07
20 *Contre Sainte-Beuve*, pp. 158–9
21 *Remembrance of Things Past*, 3, p. 506
22 *Contre Sainte-Beuve*, p. 786
23 Letter from Gaston Calmette, 1.2.07
24 Letter to Gaston Calmette, 1.2.07
25 Letter to Reynaldo Hahn, 6.2.07
26 Letter to Robert Dreyfus, 3.2.07
27 Letter to Lucien Daudet, 1st days of 2.07
28 Letter to Robert Dreyfus, 3.2.07
29 Letter to Mme Catusse, 2.07
30 Letter to Louisa de Mornand, 1.1.07

31 Letter to Louisa de Mornand, 2.1.07
32 Letters to Louisa de Mornand, shortly after 4.3. and shortly after 5.3.07
33 *Contre Sainte-Beuve*, p. 543
34 Ibid., pp. 542–3
35 Letter to Montesquiou, 15.5.07
36 Letter to Reynaldo Hahn, 7.1.07
37 Letter from Reynaldo Hahn to Montesquiou, 8 or 9.1.07
38 Letter from Montesquiou, 23.3.07
39 Letter to Montesquiou, 8.5.07
40 Letter to Georges de Lauris, 10.2.07
41 Letter to Georges de Lauris, 16.2.07
42 Letter to Georges de Lauris, 18.2.07
43 Letter to Georges de Lauris, shortly after 18.2.07
44 *Contre Sainte-Beuve*, p. 532
45 Letter to Georges de Lauris, shortly after 20.3.07
46 Letter to Reynaldo Hayn, 6.2.07
47 Letter to Paul Bacart, 15.2.07
48 Letter to Mme Straus, middle of 3.07
49 Letter to Francis de Croisset, middle of 5.07
50 Letters to Montesquiou, 3.6 and 10.6.07
51 Letter to Mme Straus, 1.4.07
52 Letter to Georges de Lauris, 7.5.07
53 Letter to Montesquiou, 11.5.07
54 Letter to Mme Straus, *ca* 26.6.07
55 Letter to Reynaldo Hahn, 3.7.07
56 Élisabeth de Gramont, p. 105
57 Letter to Reynaldo Hahn, 3.7.07
58 Ibid.
59 Letter to Mme Straus, 3 or 4.7.07
60 Letter to Robert Proust, 7.07
61 Letter to Robert de Flers, 21.7.07
62 *Contre Sainte-Beauve*, p. 545
63 Ibid., pp. 547–8.
64 Letter to Robert de Flers, shortly after 23.7.07
65 Letter to Reynaldo Hahn, 1.8.07
66 Letter to Mme de Caraman–Chimay, 8.07

Chapter 17

1 Gimpel, p. 173
2 Letter to Reynaldo Hahn, 6.8.07
3 Ibid.
4 Letter to Émile Mâle, 8.8.07
5 *Remembrance of Things Past*, 3, p. 698

6 Letter to Mme de Caraman-Chimay, 8.07
7 Gimpel, pp. 173-4
8 Letter to Émile Mâle, 8.8.07
9 Letter to Emmanuel Bibesco, shortly before middle of 8.07
10 Letter to Georges de Lauris, shortly before middle of 8.07
11 Clermont-Tonnerre, *Robert de Montesquiou et Marcel Proust*, pp. 101-2
12 Duc de Gramont, Bulletin, p. 173
13 Letter to Georges de Lauris, 7.10.08
14 *Contre Sainte-Beuve*, p. 63
15 Ibid., p. 64
16 Ibid., pp. 64-6
17 Letter to Georges de Lauris, 27.8.07
18 Letter to Reynaldo Hahn, 2nd half of 8.07
19 Letter to Mme de Caraman-Chimay, 8.07
20 Letter to Georges de Lauris, 27.8.07
21 Ibid.
22 Letter to Émile Mâle, shortly after middle of 8.07
23 Letter to Paul Helleu, end of 2.08
24 Letter to Robert de Billy, early 10.07
25 Letter to Francis de Croisset, 9.10.07
26 Letter to Montesquiou, 7.9.07
27 Letter to Mme de Clermont-Tonnerre, 10.07
28 Letter to Mme de Clermont-Tonnerre, beginning of 10.07
29 Letter to Mme Straus, 8.10.07
30 Ibid.
31 Letter to Antoine Bibesco, 10.07.
32 Letter to Robert Dreyfus, 19.10.07
33 Letter to Auguste Marguillier, late in 07
34 Letter to Mme Catusse, 7.11.07
35 Letter to Montesquiou, shortly after 8.11.07

Chapter 18

1 Letter to Mme Straus, 2.2.08
2 *Cahiers Marcel Proust*, new series, no. 8 (Paris, 1976), p. 47
3 Ibid.
4 Letter to Auguste Marguillier, shortly before 8.1.08
5 *Cahiers Marcel Proust*, new series, no. 8, pp. 11-13, 56 and 141
6 *Contre Sainte-Beuve*, pp. 688-91
7 Letter to Mme Straus, 9.98
8 Letter to Reynaldo Hahn, 1906
9 Letter to princesse Bibesco, 3.08 or 09; *Contre Sainte-Beuve*, p. 691

10   Letter to Ramon Fernandez, 1919; *Le Divan*, 10–12.48; *Contre Sainte-Beuve*, pp. 690–1
11   *Contre Sainte-Beuve*, pp. 8–10
12   Ibid., pp. 24–6
13   Letter to Anna de Noailles, shortly after 22.2.08
14   Letters to Paul Helleu, end of 2.08
15   Letter to Mme Catusse, first days of 3.08
16   Letter to Robert Dreyfus, 21.3.08
17   *Contre Sainte-Beuve*, pp. 13–17
18   Ibid., p. 32
19   Ibid., p. 38
20   Letter to Robert Dreyfus, 21.3.08
21   Ibid.
22   Letter to Maurice de Fleury, 3 or 4.08
23   Letter to Mme Gaston de Caillavet, 14.4.08
24   Letter to Georges de Lauris, towards end of 4.08
25   Letter from Anna de Noailles, 21.3.08
26   Chateaubriand, *Mémoires d'outre-tombe*, vol. 1 (Paris, 1948), p. 519
27   Noticed by Kolb, *Correspondance*, 7, pp. x–xi
28   Letter to Albufera, 15.4.08
29   Letter to Albufera, 26.3.08
30   Letter to Albufera, 21.4.08
31   Letter to Albufera, 15.4.08
32   Letter to Georges de Lauris, towards end of 4.08
33   Letter to Louis de la Salle, 13 or 14.4.08
34   Letter to Albufera, 18.7.08
35   Letter to Mme Catusse, shortly before 29.3.08
36   Letter to Georges de Lauris, towards end of 4.08
37   Kolb's conjecture, *Correspondance*, 7, p. 193
38   Francis and Gontier, p. 207
39   *Remembrance of Things Past*, 3, p. 609
40   Letter to Albufera, 5 or 6.5.08
41   Letter to Robert Dreyfus, 16.5.08
42   Letter to Mme Robert de Billy, 16.5.08
43   Letter to Pierre Lavallée, shortly after 19.6.08
44   Letter to Albufera, 29.5.08
45   Ibid.
46   Letter to Mme de Caraman-Chimay, 8.6.08
47   *Le Figaro*, 14.6.08
48   Letter to vicomte de Paris, 12.6.08
49   Letter to Reynaldo Hahn, 22.6.08
50   Letter to Albufera, 22.6.08
51   Ibid.
52   Letter to Mme Straus, 22.6.08

53 Letter to Albufera, 22.06.08
54 Letter to Albufera, 1.7.08
55 Larcher, p. 46
56 Letter to vicomte de Paris, 1st half of 7.08
57 First notebook, Bibliothèque Nationale
58 *Le Carnet de 1908*, p. 50
59 Ibid.
60 *Remembrance of Things Past*, 2, pp. 787–8
61 Letter to Henri Bernstein, shorltly after 18.7.08
62 Georges de Lauris, p. 29
63 Letter to Henri Bernstein, shortly after 18.7.08
64 Albaret, pp. 83–4
65 Letter to Georges de Lauris, 15 or 16.7.08
66 Letter to Robert de Billy, towards end of 7.08
67 *Contre Sainte-Beuve*, p. 550
68 Letter to Lucien Daudet, towards 1.8
69 Kolb, *Correspondance*, 8, p. xxi
70 Letter to Céline Cottin, *ca* 11 or 12.8.08
71 Letter to Reynaldo Hahn, 7.08
72 Letter to Robert de Billy, towards end of 7.08
73 Letter to Louisa de Mornand, 1st half of 8.08
74 First notebook, pp. 55–7
75 Letter to Louisa de Mornand, shortly before 25.8.08
76 Ibid.
77 Painter, vol. 2, pp. 109–10
78 Letter to Marcel Plantevignes, undated
79 Plantevignes, pp. 98–114
80 *À un ami*, pp. 147–52
81 *Carnets de 1908*, p. 60
82 Ibid., pp. 60–1
83 Letter to Robert de Billy, *Cahiers Marcel Proust*, 1, p. 31
84 *Carnets de 1908*, p. 61
85 *Remembrance of Things Past*, 1, pp. 883–6
86 Letter to Georges de Lauris, 7.10.08
87 *Le Carnet de 1908*, p. 62
88 Letter to Marcel Plantevignes, 2 or 3.10.08
89 Letter to Max Daireaux, shortly after 6.10.08
90 Letter to Robert de Billy, 10.08
91 Letter to Robert de Flers, 9.10.08
92 Letter to Abel Desjardins, 11.10.08
93 Letter to Mme de Pierrebourg, 23.10.08
94 Letter to Mme Straus, 27.10.08
95 Letter to Marie Nordlinger, *ca* 18.10.08
96 Letter to Robert de Flers, 9.10.08
97 Letter to Albufera, 12 or 13.10.08

98 Letter to Mme Straus, 27.10.08
99 Ibid.
100 *Carnets de 1908*, p. 69
101 Letter to Charles d'Alton, 30.10.08
102 Letter to Georges de Lauris, 8.11.08

Chapter 19

1   Letter to Henri Ghéon, 2.1.14
2   Letter to Georges de Lauris, 8.11.08
3   Letter to Joseph Primoli, 25.12.08
4   Letter to Albufera *ca* 11.11.08
5   Letter to Lionel Hauser, 5 or 6.11.08
6   Letters to Emmanuel Bibesco, 11.08
7   Letter to Mme Straus, 6.11.08
8   Letter to Albufera, 6 or 7.12.08
9   Letter to Mme Catusse, towards end of 11.08 or 12
10 Letter to Lionel Hauser, 1.12.08
11 Letter to Albufera, 6 or 7.12.08
12 Letter to Georges de Lauris, shortly after middle of 12.08
13 Letter to Georges de Lauris, towards end of 12.08
14 Letters to Anna de Noailles and Georges de Lauris, middle of 12.08
15 Letters to Georges de Lauris, shortly after middle of 12 and towards end of 12.08
16 Letter to Georges de Lauris, towards end of 12.08
17 Letter to Georges de Lauris, *ca* 12.08
18 Letters to Montesquiou, 10.2.09, and Maurice Barrès, 17.2.09
19 Letter to Georges de Lauris, *ca* 15.1.09
20 Letter to Lionel Hauser, 1.2.09
21 Letter to Georges de Lauris, *ca* 15.1.09; quoted by Sainte-Beuve in *Portraits littéraires*, 2, p. 307
22 Letter to Georges de Lauris, 15.1.09
23 Letter from Lionel Hauser, 5.1.17
24 Letter to Max Daireaux, *ca* 5.09
25 Letter to Maurice Barrès, shortly after 9 or 16.11.08
26 Letter from Montesquiou, 6.3.08
27 Letter to Henri Bordeaux, shortly after 3.3.09
28 Kolb, *Correspondance*, 9, pp. vii–viii
29 Letter to Georges de Lauris, shortly after 6.3.09
30 *Contre Sainte-Beuve*, p. 219
31 *Against Sainte-Beuve*, pp. 3–4
32 Esquisses 13 and 14 in *À la recherche*, 1, p. 87
33 *Remembrance of Things Past*, 1, p. 50
34 Doubrovsky, passim

35 *Contre Sainte-Beuve*, p. 220
36 Ibid., p. 224
37 Letter to Lionel Hauser, Illinois collection
38 Notebook, Bibliothèque Nationale
39 *Contre Sainte-Beuve*, p. 221 – Sainte-Beuve's article of 22.7.1862
    reprinted in vol. 3 of *Nouveaux lundis*
40 *Contre Sainte-Beuve*, pp. 224–8
41 *Remembrance of Things Past*, 1, p. 6
42 Notebook, Bibliothèque Nationale
43 Cahier 42
44 *Contre Sainte-Beuve*, p. 299
45 Letter to Paul Souday, 11.20, CG, 3, p. 85
46 *By Way of Sainte-Beuve*, p. 64
47 *Remembrance of Things Past*, 1, p. 615
48 Ibid., 2, p. 348
49 Letter to Georges de Lauris, 23.5.09
50 Letter to Georges de Lauris, shortly after 23.5.09
51 Letter to Robert Dreyfus, 22 or 23.3.09
52 Letter to Maurice Duplay, 1st days of 4.09
53 Letter to Lucien Daudet, 5.09
54 Kolb, *Correspondance*, 4, p. 281, n. 3
55 Letter to Max Daireaux, *ca* 5.09
56 Letter to Lionel Hauser, 9.5.09
57 Letter to Reynaldo Hahn, 9–10.5.09
58 Letter to Montesquiou, 19.6.09
59 Letter to Louisa de Mornand, 6 or 7.09
60 Letter to Georges de Lauris, shortly before 23.6.09
61 Letter to Georges de Lauris, 23.6.09
62 Letter to Georges de Lauris, shortly after 2.7.09
63 Ibid.
64 Letter to Robert Dreyfus, 7.7.09
65 Ibid.
66 Letter to Céline Cottin, 12.7.09
67 *Remembrance of Things Past*, 1, p. 20
68 Ibid., 1, p. 195
69 Ibid., p. 78
70 Ibid., pp. 208–13
71 Letter to Reynaldo Hahn, 17 or 18.7.09
72 Letter to Georges de Lauris, shortly before middle of 8.09
73 Letter to Alfred Vallette, *ca* middle of 8.09
74 Ibid.
75 Letter to Max Daireaux, early 7.10
76 Letter to Georges de Lauris, shortly after 14.8.09
77 Letter to Anna de Noailles, 10.09
78 Letter to Max Daireaux, towards 31.12.09

79   Letter to Mme Straus, towards 16.8.09
80   Letter to Georges de Lauris, shortly after 26.8.09
81   Letters to Georges de Lauris, shortly after 14.8 and 1st days of
     10.09
82   Letter to Mme Straus, shortly after 16.8.09
83   Cahier 51, p. 66; *Matinée chez la princesse de Guermantes*, p. 33
84   Cahier 51, p. 63
85   *Contre Sainte-Beuve*, p. 557
86   Letter to Georges de Lauris, shortly after 16.8.09
87   Letter to Reynaldo Hahn, shortly after 25.8.09
88   Letter to Robert Dreyfus, towards end of 8.09, and letter to
     Mme Straus, 1912?
89   Letter to Francis de Croisset, shortly after 26.8.09
90   Letter to Georges de Lauris, 26.9.09
91   Letter to Georges de Lauris, beginning of 10.09

Chapter 20

1   Letter to Antoine Bibesco, 2.11.09
2   *Remembrance of Things Past*, 2, pp. 424–5
3   Letter to Montesquiou, shortly before middle of 12.09
4   Morand, *Visiteur du soir*, p. 26
5   *Remembrance of Things Past*, 1, p. 162
6   Ibid., p. 412
7   Letter to Anna de Noailles, 10.09
8   Letter to Lucien Daudet, 16.10.09
9   Letter to Lionel Hauser, 13 or 14.11.09, and letter to Georges de
     Lauris, 27.4.10
10   Letter to Antoine Bibesco, 2.11.09
11   Letter to Lionel Hauser, 13 or 14.11.09
12   Letter to Georges de Lauris, shortly after 27.11.09
13   Letter to Anna de Noailles, 11.09
14   Michel-Thiriet, p. 209
15   Letters to Georges de Lauris, shortly before 27.11, and to
     Reynaldo Hahn, 26.11.09
16   *Remembrance of Things Past*, 1, p. 151
17   Ibid., pp. 53–76
18   Ibid., p. 164
19   Ibid., p. 232
20   Ibid., pp. 98–9
21   Ibid., p. 466
22   Ibid., p. 793
23   Ibid., p. 941, and 2, pp. 297–8
24   Ibid., 2, pp. 638–9
25   Duplay, pp. 55–6

26 *Remembrance of Things Past*, 1, p. 142
27 Letter to Georges de Lauris, shortly before 27.11.09
28 Letter to Reynaldo Hahn, 26.11.09
29 Letter to Georges de Lauris, towards 13.12.09

Chapter 21

1   *Cahiers Marcel Proust*, 1, p. 19
2   *Carnet de 1908*, p. 108
3   *Remembrance of Things Past*, 1, p. 790
4   Ibid., 2, p. 414
5   Ibid., 3, p. 700
6   Ibid., p. 909
7   Ibid., pp. 18–19
8   Victor Graham, 'The Imagery of Proust', *Literature Through Art*, ed. Helmut Hatzfield (Oxford, 1952)
9   Notebooks, Bibliothèque Nationale
10 Cahier 57
11 Inscription in Gautier-Vignal's copy of *Les Plaisirs et les jours*; Gautier-Vignal, p. 140
12 Letter to Montesquiou, 20–21.2.10
13 Straus, p. 71
14 Morand, *Visiteur du soir*, p. 24
15 Letter to Reynaldo Hahn, shortly after middle of 1.10
16 Letter to Mme Gaston de Caillavet, shortly after middle of 1.10
17 Letter from Anatole France, shortly after 13.1.10
18 Letter to Lionel Hauser, shortly after 25.1.10
19 *Le Journal des Débats*, 23 and 25.1.10
20 Letter to Robert Dreyfus, 31.1.10 and to Simonne de Caillavet, *ca* 28 or 29.1.10
21 Letters to Georges de Lauris, 15.2.10, and Reynaldo Hahn, 21.2.10
22 Letter to Montesquiou, 20–21.2.10
23 Letter to Georges de Lauris, 15.2.10
24 Letter to Robert de Billy, 3.10
25 Ibid.
26 *Gil Blas*, 9.3.10
27 Letter to Montesquiou, 9.3.10
28 Letters to Louisa de Mornand, shortly after 9.4.10, and to Albufera, 12.4.10
29 Letter to Georges de Lauris, 21 or 22.4.10
30 Letter to Georges de Lauris, 27.4.10
31 Letter to Fernand Gregh, 5.6.10
32 Letter to Mme Straus, 14.4.10
33 Letter to Georges de Lauris, 27.4.10

34 Letter to Gabriel Mourey, 30.4.10
35 Letter to Georges de Lauris, shortly after 6.5.10
36 Letter to Lionel Hauser, 13 or 14.5.10
37 Letter to Antoine Bibesco, shortly before 22.5.10
38 Letter to Mme Greffulhe, *ca* 10.6.10
39 Cahier 51, p. 60
40 Letter to Reynaldo Hahn, towards beginng of 7.10
41 Letter to Max Daireaux, 1st days of 7.10
42 Letter to Georges de Lauris, 13.7.10
43 Letter to Jean-Louis Vaudoyer, 18.7.10
44 Letter to Reynaldo Hahn, 18.7.10
45 Letter to Jean-Louis Vaudoyer, 18.7.10
46 Letter to Reynaldo Hahn, 18.7.10
47 Letter to Maurice Duplay, shortly after 8.9.10
48 Letter to Jean-Louis Vaudoyer, 18.8.10
49 Letter to Georges de Lauris, 15 or 16.7.10
50 Valentine Thomson, 'My Cousin Marcel Proust', in *Harper's Magazine*, 5.32
51 Letter to Reynaldo Hahn, 4.8.10
52 *L'Intransigeant*, 21.9.10
53 Letter to Georges de Lauris, *ca* 8.10
54 Letter to Robert Dreyfus, 6 or 7.10.10
55 Letter to Robert Dreyfus, 8.10.10
56 Letter to Georges de Lauris, 1.11.10
57 Letter to Robert de Flers, 2.11.10
58 Letter to Louisa de Mornand, 30.10.10
59 Ibid.
60 Letter to Louisa de Mornand, 1.3.96
61 Letter to Robert de Flers, 3.11.10
62 Letter to Robert Dreyfus, 10.11.10
63 Letter to Robert Dreyfus, 21.11.10
64 Letter to Robert Dreyfus, 7.12.10
65 Letter to Mme Catusse, *ca* 11.10
66 Letter to Montesquiou, 14.12.10
67 Letter to Jean Cocteau, 12.10
68 Letter to Jean Cocteau, shortly before 25.12.10
69 Letter from Anna de Noailles, 30.1.11
70 Letter to Jean Cocteau, 30 or 31.1.11
71 Letter to Lucien Daudet, 10.1.11
72 *Le Tout Paris*, 1911
73 Letter to Georges de Lauris, shortly after 21.2.11
74 Letter to Reynaldo Hahn, 4.3.11
75 Ibid.
76 Letter to Antoine Bibesco, towards end of 3.11
77 Letter to Reynaldo Hahn, shortly after 4.3.11

78 Letter to Antoine Bibesco, 3.11
79 Letter to Louis de Robert, shortly after 24.3.11
80 Letter to Antoine Bibesco, towards end of 3.11
81 Letter to Mme Straus, shortly after 21.5.11
82 Marthe Bibesco, *Au Bal avec Marcel Proust*, p. 80
83 Letter to Reynaldo Hahn, 23.5.11
84 Letter to Montesquiou, 1.?6.11

Chapter 22

1   Letter to Albert Nahmias, 2nd half of 6.12
2   Fay, p. 91
3   Cp 'La Voix de Marcel Proust', in Gallimard, *Hommages à Marcel Proust* (Paris, 1927), and 'Nous deux Marcel' in *Opium*, both reprinted in Cocteau, *Poésie critique*, vol. 1 (Paris, 1959)
4   Letters to Francis de Croisset, 2nd half of 5 and 1.6.11
5   Letter to Francis de Croisset, 1st half of 7.11
6   Ibid.
7   Letter to Young Man, late 6 or early 7.11
8   Letter to René Gimpel, 7–8.11
9   Letter to Young Man, middle of 7.11
10 Letter to Robert de Billy, 18.7.11
11 Letter to Young Man, middle of 7.11
12 Letter to René Gimpel, 7–8.11
13 Letter to Antoine Bibesco, 11.8.11
14 Letter to Reynaldo Hahn, 25.7.11
15 Letter to Reynaldo Hahn, 17 or 18.8.11
16 *Remembrance of Things Past*, 1, p. 507
17 Letter to Reynaldo Hahn, 17 or 18.8.11
18 Letter to Georges de Lauris, 23 or 4.8.11
19 Ibid.
20 Letter from the Ministry of War, 6.9.11, and letter to Gaston Calmette, 16.9.11
21 Letter to Mme Nathan, 2.10.11
22 Letter to Zadig, Reynaldo Hahn's dog, shortly after 3.11.11
23 *NRF* review by Louis Dumont-Wilson of *La Maîtresse servante* by Jerome and Jean Tharaud
24 Letter to Maurice Barrès, 1.10.11
25 Letter to Lucien Daudet, towards the beginning of 12.11
26 Letter to Lucien Daudet, beginning of 12.11
27 Letter to Reynaldo Hahn, shortly before 24.12.11
28 Ibid.
29 Ibid.
30 Letter to Reynaldo Hahn, shortly before middle of January 1912

31   Letters to Jean-Louis Vaudoyer, shortly after 21.3.12, to Georges de Lauris, *ca* 24.3.12, to Jean-Louis Vaudoyer, 5 or 6.12
32   Letter to Albert Nahmias, shortly before 23.2.12
33   Letter to Albert Nahmias, between 2 and 11.1.12
34   Letter to Robert de Billy, 19.1.12
35   Letter to Jean-Louis Vaudoyer, shortly after 21.3.12
36   Letter to Jean-Louis Vaudoyer, 4 or 5.12
37   Letter to Albert Nahmias, shortly before 23.2.12
38   Letter to Robert de Billy, 1st days of 2.12
39   Letter to Mme Nathan, shortly after 20.1.12
40   Letter to Jean-Louis Vaudoyer, shortly after 21.3.12
41   Letter to Georges de Lauris, *ca* 24.3.12
42   Letter to Montesquiou, shortly before 20.2.12
43   Letter to Albert Nahmias, between 2 and 11.1.12
44   Letter to Jean-Louis Vaudoyer, shortly after 21.3.12
45   Quoted in letter to Mme Catusse, 11.14
46   Letter to Albert Nahmias, shortly after 13.5.12
47   Letter to Albert Nahmias, 4.12
48   Letter to Mme Straus, 4.6.12
49   Ibid.
50   Letter to Mme de Caillavet, shortly before 4.12.12
51   Letter to Robert de Billy, shortly after 24.5.12
52   Letter to Mme de Caillavet, shortly after 4.12.12
53   Letter to Mme Greffulhe, 26/27.5.12
54   Letter to Mme de Caillavet, shortly before 4.6.12
55   Letter to Anna de Noailles, 3.6.12
56   Letter to Reynaldo Hahn, 13.7.12
57   Letter to Reynaldo Hahn, shortly after 19.8.12
58   Letter to Charles d'Alton, *ca* end of 4.12
59   Letter to Reynaldo Hahn, 17 or 18.8.12
60   Scheikévitch, pp. 131–2
61   Letter to Reynaldo Hahn, shortly after 18.8.12
62   Letter to Albert Nahmias, 20.8.12
63   Letter to Mme Straus, shortly after 23.8.12
64   Letter to Mme Straus, shortly after 28.10.12
65   Letter to Louis de Robert, 28.10.12
66   Letter to Antoine Bibesco, shortly before 25.10.12
67   Letter to Mme Straus, shortly before 26.10.12
68   Letter to Louis de Robert, shortly after 28.10.12
69   Letter to Louis de Robert, shortly before 28.10.12
70   Letter to Louis de Robert, 28.10.12
71   Pierre-Henri Roeser, *Vieillesse et longevité* (Paris, 1910)
72   Letter to Mme Straus, shortly before 26.10.12
73   Henri Bergson, *Creative Evolution*, chs 1 and 4 (trans. Arthur Mitchell, London, 1912); cp. Kolb, *Correspondance*, 8, p. 106

74 Letter from Gaston Calmette to Eugène Fasquelle, 26.10.12
75 Letter to Mme Straus, 28.10.12
76 Letter from Gaston Calmette to Mme Straus, 28.10.12
77 Letter to Eugène Fasquelle, 28.10.12
78 Letter to Euguène Fasquelle, shortly after 28.10.12
79 Letter to Gaston Gallimard, shortly after 5.11.12
80 Ibid.
81 Letter to Jacques Copeau, shortly after 7.11.12
82 Letter to Mme Straus, 10.11.12
83 Ibid.
84 Letter to Mme Beaunier, 10.11.12
85 Letters to Albert Nahmias, *ca* 18.12.12, and to Louis de Robert, shortly after 24.12.12
86 Letter to Mme Straus, 18.12.12
87 Letter to Louis de Robert, shortly after 24.12.12
88 Letter to Mme Straus, *ca* 22.12.12

Chapter 23

1 Letter to Mme Straus, 26.12.12
2 Letter to Louis de Robert, shortly after 24.12.12
3 Letter to Eugène Fasquelle, shortly after 24.12.12
4 Letter to Louis de Robert, 1st days of 1.13
5 Letter to Louis de Robert, 25.1.13
6 Letter to Émile Mâle, *L'Art religieux du XIIIe siècle en France* (Paris, 1910)
7 Letter to Mme Straus, 14.1.13
8 *Remembrance of Things Past*, 1, pp. 898–900
9 Letter to Louis de Robert, 30.1.13
10 Letter to Louis de Robert, 25.1.13
11 Letter to Reynaldo Hahn, 1.2.13
12 Letter to Mme Straus, 14.1.13
13 Letter to Reynaldo Hahn, 1.2.13
14 Letter to Mme Straus, 14.1.13
15 Letter to Louis de Robert, 25.1.13
16 Letter to Georges de Lauris, *ca* 20.11.13
17 Letter to Louis de Robert, 30.1.13
18 Letter to René Blum, 23.12.13
19 Letter to Mme Straus, middle of 3.13
20 Letter to Jean Cocteau, 3 or 4.2.13
21 Letter to Albert Nahmias, beginning of 12.13
22 Letter to Anna de Noailles, middle of 2.13
23 De Robert, p. 14
24 Letter to Louis de Robert, *ca* 21.2.13
25 Letter to Louis de Robert, 1st week of 5.13

26 Letter to Louis de Robert, *ca* 19.2.13
27 Letter to René Blum, *ca* 20.2.13
28 Letter to Louis de Robert, *ca* 21.2.13
29 Letter to René Blum, 23.2.13
30 Letter to Bernard Grasset, 24.2.13
31 Letters to Bernard Grasset, shortly after 24.2 and shortly before 11.3.13
32 Letter to Bernard Grasset, 11.3.13
33 Letter to Bernard Grasset, shortly after 24.2.13
34 Letter to Jean-Louis Vaudoyer, shortly after 19.3.13
35 Letter to René Blum, 14.3.13
36 Letter to Mme Straus, middle of 3.13
37 Letter to Robert de Billy, *ca* 4.13
38 Letter to Antoine Bibesco, 19.4.13
39 *Remembrance of Things Past*, I, pp. 382–3
40 Albaret, p. 3
41 Ibid., pp. 5–6
42 Letter to Bernard Grasset, 2nd half of 5.13
43 Letter to Jean Cocteau, 22.5.13
44 Letter to Louis de Robert, 7.13
45 Maurice Rostand, *Confessions d'un demi-siècle*, p. 175 (Paris, 1948)
46 Letter to Mme Scheikévitch, 2nd half of 5.13
47 Letter to Maurice Duplay, shortly after 23.5.13
48 Letter to Louis de Robert, 2nd half of 6.13

Chapter 24

1   Letter to Émile Straus, 6 or 7.6.14
2   Letter to Louis de Robert, late 6.14
3   *Remembrance of Things Past*, 3, p. 3
4   Ibid., p. 102
5   Ibid., pp. 15–16
6   Letter to Émile Straus, 3.6.14
7   Letter to Louis de Robert, 7.13
8   Letter to Max Daireaux, shortly after 18.6.13
9   Letter to Bernard Grasset, 7.13
10 Ibid.
11 Letter to Reynaldo Hahn, 26?7.13
12 Letter to Reynaldo Hahn, 26?6.13
13 Letters to Charles d'Alton, shortly after 4.8.13, and to Georges de Lauris, shortly after 11.8.13
14 Letter to Charles d'Alton, shortly after 4.8.13
15 Letter to Anna de Noailles, 11.8.13
16 Letter to Georges de Lauris, shortly after 4.8.13

17 Letters to Anna de Noailles, 11.8.13, and to Georges de Lauris, shortly after 11.8.13
18 Letter to Mme de Pierrebourg, towards end of 11.13
19 Letter to Georges de Lauris, shortly after 11.8.13
20 Letter to Charles d'Alton, *ca* middle of 8.13
21 Letter to Lucien Daudet, towards end of 8.13
22 Note by Lucien Daudet, *Cahiers*, 5, p. 67
23 Letter to Lucien Daudet, early 9.13
24 Letter to Lucien Daudet, between middle of 10.13 and middle of 11.13
25 Letter to Jean-Louis Vaudoyer, 4.11.13
26 Letter to Robert de Flers, 6, 7 or 8.11.13
27 Letter to René Blum, 5, 6 or 7.11.13
28 Albaret, p. 190
29 *Remembrance of Things Past*, 3, p. 425
30 Letter to Albert Nahmias, *ca* 1 or 2.12.13
31 Telegrams to Albert Nahmias, 3–7.12.13
32 *Remembrance of Things Past*, 3, p. 438
33 Telegram to Albert Nahmias, 3.12.13
34 Telegram to Albert Nahmias, 7.12.13
35 Letter to Gabriel Astruc, 2nd half of 12.13
36 Letters to Mme Straus and Bernard Grasset, 5.1.14
37 Letter to Montesquiou, 1.14
38 Letter to Antoine Bibesco, 1.14
39 Letter to Mme Straus, 5.1.14
40 Letter to André Gide, 6 or 7.4.14
41 Letter to Bernard Grasset, 28.3.14
42 *New York Herald*, 31.5.14
43 Quoted in letter to Émile Straus, 3.6.14
44 Letter to Émile Straus, 3.6.14
45 Ibid.
46 *Remembrance of Things Past*, 3, p. 477
47 Kolb, 'The Making of a Novel', in Quennell, p. 33
48 Cahiers 46 and 71, draft of *La Prisonnière*; draft of *La Fugitive*, in cahiers 54 and 71
49 G. Cattaui, 'Albertine Retrouvée', *Adam International* (1957), no. 260, p. 81
50 Letter to Émile Straus, 3.6.14
51 Letters to Montesquiou, shortly after 6.6.14, and to Émile Straus, 7.6.14
52 Letter to Mme Catusse, 27.5.15

Chapter 25

1   Letter to Robert de Flers, 6, 7 or 8.11.13
2   Letter to Calmette, 12.11.13
3   *Le Figaro*, 16.11.13
4   *Le Temps*, 13.11.13
5   *Excelsior*, 23.11.13
6   *Le Figaro*, 27.11.13
7   Albaret, pp. 5–8
8   Ibid., pp. 14–15
9   Letter to Anna de Noailles, shortly after middle of 11.3.14
10   Letter to Mme Hugo Finaly, *ca* 24.11.13
11   Letter from Francis Jammes, *ca* 8.9.13
12   *Le Temps*, 9.12.13
13   *Gil Blas*, 15.12.13
14   Letter to Gabriel Astruc, 9.12.13, letter from him, and letter to him, 2nd half of 12.13
15   Advertisment in the *Mercure de France*, 16.12.13
16   Letter to Jacques Rivière, early 7.14
17   *NRF*, 1.1.14
18   Letter to Henri Ghéon, 2.1.14
19   Ibid.
20   Letter to Henri Ghéon, 6.1.14
21   Letter from André Gide, 11.1.14
22   Letter to André Gide, 12 or 13.1.14
23   Letter to André Gide 18.1.14
24   Letter to Lucien Daudet, 25.1.14
25   Letter to Henry Bordeaux, 5.3.14
26   Letter to Lionel Hauser, 25.1.14
27   Letter to Albert Nahmias, towards end of 1.14
28   Letter to Lionel Hauser, 6.5.14
29   Letter to André Gide, 22.3.14
30   Edith Wharton, *A Backward Glance* (New York, 1934), pp. 323–4
31   Cp. Rilke, *Letters* (London, 1950), p. 280
32   Letter to Montesquiou, 2.14
33   Letter to Antoine Bibesco, between 16 and 23.5.14
34   Letter to Jacques Rivière, 6.2.14
35   *NRF*, 1.4.25
36   Letter to Henry Bordeaux, shortly after 14.2.14
37   Letter to André Gide, 6.3.14
38   Interview with Jules Huret in Jules Huret, *Enquête sur l'évolution littéraire* (Paris, 1891), p. 64
39   Letter to André Gide, 6.3.14
40   Letter to Mme Straus, 17–18.3.14
41   Ibid.
42   Letter from André Gide, 20.3.14

43 Letter to André Gide, 21.3.14
44 Letter from Paul Claudel to André Gide, 2.3.14
45 Letter to André Gide, 22.3
46 Letter from Bernard Grasset, 26.3.14
47 Letter to Bernard Grasset, 3.4.14
48 Letter from Bernard Grasset, 4.4.14
49 Letter to André Gide, 6 or 7.4.14
50 *L'Écho de Paris*, 15.4.14
51 Letter to Jacques Rivière, 30.4 or 1.5.14
52 Letters to Jacques Rivière, *ca* 9.5.14 and 12 or 13.5.14
53 Letter from Jacques Rivière, between 15 and 21.5.14
54 Letter to Bernard Grasset, 3.5.14
55 Letter from Bernard Grasset, 4.5.14
56 Letter to André Gide, 19.6.14
57 Letter to Émile Straus, 3.6.14
58 Letter to Robert de Flers, between 4 and 25.5.14
59 Letter to Robert de Flers, early 7.14
60 Letter to André Gide, 6 or 7.4.14
61 Letter from André Gide, 6.6.14
62 Letter to André Gide, 10 or 11.6.14
63 Letter from André Gide, 14.6.14

Chapter 26

1   Letter to Lionel Hauser, *ca* 28.7.14
2   Letter to Lionel Hauser, 2.8.14
3   Ibid.
4   Letter to Mme Straus, shortly after 16.8.14
5   Albaret, pp. 23–8
6   Letter to Reynaldo Hahn, 30.10.14
7   Ibid.
8   Letter to Louis d'Albufera, shortly after 8.3.15
9   Albaret, pp. 29–30
10 *Cahiers Marcel Proust*, 7, pp. 125–32
11 Letter to Mme Catusse, 7.9.14, and Albaret, p. 30
12 *Cahiers Marcel Proust*, 7, p. 130
13 Ibid., pp. 132–3
14 Albaret, p. 29
15 *Cahiers Marcel Proust*, 7, p. 134
16 Ibid., p. 135
17 Albaret, pp. 32–3
18 Letter to Mme de Madrazo, early 15
19 Letter to Lucien Daudet, shortly after 21.11.14
20 Painter, 2, p. 282
21 Albaret, p. 36

22 Ibid., p. 37
23 Letters to Mme Catusse, 17.10, and to Mme Straus, *ca* 22, 23 or 24.10.14
24 Letter to Reynaldo Hahn, shortly after 24.10.14
25 Ibid.
26 Letter of 3.15, Tadié, *Proust* (Paris 1983), p. 283
27 Albaret, p. 38
28 Letter to Lionel Hauser, 7.5.16
29 Letter to Reynaldo Hahn, shortly after 28.10.14
30 Letter to Lionel Hauser, 13.9.16
31 Letter to Lucien Daudet, 16.11 or shortly after
32 *Remembrance of Things Past*, 3, pp. 895–7
33 Letter to Charles d'Alton, shortly after 12.5.14
34 Letters to Lucien Daudet, 7.3 and 11.3.15, and letter to Louis de Robert, 3.1.15
35 *Le Figaro*, 15.3.15
36 Letter to Jeanne de Caillavet, 14.1.15
37 Letter to Lucien Daudet, 30 or 31.1.15
38 Letter to Jacques-Émile Blanche, 1st half of 5.15
39 Letter from Marcel Delanney, 8.4.15
40 Letter from Dr Bize, 10.4.15
41 Letter to Robert de Billy, 3.15
42 Letter to Lionel Hauser, 27.8.15
43 Albaret, pp. 72–3
44 Gimpel, pp. 179 and 265
45 Albaret, pp. 70–80
46 Duc de Gramont, *Bulletin*
47 Letter to Mme de Caillavet, 20.4.15
48 Morand, *Journal*, p. 306
49 Ibid., p. 136
50 Letter to Jean Cocteau, 23.4.15
51 Albaret, pp. 183–4
52 Letter to Mme Catusse, 27.5.15
53 Ibid.
54 Letter to Jacques-Émile Blanche, shortly before 7.7.15
55 Letter to Mme de Madrazo, 27.6.15
56 Letter to Jacques Boulenger, towards end of 6.21
57 Letters to Lucien Daudet, 8.8.15, and Lionel Hauser, 23.8.15
58 Letter to Jacques-Émile Blanche, 1st week of 8.15
59 Letters to Lionel Hauser, 28.8.15, and to Lucien Daudet, 9.15
60 Letter to Lionel Hauser, 1st days of 9.15
61 Letter to Camille Plantevignes, 6.12.15
62 Letter to Lionel Hauser, middle of 9.15
63 Letter to Camille Plantevignes, 6.12.15
64 Letter to Nicolas Cottin, 22.10.15

65 Letter to Lionel Hauser, 22.10.15
66 Letter from Lionel Hauser, 26.10.15
67 Letter to Lionel Hauser, shortly after 14.5.17; Montaigne, *Essais*, 39, 'De la Solitude'
68 Letter from Lionel Hauser, 4.11.15
69 Racine, *Athalie*, Act 3, sc. 7
70 Letter to Albert Nahmias, 28 or 29.9.15
71 Letter to Mme Catusse, 10.10.15
72 Painter, 2, p. 225
73 Letter to Mme Catusse, 10.10.15
74 Scheikévitch, p. 145
75 Letter to Mme Scheikévitch, 2 or 3.11.15
76 Letter to Mme Scheikévitch, shortly after 3.11.15, but he began the summary in the summer
77 Letter to Lucien Daudet, shortly after middle of 11.15
78 Ibid.
79 Letter to Emmanuel Berl, 16
80 Albaret, pp. 63–125
81 Letter to René Blum, 30.5.16
82 Letter to Georges de Lauris, 8.16
83 Letter to Charles d'Alton, 14.2.16
84 Letter to René Blum, 29.5.16
85 Letter to Lionel Hauser, 29.5.16
86 Letter to Mme de Madrazo, 17.2.16
87 Letter to Mme de Madrazo, 9.3.16
88 *Remembrance of Things Past*, 3, p. 661
89 Letters to Mme Catusse, shortly after 22.3.16, and to Mme Albert Hecht, 7.3.16
90 Letter to Robert Dreyfus, 16.3.16
91 Letters to Lionel Hauser, shortly after 22.3.16, and to Mme Catusse shortly after 22.3.16
92 Letters to Raymond Pétain, shortly after 14.4.16 and 20 or 27.4.16
93 Letter to Gaston Gallimard, shortly before 30.5.15
94 Letter to René Blum, 30.5.16
95 Letter to Lionel Hauser, 26.6.16
96 Letters to Lionel Hauser, 4.7.16, and to Albert Nahmias, *ca* 8.16
97 Letter to René Blum, *ca* 6.7.16
98 Letters to René Blum, 30.5.16, 6.7.16 and 14.8.16
99 Letter to Gaston Gallimard, shortly before 30.5.16
100 Letter from Bernard Grasset to René Blum, 1.8.16
101 Letter to Lionel Hauser, 4 or 5.8.16
102 Letter to René Blum, 14.8.16
103 Letter to Albert Nahmias, *ca* 8.16
104 Letter to René Blum, 14.8.16

105   Letter to Bernard Grasset, 14.8.16
106   Letters to Lucien Daudet, ca 20.8.16, and to Lionel Hauser, 27.8.16
107   Letter from Lionel Hauser, 15.9.16
108   Letter to Lionel Hauser, 27.9.16
109   Letter to Bernard Grasset, 14.9.16
110   Letter to Mme Greffulhe, 10.10.16
111   Letter from Mme Greffulhe, 10.16
112   Letter to Mme Greffulhe, 10.16
113   Letter to Charles d'Alton, ca 2.17
114   Letter to Lionel Hauser, 8.11.16
115   Letter to Montesquiou, 16.12.16
116   Mme Daudet, *Souvenir de famille et de guerre* (Paris, 1920), p. 161

Chapter 27

1   Letter to Lucien Daudet, 1st days of 1.17
2   Letter to Lionel Hauser, 6.3.17
3   Letter to Paul Morand, ca 1 or 2.17
4   Colette, p. 85
5   Clermont-Tonnerre, *Robert Montesquiou et Marcel Proust*, p. 140
6   Gimpel, pp. 180 and 264–5
7   Morand, *Visiteur du soir*, pp. 11–12
8   Morand, *Journal*, pp. 202–3
9   Letter to Lucien Daudet, 15.2.17
10   Letters to Paul Morand, 22.2.17 and 1.3.17
11   Letter to Robert de Flers, 12.11.17
12   Morand, *Journal*, pp. 185–6, 111–13, 161, 203 and 300, and *Visiteur du soir*, pp. 9–30, 36–7, 48–9 and 53
13   Letter to Paul Morand, 16.3.17
14   *Visiteur du soir*, pp. 17–19
15   Letter to Mme de Caillavet, shortly before 8.10.18
16   Letter to Lionel Hauser, shortly after 22.3.17
17   Letter to Antoine Bibesco, 2.4.17
18   Gautier-Vignal, pp. 58 and 110
19   Letter to Mme de Caraman-Chimay, 23.8.17
20   Letter to Mme Soutzo, 3.9.17
21   Morand, *Journal*, p. 243, and fragment of letter to Mme de Chevilly, 22.4.17
22   Painter, 2, p. 257
23   Sylvain Bonmariage, 'Document sur la personnalité de M. de Charlus', *Bulletin Le Rouge et Le Noir* (1930)
24   Duplay, pp. 138–9
25   Bonnet, *Les Amours*, pp. 84–5
26   Duplay, p. 72

27 Bonnet, *Les Amours*, p. 80
28 Gide, 'Ainsi soit-il', in vol. 2 of *Journal*
29 Letter to Mme Straus, 31.5.18
30 Letter to Clément de Maugny, 18
31 Winton, 1, pp. 134–5
32 Léon Daudet, *Salons et journaux*, pp. 298–9
33 Letter to Léon Daudet, 1st days of 3.17
34 Letter to Lionel Hauser, shortly after 14.5.17
35 *Remembrance of Things Past*, 1, p. 959
36 Letters to Lionel Hauser, shortly after 14.5.17, to Jacques Truelle, 15.5.17, and to Antoine Bibesco, shortly after 15.5.17
37 Letter to Lucien Daudet, *ca* 1.5.17
38 Letter to Mme de Guiche, 30.5.17
39 Letter to Jacques Truelle, 15.5.17
40 *Correspondance* (1917), p. 132, n. 24
41 Letter to Mme Scheikévitch, 23.6.17
42 Letter to Mme de Clermont-Tonnerre, 11.6.17
43 Ibid.
44 Letter to Jacques Truelle, *ca* 12.17
45 Gautier-Vignal, p. 48
46 Letter to Louisa de Mornand, *ca* 6.17
47 Letter to Charles d'Alton, shortly after 5.7.17
48 Letter to Mme Straus, towards end of 7.17
49 Morand, *Visiteur du soir*, letter of 28.7.17
50 Letter to Mme Straus, towards end of 7.17
51 Morand, *Visiteur du soir*, letter of 28.7.17
52 Letter to Mme Straus, towards end of 7.17
53 Ibid.
54 *Remembrance of Things Past*, 3, p. 782
55 Letter to Paul Morand, 17.8.17
56 Letter to Mme de Caraman-Chimay, shortly after 23.8.17
57 Marthe Bibesco, *Au Bal avec Marcel Proust*, p. 102
58 Letter to Antoine Bibesco, shortly after 15.9.17
59 Letter to André Gide, ?10.17
60 Gide, *Les Nourritures terrestres*, (Paris, 1897), p. 186
61 Rémy de Gourmont, *Le Livre des masques* (Paris, 1896)
62 Letter to Mme Catusse, 13.10.17
63 Letter to Paul Morand, last days of 10.17
64 Letter to Lucien Daudet, 3.11.17
65 Letter to Mme Soutzo, 23.11.17
66 Letter to Louis Gautier-Vignal, 10 or 11.17
67 Letter to Guiche, 14.11.17
68 Letter from Céleste Albaret to Mme Soutzo, 16.11.17
69 Letter to Walter Berry, 14.11.17
70 Letter to Mme Scheikévitch, 23.11.17

71   Letter to Robert de Flers, 12.11.17
72   Letter to Mme Scheikévitch, 1.19
73   Letter to Mme Catusse, 23.11.17
74   Letter from Mme Scheikévitch, 26.11.17
75   Letter to Mme Catusse, last days of 11.17
76   Letter to Mme Soutzo, 1.12.17
77   Ibid.
78   Letter to Mme Soutzo, 1st days of 12.17
79   *Remembrance of Things Past*, 2, p. 139
80   Letter to Jacques de Lacretelle, 14.12.17
81   Letter to Mme Catusse, 22.12.17
82   Letter to Mme Straus, 29.12.17
83   Letter to Maurice Bize, 16 or 17

Chapter 28

1   *Remembrance of Things Past*, 3, p. 757
2   Letter to Walter Berry, 1.18
3   Letter to Walter Berry, 6.1.18
4   Letter to Walter Berry, undated, in CG, vol. 5
5   Letter to Mme Straus, *ca* spring 18
6   Morand, *Visiteur du soir*, p. 82
7   Letter to Clément de Maugny, 4.18
8   Mauriac, *Proust's Way*, p. 9
9   Letter to Lucien Daudet, 8.4.18
10   *Remembrance of Things Past*, 3, p. 1090
11   Letter to Mme de Maugny, 18
12   Inscription to Jacques de Lacretelle, 20.4.18
13   *Contre Sainte-Beuve*, pp. 572–3
14   Ibid., p. 575
15   Letter to Mme Straus, *ca* spring 18
16   *Contre Sainte-Beuve*, p. 571
17   Letter to Mme Sheikévitch, 29.5.18
18   Letter to Clément de Maugny, 5.18
19   Letter to Mme Straus, 14 or 15.6.18
20   Letter to Robert Dreyfus, 7.18
21   Letter to Mme Straus, 19.10.18
22   Ibid.
23   Letter to Jacques-Émile Blanche, *ca* 8 or 9.10.18
24   Letter to Mme Straus, shortly after 20.11.18
25   Letter to Jean-Louis Vaudoyer, 18 (incorrectly dated 1919)
26   Albaret, p. 188
27   Letter to Mme Straus, 31.7.18
28   Letter to Mme Straus, 11.11.18
29   Ibid.

30 Ibid.
31 Letter to Mme Straus, *ca* 11.18
32 Ibid.
33 *Remembrance of Things Past*, 3, pp. 1007–8
34 *Chips: The Diaries of Sir Henry Channon*, ed. Robert Rhodes James (London, 1967)
35 Henry Channon, diary entry for 16.11.18
36 Violet Schiff, 'A Night with Proust', *London Magazine*, 9.56
37 Letter to Walter Berry, undated, CG, 5
38 Letter to Clément de Maugny, 18
39 Letter to Mme Straus, 12.18
40 Letter to Mme Straus, *ca* spring 19
41 Marthe Bibesco, *Au Bal avec Marcel Proust*, p. 157
42 *Contre Sainte-Beuve*, p. 48
43 Letter to Walter Berry, 3.19
44 Albaret, p. 319
45 Letter to Mme Scheikévitch, 1.1.19
46 Letters to Mme Soutzo and Mme Scheikévitch, 1.2.19
47 *Contre Sainte-Beuve*, p. 48
48 Harold Nicolson, *Peacemaking* (London, 1933), pp. 275–6, 318–19
49 Letter to Mrs Sydney Schiff, undated, CG, 3
50 Albaret, p. 314–15
51 Tadié, *Proust*, p. 305
52 Ibid.
53 Letter to Walter Berry, 19
54 Letter to Mme Catusse, 4–5.18
55 Letter to Mme Catusse, 11.5.18
56 Ibid.
57 Ibid.
58 Letters to Jean-Louis Vaudoyer and Mme Catusse, 5.19
59 Inscription in copy of *Jeunes Filles*, CG, 6, p. 262
60 Albaret, p. 322
61 Letter to Mme Catusse, undated, *Lettres à Mme C*, pp. 193–4
62 Letters to Robert de Flers and Robert Dreyfus, 6–7.18
63 Letter to Paul Souday, 10.11.18
64 Letter to comte de Gaigneron, 2.8.18
65 Letter to Walter Berry, 17.6.18
66 Letter to Robert Dreyfus, 24.7.18
67 Ibid.
68 Letter to Robert Dreyfus, 28.7.18
69 Letter to Mr and Mrs Sydney Schiff, undated, CG, 3
70 Letters to Montesquiou, to Robert Dreyfus, 7.18, to Mme Catusse, 7–8.18 and to Mme Scheikévitch, 26.12.18
71 Letter to Paul Souday, 10.11.18
72 Letter to Jacques Rivière, undated, *Lettres à la NRF*

73   Letter to Robert de Flers, 7.19
74   Letter to Robert Dreyfus, 7.19
75   Letters to Walter Berry, undated, CG, 5
76   Jacques-Émile Blanche, *Propos de peintre*, 3 vols, (Paris, 1919–28) vol. 2, pp. xxxvii–l

Chapter 29

1   Gautier-Vignal, p. 112
2   Albaret, pp. 324–5
3   Letter to Paul Souday, 10.11.19
4   Letter to Mme Straus, 25.12.19
5   Albert Thibaudet, 'Réflexions sur la litérature lettre à M. Marcel Proust', *NRF*, 3.20
6   *Contre Sainte-Beuve*, p. 586
7   Ibid., pp. 594–5
8   Ibid., p. 599
9   Letter to Jacques Boulenger, 21.12.19
10   *Excelsior*, 11.12.19
11   Letter to Jacques-Émile Blanche, end of 12.19
12   Albaret, p. 305
13   Harold Nicolson in *Travelers Library*, compiled by W. Somerset Maugham (New York, 1933)
14   Letter to Mme Catusse, 20
15   *L'Opinion*, 19.12.19
16   Letters to Jacques Boulenger, 10–11.1.20 and 13.1.20
17   Letter to Jacques Boulenger, 11.19
18   Letter to Jean-Louis Vaudoyer, 20
19   *Contre Sainte-Beuve*, p. 601
20   Ibid., p. 615
21   Letter from Jacques Rivière to Proust, 23.3.20
22   Letter to Jacques Rivière, 26.4.20
23   Painter, 2, p. 293
24   Ibid.
25   Letter to Walter Berry, 7.8.20
26   Letter to Sydney Schiff, CG, 3, p. 44
27   Letter to Mme Straus, 20.3.20
28   *Remembrance of Things Past*, 3, pp. 1058–9, 1070–4
29   Letter to Jacques Rivière, 20–28.5.20
30   Letter from Jacques Rivière, 29.5.20
31   *Revue de Paris* 9.48
32   Letter from Jacques Rivière, 29.6.20
33   Letter to Jacques Rivière, 3–12.7.20
34   Letter from Jacques Rivière, 13.7.20
35   Ibid.

36 Letter to Jacques Rivière, 25 or 26.7.20
37 *NRF*, 1.9
38 Letter to Jacques Boulenger, 4.5.21
39 Painter, 25, p. 298
40 Jaloux, pp. 18–19
41 *Contre Sainte-Beuve*, p. 607
42 Ibid., p. 615
43 Letter to Jacques Boulenger, 23.11.20
44 Marthe Bibesco, *Au Bal avec Marcel Proust*, pp. 108–9
45 Letter to Paul Souday, 9.20
46 Letter to Robert Dreyfus, 2.10.20
47 Letters to Mme Straus, shortly before 23.10, and to Mme Catusse, 20.10.20
48 Letter to Jacques Rivière, 23 or 24.7.20
49 Albaret, pp. 355–6
50 Letter to Jean-Louis Vaudoyer, 13.8.20
51 Letter to Bernard Fay, Fay, p. 104
52 Letter to Jean-Louis Vaudoyer, 20
53 Letter to Clément de Maugny, 20
54 Letter to Sydney Schiff, CG, 3, p. 49
55 Letter to Jean-Louis Vaudoyer, 20
56 *NRF*, 11.20; Rivière, pp. 153–4
57 Letter to Jacques Rivière, 7 or 8.11.20
58 *Le Temps*, 4.11.20
59 Letter to Paul Souday, 11.20
60 Letter to Jacques Boulenger, 4.12.20
61 Letter to Jacques Rivière, 6.1.21
62 Letters to Jacques Rivière, 14.1.21, to Mme Catusse, 18.1.21, and to Jacques-Émile Blanche, 16.1.21
63 Letter to Gaston Gallimard, 11.1.21
64 Tadié, *Proust*, p. 310
65 Letter from Montesquiou, undated
66 Letter to Montesquiou, undated
67 Letter to Montesquiou, undated
68 Letter to Jacques Boulenger, 18.4.21
69 Letter to Jacques Boulenger, end of 6.21
70 Letter to Jacques Boulenger, 12.7.21
71 Letter to Louis Martin-Chauffier, undated
72 Letter to Jacques Boulenger, 12.4.21
73 Letter to Jacques Rivière, 21.4.21
74 *Contre Sainte-Beuve*, p. 633
75 Ibid., pp. 628–9
76 Ibid., p. 622
77 Baudelaire, *Selected Writings on Art and Artists* (Harmondsworth, 1972), p. 423

78   Ibid., p. 427
79   Ibid.
80   *Remembrance of Things Past*, 3, p. 386
81   Ibid., p. 387
82   Ibid., pp. 386–7
83   Letter to Jacques Rivière, 22.4.21
84   *Contre Sainte-Beuve*, p. 624
85   Letter to Jacques Boulenger, 26.5.21
86   *NRF*, 6.21
87   Jacques Boulenger's footnote on p. 252 of CG, 3
88   *NRF*, 7.21
89   Jacques Boulenger's footnote on p. 262 of CG, 3; *Contre Sainte-Beuve*, p. 599

Chapter 30

1   Letter to Mme Scheikévitch, 6.21
2   Letter to Jacques Boulenger, 3.21
3   Letter to Jacques Boulenger, 1.9.21
4   Letter to Jacques Boulenger, 20
5   Letter to Clément de Maugny, 20
6   Letter to Sir Philip Sassoon, 22
7   Letter to Clément de Maugny, 19 or 20
8   Letter to Jean-Louis Vaudoyer, 13.8.21
9   *Contre Sainte-Beuve*, p. 606
10   *Remembrance of Things Past*, 3, pp. 1100–1
11   Albaret, pp. 334–5 and 338
12   *Remembrance of Things Past*, 3, pp. 180–5
13   Ibid., p. 186
14   *NRF*, 5.21
15   Letter to Jacques Boulenger, 17.5.21
16   Gide, *Journal*, 1889–1939, 14 and 18.5.21
17   Letter to Jacques Rivière, 24.4.21
18   *NRF*, 9.21
19   Mauriac, *Proust's Way*, pp. 28–9
20   Natalie Barney, *Aventures de l'esprit* (Paris, 1929) pp. 51–64
21   *Remembrance of Things Past*, 3, pp. 990–3
22   Ibid., pp. 1114–17
23   Ibid., pp. 366–7
24   Bernard Fay, *Les Précieux*, pp. 93–104
25   Letter to Jacques Boulenger, 1st days of 8.21
26   Letter to Montesquiou, undated
27   Letter to Louis Martin-Chauffier, undated
28   Letter to Clément de Maugny, undated
29   Letter to Jacques Boulenger, 4.5.21

30 Francis and Gontier, p. 167
31 Ibid., pp. 166–8
32 Letter to Jean-Louis Vaudoyer, 22
33 Marthe Bibesco, *Voyageur voilé*, p. 99
34 Letter to Montesquiou, undated
35 Letter to Jacques Boulenger, 4.5.21
36 *La Revue de France*, 15.6.21
37 Letter to Gustave Tronche, between middle of 6 and 12.7.21
38 Morand, *Visiteur du soir*, pp. 123–4
39 Letter to Jacques Boulenger, 30.8.21
40 *Remembrance of Things Past*, 2, p. 67
41 Ibid., pp. 488–9
42 Painter, 2, p. 307
43 Cocteau, *Opium*, p. 165, and *Poésie critique*, pp. 125 and 130
44 Marthe Bibesco, *Voyageur voilé*, p. 110
45 Letter to Clément de Maugny, undated, CG, 5, pp. 113–15
46 Letter to Sydney Schiff, CG, 3, p. 30
47 Letter to Gaston Gallimard, 9.21
48 Clermont-Tonnerre, *Robert de Montesquiou et Marcel Proust*, pp. 212–16 and 240–3
49 Ibid., p. 239
50 Jullian, p. 266
51 Letter to Clermont-Tonnerre, *Robert de Montesquiou et Marcel Proust*, p. 239
52 Painter, 2, p. 326
53 Letter to André Lang, *ca* 11–12.21
54 Letter to Camille Vettard, CG, 3, p. 195
55 Letter to Sydney Schiff, CG, 3, p. 44
56 Letter from Mme Straus, 13.5.21
57 Letter to Walter Berry, 6.1.22
58 Morand, *Visiteur du soir*, pp. 125–6
59 Letter to Sydney Schiff, CG, 3, p. 35 and p. 49
60 Letters to Sydney and Violet Schiff, CG, 3, pp. 50, 51 and 55
61 Letter to Gaston Gallimard, early 22
62 *Les Écrits nouveaux*, 7.21
63 Morand, *Visiteur du soir*, pp. 125–6
64 Roger Martin du Gard, *Les Mémorables* (Paris, 1957), vol. 1, pp. 195–202
65 Letter to Jacques Boulenger, undated
66 *Neue Merkur*, 2.22
67 *NRF*, 8.22
68 Albaret, pp. 336–7
69 Gautier-Vignal, p. 168
70 Jaloux, p. 11
71 Letter to Sydney Schiff, CG, 3, p. 43

72 Letter to Laure Hayman, 19.5.22
73 Richard Ellmann, *James Joyce* (New York, Oxford and Toronto, 1982), pp. 508–9
74 Letter to Lionel Hauser, 19.5.22
75 *Le Gaulois*, 27.5.22
76 *Contre Sainte-Beuve*, p. 642
77 *Lettres à la NRF*, pp. 213–14
78 Violet Schiff, *London Magazine*, 9.56
79 Letter to Jacques Rivière, 8.6.22
80 Letter to Walter Berry, 11.6.22
81 Letter to Camille Vettard, CG, 3, p. 190
82 Pouquet, pp. 94–5
83 Lucien Daudet, pp. 27 and 241, and Albaret, p. 338
84 *Lettres à la NRF*
85 Benoist-Méchin, pp. 154–5
86 Letter to Jacques Rivière, between 19 and 24.6.22
87 Letter to Edmond Jaloux, 15.7.22
88 Jaloux and *Lettres à la NRF*
89 *Lettres à la NRF*
90 Letter to Gaston Gallimard, 7.22
91 *Contre Sainte-Beuve*, p. 645
92 Ibid.
93 Letter to Jacques Rivière, 4–9.9.22
94 Letter to Ernst Curtius, posted 18.9.22
95 Letter to Sydney Schiff, CG, 3, p. 56
96 Letter to Jacques Rivière, 20 or 21.9.22
97 Cp. Marthe Bibesco, Jaloux, Kolb, *Correspondance*, and Scheikévitch
98 Letter to Jacques Rivière, 23 or 24.9.22
99 Letter to Sydney Schiff, CG, 3, p. 34
100 Cp. Winton, and Painter, 2, p. 347
101 *Remembrance of Things Past*, 2, p. 56
102 Letter to Sydney Schiff, CG, 3, p. 57
103 Albaret, pp. 345–9
104 Letter to Gaston Gallimard, 8.22
105 Letter to Gaston Gallimard, 3.2.22
106 Letter to Gaston Gallimard, 22.6.22

Chapter 31

1 Cahier, p. 139
2 Letter to Ernst Forssgren, postmarked 19.9 3, *Cahiers Marcel Proust*, new series, vol. 6, no. 1, p. 139
3 Ibid.
4 Albaret, pp. 344–5

5 Ibid., p. 348
6 Scheikévitch, p. 164
7 Letter to Jacques Rivière, 1st weeks of 11.22
8 Francis and Gontier, p. 170
9 Ibid., pp. 171–2
10 Albaret, p. 347
11 Cattaui, *Marcel Proust*, p. 138; Scheikévitch, p. 165
12 Albaret, p. 349
13 Ibid., pp. 351–2
14 Ibid., pp. 145, 154–5 and 166
15 Ibid., pp. 350–1
16 Francis and Gontier, p. 173
17 Albaret, pp. 352–60
18 Ibid., pp. 27–8
19 Ibid., p. 361

BIBLIOGRAPHY

By Proust

À la recherche du temps perdu, ed. Jean-Yves Tadié, 4 vols (Paris, 1987–9)
Chroniques, (Paris, 1927)
Albertine disparue, texte établie par Nathalie Mauriac et Étienne Wolff
(Paris, 1987)
Matinée chez la Princesse de Guermantes: Cahiers du Temps Retrouvé, texte
établie par Henri Bonnet et Bernard Brun (Paris, 1982)
Contre Sainte-Beuve, précédé de *Pastiches et mélanges* et suivi de *Essais et
articles*, ed. Pierre Clarac and Yves Sandré (Paris, 1971)
Jean Santeuil, précédé de *Les Plaisirs et les jours* (Paris, 1971)
Les Plaisirs et les jours (Paris, 1924)
Textes retrouvés, recueillis et présentés par Philip Kolb et L. B. Price
(Urbana, Chicago and London, 1968)
L'Indifférent (Paris, 1978)
Le Carnet de 1908, établi et présenté par Philip Kolb (Paris, 1976)

Translations
Ruskin, John, *La Bible d'Amiens* (Paris, 1947)
——, *Sésame et les lys* (Paris, 1935)

Correspondence
Correspondance de Marcel Proust, tomes 1–17, texte établi, présenté et
annoté par Philip Kolb (Paris, 1970–89)
Correspondance générale, 6 vols (Paris, 1930–6)
À un ami (Paris, 1948)
Choix de lettres, présentées et datées par Philip Kolb (Paris, 1954)
Lettres à la NRF (Paris, 1932)
Lettres à Mme C[atusse] (Paris, 1946)
Lettres à Reynaldo Hahn (Paris, 1956)
Lettres à une amie [Marie Nordlinger] (Manchester, 1942)
Lettres retrouvées, présentées et annotées par Philip Kolb (Paris, 1966)
Marcel Proust et Jacques Rivière: Correspondance 1914–1922, présentées et
annotées par Philip Kolb (Paris, 1955)
Correspondance avec sa mère (Paris, 1953)
Lettres à André Gide (Neuchâtel, 1949)

Lettres de Marcel Proust à Bibesco (Clairefontainée, 1949)

Bibesco, Marthe, *Au Bal avec Marcel Proust* (Paris, 1971)
——, *Le Voyageur voilé* (Geneva, 1949)
Daudet, Lucien, *Autour de soixante lettres de Marcel Proust* (Paris, 1929)
Dreyfus, Robert, *Souvenirs sur Marcel Proust* (Paris, 1926)
Gregh, Fernand, *Mon amitié avec Marcel Proust* (Paris, 1958)
Morand, Paul, *Le Visiteur du soir* (Geneva, 1949)
Pouquet, Jeanne Maurice, *Quelques Lettres de Marcel Proust* (Paris, 1928)
Proust, Marcel, et Gallimard, Gaston *Correspondance 1912–1922* (Paris, 1989)
Robert, Louis de, *Comment débuta Marcel Proust* (Paris, 1969)

In English
Remembrance of Things Past, trans. C. K. Scott-Moncrieff and Terence Kilmartin (London, 1981)
Albertine Gone, trans. Terence Kilmartin (London, 1989)
Jean Santeuil, trans. Gerard Hopkins (London, 1955)
Pleasures and Regrets, trans. Louise Varese (London, 1986)
By Way of Sainte-Beuve, trans. Sylvia Townsend Warner (London, 1958)
Against Sainte-Beuve and Other Essays, trans. John Sturrock (London, 1988)
On Reading Ruskin, trans. Jean Autret, William Burford and Phillip J. Wolfe (New Haven and London, 1987)
Selected Letters vol. 1: 1880–1903, ed. Philip Kolb, trans. Ralph Manheim (London, 1983)
Selected Letters, vol. 2: 1904–1909, ed. Philip Kolb, trans. Terence Kilmartin (London, 1989)

On Proust

Adams, William Howard, *A Proust Souvenir: Period Photographs by Paul Nadar* (London, 1984)
Albaret, Céleste, *Monsieur Proust* (London, 1976)
Bardèche, Maurice, *Marcel Proust, romancier*, 2 vols (Paris, 1971)
Barthes, Roland et al., *Recherches de Proust* (Paris, 1980)
Beckett, Samuel, *Proust* (London, 1931)
Bell, William Stewart, *Proust's Nocturnal Muse* (New York and London, 1962)
Benjamin, Walter, 'The Image of Proust', in *Illuminations* (London, 1970)
Benoist-Méchin, Jacques, *Avec Marcel Proust* (Paris, 1977)
Berl, Emmanuel, *Sylvia* (Paris, 1952)
Bersani, Leo, *Marcel Proust: The Fictions of Life and Art* (New York, 1965)

Billy, Robert de, *Marcel Proust: Lettres et conversations* (Paris, 1930)

Bonnet, Henri, *Le Progrès spirituel dans l'oeuvre de Marcel Proust*, 2 vols (Paris, 1946–9)

——, *Marcel Proust de 1907 à 1914* (Paris, 1971)

——, *Les Amours et la sexualité de Marcel Proust* (Paris, 1985)

Bowie, Malcolm, *Freud, Proust and Lacan: Theory as Fiction* (Cambridge, 1987)

Brasillach, Robert, *Portraits* (Paris, 1935)

Brée, Germaine, *The World of Marcel Proust* (London, 1967)

Buisine, Alain, *Proust et ses lettres* (Lille, 1983)

Butor, Michel, 'The Imaginary Works of Art in Proust', in *Inventory* (London, 1970)

Cattaui, George, *L'Amitié de Proust* (Paris, 1935)

——, *Proust* (London, 1987)

Clarac, Pierre, and Ferré, André, *Album Proust* (Paris, 1965)

Clermont-Tonnerre, Élisabeth de (see also Gramont, Elisabeth de), *Robert de Montesquiou et Marcel Proust* (Paris, 1925)

Cocking, J. M., *Proust* (London, 1956)

Colette, *En pays connu* (Paris, 1950)

Coulon, Bernard, *Promenades en Normandie avec un guide nommé Marcel Proust* (Condé-sur-Noireau, 1986)

Deleuze, Gilles, *Proust and Signs* (London, 1973)

Doubrovsky, Serge, *La Place de la madeleine* (Paris, 1974)

Duplay, Maurice, *Mon ami Marcel Proust* (Paris, 1972)

Fay, Bernard, *Les Précieux* (Paris, 1941)

Ferré, André, *Les Années de collège de Marcel Proust* (Paris, 1959)

Feuillerat, Albert, *Comment Marcel Proust a composé son roman* (New Haven, 1934)

Francis, Claude and Gontier, Fernande, *Marcel Proust et les siens suivi des souvenirs de Suzy Mante-Proust* (Paris, 1981)

Gautier-Vignal, Louis, *Proust connu et inconnu* (Paris, 1976)

Gide, André, *Incidences* (Paris, 1924)

——, *Journal* (Paris, 1951)

Gimpel, René, *Diary of an Art Dealer* (New York and London, 1966)

Girard, René, 'Narcissism: The Freudian Myth Demythified by Proust', in *Literature and Psychoanalaysis*, ed. William Phillips and Edith Kurzweil (New York, 1983)

Graham, Victor, *The Imagery of Proust* (Oxford, 1966)

Gramont, Duc de, 'Souvenirs sur Marcel Proust', *Bulletin des Amis de Marcel Proust*, no. 6

Gramont, Élisabeth de, *Marcel Proust* (Paris, 1948)

Hahn, Reynaldo, *Journal d'un musicien* (Paris, 1933)

Halévy, Daniel, *Pays parisiens* (Paris, 1932)

Henry, Anne, *Proust romancier* (Paris, 1983)

Jaloux, Edmond, *Avec Marcel Proust* (Geneva, 1953)

Josipovici, Gabriel, 'Proust: A Voice in Search of Itself', in *The World and the Book* (London, 1971)

Jullian, Philippe, *Robert de Montesquiou* (London, 1965)

Kilmartin, Terence, *A Guide to Proust* (London, 1983)

Kolb, Philip, *La Correspondance de Marcel Proust: Chronologie et commentaire critique* (Urbana, 1949)

Larcher, P.-L., *Le Parfum de Combray* (Illiers, 1971)

Lindner, Gladys Dudley (ed.), *Marcel Proust: Reviews and Estimates in English* (New York, 1942)

March, Harold, *The Two Worlds of Marcel Proust* (London, 1948)

Marc-Lipiansky, M., *La Naissance du monde proustien dans Jean Santeuil* (Paris, 1974)

Mauriac, François, *Proust's Way* (New York, 1950)

——, *Mémoires intérieures* (London, 1959)

Maurois, André, *À la recherche de Marcel Proust* (Paris, 1970)

Mein, Margaret, *A Foretaste of Proust* (Farnborough, 1974)

Michel-Thiriet, Philippe, *The Book of Proust* (London, 1989)

Miller, Milton L., *Nostalgia: A Psychoanalytic Study of Marcel Proust* (Port Washington and London, 1956)

Morand, Paul, *Journal d'un attaché d'ambassade* (Paris, 1949)

Moss, Howard, *The Magic Lantern of Marcel Proust* (London, 1963)

Nabokov, Vladimir, *Lectures on Literature* (New York, 1980)

Painter, George, *Marcel Proust: A Biography* (London, 1959–65)

Pierre-Quint, Léon, *Marcel Proust: Sa vie, son oeuvre* (Paris, 1925)

Plantevignes, Marcel, *Avec Marcel Proust* (Paris, 1966)

Poulet, Georges, *Proustian Space* (Baltimore and London, 1977)

Price, L. B. (ed.), *Marcel Proust: A Critical Panorama* (Urbana, Chicago and London, 1973)

Pugh, Anthony, *The Birth of À la recherche du temps perdu* (Lexington, Kentucky, 1987)

Quennell, Peter, (ed.), *Marcel Proust 1871–1922: A Centenary Volume* (London, 1971)

Revel, Jean-François, *Sur Proust* (Paris, 1970)

Richard, Jean-Pierre, *Proust et le monde sensible* (Paris, 1974)

Rivière, Jacques, *Quelques progrès dans l'étude du coeur humain* (Paris, 1985)

Sansom, William, *Proust* (London, 1973)

Scheikévitch, Marie, *Souvenirs d'un temps disparu* (Paris, 1935)

Shattuck, Roger, *Proust's Binoculars* (London, 1964)

——, *Proust* (London, 1974)

Splitter, Randolph, *Proust's Recherche: A Psychoanalytic Interpretation* (Boston, London and Henley, 1981)

Stambolian, George, *Marcel Proust and the Creative Encounter* (Chicago and London, 1972)

Straus, Bernard, *The Maladies of Marcel Proust* (New York, 1980)

Tadié, Jean-Yves, *Proust et le roman* (Paris, 1971)
——, *Lectures de Proust* (Paris, 1971)
——, *Proust* (Paris, 1983)
Turnell, Martin, *The Novel in France* (London, 1950)
Winton, Alison, *Proust's Additions: The Making of À la recherche du temps perdu*, 2 vols (Cambridge, 1977)

PICTURE ACKNOWLEDGMENTS

1 Paul Nadar/Service des Archives de la Caisse Nationale des Monuments Historiques et des Sites, Paris.
2 Paul Nadar/Service des Archives de la Caisse Nationale des Monuments Historiques et des Sites, Paris.
3 Roger-Viollet Agency, Paris.
4 Mante-Proust collection.
5 Paul Nadar/Service des Archives de la Caisse Nationale des Monuments Historiques et des Sites, Paris.
6 Mante-Proust collection.
7 Albert Bernard/French Cultural Services, New York.
8 Jacques-Emile Blanche/French Cultural Services, New York.
9 Madeleine Lemaire/British Museum.
10 Paul Nadar/Service des Archives de la Caisse Nationale des Monuments Historiques et des Sites, Paris.
11 French Cultural Services, New York.
12 Paul Nadar/Service des Archives de la Caisse Nationale des Monuments Historiques et des Sites, Paris.
13 Paul Nadar/Service des Archives de la Caisse Nationale des Monuments Historiques et des Sites, Paris.
14 Paul Nadar/Service des Archives de la Caisse Nationale des Monuments Historiques et des Sites, Paris.
15 French Cultural Services, New York.
16 Paul Nadar/Service des Archives de la Caisse Nationale des Monuments Historiques et des Sites, Paris.
17 Paul Nadar/Service des Archives de la Caisse Nationale des Monuments Historiques et des Sites, Paris.
18 Bibliothèque Nationale, Paris.
19 Courtesy of Madame Saint-Cyr.

INDEX

note: P = Marcel Proust

Also available in Minerva

ANNIE COHEN-SOLAL

Sartre

'This biography places him meticulously. Sartre the intense but anarchic Paris student is here; Sartre the friendly, bohemian lycée teacher in Le Havre, outraging the parents on speech-day; Sartre the café-dwelling chieftain of his little Paris clan; Sartre the prime Existentialist, unsuitably jolly prophet of a pessimistic doctrine; and Sartre the vociferous political pundit, travelling the world to give excitable lectures in favour of revolution and of a proletariat entirely of his own making' *Observer*

'Cohen-Solal fills a real need. Her long, careful and loving portrait of Sartre turns a remote and puzzling mandarin into a true existential being, warts and all' *Newsweek*

'Annie Cohen-Solal brings us to the heart of the only subject that counts: how an extraordinary spirit brings others closer to the real by means of his own imagination. She does it all with detail, equity, *élan*' *Le Monde*

'A fine biography: rigorous, irreverent, complete, lucid' *L'Express*

'The life and works of Sartre . . . form a deliberate, radical continuum. Annie Cohen-Solal's biography, reading like something halfway between an adventure story and a documentary of the century, records everything with consummate clarity' *El Pais*

PIETRO CITATI

Kafka

'We are conducted gracefully but irresistibly into the depth of a soul. Citati knows the diaries and letters so well that he can set out scenes as a novelist would; we are in Kafka's room, watching him work, or walking with him and Felice, or sharing with him an all-too-brief idyll in the mountains, where he had gone for the sake of his ruined lungs. Between these short "biographical" passages Citati considers the stories and the novels, subjecting them to an extraordinarily close and illuminating reading. He is such a good critic that these expository chapters are far more exciting than would have been mere tittle-tattle about the life' John Banville, *Irish Times*

'One of the few biographies I have read which would in all likelihood be admired and endorsed by its subject. And he was a hard artist to please' *Sunday Times*

'An assured and dazzling performance . . . can be recommended to anyone intrigued but baffled by Kafka' *Listener*

'An amazing piece of virtuoso writing . . . one could almost be reading Kafka himself – or, dare I say it, thinking with Kafka himself . . . This book forced me to re-read Kafka' *Glasgow Herald*

A Selected List of Titles Available from Minerva

While every effort is made to keep prices low, it is sometimes necessary to increase prices at short notice. Mandarin Paperbacks reserves the right to show new retail prices on covers which may differ from those previously advertised in the text or elsewhere.

The prices shown below were correct at the time of going to press.

Fiction
☐	7493 9026 3	**I Pass Like Night**	Jonathan Ames	£3.99	BX
☐	7493 9006 9	**The Tidewater Tales**	John Bath	£4.99	BX
☐	7493 9004 2	**A Casual Brutality**	Neil Blessondath	£4.50	BX
☐	7493 9028 2	**Interior**	Justin Cartwright	£3.99	BC
☐	7493 9002 6	**No Telephone to Heaven**	Michelle Cliff	£3.99	BX
☐	7493 9028 X	**Not Not While the Giro**	James Kelman	£4.50	BX
☐	7493 9011 5	**Parable of the Blind**	Gert Hofmann	£3.99	BC
☐	7493 9010 7	**The Inventor**	Jakov Lind	£3.99	BC
☐	7493 9003 4	**Fall of the Imam**	Nawal El Saadewi	£3.99	BC

Non-Fiction
☐	7493 9012 3	**Days in the Life**	Jonathon Green	£4.99	BC
☐	7493 9019 0	**In Search of J D Salinger**	Ian Hamilton	£4.99	BX
☐	7493 9023 9	**Stealing from a Deep Place**	Brian Hall	£3.99	BX
☐	7493 9005 0	**The Orton Diaries**	John Lahr	£5.99	BC
☐	7493 9014 X	**Nora**	Brenda Maddox	£6.99	BC

All these books are available at your bookshop or newsagent, or can be ordered direct from the publisher. Just tick the titles you want and fill in the form below. Available in:
BX: British Commonwealth excluding Canada
BC: British Commonwealth including Canada

Mandarin Paperbacks, Cash Sales Department, PO Box 11, Falmouth, Cornwall TR10 9EN.

Please send cheque or postal order, no currency, for purchase price quoted and allow the following for postage and packing:

UK   80p for the first book, 20p for each additional book ordered to a maximum charge of £2.00.

BFPO   80p for the first book, 20p for each additional book.

Overseas   £1.50 for the first book, £1.00 for the second and 30p for each additional book
including Eire   thereafter.

NAME (Block letters) ....

ADDRESS ....

....

....